THE UNFINISHED JOURNEY

THE UNFINISHED JOURNEY

America Since World War II

Sixth Edition

WILLIAM H. CHAFE
Duke University

New York   Oxford
OXFORD UNIVERSITY PRESS
2007

Oxford University Press, Inc., publishes works that further Oxford University's
objective of excellence in research, scholarship, and education.

Oxford   New York
Auckland   Cape Town   Dar es Salaam   Hong Kong   Karachi
Kuala Lumpur   Madrid   Melbourne   Mexico City   Nairobi
New Delhi   Shanghai   Taipei   Toronto

With offices in
Argentina   Austria   Brazil   Chile   Czech Republic   France   Greece
Guatemala   Hungary   Italy   Japan   Poland   Portugal   Singapore
South Korea   Switzerland   Thailand   Turkey   Ukraine   Vietnam

Published by Oxford University Press, Inc.
198 Madison Avenue, New York, New York 10016
http://www.oup.com

Oxford is a registered trademark of Oxford University Press

Library of Congress Cataloging-in-Publication Data

Chafe, William Henry.
    The unfinished journey : America since World War II / William H. Chafe.—6th ed.
        p. cm.
    Includes bibliographical references and index.
    ISBN-13: 978-0-19-531537-0 (alk. paper)
        1. United States—Politics and government—1945–1989.   2. United States—Politics and
government—1989–   3. United States—Social conditions—1945–   I. Title.
E743.C43 2007
973.92—dc22

                                                                           2006048344

Printing number: 9 8 7 6 5 4 3

Printed in the United States of America
on acid-free paper

To those who tried to create

"the beloved community,"

and who continue that effort today

CONTENTS

PREFACE

This is a book about how America has come to be what it is today.

Ironically, most of us know less about the decades that have shaped our immediate lives than we do about the era of the American Revolution. Although we instantly recognize the faces of John Kennedy, Martin Luther King, Jr., or Richard Nixon when they flash on our television screens, we have little sense of the underlying patterns that have produced the world we live in. The history courses most of us have taken in high school or college end at the New Deal or World War II. We may speak with familiarity about FDR or the "flapper" of F. Scott Fitzgerald's novels, but most of the realities that have defined our existence over the past half century—the atom bomb, Cold War tensions, the two-income household, school desegregation, women's liberation, the "culture wars," and birth of the new right—are developments that occurred after the 1930s. Indeed, despite inevitable continuities, the America that has emerged in the years since World War II is in many ways a new society, one whose tensions, complexity, and conflicts compel us to make the best effort possible to understand who we are, where we are, and how we got here.

The pages that follow reflect a conceptual framework that is also the product of the social changes that have occurred in the last few decades. Through a variety of circumstances, American historians have discovered the importance of viewing history from the perspective of groups in our society who, in the past, were either ignored or perceived as passive objects of action by others. Histories of women, the family, workers, and minorities have assumed a central place in what is now called the "new social history." Consistent with these shifts in perspective, this book begins with the conviction that gender, class, and race constitute fundamental reference points for understanding how power and resources are divided in our society and what degree of change can be said to have occurred in a given period.* For most of American history, a person's condition of birth—whether male or female, white or black, rich or poor—largely shaped one's life experience

*It should be noted that, while the category of race covers a wide variety of ethnic backgrounds, this book focuses primarily on African-Americans in highlighting the importance of race in American society.

and chances, notwithstanding the traditional belief that America is a society of individuals, not groups. Certainly, until recent decades, barriers of discrimination based on race and gender have severely limited the opportunities available to most women and virtually all African-Americans—a clear majority of the population. Many historians would agree that distinctions based on class have been just as powerful, though perhaps less visible. Hence, the issue of whether substantive social change has occurred must focus on these issues. Gender, class, and race are not emphasized here to the exclusion of political and diplomatic history—far from it. But these themes help to place that history in a different context, serving as basic categories against which to measure the degree and kind of progress that has occurred in American society. In the best sense, this book seeks to integrate social and political history, each helping to reflect the dynamics of the interaction between the two.

Within this framework, *The Unfinished Journey* argues that World War II was a turning point in our history. In the most obvious instance, the war led directly to America's role in international affairs in the postwar world, with all the attendant problems associated with nuclear weapons, the Cold War, and military conflicts ranging from Korea to Vietnam. But the war also provided the economic foundations for the prosperity of the postwar world. Technological innovations, accumulated savings from wartime wages, the G.I. Bill, housing loans from the Veterans Administration—all proved critical to the period of unparalleled economic growth that followed after 1945, and all would have been unlikely, if not impossible, had it not been for the war. Just as important, critical changes in the lives of American blacks and American women were set in motion during the war. And although the ultimate evolution of these changes took a shape and character that were full of paradox, wartime changes helped to create the structural preconditions for long-range developments that would, potentially at least, change the social landscape of America more than almost any event since the Industrial Revolution.

A second, and more complicated, argument of *The Unfinished Journey* is that 1968 constituted a pivotal dividing line during the postwar years. With the civil rights movement as a driving force, American social reform movements in the 1960s achieved an energy and critical thrust that had the potential to transform American society and to alter fundamental values of the dominant culture. For some activists, reform instincts turned into radicalism, and with the Vietnam war as a fulcrum, political rebellion, both inside and outside the established political process, became a central theme in American society. Simultaneously, those who believed devoutly in the traditional American values of hard work, the nuclear family, good manners, and patriotism rallied in defense of the institutions and beliefs they cherished. Whether the changes considered necessary by social activists could have occurred without rending the basic fabric of American society was never tested. Instead, assassinations, political disarray, cultural anarchy, and the election of Richard Nixon brought an end to the dominance of reform forces and ushered in an era of political, economic, and cultural conservatism that remained dominant for more than two decades. If the twenty years after 1948 represented the dominance of a "liberal consensus" in American politics, the twenty-plus years after 1968 saw the triumph of a "conservative consensus."

With the end of the Cold War in the early 1990s, a third major turning point occurred. For nearly 50 years, the fight against communism had shaped both domestic and foreign policy. The Cold War defined the limits of political dialogue (there could be no real *left* in America amidst the politics of anticommunism), the allocation of resources (military spending had to come first), and which issues would garner the most attention (universal health insurance could not be discussed because it represented socialized medicine). Inevitably, therefore, the conclusion of the Cold War had ramifications for the way Americans understood and interacted with the world. A new president was elected in 1992 who began his administration with an insistence that domestic concerns, not foreign policy issues, should occupy center stage. Although Bill Clinton was not as successful as he had hoped in transforming domestic politics, issues of the economy, education, and health care clearly dominated his own political agenda. Yet, as the horrors of genocide in Bosnia and Rwanda, the outbreak of civil war in Somalia, and the problem of nuclear proliferation in North Korea, Iran, Pakistan, and India have shown, the end of the Cold War neither solved nor ended the problem of being the most powerful nation in the world.

Nothing confirmed more the centrality of cultural and global conflict than the terrorist attacks on the United States on September 11, 2001. As American citizens and the world watched in disbelief, the collapse of the two towers of the World Trade Center in downtown Manhattan, with the loss of nearly 3,000 lives, confirmed that the world had entered a new era. No one, not even the greatest military power, was invulnerable. People who hated the values, economic institutions, and cultural beliefs associated with Western capitalism could attack at any place and at any time, using weapons of modern technology, including America's own commercial airliners, to try to shatter a way of life and a people. Not only did the United States have to grapple with the ongoing flaws and unfinished business of its own society; it now also had to grapple with the new threat of worldwide terrorism not organized into a nation-state alliance like the Soviet Union, but spread through countries everywhere in cells of zealous revolutionaries who viewed suicidal bombing missions as the highest form of virtue and sacrifice. For the first time, Americans had to come to grips with the cultural chasms that divided some Muslim fundamentalists from Christians and Jews, the poor from the rich, the secular from the religious. As America's journey continued, therefore, the challenges became even greater and more complicated.

Recently, a colleague who writes on literary topics asked why I wrote history books and what use they were. I answered that history offered a way of engaging and understanding what mattered in the past, because only in that way can we engage and understand where we are today and where we may seek to go in the future.

This seems all the more so as we enter a new millennium. There is something humbling about contemplating the meaning of all the history that has passed since the ancient Greeks first started to record the experience of what it meant to be human. If nothing else, entering a new millennium should heighten our own sense of how important it is that we use our brief moment on this planet as best we can, seeking whatever way possible to make a difference in the world we bequeath to our children and grandchildren.

Acknowledgments

Any book such as this, of course, depends on the scholarship of hundreds of historians. My own primary research has focused on the civil rights movement, women's history, and the the politics of the 1960s. But in these areas, as well as in others, I have relied on the works of countless colleagues who have written the monographs that make books of synthesis possible. I am also deeply indebted to friends who have taken the time to read this manuscript in various forms and the wonderful students who have helped to shape, and reshape, the ideas contained here.

At various stages, I have been helped in the writing or revision of *The Unfinished Journey* by grants from the Rockefeller Foundation, the National Endowment for the Humanities, the National Humanities Center, and the Center for Advanced Study in the Behavioral Sciences. I have benefitted at every turn from superb help from staff and research assistants, and I want to offer special thanks to Mary Jacobs, Joan Shipman, Vivian Jackson, and Andrea Franzius. Lorna, Christopher, and Jennifer Chafe have always kept me aware of what really counts. Finally, I owe a great debt to the editors I have worked with at Oxford—Sheldon Meyer, Nancy Lane, Gioia Stevens, Peter Coveney, and Brian Wheel. They have been excellent critics as well as warm and gracious friends.

Georgetown, Maine
December, 2005

1

The War Years

When Japanese bombers unleashed their terror on Pearl Harbor the morning of December 7, 1941, the event shook America with the devastation of a massive earthquake. Just fourteen months earlier Franklin Roosevelt had assured his fellow citizens that "your boys are not going to be sent into any foreign wars." During the intervening year, of course, those words became increasingly hard to believe. With German Panzer divisions terrorizing France, Belgium, and Holland, and the English forced back to their island fortress, neutrality seemed a less and less likely possibility. In December 1940 America had begun its Lend-Lease plan of sending arms to Britain (when your neighbor's house is ablaze, FDR had said, you have to lend him a hose to put out the fire), and the country prepared to impose sanctions on oil deliveries in an effort to block Japanese aggression in the South Pacific. Still, war seemed so far away, with millions retaining the fervent hope that somehow America could be spared direct involvement in this new worldwide conflagration. Now, with the sudden assault on America's entire Pacific fleet, that hope was shattered.

In the immediate aftermath of Pearl Harbor, panic spread through the country as word seeped out of the catastrophic losses American naval forces had sustained. Rumors were rife—that Japanese diplomats in Honolulu had plied American soldiers with liquor to prevent them from responding to the attack, that thousands of Japanese who had once lived in the States were preparing an invasion of the West Coast. The night after Pearl Harbor military officials in San Francisco sounded an alarm in response to a phantom Japanese air raid. In New York Mayor Fiorello La Guardia called out security guards to police all bridges, tunnels, and factories in the city. And in Seattle a hysterical mob hurled rocks and bottles at a glaring neon sign in the middle of the city that symbolized, like an enemy hidden within, a treasonous attempt to subvert the blackout that had been declared. "This is war," one woman declared. "They don't realize that one light in the city might betray us."

Within weeks, wartime mobilization set in motion developments that would help transform American society—for the next four years, and for generations to come. More than 5.6 million Americans enrolled in civil defense programs to do their part on the home front. Young men rushed to enlist. The government declared that the only answer to the manpower crisis was to "employ women on a scale hitherto unknown," reversing a decade of official policy discrimination against women workers. As industrialists geared up for levels of unprecedented productivity, workers prepared to leave their homes to go where the jobs were, beginning a mass migration that would eventually see 20 million Americans change their county of residence during the war. Black Americans, already enlisting at rates far higher than their proportion of the population, pondered how to fight racism at home as well as tyranny abroad. And Japanese Americans wondered what their fate would be in a country singing the popular song, "You're a sap, Mr. Jap, to make a Yankee crankie . . . Uncle Sam is going to spanky." As the next four years unfolded, the country would be tested as never before. Breakthroughs in the areas of technology and productivity paved the way for postwar prosperity, while controversies over economic equity and sex roles helped to shape the social agenda for decades to come. For most Americans, this was to be the last "good war," with almost every citizen joined in a united commitment to defeat a tyrannical enemy and to defend a way of life decent in its aspirations and in its values. Whether the war's results would be as "good" as the objectives for which it was fought could not yet be known. But the fact of the war itself would decisively alter the nation's history.

Making the War Real on the Homefront

One of the greatest problems American leaders faced was how to make the war real at home. Despite rumors of impending invasion and Japanese submarine attacks, the nearest battlefield was three thousand miles away. As one British visitor commented: "no one fresh from London . . . could fail to be overwhelmed by the contrast. . . . Here, if anywhere, was normality—hundreds of miles of it and not a sight or sound to remind one that this was a country at war." How to make the connection, how to convey a vivid sense of involvement, how to tie American families in Iowa City or Oshkosh to soldiers in foxholes—all these posed a dilemma for a nation that had never experienced foreign invasion, a sudden bombing attack, or sabotage on its own soil.

The first link occurred through propaganda—the public portrayal of soldiers and war issues through advertising, the mass media, music and songs. The Office of War Information (OWI), formed shortly after the war began, produced films, posters, and radio broadcasts of its own, while offering guidelines to magazines and networks on how they might expedite the process of mobilizing the homefront. In one of its most popular manifestations, this campaign took the form of vivid reminders that what took place in war factories and kitchens directly affected the fate of GI Joe. One hard-line ad asked, "Are you comfortable, brother? That's good, brother.

Just sleep right through this war . . . what's it to you that a kid just got bumped off in the Solomons . . . because *you* couldn't be bothered with scrap collection?" In another version of the same theme, a short film from Bataan featured a wounded GI exhorting his family not to waste food. "We haven't had anything but a little horsemeat and rice for days," the soldier says, "and kitchen fats mom. Don't waste any. Kitchen fats make glycerin and glycerin makes explosives. Two pounds of fat can fire five anti-tank shells." Lest the message be lost, the film ended with the announcement that the soldier had died in the hospital after making the film.

For those perplexed by the distance between America and its foreign allies, comparisons between our way of life and theirs provided a critical connection. The Russians were not dangerous revolutionaries, but jovial democrats. In a clear effort to evoke images of America's own rural electrification program, one propaganda broadcast described a Russian worker's response to a new power dam: "I helped it grow from bank to bank. I saw electric power spreading out over the country. I'll never forget my father's face when he saw the electric lights first go on in our little house. He cried for joy." The same theme was reinforced by *Mission to Moscow,* a movie which celebrated the common characteristics of two great peoples, and even went so far as to excuse Stalin's purge and slaughter of up to 5 million Russians during the late 1930s.

Perhaps the most effective bond between the homefront and the combat zone occurred in personal, emotional images of sacrifice and humanity. In one radio drama a father whose son had been killed in the war strove to find meaning and justification for the loss he had suffered. Why did his son die? For democracy:

> The House I live in,
> A plot of earth, a street,
> the grocer and the butcher
> and the people that I meet;
> The children in the playground,
> the faces that I see;
> All races, all religions,
> That's America to me.

And if Americans at home worried about the demands they faced, they were urged to remember the anxiety of those going off to face the possibility of death. An ad entitled "The Kid in Upper Four" captured the tearful homesickness of the young man going to war. "Wide awake . . . listening . . . staring into blackness," the young soldier thought about "the taste of hamburgers and pop . . . the feel of driving a roadster over a six-lane highway . . . there is a lump in his throat, and maybe a tear fills his eye. It doesn't matter, kid. Nobody will see . . . it's too dark. . . ." If Americans had to stand the next time they took a train, the advertisement concluded, they should think of the Kid in Upper Four.

The same theme of common humanity gradually came to characterize the portrayal of the soldiers themselves, further strengthening ties to the homefront. To be sure, there were stories of exaggerated heroism, especially in the beginning when rewrite men in the home office tried to gloss over defeats with stories of superhuman effort and smashing victories. As one observer noted, some of these early stories "gave the impression that any American could lick any twenty Japs." But soon a new realism and humanity emerged, embodied in the reports of people like Ernie Pyle and Bill Mauldin. Pyle wrote, not about the romance of war, but about the individual details of death and dying, loyalty and friendship. Nothing brought the battlefield closer to home than a portrait of one enlisted man, squatting beside the body of his dead captain:

> He reached and took the captain's hand, and sat there for a full five minutes holding the dead hand in his own and looking intently into the dead face. And he never uttered a sound all the time he sat there. Finally he put the hand down and he reached up and gently straightened the points of the captain's shirt collar, and then he sort of re-arranged the tattered edges of his uniform around the wound, and then he got up and walked away down the road in the moonlight.

As Pyle later wrote, "certainly there were great tragedies," but most days were spent "just toiling . . . in a world full of insecurity, discomfort, homesickness, and a dull sense of danger. . . . I knew of only twice that the war would be romantic to the men: once when they could see the Statue of Liberty and again on their first day back in their home towns with their folks." These were soldiers one could recognize and identify with—one's children, neighbors, friends. And in conveying their reality, correspondents like Pyle did as much as anyone could to preserve a sense of continuity in the face of tragedy and chaos.

War bonds also offered a direct means by which citizens at home could invest personally in the military struggle. As the historian John Blum has pointed out, there were other more effective ways of raising money for the war than government bonds. Yet Henry Morgenthau, Jr., Secretary of the Treasury, had the genius to understand the psychological value of involving citizens directly in the process of financing military procurement. America would "use *bonds* to sell the *war*, rather than *vice versa*." With a national sales campaign behind the effort, purchase of war bonds would "give everyone of you a chance to have a financial stake in American democracy—an opportunity to contribute toward the defense of that democracy." Millions of people wondered what they could do, Morgenthau told the press. "Right now, other than going in the army and navy or working in a munitions plant, there isn't anything to do. . . . Sixty percent of the reasons that I want [the bond program] is . . . to give the people an opportunity to do something."

The drive to sell bonds involved everyone. Hollywood became the spearhead of the operation. Hedy Lamarr offered a personal kiss to anyone who bought a $25,000 bond. Carole Lombard died as a result of a plane crash while on a tour to sell bonds, and Greer Garson fainted from nervous exhaustion. Hollywood stars alone sold almost $1 billion worth of bonds in 1942. A year later, in a fête that anticipated subsequent marathon drives for charity, Kate Smith spoke on CBS radio sixty-five times over an eighteen-hour period, raising $39 million for the war effort. School children purchased more than a billion dollars worth of stamps and bonds—an average of $21 per child per year—and Boy and Girl Scouts helped sell another $8 billion worth. As Morgenthau had foreseen, there was no better way to "make the country war-minded."

Through all these means—and others—the huge gap between the fighting men abroad and Americans secure at home was partially bridged. With Edward R. Murrow broadcasting from a flying fortress on a bomb raid over Berlin, movies like *This Is the Army* and *Thirty Seconds over Tokyo* conveying some of the spirit of army life, and songs such as "They're Going to be Playing Taps on the Japs" to inject scornful humor, there was little chance that Americans would forget what was going on overseas. But in the long run, what took place in America's factories, families, and cities at home would have as much to do with the war effort—and the future—as what occurred on the battlefield.

Mobilizing the Economy

World War II ended the depression and created the framework for the next thirty years of economic development. Notwithstanding the achievements of the New Deal, the American economy remained almost moribund at the end of the 1930s. Although unemployment had fallen from 25 to 17 percent, the depression, in many respects, reached a nadir in 1938 with unexpected new layoffs and another round of economic instability. Moreover, the New Deal itself appeared dead, the Roosevelt coalition broken, with neither optimism nor new ideas for reversing a decade of suffering.

Almost overnight, the defense crisis changed all that. Under the impact of the Nazi invasion of Poland and the Blitzkrieg against Belgium, Holland, and France in the spring of 1940, military preparedness spending skyrocketed, reaching almost $75 million a day by December 1941. Within two years the federal budget alone was larger than the total Gross National Product (GNP) a decade earlier. Unemployment was virtually eliminated as workers flocked to new jobs—17 million of them during the war—and for the first time, Keynesian economics (the use of deficit spending to prime the economy during periods of economic downturn) were put into practice. With half of wartime expenditures funded by borrowing, the economy boomed and capital investment reached a new height.

Nowhere was the miracle of wartime production more clear than in the aircraft and shipbuilding industries. On the eve of Pearl Harbor, America had fewer than three thousand military planes, most of them outmoded. When President Roosevelt announced a wartime goal of fifty thousand planes a year, most people accused him of indulging in fantasy. Yet between Pearl Harbor and D-Day, U.S. aircraft factories built nearly seventy thousand planes per year, supplying not only United States needs, but those of Great Britain and the Soviet Union as well. A similar transformation occurred in shipbuilding. When the war began, experts hoped at best that the shipping industry could produce one ship every six months. By 1943 the Kaiser Company—brought into existence by the war—had reduced the time to fifty-six days, with one Liberty ship even being completed in fourteen days. By the end of the war Kaiser was launching a new ship every twelve days.

The military crisis also produced rapid-fire breakthroughs in productivity and technology. With cost-plus contracts guaranteeing all expenses paid, industries poured millions into research and technology. New industries like those manufacturing synthetic rubber sprung up almost overnight. Electronics and chemical companies surged forward in response to new demands, and increased mechanization led to record levels of productivity. According to economic models based on nineteenth-century experience, it was assumed that productivity would increase only one-third as fast as capital expenditure. But between 1909 and 1949, productivity increased more than three times as fast, or nine times the overall anticipated rate. Much of this change occurred during World War II, in large part because of new technology and investment.

All these changes benefited mostly those who already occupied a dominant position in the economy. Companies like Kaiser and Boeing thrived. As "dollar a year" executives came to Washington to run the war production agencies, the corporations from which they came boomed. One hundred companies received $160 billion of the $240 billion spent on war contracts, and ten companies received 30 percent of the total. In 1943 Kaiser alone was producing 30 percent of the total national output in defense building.

But large corporations were not the only ones to benefit from wartime prosperity. Mobilization of the economy also brought unprecedented gains for American workers. In 1941, forty percent of all American families lived on less than the $1,500 per year defined as necessary for a modest standard of living by the Works Progress Administration. Almost 8 million workers earned below the legal minimum wage, and the median income nationwide was only $2,000 per year.

Suddenly, all that changed. Between 1939 and 1944 salaries and wages more than doubled. Although the wartime boom produced inflation—food prices, for example, rose 47 percent between 1939 and 1943—it also generated a massive increase in earnings. Overtime pay and the expansion of jobs led to a 70 percent increase in average weekly earnings during the war. In those areas most affected by mobilization average incomes skyrocketed—

from $2,207 to $5,208 in Hartford, $2,227 to $5,316 in Washington, D.C., $2,031 to $3,469 in Los Angeles.

Trade unions flourished as well, contributing to—and benefiting from—wartime prosperity. After the disastrous labor decade of the 1920s, national union membership had fallen to 2.5 million. During the New Deal, however, unions fought back with the 1935 Wagner Act, which provided government protection for labor activists. Led by the Congress of Industrial Organization (CIO), workers sat in at factories and successfully organized such industries as steel, automobiles, and electronics. As a result union membership swelled to 10 million by 1940. Still, wartime gains were themselves amazing. Between 1941 and 1945 membership in organized labor leaped by 50 percent to nearly 15 million workers. Because the War Labor Board sought labor-management peace, new workers were tacitly encouraged to participate in existing labor organizations, thereby receiving all the benefits of union membership, including higher wages, better fringe benefits, and the better working conditions being negotiated by union leadership. Under the protective umbrella of the War Labor Board, trade unions achieved a new level of power and influence—at least for the duration of the fighting.

Although not typical, the Jahco plant in Cleveland represented the model of what a unionized work force could enjoy under enlightened management. Because of ample fringe benefits such as free meals, medical care, and recreational facilities, workers seemed happy on the job and the absentee rate was almost nonexistent. The opportunity for abundant overtime at higher wages created a situation where some workers took home as much as $7,600 per year. Clearly, not all factories offered the benefits or demanded the hours of the Jahco plant. Nevertheless, with full employment, higher wages, and social welfare benefits provided under government regulations, American workers experienced a level of well-being that, for many, had never occurred before.

Not surprisingly, the new prosperity immediately affected spending for entertainment and consumer goods. The average purchase at department stores increased fivefold, from $2 before the war to $10 in 1944. Nightclub income leaped 35 percent, sales of playing cards surged by up to 1,000 percent, and attendance at horse races scaled new heights, with New Yorkers in 1944 betting an average of $2.2 million per day. Advertisers seized the occasion of the war to identify their products with the country's struggle against the axis. Formfit bras, one sales pitch said, were perfect "for the *support* you need [during] these hectic days of added responsibility." As a result of the new prosperity, consumer expenditures increased nearly 50 percent, from $61.7 billion at the beginning of the war to $98.5 billion by 1944.

But the most notable reality of wartime was the relative absence of consumer goods because of wartime rationing. By the spring of 1942 the Office of Price Administration (OPA) had started restricting the availability of 90 percent of the goods sold in more than 600,000 retail stores across the country. Everyone was exhorted to save. Tires, gas, sugar, coffee—all were rationed. Government rules controlled the fabric used in dresses, the leather used in shoes, and the rubber used in undergarments. One ad declared: "No girdle required for this dress of tobacco brown spun rayon, with no fastenings (zippers gone to war), adjustable at waist and bust." From the point of view of the *Wall Street Journal*, sometimes less was better. "The two piece bathing suit now is tied in with the war as closely as a zipperless dress and the pleatless skirt." Everyone complained, and black market operations—selling restricted goods at exorbitant prices illegally—allegedly affected one out of every five stores in the country. But rationing had the positive impact of giving people on the homefront a sense of investment in the war, as well as storing up for future use an endless demand for goods that were "out of stock for the duration."

Indeed, perhaps the greatest consequence of wartime prosperity was not the standard of living it produced during the war, but what it portended for future economic development. For the first time—and as it would turn out, the only time in the twentieth century—a redistribution of income took place during the war years toward greater equality, with the top 5 percent of the nation's wage earners declining in their share of total income (from 22 to 17 percent) and the bottom 40 percent increasing their share of the pie. Just as important, liquid savings skyrocketed, increasing by nearly 300 percent from May 1941 to March 1945. By the end of the war $140 billion was available for spending, as opposed to $50 billion at the time of Pearl Harbor. For the first time that many families could remember, money was available to purchase homes, automobiles, refrigerators—all the things that for over a decade had seemed beyond reach.

None of this economic transformation, of course, took place without stress, dislocation, and pain. To secure new jobs, millions of people left home. By March 1945 the Census Bureau estimated that at least 15.3 million people were living in counties different from those in which they resided on Pearl Harbor Day. As migrants poured into places like Mobile County, Alabama, Detroit, Chicago, or Newport News, facilities burst under the pressure. Without available housing, a whole series of "New Hoovervilles"—trailer camps, tent settlements, shanty towns—sprung up to house the homeless. In towns like Mobile, people slept in "hot beds" for eight-hour shifts, moving on to make room for the next customer. Washington witnessed such an influx of people that hotels placed a three-day limit on the time a guest could stay. Educational facilities collapsed under the influx of migrants, juvenile delinquency increased 56 percent, and thousands wondered why they had left home and friends for the alienation and anxiety of new and strange social settings.

But if these were the consequences of having a steady paycheck and being able to dream of a better life, most people were willing to pay the price. The war had brought, for the moment at least, a conclusion to want

and unemployment. For millions more, the war brought something else—
a sense of possibility and optimism for the first time in a generation.

Women

No class of people experienced more change as a consequence of the war
than American women. All through the 1930s, government, labor, and business officials had preached that women workers should return to the home
to guarantee stability in society and an income for male breadwinners.
Women teachers who married were fired, federal legislation prohibited
more than one member of the same family from working in the civil service,
and 82 percent of the respondents to a Gallup Poll declared that wives
should not be employed if their husbands worked. As *McCall's* magazine argued, only as a wife and mother could the American woman "arrive at her
true eminence."

Now, suddenly, the mood shifted. The eruption of hostilities abroad
generated an unprecedented demand for new workers to replace men gone
to fight the war. In response, over 6 million women took jobs, increasing the
size of the female labor force by 57 percent. Wages leaped upward, the
number of wives holding jobs doubled, and the unionization of women
grew fourfold. Instead of frowning on women who worked, government
and the mass media embarked on an all-out effort to encourage them to
enter the labor force. As one OWI filmstrip declared: "men are needed at
the battlefront. Women are needed at the homefront. Men are needed with
minds clear and hands steady. Women are needed with attention for their
work undivided." Acknowledging that "getting these women into industry is
a tremendous sales proposition," the head of the War Manpower Commission directed defense agencies to make an all-out effort to secure women
employees. Rosie the Riveter became a national heroine, and almost every
issue of national publications contained some laudatory article on women's
war contribution, praising a woman parachute maker in California, a female taxi driver, or a woman pilot. "Woman power!" one ad announced.
"The power to create, and sustain life. The power to inspire men to bravery,
to give security to little children, a limitless, ever-flowing source of moral
and physical energy—working—for victory! *That* is woman power!"

Women responded to the labor crisis with skill and ingenuity. A former
beautician became a switch woman for six hundred Long Island railroad
trains. In Gary, Indiana, women operated giant overhead cranes and
cleaned blast furnaces. A former cosmetics saleswoman from Philadelphia
worked with a 1700-ton keel binder. Women maintained road beds, greased
locomotives, and took the place of lumberjacks toppling giant redwoods.
Those who did not go directly into war industry found other ways of helping, from the grandmothers who took over the police radio in Montgomery

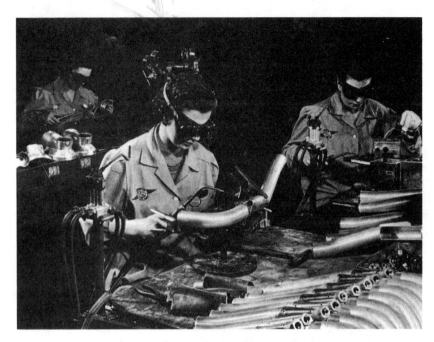

Women did work previously limited to men only as the labor crisis intensified during the war. Here women are welding aluminum alloy parts in a munitions factory. *(National Archives)*

County, Maryland, to the two thousand volunteers who helped save a million gallon strawberry crop in Tennessee.

The greatest changes, inevitably, occurred in those areas where war industries were concentrated. In Detroit the female labor force soared from 182,000 to 387,000, in San Francisco from 138,000 to 275,000. A few months after Germany invaded Poland, a total of 36 women were involved in the construction of ships. By December 1942 over 160,000 were employed welding hatches, riveting gun emplacements, and binding keels. When the Women's Bureau visited seven airplane factories in April 1941, it found 143 women employees. Eighteen months later, the same seven plants employed over 65,000 women. Nearly one million women went to work for Uncle Sam alone, most of them doing clerical work with the War Department and other agencies. By the end of the war they comprised 38 percent of all federal workers, more than twice the percentage of the last prewar year.

Patriotism offered one reason for joining the labor force, higher wages and occupational mobility another. War industries, for example, attracted almost 700,000 women from other occupations. The assembly line of one airplane factory represented a composite of the female population. Former salespeople worked alongside filing clerks, stenographers beside seamstresses. One Women's Bureau survey showed that two-thirds of women who had held jobs in eating and drinking establishments at the beginning of the war had transferred to other work by the end. Over six hundred laundries were forced to shut down in 1942 because they could not find women who were willing to shake clothes and run hot steam irons. Indeed, wages in munitions plants and aircraft factories ran an average of 40 percent higher than those in nondefense factories. A woman shipbuilder in Mobile took home $37 a week, a saleswoman $21, and a waitress $14. Not surprisingly, over half the women employed in Mobile in 1940 had changed jobs by 1944.

Perhaps the most important change brought by the war was in the demographic characteristics of the new recruits to the labor force. If it was significant that women were doing jobs that they had never performed before, it was even more important that most of them were married and middle-aged. From the very beginning of industrialization, the average employed woman was young, single, and poor. Now working women more and more frequently were married and middle-aged. By the end of the war it was just as likely that a wife over forty would be employed as a single woman under twenty-five. Almost 75 percent of those who took jobs for the first time during the war were married. Over 60 percent were over thirty-five. By the end of the war, wives for the first time comprised almost the majority of women workers. Indeed, nearly 4 million of the 6.5 million women who joined the labor force during the war listed themselves as former housewives, many of them with children of school or preschool age.

All of this led some observers to conclude that a revolution had occurred. *Life* magazine editorialized that "the status of women in America, which was changing fast enough before the war, is changing with lightning speed during it." Margaret Hickey, head of the Women's Advisory Committee to the War Manpower Commission, declared that "employers, like other individuals, are finding it necessary to weigh old values, old institutions, in terms of a world at war." At the height of the depression, over 80 percent of the American people had strongly opposed work by married women. By 1942, in contrast, 60 percent believed that wives should be employed in war industries and 71 percent asserted that there was a need for more married women to take jobs. "In the long years ahead," Erwin Canham of the *Christian Science Monitor* wrote, "we will remember these short years of ordeal as a period when women rose to full stature." Echoing the same theme, labor leader Jennie Matyas declared: "We are building up an entirely different social climate . . . what we didn't consider the nice thing to do after the last war will become the regular thing to do after this one."

But if there were reasons for celebrating progress, there were others, just as powerful, for remaining skeptical. Despite breakthroughs in war industries and skilled jobs of all kinds, discrimination continued almost unabated. The Army refused to commission women doctors until 1943, and an act of Congress was required to correct the injustice. In most factories, women worked in sex-segregated occupations, particularly those that involved more menial, routinized work. Almost without exception, women were excluded from the top policymaking bodies involved in running the war. Although a Women's Advisory Committee was appointed as an adjunct to the War Manpower Commission, it had little influence. All the decisions affecting women were made in a group composed entirely of men, and there seemed ample justification for Mary Anderson's conclusion that the WAC had been created as a calculated device to put women "off in a corner" while denying them any real power. "You can [only] make yourself felt . . . if you are where a thing happens," one WAC member observed, "[and] they apparently don't happen [here]."

A double standard was also obvious in the area of wages. Although the War Manpower Commission urged a uniform pay scale for women and men and the National War Labor Board (NWLB) endorsed the principle of equal pay in 1942, the policy was rarely implemented. One company was allowed to pay women less than men for the same work because the women were given an extra rest period. In another case the board determined that equal pay did not apply to jobs that were "historically" women's. (This, of course, was ultimately the cause of the problem since occupational segregation—by sex—served as the primary source, and rationale, for low wages for women.) Employers also had great flexibility in devising ways to avoid the equal pay principle. General Motors, for example, paid women less than men simply by substituting the categories "heavy" and "light" for "male" and "female." When the Brooklyn Navy Yard began to use women to replace men, it called them "helper trainees" instead of "mechanic learners" and assigned them a lower wage. As a result, in 1945 as in 1940, women who were employed in manufacturing earned only 65 percent of what men received.

Besides job pay, another area central to securing equality for women involved the provision of child-care centers and community services for women workers. Only if women had some assistance in carrying forward two full-time jobs would it be possible for them to function independently and as equals in the labor force. Moreover, the absence of such services proved detrimental to the war effort. For every two women workers hired in war production factories in June 1943, one quit. A 1943 survey of war plants showed that 40 percent of all women who left work cited marital, household, and associated difficulties as the reason, but only 9 percent spoke of poor wages or working conditions. In another study, the National Industrial Conference Board reported that, after illness, family needs ranked as the cause most often given for women's absenteeism.

The issue of child-care centers crystallized the problem. The War Manpower Commission estimated in 1943 that as many as 2 million youngsters needed some form of assistance. Surveys of Buffalo, San Diego, Los Angeles, and Baltimore established that 25 percent of the new members of the female labor force had at least one child that required supervision during the day. In Washington, government officials concluded that 2 million working hours a year were lost in federal agencies as a result of women who stayed home to care for children who were sick or in need of assistance.

Starkly, the West Coast Air Production Council summarized the consequences for the war effort: "One child care center adds up to eight thousand man-hours a month, and ten weeks is equal to one four-engine bomber. Lack of twenty-five child-care centers can cost ten bombers a month."

But the idea of child-care centers violated some of the most powerful underlying values of American culture. Although war production officials pushed for the employment of all women, including mothers of small children, many policymakers agreed with the Children's Bureau when it declared that "A mother's primary duty is to her home and children. This duty is one that she cannot lay aside, no matter what the emergency." "We have what amounts to a national policy," one WPA official declared, "that the best service a mother can do is to rear her children in the home." New York Mayor Fiorello La Guardia agreed, declaring in 1943 that the worst mother was better than the best nursery. Summarizing such attitudes, the Women's Bureau observed that "in this time of crisis . . . mothers of young children can make no finer contribution to the strength of the nation than to assure their children the security of the home, individual care and affection."

Largely because of the strength of such values, the government proved reluctant to embark quickly on a program of community services and child-care centers. When Lanham Act funds for the construction of wartime facilities were finally allocated to build and operate day-care centers in 1943, bureaucratic squabbles, ideological conflicts, and citizen ambivalence prevented the program from ever becoming effective. At its high point, the government's child-care program provided supervision for only 10 percent of the children needing it—offering care to only one-third the number of children cared for in Great Britain, a country with less than half the population of the United States. Thus, in an area crucial to any long-term progress toward sex equality, little change occurred.

Nor was there significant evidence of commitment to sex equality on the part of official leaders. "We know that actual equality under the law for men and women is not wholly possible," the Women's Bureau declared in 1944, "because the sexes are not equal biologically or functionally." Supporting the same position, Secretary of Labor Frances Perkins declared that "legal equality . . . between the sexes is not possible because men and women are not identical in physical structure or social function, and therefore their needs cannot be identical." Ironically, women government officials frequently invoked traditional stereotypes of women to explain and justify their employment. "Women adapt themselves readily to repetitive jobs requiring constant alertness, if not skill," Mary Anderson of the Women's Bureau declared. "Women excel at processes of a painstaking or repetitive nature—those requiring finger dexterity—the ability to stick at a tedious job without flagging." It was perhaps not surprising, then, that a 1945 Women's Bureau position paper denounced "the extreme feminists . . . who seek to nourish grievances and create sex antagonism" and called them

Even as women took on dramatically different economic roles during the war, government propagandists attempted to persuade the women—and the country at large—that no basic shift was occurring and that women were simply carrying out in a new location their traditional roles. The text accompanying this photograph, for example, read: "Dishwashing. One woman dries while the other washes. Parts being cleaned for welding do for dishes and the 'sink' is full of Oakite." The photograph is part of the "Women's Work Is Just Like In The Home" series of the Women's Bureau. *(National Archives)*

"a small but militant group of leisure class women [giving vent] to their resentment at not having been born men."

The balance sheet on women's experience during the war was thus uneven. Millions had taken jobs that otherwise would never have been available. Most found they enjoyed the experience. Looked at from one perspective, the results were revolutionary. As Elinor Herrick declared,

"Women must get it out of their heads [that they belong in the home]. We are in the throes of a stupendous social revolution. Because of their work in the war, [women] will come to feel that they are socially useful. They will want to continue that feeling of independence." Looked at from another perspective, however, the persistence of inequality in wages, the absence of opportunities in executive positions, the failure to provide child-care and community services, and the perpetuation of traditional definitions of women's place suggested that the wartime experience might well prove to be a temporary hiatus in a long-term pattern of continued oppression. Clearly, some changes had begun. What was less clear was whether, when the war came to an end, they would persist.

Black Americans

The war also brought massive changes to American blacks. As late as 1940, 75 percent of all blacks lived in the rural South. During the next decade, more than 2 million moved to northern and western industrial areas. During the 1930s, lynching not only still occurred in the South, but frequently failed even to elicit condemnation from federal officials. A decade later, antiblack terrorism still took place, but no longer did the White House keep silent. Throughout the depression, virtually no one challenged a "separate but equal" educational system that allocated three times as many dollars to white pupils as to black pupils. By the end of the 1940s, however, Jim Crow schools increasingly came under direct attack. Although the record was mixed, World War II served as a crucial catalyst aiding black Americans in their long struggle for freedom.

Black determination to challenge white racism first became obvious with the March on Washington Movement (MOWM) in 1941 led by A. Philip Randolph. For years, Randolph had labored—ultimately with success—to construct an all-black trade union. As head of the Brotherhood of Sleeping Car Porters union, Randolph knew what organization was all about. Now he insisted that black Americans challenge the employment policies of the federal government and demand equal treatment in the work force, particularly in defense industries. "I suggest that ten thousand Negroes march on Washington," he declared. "WE LOYAL NEGRO AMERICANS DEMAND THE RIGHT TO WORK AND FIGHT FOR OUR COUNTRY." Threatening to bring his marchers to the capital in the midst of a congressional debate on military preparedness, Randolph brilliantly used the lever of the war crisis to drive home his demands. In response, Roosevelt promulgated Executive Order 8802 in June 1941, establishing the President's Committee on Fair Employment Practices (FEPC) "to receive and investigate complaints of discrimination" so that "there shall be no discrimination in the employment of workers in defense industries or government because of race, creed, color, or national origin."

As a result of the wartime crisis, black employment increased dramatically. The number of black workers in shipyards leaped from 6,000 to 14,000, in aircraft factories from 0 to 5,000, in government service from 60,000 to 200,000. Overall, the number of Negroes employed in manufacturing grew from 500,000 to 1.2 million, with the proportion of blacks in the iron and steel industries growing to more than 25 percent. Black women in particular experienced change. During the 1930s over 70 percent of employed black women worked as domestic servants in private homes. Now, in response to the call for new workers, over 400,000 domestics left their former jobs. The number of black women who held positions as servants fell from 72 percent to 48 percent, while the proportion who were employed as operators in factories grew from 7.3 percent to 18.6 percent. Overall, the number of blacks employed as skilled craftsmen and foremen doubled from 1940 to 1944, as did black membership in labor unions.

But there was a negative side as well, all the more powerful given the promise of equal opportunity. Thirteen national trade unions, including some of the most powerful in the country, excluded blacks from membership. Despite some improvement in job opportunities, most openings were at low levels, with blacks primarily hired as janitors or scrubwomen rather than as technicians, secretaries, or skilled craftsmen. Indeed, when attempts were made to upgrade black employees, whites frequently rebelled, as when twenty thousand white workers in Mobile walked off their jobs and rioted when efforts were made to hire twelve blacks as welders in a shipyard. A similar strike occurred when the Philadelphia Transit Company upgraded eight black porters to the rank of driver. Overall, the proportion of blacks holding decent jobs in manufacturing and mechanical positions rose to 8 percent—but that figure was only 0.7 percent higher than it had been prior to the depression.

Even the FEPC represented, at least in retrospect, a hollow concession. The agency lacked all enforcement power and served primarily the purposes of exhortation and propaganda. The FEPC budget was only $80,000, its leadership proved less than assertive, and it received little support from the White House. On one occasion administration officials advised the FEPC not to publish a summary of hearings on discrimination, leaving enforcement to "private persuasion." Throughout, the administration emphasized the importance of filling labor needs as quickly as possible, even if that involved sanctioning racial prejudice. The FEPC failed to persuade Southern railroads to hire blacks as engineers or conductors, and even proved ineffective in securing integration of blacks on the transit system in Washington, D.C. Overall, the agency resolved successfully only 20 percent of the complaints brought to it from the South.

The same paradox of small progress in the midst of massive racism existed in the Armed Forces as well. There, the struggle was perhaps the hardest. Although blacks enlisted at a rate 60 percent higher than their proportion of the population, they met immediate segregation and prejudice.

When blacks in Tennessee demanded that the governor appoint Negroes to the State Draft Board, he responded: "This is a white man's country . . . the Negro had nothing to do with the settling of America." Training camps, especially in the South, became infamous for their persecution of blacks. When an on-duty Negro MP was shot by a white law-enforcement officer, a local jury found the sheriff innocent. A black private at Fort Benning, Georgia, was lynched; military officials refused to act when a black Army nurse was brutally beaten for defying Jim Crow seating on a Montgomery, Alabama, bus; and religious services were segregated, the sign at one base proclaiming separate worship for "Catholics, Jews, Protestants, and Negroes."

Stories of racism were legion. The Red Cross, for example, segregated "white" and "colored" bottles of blood plasma (ignoring the fact that a black scientist, Dr. Charles Drew, had perfected the method of preserving blood plasma). Congressman John Rankin of Mississippi denounced "the crackpots, the communists, and the parlor pinks of this country" for attempting to change the labeling system so that "it will not show whether it is Negro blood or white blood. That seems to be one of the schemes of these fellow travellers to try to mongrelize this nation." A comparable example of stupidity occurred when black soldiers entered a lunch room in Salina, Kansas. "You boys know we don't serve colored here," the manager said. Indeed, the soldiers did know. So they just stood there "inside the door, staring at what we had come to see—German prisoners of war who were having lunch at the counter. . . . It was no jive talk. The people of Salinas served these enemy soldiers and turned away black American GI's."

But even in the armed services, a few positive changes occurred. Despite Secretary of War Henry Stimson's conviction that "leadership is not imbedded in the Negro race yet," more and more blacks were trained for combat positions, some integration took place on an experimental basis, and the Army agreed to train black pilots. Above all, thousands upon thousands experienced a taste of life without prejudice, particularly in places like France and Hawaii. If nothing else, government propaganda that emphasized America's fight against racism abroad helped to highlight the hypocrisy of racism at home, and the need to struggle against it.

Change also came as a consequence of the accelerated migration of blacks from the South, and within the South from farm to city. Whether lured by a specific job in a munitions plant, ordered by a directive from the selective service, or simply beckoned by the hope of a better life elsewhere, hundreds of thousands of blacks boarded trains and buses and headed north and west. When they arrived at their destination, they found living situations often less attractive than they had expected. The urban ghetto, with its overcrowded housing, hard-pressed social facilities, and oppressive discrimination, was not much better than what they had left behind. Yet there was also a difference. A Northern urban political machine sought votes and offered some political recognition in return. There was more psychological space, more opportunity to talk freely. The community was new, the imminent tyranny of small-town authority was removed, and different ground rules applied. The very act of physical mobility brought independence from the overwhelming social constraints that had been enforced in small rural Southern communities. If racist control still existed in new forms, there was now at least the possibility of a different response, as well as a heightened sense of what might be done to achieve a better life.

Significantly, all these changes exhibited a common theme: the interaction of some improvement together with daily reminders of ongoing oppression. The chemistry of the process was crucial. Simultaneous with new exposure to travel, the prospect of better jobs, and higher expectations came the reality of day-to-day contact with Jim Crow in the Armed Forces, housing, and on the job. The juxtaposition could not help but spawn anger and frustration. The possibility of some improvement generated the expectation for still more, and when those expectations were dashed, a rising tide of protest resulted.

The racial situation in Detroit encapsulated the entire process. As blacks migrated north to the nation's leading industrial city, they met constant frustration and discrimination. At almost a third of the war plants in the city, fewer than one percent of the employees were black. When three black workers were promoted at one factory, three thousand whites walked out in protest. Housing was virtually impossible to find, and blacks were forced to crowd together in Paradise Valley, the black slum, where rents were high, housing substandard, and recreation almost impossible to find. (According to a 1941 survey, 50 percent of all black dwellings were substandard in contrast to only 14 percent of white dwellings.) When blacks finally were given some space at the Sojourner Truth Homes—a new housing project—they had to be protected by troops. It was not surprising, then, that on a hot summer day in 1943, the racial situation exploded. Whites started to stone a black swimmer at Belle Isle Park when he wandered into the white swimming area. As rumors spread of murderous attacks by each race on the other, violence swept the city until hundreds were injured, more than seventy killed, and federal troops were called out—too late—to quell the killing and looting.

To many, the Detroit race riots symbolized not only the rawness of race relations in America, but also a new spirit of militancy and assertiveness among American blacks. War had provided a forge within which anger and outrage, long suppressed, were seeking new expression. The searing contradiction between the rhetoric of fighting for democracy and the reality of racism at home galvanized black anger. "Our war is not against Hitler and Europe," one black columnist proclaimed, "but against the Hitlers in America." Another black wrote to the president: "If there is such a thing as God he must be a white person, according to the conditions we colored people are in . . . . Hitler has not done anything to the colored people—it's the people right here in the United States who are keeping us out of work and keeping us down." Epitomizing the ideological irony at the heart of America's war was a slogan that circulated among black draftees: "Here lies a black man killed fighting a yellow man for the glory of a white man."

In the face of such absurdity, black protest mounted. Local NAACP chapters tripled in number, while national membership increased 900 percent to over 500,000 people. As black newspapers took up the cry for a "Double V" campaign—victory at home as well as victory abroad—their circulation increased by 40 percent. Roy Wilkins of the NAACP returned from a visit to North Carolina declaring that "Negroes are organizing all over the state to secure their rights. They are not frightened." In Washington, D.C., an interracial group of students began to sit-in at restaurants and picket against segregation. "We die together," their signs read. "Let's eat together." As if to illustrate the changes that were occurring, Southern black leaders meeting in Durham, North Carolina, in October 1942 demanded complete equality for the Negro in American life. "We are fundamentally opposed to the principle and practice of compulsory segregation in our American society," the Durham meeting declared. Ten years earlier such a statement would have been inconceivable.

It was too soon to say what it all meant. Certainly, administration officials offered no reason for optimism. Roosevelt's general approach was embodied in a statement by the Office of War Information that "the long-range problems of racial and minority-majority antagonisms cannot be settled during the war. . . . The war must be won first." The president himself failed to endorse abolition of the poll tax, refused to have the Justice Department join the legal challenge to the "white primary," and after the Supreme Court had invalidated such techniques of disfranchisement, refused to instruct his Attorney General to prosecute vigorously those who sought to enact new obstacles to voting rights. As the historian Harvard Sitkoff has observed, "to Roosevelt, the Negro had always remained an unfortunate ward of the nation—to be treated kindly with charity as a reward for good behavior." But there was clearly a new air of militancy abroad in the land, and as black protest built on the anxiety generated by racial violence in Detroit and Harlem, some white and black leaders began talking together about the need to develop a legislative and political coalition that would seek, through gradual change, to address the long overdue issue of racial injustice.

Other Minorities

Tragically, other minorities fared even less well than black Americans. Japanese citizens experienced the most grotesque forms of injustice. After Pearl Harbor, rumors of conspiracy and sabotage spread through the country. One story told of Japanese-American fishing trawlers that were mining harbors, another of Japanese farmers poisoning vegetables on truck farms. As Japanese troops advanced across the Pacific, paranoia in the United

States mounted about "the enemy within." "A Jap is a Jap," one general said in early 1942. "It makes no difference whether he is an American citizen or not . . . I don't want any of them. . . . There is no way to determine their loyalty." Given the hysteria that prevailed, the absence of any sabotage became, in a perverted way, evidence of how clever the Japanese were in plotting their ultimate attack.

In the face of such emotion, pressure increased to remove the Japanese from other Americans, to isolate them somewhere away from strategic areas, and to incarcerate them for the duration. "Herd 'em up, pack 'em off . . . let 'em be pinched, hurt, hungry," wrote one columnist. More than 90 percent of the 127,000 Japanese-Americans lived on the West Coast. And it was California leaders who led the outcry for their removal, including—to his everlasting regret—California Attorney General Earl Warren. Responding to political and military pressure, President Roosevelt issued Executive Order 9066 on February 19, 1942, authorizing the relocation of Japanese Americans to areas removed from positions of military vulnerability. The military justification: "The continued pressure of a large, unassimilated, tightly knit racial group, bound to an enemy nation by strong ties of race, culture, custom and religion along a frontier vulnerable to attack, constituted a menace which had to be dealt with."

Within two months, more than 100,000 Japanese-Americans were relocated in America's own version of concentration camps. The victims— 47,000 Issei, Japanese who were ineligible for naturalization under the immigration act of 1924, and 80,000 Nisei, Japanese-Americans born in the United States—were forced to leave behind or sell cheaply their possessions, gather together at removal stations, and board trains and buses for the internment centers. Although some newspapers insisted that the Japanese-Americans were "coddled" and "pampered," life in the concentration camps was bleak. In one Wyoming center, 11,000 people were gathered in 456 barracks. A barbed wire fence surrounded the camp, and watchtowers at each corner kept the prisoners under surveillance. There were no private toilets, no private dining facilities. People who had spent their lives fishing the waters of the Pacific, or toiling in the rich fields of California's greenbelt, now huddled against the wind, dust, and cold of Wyoming winters.

Although anxiety about Japanese sabotage may have been understandable in the aftermath of Pearl Harbor, there is no way to ignore the racism involved in the treatment of Japanese-Americans. Neither German- nor Italian-Americans experienced anything remotely resembling the incarceration and persecution of the Japanese. The portrayal of "Japs" in war movies, the popular songs that referred to "those little yellow bellies," and promises to slap "the Jap right off the map"—all this conveyed a flavor of racial animosity never applied to America's white adversaries. The racism embodied in Roosevelt's executive order was simply a polite version of that expressed by the governor of Idaho: "the Japs live like rats, breed like rats, and act like rats. We don't want them." Ironically, even the liberal repositories of Amer-

Dust storm at a Japanese-American "War Relocation Center" during World War II.
(Photograph by Dorothea Lange, National Archives)

ica's conscience acquiesced, including magazines like the *New Republic* and
the *Nation*. The United States, Justice Frank Murphy declared in his lonely
dissent to the Supreme Court's approval of the wartime relocation, had engaged in the "legalization of racism." There was no other way to describe it.

As the war also showed, American immigration policies were closely
bound to the state of the economy. Mexican-American farm workers had
been deported during the Depression. But war-related labor shortages on
the farms, railroads, and factories in the American West, aggravated by the
internment of Japanese Americans, forced America to open its doors again
to Hispanic immigrants. In 1942, the U.S. and Mexican governments negotiated the so-called bracero agreement to meet the growing demands of
the U.S. labor market and to alleviate poverty in Mexico. The 200,000 Mexicans who entered the United States between 1942 and 1947 as agricultural
contract laborers contributed to a rapid expansion of Mexican-American
neighborhoods in American West Coast cities. Increasing racism and discrimination against the immigrants erupted in the summer of 1943 in the
so-called zoot suit riots in Los Angeles, when American sailors attacked
gangs of second-generation Mexican Americans who showed their alienation from the dominant culture by wearing large stylish suits that flew in

the face of rules limiting the amount of wool that could be used in clothes. The zoot suit riots represented, on the one hand, Mexican-American disaffection from wartime customs and, on the other, the sailors' wish to punish a new minority for its alleged lack of patriotism.

During the war, the U.S. army and the war industry recruited both Hispanics and Native Americans. Three hundred thousand Mexican Americans and thousands of Native Americans served in combat, and Navajos were successfully employed as code talkers in the Pacific theater. With government subsidies dwindling and pressure for assimilation increasing, but also eager to contribute to the war effort, over 40,000 Native Americans—about half of the men who did not serve in the military and a fifth of the women—left their reservations for war-related work. Native American women not only worked as riveters, inspectors, and machinists in the war plants, but also began to serve as teachers in the reservations' schools. They conveyed positive messages about their traditional culture and about life outside the reservations. In support of the war effort, many Native American tribes donated money, organized fund raisers, and purchased an estimated $50 million in war bonds and stamps, a total that far exceeded the contributions of any other minority group. But the war and the opening of Native American reservations to the outside world also led to more problematic developments. Native Americans lost hundreds of thousands of acres to the military's need for bombing and gunnery ranges and were forced to comply with the government's plan to relocate Japanese Americans—nearly one-quarter of all detainees—on Native American lands.

Tragically, anti-Semitism also remained a corrosive presence in America. The FEPC found a significant pattern of employment discrimination against Jews in New York; *Fortune* magazine insisted on talking about Jewish "klannishness"; and numerous right-wing politicians defended violence against Jews in America and insisted that the war itself was a Jewish plot. "The white Gentiles of this country still have some rights left," Congressman John Rankin declared, "and should be protected from the persecution they are now compelled to endure. . . . Remember that something like 98 percent of the men who are dying on the high seas and the battlefronts of the world to protect American institutions in this war are white Gentiles."

But the most devastating impact of anti-Semitism appeared in acts of omission rather than commission. Beginning in 1942, word about Hitler's "final solution" of exterminating the Jews had become public knowledge. State Department officials in Bern, Switzerland, confirmed the mass murders of Jews in Poland and the starvation of Jews in Romania. Congress denounced the Nazi policy of genocide, American Jewish organizations held rallies demanding action, and individual leaders pleaded with people like Eleanor Roosevelt to intervene to get the State Department to do something to help those searching for a way to escape.

And there were ways to escape—not for most, but certainly for some. If America had relaxed its own visa policy, helped to provide sanctuaries for Jewish refugees in Latin America or the British Commonwealth, or offered transportation support to relocate Jewish refugees in neutral countries, thousands of lives could have been saved. In the summer of 1943, Romania offered to allow the evacuation of 70,000 Jews in return for a bribe of $170,000. Six months later, nothing had been done to implement the plan.

Although part of the problem was bureaucratic, the underlying issue was a failure of will. Assistant Secretary of State Breckinridge Long consistently obstructed efforts to facilitate a more flexible visa policy. Occasionally, Eleanor Roosevelt secured action for an individual or a few people. But the masses of Jewish refugees who might have escaped if the U.S. government had adopted a policy committed to saving lives were never given the assistance necessary. State Department officials who protested found themselves transferred or silenced. Long received backing from above, and the president himself never made the issue of saving Jews a high enough priority to insist on action. Finally, in January 1944, Roosevelt created the war refugee board that began to take some of the steps proposed eighteen months earlier. But in the meantime, indifference, prejudice, and callous racism had deprived thousands—perhaps hundreds of thousands—of a way to escape the gas chamber. The government study that documented this record of abomination was entitled appropriately: "Report to the Secretary on the Acquiescence of This Government in the Murder of the Jews."

Politics at Home

In the meantime, a different war was being waged at home for the soul of the New Deal. The high tide of reform had come in 1935–36 when the Social Security Act, the Wagner Labor Relations Act, the Holding Company Act, and the Works Progress Administration represented hallmarks of the government's concern for the poor and for social reform. Denouncing the corporate leadership of the country as "economic royalists" and "malefactors of wealth," FDR had ridden to tumultuous victory in 1936 with a promise to complete the agenda of social and economic change. Then, within two years, the New Deal coalition had fallen apart. First, a divisive battle over adding new judges to the Supreme Court had riven the New Deal coalition. Then came the unsuccessful effort in 1938 to purge Congress of reactionary members. By the late 1930s, the prospect of getting new reform legislation through Congress had become almost nonexistent. The question was whether the war would see a resumption of the social idealism associated with the mid-thirties, or the institutionalization of a new conservative ethos.

On that issue, as so many others, the record was mixed. As we have seen, the war brought significant economic progress for the average worker, as well as beneficial changes—at least for the moment—to women and some blacks. Some people even believed, in the words of *New York Herald Tribune's* Mark Sullivan, that the administration was "trying to do two things at the same time—carry on a social revolution and conduct a war." The Office of War Information frequently used pamphlets and radio programs to advance the causes of greater social equity, particularly in the area of race, and liberals like Vice-President Henry Wallace talked about the war as the occasion for carrying forward an agenda of social justice. In contrast to *Life* magazine, which viewed the "American Century" as one of American political, economic, and religious dominance, Wallace declared that "the century which will come out of this war . . . must be the century of the common man. . . . The people's revolution is on the march, and the devil and all his angels cannot prevail against it. They cannot prevail for on the side of the people is the Lord."

The 1942 congressional election, however, appeared to inaugurate a reign of conservative withdrawal from New Deal programs. Republicans picked up forty seats in the House and five in the Senate, leaving them only thirteen seats short of a majority in the lower chamber. With the President choosing a bi-partisan cabinet to wage the war, and with "dollar-a-year" business executives hurrying to Washington to manage the mobilization effort, the administration took on a conservative aura. Antitrust laws were waived, liberal leaders like Henry Wallace lost internecine wars to their conservative foes, and the president himself announced the retirement of "Dr. New Deal" so that "Dr. Win the War" could take over.

When the 78th Congress arrived in Washington in January 1943, a systematic assault against New Deal programs began. Almost immediately the Works Progress Administration and the Civilian Conservation Corps were abolished. With the onset of war, it was argued, such relief agencies no longer had a place. More difficult to justify was the assault on the Farm Security Administration (FSA), the Rural Electrification Administration (REA), and the National Youth Administration (NYA). Each had been in the vanguard of liberal change during the thirties. The FSA virtually provided the only arm of the government committed to defending the interest of poor farmers and sharecroppers. The NYA, in turn, served to train thousands of young white and black Americans who otherwise would have been without job skills or education, and represented perhaps the most progressive of all the New Deal agencies. Now, each suffered mortal blows. Congress liquidated the NYA, cut the FSA budget almost to the point of extinction, and abolished the REA.

Other progressive agencies also suffered. The domestic branch of the Office of War Information came under sharp attack for its "liberal" propaganda about social justice at home. A similar fate greeted the National Resources Planning Board (NRPB) which symbolized that part of the New Deal most committed to using long-range planning for the purpose of reconstructing society. When the NRPB published two controversial pamphlets (one called "After the War—Full Employment," the other "After the War—Toward Security"), it was denounced as a tool of socialism. The NRPB's agenda, the *Wall Street Journal* charged, represented a "totalitarian plan" to use the emergency power of war to transform America's social fabric. "There are no lengths to which these planners will not go," the paper announced. "They even propose that in time to come every American man and woman who so chooses will be a college graduate at public expense!" That clearly was too much, and the NRPB's budget was cut from $1 million to $200,000.

Organized labor also experienced setbacks. Inflamed by wartime strikes in the coal fields by John L. Lewis's United Mine Workers, Congress enacted the Smith-Connally Bill authorizing the president to seize plants where strikes interfered with wartime production. The legislation also prohibited strike activity in plants or mines seized by the government, banned political contributions by labor unions, and established a thirty-day "cooling off" period for negotiations prior to any strike. Although Roosevelt rejected the measure, it was passed handily over his veto, suggesting the degree to which Congress was tired of labor militancy.

On the other hand, New Deal liberals could take renewed sustenance from the resurgence of progressive rhetoric by Roosevelt during the last eighteen months of his life. Although he later backed down from his attack on Congress, FDR denounced the tax bill passed in 1943 as one "providing relief not to the needy, but for the greedy." The measure, he said, was "replete with provisions which not only afford special privileges for favorite groups but set dangerous precedents for the future." During the fall of 1943 the president asked Congress for substantially liberalized unemployment, Social Security, and educational benefits for veterans, and in his State of the Union message in 1944 called for "a second bill of rights under which a new basis of security and prosperity can be established for all." This "bill of rights" represented a litany of treasured New Deal priorities: useful employment, adequate earnings for food, clothing, and recreation, decent housing, protection from the fears of old age and sickness, a good education. Even Roosevelt's primary political antagonist, Wendell Willkie, seemed to endorse liberalism, advocating full protection of minorities and guarantees against unemployment. Willkie denounced the more reactionary wing of his party as "a bunch of political liabilities, anyway."

The election of 1944 seemed to offer liberals further reason for hope. After Willkie suffered a fatal heart attack, the Republicans nominated Thomas Dewey, described by one of his critics as "the boy orator of the platitude" and a man who could "strut sitting down." Roosevelt went on the attack, campaigning for his bill of rights, promising more hospitals, better airports, sixty million jobs, a permanent FEPC, better health care—in short, all the good things that the war was supposedly about. Aided by strong support from the CIO's political action committee, Roosevelt swept thirty-six states,

55 percent of the vote, and 432 electoral votes, while the Democratic Party regained twenty-two seats in the House of Representatives. Although some worried about the health of both the president and his New Deal principles, the campaign appeared to revive both. Denouncing Republicans for attacking his dog "Fala" and campaigning against Republicans as though they were all imitations of Herbert Hoover, FDR revived progressive hopes and seemed to promise that the end of the war would bring a return to the social and economic agenda of the liberal New Deal. Thus, it was a time for liberal optimism as well as concern.

Conclusion

As the American people sensed impending victory in the spring of 1945, they could not help but wonder at the massive changes that had taken place during the preceding four years, even as they approached with anxiety the unknown future of a world without a war. Factories bustled with triple shifts, and virtually every American who wanted a job was employed. Millions of people had secured a new start, a new bank account, perhaps a new family. The country had absorbed, and then overcome, one of the most severe attacks ever launched on its values and survival. So much had changed. Yet so much remained uncertain. What would happen to the economy, the family, morality, and politics in the new world that was unfolding?

The world of the family and women's role within it highlighted the uncertainties facing American society. Most of the 6 million women who took jobs during the war had believed, when they first entered the labor force, that they would joyfully resume the traditional life of homemaker when the war ended. But three years later they had changed their minds. A Women's Bureau survey of ten areas showed that 75 percent of the women who had taken jobs wished to continue working. "War jobs have uncovered unsuspected abilities in American women," one worker said in explaining her desire to remain employed. "Why lose all these abilities because of a belief that a 'woman's place is in the home.' For some it is, for others it is not."

Some observers feared that, as a consequence of wartime changes, the institution of the family would be threatened. The sociologist Willard Waller charged that women had "gotten out of hand" during the war with the result that the very survival of the home was in danger. The only solution, he asserted, was the restoration and strengthening of the patriarchal family. "Women must bear and rear children; husbands must support them." Yet would women accept such reasoning? After four years of earning their own money, performing a job valued by society, and enjoying the world of the workplace, the *Saturday Evening Post* observed, "millions of the sex are going to sniff at postwar bromides about women's place." Thus, one question facing the country as the war hurtled toward a climax was whether, as the Women's Bureau's Mary Anderson said, the nation would "meet the days to come in terms of the future, or . . . try to keep the world bound to an outworn order?"

The same issue galvanized black Americans. During the war black protest had achieved new levels of militancy. The context had changed, and as blacks moved to cities from farms, to assembly lines from custodial positions, they found new opportunities—and new reasons—to articulate their anger and insist on freedom. If the resistance to oppression had been there all along, there now was a new occasion for expressing it—through mass marches like that envisioned by A. Philip Randolph, through more aggressive court cases such as those instituted by the NAACP, through political action such as voter registration and bloc voting. No longer could Northern politicians ignore those who held the balance of power in local as well as national elections.

As Eleanor Roosevelt indicated, "a wind [is] rising throughout the world of free men everywhere, and they will not be kept in bondage." Black Americans were part of that rising wind, from Southern black leaders who readied themselves to demand the right to vote and challenge school segregation, to the returning veterans intent on claiming their full citizenship. "World War II has immeasurably magnified the Negro's awareness of the disparity between the American profession and practice of democracy," the NAACP's Walter White wrote. "The majority will return home convinced that whatever betterment of their lot is achieved must come largely through their own efforts." The unanswered question was how white America would respond.

Uncertainty also clouded the economy. During the war wages had more than doubled. Consumer expenditures increased by 50 percent, and individual savings accounts had climbed almost sevenfold. But could the economy sustain the impact of 11 million soldiers returning home? Memories of the Depression were traumatic. As *Fortune* magazine commented, "the American soldier is depression conscious . . . worried sick about post-war joblessness." Public opinion surveys showed that seven out of ten Americans expected to be personally worse off after the war, and six out of ten expected lower wages. Only 37 percent believed that their children would have a better opportunity after the war than they themselves had enjoyed.

Nowhere were postwar fears and hopes more sharply counterbalanced. With savings accounts overflowing, consumers could hardly wait to buy better radios, a new dishwasher, an automatic toaster, a car, or a house. Advertisements boasted of the good life that would come through automatic appliances, and surveys of bank depositors showed the people ready and eager to spend their savings. But what would happen if the economy collapsed, food lines resumed, and relief rolls mounted? Union membership was 50 percent higher than it had ever been before, but could labor remain strong and defend workers' interests when there no longer was a war to fight. No one knew.

All of these issues ultimately telescoped into a simple series of questions: Which direction would America follow in the postwar years, which values would it embrace, and what would it stand for? For sixteen years the country had been in crisis, preoccupied with economic disaster and military threat. Now, there was a chance for a new beginning. As the historian Allen Nevins wrote, "Americans suddenly seemed to stand, as the war closed, beholding a new heaven and a new earth, to which they somewhat dazedly tried to adjust themselves." Would the movement toward redistribution of income that had begun during the war be continued or lapse? Would the politics of the postwar years resemble Franklin Roosevelt's 1944 economic bill of rights, or the conservatism of the 78th Congress? Would America move toward new measures to correct the ancient injustices of discrimination based on race and sex, or would it resume old attitudes of neglect, racism, and complicity in oppression?

These were some of the issues on the nation's agenda as the end of the war finally came in view. It was a time of anxiety and fear. It was also a moment of possibility.

2

Origins of
the Cold War

In the spring of 1945 most American people looked to the world beyond their borders with an air of optimism. Nearly 80 percent endorsed U.S. involvement in the United Nations. Fewer than one-third anticipated another world war during the next quarter-century. Sixty-four percent expressed satisfaction with relationships among Britain, the Soviet Union, and the United States. Interestingly enough, the Soviet Union ranked higher in popularity among the American people than England.

Yet within a brief time, such optimism had vanished. In a few months, American and Soviet diplomats were waging a battle of angry words. By the spring of 1948 General Lucius Clay, the American military governor of Berlin, was warning that "war . . . may come with dramatic suddenness." President Harry Truman charged that the Soviet Union was engaged in a "ruthless course of action . . . [seeking to] extend [its rule] over Europe." By 1950, the National Security Agency—America's highest authority on military and foreign policy—concluded that the world faced a "polarization of power" in which a "slave society" was seeking to triumph over "the free." The Cold War had become a reality.

The Historical Context

The animosity of postwar Soviet-American relations drew on a deep reservoir of mutual distrust. Soviet suspicion of the United States went back to America's hostile reaction to the Bolshevik revolution itself. At the end of World War I, President Woodrow Wilson had sent more than ten thousand American soldiers as part of an expeditionary allied force to overthrow the new Soviet regime by force. When that venture failed, the United States nevertheless withheld its recognition of the Soviet government. Back in the United States, meanwhile, the fear of Marxist radicalism reached an hysterical pitch with the Red Scare of 1919–20. Attorney General A. Mitchell Palmer ordered government agents to arrest 3,000 purported members of the Communist party, and then attempted to deport them. American attitudes toward the Soviet Union seemed encapsulated in the comments of one minister who called for the removal of communists in "ships of stone with sails of lead, with the wrath of God for a breeze and with hell for their first port."

American attitudes toward the Soviet Union, in turn, reflected profound concern about Soviet violation of human rights, democratic procedures, and international rules of civility. With brutal force, Soviet leaders had imposed from above a revolution of agricultural collectivization and industrialization. Millions had died as a consequence of forced removal from their lands. Anyone who protested was killed or sent to one of the hundreds of prison camps which, in Alexander Solzhenitsyn's words, stretched across the Soviet Union like a giant archipelago. What kind of people were these, one relative of a prisoner asked, "who first decreed and then carried out this mass destruction of their own kind?" Furthermore, Soviet foreign policy seemed committed to the spread of revolution to other countries, with international coordination of subversive activities placed in the hands of the Comintern. It was difficult to imagine two more different societies.

For a brief period after the United States granted diplomatic recognition to the Soviet Union in 1933, a new spirit of cooperation prevailed. But by the end of the 1930s suspicion and alienation had once again become dominant. From a Soviet perspective, the United States seemed unwilling to join collectively to oppose the Japanese and German menace. On two occasions, the United States had refused to act in concert against Nazi Germany. When Britain and France agreed at Munich to appease Adolph Hitler, the Soviets gave up on any possibility of allied action against Germany and talked of a capitalist effort to encircle and destroy the Soviet regime.

Yet from a Western perspective, there seemed little basis for distinguishing between Soviet tyranny and Nazi totalitarianism. Between 1936 and 1938 Stalin engaged in his own holocaust, sending up to 6 million Soviet citizens to their deaths in massive purge trials. Stalin "saw enemies everywhere," his daughter later recalled, and with a vengeance frightening in its irrationality, sought to destroy them. It was an "orgy of terror," one historian said. Diplomats saw high officials tapped on the shoulder in public places, removed from circulation, and then executed. Foreigners were subject to constant surveillance. It was as if, George Kennan noted, outsiders were representatives of "the devil, evil and dangerous, and to be shunned."

On the basis of such experience, many Westerners concluded that Hitler and Stalin were two of a kind, each reflecting a blood-thirsty obsession with power no matter what the cost to human decency. "Nations, like individuals," Kennan said in 1938, "are largely the products of their environment." As Kennan perceived it, the Soviet personality was neurotic, conspiratorial, and untrustworthy. Such impressions were only reinforced when Stalin suddenly announced a nonaggression treaty with Hitler in August 1939, co-attacked Poland with Hitler in September, and later that year invaded the small, neutral state of Finland. It seemed that Stalin and Hitler deserved each other. Hence, the reluctance of some to change their attitudes toward the Soviet Union when suddenly, in June 1941, Germany invaded Russia and Stalin became "Uncle Joe."

Compounding the problem of historical distrust was the different way in which the two nations viewed foreign policy. Ever since John Winthrop had spoken of Boston in 1630 as "a city upon a hill" that would serve as a beacon for the world, Americans had tended to see themselves as a chosen people with a distinctive mission to impart their faith and values to the rest of humankind. Although all countries attempt to put the best face possible on their military and diplomatic actions, Americans have seemed more committed than most to describing their involvement in the world as pure and altruistic. Hence, even ventures like the Mexican War of 1846–48— clearly provoked by the United States in an effort to secure huge land masses—were defended publicly as the fulfillment of a divine mission to extend American democracy to those deprived of it.

Reliance on the rhetoric of moralism was never more present than during America's involvement in World War I. Despite its official posture of neutrality, the United States had a vested interest in the victory of England and France over Germany. America's own military security, her trade lines with England and France, economic and political control over Latin America and South America—all would best be preserved if Germany were defeated. Moreover, American banks and munition makers had invested millions of dollars in the allied cause. Nevertheless, the issue of national self-interest rarely if ever surfaced in any presidential statement during the war. Instead, U.S. rhetoric presented America's position as totally idealistic in nature. The United States entered the war, President Wilson declared, not for reasons of economic self-interest, but to "make the world safe for democracy." Our purpose was not to restore a balance of power in Europe, but to fight a war that would "end all wars" and produce "a peace without victory." Rather than seek a sphere of influence for American power, the United States instead declared that it sought to establish a new form of internationalism based on self-determination for all peoples, freedom of the seas, the end of all economic barriers between nations, and development of a new international order based on the principles of democracy.

America's historic reluctance to use arguments of self-interest as a basis for foreign policy undoubtedly reflected a belief that, in a democracy, people would not support foreign ventures inconsistent with their own sense of themselves as a noble and just country. But the consequences were to limit severely the flexibility necessary to a multifaceted and effective diplomacy, and to force national leaders to invoke moral—even religious—idealism as a basis for actions that might well fall short of the expectations generated by moralistic visions.

The Soviet Union, by contrast, operated with few such constraints. Although Soviet pronouncements on foreign policy tediously invoked the rhetoric of capitalist imperialism, abstract principles meant far less than national self-interest in arriving at foreign policy positions. Every action that the Soviet Union had taken since the Bolshevik revolution, from the peace treaty with the Kaiser to the 1939 Nazi-Soviet pact and Russian occupation of the Baltic states, reflected this policy of self-interest. As Stalin told British Foreign Minister Anthony Eden during the war, "a declaration I regard as algebra . . . I prefer practical arithmetic." Or, as the Japanese ambassador to Moscow later said, "the Soviet authorities are extremely realistic and it is most difficult to persuade them with abstract arguments." Clearly, both the United States and the Soviet Union saw foreign policy as involving a combination of self-interest and ideological principle. Yet the history of the two countries suggested that principle was far more a consideration in the formulation of American foreign policy, while self-interest—purely defined—controlled Soviet actions.

The difference became relevant during the 1930s as Franklin Roosevelt attempted to find some way to move American public opinion back to a spirit of internationalism. After World War I, Americans had felt betrayed by the abandonment of Wilsonian principles. Persuaded that the war itself represented a mischievous conspiracy by munitions makers and bankers to get America involved, Americans had preferred to opt for isolation and "normalcy" rather than participate in the ambiguities of what so clearly appeared to be a corrupt international order. Now, Roosevelt set out to reverse those perceptions. He understood the dire consequences of Nazi ambitions for world hegemony. Yet to pose the issue strictly as one of self-interest offered little chance of success given the depth of America's revulsion toward internationalism. The task of education was immense. As time went on, Roosevelt relied more and more on the traditional moral rhetoric of American values as a means of justifying the international involvement that he knew must inevitably lead to war. Thus, throughout the 1930s he repeatedly discussed Nazi aggression as a direct threat to the most cherished American beliefs in freedom of speech, freedom of religion, and freedom of occupational choice. When German actions corroborated the president's simple words, the opportunity presented itself for carrying the nation toward another great crusade on behalf of democracy, freedom, and peace. Roosevelt wished to avoid the errors of Wilsonian overstatement, but he understood the necessity of generating moral fervor as a means of moving the nation toward the intervention he knew to be necessary if both America's self-interest—and her moral principles—were to be preserved.

The Atlantic Charter represented the embodiment of Roosevelt's quest for moral justification of American involvement. Presented to the world after the president and Prime Minister Churchill met off the coast of Newfoundland in the summer of 1941, the Charter set forth the common goals that would guide America over the next few years. There would be no secret commitments, the President said. Britain and America sought no territorial aggrandizement. They would oppose any violation of the right to self-government for all peoples. They stood for open trade, free exchange of ideas, freedom of worship and expression, and the creation of an international organization to preserve and protect future peace. This would be a war fought for freedom—freedom from fear, freedom from want, freedom of religion, freedom from the old politics of balance-of-power diplomacy.

Roosevelt deeply believed in those ideals and saw no inconsistency between the moral principles they represented and American self-interest. Yet these very commitments threatened to generate misunderstanding and conflict with the Soviet Union whose own priorities were much more directly expressed in terms of "practical arithmetic." Russia wanted security. The Soviet Union sought a sphere of influence over which it could have unrestricted control. It wished territorial boundaries that would reflect the concessions won through military conflict. All these objectives—potentially—ran counter to the Atlantic Charter. Roosevelt himself—never afraid of inconsistency—often talked the same language. Frequently, he spoke of guaranteeing the U.S.S.R. "measures of legitimate security" on territorial questions, and he envisioned a postwar world in which the "four policemen"—the superpowers—would manage the world.

But Roosevelt also understood that the American public would not accept the public embrace of such positions. A rationale of narrow self-interest was not acceptable, especially if that self-interest led to abandoning the ideals of the Atlantic Charter. In short, the different ways in which the Soviet Union and the United States articulated their objectives for the war—and formulated their foreign policy—threatened to compromise the prospect for long-term cooperation. The language of universalism and the language of balance-of-power politics were incompatible, at least in theory. Thus, the United States and the Soviet Union entered the war burdened not only by their deep mistrust of each other's motivations and systems of government, but also by a significantly different emphasis on what should constitute the major rationale for fighting the war.

The War Years

Whatever tensions existed before the war, conflicts over military and diplomatic issues during the war proved sufficiently grave to cause additional mistrust. Two countries that in the past had shared almost no common ground now found themselves intimately tied to each other, with little foundation of mutual confidence on which to build. The problems that resulted clustered in two areas: (1) how much aid the West would provide to alleviate the disproportionate burden borne by the Soviet Union in fighting the war; and (2) how to resolve the dilemmas of making peace, occupying conquered territory, and defining postwar responsibilities. Inevitably, each issue became inextricably bound to the others, posing problems of statecraft and good faith that perhaps went beyond the capacity of any mortal to solve.

The central issue dividing the allies involved how much support the United States and Britain would offer to mitigate, then relieve, the devastation being sustained by the Soviet people. Stated bluntly, the Soviet Union bore the massive share of Nazi aggression. The statistics alone are overwhelming. Soviet deaths totaled more than 18 million during the war—sixty times the three hundred thousand lives lost by the United States. Seventy thousand Soviet villages were destroyed, $128 billion dollars worth of property leveled to the ground. Leningrad, the crown jewel of Russia's cities, symbolized the suffering experienced at the hands of the Nazis. Filled with art and beautiful architecture, the former capital of Russia came under siege by German armies almost immediately after the invasion of the Soviet Union. When the attack began, the city boasted a population of 3 million citizens. At the end, only 600,000 remained. There was no food, no fuel, no hope. More than a million starved, and some survived by resorting to cannibalism. Yet the city endured, the Nazis were repelled, and the victory that came with survival helped launch the campaign that would ultimately crush Hitler's tyranny.

Such suffering provided the backdrop for a bitter controversy over whether the United States and Britain were doing enough to assume their own just share of the fight. Roosevelt understood that Russia's battle was America's. "The Russian armies are killing more Axis personnel and destroying more Axis matériel," he wrote General Douglas MacArthur in 1942, "than all the other twenty-five United Nations put together." As soon as the Germans invaded Russia, the president ordered that lend-lease material be made immediately available to the Soviet Union, instructing his personal aide to get $22 million worth of supplies on their way by July 25—one month after the German invasion. Roosevelt knew that, unless the Soviets were helped quickly, they would be forced out of the war, leaving the United States in an untenable position. "If [only] the Russians could hold the Germans until October 1," the president said. At a Cabinet meeting early in August, Roosevelt declared himself "sick and tired of hearing . . . what was on order"; he wanted to hear only "what was on the water." Roosevelt's commitment to lend-lease reflected his deep conviction that aid to the Soviets was both the most effective way of combating German aggression and the strongest means of building a basis of trust with Stalin in order to facilitate postwar cooperation. "I do not want to be in the same position as the English," Roosevelt told his Secretary of the Treasury in 1942. "The English promised the Russians two divisions. They failed. They promised them to help in the Caucasus. They failed. Every promise the English have made to the Russians, they have fallen down on. . . . The only reason we stand so well . . . is that up to date we have kept our promises." Over and over again Roosevelt intervened directly and personally to expedite the shipment of supplies. "Please get out the list and please, with my full authority, use a heavy hand," he told one assistant. "Act as a burr under the saddle and get things moving!"

But even Roosevelt's personal involvement could not end the problems that kept developing around the lend-lease program. Inevitably, bureaucratic tangles delayed shipment of necessary supplies. Furthermore, German submarine assaults sank thousands of tons of weaponry. In just one month in 1942, twenty-three of thirty-seven merchant vessels on their way to the Soviet Union were destroyed, forcing a cancellation of shipments to Murmansk. Indeed, until late summer of 1942, the Allies *lost* more ships in submarine attacks than they were able to *build*.

Above all, old suspicions continued to creep into the ongoing process of negotiating and distributing lend-lease supplies. Americans who had learned during the purges to regard Stalin as "a sort of unwashed Genghis Khan with blood dripping from his fingertips" could not believe that he had changed his colors overnight and was now to be viewed as a gentle friend. Many Americans believed that they were saving the Soviet Union with their supplies, without recognizing the extent of Soviet suffering or appreciating the fact that the Russians were helping to save American lives by their sacrifice on the battlefield. Soviet officials, in turn, believed that their American counterparts overseeing the shipments were not necessarily doing all that they might to implement the promises made by the president. Americans expected gratitude. Russians expected supplies. Both expectations were justified, yet the conflict reflected the extent to which underlying distrust continued to poison the prospect of cooperation. "Frankly," FDR told one subordinate, "if I was a Russian, I would feel that I had been given the runaround in the United States." Yet with equal justification, Americans resented Soviet ingratitude. "The Russian authorities seem to want to cover up the fact that they are receiving outside help," American Ambassador Standley told a Moscow press conference in March 1943. "Apparently they want their people to believe that the Red Army is fighting this war alone." Clearly, the battle against Nazi Germany was not the only conflict taking place.

Yet the disputes over lend-lease proved minor compared to the issue of a second front—what one historian has called "the acid test of Anglo-American intentions." However much help the United States could provide in the way of war matériel, the decisive form of relief that Stalin sought was the actual involvement of American and British soldiers in Western Europe. Only such an invasion could significantly relieve the pressure of massive German divisions on the eastern front. During the years 1941–44, fewer than 10 percent of Germany's troops were in the west, while nearly three hundred divisions were committed to conquering Russia. If the Soviet Union was to survive, and the Allies to secure victory, it was imperative that American and British troops force a diversion of German troops to the west and help make possible the pincer movement from east and west that would eventually annihilate the fascist foe.

Roosevelt understood this all too well. Indeed, he appears to have wished nothing more than the most rapid possible development of the second front. In part, he saw such action as the only means to deflect a Soviet push for acceptance of Russia's pre-World War II territorial acquisitions, particularly in the Baltic states and Finland. Such acquisitions would not only be contrary to the Atlantic Charter and America's commitment to self-determination; they would also undermine the prospect of securing political support in America for international postwar cooperation. Hence, Roosevelt hoped to postpone, until victory was achieved, any final decisions on issues of territory. Shrewdly, the president understood that meeting Soviet demands for direct military assistance through a second front would offer the most effective answer to Russia's territorial aspirations.

Roosevelt had read the Soviet attitude correctly. In 1942, Soviet foreign minister Molotov readily agreed to withdraw his territorial demands in deference to U.S. concerns because the second front was so much more decisive an issue. When Molotov asked whether the Allies could undertake a second front operation that would draw off forty German divisions from the eastern front, the president replied that it could and that it would. Roosevelt cabled Churchill that he was "more anxious than ever" for a cross-channel attack in August 1942 so that Molotov would be able to "carry back some real results of his mission and give a favorable report to Stalin." At the end of their 1942 meeting, Roosevelt pledged to Molotov—and through him to Stalin—that a second front would be established *that* year. The president then proceeded to mobilize his own military advisors to develop plans for such an attack.

But Roosevelt could not deliver. Massive logistical and production problems obstructed any possibility of invading Western Europe on the timetable Roosevelt had promised. As a result, despite Roosevelt's own best intentions and the commitment of his military staff, he could not implement his desire to proceed. In addition, Roosevelt repeatedly encountered objections from Churchill and the British military establishment, still traumatized by the memory of the bloodletting that had occurred in the trench fighting of World War I. For Churchill, engagement of the Nazis in North Africa and then through the "soft underbelly" of Europe—Sicily and Italy—offered a better prospect for success. Hence, after promising Stalin a second front in August 1942, Roosevelt had to withdraw the pledge and ask for delay of the second front until the spring of 1943. When that date arrived, he was forced to pull back yet again for political and logistical reasons. By the time D-Day finally dawned on June 6, 1944, the Western Allies had broken their promise on the single most critical military issue of the war three times. On each occasion, there had been ample reason for the delay, but given the continued heavy burden placed on the Soviet Union, it was perhaps understandable that some Russian leaders viewed America's delay on the second front question with suspicion, sarcasm, and anger. When D-Day arrived, Stalin acknowledged the operation to be one of the greatest military ventures of human history. Still, the squabbles that preceded D-Day contributed substantially to the suspicions and tension that already existed between the two nations.

Another broad area of conflict emerged over who would control occupied areas once the war ended? How would peace be negotiated? The principles of the Atlantic Charter presumed establishment of democratic, freely elected, and representative governments in every area won back from the Nazis. If universalism were to prevail, each country liberated from Germany would have the opportunity to determine its own political structure through democratic means that would ensure representation of all factions of the body politic. If "sphere of influence" policies were implemented, by contrast, the major powers would dictate such decisions in a manner consistent with their own self-interest. Ultimately, this issue would become the decisive point of confrontation during the Cold War, reflecting the different state systems and political values of the Soviets and Americans; but even in the midst of the fighting, the Allies found themselves in major disagreement, sowing seeds of distrust that boded ill for the future. Since no plans were established in advance on how to deal with these issues, they were handled on a case by case basis, in each instance reinforcing the suspicions already present between the Soviet Union and the West.

Notwithstanding the Atlantic Charter, Britain and the United States proceeded on a de facto basis to implement policies at variance with universalism. Thus, for example, General Dwight Eisenhower was authorized to reach an accommodation with Admiral Darlan in North Africa as a means of avoiding an extended military campaign to defeat the Vichy, pro-fascist collaborators who controlled that area. From the perspective of military necessity and the preservation of life, it made sense to compromise one's ideals in such a situation. Yet the precedent inevitably raised problems with regard to allied efforts to secure self-determination elsewhere.

The issue arose again during the Allied invasion of Italy. There, too, concern with expediting military victory and securing political stability caused Britain and the United States to negotiate with the fascist Badoglio regime. "We cannot be put into a position," Churchill said, "where our two armies are doing all the fighting but Russians have a veto." Yet Stalin bitterly resented being excluded from participation in the Italian negotiations. The Soviet Union protested vigorously the failure to establish a tripartite commission to conduct all occupation negotiations. It was time, Stalin said, to stop viewing Russia as "a passive third observer. . . . It is impossible to tolerate such a situation any longer." In the end, Britain and the United States offered the token concession of giving the Soviets an innocuous role on the advisory commission dealing with Italy, but the primary result of the Italian experience was to reemphasize a crucial political reality: when push came to shove, those who exercised military control in an immediate situation would also exercise political control over any occupation regime.

The shoe was on the other foot when it came to Western desires to have a voice over Soviet actions in the Balkan states, particularly Romania. By not giving Russia an opportunity to participate in the Italian surrender, the West—in effect—helped legitimize Russia's desire to proceed unilaterally in Eastern Europe. Although both Churchill and Roosevelt were "acutely conscious of the great importance of the Balkan situation" and wished to "take advantage of" any opportunity to exercise influence in that area, the simple fact was that Soviet troops were in control. Churchill—and privately Roosevelt as well—accepted the consequences. "The occupying forces had the power in the area where their arms were present," Roosevelt noted, "and each knew that the other could not force things to an issue." But the contradiction between the stated idealistic aims of the war effort and such *Realpolitik* would come back to haunt the prospect for postwar collaboration, particularly in the areas of Poland and other east European countries.*

Moments of conflict, of course, took place within the context of day-to-day cooperation in meeting immediate wartime needs. Sometimes, such cooperation seemed deep and genuine enough to provide a basis for overcoming suspicion and conflict of interest. At the Moscow foreign ministers conference in the fall of 1943, the Soviets proved responsive to U.S. concerns. Reassured that there would indeed be a second front in Europe in 1944, the Russians strongly endorsed a postwar international organization to preserve the peace. More important, they indicated they would join the war against Japan as soon as Germany was defeated, and appeared willing to accept the Chiang Kai-shek government in China as a major participant in world politics. In some ways, these were a series of *quid pro quos*. In exchange for the second front, Russia had made concessions on issues of critical importance to Britain and the United States. Nevertheless, the results were encouraging. FDR reported that the conference had created "a psychology of . . . excellent feeling." Instead of being "cluttered with suspicion," the discussions had occurred in an atmosphere that "was amazingly good."

The same spirit continued at the first meeting of Stalin, Churchill, and Roosevelt in Tehran during November and early December 1943. Committed to winning Stalin as a friend, FDR stayed at the Soviet Embassy, met privately with Stalin, aligned himself with the Soviet leader against Churchill on a number of issues, and even went so far as to taunt Churchill "about his Britishness, about John Bull," in an effort to forge an informal "anti-imperial" alliance between the United States and the Soviet Union. A spirit of cooperation prevailed, with the wartime leaders agreeing that the Big Four would have the power to police any postwar settlements (clearly consistent with Stalin's commitment to a "sphere of influence" approach), reaffirming plans for a joint military effort against Japan, and even—after much difficulty—appearing to find a common approach to the difficulties of Poland and Eastern Europe. When it was all over, FDR told the American people: "I got along fine with Marshall Stalin . . . I believe he is truly representative of the heart and soul of Russia; and I believe that we are going to get along very well with him and the Russian people—very well indeed." When pressed on what kind of a person the Soviet leader was, Roosevelt responded: "I would call him something like me, . . . a realist."

The final conference of Stalin, Churchill, and Roosevelt at Yalta in February 1945 appeared at the time to carry forward the partnership, although

* Poland will be discussed at length in a subsequent section.

The three leaders of the wartime alliance meet at Yalta to shape postwar plans. From left to right, they are Winston Churchill, Franklin Delano Roosevelt, and Josef Stalin. *(National Archives)* When released to the public, this photograph was accompanied by a government text which read: "During the historic Crimea conference, Prime Minister Churchill, President Roosevelt, and Marshall Stalin came to complete agreement on matters of both war and peace."

in retrospect it would become clear that the facade of unity was built on a foundation of misperceptions rooted in the different values, priorities, and political ground rules of the two societies. Stalin seemed to recognize Roosevelt's need to present postwar plans—for domestic political reasons—as consistent with democratic, universalistic principles. Roosevelt, in turn, appreciated Stalin's need for friendly governments on his borders. The three leaders agreed on concrete plans for Soviet participation in the Japanese war, and Stalin reiterated his support for a coalition government in China with Chiang Kai-shek assuming a position of leadership. Although some of Roosevelt's aides were skeptical of the agreements made, most came back confident that they had succeeded in laying a basis for continued partnership. As Harry Hopkins later recalled, "we really believed in our hearts that this was the dawn of the new day we had all been praying for. The Russians have proved that they can be reasonable and far-seeing and there wasn't any doubt in the minds of the president or any of us that we could live with them and get along with them peacefully for as far into the future as any of us could imagine."

In fact, two disquietingly different perceptions of the Soviet Union existed as the war drew to an end. Some Washington officials believed that the mystery of Russia was no mystery at all, simply a reflection of a national history in which suspicion of outsiders was natural, given repeated invasions from Western Europe and rampant hostility toward communism on the part of Western powers. Former Ambassador to Moscow Joseph Davies believed that the way to cut through that suspicion was to adopt "the simple approach of assuming that what they say, they mean." On the basis of his personal negotiations with the Russians, presidential aide Harry Hopkins shared the same confidence.

The majority of well-informed Americans, however, endorsed the opposite position. It was folly, one newspaper correspondent wrote, "to prettify Stalin, whose internal homicide record is even longer than Hitler's." Hitler and Stalin were two of the same breed, former Ambassador to Russia William Bullitt insisted. Each wanted to spread his power "to the ends of the earth. Stalin, like Hitler, will not stop. He can only *be* stopped." According to Bullitt, any alternative view implied "a conversion of Stalin as striking as the conversion of Saul on the road to Damascus." Senator Robert Taft agreed. It made no sense, he insisted, to base U.S. policy toward the Soviet Union "on the delightful theory that Mr. Stalin in the end will turn out to have an angelic nature." Drawing on the historical precedents of the purge trials and traditional American hostility to communism, totalitarianism, and Stalin, those who held this point of view saw little hope of compromise. "There is as little difference between communism and fascism," Monsignor Fulton J. Sheen said, "as there is between burglary and larceny." The only appropriate response was force. Instead of "leaning over backward to be nice to the descendents of Genghis Khan," General George Patton suggested, "[we] should dictate to them and do it now and in no uncertain terms." Within such a frame of reference, the lessons of history and of ideological incompatibility seemed to permit no possibility of compromise.

But Roosevelt clearly felt that there was a third way, a path of mutual accommodation that would sustain and nourish the prospects of postwar partnership without ignoring the realities of geopolitics. The choice in his mind was clear. "We shall have to take the responsibility for world collaboration," he told Congress, "or we shall have to bear the responsibility for another world conflict." President Roosevelt was neither politically naive nor stupid. Even though committed to the Atlantic Charter's ideals of self-determination and territorial integrity, he recognized the legitimate need of the Soviet Union for national security. For him, the process of politics—informed by thirty-five years of skilled practice—involved striking a deal that both sides could live with. Roosevelt acknowledged the brutality, the callousness, the tyranny of the Soviet system. Indeed, in 1940 he had called Russia as absolute a dictatorship as existed anywhere. But that did not mean a solution was impossible, or that one should withdraw from the struggle to find a basis for world peace. As he was fond of saying about negotiations with Russia, "it is permitted to walk with the devil until the bridge is crossed."

The problem was that, as Roosevelt defined the task of finding a path of accommodation, it rested solely on his shoulders. The president possessed an almost mystical confidence in his own capacity to break through policy differences based on economic structures and political systems, and to develop a personal relationship of trust that would transcend impersonal forces of division. "I know you will not mind my being brutally frank when I tell you," he wrote Churchill in 1942, "[that] I think I can personally handle Stalin better than either your Foreign Office or my State Department. Stalin hates the guts of all your top people. He thinks he likes me better, and I hope he will continue to do so." Notwithstanding the seeming naiveté of such statements, Roosevelt appeared right, in at least this one regard. The Soviets *did* seem to place their faith in him, perhaps thinking that American foreign policy was as much a product of one man's decisions as their own. Roosevelt evidently thought the same way, telling Bullitt, in one of their early foreign policy discussions, "it's my responsibility and not yours; and I'm going to play my hunch."

The tragedy, of course, was that the man who perceived that fostering world peace was his own personal responsibility never lived to carry out his vision. Long in declining health, suffering from advanced arteriosclerosis and a serious cardiac problem, he had gone to Warm Springs, Georgia, to recover from the ordeal of Yalta and the congressional session. On April 12, Roosevelt suffered a massive cerebral hemorrhage and died. As word spread across the country, the stricken look on people's faces told those who had not yet heard the news the awful dimensions of what had happened. "He was the only president I ever knew," one woman said. In London, Churchill declared that he felt as if he had suffered a physical blow. Stalin greeted the American ambassador in silence, holding his hand for thirty seconds. The leader of the world's greatest democracy would not live to see the victory he had striven so hard to achieve.

Cold War Issues

Although historians have debated for years the cause of the Cold War, virtually everyone agrees that it developed around five major issues: Poland, the structure of governments in other Eastern European countries, the future of Germany, economic reconstruction of Europe, and international policies toward the atomic bomb and atomic energy. All of these intersected, so that within a few months, it became almost impossible to separate one from the other as they interacted to shape the emergence of a bipolar world. Each issue in its own way also reflected the underlying confusion and conflict surrounding the competing doctrines of "universalist" versus "sphere-of-influence" diplomacy. Examination of these fundamental questions is essential if we are to comprehend how and why the tragedy of the Cold War evolved during the three years after Germany's defeat.

Poland constituted the most intractable and profound dilemma facing Soviet-U.S. relations. As Secretary of State Edward Stettinius observed in 1945, Poland was "*the big apple in the barrel.*" Unfortunately, it also symbolized, for both sides, everything that the war had been fought for. From a Soviet perspective, Poland represented the quintessence of Russia's national security needs. On three occasions, Poland had served as the avenue for devastating invasions of Russian territory. It was imperative, given Russian history, that Poland be governed by a regime supportive of the Soviet Union. But Poland also represented, both in fact and in symbol, everything for which the Western Allies had fought. Britain and France had declared war on Germany in September 1939 when Hitler invaded Poland, thus honoring their mutual defense pact with that victimized country. It seemed unthinkable that one could wage war for six years and end up with another totalitarian country in control of Poland. Surely if the Atlantic Charter signified anything, it required defending the right of the Polish people to determine their own destiny. The presence of 7 million Polish-American voters offered a constant, if unnecessary, reminder that such issues of self-determination could not be dismissed lightly. Thus, the first issue confronting the Allies in building a postwar world would also be one on which compromise was virtually impossible, at least without incredible diplomatic delicacy, political subtlety, and profound appreciation, by each ally, of the other's needs and priorities.

Roosevelt appears to have understood the tortuous path he would have to travel in order to find a peaceful resolution of the conflict. Given his own commitment to the Atlantic Charter, rooted in both domestic political reasons and personal conviction, he recognized the need to advocate an independent and democratic government for the Polish people. "Poland must be reconstituted a great nation," he told the country during the 1944 election. Yet the president also repeatedly acknowledged that the Russians must have a "friendly" government in Warsaw. Somehow, Roosevelt hoped to find a way to subordinate these two conflicting positions to the higher priority of postwar peace. "The President," Harry Hopkins said in 1943, "did not intend to go to the Peace Conference and bargain with Poland or the other small states; as far as Poland is concerned, the important thing [was] to set it up in a way that [would] help maintain the peace of the world."

The issue was first joined at the Tehran conference. There, Churchill and Roosevelt endorsed Stalin's position that Poland's eastern border, for security reasons, should be moved to the west. As Roosevelt had earlier explained to the ambassador from the Polish government-in-exile in London, it was folly to expect the United States and Britain "to declare war on Joe Stalin over a boundary dispute." On the other hand, Roosevelt urged Stalin to be flexible, citing his own need for the Polish vote in the 1944 presidential election and the importance of establishing cooperation between the London Poles and the Lublin government-in-exile situated in Moscow. Roosevelt had been willing to make a major concession to Russia's security needs by accepting the Soviet definition of Poland's new boundaries. But he also expected some consideration of his own political dilemma and of the principles of the Atlantic Charter.

Such consideration appeared to be forthcoming in the summer of 1944 when Stalin agreed to meet the prime minister of the London-Polish government and "to mediate" between the two opposing governments-in-exile. But hopes for such a compromise were quickly crushed as Soviet troops failed to aid the Warsaw Polish resistance when it rose in massive rebellion against German occupation forces in hopes of linking up with advancing Soviet forces. The Warsaw Poles generally supported the London government-in-exile. As Red Army troops moved to just six miles outside of Warsaw, the Warsaw Poles rose en masse against their Nazi oppressors. Yet when they did so, the Soviets callously rejected all pleas for help. For eight weeks they even refused to permit American planes to land on Soviet soil after airlifting supplies to the beleaguered Warsaw rebels. By the time the rebellion ended, 250,000 people had become casualties, with the backbone of the pro-London resistance movement brutally crushed. Although some Americans, then and later, accepted Soviet claims that logistical problems had prevented any assistance being offered, most Americans endorsed the more cynical conclusion that Stalin had found a convenient way to annihilate a large part of his Polish opposition and facilitate acquisition of a pro-Soviet regime. As Ambassador Averell Harriman cabled at the time, Russian actions were based on "ruthless political considerations."

By the time of the Yalta conference, the Red Army occupied Poland, leaving Roosevelt little room to maneuver. When one American diplomat urged the president to force Russia to agree to Polish independence, Roosevelt responded: "Do you want me to go to war with Russia?" With Stalin having already granted diplomatic recognition to the Lublin regime, Roosevelt could only hope that the Soviets would accept enough modification of the status quo to provide the *appearance* of representative democracy. Spheres of influence were a reality, FDR told seven senators, because "the occupying forces [have] the power in the areas where their arms are present." All America could do was to use her influence "to ameliorate the situation."

Nevertheless, Roosevelt played what cards he had with skill. "Most Poles," he told Stalin, "want to save face. . . . It would make it easier for me at home if the Soviet government could give something to Poland." A government of national unity, Roosevelt declared, would facilitate public acceptance in the United States of full American participation in postwar arrangements. "Our people at home look with a critical eye on what they consider a disagreement between us. . . . They, in effect, say that if we cannot get a meeting of minds now . . . how can we get an understanding on even more vital things in the future?" Although Stalin's immediate response was to declare that Poland was "not only a question of honor for Russia, but one of life and death," he finally agreed that some reorganization of the Lublin regime could take place to ensure broader representation of all Poles.

In the end, the Big Three papered over their differences at Yalta by agreeing to a Declaration on Liberated Europe that committed the Allies to help liberated peoples resolve their problems through democratic means and advocated the holding of free elections. Although Roosevelt's aide Admiral William Leahy told him that the report on Poland was "so elastic that the Russians can stretch it all the way from Yalta to Washington without ever technically breaking it," Roosevelt believed that he had done the best he could under the circumstances. From the beginning, Roosevelt had recognized, on a de facto basis at least, that Poland was part of Russia's sphere of influence and must remain so. He could only hope that Stalin would now show equal recognition of the U.S. need to have concessions that would give the appearance, at least, of implementing the Atlantic Charter.

The same basic dilemmas, of course, occurred with regard to the structure of postwar governments in all of Eastern Europe. As early as 1943, Roosevelt had made clear to Stalin at Tehran that he was willing to have the Baltic states controlled by the Soviets. His only request, the president told Stalin, was for some public commitment to future elections in order to satisfy his constituents at home for whom "the big issues . . . would be the question of referendum and the right of self-determination." The exchange with Stalin accurately reflected Roosevelt's position over time.

Significantly, Roosevelt even sanctioned Churchill's efforts to divide Europe into spheres of influence. With Roosevelt's approval, Churchill journeyed to Moscow in the fall of 1944. Sitting across the table from Stalin, Churchill proposed that Russia exercise 90 percent predominance in Romania, 75 percent in Bulgaria, and 50 percent control, together with Britain, in Yugoslavia and Hungary, while the United States and Great Britain would exercise 90 percent predominance in Greece. After extended discussion and some hard bargaining, the deal was made. (Poland was not even included in Churchill's percentages, suggesting that he was acknowledging Soviet control there.) At the time, Churchill suggested that the arrangements be expressed "in diplomatic terms [without use of] the phrase 'dividing into spheres,' because the Americans might be shocked." But in fact, as Robert Dallek has shown in his superb study of Roosevelt's diplomacy, the American president accepted the arrangement. "I am most pleased to know," FDR wrote Churchill, "you are reaching a meeting of your two minds as to international policies." To Harriman he cabled: "My active interest at the present time in the Balkan area is that such steps as are practicable should be taken to insure against the Balkans getting us into a future international war." At no time did Roosevelt protest the British-Soviet agreement.

In the case of Eastern Europe generally, even more so than in Poland, it seemed clear that Roosevelt, on a de facto basis, was prepared to live with spheres-of-influence diplomacy. Nevertheless, he remained constantly sensitive to the political peril he faced at home on the issue. As Congressman John Dingell stated in a public warning in August 1943, "We Americans are not sacrificing, fighting, and dying to make permanent and more powerful the communistic government of Russia and to make Joseph Stalin a dictator over the liberated countries of Europe." Such sentiments were widespread. Indeed, it was concern over such opinions that led Roosevelt to urge the Russians to be sensitive to American political concerns. In Eastern Europe for the most part, as in Poland, the key question was whether the United States could somehow find a way to acknowledge spheres of influence, but within a context of universalist principles, so that the American people would not feel that the Atlantic Charter had been betrayed.

The future of Germany represented a third critical point of conflict. For emotional as well as political reasons, it was imperative that steps be taken to prevent Germany from ever again waging war. In FDR's words, "We have got to be tough with Germany, and I mean the German people not just the Nazis. We either have to castrate the German people or you have got to treat them in such a manner so they can't just go on reproducing people who want to continue the way they have in the past." Consistent with that position, Roosevelt had agreed with Stalin at Tehran on the need for destroying a strong Germany by dividing the country into several sectors, "as small and weak as possible."

Still operating on that premise, Roosevelt endorsed Secretary of the Treasury Henry Morgenthau's plan to eliminate all industry from Germany and convert the country into a pastoral landscape of small farms. Not only would such a plan destroy any future war-making power, it would also reassure the Soviet Union of its own security. "Russia feared we and the British were going to try to make a soft peace with Germany and build her up as a possible future counter-weight against Russia," Morgenthau said. His plan would avoid that, and simultaneously implement Roosevelt's insistence that "every person in Germany should realize that this time Germany is a defeated nation." Hence, in September 1944, Churchill and Roosevelt approved the broad outlines of the Morgenthau plan as their policy for Germany.

Within weeks, however, the harsh policy of pastoralization came unglued. From a Soviet perspective, there was the problem of how Russia could exact the reparations she needed from a country with no industrial base. American policymakers, in turn, objected that a Germany without industrial capacity would prove unable to support herself, placing the entire burden for maintaining the populace on the Allies. Rumors spread that the Morgenthau plan was stiffening German resistance on the western front. American business interests, moreover, suggested the importance of retaining German industry as a key to postwar commerce and trade.

As a result, Allied policy toward Germany became a shambles. "No one wants to make Germany a wholly agricultural nation again," Roosevelt insisted. "No one wants 'complete eradication of German industrial production capacity in the Ruhr and the Saar.'" Confused about how to proceed, Roosevelt—in effect—adopted a policy of no policy. "I dislike making detailed plans for a country which we do not yet occupy," he said. When Churchill, Stalin, and Roosevelt met for the last time in Yalta, this failure to plan prevented a decisive course of action. The Russians insisted on German reparations of $20 billion, half of which would go to the Soviet Union. Although FDR accepted Stalin's figure as a basis for discussion, the British and Americans deferred any settlement of the issue, fearing that they would be left with the sole responsibility for feeding and housing the German people. The only agreement that could be reached was to refer the issue to a new tripartite commission. Thus, at just the moment when consensus on a policy to deal with their common enemy was most urgent, the Allies found themselves empty handed, allowing conflict and misunderstanding over another central question to join the already existing problems over Eastern Europe.

Directly related to each of these issues, particularly the German question, was the problem of postwar economic reconstruction. The issue seemed particularly important to those Americans concerned about the postwar economy in the United States. Almost every business and political leader feared resumption of mass unemployment once the war ended. Only the development of new markets, extensive trade, and worldwide economic cooperation could prevent such an eventuality. "The capitalistic system is essentially an international system," one official declared. "If it cannot function internationally, it will break down completely." The Atlantic Charter had taken such a viewpoint into account when it declared that all states should enjoy access, on equal terms, to "the raw materials of the world which are needed for their economic prosperity."

To promote these objectives, the United States took the initiative at Bretton Woods, New Hampshire, in 1944 by creating a World Bank with a capitalization of $7.6 billion and the International Monetary Fund with a capitalization of $7.3 billion. The two organizations would provide funds for rebuilding Europe, as well as for stabilizing world currency. Since the United States was the major contributor, it would exercise decisive control over how the money was spent. The premise underlying both organizations was that a stable world required healthy economies based on free trade.

Attitudes toward economic reconstruction had direct import for postwar policies toward Germany and Eastern Europe. It would be difficult to have a stable European economy without a significant industrial base in Germany. Pastoral countries of small farms rarely possessed the wherewithal to become customers of large capitalist enterprises. On the other hand, a prosperous German economy, coupled with access to markets in Eastern and Western Europe, offered the prospect of avoiding a recurrence of depression and guaranteed a significant American presence in European politics as well. Beyond this, of course, it was thought that if democracy was to survive, as it had not after 1918, countries needed a thriving economy.

Significantly, economic aid also offered the opportunity either to enhance or diminish America's ties to the Soviet Union. Averell Harriman, the American ambassador to Moscow after October 1943, had engaged in extensive business dealings with the Soviet Union during the 1920s and believed firmly in the policy of providing American assistance to rebuild the Soviet economy. Such aid, Harriman argued, "would be in the self-interest of the United States" because it would help keep Americans at work producing goods needed by the Russians. Just as important, it would provide "one of the most effective weapons to avoid the development of a sphere of influence of the Soviet Union over eastern Europe and the Balkans."

Proceeding on these assumptions, Harriman urged the Russians to apply for American aid. They did so, initially, in December 1943 with a request for a $1 billion loan at an interest rate of one-half of 1 percent, then again in January 1945 with a request for a $6 billion loan at an interest rate of 2.25 percent. Throughout this period, American officials appeared to encourage the Soviet initiative. Secretary of the Treasury Morgenthau had come up with his own plan for a $10 billion loan at 2 percent interest. When Chamber of Commerce head Eric Johnson visited Moscow, Stalin told him: "I like to do business with American businessmen. You fellows know what you want. Your word is good, and, best of all, you stay in office a long time—just like we do over here." So enthusiastic were some State Department officials about postwar economic arrangements that they predicted exports of as much as $1 billion a year to Russia. Molotov and Mikoyan encouraged such optimism, with the Soviets promising "a voluminous and stable market such as no other customer would ever [offer]."

As the European war drew to a close, however, the American attitude shifted from one of eager encouragement to skeptical detachment. Harriman and his aides in Moscow perceived a toughening of the Soviet position on numerous issues, including Poland and Eastern Europe. Hence, they urged the United States to clamp down on lend-lease and exact specific concessions from the Russians in return for any ongoing aid. Only if the Soviets "played the international game with us in accordance with our standards," Harriman declared, should the United States offer assistance. By April 1945, Harriman had moved to an even more hard-line position. "We must clearly recognize," he said, "that the Soviet program is the establishment of totalitarianism, ending personal liberty and democracy." A week later he urged the State Department to view the Soviet loan request with great suspicion. "Our basic interest," he cabled, "might better be served by increasing our trade with other parts of the world rather than giving preference to the Soviet Union as a source of supply."

Congress and the American people, meanwhile, seemed to be turning against postwar economic aid. A public opinion poll in December 1944 showed that 70 percent of the American people believed the Allies should repay their lend-lease debt in full. Taking up the cry for fiscal restraint, Senator Arthur Vandenberg told a friend: "We have a rich country, but it is not

rich enough to permit us to support the world." Fearful about postwar recession and the possibility that American funds would be used for purposes
it did not approve, Congress placed severe constraints on continuation of
any lend-lease support once the war was over and indicated that any request
for a postwar loan would encounter profound skepticism.

Roosevelt's response, in the face of such attitudes, was once again to
procrastinate. Throughout the entire war he had ardently espoused a generous and flexible lend-lease policy toward the Soviet Union. For the most
part, FDR appeared to endorse Secretary Morgenthau's attitude that "to get
the Russians to do something [we] should . . . do it nice. . . . Don't
drive such a hard bargain that when you come through it does not taste
good." Consistent with that attitude, he had rejected Harriman's advice to
demand *quid pro quos* for American lend-lease. Economic aid, he declared,
did not "constitute a bargaining weapon of any strength," particularly since
curtailing lend-lease would harm the United States as much as it would in-
jure the Russians. Nevertheless, Roosevelt accepted a policy of postpone-
ment on any discussion of postwar economic arrangements. "I think it's very
important," the president declared, "that we hold back and don't give
[Stalin] any promise until we get what we want." Clearly, the amount of
American aid to the Soviet Union—and the attitude which accompanied
that aid—could be decisive to the future of American-Soviet relations. Yet in
this—as in so many other issues—Roosevelt gave little hint of the ultimate
direction he would take, creating one more dimension of uncertainty
amidst the gathering confusion that surrounded postwar international
arrangements.

The final issue around which the Cold War revolved was that of the
atomic bomb. Development of nuclear weapons not only placed in human
hands the power to destroy all civilization, but presented as well the critical
question of how such weapons would be used, who would control them, and
what possibilities existed for harnessing the incalculable energy of the atom
for the purpose of international peace and cooperation rather than destruction. No issue, ultimately, would be more important for human survival. On the other hand, the very nature of having to build the A-bomb in
a world threatened by Hitler's madness mandated a secrecy that seriously
impeded, from the beginning, the prospects for cooperation and international control.

The divisive potential of the bomb became evident as soon as Albert Ein-
stein disclosed to Roosevelt the frightening information that physicists had
the capacity to split the atom. Knowing that German scientists were also pursuing the same quest, Roosevelt immediately ordered a crash program of research and development on the bomb, soon dubbed the "Manhattan Project." British scientists embarked on a similar effort, collaborating with their
American colleagues. The bomb, one British official noted, "would be a terrific factor in the postwar world . . . giving an absolute control to whatever
country possessed the secret." Although American advisors urged "restricted

interchange" of atomic energy information, Churchill demanded and got full cooperation. If the British and the Americans worked together, however, what of the Soviet Union once it became an ally?

In a decision fraught with significance for the future, Roosevelt and Churchill agreed in Quebec in August 1943 to a "full exchange of information" about the bomb with "[neither] of us [to] communicate any information about [the bomb] to third parties except by mutual consent." The decision ensured Britain's future interests as a world power and guaranteed maximum secrecy; but it did so in a manner that would almost inevitably provoke Russian suspicion about the intentions of her two major allies.

The implications of the decision were challenged just one month later when Niels Bohr, a nuclear physicist who had escaped from Nazi-occupied Denmark, approached Roosevelt (indirectly through Felix Frankfurter) with the proposal that the British and Americans include Russia in their plans. Adopting a typically Rooseveltian stance, the president both encouraged Bohr to believe that he was "most eager to explore" the possibility of cooperation and almost simultaneously reaffirmed his commitment to an exclusive British-American monopoly over atomic information. Meeting personally with Bohr on August 26, 1944, Roosevelt agreed that "contact with the Soviet Union should be tried along the lines that [you have] suggested." Yet in the meantime, Roosevelt and Churchill had signed a new agreement to control available supplies of uranium and had authorized surveillance of Bohr "to insure that he is responsible for no leakage of information, particularly to the Russians." Evidently, Roosevelt hoped to keep open the possibility of cooperating with the Soviets—assuming that Bohr would somehow communicate this to the Russians—while retaining, until the moment was right, an exclusive relationship with Britain. Implicit in Roosevelt's posture was the notion that sharing atomic information might be a *quid pro quo* for future Soviet concessions. On the surface, such an argument made sense. Yet it presumed that the two sides were operating on the same set of assumptions and perceptions—clearly not a very safe presumption. In this, as in so many other matters, Roosevelt appears to have wanted to retain all options until the end. Indeed, a meeting to discuss the sharing of atomic information was scheduled for the day FDR was to return from Warm Springs, Georgia. The meeting never took place, leaving one more pivotal issue of contention unresolved as the war drew to a close.

Conclusion

Given the nature of the personalities and the nations involved, it was perhaps not surprising that, as the war drew to an end, virtually none of the critical issues on the agenda of postwar relationships had been resolved. Preferring to postpone decisions rather than to confront the full dimension of the conflicts that existed, FDR evidently hoped that his own political genius, plus the exigencies of postwar conditions, would pave the way for a mutual accommodation that would somehow satisfy both America's commitment to a world of free trade and democratic rule, and the Soviet Union's obsession with national security and safely defined spheres of influence. The Russians, in turn, also appeared content to wait, in the meantime working militarily to secure maximum leverage for achieving their sphere-of-influence goals. What neither leader nor nation realized, perhaps, was that in their delay and scheming they were adding fuel to the fire of suspicion that clearly existed between them and possibly missing the only opportunity that might occur to forge the basis for mutual accommodation and coexistence.

3

Truman and
the Cold War

The man who would inherit these prickly issues was a former haber-dasher from Missouri who had had virtually no experience in foreign affairs. Harry Truman had been born on a small farm in Lamar, Missouri. After serving as the captain of an artillery unit during World War I, he had entered the clothing business and failed. Well liked by his peers, he next decided to run for office as a county executive. Comfortably ensconced as part of the Pendergast machine in Kansas City, Truman was selected as a candidate for the U.S. Senate in 1934 after other Missouri Democrats had turned the offer down. In a three-way race, Truman won. In the Senate, Truman played the role of a moderate, supporting most New Deal measures, but with less fervor than such liberals as Robert Wagner. His major achievement in the Senate was as chairman of the Special Committee to Investigate the National Defense Program where he earned a reputation for fairness and toughness.

Truman's selection as vice-presidential nominee in 1944 was almost a rerun of his choice in the U.S. Senate nomination. Henry Wallace, Roosevelt's running mate in 1940, was a classic liberal who wanted to run again. But faced with a mounting controversy over a fourth term as well as the conservative inclinations of Congress, Roosevelt searched for a more acceptable alternative. His own favorite was James Byrnes, director of the Office of War Mobilization and a man who had been "assistant president" in charge of running domestic affairs during the war. But Byrnes was a Southerner, hostile to labor, and unacceptable to northern liberals, civil rights advocates, and urban bosses. Truman became the perfect compromise. Although Roosevelt observed that "I hardly know [him]" the man from Missouri had all the right credentials. He was from a border state, had alienated no one, and was sufficiently popular with his colleagues that he might prove useful in furthering Roosevelt's legislative program for the postwar years. When Truman balked at the idea of running, Roosevelt declared: "If he wants to break up the Democratic Party in the middle of the war, that's his responsibility." "Oh, shit," Truman said, "if that is the situation, I'll have to say yes." Less than four months after taking office, a call came from White House Press Secretary Stephen Early asking Truman to come to the White

House. When the vice-president walked into the room, he knew that the worst had happened. Mrs. Roosevelt placed her hand on his shoulder and said, "Harry, the President is dead."

The Challenge of the Presidency

Few people were less prepared for the challenge of becoming president. Although well-read in history, Truman's experience in foreign policy was minimal. His most famous comment on diplomacy had been a statement to a reporter in 1941 that "if we see that Germany is winning [the war] we ought to help Russia, and if Russia is winning we ought to help Germany and that way let them kill as many as possible, although I don't want to see Hitler victorious under any circumstances." As vice-president, Truman had been excluded from all foreign policy discussions. He knew nothing about the Manhattan Project. The new president, Henry Stimson noted, labored under the "terrific handicap of coming into . . . an office where the threads of information were so multitudinous that only long previous familiarity could allow him to control them." More to the point were Truman's own comments: "They didn't tell me anything about what was going on. . . . Everybody around here that should know anything about foreign affairs is out." Faced with burdens sufficiently awesome to intimidate any individual, Truman had to act quickly on a succession of national security questions, aided only by his native intelligence and a no-nonsense attitude reflected in the now-famous slogan that adorned his desk: "The Buck Stops Here."

Truman's dilemma was compounded by the extent to which Roosevelt had acted as his own secretary of state, sharing with almost no one his plans for the postwar period. Roosevelt placed little trust in the State Department's bureaucracy, disagreed with the suspicion exhibited toward Russia by most foreign service officers, and for the most part appeared to believe that he alone held the secret formula for accommodation with the Soviets. Ultimately that formula presumed the willingness of the Russian leadership "to give the Government of Poland [and other Eastern European countries] an *external appearance* of independence [italics added]," in the words of Roosevelt's aide Admiral William Leahy. In the month before his death, FDR had evidently begun to question that presumption, becoming increasingly concerned about Soviet behavior. Had he lived, he may well have adopted a significantly tougher position toward Stalin than he had taken previously. Yet in his last communication with Churchill, Roosevelt was still urging the British prime minister to "minimize the Soviet problem as much as possible . . . because these problems, in one form or another, seem to arrive everyday and most of them straighten out." If Stalin's intentions still remained difficult to fathom, so too did Roosevelt's. And now Truman was in charge, with neither Roosevelt's experience to inform him, nor a clear sense of Roosevelt's perceptions to offer him direction.

Without being able to analyze at leisure all the complex information that was relevant, Truman solicited the best advice he could from those who were most knowledgeable about foreign relations. Hurrying back from Moscow, Averell Harriman sought the president's ear, lobbying intensively with White House and State Department officials for his position that "irreconcilable differences" separated the Soviet Union and the United States, with the Russians seeking "the extension of the Soviet system with secret police, [and] extinction of freedom of speech" everywhere they could. Earlier, Harriman had been well disposed toward the Soviet leadership, enthusiastically endorsing Russian interest in a postwar loan and advocating cooperation wherever possible. But now Harriman perceived a hardening of Soviet attitudes and a more aggressive posture toward control over Eastern Europe. The Russians had just signed a separate peace treaty with the Lublin (pro-Soviet) Poles, and after offering safe passage to sixteen pro-Western representatives of the Polish resistance to conduct discussions about a government of national unity, had suddenly arrested the sixteen and held them incommunicado. America's previous policy of generosity toward the Soviets had been "misinterpreted in Moscow," Harriman believed, leading the Russians to think they had carte blanche to proceed as they wished. In Harriman's view, the Soviets were engaged in a "barbarian invasion of Europe." Whether or not Roosevelt would have accepted Harriman's analysis, to Truman the ambassador's words made eminent sense. The international situation was like a poker game, Truman told one friend, and he was not going to let Stalin beat him.

Just ten days after taking office, Truman had the opportunity to play his own hand with Molotov. The Soviet foreign minister had been sent by Stalin to attend the first U.N. conference in San Francisco both as a gesture to Roosevelt's memory and as a means of sizing up the new president. In a private conversation with former Ambassador to Moscow Joseph Davies, Molotov expressed his concern that "full information" about Russian-U.S. relations might have died with FDR and that "differences of interpretation and possible complications [might] arise which would not occur if Roosevelt lived." Himself worried that Truman might make "snap judgments," Davies urged Molotov to explain fully Soviet policies vis-à-vis Poland and Eastern Europe in order to avoid future conflict.

But based on the information he had received, Truman had already decided to "[lay] it on the line with Molotov." "We must stand up to the Russians," he told his secretary of state. "We have been too easy with them." Over and over again in the period leading up to the meeting with Molotov, Truman repeated his determination to be "tough." It might be unreasonable to expect the Soviets to give in a hundred percent of the time, he noted, but surely the United States should get about eighty-five percent of what it wanted. At a meeting of advisors just before the scheduled session with Molotov, only Secretary of War Henry Stimson and General George Marshall took issue with the president's proposed approach. Adopting essentially what appears to have been Roosevelt's private position, Stimson told the president that peace was too important to be endangered by the Polish issue, and declared that Russia was perhaps being more realistic about her own security needs than the United States. Now was not the time for a rash break with the Soviets, Stimson warned. But Truman had already made up his mind. "Our agreements with the Soviet Union so far [have been] a one-way street," he said. The time had come to talk to the Russians "in words of one syllable."

When Molotov walked in, the president took little time to assert his authority. While the Soviet minister engaged in diplomatic chitchat, seeking to feel out the man he had never met before, Truman got right to the point. Poland, he told Molotov, was the most important problem facing the Allies. Thus far, the president said, the Soviet Union had not lived up to its agreements at Yalta to bring more democracy to the countries of liberated Europe. This failure called into question the whole basis of postwar cooperation. When Molotov protested that he had "never been talked to like that in my life," Truman retorted: "Carry out your agreements and you won't get talked to like that." At that point, a Truman aide recalled, Molotov turned "a little ashy." Then the president said: "That will be all, Mr. Molotov. I would appreciate it if you would transmit my views to Marshall Stalin." Later, recounting the conversation, Truman told a friend: "I gave him the one-two, right to the jaw."

Truman implemented the same no-nonsense approach when it came to decisions about the atomic bomb. Astonishingly, it was not until the day after Truman's meeting with Molotov that he was first briefed about the bomb. By that time, $2 billion had already been spent on what Stimson called "the most terrible weapon ever known in human history." Immediately, Truman grasped the significance of the information. "I can't tell you what this is," he told his secretary, "but if it works, and pray God it does, it will save many American lives." Here was a weapon that might not only bring the war to a swift conclusion, but also provide a critical lever of influence in all postwar relations. As James Byrnes told the president, the bomb would "put us in a position to dictate our own terms at the end of the war."

In the years subsequent to Hiroshima and Nagasaki, historians have debated the wisdom of America's being the first nation to use such a horrible weapon of destruction and have questioned the motivation leading up to that decision. Those who defend the action point to ferocious Japanese resistance at Okinawa and Iwo Jima, and the likelihood of even greater loss of life if an invasion of Japan became necessary. Support for such a position comes even from some Japanese. "If the military had its way," one military expert in Japan has said, "we would have fought until all 80 million Japanese were dead. Only the atomic bomb saved me. Not me alone, but many Japanese. . . ." Those morally repulsed by the incineration of human flesh that resulted from the A-bomb, on the other hand, doubt the necessity of dropping it, citing later U.S. intelligence surveys which concluded that "Japan would have surrendered even if the atomic bombs had not been dropped, even if Russia had not entered the war, and even if no invasion had been planned or contemplated." Distinguished military leaders such as Dwight Eisenhower later opposed use of the bomb. "First, the Japanese were ready to surrender, and it wasn't necessary to hit them with that awful thing," Eisenhower noted. "Second, I hated to see our country be the first to use such a weapon." In light of such statements, some have asked why there was no effort to communicate the horror of the bomb to America's adversaries either through a demonstration explosion or an ultimatum. Others have questioned whether the bomb would have been used on non-Asians, although the fire-bombing of Dresden claimed more victims than Hiroshima. Perhaps most seriously, some have charged that the bomb was used primarily to intimidate the Soviet Union rather than to secure victory over Japan.

Although revulsion at America's deployment of atomic weapons is understandable, it now appears that no one in the inner circles of American military and political power ever seriously entertained the possibility of *not* using the bomb. As Henry Stimson later recalled, "it was our common objective, throughout the war, to be the first to produce an atomic weapon and use it. . . . At no time, from 1941 to 1945, did I ever hear it suggested by the president, or by any other responsible member of the government, that atomic energy should not be used in the war." As historians Martin Sherwin and Barton Bernstein have shown, the momentum behind the Manhattan Project was such that no one ever debated the underlying assumption that, once perfected, nuclear weapons would be used. General George Marshall told the British, as well as Truman and Stimson, that a land invasion of Japan would cause casualties ranging from five hundred thousand to more than a million American troops. Any president who refused to use atomic weapons in the face of such projections could logically be accused of needlessly sacrificing American lives. Moreover, the enemy was the same nation that had unleashed a wanton and brutal attack on Pearl Harbor. As Truman later explained to a journalist, "When you deal with a beast, you have to treat him as a beast." Although many of the scientists who had seen the first explosion of the bomb in New Mexico were in awe of its destructive potential and hoped to find some way to avoid its use in war, the idea of a demonstration met with skepticism. Only one or two bombs existed. What if, in a demonstration, they failed to detonate? Thus, as horrible as it may seem in retrospect, no one ever seriously doubted the necessity of dropping the bomb on Japan once the weapon was perfected.*

---

* The decision to drop a second bomb, two days after Hiroshima, of course, raises other questions. Why, once the horror of the weapon had been displayed, was it necessary to use it again so quickly, before the Japanese even had time to consider the awesome implications of its power? The only answer seems to be the bureaucratic and organizational momentum of decisions already made in the first instance that were never re-examined. Others have asked why the United States did not wait to see whether Russia's entry into the war on August 6 was sufficient to cause a Japanese surrender. What was the hurry, these historians ask, unless one purpose in dropping the bomb was to intimidate Russia.

On the Russian issue, however, there now seems little doubt that administration officials thought long and hard about the bomb's impact on postwar relations with the Soviet Union. Faced with what seemed to be the growing intransigence of the Soviet Union toward virtually all postwar questions, Truman and his advisors concluded that possession of the weapon would give the United States unprecedented leverage to push Russia toward a more accommodating position. Senator Edwin Johnson stated the equation crassly, but clearly. "God Almighty in his infinite wisdom," the Senator said, "[has] dropped the atomic bomb in our lap . . . [now] with vision and guts and plenty of atomic bombs, . . . [the U.S. can] compel mankind to adopt a policy of lasting peace . . . or be burned to a crisp." Stating the same argument with more sophistication prior to Hiroshima, Stimson told Truman that the bomb might well "force a favorable settlement of Eastern European questions with the Russians." Truman agreed. If the weapon worked, he noted, "I'll certainly have a hammer on those boys."

Use of the bomb as a diplomatic lever played a pivotal role in Truman's preparation for his first meeting with Stalin at Potsdam. Not only would the conference address such critical questions as Eastern Europe, Germany, and Russia's involvement in the war against Japan; it would also provide a crucial opportunity for America to drive home with forcefulness its foreign policy beliefs about future relationships with Russia. Stimson and other advisors urged the president to hold off on any confrontation with Stalin until the bomb was ready. "Over any such tangled wave of problems," Stimson noted, "the bomb's secret will be dominant. . . . It seems a terrible thing to gamble with such big stakes and diplomacy without having your master card in your hand." Although Truman could not delay the meeting because of a prior commitment to hold it in July, the president was well aware of the bomb's significance. Already noted for his brusque and assertive manner, Truman suddenly took on new confidence in the midst of the Potsdam negotiations when word arrived that the bomb had successfully been tested. "He was a changed man," Churchill noted. "He told the Russians just where they got on and off and generally bossed the whole meeting." Now, the agenda was changed. Russian involvement in the Japanese war no longer seemed so important. Moreover, the United States had as a bargaining chip the most powerful weapon ever unleashed. Three days later, Truman walked up to Stalin and casually told him that the United States had "perfected a very powerful explosive which we're going to use against the Japanese." No mention was made of sharing information about the bomb, or of future cooperation to avoid an arms race.

Yet the very nature of the new weapon proved a mixed blessing, making it as much a source of provocation as of diplomatic leverage. Strategic bombing surveys throughout the war had shown that mass bombings, far from demoralizing the enemy, often redoubled his commitment to resist. An American monopoly on atomic weapons would, in all likelihood, have the same effect on the Russians, a proud people. As Stalin told an American diplomat later, "the nuclear weapon is something with which you frighten people [who have] weak nerves." Yet if the war had proven anything, it was that Russian nerves were remarkably strong. Rather than intimidate the Soviets, Dean Acheson pointed out, it was more likely that evidence of Anglo-American cooperation in the Manhattan Project would seem to them "unanswerable evidence of . . . a combination against them. . . . It is impossible that a government as powerful and power conscious as the Soviet government could fail to react vigorously to the situation. It must and will exert every energy to restore the loss of power which the situation has produced."

In fact, news of the bomb's development simply widened the gulf further between the superpowers, highlighting the mistrust that existed between them, with sources of antagonism increasing far faster than efforts at cooperation. On May 11, two days after Germany surrendered—and two weeks after the Truman-Molotov confrontation—America had abruptly terminated all lend-lease shipments to the Soviet Union that were not directly related to the war against Japan. Washington even ordered ships in the mid-Atlantic to turn around. The action had been taken largely in rigid bureaucratic compliance with a new law governing lend-lease just enacted by Congress, but Truman had been warned of the need to handle the matter in a way that was sensitive to Soviet pride. Instead, he signed the termination order without even reading it. Although eventually some shipments were resumed, the damage had been done. The action was "brutal," Stalin later told Harry Hopkins, implemented in a "scornful and abrupt manner." Had the United States consulted Russia about the issue "frankly" and on "a friendly basis," the Soviet dictator said, "much could have been done"; but if the action "was designed as pressure on the Russians in order to soften them up, then it was a fundamental mistake."

Russian behavior through these months, on the other hand, offered little encouragement for the belief that friendship and cooperation ranked high on the Soviet agenda. In addition to violating the spirit of the Yalta accords by jailing the sixteen members of the Polish underground and signing a separate peace treaty with the Lublin Poles, Stalin seemed more intent on reviving and validating his reputation as architect of the purges than as one who wished to collaborate in spreading democracy. He jailed thousands of Russian POWs returning from German prison camps, as if their very presence on foreign soil had made them enemies of the Russian state. One veteran was imprisoned because he had accepted a present from a British comrade in arms, another for making a critical comment about Stalin in a letter. Even Molotov's wife was sent to Siberia. In the meantime, hundreds of thousands of minority nationalities in the Soviet Union were removed forcibly from their homelands when they protested the attempted obliteration of their ancient identities. Some Westerners speculated that Stalin was clinically psychotic, so paranoid about the erosion of his control over the Russian people that he would do anything to close Soviet borders and prevent the Russian people from getting a taste of what life in a more open society would be like. Winston Churchill, for example, wondered whether Stalin might not be more fearful of Western friendship than of Western hostility, since greater cooperation with the noncommunist world could well lead to a dismantling of the rigid totalitarian control he previously had exerted. For those American diplomats who were veterans of service in Moscow before the war, Soviet actions and attitudes seemed all too reminiscent of the vise-like terror they remembered from the worst days of the 1930s.

When Truman, Stalin, and Churchill met in Potsdam in July 1945, these suspicions were temporarily papered over, but no progress was made on untying the Gordian knots that plagued the wartime alliance. Truman sought to improve the Allies' postwar settlement with Italy, hoping to align that country more closely with the West. Stalin agreed on the condition that changes favorable to the Soviets be approved for Romania, Hungary, Bulgaria, and Finland. When Truman replied that there had been no free elections in those countries, Stalin retorted that there had been none in Italy either. On the issue of general reparations the three powers agreed to treat each occupation zone separately. As a result, one problem was solved, but in the process the future division of Germany was almost assured. The tone of the discussions was clearly not friendly. Truman raised the issue of the infamous Katyn massacre, where Soviet troops killed thousands of Polish soldiers and bulldozed them into a common grave. When Truman asked Stalin directly what had happened to the Polish officers, the Soviet dictator responded: "they went away." After Churchill insisted that an iron fence had come down around British representatives in Romania, Stalin dismissed the charges as "all fairy tales." No major conflicts were resolved, and the key problems of reparation amounts, four-power control over Germany, the future of Eastern Europe, and the structure of any permanent peace settlement were simply referred to the Council of Foreign Ministers. There, not surprisingly, they festered, while the pace toward confrontation accelerated.

The first six months of 1946 represented a staccato series of Cold War events, accompanied by increasingly inflammatory rhetoric. In direct violation of a wartime agreement that all allied forces would leave Iran within six months of the war's end, Russia continued its military occupation of the oil-rich region of Azerbaijan. Responding to the Iranian threat, the United States demanded a U.N. condemnation of the Soviet presence in Azerbaijan and, when Russian tanks were seen entering the area, prepared for a direct confrontation. "Now we will give it to them with both barrels," James Byrnes declared. Unless the United States stood firm, one State Department official warned, "Azerbaijan [will] prove to [be] the first shot fired in the Third World War." Faced with such clear-cut determination, the Soviets ultimately withdrew from Iran.

Yet the tensions between the two powers continued to mount. In early February, Stalin issued what Supreme Court Justice William Douglas called the "Declaration of World War III," insisting that war was inevitable as long as capitalism survived and calling for massive sacrifice at home. A month later Winston Churchill—with Truman at his side—responded at Fulton, Missouri, declaring that "from Stetting in the Baltic to Trieste in the Adriatic, an iron curtain has descended across the [European] continent." Claiming that "God has willed" the United States and Britain to hold a monopoly over atomic weapons, Churchill called for a "fraternal association of the English speaking people" against their common foes. Although Truman made no public statement, privately he had told Byrnes in January: "I'm tired of babying the Soviets. They [must be] faced with an iron fist and strong language. . . . Only one language do they understand—how many divisions have you?" Stalin, meanwhile, charged Britain and the United States with repressing democratic insurgents in Greece, declaring that it was the western Allies, not the Soviet Union, that endangered world peace. "When Mr. Churchill calls for a new war," Molotov told a foreign ministers' meeting in May, "and makes militant speeches on two continents, he represents the worst of twentieth-century imperialism."

During the spring and summer, clashes occurred on virtually all the major issues of the Cold War. After having told the Soviet Union that the State Department had "lost" its $6 billion loan request made in January 1945, the United States offered a $1 billion loan in the spring of 1946 as long as the Soviet Union agreed to join the World Bank and accept the credit procedures and controls of that body. Not surprisingly, the Russians refused, announcing instead a new five-year plan that would promote economic self-sufficiency. Almost paranoid about keeping Westerners out of Russia, Stalin had evidently concluded that participation in a Western-run financial consortium was too serious a threat to his own total authority. "Control of their border areas," the historian Walter LaFeber has noted, "was worth more to the Russians than a billion, or even ten billion dollars." A year earlier the response might have been different. But 1946 was a "year of cement," with little if any willingness to accept flexibility. In Germany, meanwhile, the Russians rejected a Western proposal for unifying the country and instead determined to build up their own zone. The United States reciprocated by declaring it would no longer cooperate with Russia by removing reparations from the west to the east. The actions guaranteed a permanent split of Germany and coincided with American plans to rebuild the West German economy.

The culminating breakdown of U.S.-Soviet relations came over the failure to secure agreement on the international control of atomic energy. After Potsdam, some American policymakers had urged the president to take a new approach on sharing such control with the Soviet Union. The atom bomb, Henry Stimson warned Truman in the fall of 1945, would dominate America's relations with Russia. "If we fail to approach them now and continue to negotiate with . . . this weapon rather ostentatiously on our hip, their suspicions and their distrust of our purposes and motives will increase." Echoing the same them, Dr. Harold Urey, a leading atomic scientist, told the

Senate that by making and storing atomic weapons, "we are guilty of begin-ning the arms race." Furthermore, there was an inherent problem with the "gun on our hip" approach. As the scientist Vannevar Bush noted, "there is no powder in the gun, [nor] could [it] be drawn," unless the United States were willing to deploy the A-bomb to settle diplomatic disputes. Recognizing this, Truman set Dean Acheson and David Lilienthal to work in the winter of 1945–46 to prepare a plan for international control.

But by the time the American proposal had been completed, much of the damage in Soviet-American relations seemed irreparable. Although the Truman plan envisioned ultimate sharing of international control, it left the United States with an atomic monopoly—and in a dominant position—until the very last stage. The Soviets would have no veto power over inspec-tions or sanctions, and even at the end of the process, the United States would control the majority of votes within the body responsible for devel-oping peaceful uses of atomic energy inside the Soviet Union. When the Russians asked to negotiate about the specifics of the plan, they were told they must either accept the entire package or nothing at all. In the context of Soviet-American relations in 1946, the result was predictable—the genie of the atomic arms race would remain outside the bottle.

Not all influential Americans were pleased by the growing polarization. Averell Harriman, who a year earlier had been in the forefront of those de-manding a hardline position from Truman, now pulled back somewhat. "We must recognize that we occupy the same planet as the Russians," he said, "and whether we like it or not, disagreeable as they may be, we have to find some method of getting along." The columnist Walter Lippmann, deeply concerned about the direction of events, wondered whether the in-experience and personal predilections of some of America's negotiators might not be part of the problem. Nor were all the signs negative. After his initial confrontation with Molotov, Truman appeared to have second thoughts, sending Harry Hopkins to Moscow to attempt to find some com-mon ground with Stalin on Poland and Eastern Europe. The Russians, in turn, had not been totally aggressive. They withdrew from Hungary after free elections in that country had led to the establishment of a noncom-munist regime. Czechoslovakia was also governed by a coalition govern-ment with a Western-style parliament. The British, at least, announced themselves satisfied with the election process in Bulgaria. Even in Romania, some concessions were made to include elements more favorably disposed to the West. The Russians finally backed down in Iran—under considerable pressure—and would do so again in a dispute over the Turkish straits in the late summer of 1946.

Still, the events of 1946 had the cumulative effect of creating an aura of inevitability about bipolar confrontation in the world. The preponder-ance of energy in each country seemed committed to the side of suspicion and hostility rather than mutual accommodation. If Stalin's February pre-diction of inevitable war between capitalism and communism embodied in

An atomic test at Bikini Island in 1946 produces a "mushroom-shaped cloud" that soon became synonymous with the threat of radioactive poisoning. Not only did atomic weapons transform foreign policy and military strategy. They also raised the specter of radiation disease carried through the atmosphere hundreds and even thousands of miles from the site of an explosion. *(National Archives)*

its purest form Russia's jaundiced perception of relations between the two countries, an eight-thousand-word telegram from George Kennan to the State Department articulated the dominant frame of reference within which Soviet actions would be perceived by U.S. officials. Perhaps *the* preeminent expert on the Soviets, and a veteran of service in Moscow in the thirties as well as the forties, Kennan had been asked to prepare an analysis of Stalin's speech. Responding in words intended to command attention to

Washington, Kennan declared that the United States was confronted with a "political force committed fanatically to the belief that [with the] United States there can be no permanent *modus vivendi,* that it is desirable and necessary that the internal harmony of our society be broken if Soviet power is to be secure." According to Kennan, the Russians truly believed the world to be divided permanently into capitalist and socialist camps, with the Soviet Union dedicated to "ever new heights of military power" even as it sought to subvert its enemies through an "underground operating directorate of world communism." The analysis was frightening, confirming the fears of those most disturbed by the Soviet system's denial of human rights and hardline posture toward Western demands for free elections and open borders in occupied Europe. Almost immediately, the Kennan telegram became required reading for the entire diplomatic and military establishment in Washington.

Declaration of the Cold War

In late February 1947, a British official journeyed to the State Department to inform Dean Acheson that the crushing burden of Britain's economic crisis prevented her from any longer accepting responsibility for the economic and military stability of Greece and Turkey. The message, Secretary of State George Marshall noted, "was tantamount to British abdication from the Middle East, with obvious implications as to their successor." Conceivably, America could have responded quietly, continuing the steady stream of financial support already going into the area. Despite aid to the insurgents from Yugoslavia and Bulgaria, the war going on in Greece was primarily a civil struggle, with the British side viewed by many as reactionary in its politics. But instead, Truman administration officials seized the moment as the occasion for a dramatic new commitment to fight communism. In their view, Greece and Turkey could well hold the key to the future of Europe itself. Hence they decided to ask Congress for $400 million in military and economic aid. In the process, the administration publicly defined postwar diplomacy, for the first time, as a universal conflict between the forces of good and the forces of evil.

Truman portrayed the issue as he did, at least in part, because his aides had failed to convince congressmen about the merits of the case on grounds of self-interest alone. Americans were concerned about the Middle East for many reasons—preservation of political stability, guarantee of access to mineral resources, a need to assure a prosperous market for American goods. Early drafts of speeches on the issue had focused specifically on economic questions. America could not afford, one advisor noted, to allow Greece and similar areas to "spiral downward into economic anarchy." But such arguments, another advisor noted, "made the whole thing sound like an investment prospectus." Indeed, when Secretary of State Marshall used such arguments of self-interest with congressmen, his words fell on deaf ears, particularly given the commitment of Republicans to cut government spending to the bone. It was at that moment, Dean Acheson recalled, that "in desperation I whispered to [Marshall] a request to speak. This was my crisis. For a week I had nurtured it."

When Acheson took the floor, he transformed the atmosphere in the room. The issue, he declared, was the effort by Russian communism to seize dominance over three continents, and encircle and capture Western Europe. "Like apples in a barrel infected by the corruption of one rotten one, the corruption of Greece would infect Iran and alter the Middle East . . . Africa . . . Italy and France." The struggle was ultimate, Acheson concluded. "Not since Rome and Carthage has there been such a polarization of power on this earth. . . . We and we alone are in a position to break up" the Soviet quest for world domination. Suddenly, the congressmen sat up and took notice. *That* argument, Senator Arthur Vandenberg told the president, would be successful. If Truman wanted his program of aid to be approved, he would—like Acheson—have to "scare hell" out of the American people.

By the time Truman came before Congress on March 12, the issue was no longer whether the United States should extend economic aid to Greece and Turkey on a basis of self-interest, but rather whether America was willing to sanction the spread of tyrannical communism everywhere in the world. Facing the same dilemma Roosevelt had confronted during the 1930s in his effort to get Americans ready for war, Truman sensed that only if the issues were posed as directly related to the nation's fundamental moral concern—not just self-interest—would there be a possibility of winning political support. Hence, as Truman defined the question, the world had to choose "between alternative ways of life." One option was "free," based on "representative government, free elections, guarantees of individual liberty, and freedom of speech and religion." The other option was "tyranny," based on "terror and oppression, a controlled press and radio, . . . and a suppression of personal freedoms." Given a choice between freedom and totalitarianism, Truman concluded, "it must be the policy of the United States to support free peoples who are resisting attempted subjugation by armed minorities."

Drawing on the "worst case" scenario implicit in Kennan's telegram, Truman, in effect, had presented the issue of American-Soviet relations as one of pure ideological and moral conflict. There were some who criticized him. Senator Robert Taft, for example, wondered whether, if the United States took responsibility for Greece and Turkey, Americans could object to the Russians continuing their domination over Eastern Europe. Secretary of State Marshall was disturbed at "the extent to which the anticommunist element of the speech was stressed." And George Kennan, concerned over how his views had been used, protested against the president's strident tone. But Truman and Acheson had understood the importance of defining the issue on grounds of patriotism and moral principle. If the heart of the question was the universal struggle of freedom against tyranny—not taking sides in a civil war—who could object to what the government proposed? It was, Senator Arthur Vandenberg noted, "almost like a presidential request for a declaration of war. . . . There is precious little we can do except say yes." By mid-May, Truman's aid package had passed Congress over-whelmingly.

On the same day the Truman Doctrine received final approval, George Marshall and his aides at the State Department were busy shaping what Truman would call the second half of the same walnut—the Marshall Plan of massive economic support to rebuild Western Europe. Britain, France, Germany, Italy, Belgium—all were devastated by the war, their cities lying in rubble, their industrial base gutted. It was difficult to know if they could survive, yet the lessons of World War I suggested that political democracy and stability depended on the presence of a healthy and thriving economic order. Already American officials were concerned that Italy—and perhaps France—would succumb to the political appeal of native communists and become victims of what William Bullitt had called the "red amoeba" spreading all across Europe. Furthermore, America's selfish economic interests demanded strong trading partners in Western Europe. "No nation in modern times," Assistant Secretary of State Will Clayton had said, "can long expect to enjoy a rising standard of living without increased foreign trade." America imported from Europe only half of what it exported, and Western Europe was quickly running out of dollars to pay for American goods. If some form of massive support to reconstruct Europe's economy were not developed, economic decay there would spread, unemployment in America would increase, and political instability could well lead to communist takeovers of hitherto "friendly" countries.

The chief virtue of the plan Marshall and his aides were crafting was its fusion of these political and economic concerns. As Truman told a Baylor University audience in March 1947, "peace, freedom, and world trade are indivisible. . . . We must not go through the '30s again." Since free enterprise was seen as the foundation for democracy and prosperity, helping European economies would both assure friendly governments abroad and additional jobs at home. To accomplish that goal, however, the United States would need to give economic aid directly rather than through the United Nations, since only under those circumstances would American control be assured. Ideally, the Marshall Plan would provide an economic arm to the political strategy embodied in the Truman Doctrine. Moreover, if presented as a program in which even Eastern European countries could participate, it would provide, at last potentially, a means of including pro-Soviet countries and breaking Stalin's political and economic domination over Eastern Europe.

On that basis, Marshall dramatically announced his proposal at Harvard University's commencement on June 5, 1947. "Our policy is directed not against any country or doctrine," Marshall said, "but against hunger,

At the end of World War II, much of Western Europe was in rubble as a consequence of wartime bombing. The devastation was such that some wondered whether the societies and economies of the war-struck countries could ever revive. It was this concern that helped to prompt the Marshall Plan. Pictured here is Cologne, with only the famous Cathedral intact after the bombing. *(National Archives)*

poverty, desperation, and chaos. Its purpose should be revival of a working economy. Any government that is willing to assist in the task of recovery will find full cooperation . . . on the part of the United States government." Responding, French Foreign Minister George Bidault invited officials throughout Europe, including the Soviet Union, to attend a conference in Paris to draw up a plan of action. Poland and Czechoslovakia expressed interest, and Molotov himself came to Paris with eighty-nine aides.

Rather than inaugurate a new era of cooperation, however, the next few days simply reaffirmed how far polarization had already extended. Molotov urged that each country present its own needs independently to the United States. Western European countries, on the other hand, insisted that all the countries cooperate in a joint proposal for American consideration. Since the entire concept presumed extensive sharing of economic data on each country's resources and liabilities, as well as Western control over how the aid would be expended, the Soviets angrily walked out of the deliberations. In fact, the United States never believed that the Russians would participate in the project, knowing that it was a violation of every Soviet precept to open their economic records to examination and control by capitalist outsiders. Furthermore, U.S. strategy was premised on a major rebuilding of German industry—something profoundly threatening to the Russians. Ideally, Americans viewed a thriving Germany as the foundation for revitalizing the economies of all Western European countries, and providing the key to prosperity on both sides of the Atlantic. To a remarkable extent, that was precisely the result of the Marshall Plan. Understandably, such a prospect frightened the Soviets, but the consequence was to further the split between East and West, and in particular, to undercut the possibility of promoting further cooperation with countries like Hungary and Czechoslovakia.

In the weeks and months after the Russians left Paris, the final pieces of the Cold War were set in place. Shortly after the Soviet departure from Paris the Russians announced the creation of a series of bilateral trade agreements called the "Molotov Plan," designed to link Eastern bloc countries and provide a Soviet answer to the Marshall Plan. Within the same week the Russians created a new Communist Information Bureau (Cominform), including representatives from the major Western European communist parties, to serve as a vehicle for imposing Stalinist control on anyone who might consider deviating from the party line. Speaking at the Cominform meeting in August, André Zhdanov issued the Soviet Union's rebuttal to the Truman Doctrine. The United States, he charged, was organizing the countries of the Near East, Western Europe, and South America into an alliance committed to the destruction of communism. Now, he said, the "new democracies" of Eastern Europe—plus their allies in developing countries—must form a counter bloc. The world would thus be made up of "two camps," each ideologically, politically, and, to a growing extent, militarily defined by its opposition to the other.

To assure that no one misunderstood, Russia moved quickly to impose a steel-like grip on Eastern Europe. In August 1947 the Soviets purged all left-wing, anticommunist leaders from Hungary and then rigged elections to assure a pro-Soviet regime there. Six months later, in February 1948, Stalin moved on Czechoslovakia as well, insisting on the abolition of independent parties and sending Soviet troops to the Czech border to back up Soviet demands for an all new communist government. After Foreign Minister Jan Masaryk either jumped or was pushed from a window in Prague, the last vestige of resistance faded. "We are [now] faced with exactly the same situation . . . Britain and France faced in 1938–39 with Hitler," Truman wrote. The Czech coup coincided with overwhelming approval of the Marshall Plan by the American Congress. Two weeks later, on March 5, General Lucius Clay sent his telegram from Germany warning of imminent war with Russia. Shortly thereafter, Truman called on Congress to implement Universal Military Training for all Americans. (The plan was never put in place.) By the end of the month Russia had instituted a year-long blockade of all supplies to Berlin in protest against the West's decision to unify her occupation zones in Germany and institute currency reform. Before the end of spring, the Brussels Pact had brought together the major powers of Western Europe in a mutual defense pact that a year later would provide the basis for NATO. If the Truman Doctrine, in Bernard Baruch's words, had been "a declaration of ideological or religious war," the Marshall Plan, the Molotov Plan, and subsequent developments in Eastern Europe represented the economic, political, and military demarcations that would define the terrain on which the war would be fought. The Cold War had begun.

Causes and Interpretations

Any historian who studies the Cold War must come to grips with a series of questions, which, even if unanswerable in a definitive fashion, nevertheless compel examination. Was the Cold War inevitable? If not, how could it have been avoided? What role did personalities play? Were there points at which different courses of action might have been followed? What economic factors were central? What ideological causes? Which historical forces? At what juncture did alternative possibilities become invalid? When was the die cast? Above all, what were the primary reasons for defining the world in such a polarized and ideological framework?

The simplest and easiest response is to conclude that Soviet-American confrontation was so deeply rooted in differences of values, economic systems, or historical experiences that only extraordinary action—by individuals or groups—could have prevented the conflict. One version of the inevitability hypothesis would argue that the Soviet Union, given its commitment to the ideology of communism, was dedicated to worldwide revolution and would use any and every means possible to promote the demise of the West. According to this view—based in large part on the rhetoric of Stalin and Lenin—world revolution constituted the sole priority of Soviet policy. Even the appearance of accommodation was a Soviet design to soften up capitalist states for eventual confrontation. As defined, admittedly in oversimplified fashion, by George Kennan in his famous 1947 article on containment, Russian diplomacy "moves along the prescribed path, like a persistent toy automobile, wound up and headed in a given direction, stopping only when it meets some unanswerable force." Soviet subservience to a universal, religious creed ruled out even the possibility of mutual concessions, since even temporary accommodation would be used by the Russians as part of their grand scheme to secure world domination.

A second version of the same hypothesis—argued by some American revisionist historians—contends that the endless demands of capitalism for new markets propelled the United States into a course of intervention and imperialism. According to this argument, a capitalist society can survive only by opening new areas for exploitation. Without the development of multinational corporations, strong ties with German capitalists, and free trade across national boundaries, America would revert to the depression of the prewar years. Hence, an aggressive internationalism became the only means through which the ruling class of the United States could retain hegemony. In support of this argument, historians point to the number of American policymakers who explicitly articulated an economic motivation for U.S. foreign policy. "We cannot expect domestic prosperity under our system," Assistant Secretary of State Dean Acheson said, "without a constantly expanding trade with other nations." Echoing the same theme, the State Department's William Clayton declared: "We need markets—big markets—around the world in which to buy and sell. . . . We've got to export three times as much as we exported just before the war if we want to keep our industry running somewhere near capacity." According to this argument, economic necessity motivated the Truman Doctrine, the Marshall Plan, and the vigorous efforts of U.S. policymakers to open up Eastern Europe for trade and investment. Within such a frame of reference, it was the capitalist economic system—not Soviet commitment to world revolution—that made the Cold War unavoidable.

Still a third version of the inevitability hypothesis—partly based on the first two—would insist that historical differences between the two superpowers and their systems of government made any efforts toward postwar cooperation almost impossible. Russia had always been deeply suspicious of the West, and under Stalin that suspicion had escalated into paranoia, with Soviet leaders fearing that any opening of channels would ultimately destroy their own ability to retain total mastery over the Russian people. The West's failure to implement early promises of a second front and the subsequent divisions of opinion over how to treat occupied territory had profoundly strained any possible basis of trust. From an American perspective, in turn, it stretched credibility to expect a nation committed to human rights to place confidence in a ruthless dictator, who in one Yugoslav's words, had single-handedly been responsible for more Soviet deaths than all the armies of Nazi Germany. Through the purges, collectivization, and mass imprisonment of Russian citizens, Stalin had presided over the killing of 20 million of his own people. How then could he be trusted to respect the rights of others? According to this argument, only the presence of a common enemy had made possible even short-term solidarity between Russia and the United States; in the absence of a German foe, natural antagonisms were bound to surface. America had one system of politics, Russia another, and as Truman declared in 1948, "a totalitarian state is no different whether you call it Nazi, fascist, communist, or Franco Spain."

Yet, in retrospect, these arguments for inevitability tell only part of the story. Notwithstanding the Soviet Union's rhetorical commitment to an ideology of world revolution, there is abundant evidence of Russia's willingness to forego ideological purity in the cause of national interest. Stalin, after all, had turned away from world revolution in committing himself to building "socialism in one country." Repeatedly, he indicated his readiness to betray the communist movement in China and to accept the leadership of Chiang

Kai-shek. George Kennan recalled the Soviet leader "snorting rather contemptuously . . . because one of our people asked them what they were going to give to China when [the war] was over." "We have a hundred cities of our own to build in the Soviet Far East," Stalin had responded. "If anybody is going to give anything to the Far East, I think it's you." Similarly, Stalin refused to give any support to communists in Greece during their rebellion against British domination there. As late as 1948 he told the vice-premier of Yugoslavia, "What do you think, . . . that Great Britain and the United States . . . will permit you to break their lines of communication in the Mediterranean? Nonsense . . . the uprising in Greece must be stopped, and as quickly as possible."

Nor are the other arguments for inevitability totally persuasive. Without question, America's desire for commercial markets played a role in the strategy of the Cold War. As Truman said in 1949, devotion to freedom of enterprise "is part and parcel of what we call America." Yet was the need for markets sufficient to force a confrontation that ultimately would divert precious resources from other, more productive use? Throughout most of its history, Wall Street has opposed a bellicose position in foreign policy. Similarly, although historical differences are important, it makes no sense to regard them as determinative. After all, the war led to extraordinary examples of cooperation that bridged these differences; if they could be overcome once, then why not again? Thus, while each of the arguments for inevitability reflects truths that contributed to the Cold War, none offers an explanation sufficient of itself, for contending that the Cold War was unavoidable.

A stronger case, it seems, can be made for the position that the Cold War was unnecessary, or at least that conflicts could have been handled in a manner that avoided bipolarization and the rhetoric of an ideological crusade. At no time did Russia constitute a military threat to the United States. "Economically," U.S. Naval Intelligence reported in 1946, "the Soviet Union is exhausted. . . . The U.S.S.R. is not expected to take any action in the next five years which might develop into hostility with Anglo Americans." Notwithstanding the Truman administration's public statements about a Soviet threat, Russia had cut its army from 11.5 to 3 million men after the war. In 1948, its military budget amounted to only half of that of the United States. Even militant anticommunists like John Foster Dulles acknowledged that "the Soviet leadership does not want and would not consciously risk" a military confrontation with the West. Indeed, so exaggerated was American rhetoric about Russia's threat that Hanson Baldwin, military expert of the *New York Times*, compared the claims of our armed forces to the "shepherd who cried wolf, wolf, wolf, when there was no wolf." Thus, on purely factual grounds, there existed no military basis for the fear that the Soviet Union was about to seize world domination, despite the often belligerent pose Russia took on political issues.

A second, somewhat more problematic, argument for the thesis of avoidability consists of the extent to which Russian leaders appeared ready to abide by at least some agreements made during the war. Key, here, is the understanding reached by Stalin and Churchill during the fall of 1944 on the division of Europe into spheres of influence. According to that understanding, Russia was to dominate Romania, have a powerful voice over Bulgaria, and share influence in other Eastern European countries, while Britain and America were to control Greece. By most accounts, that understanding was implemented. Russia refused to intervene on behalf of communist insurgency in Greece. While retaining rigid control over Romania, she provided at least a "fig-leaf of democratic procedure"—sufficient to satisfy the British. For two years the U.S.S.R. permitted the election of noncommunist or coalition regimes in both Hungary and Czechoslovakia. The Finns, meanwhile, were permitted to choose a noncommunist government and to practice Western-style democracy as long as their country maintained a friendly foreign policy toward their neighbor on the east. Indeed, to this day, Finland remains an example of what might have evolved had earlier wartime understandings on both sides been allowed to continue.

What then went wrong? First, it seems clear that both sides perceived the other as breaking agreements that they thought had been made. By signing a separate peace settlement with the Lublin Poles, imprisoning the sixteen members of the Polish underground, and imposing—without regard for democratic appearances—total hegemony on Poland, the Soviets had broken the spirit, if not the letter, of the Yalta accords. Similarly, they blatantly violated the agreement made by both powers to withdraw from Iran once the war was over, thus precipitating the first direct threat of military confrontation during the Cold War. In their attitude toward Eastern Europe, reparations, and peaceful cooperation with the West, the Soviets exhibited increasing rigidity and suspicion after April 1945. On the other hand, Stalin had good reason to accuse the United States of reneging on compacts made during the war. After at least tacitly accepting Russia's right to a sphere of influence in Eastern Europe, the West seemed suddenly to change positions and insist on Western-style democracies and economies. As the historian Robert Dallek has shown, Roosevelt and Churchill gave every indication at Tehran and Yalta that they acknowledged the Soviet's need to have friendly governments in Eastern Europe. Roosevelt seemed to care primarily about securing token or cosmetic concessions toward democratic processes while accepting the *substance* of Russian domination. Instead, misunderstanding developed over the meaning of the Yalta accords, Truman confronted Molotov with demands that the Soviets saw as inconsistent with prior understandings, and mutual suspicion rather than cooperation assumed dominance in relations between the two superpowers.

It is this area of misperception and misunderstanding that historians have focused on recently as most critical to the emergence of the Cold War. Presumably, neither side had a master plan of how to proceed once the war ended. Stalin's ambitions, according to recent scholarship, were ill-defined, or at least amenable to modification depending on America's posture. The United States, in turn, gave mixed signals, with Roosevelt implying to every group his agreement with their point of view, yet ultimately keeping his personal intentions secret. If, in fact, both sides could have agreed to a sphere-of-influence policy—albeit with some modifications to satisfy American political opinion—there could perhaps have been a foundation for continued accommodation. Clearly, the United States intended to retain control over its sphere of influence, particularly in Greece, Italy, and Turkey. Moreover, the United States insisted on retaining total domination over the Western hemisphere, consistent with the philosophy of the Monroe Doctrine. If the Soviets had been allowed similar control over their sphere of influence in Eastern Europe, there might have existed a basis for compromise. As John McCloy asked at the time, "[why was it necessary] to have our cake and eat it too? . . . To be free to operate under this regional arrangement in South America and at the same time intervene promptly in Europe." If the United States and Russia had both acknowledged the spheres of influence implicit in their wartime agreements, perhaps a different pattern of relationships might have emerged in the postwar world.

The fact that such a pattern did not emerge raises two issues, at least from an American perspective. The first is whether different leaders or advisors might have achieved different foreign policy results. Some historians believe that Roosevelt, with his subtlety and skill, would have found a way to promote collaboration with the Russians, whereas Truman, with his short temper, inexperience, and insecurity, blundered into unnecessary and harmful confrontations. Clearly, Roosevelt himself—just before his death— was becoming more and more concerned about Soviet intransigence and aggression. Nevertheless, he had always believed that through personal pressure and influence, he could find a way to persaude "uncle Joe." On the basis of what evidence we have, there seems good reason to believe that the Russians did place enormous trust in FDR. Perhaps—just perhaps—Roosevelt could have found a way to talk "practical arithmetic" with Stalin rather than algebra and discover a common ground. Certainly, if recent historians are correct in seeing the Cold War as caused by both Stalin's undefined ambitions and America's failure to communicate effectively and consistently its view on where it would draw the line with the Russians, then Roosevelt's long history of interaction with the Soviets would presumably have placed him in a better position to negotiate than the inexperienced Truman.*

The second issue is more complicated, speaking to a political problem which beset both Roosevelt and Truman—namely, the ability of an American president to formulate and win support for a foreign policy on the basis of national self-interest rather than moral purity. At some point in the past, an American diplomat wrote in 1967:

> [T]here crept into the ideas of Americans about foreign policy . . . a histrionic note, . . . a desire to appear as something greater perhaps than one ac-

---

* It should go without saying that, on the other side, a leader other than Stalin could have made a significant difference in the Soviet posture. Stalin's ruthlessness, his cruelty, his isolation, and his possible paranoia all contributed substantially to Soviet responsibility for the Cold War.

tually was. . . . It was inconceivable that any war in which we were involved could be less than momentous and decisive for the future of humanity. . . . As each war ended, . . . we took appeal to universalistic, utopian ideals, related not to the specifics of national interest but to legalistic and moralistic concepts that seemed better to accord with the pretentious significance we had attached to our war effort.

As a consequence, the diplomat went on, it became difficult to pursue a policy not defined by the language of "angels or devils," "heroes" or "blackguards."

Clearly, Roosevelt faced such a dilemma in proceeding to mobilize American support for intervention in the war against Nazism. And Truman encountered the same difficulty in seeking to define a policy with which to meet Soviet postwar objectives. Both presidents, of course, participated in and reflected the political culture that constrained their options. Potentially at least, Roosevelt seemed intent on fudging the difference between self-interest and moralism. He perceived one set of objectives as consistent with reaching an accommodation with the Soviets, and another set of goals as consistent with retaining popular support for his diplomacy at home. It is difficult to avoid the conclusion that he planned—in a very Machiavellian way—to use rhetoric and appearances as a means of disguising his true intention: to pursue a strategy of self-interest. It seems less clear that Truman had either the subtlety or the wish to follow a similarly Machiavellian course. But if he had, the way might have been opened to quite a different—albeit politically risky—series of policies.

None of this, of course, would have guaranteed the absence of conflict in Eastern Europe, Iran, or Turkey. Nor could any action of an American president—however much rooted in self-interest—have obviated the personal and political threat posed by Stalinist tyranny and ruthlessness, particularly if Stalin himself had chosen, for whatever reason, to act out his most aggressive and paranoid instincts. But if a sphere-of-influence agreement had been possible, there is some reason to think—in light of initial Soviet acceptance of Western-style governments in Hungary, Czechoslovakia, and Finland—that the iron curtain might not have descended in the way that it did. In all historical sequences, one action builds on another. Thus, steps toward cooperation rather than confrontation might have created a momentum, a frame of reference and a basis of mutual trust, that could have made unnecessary the total ideological bipolarization that evolved by 1948. In short, if the primary goals of each superpower had been acknowledged and implemented—security for the Russians, some measure of pluralism in Eastern European countries for the United States, and economic interchange between the two blocs—it seems conceivable that the world might have avoided the stupidity, the fear, and the hysteria of the Cold War.

As it was, of course, very little of the above scenario did take place. After the confrontation in Iran, the Soviet declaration of a five-year plan,

Churchill's Fulton, Missouri, speech, and the breakdown of negotiations on an American loan, confrontation between the two superpowers seemed irrevocable. It is difficult to imagine that the momentum building toward the Cold War could have been reversed after the winter and spring of 1946. Thereafter, events assumed an almost inexorable momentum, with both sides using moralistic rhetoric and ideological denunciation to pillory the other. In the United States it became incumbent on the president—in order to secure domestic political support—to defend the Truman Doctrine and the Marshall Plan in universalistic, moral terms. Thus, we became engaged, not in an effort to assure jobs and security, but in a holy war against evil. Stalin, in turn, gave full vent to his crusade to eliminate any vestige of free thought or national independence in Eastern Europe. Reinhold Niebuhr might have been speaking for both sides when he said in 1948, "we cannot afford any more compromises. We will have to stand at every point in our far flung lines."

The tragedy, of course, was that such a policy offered no room for intelligence or flexibility. If the battle in the world was between good and evil, believers and nonbelievers, anyone who questioned the wisdom of established policy risked dismissal as a traitor or worse. In the Soviet Union the Gulag Archipelago of concentration camps and executions was the price of failing to conform to the party line. But the United States paid a price as well. An ideological frame of reference had emerged through which all other information was filtered. The mentality of the Cold War shaped everything, defining issues according to moralistic assumptions, regardless of objective reality. It had been George Kennan's telegram in February 1946 that helped to provide the intellectual basis for this frame of reference by portraying the Soviet Union as "a political force committed fanatically" to confrontation with the United States and domination of the world. It was also George Kennan twenty lears later who so searchingly criticized those who insisted on seeing foreign policy as a battle of angels and devils, heroes and blackguards. And ironically, it was Kennan yet again who declared in the 1970s that "the image of a Stalinist Russia, poised and yearning to attack the west, . . . was largely a product of the western imagination."

But for more than a generation, that image would shape American life and world politics. The price was astronomical—and perhaps—avoidable.

4

"The Other Half of the Walnut"

Social Reform and Activism
in the Postwar Years

At home, at least some Americans hoped that the end of the war would bring new opportunities for social reform and the chance to build on gains made during the war. Although women war workers in 1942 had overwhelmingly declared their desire to return to the role of housewife after the war, the vast majority now expressed a determination to hold onto their wartime jobs. Black Americans, especially in the South, seemed intent on continuing the militancy of the war years. "The old southern Uncle Toms," one newspaper noted, "have had to concede ground to these new southern Negroes who are aligning themselves with liberal whites in the labor movement and in the intellectual fields." Union members, too, looked forward optimistically to the future. Having achieved unprecedented strength during the war (15 million members by 1945), labor leaders were ready to forge ahead further. The CIO's "Operation Dixie" even ventured to organize the almost totally nonunion South.

Five years later, that optimism, too, appeared misplaced and naive. Social reform forces everywhere felt embattled. Although the number of women employed remained virtually the same as at the end of the war, the jobs they held paid far lower wages and offered far less status and prestige. Black Americans had ridden a roller coaster of hope and despair, with some significant legal advances made by the Truman administration; but in the end the government's rhetoric of commitment to racial change was often not matched by performance. In the meantime, organized labor reeled from a series of legislative and political defeats, with internal divisions sapping almost all the energies displayed in the immediate aftermath of the war. Surrounding all these developments was a pervasive aura of anticommunism—a new Red Scare—so powerful that many social causes identified with liberal principles could be tarred by opponents with the fatal brush of being subversive. While for many Americans the postwar years brought unparalleled prosperity and good fortune, for those most concerned with dramatic progress on issues of equality, the same years brought a shrinking of vision and a sharply reduced sense of possibility.*

The Politics of 1945–46

All of this took place within a political framework that, initially at least, seemed hospitable toward liberalism. Despite the elimination of New Deal programs like the Works Progress Administration (WPA) and the National Youth Administration (NYA) during the war, most liberals believed that FDR would resurrect and revitalize the New Deal as soon as the war ended. His 1944 pledge to enact an economic "bill of rights" for all Americans, including decent housing, education, and health care, helped nurture this conviction. New Dealers still talked about helping "the degraded and impoverished . . . the disinherited and despised," and although FDR had sometimes turned his back on these people, they trusted him, believing—almost with religious faith—that he would deliver on his promise of social redemption. As one Georgia black said while waiting for FDR's funeral train to pass by, "he made a way for folks when there wasn't no way."

In *Tomorrow Without Fear*, a book published in 1946, Chester Bowles articulated the liberal vision of what America could be like if it followed the tenets of FDR's program. Wartime spending, Bowles argued, had turned the economy around, improving everyone's standard of living and showing that government investment in such socially beneficial causes as education and health services could keep the economy booming. If the government guaranteed "full production and full employment," consumerism would increase, tax revenues would finance social improvements for "the disinherited," and all Americans would learn "to live constantly better." No one would suffer, everyone would gain, and poverty, sickness, and malnutrition could be eliminated.

In the immediate aftermath of FDR's death, many liberals believed that Harry Truman would carry forward such a program. A loyal supporter of Roosevelt throughout his years in the Senate, Truman pledged to carry forward the policies of the fallen president. "Franklin Roosevelt is not dead,"

---

* This chapter deals primarily with the obstacles that prevented social activists from achieving the reforms they hoped for in 1945. The next chapter focuses on all the positive changes that occurred in the postwar years—changes that brought a better life for millions of Americans and helped lessen the concern with problems of discrimination, which remained. Stated succinctly, though in an oversimplified fashion, these chapters argue that social reform must be distinguished from social change, and that there were two reasons for an absence of greater social reform in the immediate postwar years: (1) the negative response to social activists, partly based on the ascendancy of the politics of anticommunism; and (2) the positive changes in housing, prosperity, and consumerism which occupied the attention and energies of millions of Americans who were enjoying a better life than ever before.

former New York Mayor Fiorello La Guardia declared. "His ideals live." That Truman shared these ideals seemed evident in the sweeping legislative program of social reforms that he proposed to Congress in 1945—a full employment bill, a higher minimum wage, and national housing legislation. Truman's legislative agenda, a political aide observed, "was a reminder to the Democratic Party, to the Congress, to the country, that there was continuity between the new national leadership and the old." Moreover, Truman had "a very personal stake" in the program—to destroy the complacent assumption of his opponents that "with 'that man' gone, the White House would be 'reasonable,' 'sound,' and 'safe.'"

As time passed, however, the same liberals found cause for concern. Truman's tactics and political style appeared to contradict the vision of his legislative program. Attempting to repair some of the erosion of relationships between the executive branch and the congress that had occurred under Roosevelt, he appointed to his cabinet conservatives and moderates well thought of on Capitol Hill—people like James Byrnes, Fred Vinson, Tom Clark, and Clinton Anderson. By late summer, only Harold Ickes and Henry Wallace remained from Roosevelt's cabinet. In the meantime, Congress did little to cope with the human problems inherent in demobilization and reconversion, instead appropriating $5 billion to aid business and industry. As Roosevelt's Secretary of Labor Frances Perkins wrote to Henry Wallace after she left the Truman cabinet, "I find myself wondering profoundly about the . . . political future."

The fate of the Full Employment Act highlighted these concerns. Introduced initially in January 1945, the measure aspired to be the centerpiece of liberal hopes for a prosperous, just society. As originally drawn, it would have made the federal government responsible for providing employment for everyone who was "able to work and seeking work," with the president recommending programs to sustain employment whenever his economic experts projected a dip in the economy. Although such programs might cause short-term budget deficits, supporters believed that in the long run full employment would generate sufficient taxes both to balance the budget and finance social welfare programs such as increased minimum wages and national health insurance.

By the time Congress finally acted on the measure, however, most of its key provisions had been gutted. Truman himself delayed submitting his own version of the bill. Then amendments from conservatives crippled its intent. Instead of "full" employment, the legislation called for "maximum" employment—a phrase that conceivably could justify a jobless rate of 5 or 6 percent. Other amendments provided that federal responsibility for employment should be shared with additional private and governmental bodies, thereby relieving Washington of specific responsibility. By the time the measure was finally passed, it represented a vague statement of principles rather than a plan for action, its most significant reform being the creation of a Council of Economic Advisors to provide recommendations to the president and Congress regarding long-range economic developments. In the meantime, Congress had failed to act on increasing minimum wages or extending Social Security. What had begun as an effort to "fine tune" the economy and provide a foundation for revitalizing the New Deal turned out to be little more than an empty shell.

Although Truman bore only partial responsibility for these setbacks, liberals felt increasingly betrayed by the new president. "The path Franklin Roosevelt charted," Elliott Roosevelt said, "has been grievously—and deliberately—forsaken." Truman's rhetoric was fine. Repeatedly, he urged Congress to enact an agenda of reform. But all too often, the president's words did not translate into action. Nor were liberals reassured by Truman's appointments. In February 1946, Harold Ickes left the cabinet in protest over Truman's selection of a subcabinet officer who had been involved in suspicious oil deals in the southwest. According to the journalist Howard K. Smith, 80 percent of Truman's most important appointments in his first two years had gone to businessmen, corporate lawyers, bankers, and military men. "The effective locus of government," Smith declared, "seems to have shifted from Washington to some place equidistant between Wall Street and West Point."

By the fall election of 1946, liberal hopes for the Truman administration and a progressive Congress seemed crushed. Only 32 percent of the electorate approved of Truman's performance according to an October poll. The end of most price controls in June had prompted a surge of inflation. Labor unrest, in turn, led to massive strikes. Although much of this was not Truman's fault, and many of the defeats of liberal measures could be traced to the same conservative coalition that had frustrated FDR ever since 1937, Truman's own vacillation and ineptitude received much of the blame. "To err is Truman," became the joke of the day. On election day, the voters offered a resounding yes to the Republican question "Had Enough?" and, in a landslide, Republicans won control of the new House of Representatives, 246 to 188, and of the new Senate 51 to 45. Among the victors were Richard Nixon and Joseph McCarthy. So stunned were some Democrats that Senator J. William Fulbright of Arkansas urged Truman to name a Republican as Secretary of State and then resign so that, in the order of constitutional succession in place at the time, a Republican could ascend to the presidency. From the point of view of those committed to rapid social reform, the politics of 1945 and 1946 had proved to be a bitter disappointment.

The Experience of Women

Those women who hoped to consolidate and expand the advances they had made during the war also encountered frustration. Significantly, the vast majority of those who had taken jobs in the midst of the war wished to continue working. In New York the figure was 80 percent, in Detroit 75 percent.

A woman steel worker angrily rejected the idea that women should go back home. "If [women] are capable," she asserted, "I don't see why they should give up their position to men. . . . The old theory that a woman's place is in the home no longer exists. Those days are gone forever." Women over forty-five were particularly committed to retaining their positions. "These are the women who have been developing new skills during the war," one government official noted.

The desire to build on wartime gains was not without support in official Washington. The Women's Advisory Committee, an arm of the War Manpower Commission, urged establishment of a family assistance program and child-care facilities to help women workers. "No society can boast of democratic ideals if it utilizes woman power in a crisis and neglects it in peace," the committee asserted. "To take for granted that a woman does not need work and use this assumption as a basis for dismissal is no less unfair than if the same assumption were used as a basis for dismissal of a man." The War Department, in turn, distributed a pamphlet urging soldiers to share housework and support such innovations as a family allowance, community laundries, and child-care centers. "Family problems are produced by social change," the pamphlet said, "and often can be solved only by further changes." Many magazines and newspapers also supported continued employment for women. "Women have every right to resent the idea," the *Cincinnati Post* editorialized, "that it's their 'duty' to work in times like the present, but that unlike men, they should stay meekly at home when jobs are scarce."

Nevertheless, the dominant theme of postwar popular writing consisted of exhortations insisting that women return to their rightful place in the home. Congress should force "wives and mothers back to the kitchen," one southern senator declared, in order to insure jobs for the millions of veterans who would be returning. Ironically, even the wartime propaganda that had propelled women into the job market now offered a rationalization for their returning to the home. As Leila Rupp has shown, war ads appealed to a "a concept of extended motherhood," urging women to take jobs in order to serve their men who were away fighting. By implication, once the men returned, women should resume their traditional way of serving their loved ones.

One advertisement toward the end of the war highlighted the dual message being sent to women. As a mother in overalls left the house for her job, her daughter asked in a pleading voice: "Mother, when will you stay home again?" The answer was clear. "Some jubilant day," the woman responds, "mother will *stay home again,* doing the job she likes best—making a home for you and daddy, when he gets back." Such ads represented a solution for all seasons. Children need mothers at home; women must take jobs in order to help their men when they are away; and once the men come back, women will turn again to the job they "like best." Against such a portrait, one journalist observed in 1947, the woman who wished to continue working appeared "thoughtless and greedy, . . . extravagant, a poor mate for her husband and a bad housekeeper."

In the face of such cultural assumptions, it was not surprising that many women lost their jobs. Under the Selective Service Act veterans took priority over wartime workers in the competition for their old jobs. Hence, as war plants reconverted to peacetime production, women who were last hired were also first fired. Over 800,000 workers were laid off in the aircraft industry after VJ-Day—most of them women. In the automobile industry women fell from 25 percent of workers in 1944 to 7.5 percent in April of 1946. Overall, women workers were laid off at a rate 75 percent higher than men. With the wartime labor crisis over, some companies reinstituted age requirements which threw women over forty-five out of work, while others such as Detroit-Edison and IBM reimposed earlier restrictions against the hiring of married women.

Despite these developments, a large number of women returned to work after the immediate disruption of demobilization. Between September 1945 and November 1946, 3.25 million women were either laid off or left their jobs; yet in the same period, nearly 2.75 million were hired. Two years after the war ended, women's employment rates had begun to return to wartime peaks. Although the total number of women in manufacturing had declined by nearly a million, there were still 1 million more women in the nation's factories in late 1946 than there had been in 1940. By the end of the decade, the proportion of women at work had increased to 32 percent as opposed to 27 percent a decade earlier. The change was greater than that for the entire preceding thirty years. Moreover, the greatest increase— 77 percent—occurred among women forty-five to fifty-four years old, the group most committed to retaining wartime jobs. By 1950, such women comprised 40 percent of the total number of women at work.

Behind the statistics of continued growth in women's employment, however, lay a story of disappointment and frustration in the fight for economic equality. Although wartime clerical employees had for the most part stayed on the job, those who had worked in the high-paying durable goods areas had lost their jobs, being forced to resume work as waitresses, service workers, or maids instead of working in an aircraft assembly plant or a steel mill. In one survey of Baltimore war workers, women's average weekly wages fell from $50 to $37. At the end of the war, women in manufacturing earned 66 percent of what men were paid. Five years later, the Bureau of Labor Statistics disclosed that women's median earnings were only 53 percent of men's. Far from expanding on the gains they had made during the war, most women still employed in 1950 were back in low-paying jobs with little possibility of promotion and even less public recognition. Only 17 percent of collective bargaining agreements involving women had equal pay clauses. Women might be working in record numbers, but there was little reason to believe that any basic change had occurred in the assumption that their work was worth less than men.

Other barometers of attitudes toward sex equality offered even less reason for optimism. The number of women doctors, lawyers, and superintendents of schools continued to decline. Medical schools imposed a quota of 5 percent on female admissions; 70 percent of all hospitals refused to accept women interns; and medical associations like the New York Obstetrical Society rejected women members. Despite repeated pleas from social welfare advocates, all federal support for child-care facilities ended, with those mothers who needed such centers dismissed as "only [trying] to satisfy their desire for a career." Indeed, said one well-known psychiatrist, women with small children who wished to work were "stimulated by neurotic competition."

Finally, the Equal Right Amendment continued to lack the necessary votes for passage. Although Congress talked of approving the amendment as a means of thanking women for their "magnificent wartime performance," too many people disagreed vociferously over the amendment's implication for protective legislation. Prominent leaders like Eleanor Roosevelt and Mary Anderson insisted that retaining laws that offered special assistance to women was more important than establishing an abstract principle of legal rights. Their attitude was clearly manifested in the Women's Bureau memorandum that dismissed ERA supporters as "a small but militant group of leisure class women [venting] their resentment of not having been born men."

At best, therefore, working women's experience in the five years after World War II proved ambivalent. Although many of the statistical advances made during the war in women's employment had been maintained, the jobs women held bore little resemblance to those popularized by "Rosie the Riveter" during the war. Indeed, the revival of traditional attitudes toward women's "place" created a context in which women who wished employment could find it only by accepting the inequality produced by such attitudes. In the meantime, there seemed little reason for optimism that a successful challenge could be mounted against traditional definitions of women's proper role. Feminism had little support, and there was no evidence of widespread challenge to traditional definitions of masculinity and femininity. Although some change had occurred, it was within a structure of assumptions and values that perpetuated massive inequality between the sexes.

The Black Experience

Perhaps more than any other group, black Americans in 1945 looked forward to advancing their fight for freedom. During the war their share of defense jobs increased from 3 to 8 percent as a result of pressure from labor and civil rights groups. Almost half a million people belonged to the NAACP. Despite persistent racism and continued government indifference, a new sense of ferment and protest was abroad in the land. Whether in

Northern cities or Southern towns, black Americans—together with some white allies—were committed to building on the energies of the war years, seeking to secure a permanent FEPC, to abolish the poll tax, to achieve the basic right of citizenship involved in voter registration, and to outlaw forever the terrorism of lynching. Over a million black soldiers had fought in a war to preserve democracy. Now, many refused to accept passively a return to the status quo of racism.

As in the case of women, the possibility of change depended both on insurgency from below and on a positive response from above. But in contrast to women who lacked a broad-based protest movement, black Americans engaged in a frontal assault on traditional patterns in the culture. Veterans led the way. Sometimes before they even took off their uniforms, they headed for the voter registration office at the county courthouse. In the heart of Mississippi Medgar Evers went to cast his ballot even though whites warned they would shoot him if he tried. In Terrell County, Georgia (long known as "terrible Terrell"), soldiers came back intent on challenging the most oppressive structure of power in the country. In Columbia, Tennessee, black veterans rejected "business as usual," insisting that there would have to be "a new deal" in the jobs they held and the way they were treated. Cities like Winston-Salem, Greensboro, and Altanta even witnessed the building of black political machines which chose candidates to run for citywide office.

The movement from below brought some success. More than 18,000 blacks registered to vote in Atlanta in 1946. In Winston-Salem 3,000 new black voters helped to choose the first black alderman in that city's history in 1947. A few miles away in Greensboro, North Carolina, a voter registration drive doubled the number of blacks on the voting rolls and citizen groups mounted a campaign against the political chicanery whereby whites bought black votes and then ignored black interests. As a result of these efforts, the number of Negroes registered to vote in the south increased from 2 percent in 1940 to 12 percent in 1947.

Yet such successes paled when placed beside the overwhelming intransigence of whites. When Medgar Evers and five other veterans went to vote, white men with pistols drove them away. In Georgia Eugene Talmadge won his race for governor proclaiming that "no Negro will vote in Georgia for the next four years." Afterward, the only black to vote in one district was killed in his front yard by four white men. Nearby, in Walton County, whites shot and killed two other blacks. When one of the victims' wives recognized a member of the shooting gang, the two wives were murdered also. As Isaac Woodward got off the bus in South Carolina, still wearing his uniform, policemen blinded him with billy clubs. And in Columbia, Tennessee, whites rioted in protest against "uppity" blacks insisting on their rights. Seventy Negroes were arrested, and a mob broke into the jail to murder two of the prisoners. All this took place in the first eight months of 1946.

Behind such repression lay a hundred more subtle ways of quelling dissent. Blacks knew that when a registrar asked a Negro to explain the mean-

Despite the successful conclusion of America's war for democracy, blacks in the South still had to cope with the daily indignities of segregation, as reflected in this 1945 photograph of a "Colored Only" store in Belle Glade, Florida. *(National Archives)*

ing of "habeas corpus," the real message was, "habeas corpus—that means that this black man ain't going to register today." The head of the White Citizens Council in Mississippi pointed out that 95 percent of blacks were employed by whites. Hence anyone who dared to register to vote could simply be told "take a vacation." Insurance policies could be cancelled, credit lines cut off, sharecroppers evicted from their land if Negroes dared attempt to register. In Alabama, a black voter applicant had to get two whites to vouch for his citizenship in order to be enrolled. The chances of doing so were summed up by a former president of the Alabama Bar Association: "No Negro is good enough and no Negro will ever be good enough to participate in making the law under which the white people in Alabama have to live." For those who did not get the message, Mississippi's Senator Theodore Bilbo made it crystal clear. "If there is a single man or woman serving [as a registrar]," Bilbo said during his re-election campaign in 1946, "who cannot think up questions enough to disqualify undesirables, then write Bilbo or any good lawyer and there are a hundred good questions which can be furnished . . . but you know and I know what is the best way to keep the nigger from voting. You do it the night before the election. I don't have to tell you anymore than that. Red-blooded men know what I mean." Bilbo winked and left the stage.

In the midst of such intimidation, protest could succeed only if the federal government was willing to intervene to provide minimum guarantees of physical security. To be sure, the system of federalism, with its concession of so much power to state governments, imposed substantial constraints on the federal government's ability to intervene in local elections. Nor had the White House demonstrated much political clout with Congress on domestic issues. Still, the federal government represented the only hope blacks had of securing their most basic freedoms.

Significantly, the person with the most power in Washington had a mixed record on civil rights. As a product of the Pendergast machine in Missouri, Harry Truman understood the importance of paying attention to the 130,000 black voters in his constituency. Not surprisingly, his Senate record reflected these political realities. Truman supported legislation to abolish the poll tax, appropriations for the FEPC, passage of antilynching legislation, and an end to the filibuster on an anti-poll-tax bill. But political astuteness did not necessarily represent personal belief. Truman reportedly told one Southern colleague: "You know I'm against this [antilynching bill], but it if comes to a vote, I have to vote for it. My sympathies are with you, but the Negro vote in Kansas City and St. Louis is too important." On another occasion, Truman held hearings on racial discrimination in the defense industry, yet a Truman aide told friends: "If anybody [thinks] the committee is going to help black bastards into a $100 a week job, they [are] sadly mistaken." The *Pittsburgh Courier,* one of America's leading black newspapers, viewed Truman's nomination as vice-president in 1944 over Henry Wallace as "an appeasement of the south." At least some Southerners agreed. After Truman ascended to the presidency, one Southern Senator remarked: "Everything is going to be alright—the new president knows how to handle the niggers."

The president's record on the controversial FEPC issue highlighted the ambiguity of his position. In a remarkable departure from Roosevelt, Truman intervened openly with Congress on behalf of legislation to create a permanent FEPC, writing the Chairman of the House Rules Committee that to abandon the FEPC was "unthinkable." Yet after saying this, the president did little else. "There is yet no evidence," the *Pittsburgh Courier* wrote in September 1945, "that he has tried to use any of his great power to bring pressure on the recalcitrant southern senators." Indeed, Truman refused to permit the wartime FEPC to order Washington's transit system to hire black operators. The act so outraged black lawyer Charles Houston that he resigned from the FEPC, protesting the government's failure "to enforce democratic practices and protect minorities in its own capital." Such evidence led one historian to question whether Truman's statements on behalf of civil rights were not simply "an attempt to curry favor with liberal groups in Congress while at the same time not antagonizing those who opposed the FEPC."

Nevertheless, in the face of brutal repression of black efforts to secure citizenship, Truman came under renewed pressure to respond. During the spring and summer of 1946 black protest groups and their white allies demanded action. "SPEAK, SPEAK, MR. PRESIDENT," pickets outside the White House demanded. After violence in Georgia, Tennessee, and South Carolina, and long before the age of mass demonstrations, 15,000 people marched to the Lincoln Memorial demanding that the Ku Klux Klan be outlawed. Eleanor Roosevelt joined other reformers in creating a National Committee for Justice in Columbia, Tennessee, and more than forty religious and civil rights organizations joined the NAACP in a National Emergency Committee Against Violence. When the president met a delegation of the committee in 1946 to discuss their demands for antilynching legislation, he seemed sympathetic. "My God," he told the group, "I had no idea it was as terrible as that. We have to do something."

In a bold response to the protest leaders' demands, Truman created a Committee on Civil Rights in December 1946. Comprised of such distinguished individuals as Charles Wilson of General Electric, Frank Porter Graham of the University of North Carolina, and Franklin Roosevelt, Jr., it surveyed the entire spectrum of race relations in America and concluded that something was desperately wrong. In its report entitled "To Secure These Rights," the committee recommended a series of actions to correct racial inequality, including establishment of a permanent civil rights division of the Justice Department, the creation of a Commission on Civil Rights, enactment of antilynching legislation, abolition of the poll tax, passage of laws to protect the rights of qualified voters, desegregation of the Armed Forces, elimination of grants-in-aid from the federal government to segregated institutions, enactment of a permanent FEPC, home rule for the District of Columbia, and support for the legal attack on segregated housing. In the meantime, Truman had become the first president to address an NAACP rally, declaring that "there is a serious gap between our ideals and some of our practices" and pledging that "this gap must be closed." "Every man," Truman said, "should have the right to a decent home, the right to an education, . . . the right to a worthwhile job, the right to an equal share in making public decisions through the ballot. . . . We must assure that these rights—on equal terms—are enjoyed by every citizen."

Black Americans were elated by Truman's posture. Clearly, the president anticipated the kind of report that would be issued by the people he appointed to the Civil Rights Commission. Moreover, he immediately endorsed the commission's recommendations, and the day after their release, ordered the Justice Department to intervene before the Supreme Court in a case seeking to invalidate restrictive covenants in housing. In a special message to Congress on February 2, 1948, Truman enthusiastically endorsed virtually all the proposals of his Civil Rights Committee.

Yet it soon became obvious that the appearance of commitment to civil rights did not necessarily translate into action. After his bold civil rights message of February, the president retreated quickly. Southern governors and senators had threatened to bolt the Democratic Party in protest, while white Southern newspapers accused the president of "stabbing the south in the back." Hoping to appease the white South while holding onto his liberal image with blacks, Truman refrained from introducing any legislation to implement the recommendations of his Civil Rights Commission. Nor did he issue the executive orders to end segregation in federal employment or in the military that the Committee had urged. "The strategy," a Truman aide later explained, "[was] to start with a bold measure and then temporize to pick up the right-wing forces. Simply stated, backtrack after the bang."

In fact, Truman's actions were shaped as much by the changing political climate as by personal convictions. In 1947, Clark Clifford, Truman's leading political advisor, had concluded that the 1948 election would hinge on winning the support of "labor and urban minorities." Over the preceding eight years, the black population in leading Northern cities had grown by almost 2 million. In states such as New York, New Jersey, Pennsylvania, Ohio, Michigan, and Illinois, the black vote constituted a potential balance of power. By championing civil rights, Truman could appeal to this essential constituency. By backing away from action on civil rights, on the other hand, he could hope to retain the loyalty of conservative Democrats in the South. As one historian has noted, Truman's tactics were designed to win some support from all sides:

> While avoiding a bruising fight, he could still make certain ritualistic gestures on behalf of a good cause. A speech here and a letter there would assure him of some liberal support and gratitude for his efforts. In this manner he could keep his lines of communication open with all factions while retaining a free hand to do exactly as he pleased in any given situation.

In the end, expressions of black protest succeeded more in generating promises of support than substantive action. Some progress did occur. It was important that Truman became the first president to address the NAACP, to identify civil rights as a moral issue, and to create a National Commission to study racial injustice. Yet symbolic action all too rarely resulted in programmatic change. Although Truman vigorously supported FEPC each year in policy messages, his tactics and follow-through were less ardent, causing some to wonder whether the entire process was simply a charade. Truman's Justice Department did little to investigate or prosecute violations of civil rights when blacks tried to register in the South. Although Truman finally issued an executive order to end discrimination in the Armed Forces in July 1948, he acted in large part because A. Philip Randolph threatened to mount a massive civil disobedience campaign if the Armed Forces remained segregated. Even then, it was not until after the Korean War that the Army was integrated. As Senator Hubert Humphrey noted at the time, it would have been more helpful to have less rhetoric and more action in the areas of lynching and voting.

Thus, by the end of the 1940s, black Americans faced a daily reality not very different from that which had existed when World War II ended, notwithstanding all the fine gestures and political speeches. On September 8, 1948, Isaac Nixon was warned not to cast his ballot in Wrightsville, Georgia. The Army veteran disregarded the advice. He was murdered before the sun had set. A few days later another band of whites drove the president of the local NAACP branch from his home and forced him to flee to Atlanta for safety. In November an all-white jury acquitted the men accused of Nixon's murder. For these black Americans, the politics of gesture was not enough.

The Experience of Labor

No group had greater reason for optimism at the end of the war than organized labor. Union membership had vaulted to 15 million—a fivefold increase over 1933. Almost every major industry had been organized, with CIO victories in steel, rubber, mining, electricity, and automobiles setting the pace. Labor's progress had been "well-nigh phenomenal," commented one union intellectual. "The amazingly rapid growth of unionism and of its power potential . . . goes beyond anything ever known." Indeed, the surge of labor organization prompted one scholar to suggest that the United States was "gradually shifting from a capitalist community to a laboristic one—that is, to a community in which employees rather than businessmen are the strongest single influence."

In their most ebullient moments, liberals envisioned organized labor as the phalanx of a movement that would transform America economically and politically. Renouncing the conservative orientation of the AFL's "business unionism," CIO leaders hoped to inaugurate a new era of "industrial democracy" wherein workers and their representatives would help shape every aspect of economic and business developments. As the historian David Brody has pointed out, this agenda struck at the heart of corporate America's most prized possession—total control over management decisions. If successful in their venture, labor leaders would become joint partners in corporate life, not simply defenders of such traditional union interests as higher wages and better working conditions.

The initial impetus to forge a new labor-management partnership emerged out of the war. If the government wished maximum production and mutual sacrifice, CIO leaders urged, industrial councils in which management and labor jointly ran industry offered the best guarantee of success. Men like Walter Reuther of the United Automobile Workers (UAW) insisted such councils were essential to successful prosecution of the war, as well as to effective industrial democracy. Rather than return to older trade union patterns when the war ended, Reuther and his CIO colleagues continued to agitate for structural change, leaving industry to conclude—accurately—that unions wished to "extend the scope of collective bargaining to include matters and functions that are clearly the responsibility of management." The fundamental issue was control of the workplace from top to bottom—not just issues of seniority, but also those of job content, production schedules, shop discipline, and finance. As one union leader declared, it was organized labor's mandate to influence the employer "at every point where his action affected the welfare of the men." The underlying economic objective of Reuther and his allies represented nothing less than a complete overhaul of the economic system, with organized labor becoming "a coequal with management." As the *Washington Post* observed in 1946, "the question [of] how far employees should have a voice in dictating to management is at present one of the hottest issues before the country."

Political action constituted the second dimension of the CIO's strategy for change. After the triumph of conservatism in the congressional elections of 1942, the CIO had created a Political Action Committee (PAC) to organize the country on behalf of liberal principles. Embracing FDR's economic "bill of rights" and Henry Wallace's call for the century of the common man, PAC hoped to work through the Democratic Party to institutionalize the social welfare state. Although some hoped that the CIO could provide the basis for a new party made up of farmers, blacks, the working class, and intellectuals, labor leaders were content for the moment to work through the traditional Democratic Party structure. With progressive forces like CIO-PAC in the vanguard, the party could provide as good a vehicle as any to secure full employment legislation, national health insurance, civil rights for blacks, and a decent education for everyone. If CIO unions could transform the economy into a partnership of management and labor, and CIO-PAC could lay the basis for full employment and a social welfare state, social democracy seemed within reach.

But it was not to be. In the immediate context of the postwar world, neither the economic nor the political agenda of CIO unionists bore fruit. Inflation and fears of recession focused the attention of most unions on traditional issues of wages and job security. American corporations fought vigorously and effectively against sharing management decisions. The Truman administration oscillated wildly between support and antipathy toward organized labor; by 1948 hopes for a progressive liberal/labor alliance had foundered on the issue of communism. At the end of the decade, trade unionism itself remained a strong presence in American society, but the vision of a world transformed had given way to traditional concerns of business unionism.

The immediate problem was simply preserving the gains made during the war. Real income had risen by 53 percent during the war years, but most of the increase occurred as a result of long hours of overtime. Under the "little steel formula" adopted by the War Labor Board in 1942, wages were set at a January 1941 level, with upward adjustments limited to cost-of-living increases. Although government regulations helped unions grow by encouraging the union shop, they also took away labor's prime weapon by forbidding strikes. Anger at the restraints of the "little steel formula" threatened to spill over when overtime ended with the close of the war and prices started to rise. While corporate profits hit all time highs, real wages dropped by approximately 12 percent in the year after the war. Indeed, when price controls ended on June 30, 1946, costs of consumer goods skyrocketed 28 percent just during the first sixteen days of July.

As price increases outpaced wages, worker frustration boiled over in a wave of strikes that swept the country. On November 20, 1945, 225,000 auto workers at General Motors went on strike. Two months later they were joined by 174,000 electrical workers, and then 800,000 steel workers. Within a year after V-J Day more than 5 million men and women had walked off the job in quest of better wages, improved working conditions, and job security, creating the greatest work stoppage in American history. The strikes involved the country's largest industries—coal, railroads, shipping, automobile, electrical companies—and caused the loss of nearly 120 million work days. At no time in the past, with the possible exception of 1919, had America's economy been so rocked by labor militancy. Yet, because of the immediate circumstances, the strikes focused on issues of wages and hours in order to combat inflation, not on the larger issues of control over the workplace and shared authority with management. In 1944, over 40 percent of work stoppages had centered on questions such as speed-ups and shop conditions, with 43 percent concerned about wages and hours. Now, strikes involving issues other than wages and hours fell to 23 percent.

Significantly, industry responded to the labor crisis with a hard-line position, eventually making some concessions on wages, but adamantly refusing any suggestion of sharing management responsibilities and prerogatives. In the face of workers' primary concern with inflation and security, labor leaders found themselves inevitably accepting the narrow and traditional definition of their role as one that should focus on wages rather than attempt to redefine the framework of industrial management. In this manner a *quid pro quo* evolved. Industry eventually accepted labor packages that involved wage increases, cost-of-living adjustments, job security, and provisions for pensions and other fringe benefits. But in return, labor leaders accepted corporate domination of industrial management, jettisoning demands to restructure control over the workplace. In this way, corporate executives retained discretion over all functions of management, with labor assuming the role of junior partner—even helping to enforce the discipline mandated from above and codified in labor-management contracts.

The UAW strike against General Motors highlighted both the challenge and the retreat of organized labor. Moved by both record-breaking corporate profits and the onset of inflation, the UAW demanded a 30 percent wage increase with no comparable rise in the price of automobiles. Simultaneously, Walter Reuther insisted that GM open its books so that the public—and workers—could see the cards that management had to play. The strike, one UAW official noted, would be "the first act of a new and significant era in American unionism, an era in which labor might break away from the bonds of business unionism, to wage an economic struggle planned to advance the welfare of the community as a whole." Corporate executives understood the dimensions of the challenge. It was, one declared, "an opening wedge whereby the unions hoped to pry their way into the whole field of management. It leads surely to the day when union bosses, under threat of strike, will seek to tell us *what* we can make, *when* we can make it."

On that issue, GM drew the line. It would not open its books, nor discuss prices. When a government fact-finding commission did review company accounts and ruled that "ability to pay" was a legitimate issue, GM stalked out of the negotiations. Adamant to the end, GM was willing to negotiate on wages, never on management prerogatives. To preserve these, David Brody has observed, GM endured a 113-day strike with losses of nearly 90 million dollars. Nothing could more eloquently dramatize the importance of labor's challenge to traditional corporate practices, nor the price management would pay to retain control over its territory.

In the face of company toughness, the UAW settled for an increase in wages. GM sweetened the package by tying wage rates to inflation and, subsequently, by guaranteeing union stability and accepting a more generous pension plan. In light of worker concern about inflation, the union was forced to reorder its priorities. On any matters "designated as within the sphere of management," Brody observes, "[GM] opposed any form of labor-management cooperation that gave the union a place . . . on management's side of the line." The company had made the union choose between long-range control of the workplace and short-term benefits. In this critical moment, the union opted for benefits. As one GM official later noted, the company policy would be to "give the union the money, the least possible . . . but don't let them take the business away from us." From that point forward, the *economic* dimensions of the CIO's hope for "industrial democracy" would be limited. Whatever gains were made would occur within the traditional context of business unionism.

By the end of 1946, it had also become clear that labor's political vision for change had little prospect of being realized. At the end of the war, CIO leaders had hoped for "a plan to keep our industries going full blast, and a president and a congress who will assume the responsibility for all the peoples' needs." But the promises held forth in FDR's economic bill of rights—national health insurance, full employment, and improved social programs—lay in shambles by the time congressional elections were held in November 1946.

In fact, Truman appeared to many labor leaders more a leader of the opposition than an ally in arms. Not only did Truman seem inadequate as a legislative leader on full employment; he also spearheaded the attack on labor militancy. After the UAW went on strike against GM in November and steel workers voted to call for a national walkout, the president requested legislation to prevent major strikes through fact-finding procedures, cooling-off periods, and federal mediation. To CIO president Philip Murray, such proposals smacked of strike breaking and a complete betrayal of FDR's labor policy. Five months later, when a nationwide railroad strike occurred, Truman told his cabinet he was going to ask for the harshest labor law in history. The government should have the power to seize vital industries, Truman told Congress, to draft strikers, and to incarcerate rebellious union leaders. Moreover, Truman pushed for his plan even *after* a settlement of the strike was announced.

Labor leaders were stunned. Mike Quill, head of the transportation workers in New York, called Truman "the number one strike breaker of the American bankers and railroads." The head of the railway trainmen described Truman's plan as "the warp and woof of fascism." Even conservatives were shocked. Republican Senator Robert Taft of Ohio charged that Truman's plan offended "every basic principle for which the American republic was established," reflecting more the values of "Hitlerism, Stalinism, [and] totalitarianism" than of freedom. Although Truman had retrieved some of the ground lost by vetoing the Case Bill, which required advance notice of strikes and outlawed secondary boycotts, labor leaders became furious again in the fall of 1946 when Truman secured an injunction against a coal miners' strike, resulting in a fine of $3.5 million against the United Mine Workers (UMW). The administration, one union official charged, was attempting "to enforce economic servitude on the miners [and] . . . give impetus to the program now being spawned by reactionary capitalism."

The situation was complicated further by the degree to which the strongest CIO unions also reflected substantial Communist Party influence. Throughout the '30s and '40s, communists were among the best organizers in the steel, automobile, and electrical industries. Mike Quill, head of the transportation workers in New York, was a member of the party. Most experts agreed that as much as 25 percent of the CIO leadership shared some loyalty to the communist cause, creating a prickly dilemma for union leaders trying to find the proper course to follow.

If labor leaders had soured on the president, however, it was by no means clear what alternative existed. Despite precedents such as the American Labor Party in New York and the Farmer-Labor Party in Minnesota, proposals for a third party failed to evoke enthusiasm. As Philip Murray had observed in 1944, such a party "would only serve to divide labor and progressive forces resulting in the election of political enemies." Nevertheless, in the aftermath of the disasters in 1946 and Truman's sacking of Henry Wallace from the cabinet, some CIO leaders, as well as other liberals, formed a group calling itself the Progressive Citizens of America, and warning in the process that if "the Democratic Party woos privilege and betrays the people it will die and deserve to die."

By late 1947, therefore, the political situation facing labor had become increasingly problematic. A new Progressive Party, with Henry Wallace as its champion, attempted to mobilize labor's battalions on behalf of traditional New Deal liberalism and a more accommodating position toward the Soviet Union on foreign policy. Truman, in the meantime, sought to recoup his losses among liberals by vetoing the Taft-Hartley Act that promised to revive government injunctions, provide an 80-day, cooling-off period prior to strikes, and safeguard the open shop. (The veto was overridden by Congress.) By defending labor and appearing as an ardent advocate of New Dealism, Truman hoped to restore his leadership of the New Deal coalition at home, even as he led the fight against Soviet expansionism abroad.

In the midst of all this, labor fell victim to a vicious internecine war prompted by the rapid spread of political anticommunism. All that could be said with certainty was that, two years after the war, the political and economic vision that had inspired progressive labor leaders no longer seemed viable. Whatever gains had been made took place within an older, more traditional structure of labor-management relations. As AFL chief George Meany would later say, trade unionists do "not seek to recast American society. . . . We seek [only] a rising standard of living," within the existing structure of society.

The Politics of Anticommunism

Like a seasonal allergy, anticommunism has recurred at regular intervals throughout twentieth-century history. The Red Scare of 1919–20 helped to quell the labor revolts of that period, as well as to provide an outlet for frustrations left over from the war. In the middle of the twenties women's groups committed to social welfare were depicted as part of a "spider web" conspiracy emanating from Moscow and determined to subvert the American family. The New Deal, not surprisingly, was seen by many as a new incarnation of the Red Menace. It was all right, Al Smith said in 1936, if the intellectuals around FDR wished "to disguise themselves as Norman Thomas or Karl Marx or Lenin," but it became blasphemy when they attempted to "march under the banner of Jefferson, Jackson or Cleveland."

By 1944 the charge had taken on new vigor. FDR's friendship with "Uncle Joe" and American propaganda supporting the "democratic" people of the Soviet Union fit neatly the preconceptions of those who saw the New Deal and communism as indistinguishable. "First the New Deal took over the Democratic Party and destroyed its very foundation," Republican vice-presidential candidate John Bricker charged in 1944. "Now these Communist forces have taken over the New Deal and will destroy the very foundations of the Republic." By the end of the 1944 campaign Thomas Dewey had a new definition of a communist—anyone "who supports the fourth term so our form of government may more easily be changed." After 1941, one writer charged, federal bureaus became "roosting places for droves of

Communist termites who utilized their position . . . to advance the interest of Soviet Russia."

In the years after World War II, the politics of anticommunism achieved a new pitch of hysteria. The House Committee on Un-American Activities (subsequently HUAC), first established in 1938 to investigate anti-American propaganda, was made a permanent standing committee. The Smith Act, passed in 1940, provided a vehicle for prosecuting anyone who even advocated communism. (At the time, the *New York Times* characterized the Smith Act as drawing together "most of the anti-alien and anti-radical legislation offered in Congress in the last twenty years.") In a postwar atmosphere suffused with fear and suspicion, opportunities were rife to use these acts for political persecution and intimidation, as well as legitimate inquiry.

Reason for legitimate inquiry did exist. Many young idealists had been drawn to communism during the depression, some of them moving on to fill government positions. Although most had left the party in the aftermath of the Nazi-Soviet pact in 1939, a few remained, some still holding sensitive government offices. Moreover, two episodes in 1945 and 1946 offered reason for concern. In June 1945 a government raid on the editorial offices of *Amerasia*, a journal friendly to the Chinese communists, uncovered a series of classified documents. Although some of these had come into the magazine's possession through the time-honored practice of government "leaks" and background briefings, others appeared to have arrived through less conventional avenues. The revelation ten months later of an atomic spy ring operating out of Canada, with American connections, provided additional credence to those who expressed concern that some individuals working for the government might be serving two masters.

Yet legitimate concerns could easily spill into political paranoia and exploitation. Republican campaigners in 1946, for example, had a field day asking voters: "Got enough inflation? . . . got enough debt? . . . got enough strikes? . . . got enough communism?" Even as distinguished a person as Robert Taft accused Truman of seeking a congress "dominated by a policy of appeasing the Russians abroad and of fostering communism at home." A young candidate in California named Richard Nixon denounced his opponent as a "lip service American" who consistently voted the Moscow line in Congress and who "fronted for un-American elements . . . by advocating increased federal control over the lives of people." The insidious character of such thinking was dramatized in congressional hearings on the appointment of David Lilienthal, former head of the Tennessee Valley Authority, to become chairman of the Atomic Energy Commission. One senator questioned Lilienthal's loyalty because his family had been born in Austria-Hungary in an area that later became part of Czechoslovakia, and, after all, Czechoslovakia had come under Soviet influence.

Ironically, the Truman administration itself bore partial responsibility for the outrages that would occur in the name of anticommunism over the next few years. Although Truman himself appeared not overly concerned in learning about the operations of the Canadian spy ring, he did appoint a temporary commission on employee loyalty in November 1946 to inquire into government procedures. That commission's report was vague and inadequate, resting almost entirely upon a single letter from the FBI that affirmed the existence of a loyalty problem. Nevertheless, Truman now moved quickly. Just nine days after the Truman Doctrine on Greece and Turkey was proclaimed, the president issued Executive Order 9835 creating a Federal Employee Loyalty Program and giving government security officials authorization to screen 2 million employees of the federal government for any hint of political deviance. The order also authorized the Attorney General to draw up a list of "totalitarian, fascist, or subversive organizations." Membership, affiliation, or even sympathy with such groups could then be used as a basis for determining disloyalty.

Truman's response reflected a combination of concerns. Clearly, there was at least some connection with the Truman Doctrine. If the country were to wage a crusade against atheistic communism abroad, a strong commitment to clean out communist subversives at home seemed a logical parallel. As late as December 1946, public opinion had been divided on the wisdom of seeking an accommodation with the Soviet Union, and recently negotiated treaties concerning Finland, Romania, Bulgaria, and Italy offered some hope that international tensions could be relaxed. If, as Senator Vandenberg said, the only way to get the Truman Doctrine through Congress was to "scare hell out of the American people" about Soviet expansionism abroad, a vigorous anticommunist program at home would serve as an appropriate complement. Just as important, leading members of the new 80th Congress launched a vehement attack on domestic subversives. Styles Bridges and John Taber, chairmen, respectively, of the Senate and House Appropriations Committees, were convinced that communists (often defined as New Dealers) riddled the federal bureaucracy. If Truman wished to get his foreign aid appropriations approved, it seemed, he would need to acknowledge the political conservatism of such power-brokers.

In so doing, however, Truman helped legitimize a form of political inquisition. All the later abuses of McCarthyism were fully anticipated by Seth Richardson, the first president of the Loyalty Review Board, when he declared that "the government is entitled to discharge any employee . . . without extending to such employee any hearing whatsoever." Indeed, any "suspicion of disloyalty, . . . however remote" could provide justification for such dismissal. Using these procedures, civil servants who at any time in their lives had expressed criticism of their society became subject to disciplinary action without the right to confront their accusers. The Attorney General's list of subversive organizations, in turn, made people objects of suspicion if they had ever belonged to such a group as the Soviet-American Friendship Society—even though during World War II such associations were perfectly consistent with national policy. Nor could civil liberatarians take solace from the fact that, during most of the Truman administration, the Attorney General was J. Howard McGrath, a man who declared that communists "are everywhere—in factories, offices, butcher stores, on street corners, and private business. And each carries in himself the death of our society." CIO president Philip Murray reflected the concern of many when he asked: "What sudden threat can warrant our throwing overboard the democratic principles of fair hearing and fair trial?"

The House Committee on Un-American Activities quickly demonstrated its own readiness to disregard civil liberties in the name of anticommunism. Acting in concert with officials such as J. Edgar Hoover of the FBI, the HUAC began in 1947 to "ferret out" communist sympathizers in the federal government, expose communist influence in the American labor movement, provide research and names to other agencies concerned with the same problem, and, in general, investigate the presence of communist sympathizers in America's educational, religious, and entertainment activites. With flamboyant politicians like John Rankin among its members (Rankin had claimed that World War II was started by "a little group of our international Jewish brethren"), the HUAC investigations inevitably attracted widespread media attention.

The committee's methods could have been a model for Joseph Heller's fictional "Catch-22," where any action one takes becomes a trap. Witnesses were called who, at one point or another, may have belonged to an organization that appeared on the Attorney General's subversive activities list. It mattered little whether or not they had been, or remained, sympathetic to communism. The purpose was to inquire about their prior associations. If they admitted being part of such groups, they were then asked to list other people with whom they had been associated. Once a witness started to answer questions, he or she was required under the rules of Congress to continue. If witnesses refused, they were subject to contempt of Congress charges and to federal prosecution. Initially, reluctant witnesses cited the "free speech" clause of the First Amendment as a basis for refusing to answer, but then the Supreme Court rejected that claim. Once that decision was made, many witnesses invoked the Fifth Amendment, refusing to answer any questions on the grounds that to do so might force them to incriminate others. In this way, they could protect their friends and prevent the smear tactics of guilt by association that inevitably followed public identification before the committee. On the other hand, "taking the 5th" quickly became synonymous in the eyes of anticommunists with confessing complicity in subversive activities. It was a no-win situation. If witnesses cooperated, they ran the danger of exposing their associates to retribution, including social ostracism and the loss of jobs. Yet if they invoked their constitutional rights and refused to cooperate, they appeared to be offering proof of their guilt.

The HUAC's investigation of communist influence in Hollywood typified the process. When witnesses like Millard Lampell (author of the folk cantata about Lincoln's funeral, *The Lonesome Train*) or Lillian Hellman (the distinguished playwright) refused to provide names and dates of meetings they had attended during the late thirties and early forties, they suddenly found themselves on a "black list," barred from employment by any major studio. Eric Johnston, president of the Motion Picture Association, announced that no one would be hired who did not cooperate with the HUAC. New movies like *The Iron Curtain* exhibited the orthodoxy of the day, teaching the American public, as *New York Times* film critic Bosley Crowther said, to "hate the Reds." With voluntary groups like *Alert,* Inc. cooperating with the HUAC, hundreds of artists defined as "liberal" or "left" found themselves out of work. The dissident writer, Bertolt Brecht said, was "not deprived of his life, only of a means of life." Everyone had to conform to the anticommunist line; no one dared deviate. The effect on free political debate was chilling.

Ironically, the Communist Party itself had fallen on hard times. With the end of the war and the enunuciation of a new party line from Moscow, the communists renounced the "popular front" strategy of the New Deal and the war years. By purging former party leader Earl Browder and giving unreserved support to all Soviet actions, the party, in effect, cut itself off from the noncommunist left. As the *New Republic* declared, "[the Communists have] lost all their following in the United States except for the humorless hard-core fanatics." A majority of delegates at the Socialist Workers Party Convention of 1946 condemned the Soviets for outdoing the Nazis in their denial of human freedom. Although the party remained active in some areas of American life, it represented only a shadow of its former strength and influence.

Such distinctions mattered little, however, to the politics of anticommunism. As the presidential election of 1948 approached, the Cold War at home loomed even larger than the Cold War abroad. Although President Truman denounced the tactics of the HUAC and charged it with "having recklessly cast a cloud of suspicion over the most loyal civil service in the world," he himself had helped to initiate the process. Now the question was what would happen to the liberal, New Deal tradition in a context where strong advocacy of viewpoints to the left of center all too often meant being labeled a supporter of communism.

The Election of 1948

The answer came in the election of 1948—an election that took place against a backdrop of apparent disintegration among the regular party constituencies in the country. In the aftermath of Henry Wallace's firing and Truman's antilabor pronouncements of 1946, a split in the Democratic Party seemed inevitable, with at least some liberal New Dealers joining the Progressive Citizens of America in support of a third party candidacy for Henry Wallace. Truman's chances for re-election appeared to be undermined further when Southern Democrats bridled at his liberal rhetoric in support of civil rights. By the fall of 1947 it seemed conceivable that Truman would receive less than a third of the vote, with Thomas Dewey coasting to a landslide victory in the face of a Democratic Party divided into three parts. Truman's ultimate triumph against all odds reflected two facts: his own shrewdness in donning anew the mantle of liberalism, and his effective use of the anticommunist mystique.

From the very beginning, Henry Wallace's candidacy generated the charge that he was a tool of the communists. Wallace's 1946 speech calling for free trade with Eastern Europe and accommodation with the Soviet Union appears, in retrospect, as a moderate statement of what would later be called détente. Indeed, it was attacked at the time by the *Daily Worker*, the Communist Party newspaper, as a paean to capitalist domination of the world. But hardliners in the Truman administration viewed the speech as an assault on their policies and effectively circulated the notion that "Henry was soft" on the Reds. That charge, together with Wallace's devotion to racial equality, social justice, and New Deal experimentation made him the logical target for those who posited a direct link between liberals and communists. Wallace himself seemed to invite such attacks by criticizing liberals who voted for the Marshall Plan, deleting from his speeches any negative references to the Soviet Union, and failing to condemn the communist coup in Czechoslovakia. When, after months of indecision, the Communist Party decided to offer support to the Progressives, many saw the action as irrefutable proof that a link between the two existed.

The emergence of a Wallace candidacy posed a particular dilemma for the CIO, caught up in its own internal war over communism. Ever since the late 1930s, liberal labor leaders like Walter Reuther and David Dubinsky had discussed the possibility of a third-party movement devoted to the social democratic policies of the Progressive platform. On the other hand, union leaders had also become sensitive to the charge that labor militancy offered an instrument for Soviet designs. Responsive to the charge of communist domination, the CIO's 1945 convention passed a resolution, with communist support, stating that the union "resents and rejects efforts of the Communist Party, or any other political party, to intervene in the affairs of the CIO." Philip Murray urged his fellow labor leaders to stop "apologizing for communism," and to "throw it the hell out" if it became a problem. Now the CIO faced the dilemma of whether to cast its lot with a new party that embodied its social democratic values, but was already tarred with the brush of being pro-communist, or accepting a compromise of political values, and sticking with an administration whose leader had seemed, all through 1946, an archenemy of labor.

Two events helped persuade CIO leaders to side with Truman. First, the president vetoed the Taft-Hartley Act of 1947, re-establishing his credentials as a champion of the working class. Although the law was passed over Truman's veto, his election seemed imperative for those who hoped to repeal the harsh antilabor act. Throughout late 1947, Truman also enthusiastically embraced liberal programs he had seemed to shun a year earlier, giving hope that the cause of New Deal liberalism could yet be salvaged within the Democratic Party. Second, a group of New Deal liberals, fearing the anti-Cold War foreign policy of the Progressive Party, formed their own association of Americans for Democratic Action (ADA). ADA included liberals like Eleanor Roosevelt, intellectuals like Reinhold Niebuhr and labor leaders like Walter Reuther—precisely the people who might have made the Progressive Party a more viable alternative. "We reject any association with communists or sympathizers with communism in the United States," the ADA proclaimed. While the Progressive Party criticized Truman's foreign policy and sought to resurrect New Deal liberalism, the ADA staunchly supported Truman's Cold War posture, especially the Marshall Plan, and believed, despite earlier misgivings, that the president himself could become the embodiment of New Deal liberalism. Certain that endorsing Wallace would both guarantee a Republican victory and ensure even more vigorous Redbaiting of the labor movement, CIO leaders embraced the ADA and by a vote of 33 to 13 rejected the Wallace candidacy.

Now, Truman's strategy began to work. In his famous election memo of 1947, presidential aide Clark Clifford had urged Truman to accept a two-pronged plan: to cultivate urban areas and minorities with his liberalism, and—if Wallace ran— "to identify him and isolate him in the public mind with the communists." Truman quickly did both. By endorsing the Civil Rights Committee report in February, he helped to erode one of Wallace's strongest claims to being the more liberal candidate, a claim Wallace made good every time he refused to speak in a segregated facility in the South. Then, one month later Truman went on the attack. "I do not want," the president declared, "and will not accept the political support of Henry Wallace and his communists. . . . These are days of high prices for anything, but any price for Wallace and his communists is too much for me."

By September the Clifford battle plan moved into full gear. When the ADA and urban liberals overturned Truman's preference for a weak civil rights plank in the party's platform (designed to keep Southerners on board), Truman interpreted the defeat as a victory for his own cause and trumpeted his devotion to eradicating "all racial, religious, and economic discrimination." Campaigning in Harlem, the president more than compensated for the defection of four Southern states to the States Rights Party* by rallying the black votes that would eventually help make the difference between victory and defeat. Democrats, meanwhile, continued to

---

* At the 1948 Democratic Convention, four Southern states walked out when a majority of delegates endorsed a strong civil rights plank (not originally supported by Truman). These four states became the rallying point for the creation of a States Rights Party, with Senator Strom Thurmond of South Carolina as it presidential nominee. Thus the Democratic Party was split into three parties in 1948.

hammer away at the Progressive Party's allegedly pro-communist sympathies. Hubert Humphrey, the man who had transformed the Democratic Convention on civil rights by saying it was time to march out of the dark shadow of discrimination into the broad sunlight of equal justice, lambasted Wallacite forces in Minnesota as fellow travelers of Moscow. "If I have to choose between being called a Red-baiter and traitor," Humphrey declared, "I'll be a Red-baiter." In the face of such attacks, Progressive Party support in the Gallup Poll fell from over 15 percent to under 4 percent.

Whistle-stopping across America, Truman seized the momentum. Using the obstructionist record of the 80th Congress as his text, Truman repeatedly charged that it was the "do-nothing" Republicans who were responsible for America's problems. Feisty, biting, and combative, Truman mocked the Republicans, Red-baited the Progressives, ignored Strom Thurmond's States Rights Party, and began to win the loyalty of the 6 million people who came to hear his stump speeches. Compared to the colorful Truman campaign, Dewey was as exciting as a piece of chalk. As one reporter said: "Dewey doesn't seem to walk, he coasts out like a man who has been mounted on casters and given a tremendous shove from behind." Six months earlier that would have been adequate for a landslide victory. By November, it had become a liability.

When the country awoke the day after the election, the "miracle of 1948" had happened. Truman was re-elected, with black votes providing the decisive difference in states like California, Illinois, and Ohio. Blue-collar voters went to Truman in unprecedented numbers. Most liberals had stuck to Truman, out of fear of a Republican victory and because groups like the ADA insisted that Wallace was a "dupe of the communists." Middle-of-the-roaders, upset with skyrocketing prices, accepted Truman's charge that the Republican Congress was at fault. And many segregationist Southerners, wanting their vote to count for something, decided to stay inside the Democratic tent and work to influence the president from within. With over-optimism, the *New Republic* proclaimed: "reaction is repudiated. The New Deal is again empowered to carry forward the promise of American life." What had happened in fact was that Truman, with Clark Clifford's strategy to guide him, had occupied America's middle ground, using civil rights and New Deal rhetoric to hold the liberals, while decimating any option on the left through the politics of anticommunism.

This formulation was later dubbed the "liberal consensus" by British journalist Godfrey Hodgson, and it provided the paradigm that guided American politics for the next two decades. As Hodgson described it, the liberal consensus consisted of five interlinked axioms: (1) capitalism was the best economic system in the world; (2) an inextricable connection existed between capitalism and democracy, the best political system in the world; (3) although some areas of imperfection persisted in America, nothing organically or structurally was wrong with American society that would require radical change; (4) where problems did exist, they could be addressed through incremental reforms, fueled by a growing economy; and (5) anchoring the entire consensus was a bipartisan commitment to anti-communism and containment of the Soviet menace. Any deviation from this anticommunist commitment would be considered the equivalent of treason.

As Truman showed in 1948, the "liberal consensus" functioned brilliantly as a political framework for moderate politics. Henry Wallace could be dismissed because he was from the left; Wallace and "his communists," as Truman called them, threatened the unanimity of opposition to Soviet positions required by the new Cold War. On the other hand, Truman was ready to acknowledge the need to correct one of the most glaring flaws in American society—racial discrimination—as well as to address other economic areas of need through his "Fair Deal." But none of this would call into question the fundamental stability of democratic capitalism or the capacity of economic growth to provide the resources to handle any remaining social problems.

Consequences

Not surprisingly, the politics of anticommunism dominated American political life in the years after 1948, both because it provided the anchor for all other aspects of the "liberal consensus" and because increasing evidence suggested that a real threat of communist subversion existed. As the Cold War deepened abroad, suspicions multiplied that fellow travelers and "fifth columnists" at home were aiding the communist conspiracy. Alger Hiss, an Ivy Leaguer who served as assistant secretary of state and as a Roosevelt advisor at Yalta, was accused by former Communist Party member Whittaker Chambers (in 1948 a *Time Magazine* editor) of being a communist spy. Initially, Hiss successfully parlayed the charge, but then Richard Nixon, a member of the House Committee on Un-American Activities, burrowed into Chambers' testimony and came up with evidence that in fact the two men had been collaborators (Chambers recalled that Hiss was an ornithologist and used the Quaker parlance of "thee and thou" to address his wife). Eventually, Chambers produced documentation that classified documents, written on Hiss' typewriter, had been passed on to him. The so-called Pumpkin Papers (they had been buried in a hollowed-out pumpkin) proved decisive in changing public opinion about Hiss, and largely due to Nixon's assiduous efforts, Hiss was convicted of perjury. Nor was he the only person believed to have served the communist cause. Harry Dexter White and Laughlin Currie, both on FDR's White House staff, were suspected of communist connections. International events, moreover, magnified the consequences of suspected disloyal activities. In 1949 the Soviet Union exploded an atomic weapon—years before American intelligence officials believed it would do so; the same year communists defeated Chiang Kai-shek in the

Chinese civil war; and new rumors of an atomic spy ring became rife, soon given credence by the arrest, trial, and conviction of Julius and Ethel Rosenberg for their role in stealing critical information about the development of America's atomic bomb and passing it on to the Soviet Union. (Significantly, new evidence from the Soviet archives, dubbed "the Verona Project," confirms the degree to which communists had made significant inroads into the American government and especially its atomic energy research.)

In such a context, visions of subversion multiplied with geometric progression. Looking for a campaign issue, Senator Joseph McCarthy of Wisconsin went to Wheeling, West Virginia, in 1950 and announced: "I have here in my hand a list of 205 [card-carrying communists] . . . who are still working and shaping policy in the State Department." By the time he had finished his four-year tirade, McCarthy had succeeded in terrorizing Washington and had pinned the Democrats with being responsible for "twenty years of treason." Even General George Marshall, he charged, was part of "a conspiracy so immense and an infamy so black as to dwarf any previous such venture in the history of man." His colleague Richard Nixon had joined him in the Senate in 1950 by denouncing the liberal reformer Helen Galagan Douglas as "a pink lady." Groups like the Chamber of Commerce insisted that anyone suspected of even the slightest sympathy for communism be fired from all agencies affecting public opinion, and the Congress in 1950 passed—over Truman's veto—the McCarran Act that required communists to register with the government, revoked the passports of those suspected of communist sympathy, and established provisions for setting up concentration camps for subversives in the event of a national emergency. The conservative mood of the time was well summarized by James Burnham, a conservative writer. America should tell the Soviet Union, he said, "here are our demands. Meet them, and you may live."

Inevitably, the divisive consequences of the anticommunist crusade had an impact on domestic politics as well, making suspect any politician, group, or cause that could be described as "leftist." Nowhere was this more clear than with the CIO. Communist Party members or those friendly to the party held leadership positions in fourteen out of thirty-one international unions, although not in the national office. The Roman Catholic Church, among others, was deeply concerned about this communist role. New York's Francis Cardinal Spellman accused communist sympathizers of "tirelessly trying to grind into the dust the blessed freedoms for which our sons have fought." The Association of Catholic Trade Unionists (ACTU) carried the same concern into the unions themselves. In the United Electrical Workers, for example, James Carey waged a lengthy battle to prevent, in his words, "our great international union [from becoming] known as a transmission belt for the American Communist Party."

Liberal labor leaders clearly faced a dilemma. Undoubtedly, Communist Party members had no compunction about using their authority within unions to render service to their party. On the other hand, union leaders who had allied with communists in the past were also deeply committed to social justice. They had provided the vanguard of courageous organizers seeking to topple the barriers of sex and race discrimination within the labor movement. The problem was to eliminate the influence of communist cynics without, in the process, destroying the insurgent forces with whom they had, in the past, been allied. If purging communist leadership also led to a destruction of the legitimate battle to organize the unorganized and achieve social justice, any victory would be hollow.

The cruel nature of the dilemma became vividly apparent in Southern organizing campaigns. During the summer of 1943 CIO organizers had helped to unionize the R. J. Reynolds Tobacco Company in Winston-Salem, the largest tobacco factory in the world. One day, after a speed-up, black women workers sat down beside their machines and refused to continue. As word spread of their action, the entire factory shut down. Together with the CIO organizers, black workers succeeded in winning a major victory. For the first time in R. J. Reynolds history a union secured company recognition. Moreover, although blacks dominated, the union was integrated—land in the South. The victory soon led to other activities as well. Union-based voter registration efforts helped to elect the first black alderman in Winston-Salem. Significantly, some of the union leaders *were* communists or were willing to cooperate with those who had communist sympathies.

It was this issue on which the company chose to mount its counter-attack. Beginning in 1947, Reynolds management embarked on a systematic Red-baiting campaign, denouncing union supporters as subservient to a worldwide communist conspiracy. The attack, using patriotism as its banner, eventually succeeded. Although there had been some communists in the union leadership, the company's real target was the union itself. Thus, using the anicommunist campaign as a wedge, the company had broken its enemy and destroyed one of the few vehicles for interracial union democracy in the South. Not for the last time, patriotism would serve as a banner for attacking democracy.

Perhaps inevitably, concern about communism became dominant in the national CIO, with legitimate fears about Communist Party influence merging into attacks on progressive trade union forces generally. The United Electrical Workers had already withdrawn from the CIO in protest against claims that it was communist dominated. With James Carey organizing a dissident union, the electrical workers became polarized into political factions. Now, in the aftermath of the 1948 election, CIO head Philip Murray led a move to expel and destroy any communist influence in his organization. Expulsion of unions with a communist taint was necessary, Murray claimed, "to fight Stalin, to fight Moscow, to fight imperialism, to fight aggression here at home." During the next year eleven unions were expelled, with a membership of over one million workers, most of them not communists. Few of those unions survived.

Wittingly, or unwittingly, the CIO had itself become a victim of the anticommunist crusade. Faced with a legitimate issue—the presence of people loyal to communist ideology in the leadership of many of its unions—the

CIO chose the course of a blanket indictment rather than action on a case-by-case basis. The price had been heavy. "Granting the desirability of eliminating communist influence," Irving Howe and Lewis Coser have written, "one might still have argued that mass expulsions were not only a poor way of achieving this end, but constituted a threat to democratic values and procedures." The result was the imposition of a new orthodoxy on trade unionism, and the suspicion of anything even remotely radical. As Paul Jacobs, a union activist who supported the purge later said, "[the expulsions brought] all serious political debate inside the CIO to a standstill. In some unions it became a habit to brand as a Communist anyone who opposed the leaders." CIO membership plummeted from 5.2 million to only 3.7 million, the union hierarchy imposed itself between workers and management, and the dynamism that had transformed labor during the late thirties and early forties evaporated into stultifying conformity. For all intents and purposes, the politics of anticommunism—together with the economic considerations discussed earlier—sapped the strength and energy of the American labor movement. In 1946 the magazine *Nation's Business* observed that "whoever stirs up needless strife in American trade unions advances the causes of Communism." After 1949, there was no need to worry.

As the decade of the 1940s drew to a close, the politics of anticommunism had exerted a chilling effect on virtually all progressive causes. Any program that deviated from one hundred percent conservative Americanism might be attacked as reflecting a Moscow party line. When women in New York fought for the retention of day-care programs, the *New York World Telegram* charged that the entire program of child care was conceived by leftists operating out of communist social work cells. The campaign for day-care centers, the newspaper declared, had "all the trappings of a Red drive, including leaflets, letters, telegrams, petitions, protest demonstrations, mass meetings, and hat passing."

Civil rights groups suffered from similar defamation. In Georgia, Governor Eugene Talmadge attributed civil rights protests to "Communist doctrines from outside the state" and pledged to restore the all-white primary in opposition to such foreign influences. In the eyes of many anticommunist crusaders, support for integration represented part of a communist conspiracy to disrupt America. Walter White, executive secretary of the NAACP, wrote Truman that government investigators "have been asking white persons whether they associate with colored people," and blacks "whether they have entertained white people in their homes." Moreover, White charged, many blacks in government were being accused of disloyalty precisely because they actively opposed segregation. So extreme did the association of civil rights and communism become that people were even asked whether they had an album of Paul Robeson's songs (Robeson was a famous black singer who had often exhibited sympathy for the Russians). One bootblack at the Pentagon was questioned seventy times by the FBI because he had once given $10 to the defense of the Scottsboro Boys, a group of black teenagers erroneously charged with rape and later represented by a communist attorney.

Ultimately, then, the most damaging effect of the politics of anticommunism was to define as perilous, unsafe, and out of bounds advocacy of substantial social reform. The process appealed to deep cultural values. If you supported day care you must be against the family and, after all, the Russians were against the family. If you believed in civil rights you were critical of America's racial customs and, therefore, an ally of those who—from abroad—also criticized American racism. If you liked modern art you were giving aid and comfort to those who wished to introduce disorder and chaos into American culture—something the Russians were expert at. And if you protested the politics of anticommunism, you must be, in Joseph McCarthy's words, one of those "egg-sucking phony liberals," one of those "communists and queers," one of those "pinkos." Machismo, patriotism, belief in God, opposition to social agitation, hatred of the Reds—these were the definitions of true Americanism. In a world where the ultimate power of politics is the power to define what is permissible and unpermissible, the crusaders for anticommunism had helped strike from the agenda of acceptable discussion many reforms of greatest significance to social activists. As one intelligence officer told a congressional subcommittee, "a liberal is only a hop, skip, and a jump from a Communist. A Communist starts as a liberal." The impact of such attitudes was devastating. It might still be possible to advocate racial reform or social justice within the "liberal consensus," but only on terms that were strictly patriotic and that could never be construed as criticizing the fundamental soundness of American society.

The Other Half of the Walnut

In 1947 Harry Truman had described the Truman Doctrine and the Marshall Plan as "two halves of the same walnut." While the Truman Doctrine provided military and economic support to regimes in immediate trouble, the Marshall Plan offered the economic foundation for rebuilding a prosperous and stable Europe. In fact, it can be argued that the politics of anticommunism at home represented "the other half of the walnut." Just nine days after the Truman Doctrine was announced, with its rhetoric of freedom against tryanny, good against evil, and democracy against totalitarianism, the federal employee loyalty program was announced at home, marking the inauguration of an anticommunist crusade within America's own borders that paralleled the Cold War abroad. In late 1946 and early 1947 the American people were still divided over the possibility of seeking an accommodation with the Soviet Union. Over 70 percent, according to a Gallup Poll, supported Henry Wallace's call in September for pursuing more friendly policies toward the Russians. Another Gallup Poll, taken a year later, showed that 76 percent the nation believed that Russia was out to rule the world, and that 63 percent expected a full-scale war within the next twenty-five years. Wittingly, or unwittingly, the Truman administration had helped to legitimize a program that "scared the hell out of the American people" at home, just as it mobilized support for the containment of communism abroad.

At the intersection of both policies was a rhetoric of moralism. The Reverend Billy Graham talked about "barbarians beating at our gates from without and moral termites from within." FBI Director J. Edgar Hoover used the same imagery. There was, out there, he proclaimed, a "force of traitorous communists, constantly gnawing away like termites at the very foundations of American society. . . ." Hoover prayed that "the Supreme architect will give us the strength, wisdom, and guidance to triumph against the onrush of Red fascism and atheistic communism." General Douglas MacArthur made the same connection. The Soviet Union, with its atomic bomb, was threatening from without, while within, "New Dealism [was] eating away the vitals of the nation." Whether most Americans believed such rhetoric was less important than the fact that those on the left who might have articulated an alternative vision no longer had cultural or political sanction. The result was a vacuum that—in the absence of any other option—those on the right readily occupied.

The American foreign policy of containment toward the Soviet Union did not necessarily require an anticommunist crusade at home to be successful. Yet, in the politics of the situation, the Truman administration chose not to take that chance. Instead, it used the anticommunist mystique at home as a means of ensuring support for the Cold War abroad. Soon little children would be taught to dive under their desks or rush to air-raid shelters in the event of a Soviet atomic attack; they were also enjoined to be on the alert for domestic deviants who might give support to communism at home. For American foreign policy the rhetoric of moralism led to rigidity, a loss of flexibility, and the elimination of any possibility for honest debate and criticism about the Cold War. But the other half of the walnut was equally, though less visibly, influential. Because of the anticommunist crusade, domestic dissent was stifled, civil liberties were compromised, and advocates of social reform risked being pilloried as agents of a foreign state. The prospect for change that had given hope to activists, blacks, labor leaders, and women after the war had shrunk before the chill wind of anticommunism. Another moment of possibility had passed.

5

The Paradox
of Change

American Society
in the Postwar Years

Although activists and liberals may have been disappointed at the slow pace of social reform after World War II, the attention of most Americans was so riveted on the astonishing new world of consumerism and prosperity that social issues—for the moment, at least—seemed relatively unimportant. Rarely has a society experienced such rapid or dramatic change as that which occurred in America after 1945. At the end of World War II only 40 percent of American families owned their own homes. Radio and movies constituted the principal form of entertainment. People purchased their food at a neighborhood grocery. Most could anticipate, at best, having just one car. As late as 1942 only 37 percent believed that their children would have better opportunities in life than their own. TV represented an eccentric idea offered by a few esoteric inventors, and airplanes were something flown by the military and a few adventurous businessmen.

Fifteen years later, a new world had come into being. Ribbons of highways connected inner cities to suburban developments that sprouted everywhere. Sixty percent of all Americans now owned their own homes. TV antennae perched on nearly every roof, families sat down to eat frozen dinners purchased at the supermarket in a nearby suburban shopping mall, and they then argued over the correct cost of the latest consumer gadget on TV's quiz show, "The Price Is Right." Jet planes had reduced coast-to-coast travel to five hours, the two-car family was as much the rule as the exception, and families of the middle class debated whether to take an out-of-state vacation or build a new addition on the house. Between 1947 and 1960 the average real income for American workers increased by as much as it had in the previous half-century, and the editors of *Fortune* magazine proclaimed that only a million families "still look really poor." Observing the world about him, the sage Walter Lippmann declared: "We talk about ourselves these days as if we were a completed society, one which has no further great business to transact."

Economic Growth

The astonishing growth of the American economy represented the single most impressive development of the postwar years. The gross national product soared 250 percent between 1945 and 1960. Expenditures on new construction multiplied nine times, while consumption of personal services increased three times. By 1960 per capita income was 35 percent higher than even the boom year of 1945. America had entered what the economist Walt Rostow called the "high mass consumption" stage of economic development. Short-term credit leaped from \$8.4 billion in 1946 to \$45.6 billion in 1958. As a result of the postwar boom, nearly 60 percent of the American people had achieved a "middle-class" standard of living by the mid-1950s (defined as incomes of \$3,000 to \$10,000 in constant dollars) in contrast to only 31 percent in the last year of prosperity before the Great Depression. By the end of the decade 75 percent of American families owned their own car, 87 percent their own TV set, and 75 percent their own washing machine. Observing developments in the postwar years, economic historian Harold G. Vatter declared that "the remarkable capacity of the U.S. economy in 1960 represents the crossing of a great divide in the history of humanity."

World War II provided the decisive catalyst for postwar growth, first through ensuring adequate purchasing power at the end of the war, and second through offering veterans benefits that helped create the foundation for sustained postwar prosperity. During the war years the proportion of the population earning less than \$3,000 (in 1968 dollars) was cut in half. Just as important, savings accounts skyrocketed, and the liquid assets of individuals increased from \$50 billion to \$140 billion. Most Americans could hardly wait to spend their accumulated savings on automobiles, washing machines, electrical appliances, and housing. With advertisers promoting fantasies of consumer indulgence, and war workers ready to release their pent-up urge to spend, the postwar economy possessed its own built-in momentum.

The GI Bill, in turn, helped to provide the ingredients for long-term prosperity. Veterans returning from the war received a panoply of benefits. Those whose schooling had been interrupted, or who wished to pursue technical or university training, received tuition as well as subsistence pay while they secured training for decent jobs. Those wishing help in establishing businesses could go to the Veterans Administration for guaranteed loans up to \$2,000. Perhaps most important, the government offered assistance in home buying. A soldier returning from the war was guaranteed access to \$2,000. Since the Federal Housing Authority (FHA) was willing to underwrite mortgages up to 80 or 90 percent of a home's value, the additional VA loan offered millions the opportunity for home ownership, at low interest rates, without ever having to make a downpayment. The GI Bill thus made possible the incredible building boom of the late 1940s and 1950s which did so much to fuel postwar prosperity, even as its educational provisions made possible the training of a generation of skilled workers and professionals to fill positions being generated by the burgeoning economy.

The government also served as primary sponsor for the technological breakthroughs that spawned new industries and facilitated productivity. With the war as an impetus, scientists made lightning breakthroughs in nuclear physics, aerospace, chemicals, and electronics. Not surprisingly, the industries that housed such enterprises experienced a parallel growth. Between 1937 and 1958 the Dow Chemical Company grew 750 percent, while electronics spurted from forty-ninth to fifth place among the nation's industries. After the war, Washington disposed of its investments in aluminum plants, aircraft factories, and machine-tool facilities, giving private businesses a headstart—in readymade facilities—in some of the nation's fastest growing industries. Moreover, government-sponsored research in areas like plastics—which grew 600 percent during the 1950s—made possible the development of whole new consumer industries. With Cold War tensions and the outbreak of fighting in Korea in 1950, government involvement in the economy remained a primary source of support for research and development, as well as new jobs. As Richard Hofstadter commented, there was a new form of "military Keynesianism" that made the government almost a guarantor of full employment. Directly and indirectly, federal funds were fueling an unprecedented era of economic growth—providing financing for mortgages, stipends for education, and investment in scientific research destined to produce massive economic dividends. In 1929, federal government expenditures had amounted to 1 percent of the gross national product. By the mid-1950s the percentage had increased seventeen times. The results were remarkable.

As a consequence of technological breakthroughs, productivity increased dramatically. From 1947 to 1956 alone, the advance was 200 percent per capita. It took 310 labor hours to make a car at the end of the war, only half of that fifteen years later. During the postwar years, corporations invested an average of $10 billion a year in new plants and machinery designed to speed up the production process.

Developments in computer technology exemplified the massive leaps being made. In collaboration with IBM, Harvard University produced the first general-purpose computer in 1944, MARK I, 50 feet long, 8 feet tall, 3 feet deep, consisting of 530 miles of wire and 765,000 parts. Two years later, the first electronic computer, ENIAC, rendered its electromechanical predecessor completely obsolete. It still weighed 30 tons and was as large as a box car. In 1950, John Neuman built the first stored program computer with government funding; at this same time, developers were ready to market computers to corporate customers, and 20 were sold in 1954. By the end of the decade, the number had increased to 2,000. Generally, computers were only useful for large-scale industrial, scientific, and military projects.

One result of such breakthroughs was to make theoretical knowledge a centerpiece of economic development, supplying the foundation for such crucial innovations as systems analysis, micro economics, and chemical engineering. So critical did theoretical and technical knowledge become that research and development (R&D) emerged as a major industry in its own right.

The inextricable links between military defense, scientific research, and the industry emerged at the beginning of the Cold War in the late 1940s and early 1950s. The Atomic Energy Act of 1946 represented one of the first steps into this direction. It established the Atomic Energy Commission to fund nuclear research, particularly in weaponry. A year later, the R&D board was formed, and in 1950 the National Science Foundation was formed to support basic research, research that often had military implications. The Soviet launch of Sputnik in 1957 was followed by the creation of NASA and the 1958 National Defense Education Act that appropriated an initial $621 million for college student loans and programs to boost scientific and foreign language instruction. Huge defense contracts established airline manufacturers such as Douglas and Boeing as integral parts of the emerging military-industrial complex. Research also furthered the development of weapons of mass destruction, including the hydrogen bomb that was first tested in 1954. With an explosive power of 15 million tons of TNT, it was 750 times more powerful than the atomic bomb. Instead of the nuclear fission that split heavy atomic nuclei, the hydrogen bomb fused the nuclei of light elements at extremely high temperatures to convert mass into energy. Atmospheric nuclear testing polluted the environment by releasing large quantities of radioactive strontium 90, which found its way into cows' milk. After protests against this practice, the United States and Soviet Union agreed to conduct underground instead of atmospheric tests. Soon, both countries produced 100-megaton bombs, each the equivalent of 100 million tons of TNT.

To an ever-increasing extent corporate prosperity depended on the genius of scientists. As Daniel Bell has noted, the "knowledge revolution" transformed the occupational structure of the country. In 1940, 2.9 million people were engaged in professional and technical occupations. By 1964 that figure had more than doubled. Engineers increased in number by 370 percent between 1930 and 1964; scientists by 930 percent.

Technology decisively affected the type of jobs available to American workers. "Automation," *Business Week* observed in the 1950s, "[is] the art and science of going through as many stages of production as possible with as little human help as possible." With industries like automobiles and steel devoting 15 to 20 percent of their budgets to labor-saving devices, productivity increased in the country's factories, but the assembly line required fewer workers to turn out the same number of goods. Thus between 1947 and 1957, the number of factory operators actually fell 4 percent. By contrast, the number of clerical workers increased 23 percent.

As one sign of the shift, the nation's economy in 1956 crossed the line from an industrial to a "post-industrial" state, with white-collar workers outnumbering blue-collar workers for the first time. The new jobs were in

As corporate America expanded, so too did white-collar jobs that employed millions of women, as in this Lever Brothers office in New York City. *(National Archives)*

occupations that served the consumer—sales personnel in automobile show rooms and appliance stores, telephone operators, government bureaucrats, bank tellers, investment counselors, advertising people. Such jobs testified to the emergence of a new economy focused on the production of services designed to enhance the quality of life, rather than on providing basic necessities.

The shift deleteriously affected the vitality of the labor movement. In a society that equated white-collar jobs with upward mobility, the unionization of clerical and sales workers proved difficult. By 1960, unions had organized less than 184,000 of 5 million public employees, only 200,000 of 8.5 million office workers, and only 12,000 of 600,000 engineers, draftsmen, and technicians. Significantly, the majority of these jobs were held by women. As the work force changed in composition, organized labor stagnated, and in the 15 years between 1945 and 1960, the unionized portion of the country's nonagricultural workers fell by 14 percent. Already weakened by anticommunism and the failure of the new organizing campaigns in the immediate postwar years, labor became more and more conservative, focusing on the traditional techniques of business unionism. As salaries of union leaders grew to more than $30,000 per year, the profile of trade union executives came more and more to resemble that of the managers with whom they negotiated for higher wages and fringe benefits. In Daniel Bell's words, labor had taken on "the grossest features of a business society," leaving behind the insurgency of the thirties and forties.

Perhaps the greatest impact of the shift in the economy was the emergence of a new managerial class. Between 1947 and 1957, the number of salaried middle-class workers rose 61 percent. The increase reflected the sharp growth of large corporations, the rapid advances in productivity, and the importance of developing specialized personnel to market and manage the corporate product. To an ever-increasing extent, the economy was dominated by a few gigantic enterprises that depended for their efficiency on the particularized knowledge of skilled experts. A marketing analyst made decisions on the sales potential of a new product, a specialist in management science coordinated personnel, and a physicist or research engineer oversaw the development of new inventions and design. In Daniel Bell's words, the proletariat was being replaced "by a salariat." Thus, in the chemical industry, the blue-collar work force increased by 3 percent between 1947 and 1952, but the white-collar force increased by 50 percent. In companies like General Motors, there were as many as 130,000 salaried workers. Indeed, companies like GM and AT&T took on the characteristic of nation states, with profits over $1 billion per year and huge bureaucracies carrying out highly differentiated tasks. The old family enterprise—even the kind of "family capitalism" represented in companies such as Ford Motors, or the Ball Glass Company—was becoming an anachronism. Ford, for example, "went public" in 1956 selling stock to over 250,000 investors.

According to many social observers, these huge corporate enterprises created a new managerial personality. In the past, sociologists William Whyte and C. Wright Mills observed, businessmen worked hard, mastered their area of professional responsibility, and looked toward internal "character" values for guidance in their daily behavior. Now, it was argued, people not only needed to have specialized skills, but also the ability to get along with thousands of co-workers in an increasingly differentiated bureaucracy. "The organization man" was as much involved in mastering the art of interpersonal relationships as in accomplishing the professional task before him. Indeed, one could rise in the corporation only by testing the environment around one's self and determining how most effectively to follow the prevailing wind.

David Riesman concluded that the new managerial class had turned its back on the "inner direction" of past generations and had donned in its place an "other-directed" personality. Instead of an interior gryoscope which one looked to for moral and personal direction, one sought "approval and direction from others." While "inner direction" was the "typical character of the old middle class," "other direction" became the "typical character of the new middle class—the bureaucrat, the salaried employee in business." C. Wright Mills noted the same characteristic. "When white collar people get jobs," he wrote, "they sell not only their time and energy, but

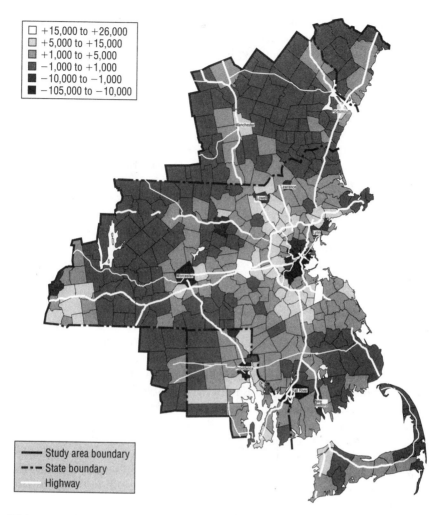

☐	+15,000 to +26,000
▨	+5,000 to +15,000
▩	+1,000 to +5,000
▦	−1,000 to +1,000
▪	−10,000 to −1,000
■	−105,000 to −10,000

Study area boundary
State boundary
Highway

This map of Boston and its suburbs highlights the rapidity with which America's population growth in the postwar period concentrated around the country's large cities. It was a mass migration comparable to that of European immigrants in the first two decades of the twentieth century. *(National Atlas of the United States, http:// nationalatlas.gov)*

their personalities as well. They sell by the week or month their smiles and their kindly gestures, and they must practice the prompt repression of resentment and aggression." By paying attention to the wishes of others, avoiding conflict, and suppressing the instinct for individual self-assertion or rebellion, the new "organization man" could move from group to group in a huge bureaucracy, sensing at any given moment which exact combination of personality characteristics and viewpoints would lead to maximum success. Only those most sensitive to signals from others could function effectively within the huge bureaucracy and move to the top. Expertise in a particular area of business was no longer sufficient; only the combination of particularized skill *plus* the generalized ability to win approval from one's peers could assure success. Indeed, in a pinch, sensitivity to others dwarfed more specialized skills in importance.

Suburbia and Consumerism

If the "organization man" came to symbolize the new corporate personality, the suburban housing development came to symbolize the middle-class lifestyle he went home to. (In the 1950s, there were virtually no "organization women.") In one of the most astounding migrations in history, suburbanites flocked to the new communities that blossomed in ever-widening circles around the nation's metropolitan areas. At the height of the great European migration in the early twentieth century, 1.2 million new citizens came to America in a single year. During the 1950s the same number moved to the suburbs every year. Irving, Texas—outside of Dallas—had a population in 1950 of 2,621; a decade later 45,000 people lived there. The Levittown communities in New York and Pennsylvania boasted of 17,000 homes apiece. During the 1950s, suburbs grew six times faster than cities. Between 1950 and 1960 alone, 18 million people moved to the suburbs. During the same decade the total population increase was only 28 million.

The move to suburbia represented a miraculous fusion of need and desire. After the war the number of marriages doubled, and most of the new households had nowhere to go. Over 2 million couples in 1948 were living with relatives. It was against such a backdrop that easy housing loans through VA and FHA combined with a booming economy to make possible a massive program of housing construction. Between 1950 and 1960 more than 13 million homes were built in America—11 million of them in the suburbs. Building contractors wanted cheap land; county governments were happy to welcome them to empty space crying for development. Overnight a new community would come into being—not necessarily the spacious manor houses that most people dreamed of when they thought of suburban domesticity, but nevertheless a comfortable four-room home with a plot of ground, the latest in gadgetry, and at least a few trees to convey a sense of the open countryside. By 1960 one-quarter of the entire population lived in such suburban areas.

The housing boom reflected in part the simplicity and ease of construction. Architectural critic Lewis Mumford acidly described suburbs as

> a multitude of uniform, unidentifiable houses, lined up inflexibly, at uniform distances, on uniform roads, in a treeless communal wasteland, inhabited by people of the same class, the same income, the same age group.

But if some suburban houses did look like boxes arranged in circles, they nevertheless represented an improvement over cramped apartments in the

During the postwar years, millions of people moved to new homes in suburbia like these in Levittown, Pennsylvania. Critics commented on the sameness of such dwellings, but to millions, these new homes represented a new opportunity to live "the good life." *(National Archives)*

inner city, and millions were delighted to have the opportunity to move and achieve home ownership. Moreover, the suburbs tended to be arranged in ascending orders of class mobility. Thus, as one's job and income improved, one could move further away from the city to a large house with more land and space. During the postwar years Americans experienced unprecedented mobility, with approximately 25 percent of the population changing their home address at least once a year. Between 1940 and 1960 migration across county lines leaped by 50 percent.

The emergence of suburbia went hand in hand with an encore performance of the automobile revolution. Between 1945 and 1960 the number of cars in the country increased by 133 percent. During the middle 1950s, almost as many cars were being junked each year as were being manufactured, and Americans raced to find the newest models with the largest fins. The boom in car sales reflected the increased tendency of suburban households to have more than one automobile so that commuters could take one to the city or the railroad station, with the other car left at home for transporting children and doing shopping. Making all of this possible was the massive construction of a new network of roads. Under the Highways Act of

1956 Congress appropriated $32 billion to build 41,000 miles of highway. It all somehow made sense. The government provided the loans for the new suburban houses. It built the highways that went to those homes. And an economy, built in large part on the consumption of new housing and automobiles, created a spiral of sustained prosperity and growth.

Consumerism represented one of the primary consequences—as well as one of the essential ingredients—of this prosperity. The initial quest for appliances, automobiles, and new furniture after the war expanded quickly into the mass consumption of services, goods, and recreational materials during the 1950s. As early as 1929, commentators had observed that America had a new idea to give to the world—the idea that labor should be looked on "not simply as workers and producers, but as *consumers* . . . pay them more, sell them more, prosper more is the equation." During the fifties the idea came to fruition. In many areas of the country weekend entertainment consisted of visiting the local "Mammoth Mart" and buying the latest gadget to make life easier, from electric carving knives to automatic shoe shiners. The use of electricity tripled during the 1950s, in large part because of the appliances purchased. Between 1945 and 1960 advertising increased 400 percent, amounting to three times the nation's annual investment in higher education. John Kenneth Galbraith pointed out that the modern economy was one in which consumer industries met a demand for products which they themselves had generated. As shopping centers proliferated and a new culture of buying took control, suburban residents were bombarded with the message that they could not enjoy the good life without a motorized lawnmower, a new convertible, or the latest imported wine.

Much of the new consumerism focused on recreation. During the 1950s the average family in suburbia earned $6,500—70 percent higher than the average income for the rest of the nation. In the richer suburbs people purchased boats (4 million during the 1950s), swimming pools, and expensive vacations. More than 8 million people traveled abroad in the 1950s, and with all the new automobiles and highways, those who stayed at home helped to create a new industry of domestic tourism, visiting national parks, camping at beaches, and providing the customers for amusement areas like Disneyland. Receipts for the motel industry alone increased 2,300 percent between 1939 and 1958, and the new inns that dotted American highways competed to provide both uniform and increasingly luxurious facilities, from large swimming pools to miniature golf courses. During nonvacation times, meanwhile, social life revolved around the outdoor barbecue, with practically every suburban household boasting its own redwood picnic table and outdoor grill.

In all of this a profound irony existed: those who left the city in order to find a private home of their own sometimes became enmeshed in a form of group living that crushed privacy and undermined individualism. In many urban apartment buildings, residents rarely interacted except by prior arrangement, or an accidental meeting at the elevator. Most social interaction occurred in a planned and formal manner. (There were many exceptions, of course, especially in ethnic and working-class neighborhoods.) But in suburbia, as one observer noted, "privacy has become clandestine." Frequently, tract houses in suburban developments faced on a common street or a shared backyard. Picture windows made everyone's movement accessible to one's neighbors. New residents were greeted by the "welcome wagon," and each evening people poured from their houses for a nighttime promenade to meet their neighbors on the street and discuss the new teacher at the school, Johnny's cold, or the latest cure for crabgrass. If a family was new to the community, its members might wait until the neighborhood congregation had assembled for its evening gossip, and then move out to become part of the group, thereby achieving with ease and informality an initiation into the neighborhood group. Those who failed to emerge from their houses might well note furtive glances being cast at their door by neighbors who wondered what kind of strange and unfriendly foreigners had come into their midst.

Togetherness and informality became watchwords of suburbia. Whether at an impromptu cookout, the neighborhood bridge game, or the morning kaffeeklatsch, people spent their time *with each other*. As one junior executive said,

> We have learned not to be so introverted. . . . Before we came here we used to live pretty much to ourselves. On Sundays, for instance, we used to stay in bed until around maybe two o'clock, reading the paper and listening to the symphony on the radio. Now we stop around and visit with people or they visit with us. I really think [the experience] has broadened us.

The very nature of suburban life encouraged cooperation and volunteerism. Young families joined together to form car pools or babysitting clubs. If a local school needed a new playground, parents banded together to construct it. From the potluck supper to the local school planning council, the vogue of togetherness and group participation reigned supreme.

Even religion reflected the new ethos. The 1950s witnessed a mass revival of religion. By 1958 church membership had leaped to 110 million, and 97 percent of the American people declared that they believed in God. As congregations proliferated to serve the new suburban constituency, the church often became a chief disciple of togetherness, running so many group activities that an ardent church member would literally have no time for anything else. A typical church bulletin read like a hectic social calendar: Monday night, the Men's Bowling Club; Tuesday, "A Couples Group"; Wednesday, The Arts and Crafts Association; Thursday, "A Family Swim"; Friday, "A Potluck"; and Saturday, "A Car Wash To Raise Funds for the Youth Group." Even on Sunday, the themes of family togetherness might prevail, with churches sponsoring re-enactment of wedding ceremonies on Family Sunday so that husbands and wives could take anew their vows to each other in celebration of the bonds that kept the community intact.

For many, the whole complex of suburban institutions represented a devastating blow to individuality, diversity, and faith. "Religion nowadays has the appearance of what the ideal modern house has been called," Lionel Trilling commented, "a machine for living." Instead of creating a community based on faith in God ("even though He slay me, yet will I trust Him"), the suburban church preached the gospel of comfort and security ("Suffer the little children to come unto me"). People might say they believed in God, MIT philosopher Houston Smith has said, "but on examination it turns out that many people believe in believing in Him." The church had lost its core, these critics believed, becoming one more manifestation of consumerism. "On weekdays one shops for food, . . . and on Sundays one shops for the Holy Ghost." Like the corporate organizations it emulated, the church had become an instrument for social adjustment, cheap therapy that guaranteed community identity. "In place of the sacraments, we have the committee meeting," theologian Gibson Winter declared. "In place of the confession, the bazaar; . . . in place of community, a collection of functions; . . . every church activity seems to lead further into a maze of superficiality which is stultifying the middle class community."

Others issued the same indictment against the social life of the neighborhood. For all the attractiveness of its informality, group interaction on the block, in the eyes of some, quickly assumed the tyranny of mindless conformity. As William Whyte perceived it, the "social ethic" of Park Forest simply represented an extension of the "organization-man" style of the corporation. To get along, one had to go along. Individualism was forbidden. Those who preferred to read Plato or listen to a symphony instead of joining the neighborhood promenade all too often were ostracized. The group controlled everything, and anyone who violated its norms risked forced exile. If a family wished to secure acceptance, it must do no more and no less than everyone else. "Not getting the balance just right," *Fortune* magazine commented, "is a source of friction, feuds, and sleepless nights in many of the newer suburban communities."

When one resident of Park Forest broke the rules and tried to impress her neighbors with a conspicuous display of material goods, she found herself stigmatized. "It's really pitiful," a friend commented. "She sits there in her beach chair out front just dying for someone to come and [have coffee] with her, and right across the street four or five of the girls will be yakking away. Every time they suddenly all laugh at some joke she thinks they are laughing at her. She came over here yesterday and cried all afternoon." This was the world one writer called *The Split-Level Trap*. From the perspective of many social critics in the 1950s, it represented a dictatorship of blandness and uniformity that killed the human spirit. In the words of one satirical song:

> They all play on the golf course
> And drink their martinis dry,
> And they all have pretty children,

And their children go to school,
And the children go to summer camp
And then to the university.
Where they are put in boxes
And they come out just the same.

In the end, however, such criticisms ignored the real achievements of suburbia. As Herbert Gans and William Dobriner have pointed out, suburbia itself was not a monolith. A significant amount of diversity existed in the lifestyle, political viewpoints, and social interaction of different neighborhoods. Perhaps more important, critics overlooked the extent to which the residents of Park Forest and Levittown exhibited imagination and courage in their effort to create communities where none had existed before. During a time of massive geographical mobility and intense pressure to "make it," the residents of suburbia were forging bonds of identity and collective commitment to sustain them. While neighborhood barbecues or hyperactive "organization" churches might represent at times a frenetic effort to find an artificial sense of belonging, they also reflected an effective attempt to develop bonds of communal solidarity where these did not exist naturally as a result of a common ethnic or regional tradition. Voluntary associations in suburbia provided means of building a community as well as establishing connections and credentials. The intimate friendships of next-door neighbors might only last for two or three years before a new promotion caused a move, but they also served to provide the emotional support and reinforcement that no longer existed (and may never have existed) in stable urban-neighborhoods surrounded by relatives. In the face of social changes that could easily have generated massive alienation, the institutions and lifestyles developing in suburban America represented an achievement that, whatever its limitations and disadvantages, could not be denied.

Family Life and Sex Roles

As much as any other part of American life, the family reflected both the themes—and the contradictions—of American society during the 1940s and 1950s. Certainly no institution enjoyed such unprecedented growth. By the end of World War II there were 2.5 million fewer single women than there had been in 1940. By 1950 nearly 60 percent of all 18- to 24-year-old women were married as opposed to only 42 percent in 1940. It was these new families, taking advantage of the opportunities offered by the postwar economy, who purchased the four-room houses in suburbia, went back to college under the GI Bill, secured good jobs, and provided the vanguard for the burgeoning consumer society of the 1950s.

The baby boom became the single largest growth industry of postwar America. During the 1940s America's population grew by 19 million, more than twice the growth of the 1930s. But in the 1950s even that figure was dwarfed as America grew by almost 30 million people and approached a level of population growth identical to that of India. Before World War II, the fertility rate was 80 and the birth rate only 19 per 100,000 people. Seventeen years later the fertility rate peaked at 123, and the birth rate at 25 per 100,000. Togetherness became more than just a slogan, as the birth rate for third children doubled between 1940 and 1960 and that for fourth children tripled. All during the 1940s school enrollments increased by only a million. Then, during the 1950s, they skyrocketed by 10 million. Instead of picturing families with two children in their advertisements, mass circulation magazines now featured family portraits of five- and six-person families, all supposedly participating in the prosperity and bliss of suburban living.

According to popular images, this "new" family was run by children. Filiality had taken the place of both patriarchy and matriarchy. During the early years of a child's life, social life revolved around play time for infants and toddlers in the backyards of suburbia. Later on, dance lessons, piano lessons, and sports events occupied parents in an endless round of chauffeuring. Given the number of four-children families, the average mother could easily have devoted her day in equal parts to diapering the baby, supervising a toddler on a swing, serving as a den mother for an eight-year-old cub scout, and transporting a ten-year-old daughter to gymnastics. According to many experts, permissiveness reigned as the dominant ethic, with children in control. "Suburban parents and teachers are prone to do for *youth* rather than to spur youth to do for itself," one observer noted. "Too zealously we shield our children from a knowledge of the realities of life."

According to the same portrait, sex roles achieved a new level of polarization in the suburban family. A commuter father left the home almost before daybreak, returning just in time for a romp with the kids, perhaps a quick swing, and then a kiss goodnight. Mothers, meanwhile, held down the fort at home, cleaned the house, transported the children to their daily activities, participated in various P.T.A. and church groups, and still found time, in the midst of it all, for kaffeeklatsching with women friends and discussing childrearing. A woman's life, one humorist commented, "was motherhood on wheels [delivering children] obstetrically once and by car forever after."

Despite its frustrations and difficulties, such a life was perceived by most opinion makers as the complete embodiment of women's highest dreams. In the years after World War II what Betty Friedan later called "the feminine mystique" became a staple of America's popular culture. College newspapers described young coeds as distraught if they were not engaged by their senior year, young women told public pollsters that they looked forward to four or more children, and women's magazines presented an image of women as "daily content in a world of bedroom, kitchen, sex, babies and home." According to a popular best-seller, *Modern Woman: The Lost Sex,* the independent woman was "a contradiction in terms." Women could secure fulfillment only by devoting themselves to homemaking, repossessing the old arts of canning, preserving, and interior decorating, and making household work into a creative adventure. According to this analysis, any women dissatisfied with such a role were neurotic, victims of feminist propaganda, "masculinized." If a woman followed the path of "normal femininity," psychiatrist Helene Deutsch declared, she accepted her distinctive sexuality, repressed her masculine strivings, and related to the outside world through identification with her husband and children. Or, as Ferdinand Lundberg and Marynia Farnham said, female happiness required that women "accept with deep inwardness and readiness . . . the final goal of [intercourse]—impregnation." With this acceptance, sexual pleasure and domestic happiness were guaranteed. Any women wishing complete fulfillment had only to extend the attributes of acceptance and love displayed during intercourse to the rest of their lives.

At the core of the feminine mystique was the notion that the "eternal female" constituted the foundation for a secure and happy society. "Modern man needs an old fashioned woman around the house," the novelist Sloan Wilson declared. Striking the same theme, another author insisted that while women "had many careers, they had only one vocation—motherhood." Women were the "cement of society, [its preservation against the] competitive, materialistic world" of men. "What modern woman has to recapture," she concluded, "is [that] just being a woman is her central task and her greatest honor. . . . Women must boldy announce that no job is more exacting, more necessary, or more rewarding than that of housewife and mother." Within such a framework, the suburban wife—a model of "efficiency, patience and charm"—became the counterpart to the organization man, helping the family to achieve new levels of fulfillment and prosperity. As Ashley Montague said: "A man needs the love of a woman to maintain him in good mental and physical health. For his complete and adequate functioning, he is more dependent on such a love than a woman is. In such a fundamental human situation, women will not dream of considering themselves anything but help mates to men."

Yet there was something profoundly suspicious about such rhetoric. The effort to reinforce traditional norms seemed almost frantic, as though in reality something very different was taking place. Indeed, all during the late 1940s and early 1950s the same magazines that celebrated women's fulfillment in suburban homes also printed articles repeatedly asking what was "the trouble with women." "Choose any set of criteria you like," Margaret Mead wrote, "and the answer is the same: women—and men—are confused, uncertain and discontented with the present definition of women's place in America." In 1946 a *Fortune* poll asked American women whether they would prefer to be born again as women or men. A startling 25 percent declared that they would prefer to be men (only 3.3 percent of the men preferred to be women). A later poll of the 1934 graduates of the best women's colleges indicated that 1 out of 3 felt frustrated and unfulfilled.

In fact, the feminine mystique represented but one side of a tug-of-war between traditional and modern roles. *Life* magazine, commenting on the tension, devoted a 13-page spread in 1947 to "American Woman's Dilemma." In the past, the magazine declared, women had only to make one big decision—their choice of a husband. Now, although women still hoped to get married and have children, they also looked forward to participating in a world beyond the home. But how could that happen when the culture provided little support for independence, and few sanctions for women's autonomy? In the face of articles that called women neurotic if they deviated from the norm and urged women college students to study the "theory and preparation of a Basque paella" instead of post-Kantian philosophy, there was little encouragement to find a more satisfying niche in society.

Charting the experience of women students at Barnard, the sociologist Mirra Komarovsky concluded that modern women faced a bewildering choice of pressures that inevitably created ambivalence and unhappiness. Taught as children to "select girls' toys and to be more restrained, sedentary, quiet and neat" than their brothers, young women also faced the pressure to work hard, get good grades, and achieve. Yet if they appeared to be "too smart" and to scare off prospective suitors, they risked the danger of losing the ultimate definition of female success—marriage and a family. Hence, 40 percent of Barnard women admitted that they "played dumb" on dates to get along with the boys. Then, after marriage, the same women found themselves frustrated at the absence of opportunities to carry forward their academic skills. As one alumna observed, "the plunge from the strictly intellectual college life to the 24-hour a day domestic one is a terrible shock. We stagger through our first years of childrearing wondering what our values are in struggling to find some compromise between our intellectual ambition and the reality of everyday living."

The price of such cultural confusion could be seen in the growing evidence of social anomie, even in those suburbs that allegedly represented the culmination of happiness. Popular writers noted the increase in alcoholism and the rise in divorce rates during the "contented" fifties. Consumption of tranquilizers skyrocketed from 462,000 pounds in 1958 to 1.15 million pounds in 1959. Magazines like *Life* wondered especially about those women who devoted themselves exclusively to the home and, as a result, found themselves increasingly removed from the world of ideas and experiences encountered by their husbands. "Once their children have grown," *Life* said, "a housewife . . . lacking outside interests and training, is faced with vacant years . . . bored stiff with numbing rounds of club meetings and card playing."

Compounding the confusion was the fact that millions of women continued to enter the job market, thereby directly contradicting the popular stereotype that all were happily ensconced in their roles as homemakers and housewives. By 1960 twice as many women were employed as in 1940, and 40 percent of all women over 16 held a job. During the 1950s female employment increased at a rate four times faster than men's. The proportion of wives at work had doubled from 15 percent in 1940 to 30 percent in 1960. Although the greatest numerical increases took place among married workers (from 7.5 million in 1947 to 10.4 million in 1952) who were over 35, the number of mothers at work leaped 400 percent—from 1.5 million to 6.6 million—and 39 percent of women with children aged 6 to 17 had jobs by the end of the fifties.

Clearly, these women were not pursuing careers or achieving equality in the job place. Many worked part-time, and the majority were concentrated in clerical and white-collar positions that were underpaid and offered little possibility for promotion. In 1950, for example, women comprised 64 percent of the workers in the insurance industry, but only 20 percent of those in higher level positions. In banking, the figures were 46 percent of the work force, but only 15 percent in upper-level jobs. A survey of academic jobs came to the same conclusion. "Women scholars are not taken seriously," a 1959 study concluded, "and cannot look forward to a normal professional career . . . because they are outside the prestige system entirely. . . . In the world of ideas, women simply do not count."

Nevertheless, a major change had occurred. In the past, single women and married women from lower income families had predominated in the female labor force. Now, the increase came primarily from married women who were either in, or entering, the middle class. In households where the husband earned from $7,000 to $10,000 a year, the rate of women's participation in the job market rose from 7 percent in 1950 to 25 percent in 1960. By the early sixties over 53 percent of women college graduates were employed in contrast to only 36 percent of those with just a high school diploma. In short, not only was the increase in women's employment continuing, it was also being led by the same middle-class wives and mothers who allegedly had found new contentment in domesticity.

In fact, the expansion of women's economic roles represented, in many cases, the indispensable prerequisite to families achieving middle-class status. In the 1960s, census bureau officials noted that the number of households earning $15,000 or more would be cut in half if women's incomes were excluded. The trend had begun a decade earlier. By 1960 both husbands and wives worked in over 10 million homes (an increase of 330 percent over 1940). Many of these families could buy a new house or enjoy the benefits of consumer affluence only because of the wife's income. A survey in Illinois, for example, revealed that two-income families spent 45 percent more on gifts and recreation, 95 percent more on restaurant meals, and 23 percent more on household equipment than single-earner families. Clearly, if there was a margin between the comfort of the middle class and remaining part of a working-class lifestyle, women's employment often provided it.

In all of this, there was a certain cultural and economic logic. The greatest increase in women's employment came among women over 35 who had completed the primary childrearing responsibilities, and either had no children at home or had already sent their last child off to school. Such women were not challenging the most sacrosanct definition of women's "place," nor were they competing with men for jobs or seeking careers. Because they were "helping the family" to achieve comfort and security, their activities could be seen as consistent with traditional family norms. At the same time, these women found a partial answer to the absence of a culturally sanctioned role of independence. Almost 90 percent of working women interviewed in two cities during the late 1950s stated that they enjoyed their jobs, particularly the opportunity to be with other people and to receive recognition for their work. In one survey, almost two-thirds of married women workers referred to their jobs as a basis for feeling "important" or "useful," while only one-third cited the socially sanctioned activity of housekeeping.

In the end, family life and sex roles reflected many of the same contradictions and ambiguities that characterized suburban lifestyle generally. Although a majority of those who lived in the new housing developments surrounding American cities enacted stereotypic roles—husbands working away from home all day and women tending the children—a significant minority engaged in a different pattern. In these cases, women worked before bearing children, helping to make possible the downpayment on the home and the entrance into a middle-class life. After spending a few years raising the children, the same women re-entered the job market after the age of 35, providing critical resources for the ongoing prosperity of the family. Simultaneously, these women were carving out one of the only paths available within the existing culture for resolving the contradiction between traditional and modern definitions of women's "place."

In the end, perhaps only two things could be said with certainty. The nature of family life, particularly in suburbia, was far more complicated and tension-filled than the stereotypes of the fifties would have us believe. And much of the lifestyle of "affluence" that we associate with that era rested on the employment of women who, in the past, had not held jobs and who were now reflecting both the economic pressures of their society and the social pressures of a culture that offered no sanction for sex equality or a life of independence and free choice for women.

TV and Popular Culture

Not surprisingly, popular culture reflected the same patterns of growth and tension that existed in the rest of society. Within fifteen years after World War II, the number of symphony orchestras had doubled, book sales increased by 250 percent, and art museums emerged in every moderately sized city in the country. Abstract Expressionism ceased to be an eccentricity indulged in by only a few, and its leading exponent, Jackson Pollock, became a cult hero of sorts after a tragic automobile crash that ended his life. So much did the art world become a part of consumer culture that, in 1960, one of New York's most prestigious galleries held an auction for a nationwide audience linked by closed-circuit TV. As works by Cézanne and Utrillo went to the highest bidder, the auctioneer incited potential customers not to let down their respective constituencies. "Come on, Chicago, you're not going to let Dallas get it, are you?"

Every other instrument of popular culture, of course, paled in comparison to the astonishing growth of TV. Although TV had been invented in the 1920s, few stations were licensed and no one anticipated a significant commercial market. Then, suddenly, everything changed. With the FCC resuming commercial licensing, the number of stations skyrocketed from 6 in 1946 to 442 in 1956. Two years after the war 7,000 TV sets were sold. Three years later the figure had leaped to 7 million. By the middle of the 1950s, 66 percent of all homes boasted their own television. As Max Lerner declared, TV had become "the poor man's luxury because it is his psychological necessity." A 1950 survey showed that junior high school students with TVs in the home watched the set 27 hours a week. Advertisers, meanwhile, discovered that TV offered a magic carpet to success. When Hazel Bishop, the lipstick maker, started to use TV advertising, the company had an annual business of $50,000 a year. Two years later its sales soared to $4.5 million.

The emergence of a standardized mass culture appeared in the consolidation of TV networks and the media in general. Three networks, ABC, CBS, and NBS, controlled early television, which, in turn, altered the shape of the culture, bringing people from the most disparate backgrounds together in a common experience. In 1950 only 3 percent of America's rural homes had a television. By 1960 the figure had leaped to 80 percent. In *Understanding Media*, Marshall McLuhan celebrated the new media and especially television as a "quantum leap" in human communication. Considering the medium itself the message, McLuhan suggested that a change of perception, initiated by the new media, would change the world. Americans watched together as John Cameron Swayze came on each evening with the *Camel News Caravan*, fascinated as the upbeat commentator took his audience "hopscotching around the world."

The World Series became a tangible reality for millions who had never seen a major league ballpark as the Zoomar lens showed Don Larsen pitching a perfect game against the Dodgers, or Bobby Thomson hitting the miracle home run in the playoff that sent the New York Giants into the series. With the introduction of frozen TV dinners in 1954, families even gathered around the set at mealtime, conversation hushed by the new miracle invention that held everyone spellbound. Nightclubs darkened as former customers stayed home on Saturday to watch Sid Ceasar and Imogene Coca in "Your Show of Shows," and the average weekly attendance at movies plummeted from 90 million to 47 million in the ten years after 1946. Toledo, Ohio, officials, not surprisingly, noted a massive increase in water consumption, coinciding with a three-minute break for commercials between TV shows.

As a result of TV, a whole generation grew up with new heros. Youngsters dissolved in laughter as they talked about Milton Berle being hit by a cream puff, or Jackie Gleason—acting the part of Ralph Kramden in the

"Honeymooners"—waving his fist and saying, "One of these days, Alice, one of these days—*pow*—right in the kisser." Gorgeous George, the wrestler with marcelled hair (in real life a psychiatric resident at New York's Bellevue Hospital) entertained millions with his antics in the ring, while Lucille Ball in "I Love Lucy" kept an entire nation on the edge of its seat as it watched her live through her pregnancy on the TV series. When the baby arrived, nearly 70 percent of the nation's TV sets were tuned in, with the news of the birth competing for headlines with Eisenhower's inaugural. A whole new form of suspense emerged with the "$64,000 Question," a game show that combined the nation's fascination with consumerism, upward mobility, and brains. The quiz show, sponsored by Revlon, pitted contestants against each other in isolation booths. With staccato music building tension, the contestants furrowed their brows, searching for the right answer. Charles Van Doren soon became the 1950s version of Charles Lindbergh as he swept the board with his brilliance. (Only later would it be revealed that the entire show was fixed in advance.) Thus, from Lucy to Van Doren, from Clint Walker of "Cheyenne" to James Garner of "Maverick," Americans beheld a new pantheon of folk heros. Even Ronald Reagan became a byword through his role hosting "Death Valley Days" and the "General Electric Theatre."

For the most part, television reinforced the conservative, celebratory values of the dominant culture. "I Remember Mama" offered a vision of immigrant life designed to warm every American heart with its depiction of assimilation, upward mobility, and ethnic nostalgia. The show hinted at nothing like the 84-hour work week in Pittsburgh, or the sweatshops of New York. Shows like "Father Knows Best," in turn, reassured Americans that traditional male authority and female subservience offered the only way to true happiness. In one episode, Margaret worried that her husband might be attracted to an old high school flame who had gone off to become a medical doctor, and then a world-renown missionary, while she, Margaret, had done "nothing." She was quickly reassured by the returning doctor that no, it was Margaret who had triumphed, and the doctor who had failed, because *she* had given up the possibility of true happiness through marriage and motherhood.

Much more insidious was the effort by anticommunists to control the airwaves and those who would appear on them. Ever since the HUAC hearings investigating the political sympathies of Hollywood writers in 1947, entertainers had found themselves objects of microscopic examination by members of the right wing who believed that TV and movies were in the vanguard of a Moscow plot to subvert America. The techniques were familiar. Find a name, link it to other names, locate some moment of intersection with a group that someone else had called subversive, and then blacklist the entire roster. Sometimes the rationale for calling something communist was transparently ludicrous, as when Jack Warner described as communist propaganda those scripts which poked "fun at our political system" or made critical remarks about the rich. A favorite tactic of communist sympathizers,

Warner said, was "the routine of the Indians and the Colored folks. That is always their setup." But the results of such logic were deadly serious.

The blacklist reached a new height of effectiveness in 1950 when an anticommunist group called "Counter-Attack" published a 215-page book entitled *Red Channels: The Report of Communist Influence in Radio and Television*. Included in the book was a list of 151 people who were "potential subversives." The list contained composers Leonard Bernstein and Aaron Copland, actors Lee Cobb and Will Geer, singers Lena Horne and Burl Ives, and announcers Alexander Kendrick and Ben Grauer—a virtual "Who's Who" of the entertainment industry. Their crime? Alleged participation in one or another group that might at some point in the past have been linked, however distantly, with organizations friendly to Russia, the United Nations, or other progressive causes. Almost immediately *Red Channels* took its toll. When NBC announced that the "Aldridge Family" would make its TV debut in the summer of 1950, starring Jean Muir as the mother, a rash of phone calls reached the sponsor protesting the decision. Muir, it turned out, was on the blacklist. Three days before the opening telecast, the first show was postponed. Later, Muir's contract was cancelled and she never appeared in the series.

By the end of 1950 the whole industry was terrorized by professional anticommunists. Laurence Johnson, an official in the National Association of Supermarkets, took it upon himself to examine the casting list of proposed programs. Together with Vincent Hartnett, a man who called himself "the nation's top authority on communism and communications," Johnson pressured advertisers of products sold in supermarkets to boycott any program proposing to use an actor listed by *Red Channels* or "Counter-Attack." Thus, when the TV series "Danger" cast a suspect actor in one of its programs, Johnson called the sponsor, saying he would advertise the sponsor's product, Amni-dent, side by side with its competitor Chlorodent. In front of Chlorodent would be a sign saying that its programs used only pro-American artists and shunned "Stalin's little creatures." The Amni-dent sign could then explain to potential customers why programs it sponsored used subversives. Needless to say, the actors in question were removed from the program, posthaste. By 1951, to avoid such potential conflict, the major networks had set up their own blacklist offices to clear—in private—all actors with people like Hartnett and Johnson. As Erik Barnouw, the broadcast historian, has noted, phone calls were used to convey approval or disapproval. "Memoranda and face to face meetings were avoided. The voice at the other end would go down the list of proposed [actors] with 'yes,' 'no' and 'yes' and 'no.' Questions were not to be asked." So powerful had the anticommunists become that two supporters of Senator Joseph McCarthy were named by Dwight Eisenhower to the Federal Communications Commission. The chilling effect of such actions could hardly be overstated.

In the face of this onslaught, TV still achieved some major creative breakthroughs. The early drama programs—"Kraft Television Theatre," the

"Philco Television Playhouse," "Playhouse 90"—offered a vehicle for new writers, directors, and actors to make their mark. Individuals like Paul Newman, Rod Steiger, Arthur Penn, and Reginald Rose built solid reputations on the basis of hour-long live theatre productions, which despite the constraints of a television format, offered an effective new arena for talents to triumph. Sometimes, as in Reginald Rose's *Thunder on Sycamore Street,* the dramas even registered a significant political statement. In *Sycamore Street,* Rose portrayed a suburban neighborhood that organized—vigilante style— to expel a new, "foreign" family on the block. Although the network rejected Rose's initial script that defined the new family as black, he ingeniously rewrote the play so that no one knew until the very last act what it was that made the new family "different." The theme remained intact—the use of extralegal and prejudiced group action to deny individuals their fair right to live alongside other Americans. Viewers were left to guess whether the family in question were Jews, Russians, Blacks, or Asians, and when at the end the audience discovered that the family was headed by an ex-convict, it was too late to dilute the message about conformity and prejudice that the drama had already communicated.

But it was Edward R. Murrow who provided television's finest hour. The CBS newsman who had broadcast nightly from London during the war had returned to America and begun a TV series called *See It Now,* focusing on a particular news event or personality. Late in 1953, Murrow read about an Air Force lieutenant—Milo Radulovich—who had been asked to resign because his sister and father had been accused by someone—unnamed—of reading "subversive newspapers." Radulovich himself pointed out that "the actual charge against me is that I had maintained a close and continuing relationship with my dad and my sister over the years." Murrow and his producer, Fred Friendly, decided to spotlight the case, knowing that in the process they were taking on the entire phenomenon of guilt by association. After offering the Air Force a chance to comment (it refused), Murrow went on the air, with Radulovich himself raising the basic issues. "If I'm going to be judged by my relatives," he said, "are my children going to be asked to denounce me?" When the network refused to pay for an advertisement for the program, Murrow and Friendly forked up the money from their own pockets. "Things will never be the same around here after tonight," Murrow commented.

Indeed, they were not. Just a few months later Murrow and Friendly concluded that it was time to confront McCarthyism directly. Recognizing that McCarthy had reached his ascendancy by the technique of the "big lie," with the senator constantly shifting ground and using new and bigger charges to deflect those who protested the absence of documentation, Murrow and Friendly determined to let the evidence speak for itself. Using a compilation of footage from McCarthy's own statements, they allowed the TV audience to see how the junior senator from Wisconsin recklessly assaulted people's integrity, destroyed careers, and used character assassination to seize control of the political process. At the end of the film footage, with his customary cigarette in hand, Murrow faced the cameras.

> As a nation we have come into our full inheritance at a tender age. We proclaim ourselves—as indeed we are—the defenders of freedom, what's left of it, but we cannot defend freedom abroad by deserting it at home. The actions of the Junior Senator from Wisconsin have caused alarm and dismay amongst our allies abroad and given considerable comfort to our enemies, and whose fault is that? Not really his. He didn't create this situation of fear; he merely exploited it, and rather successfully. Cassius was right: "the fault, dear Brutus, is not in our stars but in ourselves. . . ." Goodnight, and good luck.

It was a moment that broadcasters would honor as long as the industry existed. Although McCarthy denounced Murrow as "the leader and cleverest of the jackal pack which is always found at the throat of anyone who dares to expose individual communists and traitors," his own rebuttal simply exemplified the basic points that Murrow had made. The smear tactic had suffered its first major reversal. Others could now speak up for decency and integrity. Two courageous newspeople had taken a stand.

American films reflected some of the same tendencies as television. As in the TV world, consolidation ruled. Five film studios, MGM, Paramount, Warner Brothers, RKO, and Twentieth Century Fox, produced nearly all the movies and controlled a large cinema network. In the immediate postwar era, Hollywood produced a significant number of movies dealing with social problems. *Pinkie,* for example, addressed the issue of light-skinned blacks "passing" into white society. But then came the HUAC hearings, the blacklist, and a flood of films almost saccharine in their sweetness. The early fifties were the era of *An American in Paris, The Greatest Show on Earth,* and others designed to entertain, not provoke thought. Only later in the decade, with films like the *Defiant Ones* and *Twelve Angry Men,* did Hollywood return, at least to some degree, to examining harsher issues of bigotry, prison life, and race relations.

More interesting, perhaps, was the perception of women, and their relationship to men and society, that emerged from the postwar era of films. Right after the war, films reflected some of the confusion in the dominant culture about women's roles. Women were portrayed as powerful, unpredictable, possessed of a mysterious power—rooted in their sex and their personality—that eluded control. Rita Hayworth's *Gilda* communicated the dual image of sexual allure and the potential, at least, that she could be persuaded to settle down to domestic fulfillment. (In the movie, a woman is said to have burned down Chicago and to have caused an earthquake in San Francisco. Later, the H bomb dropped on Bikini Island was dubbed Gilda.) As Michael Wood has pointed out, Gilda both was and was not "decent"—"the star of that heroic and much-cherished male dream: the roaring, sexy woman that you alone can conquer and keep." If in the end her "decent" side prevailed, the tantalizing question of whether she would break away from convention into passionate rebellion spoke to larger fears present in the culture about women's "place."

By the 1950s, however, innocence had reasserted itself. Even Marilyn Monroe, the all-time sex symbol, was naive. Never would she manipulate, scheme, or threaten. Whatever she was, Michael Wood observes, "she couldn't help it. . . . She and the '50s were a peak in American self-deception; they were a world wiped entirely clean." While Monroe replaced Hayworth, Doris Day replaced Greer Garson and Katharine Hepburn. Women were in their place and men could be secure.

Most pictures, meanwhile, celebrated a male culture of individualism, courage, and strength. Despite the vogue of togetherness, the ideal depiction of community was not of women and men living in families, but of soldiers or cowhands joining, through the bond of male camaraderie, to confront the evil of the world. Families were something that men felt nostalgic about, or fought over; the real story was the bravado and courage of their fighting. As Humphrey Bogart tells Ingrid Bergman in *Casablanca,* an earlier 1943 movie, "Where I'm going, you can't follow . . . what I've got to do, you can't be any part of." Gary Cooper goes off by himself to meet the gunslinger in *High Noon,* and Glenn Ford tells the townspeople in the *Sheep Man* that "nobody is going to tell me what to do. . . . I guess I'm just stubborn." Although on occasion these paeans to individualism could be interpreted as a political protest against the conformity of McCarthyism, more often than not the "masculine mystique" was equated with patriotism and the credo of standing tough in the face of influences that would corrupt and soften a society's moral fiber.

It was the literature of the period that developed most fully the theme of the individual against the system—how to find freedom in a world where every move fits into someone else's plan, and the individual, even under the illusion of acting independently, ultimately exerts no control over his own destiny. Nowhere was the issue more profoundly illuminated than in Ralph Ellison's *Invisible Man.* There, the hero was surrounded by power—from the black college president who insists that his students dissemble and shuffle in front of white benefactors, to the Communist Party he joins in the search for a way out, to the hospital that tries to cure his "abnormality" by a frontal lobotomy, to the underground room where he ends up living, with the lighting provided by 1,369 light bulbs using free current from the Monopolated Light and Power Company. As Dr. Bledsoe, the black college president, tells him, "This is a power set up son, and I'm at the controls." Everywhere he goes, the hero meets some other institution trying to program his activities, force him into acting out prescribed roles, and making him a puppet of someone else's whims. From the white southerners who made black young people fight each other on an electrified rug for a few coins, to the communists who said that "life was all pattern and discipline," there seemed no way out. The only advice that made any sense was to "play the game without believing it," thereby at least retaining a separation between one's inner self and one's outer behavior.

The same sense of individual despair in the face of all-powerful organizations permeates *Augie March* and *Catch-22*. In *Augie March,* Saul Bellow has one of his characters say to Augie, "If you make a move you may lose, but if you sit still you will decay." No matter what one does, the result is to be part of a system over which no ultimate control can be exercised. *Catch-22* makes a parable of the same dilemma. To fly a mission in an absurd war and accept all the rules of the system means subjecting one's self to the constant risk of alienation; yet to seek escape is simply to become a victim of other circumstances that for all intents and purposes, also leave one entrapped. The only option available to both Augie March and *Catch-22*'s Yossarian is to run and dodge, to keep moving, to "barrel in over the target from all directions and every height, climbing and diving and twisting and turning, weaving . . . through the flack with every sort of extreme maneuver." Staying in motion provides neither refuge or salvation, but it offers the only meaning there is to be found.

In all of this, overtones of existentialist philosophy recur. Going back to Søren Kierkegaard, but contemporaneously embodied in the drama and fiction of Jean-Paul Sartre and Albert Camus, existentialism portrayed the human being as constantly in process. Reality, Sartre said, represented the constant tension between being *for itself* and being *in itself.* In the human condition, people were always projecting themselves from one moment in time to another, engaged in the endless quest for immortality and immutability, arriving at something permanent. Yet the very nature of consciousness—of being able to project oneself into the future—forever prevented the condition of being *in itself* from being achieved except at death. The result was that individuals were caught in a system beyond their control, puppets in a society whose institutions used and manipulated them, with no lasting redemption available. The most one could hope for was to be aware of the choices one made, to choose them with integrity, and in the process of choosing— that is, in living—retain the only remnant of integrity that could be salvaged, self-awareness of possibility. As Kierkegaard observed, "When a human existence is brought to the [point] that it lacks possibility, it is in despair. . . . Possibility is the only saving remedy."

Significantly, existentialism could lead either to a sense of powerlessness and helplessness, or to a posture of engaged commitment. Those who examined the world around them and saw how thoroughly their condition was defined by external organizations and caprice could well conclude that life had no meaning and that one should simply "go along to get along." Others, who perceived life as constant process and possibility, could recognize that it was conceivable to give meaning to life through personal decision and to shape—self-consciously—the moment of possibility.

Interestingly enough, Albert Camus offered both options in his novels. In *The Stranger* Merseault reacts to the moment as though everything is out of his control. The only basis for action is to follow one's instincts. Without will or decision, he commits murder, is put on trial, and convicted. At no point does he see a choice or believe that he has control over the world around him. Instead, Merseault resigns himself to "the benign indifference of the universe." By contrast, Dr. Rieux in *The Plague* confronts the murderous reality that surrounds him and makes a choice for life. In a metaphor for Nazism, the plague is a disease that engulfs a Mediterranean city. Everyone is either afflicted by, or in danger of falling victim to, the spreading epidemic. But instead of resigning himself to his fate, Dr. Rieux chooses to minister to the ill, to stand up against the disease, to fight for the restoration of health. In the end, his action may or may not make any difference in the ultimate fate of the universe. Yet he makes a choice and in making it finds meaning for himself. Indeed, the decision to struggle against tyranny is precisely what defines man as human rather than as animal. Self-awareness and self-consciousness require action, and in choosing action freely, one creates the meaning of one's life.

The 1940s and 1950s also witnessed the emergence of a new form of jazz that reflected the tension and anxieties under society's conformist surface: the new fast and edgy bebop expressed a musical rebellion against a mass-marketed music industry that favored commercialized easy-to-consume swing during the 1930s. But despite jazz's newly proclaimed independence from white-dominated mass culture and the marketplace, it remained deeply embedded in urban popular entertainment, and the black musicians in their quest for professionalization remained dependent on the white music industry, as well as on white and black audiences. These tensions also played a part in jazz's move away from its initial black base toward an all-encompassing ethnic universalism that eventually appealed to audiences worldwide and made the music an American classic. By the mid-1950s, during the beginning of the civil rights movement, the State Department used jazz's potentially useful political and racial implications by sending black jazz musicians such as Dizzy Gillespie, Louis Armstrong, Duke Ellington, and Randy Weston on international tours as cultural ambassadors of freedom and democracy, trying to woo Third World and Eastern bloc audiences away from communism. While Washington sponsored some artists to support its Cold War propaganda, others were silenced. More politically outspoken performers such as Josephine Baker and Paul Robeson both saw their passports revoked by the U.S. government, which also undermined the careers of Woody Guthrie and Charles Chaplin for similar reasons.

Although few of the novels, plays, or movies of the postwar era referred directly to the themes of existentialism, it nevertheless provided the intellectual milieu within which a generation sought to come to grips with its own condition. The themes of individualism against conformity, of free will against determinism, of rebellion against the organization—all derived from the broader philosophical underpinnings of existentialist philosophers and their followers. People as diverse as Humphrey Bogart, Jackson Pollock, James Dean, and Camus shared in common the image of trying to understand chaos, interpret the meaning of a world almost destroyed by war, and find a niche for individuals who wanted to create their own freedom in a world increasingly controlled by structures beyond human influence. If anything gave coherence to the cultural and social patterns of the postwar era, it was the way in which phenomena as diverse as the "organization man," the fight against McCarthyism, or the quest for meaning in suburbia were in some way related to the existentialist dilemma of finding a way to create meaning in the face of forces over which one had no control.

Politics of the Fifties

It was no accident, perhaps, that the man who presided politically over America during these years of anxiety was himself a model of serenity and security. Born in 1890 in Texas, reared in Abilene, Kansas, and trained at West Point, Dwight David Eisenhower was everyone's hero. Not given to the megalomania of Douglas MacArthur, or the dramatic tactical brilliance of George Patton, Eisenhower nevertheless was a man on whose shoulders had rested the responsibility for coordinating, mobilizing, and executing one of the greatest military ventures in history—the Allied invasion of Europe. Consummate in the art of interpersonal diplomacy and organizational management, he had brought together the disparate, divided, and often eccentric military leaders of the Allies in a brilliantly orchestrated and massively successful final effort to destroy Hitler. Although few perceived him as a military genius, virtually everyone respected his authority, his leadership, and the calm way in which he steered a steady course in the midst of conflicting pressures buffeting him from all sides. "Upon first encounter," one observer noted,

> the man instantly conveyed one quality—strength. . . . There was one feature of his face impossible to ignore or to forget—the blue eyes of a force and intensity singularly deep, almost disturbing, above all commanding. . . . Always they would speak of the moment and the mood: icy with anger, warm with satisfaction, sharp with concern, glazed with boredom. And always somehow—was it their eloquent explicitness of feeling?—they conveyed an image and a sense of strength.

In the aftermath of the war, Eisenhower was assiduously courted by politicians of every stripe. Obviously, the personality irrevocably identified with the victorious crusade in Europe would be an invaluable asset to any political cause. He was a man sufficiently committed to his soldiers that he reprimanded George Patton for slapping an infantry man, yet distant and commanding enough to make the lonely decision, in the face of weather reports predicting potential disaster on the shores of Normandy, to order the invasion to proceed. Everyone looked to him for leadership. In the dark days of the Democratic defeats in 1946 and 1947, liberal New Dealers beseeched him to come home and lead their party as its presidential nominee in 1948. But the General resisted. Military men should not become involved in politics, he declared; indeed, he had never even registered to vote.

Yet the lure of public office and the growing sense of crisis in the country caused Eisenhower to reconsider four years later, this time as a Republican. Here was a man who could unite the country and the party, and make possible—for the first time in twenty years—the defeat of the Democrats. Although the brilliant conservative, Robert Taft, was also a candidate for the Republican nomination, the Ohio senator seemed too narrow, too combative, too committed to isolationism for the East Coast, international wing of the party. Even though Republican delegates knew little of Eisenhower's social or economic philosophy, they understood the magic of the name, the attraction of the smile, the invincibility of the war hero at a time when the country was wracked by division over the Korean conflict.* Eisenhower appeared to be the perfect leader to restore stability to a troubled land. As one journalist observed, "The typical American in the ideal sense should be neither Republican nor Democrat. . . . A certain amount of vagueness is essential to the role. . . . Dwight Eisenhower as president may prove to be what the doctor ordered."

Sweeping the nomination on the second ballot, Eisenhower fulfilled the prophecy. Appeasing the right wing of the party, he selected Richard Nixon—the man who had "gotten" Alger Hiss—as his vice-president. Although the General was not entirely comfortable with the "purple, 'prosecuting-attorney' style" of the Republican platform, he pledged to carry forward its principles, albeit in a new style of "moderate" Republicanism. Despite his distress at right-wing attacks that labeled his close friend, General George Marshall, a subversive and a traitor, he refused publicly to denounce the Red-baiters and worked for their re-election. Triumphing over all subsidiary issues was a national sense of insecurity and lack of direction typified in the Republican slogan, "K1, C2"—Korea, Communism, and Corruption. The General would not only clean out the government, he would also bring peace. "If elected," he told a Detroit audience, "I shall go to Korea." Against such a promise, the Democratic candidate Adlai Stevenson could offer little but eloquent intellectualism and a defense of the Democratic administrations now being blamed for all the difficulties the country found itself in. On election day, Eisenhower was swept to office in a landslide.

The Eisenhower administration proved singularly successful in offering a respite from conflict and controversy, charting a path so close to the middle of the road that it was difficult for critics to gain an audience. Despite the notion that Eisenhower represented a dramatic departure from the Democratic administration of Truman, in fact Ike was fully within the "liberal consensus" established in 1948. For Ike, moderate Republicanism meant running the government in a businesslike fashion, giving power back

---

* Foreign policy issues will be considered in a subsequent chapter.

to private interests in the states where appropriate, but retaining the new overall responsibility of the federal government for issues of social welfare and security. As he described it, the government should be liberal when it comes to human beings, conservative when it comes to spending; and if— as Adlai Stevenson said—that meant recommending more schools "to accommodate the needs of our children, but not [providing] the money," the rhetoric nevertheless sounded right to millions of Americans tired of new departures. Even Democrats seemed to go along. As Joseph Rauh, the liberal ADA attorney, declared in 1956, "Congressional Democrats have become practically indistinguishable from the party they allegedly oppose." The Eisenhower legislative program pleased pro-business conservatives, while not being sufficiently reactionary to alienate moderates and liberals.

This conservatism surfaced most in presidential appointments and in his position on public power and natural resources. The Eisenhower cabinet, one wag said, consisted of nine businessmen and a plumber. (The "plumber" was Martin Durkin, a union official who lasted only a short while as Secretary of Labor.) Three cabinet officials had connections at General Motors, with former GM head Charles Wilson—Eisenhower's Secretary of Defense—uttering the quotable quote of the decade when he declared that "what's good for General Motors business is good for America." In his appointments to the Federal Trade Commission, the FCC, and the Federal Power Commission, Eisenhower ensured that interests sympathetic to large corporations would fight against antitrust policies and public power.

The president also pushed through Congress the Submerged Land Act, a bill which removed from federal control at least $40 billion worth of disputed offshore oil lands, returning them to the states where they could be more easily made available to oil companies. It was, the *New York Times* said, "one of the greatest and surely the most unjustified give-away program in all the history of the United States." Eisenhower also attempted to hand over Hell's Canyon in Idaho to private utilities, called the Tennessee Valley Authority an example of "creeping socialism," and in the Dixon-Yates deal, attempted to transfer authority over a power project in Memphis to a firm in which a government official had an interest. (The project was finally cancelled due to conflict of interest.) In all these areas, Eisenhower reflected the pro-business, anti-government-regulation views of the men who manned his cabinet and who provided companionship for him during his off-hour activities on the golf course and at the bridge table.

Yet for the most part, Eisenhower consolidated the social welfare programs of the New Deal, refusing to seek their dismantlement. Although his Defense Secretary announced his preference for "birddogs rather than kennel-fed dogs—you know, one who will get out and hunt for food rather than sit on his hands and yell," the Eisenhower administration acquiesced in the expansion of Social Security and unemployment compensation, and in an increase of the minimum wage. Eisenhower also established the Department of Health, Education and Welfare, appointing Oveta Culp Hobby, a rich Texan, as the second woman ever to hold a cabinet office. In addition, after the Russians shot Sputnik into outer space in 1957, Eisenhower supported enactment of the National Defense Education Act, a bill which eventually did more to pump federal dollars into the educational establishment than anything in previous history.

In the end, however, the most distinguishing quality of the Eisenhower administration was the personal style of the president himself. Projecting an image of the beneficent father, he presided over an administration notable for its refusal to engage controversial questions, its reluctance to initiate new departures in social policy, and its insistence on maintaining the politics of centrism and moderation. The secret to Eisenhower's presidential style was his socialization in the military. There, he had risen through the command structure, not by sticking his neck out or becoming involved in bitter internecine fights, but by playing it safe, waiting for all the evidence of his lieutenants to come in, and then issuing a command decision.

As president, he operated the same way, appointing a chief of staff (Sherman Adams), delegating authority to his cabinet, and having all questions thoroughly "staffed" out by his subordinates before they came to him for final decision. He insisted that the relative merits of each issue be summarized in a single page for his ultimate disposition. Many attacked him for failing to lead from above, or become embroiled in issues of controversy, or mobilize his allies against the opposition. But for him to have done so would have run counter to everything he had ever learned. As he told one critic,

> Now, look, I happen to *know* a little about leadership. I've had to work with a lot of nations, for that matter at odds with each other. And I tell you this: you do not *lead* by hitting people over the head. Any damn fool can do that, but it's usually called "assault"—not "leadership." . . . I'll tell you what leadership is. Its *persuasion*—and *conciliation*—and *patience*. Its long, slow, tough work. That's the only kind of leadership I know or believe in—or will practice.

Although some viewed Eisenhower as a bumbling, ineffectual, incompetent president, he was totally in control and knew what he was doing. Critics pointed to the ungrammatical syntax of his press conferences, or lapses in his knowledge about issues, to suggest that Ike was not really "all there." But as Murray Kempton and others have argued, Ike used these apparent gaffes to promote his own ends. He was, in fact, a highly literate man, having spent much of his time in the Army writing speeches, composing position papers, and even authoring two chapters of General Pershing's autobiography. Speech writers called him a superb editor and author. When he did seem to make mistakes, they were more often intentional than unanticipated. During one foreign policy crisis, for example, his press secretary advised him to say nothing about a particular issue. "Don't worry, Jim," Eisenhower replied. "If that question comes up, I'll just confuse them." As Eisenhower aide Arthur Larson has pointed out, it was other cabinet members—not Eisenhower—who uttered the politically damaging statements of his administration.

Yet, if Eisenhower is to be given credit for the political know-how and shrewdness of his administration, he must also bear the responsibility for having ignored or suppressed profound social problems that eventually would come home to imperil the country. The economy sputtered at a growth rate of only 2.5 percent during his administration, and despite advice to the contrary, Eisenhower refused to initiate tax cuts in the midst of two recessions. His failure on the issue of civil rights, to be discussed later, would help ensure a decade of conflict after he left office. Although in many respects he seemed the ideal president for his time, providing a symbol of serene benevolence after an era of upheaval, he failed—ultimately— to provide constructive leadership, choosing to hoard his political capital rather than spend it on behalf of critically needed moral and social departures. As with so much else during the 1950s, the appearance of comfort and complacency obscured contradictions and tensions that would inevitably surface and explode.

The Critique of Conformity

During the 1950s critics of American society were more and more upset by the cult of consensus that seemed to prevail. In politics, Democrats appeared confused and uncertain, not knowing where to attack, where to differ from Republican moderation, or who to turn to for leadership. More often than not, Stevenson seemed to resemble Eisenhower. "It is time for catching our breath," he told a Chicago audience in 1955. "Moderation is the spirit of the times." Instead of addressing the problems of corporate wealth and privilege, Democrats sounded like Republicans in stressing budgetary conservatism. An ADA analysis of key roll-call votes in Congress from 1953 to 1960 showed that liberals lost two-thirds of the time, in large part because the Democratic Party was split. As historian Richard Hofstadter said in 1956, "Liberals are beginning to find it both natural and expedient to explore the merits and employ the rhetoric of conservatism. They find themselves far more conscious of those things they would like to preserve than they are of those things they would like to change." Echoing the same theme, Walter Lippmann observed that "for the first time in history the engine of social progress has run out of the fuel of discontent." Disgruntled and concerned, some worried that the blandness and tameness of the Eisenhower mystique were extending through the entire culture. Being an "all-around person" became the norm. "What is the new loyalty?" Henry Steel Commager asked. "It is, above all, conformity. It is the uncritical and unquestioning acceptance of America as it is."

For some, the politics of consensus seemed to reflect the nation's affluence. Throughout America, people appeared to believe that economic inequality had been eliminated. As the economist Arthur Burns said in 1951, "The transformation and the distribution of our national income . . . may already be counted as one of the great social revolutions in history." With homeownership spreading, consumerism becoming the dominant lifestyle of the country, and TV advertising suggesting that everyone was taking part in the "good life," there seemed no reason for concern. "The fundamental political problems of the industrial revolution have been solved," Seymour Martin Lipset declared, "[through the] triumph of the democratic social revolution in the west."

For others, consensus simply reflected the absence of an enemy to attack. Did not the Levittowns and the Park Forests of the world suggest a new unity and homogeneity in the society? According to historian Arthur Schlesinger, Jr., there was a danger that America would become "one great and genuinely benevolent company town—the bland leading the bland." Even intellectuals appeared part of the problem. "One can have causes and passions only when one knows against whom to fight,"Daniel Bell observed. Yet the leading thinkers of the 1950s had already gone through their own revolt during their flirtation with communism a generation earlier. Now they were part of their own "counter revolt." More content with the status quo than committed to rebellion, ex-radicals of the thirties were now singing the praises of big business and capitalism.

Yet in this area, as in so many others during the 1950s, the appearance of consensus obscured mounting conflict and controversy. The very fact that poet Robert Lowell could denounce the "savage servility" of a culture where "giant finned cars nosed forward like fish" bespoke a vitality that would not—and could not—be suppressed by disciples of conformity. Some, like the critic Dwight Macdonald, might conclude that "a tepid ooze of midcult [was] spreading everywhere," but it would be difficult to place Jack Kerouac, Ken Kesey, or Joseph Heller in such a category. Beatniks prided themselves on nonconformity, rebellion, and rejection of the superficiality and hypocrisy of the consumer culture. *On the Road*, Kerouac's novel that became a Bible of the beats, celebrated individualism and the lonely quest for identity, displaying contempt for security and stability. In its manners and dress—beards, sneakers, "peasant" clothes—the new bohemianism offered a counterpoint to suburban conventionality, while its fondness for marijuana and Eastern religion suggested an openness to new modes of experience totally different from those parroted in the dominant culture as the only avenues to fulfillment.

Even within the popular culture itself there existed substantial evidence that "safety" and conformity exercised only limited appeal. While many applauded the movies of Doris Day and Rock Hudson that showcased cuteness and conventionality, the major stars of the decade were James Dean and Marlon Brando, individualists through and through. Dean's *Rebel Without a Cause* highlighted the defiant alienation of a generation that found middle-class prosperity and upward mobility both sterile and destructive. Brando, in *The Wild One*, communicated the same message. Here was a cry for the individual to reject the self-deception of consumer culture and find another way. The response of the young to rock and roll confirmed this quest for a different lifestyle. Even though lyrics like "sha-na-na-na, sha-na-na-na-na" might be dismissed as meaningless, the sensual and visceral image projected by Chuck Berry, Elvis Presley, and the Big Bopper reflected a hunger for more immediate and more vital experiences than those defined as "proper" by the "gray flannel suit" set.

Similar contradictions existed on the college campus. Although the mass media dubbed students in the 1950s as the "silent generation," committed exclusively to status seeking and what one university president called "a growing cult of yesmanship," many of these young people were raising serious questions about their culture. The Student Peace Union was born during the 1950s, reflecting a gnawing anxiety and concern among a minority of the younger generation about the horrors of nuclear war and the dangers of an uncontrolled arms race. Although few if any students of the 1950s took to the streets in protest, they were reading books like David Riesman's *The Lonely Crowd*, Erich Fromm's *Man For Himself*, and William Whyte's *The Organization Man*, and asking whether they wished to become "market personalities," doffing old personalities and putting on new ones every other year to retain an image that happened to be "in" at any given point. Although most may have been, as IBM's Tom Watson said, "more concerned with security than integrity . . . with conforming than performing, with imitating than creating," the same could be said for any generation. Moreover, against this tide, a significant minority were asking hard questions about whether they wished to be part of the bourgeois culture that surrounded them.

More and more critics, meanwhile, pointed out flaws inherent in the economic structure. Although poverty had declined significantly (in 1947, 34 percent of all families earned less than $3,000; in 1960, 22.1 percent), between one-fifth and one-fourth of the nation could not survive on the income they earned. Moreover, there had been no redistribution of income after World War II, despite optimistic proclamations to the contrary. The share of the nation's wealth held by the richest 0.5 percent of the population actually rose from 19.3 percent in 1949 to 25 percent in 1956. By the end of the 1950s the richest 1 percent owned one-third of the nation's wealth; the bottom 20 percent less than half of 1 percent. Individuals who earned more than $10,000 a year paid a lower proportion of their income in taxes than those who earned less than $2,000 per year.

Indeed, a close examination of the economy suggested as much reason for concern as for congratulation. Among the growing segment of Americans over 65, 60 percent had incomes of less than $1,000 a year in 1958. The average Social Security payment was just over $70 a month, with the majority of elderly citizens having no medical insurance. A significant minority of blue-collar workers also fared poorly, with 30 percent of those employed in industry in 1958 receiving under $3,000 a year. If a person had less than eight years of schooling, was over 65, nonwhite, or living in a female-headed household, the chances were better than even that poverty would prevail. Just as important, those who had risen to the "middle class" were far from secure. In most cases upward mobility had been financed by the government, through the GI Bill, VA loans, and FHA mortgages. Many families were barely holding on, at the cost of an astronomical increase of indebtedness. From 1952 to 1956 disposable income increased by 21 percent, but during the same period, consumer borrowing climbed 55 percent. By 1959, one survey showed, 45 percent of the nation's families had less than $200 in liquid assets. Such facts caused one observer to wonder whether the bill collector was becoming "the central figure of the good society." As time went on, critics of the economy joined other dissenters in wondering how justified was the aura of optimism and security popularized by the mass media.

Conclusion

In all of this, the 1950s seemed as much a time of complexity and contradiction as of blissful complacency. Although the era was one of unprecedented economic growth, poverty remained a significant problem and the rich increased their share of the nation's wealth. The number of Americans who called themselves middle class increased dramatically, yet much of the expansion was based on federal programs supporting housing construction, highway building, and higher education. Only through rapidly growing indebtedness and a second income were many families able to join the migration to suburbia. Surprisingly, although no area of American life seemed to exhibit more conformity than male-female relationships, there were few areas that, in fact, witnessed so much change, with millions of women departing, in their behavior at least, from the notion that, once married, a wife would spend all her time tending the household and raising children. Indeed, it is the theme of paradox that best describes the postwar era—diversity in the face of uniformity, the creation of close-knit communities despite massive mobility, changes in sex roles occurring in the face of the "feminine mystique," the emergence of cultural rebels in the midst of chilling conformity.

In the end, the 1950s represent more a time of transition than of stolidity. During the immediate aftermath of World War II, the possibilities for massive social change in the condition of workers, blacks, and women had been snuffed out. Instead, the appeal of the consumer culture, suburbanization, and a respite from political conflict became dominant, deflecting attention toward achievement of the material goods necessary for the "good life." New living patterns were forged as those seeking affluence joined large corporate organizations, moved to the developing bedroom communities that surrounded large urban areas, and attempted to put together a life that would offer meaning and fulfillment. But through all of this, tensions inherent in the social structure remained just below the surface. It required only the outbreak of protest from one aggrieved group to galvanize the energies of those critical of the dominant culture and to focus attention on the unfinished business of the society. No group had greater reason to initiate that protest than American blacks. And no group could highlight more dramatically or effectively the problems of inequality that stood at the heart of the continuing failure to make the American dream a reality for all citizens.

6

The Civil Rights Movement

"The Gods Bring Threads
to Webs Begun"

We've been buked and we've been scorned,
We've been talked about, as sure as you're born.
But we'll never turn back, no,
We'll never turn back,
Until we've all been freed and
We have equality.

The heros and heroines were legion. They came from ramshackle tenant farms in the red clay country of Georgia, from the black colleges of Atlanta and Augusta, from the churches, where each Sunday black people gathered to affirm their unity, revive sagging spirits, and find anew the assurance that God had a purpose for their lives. In the years when the law said that blacks could not vote or secure a worthwhile education, they worked within their own community to build schools, better playgrounds, and new churches. Later they attempted to push back the boundaries of control and challenge the system of segregation. From their numbers came untold stories of courage—of the simple daring required to demand a new school bus or achieve the right to vote in a place where white people took it for granted that they could shoot any Negro without risking punishment. These were the people who created the most significant social movement in all of American history.

Ella Baker was there for it all. Born in Norfolk just after the turn of the century, she grew up hearing stories of slave revolts, told by her grandmother who had been beaten for disobeying her master. Reared in the black belt area of Warren County, North Carolina, on a farm owned by her family since the 1870s, she learned from her mother the importance of assertiveness, strength, and "speaking clearly." After graduating from Shaw University, a black school started during Reconstruction, she moved to New York City where she worked for the Works Progress Administration (WPA) and helped to start consumer cooperatives. Then, in 1940, she accepted a position as Field Secretary for the NAACP. The South was her territory. Traveling from town to town, she recruited blacks to join the NAACP—an act which at the time represented bold defiance of the racial status quo and entailed the risk of immediate reprisals, economic or otherwise. On one of her organizing trips, she so impressed the young people of Greensboro, North Carolina, that they started an NAACP youth chapter. More than a decade later, that youth chapter would help provide the inspiration for four young people to decide to sit down at a Woolworth's lunch counter and ask to be served. By the end of the 1950s, Ella Baker had become the first Executive Secretary of Martin Luther King, Jr.'s Southern Christian Leadership Conference. And in 1960, she initiated the conference that started the Student Non-violent Co-ordinating Committee (SNCC). She, and the people she touched, would shape history in the 1950s and 1960s.

In Clarendon County, South Carolina, J. A. DeLaine pastored an A.M.E. Church and taught school. ("If you set out to find a place in America . . . where life among black folk had changed least since the end of slavery," Richard Kluger wrote in 1974, "Clarendon County is where you might have come.") With a decent job and an honored position in the community, DeLaine might have been expected to act with caution. But a fire was burning within him. As a youngster he had been sentenced to twenty-five lashes for pushing a white boy who had shoved his sister off the sidewalk. In the church he ministered to, DeLaine drew constant parallels between the liberation promised in scripture and the reality of contemporary life. The message of deliverance to God's chosen people took on immediate relevance in 1947 when DeLaine heard an NAACP lecturer at Allen University, a black college, ask for support. Responding, the minister decided to lead the struggle to equalize education in Clarendon County. It was, after all, an area that in 1949 spent $179 per white child in public schools and $43 per black child. Shortly thereafter, DeLaine met Thurgood Marshall, general counsel of the NAACP and a graduate of Howard University Law School. DeLaine and Marshall, too, would be heard from again.

A thousand miles away in Mississippi, Amzie Moore was ready to move as well. After returning from the war ("Here I'm being shipped overseas, and I've been segregated from this man whom I might have to save or he save my life. I didn't fail to tell it"), Moore became president of the local NAACP. The Delta region of Mississippi was not a safe place for blacks to take such action. Blacks who protested in the least bit could easily end up dead. Nearby in 1955, fourteen-year-old Emmett Till was found dead in the Tallahatchie River, lynched because he allegedly had leered at a white woman. It was Amzie Moore whom Bob Moses came to see in 1960 to talk about voter registration. Moses, a New Yorker who taught mathematics, decided to come South after the first sit-ins to do his part to win freedom for his people. Now, he and Moore began to plot how to mobilize blacks to register to vote in a state where even the hint of such action could bring devastating reprisals.

Throughout the South people like Moore and Baker and DeLaine were building a movement during the 1940s and 1950s. They tried voter registration, were beaten back, and tried again. When the federal government denied support, they sought further legislation. When politicians offered no help, they went to the courts. When the courts failed them, they went back to their communities and started all over again, this time taking their fate in their own hands. It was a story that would transform a nation and provide inspiration to the world.

The Court Fight

Although the Truman administration's endorsement of civil rights for black Americans provided a welcome change from the Roosevelt administration's silence, black leaders were increasingly frustrated by the failure of politicians to deliver on their words. "We deliberately and consciously avoided asking for a conference," Walter White wrote, "to hear Mr. Truman tell us that I am still for civil rights. . . . The time has come for him to do something . . . instead of telling us how he feels personally." Blacks had scored major victories in the legal war against disfranchisement, particularly in *Smith* v. *Alright* (1944). In that case, the Supreme Court had invalidated the "white primary"—a device used in Southern states to exclude black voters from the only election that really counted in the one-party South. Yet neither Roosevelt nor Truman had followed up on these victories through encouraging, or protecting, black voter registration. Shrewd Southern politicians simply devised new means of perpetuating black powerlessness, confident that Washington would do nothing to interfere. Until the political log jam was broken, there seemed little possibility of altering a situation where fewer than 5 percent of prospective black voters were allowed to register.

Instead, attention shifted more and more to a legal challenge of segregation. Although much of the civil rights energy in the 1940s grew out of the economic and political radicalism of the CIO, the anticommunist attack on the "left" wing of labor essentially ruled "out of order" that kind of insurgency, leaving the only safe way of making progress the process of litigation. From its founding in 1909, the NAACP had recognized the importance of waging legal war against the consequences of segregation and racism, initially through the demand that separate facilities in fact be made equal, then through challenging frontally the constitutionality of Jim Crow. The battle was long and tedious, the stakes high, the courage and patience required enormous.

With great skill, black attorneys operated initially within the framework of segregation, focusing on graduate school education—the most vulnerable area of the separate but equal doctrine. It was hard to claim that a state provided equal opportunities for legal education to its black residents if Negroes were segregated in a one-room "law school" without adequate library sources, or if they were sent out of state to another institution. Brilliantly, Charles Houston, the Harvard-educated NAACP lawyer who would train a generation of civil rights attorneys at Howard University Law School, argued before the Supreme Court that Missouri could not train someone to practice law *in* Missouri by sending them elsewhere. In *Missouri ex. rel. Gaines* (1939) the court agreed, mandating the creation of a fully equal law school for blacks in Missouri. Crucial to the NAACP victory was the principle involved. If the precedent were to hold, should not the same doctrine of *full euality* apply to high school facilities as well? Furthermore, might not new definitions of equality eventually require the eradication of so many Jim Crow institutions that segregation itself would be threatened?

The student of Charles Houston who would carry these questions to the Supreme Court was Thurgood Marshall, a man who combined the skills of a Baptist preacher, a community organizer, a legal strategist, and a political wizard. During the 1940s Marshall traveled throughout the South, organizing teachers to fight for equal pay, mobilizing parents to insist on equal bus transportation, and enlisting lawyers to risk their practices by standing up for equality. He lived with the people, rarely spending more than a dollar for a meal, never more than two dollars for a room. Wherever he went he built alliances, showing the people he worked with that here was someone they could "travel the river" with. "Everybody loved Thurgood," one NAACP staff officer said, "[he] had the common touch." While previous NAACP leaders had spoken *down* to the people, another black observed, "Thurgood Marshall was *of* the people. He knew how to get through to them. Out in Texas or Oklahoma or down the street here in Washington at the Baptist Church, he would make these rousing speeches that would have them all jumping out of their seats."

Marshall's own courage in the face of constant danger became legendary, inspiring others to follow his example. In Tennessee, in the aftermath of the Columbia riot, his car was stopped three times by police harassing him, trying to scare him away. But Marshall never wavered. As Herbert Hill of the NAACP observed, "he was a very courageous figure. He would travel to the court houses of the South, and folks would come from miles, some of them on muleback or horseback, to see 'the nigger lawyer' who stood up in white men's courtrooms." More to the point, when he got to those courtrooms he often won, demonstrating to local residents that a black man could stand up in the face of white intimidation and prevail.

It was not surprising, then, that someone like J. A. DeLaine was willing to take a chance on Marshall. The black minister from Clarendon County, South Carolina, saw in the NAACP's chief counsel an ally worth suffering for. The cost was high. Before it was over, Richard Kluger has written,

> They fired him from the school at which he had taught devotedly for ten years. And they fired his wife and two of his sisters and a niece. And they threatened him with bodily harm. And they sued him on trumped up charges and convicted him in a kangaroo court and left him with a judgment that denied him credit from any bank. And they burned his house to the ground while the fire

department stood around watching the flames consume the night. And they stoned the church at which he pastored. And fired shotguns at him out of the dark . . . all of this . . . because he was black and brave. And because others followed when he had decided the time had come to lead.

DeLaine and Marshall shared a cause; they put their lives on the line for it; and as a result, Clarendon County became one of the five cases that would eventually be called *Brown* v. *Board of Education*.

The legal struggle did not go easily. In 1950 Marshall pushed the court further than it had ever gone before on the issue of "separate but equal," arguing in *Sweatt* v. *Painter* and *McLaurin* v. *Board of Regents* that equality could not be measured by dollars or physical plant alone. The reputation of the faculty, the companionship of one's peers, the stimulation of interchange with the best minds, the quality of the library—all had to be considered as well. In light of the *Gaines* decision, Oklahoma had decided to accept George McLaurin as a student at the state law school, but "on a segregated basis." McLaurin was required to eat in a separate alcove in the cafeteria, sit in a roped off area of the class, and work at a dingy segregated desk in the library, removed from the amenities provided all the other students. Such regulations, Marshall told the court, inevitably created "a badge of inferiority which affects [McLaurin's] relationship, both to his fellow students and to his professors." The case was powerful, Marshall's arguments overwhelming, and the Supreme Court agreed. When it did so, it took a giant step toward including psychological, social, and spiritual considerations in its definition of equality.

But that was not the same thing as overturning segregation, or asking the court to reverse its own precedent in the historic 1896 case known everywhere as *Plessy* v. *Ferguson*. All the way through the *Sweatt* and *McLaurin* cases, the NAACP had brilliantly used the framework of "separate but equal" to erode the substance of the segregationist position. Now, it faced the choice of going on the offensive and persuading the court to arrive at a radically new legal position that would overturn fifty years of law. The decision was not easy. In endless debates, NAACP attorneys agonized over the alternatives. If they continued to operate on the enemy's turf, they could be relatively confident of continuing to win victories that would at least force the upgrading of black educational facilities. But if they challenged segregation itself and miscalculated the odds of winning, they took the chance of institutionalizing the legal underpinnings of American racism for another generation.

That their doubts had a basis in fact was clear in a memo written at the time by Associate Supreme Court Justice Robert Jackson:

> Since the close of the civil war the United States has been 'hesitating between two worlds—one dead, the other powerless to be born.' War brought an old order to an end, but . . . proved unequal to founding a new one. Neither north nor south has been willing really to adopt its racial practices to its professions.

Troubled, Jackson wondered whether the Supreme Court was the proper instrument to eradicate "these fears, prides, and prejudices on which segregation rests." Was it really proper for the judiciary to reverse half a century of law and take upon itself the responsibility for charting a new course for America at a time when most political forces in the country seemed intent on preserving the status quo. With all the political and legal wisdom they could command, NAACP attorneys attempted to measure the relative weight of their own powerful legal logic against the conservative and ameliorative bias inherent in the judicial system. In the end, they decided that they had no alternative but to throw down the gauntlet and challenge segregation itself.

Both inside the courtroom and in the judicial chambers, the battle was dramatic. Marshall took the Clarendon case and the four others joined in *Brown,* recited the history of inequities in per capita expenditures on pupils, books, and buildings, and spoke powerfully of the way black institutions inevitably received the short end of the stick. Only this time he made the argument not to secure more and better black facilities, but to establish that separate facilities, by definition, denied Negro Americans their rights as citizens.

Central to his argument was the cumulative stigma conferred on blacks by the process of segregation. As Negro psychologist Kenneth Clark had shown, black children educated in segregated schools developed a negative self-image and responded more positively to white dolls than to black dolls. Such data, Marshall contended, showed that segregation inevitably created low self-esteem and a permanent sense of inferiority in black children. Marshall's adversary, a distinguished, white-maned patrician from South Carolina, adopted the posture of a lawyer's lawyer. Upholding legal precedent was the important issue, he contended. Sociological tests like those of Clark were irrelevant poppycock having no place in a court of law. Only legal tradition counted, and legal tradition stood on the side of retaining segregation. Both sides had calculated their audience shrewdly, sensing the turmoil and conflict on the bench. Indeed, had the judges taken a vote immediately, they would have been deeply divided—perhaps five to four or six to three, but certainly with no unanimity on the necessity of reversing segregation. Troubled, the judges asked for reargument on the crucial issues of the intent of the framers of the Fourteenth Amendment, its history, and how specifically segregation would be dismantled if that were the court's decision.

Then Earl Warren joined the court. Chosen in 1953 by Dwight Eisenhower to be the new Chief Justice after Fred Vinson died suddenly, Warren brought to his position the leadership, compassion, sensitivity, and simplicity required to forge unity out of divisiveness. As attorney general of California during World War II, Warren had been an active participant in the decision to relocate over 100,000 Japanese-Americans in internment centers. But he had come deeply to regret that mistake, and his subsequent public life exhibited substantial evidence of a desire to redress the grievances of those unfairly treated in American society. Just as important, War-

ren's political training made him acutely aware of the need to secure unanimity in such a critical decision. Combining moral vision and political sensitivity, the new Chief Justice set out to woo potential dissenters in the *Brown*
case such as Justices Stanley Reed and Robert Jackson. The court had had
the case now for three years, and it was time to act—but only after a spirit of
harmony could be carefully nourished. Taking the cultural highground,
Warren avoided tendentious nitpicking over legalistic issues and urged his
colleagues to accept a simple affirmation of basic principle as their basis for
decision. Compromising where he could, showing respect and concern for
his colleagues' doubts, Warren marshalled the court.

Nothing about May 17, 1954 seemed particularly different as court reporters gathered for the weekly pronouncement of decisions by the court.
There had been no advance notice of any significant rulings. Then, suddenly, one hour after proceeding with the decisions in other cases, the Chief
Justice announced that he would begin reading the court's opinion in *Brown*.
Scrambling, reporters dashed to the court. Forcefully, the Chief Justice read
his first major opinion. Education, he declared, represented a central experience in life. Those things that children learned in school remained with
them for the rest of their time on earth. The critical question, then, was:
"Does segregation of children in public schools solely on the basis of
race . . . deprive the children of the minority group of equal education opportunities?" Answering, the Chief Justice declared: "We believe that it does."

> To separate [those children] from others of similar age and qualifications
> solely because of their race generates a feeling of inferiority as to their status in
> the community that may affect their hearts and minds in a way unlikely ever to
> be undone. . . . We conclude that in the field of public education the doc-
> trine of "separate but equal" has no place. Separate educational facilities are in-
> herently unequal. . . . Any language in *Plessy* v. *Ferguson* contrary to these
> findings is rejected.

Fifteen years after the *Gaines* decision in Missouri, seven years after J. A.
DeLaine agreed to challenge the Clarendon County School Board, and
sixty years after Jim Crow was legally born, segregated schools were acknowledged to be an abomination. Unanimously, the Supreme Court had
ruled that the Fourteenth Amendment required equal admission of all students to public schools. The decision, the *Chicago Defender* proclaimed, was
"a second emancipation proclamation . . . more important to our democracy than the atom bomb or the hydrogen bomb." Within five years, Thurgood Marshall predicted, all segregated schools would be abolished. "We
have won," blacks exulted. It appeared that the Supreme Court had done
what politicians had refused to do.

The Response to Brown

Initially, response to the *Brown* decision offered reason for optimism. Black
newspapers hailed the court's action, confident that the structure of segre-

gation would now quickly be dismantled. Even the white South reacted more with resignation than with rebellion. Only James Byrnes of South Carolina, Herman Talmadge in Georgia, and Hugh White in Mississippi engaged in the rhetoric of outraged resistance. More representative were comments that regretted the *Brown* decision, but called for calm acceptance of its consequences. Thus, Governor Frances Cherry of Arkansas declared: "Arkansas will obey the law. It always has." And "Big" Jim Folsom of Alabama stated: "When the Supreme Court speaks, that's the law." "The end of the world has not come for the South or for the nation," the *Louisville Courier Journal* editorialized. "The Supreme Court's ruling is not itself a revolution. It is rather an acceptance of a process that has been going on for a long time." Cities like Louisville, Kentucky, Little Rock, Arkansas, and Greensboro, North Carolina, indicated that they were ready to begin the process of compliance.

Yet the *Brown* decision by itself existed in a vacuum. It required commitment, leadership, and tangible action if it were to become more than empty rhetoric. As one legal scholar said at the time:

> The law is a landing force [of change]. It makes the beachhead. But the breakthrough, if it is to be significant, is broadened by forces from behind which take advantage of the opening to go the rest of the way. Where these forces are present, significant alteration of social practices is the result. Where they do not exist, the law has been unable to hold its beachhead and the legal action becomes a kind of military monument on which is only recorded "we were here."

Despite initial positive signs, it quickly became clear that "the forces from behind" were unwilling to act. The Supreme Court itself, as one price for securing unanimity, delayed for a year its own decision on how to implement desegregation. When the second *Brown* ruling was handed down in May 1955, it called for remanding cases to the district courts. Implementation procedures were to begin "with all deliberate speed," but no deadline was set. In the South itself, meanwhile, those willing to act decisively in support of integration suddenly found themselves alone, without reinforcement from either economic or political leaders, or from the courts. In city after city, education leaders who were ready to begin desegregation, and who had even postponed building plans because the new ruling would require integrated schools, looked in vain for pressure from above to support their initiatives. With no tangible encouragement to proceed, they decided to withdraw from the battle, forsaking the beachhead that had been won to defenders of the old order.

No one deserved more censure for the failure to follow through than the president himself. In 1954 Dwight Eisenhower enjoyed more moral authority and political strength than any president since Franklin Roosevelt at the beginning of the New Deal. His position, in some ways, was analogous to that of Andrew Johnson at the end of the Civil War. At that time, the South had been defeated, overwhelmingly. White Southerners felt helpless, resigned, waiting for cues as to how to respond. Decisive, immediate leadership in such a situation held the promise of transforming the social and political landscape.

Yet Eisenhower, like Andrew Johnson ninety years before, rejected the opportunity to act. Had he acted decisively and declared:

> The Supreme Court has spoken, integration is now the law of the land. The court's decision will be enforced by me with all the energy at my command. No resistance will be tolerated,

it is likely that school districts across the South would have commenced to desegregate. Their action would not have been without resistance, but at least in such a situation, they could have pointed to the ladder of command to deflect the negative consequences of compliance. In effect, they could have said, we have no choice but to obey the highest authority in the country.

Instead, Eisenhower waffled. Repeatedly, when asked whether he endorsed the Supreme Court's decision, he replied that he would neither express "approbation nor disapproval" of the decision. "I don't believe you can change the hearts of men with laws or decisions," the president remarked. In fact, he disapproved of the *Brown* decision vigorously. Just before the court's ruling, the president told Chief Justice Earl Warren: "All [opponents of desegregation] are concerned about is to see that their sweet little girls are not required to sit in schools alongside some big overgrown Negroes." Subsequently, he claimed that the appointment of Warren had been the "biggest damn fool mistake" he had ever made. Asked by a reporter whether he had any advice for southerners, he replied "not in the slightest." And later, he confided to an aide that "the Supreme Court decisions set back progress in the south at least fifteen years. . . . The fellow who tries to tell me that you can do these things by force is just plain nuts." In an understatement, one of the president's advisors later observed, "President Eisenhower . . . was not emotionally or intellectually in favor of combating segregation."

Central to Eisenhower's position was his conviction that the federal government should be passive on controversial social issues, and that Washington had no right to intervene in the affairs of local governments. Although he implemented desegregation in federal installations and worked effectively to bring about the integration of schools and public accommodations in the federal government's own bailiwick of Washington, D.C., he did virtually nothing to support those seeking change in the Southern states, even refusing to take action to back the federal courts. After Governor Price Daniel called out the Texas Rangers to block court-ordered integration of a high school in Mansfield, Texas, Eisenhower refused to intervene. Surely, he explained, no one wanted to see a federal police force take over local police matters. When the University of Alabama expelled its first black pupil, Autherine Lucey, in direct violation of a federal court order, the president's only response was to say: "I would certainly hope that we could avoid any interference." From Eisenhower's perspective, those who pressed for compliance with the Supreme Court decision occupied the same status as those who resisted it, and the president publicly denounced "extremists on both sides."

The president kept silent even in the face of violence. When reporters and black leaders urged Eisenhower to speak out after a Negro was murdered for urging blacks to register to vote in Mississippi and dynamite explosions rocked Clinton, Tennessee, and Bessemer, Alabama, the president refused to respond. When he was later pressed to go personally to the South in defense of law and order, he replied—in a classic non sequitur—"as you know, I insist on going for a bit of recreation every once in a while . . . I don't know what another speech would do." Ever since the presidency of Theodore Roosevelt, the historian William, E. Leuchtenburg has pointed out, the White House had been known as a "bully pulpit." Yet "when Eisenhower was president, it was an empty pulpit. It is not too much to say that a great deal of the violence, as well as the fearfully slow rate of compliance after 1954, may be laid at Eisenhower's door."

Nothing testified more dramatically to the Eisenhower administration's attitude on civil rights than the experience of E. Frederick Morrow, the only Negro on the White House staff. A Republican of long-standing, Morrow had been invited by Sherman Adams to join the administration shortly after the campaign. Then, after resigning his job with CBS, Morrow was shunted aside. His phone calls went unanswered until, belatedly, he was offered a position at the Commerce Department. Finally, in 1955, he moved to the White House only to experience further frustration. On one occasion white staff members told a "nigger story" in his presence. When, on the advice of superiors, he promised A. Philip Randolph an appointment with the president, the scheduled meeting was cancelled. Although Morrow proved a useful symbol for political purposes (Eisenhower took him to a World Series game in 1956 and had him accompany Vice-President Nixon on a tour of Africa), when it came to matters of policy, his voice was ignored. Despite repeated urgings by Morrow and others, the president refused to issue a statement deploring the breakdown of law and order in Mississippi after the lynching of Emmett Till, and when Morrow carried his concern further to urge an interracial conference under administration sponsorship to discuss civil rights, he even incurred the wrath of his principal ally, Maxwell Rabb, the official White House advisor on minorities. Blacks, according to Rabb, had not demonstrated sufficient gratitude for all that had been done for them and, instead, were being too "aggressive" in their demands for justice, showing an "ugliness and surliness" that was alienating white allies. Because blacks were being so "intemperate," Rabb declared, he could no longer argue that black support would be an asset politically. Loyal to the end, Morrow nevertheless could not help feeling angry when Eisenhower urged blacks to be "patient" in demanding their civil rights. "I feel ridiculous . . . trying to defend the administration's record on civil rights," Morrow confided to his diary.

Even those events that might be construed as favorable to blacks suggested little positive about the administration's attitudes. When Attorney General Herbert Brownell presented a four-part civil rights bill to the cabinet for consideration in 1956, only two of his colleagues supported him. The president, partly concerned with securing black votes in the election, endorsed the creation of a permanent civil rights commission, but denied approval to a section of the bill that would authorize Justice Department intervention on behalf of desegregation. Although Brownell boldly (and inaccurately) presented the entire package as having administration backing, he was ultimately sabotaged. After Senator Richard Russell of Georgia described part three of the legislation as an effort "to bring to bear the whole might of the federal government . . . to force amalgamation of white and Negro children in the state-supported schools of the south . . . and to create another reconstruction at bayonet point," Eisenhower retreated, declaring that his only objective was to assist the right to vote. Indeed, the president said, "I was reading part of that bill this morning and there were certain phrases that I didn't completely understand." As if to settle the question, the president told the reporter that "no," he did not believe the attorney general should be empowered to bring school desegregation suits.

When an emasculated version of the Civil Rights Bill was finally passed in 1957, Republican Clifford Case of New Jersey called it "a pitiful remnant" of the original measure, and Senator Richard Russell described it as "the sweetest victory in my twenty-five years as a Senator." By 1959, the legislation had not added a single Southern black to the voting rolls. Nor did Eisenhower's Justice Department investigate any of the complaints about the prevention of blacks' voting in states such as Mississippi. Three years later, another act was passed to safeguard voting rights. Yet this too lacked any real substance. Senator Harry Byrd, leader of the "massive resistance" forces, boasted that the bill was "in the main . . . a victory for the south," and Democrat Joseph Clark, a civil rights supporter, called the legislation a "crushing defeat." "Surely," he added, "in this battle on the Senate floor the roles of Grant and Lee at Appomattox have been reversed."

White Southern Resistance

Just as Andrew Johnson had given cues to former confederates that they could reassert control over the South without interference from the White House, so President Eisenhower, through his reticence and ambiguity, encouraged segregationists to believe that they had free rein to resist the Supreme Court. Within a year, the resignation that had prevailed after the first *Brown* decision had gradually changed into optimism about the possibility of preserving the status quo and, finally, into outright and systematic resistance to desegregation. Those who might have supported compliance if the president had given them no other option now found themselves competing against the rabid right for control of the political spectrum, attempting to become more racist than even the worst segregationist just to stay in office. In states like Alabama the NAACP was outlawed; elsewhere, supporters of civil rights were pilloried as agents of a communist conspiracy to take over the South. "In this atmosphere," the historian C. Vann Woodward has observed, "words began to change their meanings so that a moderate became a man who dared to open his mouth, and an extremist someone who favored eventual compliance with the law."

Resistance mushroomed in direct correlation to the growing evidence that the federal government would do nothing to counteract it. After the Supreme Court indicated in the second *Brown* decision that immediate compliance would not be necessary, state governments shifted their attention from how to comply to how to circumvent. As Eisenhower offered tacit sanction to segregationists in Texas and at the University of Alabama, state legislatures began to pass resolutions calling for massive resistance, with Virginia, Alabama, Mississippi, and Georgia claiming the right, à la John Calhoun's nullification movement of 1828, to "interpose" themselves between the people and the federal government, declaring the Supreme Court's decision "null, void, and of no effect." Nearly every state passed a pupil assignment law that transferred authority over schools to local school boards to avoid statewide suits by the NAACP. Under such legislation, criteria such as "the general welfare" were substituted for race as a basis for assigning pupils to schools. In this way segregation could be maintained in practice without mentioning the word in law, and anyone challenging the results would be forced on an individual basis to fight layers of bureaucratic control before being able to secure a court hearing. Even then, the U.S. Fourth Circuit Court ruled in 1959, parents must prove beyond a doubt that race was the basis for exclusion. Within such a structure of judicial interpretation the total burden rested with the individual plaintiff, making a mockery of any notion of far-reaching desegregation. So widespread did the atmosphere of resistance become that, in the spring of 1956, 101 of 128 congressmen from the former confederate states signed the "Southern Manifesto" promising resistance to the federal government.

The crisis at Central High School in Little Rock, Arkansas, dramatized the political forces at work. Under court order to desegregate, Little Rock school officials were prepared to comply and, in an atmosphere of relative peace and stability, had carefully mobilized community support for the desegregation process. But Orval Faubus, the governor, decided to intervene. Caught in a tight re-election battle, he chose the strategy of "out-niggering" his opponents, using the black school children of Little Rock as his foil. After creating a crisis by announcing that it would not be possible to maintain order in the face of integration (a bald-faced lie), he instructed National Guard troops to block the entry of black children into Central High. Rallied by Faubus's words, angry whites now began to act out the scenario that Faubus had predicted. Eisenhower refused to intervene, instead agreeing to meet with Faubus in an effort to find a compromise. Faubus gave his word that he would create no further problems. Then, unashamedly breaking his promise, the governor withdrew National Guard troops from the high school and left the capital. When, on Monday morning September 23, 1957, black children attempted to attend their first day of school at Central High, a shrieking crowd surrounded them chanting "two, four, six, eight, we ain't going to integrate," and "niggers, keep away from our school. Go back to the jungle."

Stunned and embarrassed, Eisenhower denounced the "disgraceful occurrence," federalized the Arkansas National Guard, and dispatched a thousand paratroopers to Little Rock. To have done otherwise, he recognized, would have been to "acquiesce in anarchy and the disillusion of the union." Yet his action was too little and too late. The time for the use of moral authority to prevent resistance had passed. Indeed, when Eisenhower was finally moved to act, it was primarily because his own sense of the military code had been breached: a lieutenant (the governor) had been guilty of insubordination. The principle of integration was quite secondary.

Nor was it possible, in the long run, to call the Little Rock episode a victory for desegregation. Despite a Supreme Court order, Governor Faubus closed the schools in Little Rock for the entire next year. Virginia cities did the same to prevent integration in that state. Indeed, during the last three years of the Eisenhower administration the number of new school districts engaged even in token desegregation fell to 49—a stark contrast to the total of 712 that had desegregated during the first three years after Brown. As one Civil Rights Commission official observed, during the last years of the 1950s, the rights of black Americans had become a "White House orphan."

Tragically, the problem was not limited to "massive resistance" states like Virginia, Alabama, and Mississippi. In fact, the process of circumvention reached its highest form of sophistication in the more "moderate" or "progressive" states. North Carolina, for example, had long been viewed as "an inspiring exception to southern racism," largely because of its fine universities and intellectual leaders like Frank Porter Graham. Yet, in reality, the Tarheel state was simply more clever at accomplishing the same goals. When the *Brown* decision was first handed down, as many as seven cities across the state, including Charlotte, Winston-Salem, Raleigh, and Greensboro, indicated a readiness to comply, and local school boards met to reconsider such issues as school bus patterns and teacher assignments in light of the *Brown* decision. For the first few months, a similar mood prevailed among state educational leaders.

But in North Carolina, as in the nation at large, "the forces from behind" failed to advance the beachhead established by law. Democratic Governor Luther Hodges was to North Carolina what Dwight Eisenhower was to the country—except that, instead of simply sanctioning the forces of resistance by inaction, Hodges marshalled them himself, all under the guise of "the politics of moderation." As the gubernatorial election of 1956 approached, Hodges proposed a plan that would authorize expenditures of state money to any white student threatened with integration who wished to attend a private school. These same tax funds would also permit any school district to close its schools if integration occurred against the wishes of the community. As Hodges presented the issue, "voluntary segregation" offered the only possibility of avoiding what he chose to describe as the equally untenable extremes of integration, on the one hand, or the shutting down of the public school system entirely, on the other.

Like Faubus in Arkansas, Hodges in large part created the issue of resistance for his own political purposes. His own staff had reported that whites in North Carolina were remarkably indifferent to the question of desegregation. Nevertheless, the governor chose to inflame racial hostility rather than stand behind the forces of compliance. Unabashedly invoking the specter of miscegenation, Hodges accused the NAACP of seeking to destroy "our interracial friendship," and of attempting the destruction of their own race by "burying it in the development of the white race." It was blacks who were responsible for the crisis, Hodges insisted. "Only the person who feels he is inferior must resort to demonstrations to prove that he is not. The person convinced of his own equality, . . . of his own race respect, needs no demonstrations to bolster his convictions." By Hodges' definition, there were two extreme groups in the state—the KKK and the NAACP. Only those who followed him could achieve the "middle way," the path of moderation.

Hodges took his plan to forestall desegregation to the voters the same summer he was waging his own re-election campaign. To white liberals, he offered the disingenuous assurance that his proposals—at least overtly—did not defy the Supreme Court, but only provided "safety valves" for those who wished to avoid desegregation. To conservative whites, he provided the guarantee that there would be virtually no integration in North Carolina under his leadership. To blacks, he offered nothing, ignoring the fact that they comprised 25 percent of the state's population. Indeed, he appeared incredulous that Negroes would dare to challenge him, urging his staff to seek blacks who had signed integration petitions in order to "ascertain their reasons" and find out "if they are in earnest." Hodges' allies in North Carolina—remarkably similar in mental outlook to Eisenhower's staff members in Washington—were upset by the "intemperance, . . . rudeness and complete self-confidence" of those blacks who insisted on their citizenship rights.

Through these tactics of "moderate" white supremacy, the initial possibilities of compliance with the *Brown* decision in North Carolina were dashed. Hodges successfully portrayed his plan as the only "enlightened" solution to the school crisis—a blend, the *Charlotte Observer* noted, of "conscience and common sense, . . . an effort to preserve the public schools and at the same time North Carolina's identity with constitutional government." As a consequence, the real issues were totally distorted. Black citizens were viewed as the cause of the crisis, white citizens as its victims. In an ultimate irony, the only people who had the law on their side were defined as outside extremists threatening the peace of the state. As one observer acidly commented: "paraphrasing Mr. Churchill, never before in human history has one man asked so many to give up so much."

It need not have been that way. Reed Sarrat, the editor of the *Winston-Salem Journal Sentinel*, concluded in 1956 that "a large number of intelligent, influential North Carolinians believed that the best way . . . is to comply." Public opinion polls showed that the vast majority of whites in the state were in the middle, between active resistance and active support for integration. They could have been led either way. "It is all so sad," one liberal wrote, "to see our beginning leadership among the southern states crushed back. Such selfishness and blind political trading: Luther Hodges had a chance for greatness." But instead, the governor had chosen the path of resistance, in the process postponing meaningful desegregation in North Carolina for more than a decade—far longer than in some states where massive resistance was practiced. By 1961, North Carolina reported a desegregation rate of 0.026 percent—less than that in Virginia, Tennessee, Arkansas, or Texas. The genius of Hodges' plan, the *Shelby Star* declared, was that it would "maintain separate school systems," but with "a tone of moderation." Recognizing what was really going on, one Little Rock school official wrote: "You North Carolinians have devised one of the cleverest techniques for perpetuating segregation that we have seen."

No people, however brave and resilient, could accept such subterfuge without frustration. All the victories that had been secured seemed hollow. National policy was ignored or contradicted by politicians given the responsibility for enforcing it. Court decisions were vitiated by legalistic manipulation. "Nothing could be worse," Justice Felix Frankfurter had said before the *Brown* decision, "than for this court to make an abstract declaration that segregation is bad and then have it evaded by tricks." Yet that is precisely what happened. Through callous disregard and distortion, black civil rights had been defined out of existence, with basic guarantees of citizenship made playthings for shrewd politicians. As much as any other group of American citizens, blacks believed in the political process, the sanctity of the judiciary, and the rule of law. Yet all of these had been turned against them. If they were victimized by the very processes they believed in, then it would be necessary for blacks to take action on their own terms and to express their convictions in ways that could no longer be ignored or misunderstood. Whatever else the history of the 1950s had shown, it was now obvious that, if America was to change its ways, blacks would have to start the process.

The Montgomery Movement

The decision to act sprung from the impatience and anger of average black Americans no longer willing to accept second-class citizenship. On a cold fall afternoon in Montgomery in 1955, Rosa Parks, a black seamstress, boarded a city bus after a long day at the sewing machine. She sat in the first row of the "colored" section of the bus, but Montgomery's Jim Crow rules provided that whenever enough white people boarded a public carrier to take up all the "white" seats, blacks must move back and give up their positions until the whites had places. As more and more whites boarded the bus that day, Mrs. Parks stared out the window. The atmosphere around her filled with tension. One black got up to give his seat, but she remained. Finally, the bus driver demanded that she move as well. No, she said, I will stay. "I felt it was just something I had to do," she later recalled. At that moment, Eldridge Cleaver subsequently noted, "somewhere in the universe a gear in the machinery shifted." Word of her arrest quickly spread through the community, and within hours, black leaders had decided that the time was right to strike a blow for freedom: they would boycott the city bus system the next Monday in protest.

The city's black leaders were ready. E. D. Nixon, president of the Alabama NAACP and head of the local chapter of the Brotherhood of Sleeping Car Porters, had long been looking for a cause around which to build a mass protest. Jo Ann Robinson, leader of the local Women's Political Council (parallel in purpose to the segregated League of Women Voters), was ready too. She had worked hard for the desegregation of drinking fountains and the hiring of black police in the city. Indeed, the infrastructure of the Montgomery movement went back to the 1940s, when Nixon and women's groups organized to demand that white officials respond to the brutal rape of a black woman by city police. Now, with Parks' arrest, Nixon and Robinson activated their telephone network and spread the word that the time had come to act—to move the struggle to a new level.

The idea of a bus boycott was not unheard of. Earlier, when other arrests had happened under similar circumstances, there had been talk of similar action. But the occasion had not been right. In one instance, the arrest victim had been an unwed mother; in another, a person from a family one of whose members was in jail. Everyone knew that in order to carry out a mass action successfully, all the circumstances had to be right. Now, they were. Rosa Parks was one of the most revered women in Montgomery. A churchgoer, secretary of the NAACP, beloved by everyone, she was a person who would unify the community. As E. D. Nixon later recalled:

> She was decent. And she was committed. First off, nobody could point no dirt at her. You had to respect her as a lady. And second, if she said she would be a certain place at a certain time, that's when she got there. . . . So when she stood up to talk, people'd shut up and listen. And when she did something people just figured it was the right thing to do.

Because she was who she was and did what she did, Rosa Parks became the rallying point for mobilizing the collective anger of Montgomery's black citizens.

That night and all the next day, E. D. Nixon set in motion the groundwork for protest. More than fifty community representatives gathered at the Dexter Avenue Baptist Church to plan the bus boycott, to rally church congregations on Sunday, and to create a transportation network among Negro taxi companies to take the place of the buses. By Monday, every black in Montgomery had received a message not to ride the city buses that day. Fearful that the boycott might not succeed, yet committed as never before to action, Montgomery's black leaders rose early to watch the buses go by. As dawn turned into morning and midday, the verdict was clear: virtually no black person in Montgomery rode the bus that day.

The bus boycott in Montgomery would last for 381 days. It provided the organizing basis for a mass movement that fought back against every legal, economic, and psychological effort to destroy it. When city leaders threatened to arrest taxi drivers for violating their chauffeur licenses, blacks created car pools instead. When whites attempted to sow seeds of dissension among leaders of the movement, the black community came together to affirm its solidarity in support of mass protest. And when white violence threatened to provoke black counterviolence and provide a basis for police action, the Negro community responded with discipline and devotion to the philosophy of nonviolence. No incident encapsulated the story of Montgomery more than the occasion when a white reporter, driving a car, stopped beside an elderly black woman walking to work. Asked if she wished a ride, the woman replied: "No, my feets is tired, but my soul is rested."

Like the first movement in a symphony, the Montgomery movement highlighted themes that would dominate the civil rights struggle for years to come. First, it demonstrated dramatically and conclusively that black Americans would sacrifice their comfort and risk their jobs to stand up for their dignity. For years, whites interested in appeasing their own conscience had insisted that "*our* black people are happy," and that any trouble of a racial nature must reflect the work of outside agitators. For 381 days, more than 90 percent of the black citizens of Montgomery demonstrated with their feet, everyday, their vivid rejection of that white illusion.

Second, the boycott exhibited how a movement, once begun, generates its own momentum, expanding the horizons of its participants and creating the basis for an ever-widening belief in, and ability to achieve, social change. Ironically, the boycott did not begin with the demand that the buses be integrated. Instead, community leaders advanced only a modest three-point agenda: (1) greater courtesy toward black passengers; (2) the hiring of Negro drivers for routes that were predominantly black; and (3) the creation of a flexible line, separating the black and white sections of the bus so that, where blacks comprised the majority of passengers, they would not be forced to move when additional whites boarded the bus. Yet Montgomery's white leadership consistently refused to respond to those demands, and as the daily sacrifice of energy generated a mass sense of self-confidence and determination, the movement decided that nothing short of complete integration would satisfy its demands. Over and over again, through the next fifteen years, the same experience of working together for a common cause would create a similar heightening of consciousness and the refusal to accept anything less than full equality.

Third, the boycott produced an articulate and persuasive leader. Martin Luther King, Jr., had been in Montgomery only six months when the boycott started. Still in his mid-twenties, he was neither a radical nor an activist. Reared in the relative prosperity of Atlanta's black middle class, King had been sheltered from many of the worst aspects of white racism. Bright, reflective, and academically successful, he seemed destined to achieve the success and comfort available to some black leaders—particularly ministers—within a Jim Crow society. There was little, on the surface at least, to suggest that he would become a protest leader. Indeed, he had turned down an invitation to become head of the local NAACP because he wished to build his congregation, to finish his doctorate, and to work his way slowly into the community.

But now a challenge came before him that he could not refuse. King's very newness made him the ideal leader to mediate between competing factions and to speak for the forces of change. As a student of existentialism, he understood how one moment of crisis could galvanize and direct an entire lifetime. Faced with that crisis, he rose mightily to the challenge, in the process forging for himself and his people a new message to America of the transforming power of Christian love. "There comes a time," King told more than 5,000 blacks on the first night of the boycott,

> when people get tired. We are here this evening to say to those who have mistreated us so long that we are tired—tired of being segregated and humiliated, tired of being kicked about by the brutal feet of oppression. . . . For many years we have shown amazing patience. . . . But we've come here tonight to be saved from that patience that makes us patient with anything less than freedom and justice. . . . If you will protest courageously and yet with dignity and Christian love, in the history books that are written in future generations, historians will have to pause and say "there lived a great people—a black people—who injected a new meaning and dignity into the veins of civilization." This is our challenge and our overwhelming responsibility.

As thousands listened, they found the meaning that would justify the sacrifices that were to come—that here in Montgomery and elsewhere throughout the South, black Americans, embodying the redemptive love of the Christian Savior, would set out to restore the wholeness of their society and redeem the sins of their oppressor.

Finally, the Montgomery bus boycott laid the foundation for the civil rights movement of the 1960s. Thousands of people had come together, and by the time the Supreme Court ruled that Montgomery's buses must integrate, they had demonstrated beyond a doubt the power of a collective body to shape a new world and a new self-confidence. On the very night the boycott ended, the white-robed Ku Klux Klan drove through black Montgomery in one more effort to splinter and intimidate. But no one ran away. Instead, blacks jeered and laughed at the invaders, highlighting their new strength and determination. Out of the bus boycott also would come the Southern Christian Leadership Conference (SCLC), headed by Dr. King, uniting black ministers throughout the South in a common determination to struggle for civil rights. The church would be the gathering place and central institution of the movement, its ministers primary spokesmen for the people.

Yet with all these accomplishments, the bus boycott itself was not enough. To a large extent, it remained a reactive strategy, depending on the right person being arrested, under the right circumstances, with the right leadership structure in place. The very genius of the boycott was also its major weakness. People could refuse to ride the bus without directly or individually placing themselves at risk. The boycott was a passive act; it was important—above all psychologically important—but not adequate to the struggle ahead. Ideal as a way of collective expression, it nevertheless was not a vehicle for individual assault against the racist status quo. It did not, for example, lend itself to the goal of seeking black admittance to previously all-white schools, hotels, lunch counters, theatres, churches, or government buildings. Boycotting a restaurant from which one was already excluded was not a viable option. For this, a new form of expression would be necessary— a form that would provide the vehicle for black Americans to topple the entire structure of Jim Crow racism.

The Sit-in Movement

On February 1, 1960, four young black freshmen at North Carolina A&T College in Greensboro set forth on a historic journey that would ignite a decade of civil rights protests. Walking into downtown Greensboro, they entered the local Woolworth's, purchased toothpaste and other small items, and then sat at the lunch counter and demanded equal service with white persons. "We do not serve Negroes," they were told. But instead of leaving, the students remained. The next day they returned, with twenty-three of their classmates. The day after that it was sixty-six. The next day, more than one hundred. By the end of the week a thousand students joined them in downtown Greensboro. The student phase of the civil rights revolution had begun.

The story of the Greensboro sit-in movement represents a microcosm of the frustration, anger, and determination that surged through black America in the years after the *Brown* decision. Three of the four young men who journeyed to Woolworth's that day had been raised in Greensboro, a city that prided itself on its progressivism, its enlightenment, its "good race relations." Thirteen or fourteen years old in 1954, these young people had come of age, intellectually and politically, in the years since the *Brown* decision. Their parents were activists, some of them belonged to the NAACP, others to churches in the forefront of efforts to build a better political and educational life for blacks. The young men attended Dudley High School, the pride of the black community, a place where teachers taught you to aspire to be the best that was in you. "We were always talking about the issues," Nell Coley, an English teacher recalled. "We might read [a poem or a novel] as a kind of pivot," but the words of a Langston Hughes or Thomas Hardy were always related to the inalienable rights of human beings to respect, freedom, and dignity. "I had to tell youngsters," Coley said, "that the way you find things need not happen . . . I don't care if they push and shove you, you must not accept [discrimination]. . . . You are who you are."

The message the young men heard at school was reinforced at home and in the church. Some went to Shiloh Baptist, whose minister had led civil rights protests at Shaw University in Raleigh, and who always provided support and encouragement to activists. Under his leadership, the local NAACP had almost doubled its membership in 1959, and it was to him that the students came for assistance with supplies and mimeographing materials after the demonstrations began. Two of the students had also belonged to the NAACP Youth Group started in 1943 after Ella Baker had visited town. At the weekly meetings, the youth chapter would discuss local and national protest activities. Students from Little Rock came to share their desegregation experience. The Montgomery bus boycott also provided a focus for discussion. "It was like a catalyst," one of the four original sit-in demonstrators recalled. "It started a whole lot of things rolling." When Martin Luther King, Jr., came to Greensboro to deliver his sermon about Christ's message for America, things began to fall into place. Dr. King's sermon was "so strong," one demonstrator recalled, "that I could feel my heart palpitating. It brought tears to my eyes."

The situation in Greensboro provided the classic example of sophisticated American racism. Although the school board had said it would desegregate schools after the *Brown* decision, its resolve dissipated when state political and economic leaders failed to offer support. Although black parents appeared at all but two school board meetings in the eighteen months after *Brown* to demand either better black facilities or substantive action on desegregation, the board did nothing. Then, in 1957, it admitted six blacks to previously all-white schools. But the action was taken, not to promote integration, but—as the school board leader later recalled—to "hold an umbrella" over the rest of the state and preserve segregation. As long as one or two school districts had token desegregation, it would be impossible for the NAACP to launch a class action suit against the entire state.

Thereafter, no matter how many black parents applied for transfer of their children to previously all-white schools, the board stood pat. Typical of its approach was its response to a 1959 court suit by black parents. Shrewdly, the NAACP had organized four parents to press for admission of their children to nearby schools rather than have them bused a mile or two away. Faced with the prospect of losing what the school board attorney called "as important a suit of litigation as has arisen in North Carolina in the whole history of the state," the board finally gave the appearance of admitting the four black applicants to the previously all-white school to which they had applied. Then, with school board initiative and encouragement, PTA leaders in that school contacted every white parent in the community to explain how they might transfer their children out of the theoretically integrated school into an all-white institution. Two months later, it officially moved every white child and every white faculty member out of the school, replacing all of them with blacks. It could then argue in court that the legal action of the black parents was "moot," because the students were in fact assigned to the schools they had initially applied to attend. One white observer called it "one of the cleverest legal maneuvers yet used in the desegregation field." More to the point was a black minister's comment: "These folks were primarily interested in evading, and they weren't even embarrassed."

Elsewhere in Greensboro, the same kind of duplicity prevailed. When blacks attempted to integrate the local golf course, they were arrested. Then mysteriously, the clubhouse burned down and the golf course was closed. Black college graduates from A&T and Bennett College were told by employers that they could apply for jobs as janitors and maids, but not as salesclerks or receptionists. In all of this, good manners and "civility" prevailed. (As one black leader said, "no one ever called me nigger here.") Greensboro's whites took pride in their paternalism, the way in which they looked out for "their" Negroes. Yet the underlying structure of racism remained. Greensboro, another black leader observed, was "a nice-nasty town."

As they discussed these conditions in their dormitory room at night, the four black students resolved to act. "We challenged each other, really," one of them later recalled. "We constantly heard about all the evils that are occurring and how blacks are mistreated and nobody was doing anything about it. . . . We used to question, 'Why is it that you have to sit in the balcony? Why do you have to ride in the back of the bus?'" Now, about to become voting-age citizens, with none of the rights of citizenship, they determined to do something. No longer were they willing to tolerate the perpetuation of the injustices that they saw all around them, particularly when the highest court in the land had condemned such practices as fundamentally unacceptable. "In 1959, 1960," one student remembered, "I don't know how many black babies had been born eighteen years ago, but I guess everybody was pretty well fed up at the same time." If whites had not been able to hear the peaceful protests and petitions offered by the older generation, perhaps they would listen to the voice of a new generation as it recorded its dissent by sitting silently at a lunch counter.

The four young men drew from each other the resolve to act. "The thing that precipitated the sit-ins," Franklin McCain declared, "was that little bit of incentive and that little bit of courage that each of us instilled in each other." On a Sunday night at the end of January, Ezell Blair, Jr., came home and asked his parents if they would be embarrassed if he got into trouble. "Why?" his parents wondered. "Because," he said, "tomorrow we're going to do something that will shake up this town." Nervous and fearful, afraid that someone might get "chicken," the four friends shored up each other's confidence until the next afternoon. "All of us were afraid," another demonstrator recalled. "But we went and did it." The result became history. "We had the confidence . . . of a Mack truck," Franklin McCain noted. "I felt better that day than I had ever felt in my life. I felt as though I had gained my manhood."

Within days it had become clear that a spontaneous action by a few had mobilized the entire community. When hundreds of students, including the A&T football team, gathered downtown on Saturday, they were met by white gangs carrying Confederate flags. Carrying their own small American flags purchased in advance by student leaders, the football players provided a wedge so that sit-in demonstrators could reach the counters. "Who do you think you are," the whites asked. "We the union army," the football players responded. Nell Coley, the teacher who had done so much to inspire black students in Greensboro, excitedly looked on. "You are never going to see this kind of thing [again]," she said,

> and I'm always happy that I [was there] because here were these black kids lined around this counter with books in their hands . . . and the white kids had confederate flags in their hands . . . and you could hardly get through [until] finally they had to close the store . . . and I was right there when the store was closed and when those black youngsters formed lines and yelled "we won."

In one town, at one moment, in a manner not planned by anyone, four people had decided to "express something that had been in their mind for a long time." In doing so, they helped the Greensboro "coffee party" take its place alongside the Boston Tea Party as an event symbolizing a new revolutionary era.

The Movement Spreads

By the time Greensboro's students had finished the first week of demonstrating, the new tactic they had discovered had already begun to transform student consciousness elsewhere. Within two months, demonstrations had broken out in fifty-four cities in nine states. It was as if an entire generation was ready to act, waiting for a catalyst. Greensboro provided the spark, but young blacks throughout the South provided the tinder for the response that followed. Although representatives of CORE, the NAACP, and SCLC traveled from flash point to flash point, there was no conspiracy or collective planning involved. Instead, each group—hearing about the actions of its comrades elsewhere—drew on the example and decided to do something. Julian Bond in Atlanta, John Lewis in Nashville, Bernard Lee in Montgomery, Cleveland Sellers in Denmark, South Carolina—all heard the news and set out to join the crusade. "My identification with the demonstrating students was so thorough," Cleveland Sellers noted, "that I would flinch every time one of the whites taunted them . . . I had a burning desire to get involved." With an electricity and speed that no one could contain, the word spread that the time had come to act.

Ella Baker understood. Sitting in her office in Atlanta where she was executive secretary of SCLC, Baker sensed the new voice and the new spirit of a younger generation. With $800 of SCLC money, she sent out a call for the student protestors to meet at her alma mater, Shaw University in Raleigh, North Carolina, on Easter weekend. There they came, from the sixty cities where sit-ins were going on, from fifty-eight southern communities in twelve states, and from colleges and universities in the North as well. In her opening remarks, Baker set forth an agenda as long as her experience in the South and as broad as her vision into the future. It was "more than a hamburger" they were after, Baker told the young people, more than a seat in a restaurant, more than a place in a pew. It was freedom—from economic squalor, from educational deprivation, from inhuman treatment. Martin Luther King addressed the crowd as well, affirming the importance of "revolt against the apathy and complacency of adults" and urging an army of volunteers "who will willingly go to jail." But it was James Lawson who galvanized the group. Recently expelled from Vanderbilt Theological Seminary because he had urged nonviolent resistance and civil disobedience, Lawson conveyed the spirit of democracy, of sacrifice, of love, and of faith that the students had experienced and helped to create. Giving voice to the credo of a generation, Lawson declared:

> We affirm the philosophical . . . ideal of non-violence as a foundation of our purpose, the presupposition of our faith, and the manner of our action. . . . Love is the central motif of non-violence. . . . Such love goes to the extreme; it remains loving and forgiving even in the midst of hostility. It matches the capacity of evil to inflict suffering with an even more enduring capacity to absorb evil, all the while persisting in love.

With Baker as its shepherd and Lawson as its moral voice, the conference declared its independence and organized itself as the vanguard of the nonviolent civil rights struggle. While King, Ralph Abernathy, and Wyatt Tee Walker assumed that the students would form themselves as an arm of the SCLC, Baker supported the students' drive for self-determination and independence. In fact, the students were deeply suspicious of their elders, fearful that King and others might try to "capture" the movement, manipulate it for their own purposes, place it in service of someone else's cause. By contrast, they sought a minimum of structure, a maximum of group participation, and the social space to create their own program of action. With Robert Moses who would become one of their spiritual leaders, they believed they should "go where the spirit" moved them, confident that with initiative and faith on their side they could topple the walls of oppression and eliminate every vestige of segregation from the earth.

The spirit of the movement was best expressed in its music. Like a circle without a break, the spirituals of slavery-time joined the freedom songs of the movement to affirm the solidarity of black people. Chanting and clapping, marchers would confront the police with the song: "Ain't Gonna Let That Sheriff Turn Me Around." In jail at night the freedom songs provided warmth and solidarity between cold cells. And in the churches, when the people gathered to restore their spirit and revitalize their strength, it was the music that imparted courage. "We'll walk hand in hand . . . we're not afraid . . . black and white together . . . we shall overcome." As Charles Sherrod recalled one such meeting:

> When the last speaker among the students, Bertha Gober, had finished, there was nothing left to say. Tears filled the eyes of hard, grown men who had seen with their own eyes merciless atrocities committed. . . . Bertha told of spending Thanksgiving in jail . . . and when we rose to sing "We Shall Overcome," nobody could imagine what kept the church on four corners. . . . I threw my head back and closed my eyes as I sang with my whole body.

The spirit and faith of "We Shall Overcome" infused those who joined SNCC. The young people were not ideological, not captive to any programmatic dream. They believed in people. As Jane Stembridge said, "Finally it all boils down to human relationships . . . the question of whether we . . . whether *I* shall go on living in isolation or whether there shall be a we. . . . Love alone is radical. Political statements are not." Living on $10 a week subsistence pay, SNCC workers found their sustenance in the people with whom they worked—and the adults they stayed with who placed their own lives and property in jeopardy by offering their homes and their food to the young civil rights workers. SNCC workers were revolutionaries for whom the word revolution meant the creation of a beloved community where people would care for each other. And they were held together by a strength that transcended any single issue—a strength evoked in one civil rights worker's description of a friend taking part in the sit-ins:

> The manager said something obscene, and grabbed her by the shoulder. "Get the hell out of here nigger." Lana was not going. I don't know whether she should have collapsed in a non-violent manner. She probably did not know. She put her hands under the counter and held. He was rough and strong. She just held and I looked down at her hands, . . . strained . . . every muscle holding. . . . All of a sudden he let go and left. I thought he knew he could not move that girl—ever.

That strength would be sorely tested in the years ahead. During the year after the Greensboro sit-ins, more than 3,600 demonstrators spent some time in jail. In Nashville, where students went to sit-in just two weeks after the Greensboro demonstrations, protestors were pelted with garbage, lighted cigarettes were ground out on their backs, and ketchup was poured over their heads. "The devil has got to come out of these people," James Bevel remarked. In Orangeburg, South Carolina, police knocked protestors off their feet with high-pressure fire hoses in subfreezing weather and then arrested over 500 young people, jamming 350 of them into a chicken coop that had no shelter from the cold. Although several hundred lunch counters were desegregated as a consequence of these and other demonstrations, the price was heavy—and it could only increase as the movement traveled south to the hard-core racist areas of Georgia, Alabama, and Mississippi.

The first sign of things to come occurred during the Freedom Rides of May 1961. Determined to test the freedom of interstate bus facilities for people of both races, James Farmer of CORE and others set out from Washington on a Greyhound bus and a Trailways bus, both bound for New Orleans. The journey through Virginia and North Carolina proceeded peacefully enough, but in Rock Hill, South Carolina, twenty whites slugged and beat John Lewis, a young veteran of the Nashville sit-ins. Then came the Mother's Day Crisis in Anniston, Alabama. A mob surrounded the Greyhound bus, cut its tires, and threw a fire bomb into a window, driving the passengers out into the assembled throng where they were beaten. An hour later, the Trailways bus—following the Greyhound—arrived. Immediately, these Freedom Riders too were assaulted, as many as six or ten men beating on a single demonstrator, pummeling them with fists and pipes. As the Southern Regional Council later observed, all the while, "police were either inactive, not present, or strangely late in arrival," even though they knew well in advance when the bus would arrive.

The Anniston beatings were sufficiently brutal to persuade most of the Freedom Riders to complete the trip to New Orleans by air. But when SNCC students in Nashville heard the news, they insisted that the rides must continue. Only in that way could the purpose of nonviolence be tested, the goal achieved. Diane Nash, Ruby Doris Smith, John Lewis—people whose names would become legendary in the movement because of all the years of struggle they would endure—journeyed to Birmingham to continue the ride for freedom. Birmingham Police Commissioner "Bull" Connor met them and transported them back to the Tennessee border—back 120 miles—and let them out. But they returned again, intent on reaching Montgomery, then Jackson, then New Orleans. When they arrived in Montgomery, the same scenario occurred, with a totally uncontrolled mob pummeling the demonstrators, even inflicting a concussion on John Siegenthaler, an assistant attorney general from the Justice Department. Still they would not stop their journey. Gathering that night at Ralph Abernathy's church, 1,200 blacks shouted "Freedom!" and refused to be intimidated when the sanctuary was surrounded by a white mob.

The next day they rode to Jackson, knowing that here—if nowhere else—rested the "heart of darkness" in the Southern white soul. After all,

Governor Ross Barnett had declared that "the Negro is different because God made him different to punish him." It was not surprising, then, that as soon as the demonstrators stepped from the buses they were immediately arrested. By August, 300 more had joined them in jail, all committed to staying there without accepting bail. At the infamous Parchman Prison the demonstrators were stripped of all personal goods and belongings and prohibited from singing or speaking in more than a whisper. When the prisoners persisted—because that was what affirmed the meaning of their suffering—their mattresses were taken away, then their sheets, then their toothbrushes, then their towels, and they slept on steel.

Mississippi was like that. Blacks earned one-third the family income of whites, feudal-style landlords kept them in poverty, and the provision of even a tar-paper shack to live in was used as an instrument for keeping "their Negroes" under control. If anyone dared to protest, food, lodging, even life, would be snuffed out. In Amite County, Herbert Lee, a black farmer who was willing to work for voter registration, had driven into town in his truck, followed by a white farmer named E. H. Hurst who lived nearby. Hurst approached Lee and started to argue with him, pulling a gun. After Lee refused to talk to the white man unless he put the gun away, Hurst slipped it inside his coat. When Lee got out of the truck, Hurst pulled the gun and shot him in the head. As Bob Moses recalled,

> Lee's body lay on the ground that morning for two hours, uncovered, until they finally got a funeral home in McComb to take it in. No one in Liberty would touch it. They had a coroner's jury that very same afternoon. Hurst was acquitted. He never spent a moment in jail. . . . I remember reading very bitterly in the papers the next morning, a little item on the front page of the McComb *Enterprise Journal* [that] said that a Negro had been shot as he was trying to attack E. H. Hurst. And that was it. Might have thought he was a bum. There was no mention that Lee was a farmer, that he had a family, nine kids, beautiful kids, and he had farmed all his life in Amite County.

Nor was it over. Three years later Lewis Allen, a black man who had told a grand jury what had actually transpired that summer day, was shot dead in his front yard, felled by three shotgun blasts.

But SNCC and the people it served would not be stopped. If they were beaten in a town like McComb, they would go back the next day in greater strength, hold a mass meeting, show that they were not intimidated. Robert Moses charged a white man who had beaten him with assault and battery—the first time such a charge had ever been brought, and even though the white man was acquitted, it was clear that there was a new determination in the air. Living in the homes of the people they worked with, going to church with them, talking to their children about the history of freedom and the struggle to achieve it, SNCC staff people shaped, and were shaped by, the movement they were building. When a black high school principal in McComb insisted that the students promise not to demonstrate, they stayed home, and when he insisted that they return or be expelled, 103 young people went to the school, deposited their books, and walked out. A revolution was happening, forged through the combined courage of the young civil rights workers and the people whose lives they touched. As Bob Moses wrote,

> You combat your own fears about beatings, shootings, and possible mob violence; you stymie by your mere physical presence the anxious fear of the Negro community . . . you create a small striking force capable of moving out when the time comes. . . . After more than six hundred lined up to receive food in Greenwood on Wednesday, 20 February, and Sam's subsequent arrest and weekend in prison on Thursday, 21 February, over one hundred people overflowed City Hall to protest at his trial, over two hundred and fifty gathered at a mass meeting that same night, and on Tuesday by 10:30 A.M. I had counted over fifty people standing in silent line in the County Court House; they say over two hundred had stood in line that day. This is a new dimension. . . . Negroes have never stood en masse in protest at the seat of power in the iceberg of Mississippi politics.

No words could describe fully the experience shared by those who put their lives on the line in Mississippi, Alabama, Georgia, and elsewhere. But the historian Howard Zinn has given us some sense of those moments in his description of his own participation in the movement. One night in Hattiesburg, Mississippi, Zinn and his fellow civil rights workers arrived in the middle of the night at a black family's house where they were to stay prior to a massive Freedom Day demonstration the next morning. Dragging a mattress into the living room, the man and his wife made their guests comfortable, and then went back to bed. Zinn woke at dawn, hearing a sound.

> At first I had thought it part of a dream, but I heard it now still, a woman's voice, pure and poignant. She was chanting softly. At first I thought it came from outside, then I realized . . . and it was his wife, praying, intoning . . . "oh, Lord, Jesus, oh, let things go well today, Jesus . . . oh, make them see, Jesus . . . show your love today, Jesus . . . oh, it's been a long, long time, oh, Jesus . . . oh, Lord, oh, Jesus."

As the lights came on, one of the civil rights workers declared: "Wake up fellows, it's Freedom Day," and Zinn, through an open doorway, could see that there was no mattress on the bed of the black couple, because they had given it to the civil rights workers.

By 1963, there were thousands of such stories of suffering, sacrifice, courage, and triumph. The nation had begun to listen. Each day, papers like the *New York Times* printed three or four pages of stories from the South, documenting the war for America's soul that was taking place there. Each night, on the network news, at least five minutes would be devoted to the latest outrages, the newest demonstrations, the most recent manifestations of nonviolent protest. As civil rights became part of the daily agenda of life for all Americans, and as more and more white students joined their black brethren in the Southern struggle, civil rights and racial equality became a focal point for the entire nation. More than any other issue, it focused on the heart of the contradiction in the American creed—equality of opportunity versus slavery and caste oppression. More than any other issue, also, it provided the ethical focus that would galvanize the discontent and contradictions of America's postwar history. Something massive and new had entered the American experience. And it came, not from above, not from the nation's political leadership, but from below, from the people themselves, who had been victims and who now said, "No more."

Not surprisingly, the black civil rights movement helped spur efforts by other minorities to remedy past grievances. Mexican Americans had long protested their marginalization. In 1929 the League of United Latin American Citizens (LULAC) was created. Following the example set by the NAACP, LULAC pursued an integrationist, "Americanization" stance. Other Mexican American groups sought to perserve an autonomous Mexican culture. World War II brought the bracero program to the United States, allowing the importation of Mexican Americans for desperately needed farm and industrial work, but tensions increased in the postwar period as illegal immigration and anti-foreign sentiment grew. As the '50s wore on, there occurred a fusion of those pursuing civil rights for Mexican Americans and improvement in the condition of Mexican aliens. The movement reached a new state of militancy with the creation of Chicanismo in the '60s—a movement rejecting assimilation and creating La Raza Unida as a political voice. Chicanas and Chicanos initiated boycotts, formed the Brown Berets, and started a student movement. They also provided crucial support for Cesar Chavez' United Farm Workers (UFW), which sought to organize grape workers and develop a national boycott of table grapes. Inspired by movements like SNCC, Hispanic students organized voter registration campaigns, engaged in organizing the barrios and ghettos to protest discrimination, and promoted Chicano pride. With the victory of Chavez over the grape growers and the rising political power of the Chicano population, the Mexican American movement achieved new stature and momentum in the late '60s and '70s.

Native Americans followed a similar progression. Their political activism and protest were triggered after World War II ended when they rebelled against unjust compensation for their lost lands by the 1946 Indian Claims Commission. Once again, tensions between assimilation and separatism were crucial, the Bureau of Indian Affairs pressing for relocation of Native Americans to urban areas. There, however, low-paying jobs, lack of advancement possibilities, and the pressures of urban life caused many to seek a return to their home reservations, where they could at least maintain their own languages and cultures. In 1961 over four hundred members of sixty-seven tribes issued a Declaration of Indian Purpose protesting the death rate of Native Americans, unemployment rates ten times higher than the national average, and the lack of respect and recognition from the federal government. By the end of the '60s the American Indian Movement

(AIM) had formed. AIM occupied Alcatraz Island, raised the banner of Red Power, and protested federal trusteeship of the Indian lands. The experience of Mexican Americans and Native Americans—like that of women (discussed in chapter 11)—charted the path set down by African Americans, working within the system for change but also challenging the notion that the strategy of assimilation alone does justice to the rich and different cultures of America's minority groups.

Conclusion

Notwithstanding significant differences among America's minority groups, the experiences of African Americans seem to exemplify the larger forces at work in the society. Although many Americans believe that the demonstrations of the 1960s represented a radical break with the past, in fact there existed remarkable continuity within the black protest movement between 1945 and 1960. The veterans who came back from World War II to demand their citizenship rights helped to provide the inspiration for those who carried forward the struggle during the 1950s, who refused to ride the buses in Montgomery, and who helped to make the sit-in movement possible in 1960. Events like World War II and the *Brown* decision were clearly important. They created new contexts, new possibilities. But the thread that linked these moments to each other was the willingness of blacks to seek change, to struggle for freedom, to act for justice.

In 1943, Ella Baker had sparked the NAACP Youth Group in Greensboro that would give birth to the sit-in movement. Seventeen years later, Ella Baker convened the conference of student demonstrators in Raleigh that more than anything else helped to give rise to the Student Non-Violent Coordinating Committee—perhaps the most important civil rights organization of the 1960s. It was E. D. Nixon who started the NAACP in Montgomery during the 1940s, and it was E. D. Nixon who organized the bus boycott of the 1950s. Medgar Evers had first challenged the tyranny of Mississippi's white racism when he went to cast his vote as a returning veteran in 1946; it was also Medgar Evers who led the struggle for voting rights and racial justice in Mississippi until his assassination in 1963. Such continuity was not incidental. It was inherent in the protest struggle.

The movement also grew out of, and depended on, the strength of black institutions. The foundation for E. D. Nixon's activism was the all-black Brotherhood of Sleeping Car Porters. The NAACP meeting that inspired J. A. DeLaine to attack segregation in Clarendon County, South Carolina, took place at Allen University, a black college. Ella Baker went to Shaw, an all-black school founded during Reconstruction, and it was at Shaw that the first meeting of SNCC took place. Black high schoolers generated the pride and aspirations that motivated the original sit-in demonstrators in Greensboro; and black colleges provided the primary base of recruitment for the movement. Ironically, many of these all-black institutions, which did so much to make possible the fight against segregation, would themselves suffer as a consequence. Yet their centrality testifies to the absolute necessity in the struggle for social change of retaining a strong home base, even as one seeks integration in the wider society.

Throughout these years, it would be difficult to overstate the failure of white political and economic leaders. With only a few exceptions, whites in positions of power refused to support the cause of civil rights unless it was directly in their self-interest to do so. Even then, the response was more often verbal than substantive. For the most part, Southern white politicians refused even to recognize the existence of blacks, or to acknowledge the extent to which the black experience created a totally different perspective on American society and politics than the white experience. All too often, the best that could be anticipated from white leaders, either in the North or the South, was paternalism. Yet from a black perspective, such an approach simply compounded the age-old problem. The time for accommodation to gestures and symbols from all-powerful white people had passed. The moment for freedom had come.

Precisely because whites refused to act on the black agenda, it became necessary for black Americans to seize the initiative, take control of their own lives, and create new vehicles for protest. As the events of the 1950s and early 1960s proved, simply to demand one's rights was not enough. The courts proved inadequate, and most politicians gave little more than lip service to racial justice. The law itself—even when clearly and simply stated—proved as much an invitation to subtle circumvention as an instrument of securing change. It seemed that only by taking new initiatives, striking at the white man's pocketbook, creating discomfort in his life, would any change occur.

In this sense, the direct-action protests manifested in the sit-in movement provided an effective new vehicle through which traditional patterns of white domination could be attacked. Direct-action protests were both a consequence and a cause of black activism. The sit-ins grew out of a tradition of protest; but they also helped to reinforce and extend that tradition, and to change the forms through which old as well as young would now express their demands for dignity and equality. Building on the lessons of the older generation, the young were forging a new method for carrying on the struggle. Thus, the student movement represented a new stage of black insurgency, reflecting the lessons as well as the frustrations of past experiences with protest. If the courts and politicians would not listen to traditional forms of expression, then new ones would have to be found. The sit-ins had created a new language, one which would have to be heard, one which would not be ignored. After 1960, the forms of communication between white and black would never again be the same. The question was whether white America would respond to the message, and how.

7

John F. Kennedy

The Reality and the Myth

For most Americans, the early 1960s evoke an image of activism and reform. The fifties had been quiet, conservative, uninteresting. But the sixties were different—or so our collective memory tells us. Full of conflict, protest, and idealism, they represented a shifting of gears in postwar America, a time when the society began to confront its unsolved ills and to embrace reforms that would redeem the nation's reputation as a leader of the "free world," both at home and abroad.

For most Americans also, the sixties are linked inextricably with the Kennedys. The decade began with the election of John F. Kennedy who boasted in his Inaugural Address that he was the first American president "born in this century." Representing "a new generation of Americans," Kennedy held his countrymen spellbound with a rhetoric and style that called forth a new epoch of heroism and sacrifice. Enjoining Americans to "Ask not what your country can do for you, but what you can do for your country," Kennedy appealed especially to the young, giving them a sense that anything was possible if only they would do their part. "We can do better," he repeatedly said. With his youthful family, the shock of hair falling over his forehead, his legendary love of touch football games, and the repeated exhortation to the new generation to pick up the "torch of the American Revolution," Kennedy seemed like a tribune at the head of a legion, his charisma intrinsically part of the social idealism and protest that would soon transform the nation. Or so it appeared.

In fact, the early 1960s—at least in Washington—were quite different. Although Kennedy would play a central role in carrying forward the Cold War, he provided little leadership initially on domestic matters. Far from being a tribune at the head of a legion, he was a follower who only reluctantly—and belatedly—joined the forces of change and protest. Despite excessive rhetoric about the "crisis" in America, he and his associates shared the consensus of the 1950s that there were no major structural problems in the country, and that the United States was well on its way to being a complete society. Because of his style, his consummate skill in shaping a distinctive public image, and our own tendency to interpret society in terms of its political leaders, we have made Kennedy synonymous with sixties' activism. But a more accurate judgment would be that John F. Kennedy was part of the politics that preceded him, a man of the center, like Eisenhower, who had to be pushed by social forces to endorse even minimal reforms, and a person whose obsession with maintaining the Cold War may eventually have done more to deflect the forces of activism than to offer them guidance. Only in the final ten months of his presidency did he act differently; only then did he offer the kind of leadership we now attribute to him in our mythology.

The Kennedy Career

The most important person in John Kennedy's early life was his father. Proud, combative, and insecure, the elder Kennedy dedicated his life to proving that an Irish-American family was as good as any WASP family descended from the Mayflower. Seemingly convinced that the only way to achieve this goal was never to stop striving for it, the elder Kennedy set out to conquer all before him. "For the Kennedys," he once told journalist Arthur Krock, "it is the shithouse or the castle—nothing in between." Making his first fortune in the shipping industry, he moved on to control the Scotch whiskey trade and to a successful career as a motion picture executive. Through it all he kept moving—with his family, from one rich community to another seeking acceptance; in his career, from brilliant business successes to public service as head of FDR's Securities and Exchange Commission and then as American ambassador to London at the Court of St. James. Yet there persisted the gnawing sense of not belonging. "When are the nice people of Boston going to accept us?" his wife asked a friend.

The ethos of competition pervaded family life. Dinnertime conversations became seminars on issues of public policy, with the children urged to engage each other and their guests in a battle of wits, both to enhance their education as citizens and to become experts at outscoring their opposition. Athletic bravado was simply an extension of the competition. "The father particularly laid it on hard trying to make the boys, and the girls, excellent in something," Supreme Court Justice William Douglas observed, "whether it was touch football, or tennis, or boating, or something else." If friends really wished acceptance, they had to surpass the roughouse football tactics of their hosts. As one associate recalled, "[You had to] show raw guts, fall on your face now and then. Smash into the house once in a while going after a pass. Laugh off twisted ankles or a big hole torn in your best suit." Anyone who pleaded injury was marked as suspect.

Such insistence on perfection posed a particularly cruel dilemma for Jack, the second oldest son. "At least one half of the days that he spent on this earth," his brother Bobby noted, "were days of intense physical pain." Jack almost died from scarlet fever as a child, suffered from a chronic weak back, and spent a substantial portion of his childhood years in bed, rarely finishing a normal school year as one ailment after another required hospitalization or diagnostic tests. Partly as a result of these illnesses, Jack became the reader of the family, voraciously devouring biographies and histories, and developing the detached, intellectual cast of mind that would later mark so strongly his political bearing.

The younger Kennedy's physical condition deteriorated further after his PT boat was struck by a Japanese destroyer during World War II. Kennedy spent hours in the water swimming to save wounded members of his crew. "There was a hole in his back that never closed up after the operation he had during the war," one friend noted; "you could look into it and see the metal plate that had been put into his spine." The pain was constant, with Kennedy spending months in hospitals seeking relief. After the war, in the course of repeated efforts to cure his back condition, doctors determined that Kennedy had Addison's disease, an adrenalin deficiency that could be contained only by massive injections of cortisone on a daily basis. At the time the disease was believed to be terminal. "I'll probably last until I'm forty-five," the young Kennedy told a friend. Although oral medication was subsequently developed that both contained the disease and offered relative assurance of a full and normal life, most of Jack's life profoundly contradicted his father's goal of health and perfection. He was "so sick," a friend noted, "that it was an irritation . . . for his father and for himself. It threatened to get in the way of everything they were trying to accomplish."

What they were trying to accomplish, of course, was to get a Kennedy elected president. Whether by choice or otherwise, Jack became the vehicle for his father's ambition after Joe Jr., the perfect embodiment of his father's vision—robust, talented, gregarious, strong, and athletic—was killed on a suicide mission during the war. In a world where their father almost always got his way, Jack became the heir apparent. "My father wanted his eldest son in politics," Jack Kennedy said. "'Wanted' isn't the right word. He demanded it." With his father prodding him, Jack became a candidate for Congress in the 11th Congressional District of Massachusetts, serving the Irish and Italian working-class districts of Charlestown, Cambridge, and Boston, as well as the Yankee enclave of Beacon Hill. Cultivating local politicians like Dave Powers, shaking hands at factory gates, and speaking to groups of veterans' mothers, the younger Kennedy learned his trade quickly and skillfully. But as he told a friend at the time, he could also "feel pappy's eyes on the back of my neck."

If Jack Kennedy ever consciously confronted the tension between his own frailty and intellectualism, on the one hand, and his father's insistence on perfection and physical prowess, on the other, he appeared to resolve the tension by emulating his father. Even in his early years, he accepted the code of physical bravado, driving himself to take part in all the sports that his elder brother played, as if to prove that he was as good—or at least as courageous—as Joe. If frequently he found himself bedridden by illnesses over which he had no control, he would—just as frequently—rise from a sick bed to join a party, attend a dance, or participate in a family outing, as if to show that nothing could keep him down. Even the choice of PT boat service—one of the riskiest, most physically demanding positions in the Navy—seemed a way of demonstrating that he could hold his own, regardless of the disabilities that afflicted him.

The younger Kennedy also embraced the values of the masculine mystique, so clearly present in his father's attitude toward women, sexuality, and weakness in men. The elder Kennedy was a notorious philanderer. He flaunted his sexual liaisons with Hollywood stars like Gloria Swanson, and even made advances to his daughter's friends. "After dinner," one noted, "he would take you home and kiss you goodnight as though he were a young so and so. One night I was visiting Eunice at the Cape and he came into my bedroom and kissed me goodnight! . . . really kissed me. It was so silly. I remember thinking, 'how embarrassing for Eunice!'" In the eyes of one Kennedy associate, such behavior inevitably posed problems for Jack. "He was a sensitive man, and I think it confused him. What kind of object is a woman? To be treated as his father treated them?"

Yet Jack Kennedy quickly became known for the same behavior. Simultaneously, he had relationships with numerous women, using his friends or inlaws to set up a rendezvous with a lover. The cortisone treatments, some said, seemed to increase his sexual appetite. Moreover, as if the value of a sexual conquest were increased by the fame of his partner or the brazenness of the circumstances, he took special delight in violating the rules, imitating his father's tendency to exhibit publicly his romantic ties. One of his earlier affairs was with a woman rumored to be a Nazi spy. Subsequently, he engaged in sexual relationships with Hollywood starlets, luxuriating in their eminence and the gossip they conveyed about other stars. Even as president, he carried on an affair—in the White House—with a woman who had formerly been a mistress to Frank Sinatra, and who continued to be intimate with leaders of organized crime. All the while, Kennedy seemed oblivious to the fact that his mistress would be under FBI surveillance. It was almost as if, having received a sentence of early death because of Addison's disease, there were no rules that mattered.

Kennedy exhibited similar "macho" values toward male politicians. He detested those who were indecisive, equating their fear of taking a strong stand with effeminacy. The way to make a difficult decision, he said, was to calculate the odds, make a choice, and "grab our balls and go." Those who vacillated were, by implication, not men. When columnist Joseph Alsop described Kennedy as a "Stevenson with balls," said Garry Wills, it was the kind of compliment Kennedy loved to hear. Kennedy displayed almost an obsession with sexually loaded imagery, as when he urged a friend to attack Arthur Krock, an old benefactor who had turned against him. "Tuck it to Krock," Kennedy said. "Bust it off in old Arthur. He can't take it, and when you go after him he folds."

The elder Kennedy also bequeathed to his son the habit of using wealth and connections to achieve success. The pernicious consequences of such a legacy were most clearly evident in the two books Kennedy published prior to his candidacy for the presidency. *Why England Slept* was Kennedy's senior thesis at Harvard. As the research paper of a maturing young mind, its primary value lay in what it revealed about Kennedy's concept of the relationship between people and government. In examining Great Britain's tardiness in mobilizing against fascist aggression, Kennedy speculated that a free press and conflicting political constituencies had severely impaired Britain's ability to respond to Hitler's dictatorship. Faced with such an enemy, Kennedy hypothesized, it might be necessary for a democracy to renounce temporarily its democratic privileges and move toward "voluntary totalitarianism." The thesis, said one professor, represented a "laborious, interesting and intelligent discussion of an interesting question."

But the project did not end there. Instead, Ambassador Kennedy determined that the thesis should be a book. Mobilizing his own resources, he sent the manuscript to Arthur Krock, a family friend (ironically, the man whom Kennedy would later turn against) who was head of the Washington Bureau of the *New York Times*. Krock took the thesis, edited it thoroughly, changed some of its major lines of argument, and enlisted his own literary agent to find a publisher. Within a short time, Kennedy's senior paper had become a major book, praised by the *New York Times Book Review* for its "mature understanding and fair mindedness" and by the *Boston Herald* for its "grasp of complex problems, its courageous frankness, its good manners, and its sound advice." More to the point, perhaps, was the response of Harold Laski, a famous English intellectual and friend of the family. "In a good university," Laski wrote Ambassador Kennedy,

> half a hundred seniors do books like this as part of their normal work in their final year. But they don't publish them for the good reason that their importance lies solely in what they get out of doing them and not out of what they have to say. I don't honestly think any publisher would have looked at that book of Jack's if he had not been your son, and if you had not been ambassador. And those are not the right grounds for publication.

If Kennedy *had* been like any other college senior, his thesis might have been the most rewarding and constructive task of his young life. Instead, the ultimate recognition attached to the work was secured through someone else's skills and connections, with the covert and insidious lesson that success would always be there as a natural consequence of wealth and power.

The same scenario repeated itself, with almost frightening parallels, when Kennedy published *Profiles in Courage* in 1955. "The concept of the book was Kennedy's," Ted Sorensen, Kennedy's closest aide, later noted. Indeed, it reflected some of the same concerns first evident in Kennedy's college years—how politicians faced up to taking positions opposed by their constituents. Yet the basic themes of the book came from an outline written by a family friend. More important, virtually all the research and writing were done by Sorensen and Jules Davids, Jacqueline Kennedy's teacher at George

Washington University. As Herbert Parmet has shown in his biography of Kennedy, the senator contributed little to the final manuscript—a few dictabelt recordings containing notes on some of the senators profiled in the book, and some paragraphs that eventually appeared in the preface and conclusion. Although Kennedy read voluminously for the project, he did not write the book. To say otherwise, Parmet concluded, would be "as deceptive as installing a Chevrolet engine in a Cadillac." Nevertheless, the book was marketed as the work of Kennedy, and Arthur Krock persuaded the 1958 Pulitzer Prize Committee to set aside the recommendations of its panel on biography in order to award the country's most distinguished literary honor to Kennedy. As a result, the junior senator from Massachusetts was once again acclaimed as a distinguished author and intellectual. Perhaps most distressing, Kennedy appears to have accepted the description as appropriate.

In the meantime, Kennedy the politician had begun to chart his views on public questions. On foreign issues particularly, his thinking was both ambivalent and prophetic. Endorsing a hard-line, anticommunist critique of Truman's and Roosevelt's foreign policy, Kennedy blamed the State Department and president for the loss of China. "What our young men have saved," Kennedy declared, "our diplomats and our president have frittered away." It was time, he said, to prevent "the onrushing tide of communism from engulfing all of Asia." On other occasions, however, Kennedy showed a keen sensitivity to the rising aspirations of Third World nations. After a trip to Southeast Asia he talked about "the fires of nationalism . . . now ablaze. . . . Colonialism is not a topic for tea-talk discussion; it is the daily fare of millions of men." America was sadly mistaken, he observed, when it ignored "civilizations striving to be born." In particular, Kennedy warned against supporting the French in Indochina. "No amount of American military assistance," he observed, "can conquer an enemy which is everywhere and at the same time nowhere, 'an enemy of the people' which has the sympathy and the covert support of the people. . . . To pour money, material, and men into the jungles of Indochina without at least a remote prospect of victory would be dangerously futile and self-destructive."

Kennedy revealed a similar ambivalence in his approach to domestic issues. A dedicated supporter of the bread-and-butter issues of greatest concern to his blue-collar constituency, Kennedy endorsed increases in the minimum wage, fought for veterans' benefits, and supported organized labor. In 1948 he introduced a housing measure that provided for slum clearance and the building of 135,000 public housing units annually. When criticized by the leadership of the American Legion, the young congressman retorted: "The leadership of the American Legion has not had a constructive thought for the benefit of this country since 1918!" But on other issues, Kennedy waffled. "I'm not a liberal at all," he told one interviewer. In particular, he avoided the commitment to domestic social welfare measures characteristic of the Americans for Democratic Action and other liberal groups. His closest friends were conservative Southerners like George

Smathers of Florida and Richard Russell of Georgia. Robert Taft was the man he most admired. Kennedy even boasted of his good personal relationships with staunch racists like John Rankin of Mississippi.

It was the issue of McCarthyism, however, that highlighted most clearly the ambiguity of Kennedy's posture. Joseph Kennedy, Sr., was an ardent admirer and strong supporter of the junior senator from Wisconsin. Frequently, his son's views sounded very much like those of McCarthy. "[I know] Joe pretty well," John Kennedy told a college class, "and he may have something." Kennedy strongly supported the anticommunist McCarran Act, declaring that we "have to get all foreigners off our backs." In a speech at the University of Notre Dame, he warned about the "ever-expanding power of the federal government," connecting it to "the scarlet thread that runs throughout the world." According to Theodore Sorensen, Kennedy was prepared to censure McCarthy for his personal excesses, but in a speech prepared for the occasion, he refused to condemn McCarthy's views. As it turned out, the speech was never delivered, and when McCarthy finally was censured, Kennedy was in a hospital recovering from back surgery. He issued no statement at the time, nor did he pair himself with an absent senator so that his views would be known. At no time did he show signs of the visceral revulsion toward McCarthy's tactics that characterized most liberals. Indeed, his views seemed to be shaped more by personality considerations than by ideology. He liked McCarthy personally, but disliked his methods. The same pattern distinguished many of his other relationships. Indeed, he even indicated that he was happy to see Richard Nixon defeat Helen Gahagan Douglas in the 1950 U.S. Senate race in California, giving Nixon a campaign contribution from his father. "It isn't going to break my heart if you can turn the Senate's loss into Hollywood's gain [by defeating Douglas]," Kennedy said.

The issue of McCarthyism would come back to haunt Kennedy after he soared to national prominence at the 1956 Democratic Convention. Widely admired for his own personal courage and reaping plaudits for his book on the courage of others, Kennedy became an increasingly popular personality. His speech nominating Stevenson for president at the 1956 convention evoked wild enthusiasm, and when Stevenson determined to make the vice-presidential nomination an open fight, Kennedy and his staff seized the occasion to focus a national spotlight on the young Massachusetts senator. Armed with a statistical chart showing that a Catholic would significantly enhance Democratic prospects for victory in the fall, Kennedy blitzed the convention, galvanizing a coalition of conservative Southerners and Northern urban bosses that almost catapulted him to victory. Narrowly defeated on the second ballot by the more liberal Estes Kefauver, Kennedy nevertheless emerged as the ultimate winner. "He probably rates as the one real victor of the entire convention," a columnist observed. "His was the one new face. . . . His charisma, his dignity, his intellectuality, and in the end his gracious sportsmanship . . . are undoubtedly what those delegates would remember." Kennedy agreed. "You know," he told Dave Powers afterward, "if we work like hell the next four years, we will pick up all the marbles."

Kennedy's basic problem was to persuade liberal democrats that—notwithstanding his waffling on McCarthyism—he deserved their support. Eleanor Roosevelt attacked him for not exhibiting the courage he wrote about, citing his reluctance to speak out against federal aid for parochial schools and his reliance on his father's money. But Kennedy struck back, mobilizing his own stable of liberal supporters. Wooing labor through his assiduous work on a labor reform bill, he succeeded in winning the backing of progressive union leaders such as Walter Reuther of the UAW. Intellectuals such as Arthur Schlesinger, Jr., came on board, creating a brains trust reminiscent of FDR's. Kennedy's brother Robert, meanwhile, organized a massively efficient delegate operation, focusing on the major industrial states. As urban bosses like Richard Daley and big state governors like David Lawrence and Michael DiSalle joined the bandwagon, Kennedy won a string of impressive primary victories, and the ingredients for victory fell into place.

By the time the Democrats gathered in Los Angeles in July 1960, the Kennedy political machine was unstoppable. The candidate was still not a liberal. Indeed, CBS commentator Eric Sevareid was probably correct in declaring that "the managerial revolution" had come to politics, with Nixon and Kennedy, "its first completely packaged products." But Kennedy had neutralized the skeptics in his own party by recruiting some of their chief advocates and endorsing a platform that called for medical care for the aged, civil rights legislation, and federal aid to education. He had used his father's wealth and connections, traveling the country in a privately owned airplane while Humphrey used a chartered bus. But he had also managed to distance himself from his father and to isolate the issue of family influence by acknowledging it, making fun of it, and then dismissing it. He even turned his sex appeal to his advantage, in reporter Murray Kempton's words, treating "southern Ohio yesterday as Don Giovanni used to treat Seville. His progress . . . was an epic of the history of the sexual instinct in the American female." In all of this, he remained cool, poised, relaxed, and full of wry humor. The question that remained was whether there was any substance behind the technique, style, and calculation. In his acceptance speech, Kennedy promised a "new frontier," with America moving to challenge "uncharted areas of science and space, unsolved problems of peace and war, unconquered pockets of ignorance and prejudice, [the] unanswered questions of poverty and surplus." The words sparkled. Whether they meant anything remained to be seen.

The Kennedy Frame of Reference

Ironically, Kennedy exhibited far more evidence of sharing the consensus approach of the previous decade than of questioning its basic assumptions. At the very moment when the civil rights movement was dramatizing basic inequities in the society, Kennedy and his associates continued to believe that most domestic problems had been solved and that the major challenges to America came from the external threat of communism. In this sense, Kennedy participated fully in Godfrey Hodgson's "liberal consensus"— confidence in capitalism as an economic system, belief in the efficacy of reform, distaste for and disapproval of "class" conflict, and dedication to social unity at home as a means of fighting communism abroad. Although "liberals" clearly preferred a more activist stance on reform than conservatives, the "liberal consensus" itself was, by definition, conservative, premised, in Hodgson's words, on "complacency about the perfectibility of American society" and virtual "paranoia about the threat of communism." Most of American politics since World War II had operated within these parameters. Indeed, the new administration's full endorsement of this world view hampered, from the beginning, its willingness to respond decisively to growing domestic problems, and propelled it into a distorted, sometimes dangerous, obsession with foreign foes.

Significantly, even the most progressive of Kennedy's supporters believed that no inherent flaws existed in America's social and economic order. "[Capitalism] works," John Kenneth Galbraith observed in *The Affluent Society* in 1958, "and in the years since World War II, quite brilliantly." In the view of Galbraith and others, the astonishing economic success of the postwar period eliminated the need to consider issues of fundamental redistribution of wealth, since an ever-expanding economic pie meant that even America's poorest citizens would eventually gain access to the benefits of capitalism. Hence, America had no need for a politics of the left committed to altering the basic economic structure. As Arthur Schlesinger, Jr., noted, New Deal concerns with "meeting stark human needs for food, clothing, shelter and employment . . . are now effectively [solved]." It was not that Kennedy or his aides were indifferent to those who had been left out of American society—only that they believed remaining inequalities could be eliminated quickly within the existing economic structure simply by making it more efficient.

For that reason, economic growth became central to Kennedy's entire domestic policy. If the Gross National Product (GNP) could increase at a sufficiently rapid rate, even the poorest members of the society would have the opportunity to participate in prosperity. Thus, productivity became a panacea for eliminating social tension or potential class conflict between the "haves" and "have nots." As Galbraith noted, "increasing aggregate output is an alternative to redistribution." Consistent with this approach, Kennedy concentrated on "fine tuning" the existing economic machinery. The American economy had already shown itself to be revolutionary in its productive potential; now the task was to maximize that potential through monetary, fiscal, and tax policies. Most of America's problems, Kennedy declared, "are *technical* problems, are administrative problems. They [involve] sophisticated judgments which do not lend themselves to the great sort of 'passionate movements' which have stirred this country so often in the past." No statement better describes Kennedy's underlying assumptions. Seemingly oblivious to the new "passionate" forces already rocking the country, Kennedy emphasized minor adjustments in the status quo. As columnist Walter Lippmann acutely observed, Kennedy was "a man of the center . . . far removed from the social struggles of the New Deal."

If acceptance of the existing domestic situation represented the first cornerstone of Kennedy's approach to politics, obsession with foreign policy issues constituted the second. Indeed, a symbiotic relationship existed between the two—an aggressive anticommunist foreign policy being premised, in the eyes of Kennedy advisors, on maintaining unity at home. According to Kennedy aide Walt Rostow, the United States could respond effectively to the "great revolutionary transformations" beyond its borders only if members of both parties avoided becoming embroiled in disputes over domestic issues. Or, stated another way, an inverse correlation existed between the amount of energy devoted to disputes at home and the administration's ability to forge and maintain a bipartisan front on foreign policy. Almost inevitably, then, a high priority on foreign policy questions led to seeking acceptance of a middle-of-the-road consensus at home. As White House aide McGeorge Bundy said, an effective foreign policy "turned upon the capacity of the Executive to take and hold the *center.*" By implication, a strong policy of anticommunism depended on minimizing those domestic problems that were most potentially divisive.

In sharp contrast to his relative equanimity about the situation at home, Kennedy insisted that the United States was facing a time of maximum peril in its relations with communist powers. "To be an American in the next decade," he said in September 1960, "will be a hazardous experience. We will live on the edge of danger." As the campaign intensified, so, too, did Kennedy's rhetoric. "Freedom and communism are locked in deadly embrace," he declared. No longer was containment "an adequate formula"; instead, the United States "must move forward to meet communism." The issue was the "preservation of civilization." "The world," he declared, "cannot exist half slave and half free."

Almost as though he believed the country faced a crisis comparable to the one he had written about in *Why England Slept,* Kennedy exhorted his fellow citizens to unite in defense of their sacred homeland. The new frontier, he declared, "holds out the promise of more sacrifice instead of more security." "Our responsibility," he told another audience, "is to be the chief defender of freedom at a time when freedom is under attack all over the globe." Nor did his depiction of the crisis moderate once he took office. In his first State of the Union Address in January 1961, he told Congress that "each day we draw nearer to the hour of maximum danger. . . . The news will be worse before it is better." On every continent, Kennedy said, America was challenged to find new ways to forestall the aggressor and seize the initiative, to "move outside the home fortress, and . . . challenge the enemy in fields of our own choosing."

Kennedy's Inaugural Address encapsulated his entire approach. Every sentence seemed designed to heighten the dimensions of the crisis facing America, to evoke the conclusion that Armageddon was imminent. The "revolutionary beliefs" for which Americans had died since the war for independence were "at issue around the globe," Kennedy declared. "Let every nation know . . . that we shall pay *any* price, bear *any* burden, meet *any* hardship, support *any* friend, oppose *any* foe, in order to assure the survival and the success of liberty." The words were ennobling, exhorting Americans to a fever pitch of moralism. It was almost as if Kennedy thought that sounding the tocsin of crisis would generate in his countrymen a surge of national purpose and confidence in a heroic leader that England had lacked in 1939. Significantly, Kennedy devoted not a paragraph of his Inaugural Address to domestic issues such as race or poverty, notwithstanding the fact that the sit-in movement had begun just eleven months before.

Through his language and his choice of emphasis, Kennedy thus charted the themes of his administration, generating in his audience a sense of the excitement of danger, the exhilaration of confrontation, and the heroism of sacrifice. By repeatedly insisting that "I welcome this challenge," and by defining his own role as "commander in chief of the Grand Alliance" at a time of maximum peril, he also evoked unrealistic expectations of what he personally could accomplish. The Inaugural Address had "that ring of command that emboldens men to renew their faith," the *New Republic* observed. Yet there was also something disturbing about the speech. In grandiloquent phrases, it evoked a sense of moral alarm about a world that for eight years had largely been at peace, while ignoring social issues at home where a rhetoric of moral fervor would have made far more sense. Through defining the world as he did, Kennedy, in effect, structured the allocation of resources and energies of his adminstration, raising hopes he could not fulfill and choosing priorities that would have to be changed before he could begin to achieve his greatest triumphs.

The third and final feature of Kennedy's frame of reference was the president's obsession with style—how to carry on the business of America. Since Kennedy accepted the broad outlines of existing domestic policy and embraced the underlying premises of the Cold War, the major area left in which he could distinguish himself involved his approach to the presidency—the way he would run the entire office, the type of people he would attract, and the image he would imprint on his administration. While Eisenhower had relied on traditional structures and had urged the new administration to establish more effective bureaucratic mechanisms for clearing decisions, Kennedy insisted on informality and short-circuiting established channels. If Eisenhower staffed his administration with corporate executives, Kennedy emphasized recruitment of young technocrats and intellectuals. And while Eisenhower abhorred "any noisy trumpeting" about national emergencies, preferring "careful calculation and balance," Kennedy relied on moral exhortation and a constant sense of urgency as primary vehicles for leadership.

Kennedy himself would be the hub of the informal decision-making process. "He wanted all the lines to lead to the White House," *Time* correspondent Hugh Sidey wrote; "he wanted to be the single nerve center." But instead of making final decisions on issues that had been thoroughly researched by layers of staff members, as in the Eisenhower years, Kennedy wanted to be part of the action itself. As the journalist Henry Fairlie observed, "the Kennedy team lived on the move, calling signals to each other in the thick of the action . . . like basketball players developing plays while the game moved on." Dismantling Eisenhower's cabinet structure, Kennedy relied on informal huddles with advisors having particular expertise on a given problem. His closest aide Theodore Sorensen celebrated the fact that "not one staff meeting was ever held, with or without the President." The emphasis was on informality, flexibility, and hard-hitting advice from energetic aides. "An awful lot of it was spit-balling," Joseph Kraft observed, "it had to be spit-ball." Those were the days, Robert Kennedy recalled, "when we thought we were succeeding because of all the stories of how hard everybody was working." The whole image of the administration was of strenuous, exciting, exalted service to a higher cause, with people competing to see who could put in the longest hours serving the country in its time of maximum need. "Senior members of [Defense Secretary McNamara's] staff," one reporter noted, "[would hurry] to the Pentagon on Sunday mornings [to] feel the hood of the Secretary's car to determine by its temperature how long he had been at work."

It was also an exhilarating time. "Washington seemed engaged in a collective effort," Arthur Schlesinger, Jr., observed, "to make itself brighter, gayer, more intellectual, more resolute. It was a golden interlude." With an aura of crisis constantly in the air, the Kennedy team, one journalist noted,

> aspired to greatness, not just occasionally, but all the time. . . . As the sun rose over the farther most shores of Cathay and began its slow process across the heavens, it was [always] one minute to midnight somewhere, and something would happen; a government would fall, there would be a significant outbreak of violence. . . . All over Washington, men would rise early to answer the bidding to crisis and to greatness, and the still slumbering public would wake in the morning to find that they had been summoned to meet danger once more; and once more to be rescued from it.

To those privileged to be part of such an atmosphere, nothing could be more rewarding. As Walt Rostow's wife said to him: "I've not seen you for years more cheerful or effective. You're an odd lot. You're not politicians or intellectuals. You're the junior officers of the Second World War come to responsibility." The metaphor was apt. With the PT commander in the White House and a new generation of Americans manning the Situation Room, the sense of shift in command was almost visceral.

Indeed, perhaps the greatest change Kennedy brought to Washington was a conviction that "the best and the brightest" of the younger generation were now in charge. Trained at Ivy League schools, veterans of World War

Nothing contributed more to the Camelot image of the Kennedy family than the youth and romance associated with the president. Here he is photographed sailing with his wife Jacqueline off the Massachusetts coast. *(National Archives)*

II or Korea, these were the cream of the crop, people who were both hard-nosed *and* brilliant—capable of solving any problem and infused with confidence that they had a special mission at a decisive moment in history. The Kennedy team, Joseph Kraft observed, "dazzled the nation by intellectual brilliance and social swank." Even White House entertainment reinforced the image of excellence. With Pablo Casals playing in the East Room, the

American Shakespeare Festival Theatre performing at a State Dinner, and André Malraux honored for his literary achievements, Kennedy seemed to be transforming Washington into a pantheon of artistic excellence, as well as governmental brilliance. Celebrating the atmosphere, Schlesinger later wrote: "Never had girls seemed so pretty, tunes so melodious, and evenings so blithe and unconstrained." The glitter was almost palpable.

Yet it was by no means clear that the emphasis on style signified any substantive departure from the past. Activism seemed almost an end in itself, with the flurry of hard work and urgent meetings providing a vehicle for process to become more important than performance. The Kennedy men, journalist Henry Fairlie observed, seemed to "have been in a constant hurry, taking last minute decisions at last minute meetings, making last minute corrections to last minute statements," but the point was not always clear; it was as though "they were always trying to catch up with events, or with each other, or even each with himself." In *Profiles in Courage* Kennedy had written that "great crises produce great men." Yet the logic was not self-evident. A more accurate statement, perhaps, would be that the appearance of great crises creates the *impression* of great men. The quality of greatness itself depended more on wisdom, experience, and reflection than on frenetic activity and a list of advanced degrees from Ivy League schools.

Perhaps most disturbing was a sense that the emphasis on crisis, heroism, and sacrifice substituted for a coherent vision of where America was, or should be going. "[When I asked the president] what he wanted to have achieved by the tme he rode down Pennsylvania Avenue with his successor," *New York Times* columnist James Reston wrote, Kennedy

> looked at me as if I were a dreaming child. I tried again: Did he not feel the need of some goal to help guide his day-to-day decisions and priorities? Again a ghastly pause. It was only when I turned the question to immediate, tangible problems that he seized the point and rolled off a torrent of statistics.

The Kennedy team may have been "an enormously, reassuringly, competent" group, as the *New Republic* noted, but they also exhibited "a certain coolness and greyness." They seemed to lack a viewpoint to give direction to their moral mission. As one of McGeorge Bundy's assistants described the National Security Advisor: "There are three kinds of people in the policy game. There are those with options who are looking for positions. There are those with positions who are looking for options. There are those with options who are looking for options. Bundy is a creature from the third species." So, too, were most of Kennedy's other aides—men, as Godfrey Hodgson has written, "who displayed a maximum of technical ingenuity with a minimum of dissent." In short, people *without* a vision of where they wanted to go.

In the end, therefore, Kennedy entered the White House more with an approach than with a direction. Relatively comfortable with the condition of the country domestically, he would emphasize "fine-tuning" the economy to maximize economic growth. Foreign policy clearly constituted his primary concern, but the repeated and inflated rhetoric of crisis conveyed little sense of how and where new departures would be made. Through it all, the overriding focus remained on image, words, style—the way one would do things, rather than what one would do. Yet style meant little without a substantive vision with goals and purposes. On the basis of all that had gone before, there was no assurance in January 1961 that John Kennedy had the capacity to develop such a vision.

The Kennedy Record

Looking back from the vantage point of the 1970s, British journalist Henry Fairlie described the Kennedy record on domestic policy as one of "absolute failure." Although that judgment is too harsh, particularly given Kennedy's legislative departures in 1963, it remains an essentially accurate assessment of Kennedy's first two years in office. Intimidated by the absence of a popular mandate, deferential and insecure in the face of the congressional power structure, and above all lacking an ideological viewpoint, Kennedy vacillated on the domestic front, hoarding his power for foreign policy ventures. Only in the late spring and summer of 1963 would he move forcefully to reverse the situation, and then only because of irresistible pressure from the civil rights movement.

Kennedy entered the White House profoundly wary of the constraints imposed by his narrow election victory. He had triumphed over Nixon by fewer than 113,000 votes out of more than 68 million cast. Although the Democrats had a two-thirds majority in the Senate and almost a one hundred vote edge in the House, the statistical superiority obscured the power of the conservative coalition of southern Democrats and Republicans. A far more accurate measure of liberal Democratic strength appeared in the House vote to enlarge the membership of the House Rules Committee—an effort to break the stranglehold over liberal legislation exercised by Virginia's reactionary Howard Smith. The Kennedy-backed reform squeaked through by a majority of only five votes, 217 to 212.

A more aggressive and venturesome president might have responded to the challenge by marshalling his allies, going over the heads of Congress to the public, and fighting steadfastly for a coherent program of change. But Kennedy lacked both the self-assurance and the sense of direction to pursue that path. Never a part of the congressional inner circle, he reacted with deference to the far older men who wielded power on Capitol Hill. Especially anxious to woo Southern support for his foreign policy, Kennedy repeatedly shied away from confronting his adversaries on domestic issues. As Joseph Kraft observed, "His motto might have been: no enemies to the right." From the perspective of some liberals, Kennedy was woefully lacking. "He could have tried to mobilize public opinion to support his convictions," one columnist observed. But Kennedy thought otherwise. "There is no sense in putting the office of the Presidency on the line . . . and then being defeated," he said.

As a result, Kennedy's legislative record for 1961 and 1962 proved mixed at best. In the tradition of Harry Truman, the president proposed an array of social programs including expansion of the minimum wage, health care for the aged, federal aid to education, increased Social Security benefits, creation of a cabinet-level Department of Housing and Urban Development (HUD), and allocation of funds to build up underdeveloped areas of the country. Some of these proposals were successful, including improvements in Social Security, expansion of the minimum wage, and passage of an Area Redevelopment Act and a Manpower Retraining Act. But even Kennedy's successes sometimes seemed like Pyrrhic victories. The final version of the minimum wage bill, for example, excluded 700,000 workers who needed assistance the most. In the meantime, Congress turned down Kennedy's tax reform proposals, vetoed the creation of a Department of Urban Affairs, rejected the president's request for stand-by authority to spend $2 billion on an antirecession public works program, and failed even to consider measures for migrant workers, youth employment, and assistance for public transportation.

No issue reflected liberal frustration more than the administration's failure to provide adequate leadership on federal aid to education. The centerpiece of the Democratic Party's platform of 1960, aid to education would have provided desperately needed federal dollars to help equalize educational opportunity throughout the country. But Kennedy vacillated, offering in one historian's words, only "inept guidance" to the bill. In a March 1961 press conference he created fatal confusion about his own position on the issue of federal funds for parochial schools, implying that some support for religiously affiliated institutions might be acceptable. From that point onward, the *New York Times'* Tom Wicker noted, Kennedy lost his capacity to provide leadership on the issue. Liberals viewed the president's position as timid and indecisive, undercutting any possibility of forging a majority coalition. Indeed, so far did Kennedy abandon the liberal platform of 1960 that tariff reduction became his primary legislative priority in 1962.

Not surprisingly, Kennedy found it easier to concentrate his attention on streamlining the economy. Convinced that rapid economic expansion offered the best vehicle for solving social problems as well as assuring a strong posture internationally, Kennedy hoped that through a combination of executive manipulations and legislation he could eliminate recessions, control inflation, and create the preconditions for sustained economic growth. During the Eisenhower years, the GNP had crept along at an average growth rate of 2.5 percent—a far cry from the Soviet Union's rate of 7 percent. Two recessions, plus an alarming increase in inflation at the end of the decade, signified the need for economic improvement. As much as anything else, it was this situation that informed Kennedy's repeated exhortation during the 1960 campaign that it was time to "get America moving again."

The person in charge of this economic agenda was Walter Heller, a University of Minnesota economist whom Kennedy named to chair the Council of Economic Advisors (CEA). From the moment he first met Kennedy in 1960, Heller preached the gospel of full employment through economic growth, controlled deficit spending, and the incentive of targeted tax cuts. "Ample employment opportunities," Heller wrote the president, "are basic requirements for making effective . . . the elimination of discrimination against certain groups of workers" and for "creating a higher standard of living." If the government could control inflation through pegging wage increases to productivity, and simultaneously encourage investment through tax policy, there was no reason, in Heller's eyes, to prevent the achievement of full employment and unbroken economic growth. Completely exemplifying the principles of the "liberal consensus," Heller saw no need for redistribution. Instead, the problems of "our less fortunate citizens" would be solved through fueling business expansion, increasing consumer spending through tax cuts, and evening out the economic cycle. Kennedy urged his CEA head to "use the White House as a pulpit for public education in economics," and Heller responded with alacrity, taking every occasion available to preach his economic message to civic and business groups outside the administration, as well as to political advisors within.

To a remarkable extent, Heller succeeded in his mission. During the first two years of the Kennedy administration, consumer cost increases were held to 1 percent, in contrast to a 3.4 percent rise in 1957. Skillfully, Heller and Kennedy pressured labor unions to accept wage contracts that called for an average hourly growth in earnings of only 3 percent a year—approximately the same level as productivity increases. Although Congress rejected the reform provisions of Kennedy's first tax bill, the Revenue Act of 1962 did encourage new investment and plant renovation through easier depreciation allowances and helped to promote a surge in economic growth.

Significantly, stability in the steel industry constituted the center-piece of the Kennedy-Heller economic strategy. "Steel bulks so large in the manufacturing sector of the economy," Heller wrote Kennedy in 1961, "that it can upset the price applecart all by itself." Looking back at the postwar years, the CEA head concluded that 40 percent of the increase in the wholesale price index from 1947 to 1958 could be traced to the fact that steel prices rose faster than other prices; stability in steel prices after 1958, in turn, led directly to the absence of inflation. According to Heller's estimates, the steel industry could continue to make profits equal to those of the previous fourteen years with no price increase whatsoever. Hence in the summer of 1961, he urged a coordinated effort by administration officials to influence both labor and management to arrive at a new contract that would permit the maintenance of price stability. When the steel union agreed in 1962 to a wage increase that would cost the companies only 2.5 percent—much more moderate than either the 1950 or 1955 contract— Kennedy officials were jubilant since the figure was less than the productivity increase to be expected during the period of the new contract.

Understandably, Kennedy was outraged when U.S. Steel and five other companies then announced a major price increase shortly after the new contract was announced. The action was a direct threat to the entire Kennedy economic policy, and thus the president responded with a degree of decisiveness and passion totally missing from his other pronouncements on domestic issues. Only on the space program, where Kennedy boldly announced that America would land a man on the moon "by the end of this decade," did the president evince comparable commitment. But space was as much a foreign policy issue as a domestic one.

In response to the steel industry's challenge, Kennedy galvanized all the resources of his administration. He denounced Roger Blough of U.S. Steel, ordered aides and cabinet members to contact other steel manufacturers to ask them to hold the line on prices, and threatened antitrust action against his enemies in the steel industry. In the urgency of the moment, an FBI agent even called steel officials in the middle of the night for information. "My father once told me that all steel men were sons-of-bitches," Kennedy was reported to have said, "and I did not realize until now how right he was." Kennedy was particularly angered by Blough's tactics. The steel magnate had walked into Kennedy's office and handed him a press release about the price increase, not even giving the president the courtesy of advance consultation. Feeling that his personal authority had been challenged, Kennedy responded as though the country were at war, creating a crisis atmosphere that ultimately forced the steel companies to retract their increases. While the president's anger was justified, perhaps the most significant aspect of his action was the fact that only on this issue—so crucial to his economic policy—did he mobilize all the forces of his administration on a question of domestic policy.*

The episode testified eloquently to the president's overall approach to domestic affairs. Challenged directly and personally in the one area he considered critical, he was capable of exercising his power aggressively and forcefully to uphold his position. The action only highlighted, however, the absence of similar commitment on other domestic issues. "We get awfully sick of this 'moderation,'" the columnist T.R.B. declared in the New Republic. "All during the Eisenhower administration there was moderation . . . and now instead of Kennedy urgency there is more moderation." Kennedy's hesitation to adopt a more activist stance had many explanations: his narrow electoral mandate, his primary commitment to foreign policy, political pragmatism, and the absence of a coherent vision for change. But whatever the reasons, the result was an acceptance of the status quo that dismayed lib-

---

* It should be noted that steel prices were permitted to rise—quickly—the next year.

eral critics. "The politics of our country have grown dangerously lopsided," journalist I. F. Stone wrote in early 1962. "There is a vocal extreme right. There is a center, which Mr. Kennedy pre-empted. There is no longer a left." The young president had mobilized substantial backing for his foreign policy positions but had refused to put his administration on the line over critical domestic issues—whether they be medicare, federal aid to education, or civil rights. "The only reason for a man to have a popularity rating of 75 percent," one observer noted, "is to bring it down to 72 percent when he does something he believes in." During the first two years of his administration, Kennedy evidently failed to find an issue on which he wished to "spend" that percentage of support. It would take the turmoil of protest from below before he finally discovered a domestic issue on which he was willing to risk his personal power.

Kennedy's Foreign Policy

Predictably, it was in the area of foreign policy that Kennedy most forcefully exhibited his penchant for activism. Here, the president was in charge. Despite the constraints potentially present in Congress's right to declare war, the commander-in-chief had a virtually unlimited range of options. From Truman's executive order to send troops to Korea to Eisenhower's order to land Marines on the beaches in Lebanon in 1958, precedent had been building for greater executive discretion in shaping America's response to her communist adversaries around the globe. Unlike Eisenhower, however, Kennedy eschewed the orderly and bureaucratic processes of making foreign policy decisions. Intentionally, he chose a secretary of state—Dean Rusk—who would serve as an obedient instrument for his own wishes, rather than as a decisive and independent figure in his own right. To Kennedy, the State Department—and all the bureaucracy it represented—was like a "bowl of jello." The way to get action was to orchestrate foreign policy from the White House itself, if need be from the Situation Room, where a few trusted aides could make rapid-fire decisions and implement them without being overly concerned with how various desk officers and their staffs at Foggy Bottom would respond. Activism was the watchword; a hard-hitting, informal team of advisors the vehicle for carrying it forward.

Because of his contempt for bureaucratic processes, Kennedy eagerly sought to cut through the "business as usual" pattern of the State and Defense departments. "The Kennedys had a romantic view of the possibilities of diplomacy," Arthur Schlesinger, Jr., later noted. "They wanted to replace protocol-minded, striped-pants officials by reform-minded missionaries of democracy who mixed with the people, spoke the native dialect, ate the food, and involved themselves in local struggles against ignorance and won." As Kennedy and his advisors saw it, imaginative departures from existing patterns of response constituted an indispensable prerequisite for combating Soviet aggression. "There is no true historical parallel to the drive of Soviet communist imperialism to colonialize the world," Robert Mc-Namara told the Armed Services Committee. Like the warring tribes of ancient history, the Russians "sought not merely conquest but the total obliteration of the enemy." To meet this threat, the United States would have to exhibit a boldness, a daring, and a degree of courage that also was unprecedented.

This commitment to innovation found many outlets, but most characteristic of the Kennedy mystique were the Peace Corps, on the one hand, and counterinsurgency, on the other. If America's fate rested on winning the "hearts and minds" of developing countries convulsed by nationalism, nothing would be more helpful than mobilizing the best of America's younger generation to work together with Third World people in achieving their own aspirations. First mentioned during the 1960 campaign, the idea of a Peace Corps fit perfectly with the view that America had a special moral mission to save the world. What could be more "American" than young people traversing the globe and living at subsistence pay in order to share their expertise with those attempting to catch up with the modern world. If nothing else, the plan represented a public relations coup, highlighting American idealism and selflessness. Almost immediately, hundreds of dedicated young people responded to the call, meeting the challenge of sacrifice on behalf of a higher, noble cause.

While the Peace Corps represented the benevolent side of Kennedy's commitment to activism, counterinsurgency embodied its more insidious dimensions. In January 1961, Nikita Khrushchev had proclaimed Soviet support for wars of national liberation all over the globe and then proceeded to boast of Russian success in such ventures. The best way to combat such a threat, Kennedy and his aides concluded, was to outperform the Soviets in the skills of infiltration, guerrilla warfare, and mobilization of indigenous nationalistic factions. Operating on the assumption that every local civil conflict was a manifestation of the larger global confrontation between the United States and the U.S.S.R., Kennedy envisioned elite fighting units like the Green Berets as winning "brush-fire" wars where traditional military units had no place. Just as the Peace Corps would recruit the best of America's young minds to wage the struggle for American superiority through education and technical expertise, the Special Forces would mobilize the most daring and tough-minded young soldiers to carry forward the military and political war against Soviet efforts to control movements for national liberation.

In this context, Vietnam became a laboratory in which to assess the potential of counterinsurgency. Although American involvement in the war there had many causes,* including the determination to use a show of strength in Southeast Asia as a counterpoint to Russian threats in Berlin and

* Vietnam will be dealt with at length in Chapters 9 and 10.

elsewhere, there could be no discounting the romantic appeal of trying out the new approach of counterinsurgency to win the struggle for "freedom" in the Third World. As American policymakers perceived it, the South Vietnamese were engaged in a valiant struggle to preserve their independence against external subversion. In such a situation, American expertise could decisively alter the balance of power and simultaneously deter Soviet aggression elsewhere by proving the efficacy of the Special Forces in combining military and political warfare. Hence, Kennedy urged that the best young officers be sent to Vietnam to see the new warfare at work and emphasized exposure to counterinsurgency as one criterion for promotion. As a result, Roswell Gilpatric of the Pentagon noted, "a lot of the more adventurous, innovative, imaginative types began to hone in on [the Indochinese War]" as an ideal spot to make their mark.

The danger of Kennedy's preferred style of foreign policy exploded for all the world to see in the Bay of Pigs operation in Cuba. Ironically, the Castro revolution against the Batista regime in Cuba represented, at its inception, the kind of democratic insurgency against totalitarian forces that Kennedy wished to identify with. But Castro had turned against the United States, had allied with the Soviet Union, and had become, as a result, a primary target of American hostility. According to the conventional wisdom at the time, Kennedy inherited a plan conceived by the Eisenhower administration to topple the Castro regime. Faced with a virtual fait accompli, Kennedy allegedly felt duty-bound to proceed, unwilling to accept the political consequences of vetoing a plan already approved by his illustrious military predecessor. According to this version, Kennedy benefited enormously from the lessons learned in the disastrous failure of the Bay of Pigs and, subsequently, became far more skeptical of the advice given him by military and intelligence officials.

In fact, the evidence suggests that Kennedy embraced the CIA plan for Castro's overthrow enthusiastically, and through his own preference for avoiding bureaucratic channels, actually contributed significantly to the final debacle. Richard Bissell, the architect of the plot to overthrow Castro, found in Kennedy a kindred spirit. Bissell's desire to circumvent the military and the State Department, Garry Wills has observed, "embodied the ideals of the new administration." Kennedy wanted action and soon discovered that the CIA was the place to go. An instant rapport developed between the two men, both committed to cutting through bureaucratic channels. As Bissell conceived the plan, the CIA would mount a classic guerrilla operation, using clandestine radio transmitters to mobilize a popular revolt against Castro in Cuba itself, while training and deploying Cuban exiles to establish an invasion beachhead that would eventually hook up with anti-Castro "freedom fighters" in Cuba. There thus ensued a vicious cycle. The radio propaganda, though generated from the United States, was used as evidence of widespread dissension against Castro in Cuba, fueling optimism that the plan would inevitably succeed, even among those who knew where the propaganda came from. The CIA's successful venture against Jacobo Arbenz in Guatemala in 1954 provided critical additional evidence, if any was needed, that such a plot could achieve its objectives, notwithstanding the fact that Arbenz had far less support than Castro. Having already agreed to exclude most relevant government officials from participation in the venture, Kennedy received little negative feedback and became a victim of the process he himself had initiated.

In retrospect, the entire venture appears to have been doomed from the start. As Wills has noted, "it was a military operation run *without* the military's control"—something Eisenhower would never have permitted. Convinced that the subterranean operation would lead to a lightning coup against Castro, Kennedy appeared unconcerned when the Joint Chiefs of Staff concluded that the chances for a successful invasion were only "fair"— a term which, in the military's mind, meant that the prospects for success were 30 for, 70 against. "The truth is," Wills has written, "that Kennedy went ahead with the Cuban action, not to complete what he had inherited from Eisenhower, but to mark his difference from Eisenhower. He would not process things through the military channels, let them penetrate Bissell's secrecy. He would be bold where he had accused Eisenhower of timidity. . . . In all this, he was the prisoner of his own rhetoric."

The rest, of course, is history. By the time the landings took place, Castro was fully aware of the invasion plan. There were no domestic insurgents against Castro ready to rise up inside of Cuba. In the meantime, Kennedy— a captive of his illusions—insisted that the exile army land at night in an obscure spot. When it became clear that the invasion force had no chance of success without large-scale American air support, Kennedy finally pulled back, unwilling to transform what he had envisioned as sophisticated subversion into an American military operation. In short, the very methods Kennedy had celebrated as vehicles for inaugurating a bold and dramatic new foreign policy became primary instruments of his own humiliation. The only appropriate course for him to have taken, General Maxwell Taylor later concluded, was to cancel the entire Bay of Pigs operation before it began because it had never cleared proper channels of review and consultation.*

Perhaps the most disastrous consequence of the Bay of Pigs, however, was that Kennedy failed to learn the lesson. Instead, those who had warned against the invasion before it happened, or who expressed concern afterward, were castigated as "soft," unmanly, and not tough enough to be counted on in a crunch. "That yellow-bellied friend of yours, Chester Bowles, is leaking all over town that he was against [the invasion]," Kennedy's press secretary Pierre Salinger told Harris Wofford. "We're going to get him." Shortly thereafter, Bowles was relieved as under-secretary of state and ap-

---

* Clayton Fritchie, a staff member of Adlai Stevenson at the United Nations, was perhaps most accurate in his assessment. "It could have been worse," he told the president. "It might have succeeded."

pointed to the honorific position of ambassador-at-large. Other critics received the presidential freeze, learning quickly that, if they were to retain their positions, the best course was to "grab their nuts" and be loyal. Far from questioning counterinsurgency, Kennedy and his chief aides redoubled their enthusiasm, blaming the innocent bystanders—the "bureaucracy"—rather than themselves for the disaster. The solution was not to reverse standard operating procedures, but to rely even more on the ad hoc crisis team. Indirectly, at least, Kennedy even appears to have given renewed support for plans to assassinate Castro.

Nor did the aura of crisis diminish in the aftermath of the Bay of Pigs. If anything, it intensified. In late April, the president went on national television, armed with charts, to warn of the impending possibility that American troops might have to be sent to Laos, although on this occasion Kennedy wisely chose negotiations over military action. When the president journeyed to Vienna in June to meet Nikita Khrushchev, the Soviet Leader's hard-line position on Berlin provoked the president into an even more belligerent response. Seemingly insecure and intimidated in his first bout at the summit, Kennedy returned to warn the nation of even more crises ahead. He called up reserve units of the Army, asked for a substantial increase in military appropriations, and in a gesture designed to mobilize popular sentiment, urged American citizens to embark on an all-out effort to build nuclear fall-out shelters. By the end of the summer, *Life* magazine was suggesting—with Kennedy's approval—that Americans could survive nuclear war, and even portrayed a happy family, living in near vacation splendor, in its underground shelter. By the fall, the Berlin crisis had been defused—largely because Khrushchev abandoned his call for a separate peace treaty with East Germany—but in the meantime, the Berlin Wall had been built, and both superpowers had announced their intention to resume the testing of nuclear weapons.

No crisis, however, could match in severity the confrontation that occurred a year later when the Soviet Union began to install intermediate-range ballistic missiles (IRBMs) in Cuba, ninety miles from America's shores. Throughout the preceding months, Republicans had been criticizing the administration for tolerating a Soviet buildup in Cuba. Kennedy had responded with the explicit assurance that the United States would accept only "defensive" additions to the Cuban arsenal. Now, intelligence photographs clearly indicated the rapid construction of missile sites for "offensive" IRBMs. In secret, Kennedy mobilized an Executive Committee—dubbed the Ex-Com—to pore over the intelligence data and devise recommendations for action, all the while giving the appearance of business as usual. Members of the Ex-Com kept their social engagements and rode to White House meetings sitting on each other's laps, lest reporters start speculating about a crisis because of all the limousines entering the White House driveway. The president himself, meanwhile, continued his normal schedule, dropping in and out of the Ex-Com's deliberations.

John F. Kennedy warning of the dangers of military confrontation if a peaceful settlement could not be found in Laos. *(National Archives)*

Kennedy's informal group of advisors outlined a series of options. The military urged a full-scale invasion to seize the entire island of Cuba and eliminate Castro's rule forever. Others advocated a surgical air strike that would knock out the missiles. Still others broached the possibility of private negotiation with either Castro or the Russians. Nearly everyone agreed that something had to be done, with the primary debate focusing on whether to pursue public as opposed to private avenues of discussion, and whether to take active and overt military measures as opposed to more passive steps such as a blockade. During a previously scheduled meeting at the White House between Soviet Foreign Minister Andrei Gromyko and the president, neither participant raised the issue. As time ran out before the actual deployment of the missiles, it became more and more evident that the response—whatever it would be—would take a public form.

During the early days of discussions, the vast majority of Ex-Com members rallied behind proposals for direct military action. Although many were not prepared to back a full-scale invasion, as favored by the Joint Chiefs of Staff, most supported a general air strike on the island. Only the dissent of Robert Kennedy blocked the idea. "I now know how Tojo felt when he was planning Pearl Harbor," the attorney general declared. Were the United States to pursue such a course, he argued, America's moral position in the world would be destroyed. In addition, Russian troops would be killed, almost certainly forcing a military response from the Kremlin. Gradually, a new consensus formed around the idea of a quarantine—legalistically distinct from a "blockade" which international law viewed as an act of war—to prevent Soviet ships from entering Cuban waters with the missiles themselves. The idea made abundant sense. While demonstrating American determination to stop the missile buildup, it would also buy time, allowing the U.S.S.R. to back down from the confrontation.

In a nationwide TV address, the president disclosed his decision to a startled world. Soviet actions, he declared, were totally unprovoked—an "unjustified change in the status quo which cannot be accepted by this country, if our courage and our commitments are ever to be trusted again either by friend or foe." Throwing down the gauntlet, Kennedy gave the Kremlin an ultimatum that the missiles must be removed. All over the world, people responded with alarm. The terrifying moment had come that everyone had always feared—direct confrontation between the two superpowers that could result in total nuclear devastation. In those cities within range of the IRBMs, Americans examined road maps, trying to find a route of escape they could pursue in advance of the missile launchings. The tension increased when Khrushchev denounced the quarantine as "outright banditry" and accused Kennedy of driving the world "to the abyss" of nuclear war. In New York, a Soviet delegate to the United Nations told a friend that "this could well be our last conversation."

Over the next few days, the world teetered on the brink of catastrophe. Although Russian ships stopped dead in the water, refusing to challenge the quarantine zone, pressure mounted for a military response. A glimmer of hope appeared five days after the crisis began, when a Soviet security official went to ABC news correspondent John Scali and proposed that the Russians remove their missiles in return for a U.S. pledge not to invade Cuba. The same day, Kennedy received a rambling, incoherent message from Khrushchev embodying the same proposal. But tensions heightened again as a Soviet ship with missiles aboard resumed its journey toward Cuba, and the Russians began to destroy classified documents at the United Nations. The next day Khrushchev sent a second note demanding that the United States withdraw its missiles in Turkey as a price for a peaceful solution in Cuba. It was, State Department's Roger Hilsman later said, "the blackest hour of the crisis." When a U-2 reconnaissance plane was shot down over Cuba, the Ex-Com was ready to strike at the Cuban missiles in retaliation.

At that point, we now know, President Kennedy himself interceded decisively. While virtually every other advisor recommended invasion and an air strike—which would almost certainly have brought military conflict with the USSR—Kennedy insisted that such action would be disastrous, especially in light of Khrushchev's "reasonable" offer to trade his missiles in Cuba for U.S. missiles in Turkey. Why invade Cuba, Kennedy asked, with the potential loss of millions of lives, "when we could have gotten [the same result] by making a deal on the missiles in Turkey." Initially the only voice resisting the rising demand for military action, Kennedy eventually won enough support to at least delay the invasion until more diplomatic efforts could occur.

In the meantime, Robert Kennedy made the critical suggestion that the president accept Khrushchev's *first* letter as a basis for agreement and ignore the second one. Khrushchev responded positively, pledging to remove the missiles under U.N. inspection in return for America's promise not to invade Cuba. *In an additional secret understanding reflecting J.F.K.'s views and his brother Robert's back-channel conversations with Soviet Ambassador Anatoly Dobrynin,* the United States also agreed to pull its missiles out of Turkey within five months. The two leaders exchanged public statements of conciliation and, for the first time in over a week, the world breathed easily.

Almost immediately, Kennedy was praised for the consummate brilliance with which he had managed the conflict. If the president did nothing else, Prime Minister Harold Macmillan of Great Britain observed, he would achieve greatness in history because of his skill in orchestrating the crisis. "It was a combination of toughness and restraint," Arthur Schlesinger, Jr., later wrote, "of will, nerve, and wisdom, so matchlessly calibrated, that [it] dazzled the world." In the most instransigent and dangerous crisis of postwar history, Kennedy had proven equal to the task.

Yet such praise seemed overstated in light of subsequent analysis about the missile crisis. First, Kennedy was disingenuous in his claim that placement of the missiles in Cuba was unprovoked. In fact, ever since the Bay of Pigs, the United States had continued to pose a significant threat to Castro's regime. Previously classified documents have revealed that the United States had moved ammunition and aircraft into position to attack Cuba *before* missile launching sites were discovered. "It is perfectly clear, now," Robert McNamara said in 1987, "that Cuban and Soviet leaders at that time believed the U.S. was intending to invade Cuba," and that therefore, deployment of missiles could be construed as an effort to protect Castro against attack rather than as an attempt to alter the balance of power in the world. Second, it was by no means clear at the time—or since—that the missiles would, in reality, have shifted the balance of power. "It makes no great difference," Secretary of Defense Robert McNamara noted, "whether you're killed by a missile fired from the Soviet Union or from Cuba. . . . A missile is a missile." Supporting McNamara, Roswell Gilpatric later observed that, "in fact, the military equation . . . was not altered."

Perhaps most important, Kennedy excluded private diplomatic negotiations as a vehicle for settling the crisis. If Gromyko had been shown the pictures of the missiles and the issue had been discussed first through diplomatic channels, there might conceivably have been a private settlement. By following this course, the terrible danger of exchanging public ultimatums could have been averted, with the option of "going public" still available if secret negotiations failed. As it was, the president chose, in Walter Lippman's words, "to suspend diplomacy," taking the enormous risk that the Soviets might refuse to back down and publicly accept humiliation. "If Khrushchev wants to rub my nose in the dirt, it's all over," Kennedy said.

In retrospect, it is clear that were it not for Robert Kennedy's conscience, John Kennedy's own belated skepticism about military force, and Nikita Khruschev's restraint, the world could easily have been destroyed. The president himself deserved substantial credit for taking his brother's advice against immediately bombing Cuba when the missiles were discovered, and for ruling out retaliation when America's U-2 spy plane was shot down and his advisors pressed for an attack. Khrushchev's own common sense in seeking a way out, first suggested to ABC's John Scali, proved to be an equally critical element on the other side. When all is said and done, however, it seems that the Kennedy administration had risked ultimate disaster in service to a crisis that was more illusory than real, at least in military terms. The key issue, Kennedy later noted, was that the missiles "would have *appeared* to [change the balance of power], and appearances contribute to reality." But that made the issue as much one of image as of substance. Although Kennedy's own temperateness and wisdom *during* the crisis had helped prevent a nuclear holocaust, his actions and rhetoric had helped precipitate it in the first place. As one historian has asked, "What . . . would have happened if Khrushchev had not backed down?" The question is terrifying.

Nevertheless, the Kennedy "victory" in the missile crisis may well have proved to be the critical event of his presidency. If throughout his career a concern with appearing "tough" and manly had been a dominant theme, the missile crisis allowed him to both show his mettle *and recognize the dangers of being too "manly."* The shrill rhetoric of crisis that had permeated his presidential campaign and the early years as president had always seemed to obscure an underlying insecurity, as though inflated words were necessary to reassure others—and perhaps himself—that he could handle any eventuality. Now, he had survived—barely—the ultimate test. If nothing else, the missile crisis may have wiped clean the slate, creating a foundation for genuine wisdom and restraint, and for charting a course that involved the substance of leadership and vision, rather than just the image.

On another front, the space age had officially begun when the Soviets launched the world's first artificial satellite, Sputnik, on October 4, 1957. Almost exactly a year later, on October 1, 1958, NASA was formed in response. NASA's charter declared that it "is the policy of the United States that activities in space should be devoted to peaceful purposes for the benefit of all mankind." Nine years later, 60 nations, among them the United States, signed a pledge to use space only for peaceful endeavors. The American development of rocket technology was initially based on captured German V-2 rockets used in World War II, but it soon followed its own path with Aerobee and Viking rockets. In 1958 NASA started the space race by successfully launching Explorer I, followed by Vanguard. But in 1961 the Soviets once more moved a step ahead of the Americans—Yuri Gagarin in

Vostok I became the first person to orbit the earth and return safely. President Kennedy immediately responded. He declared that the Americans would be the first to send a man to the moon before 1970. The Mercury and Gemini projects were the first American efforts to learn whether man could survive in space. The Apollo program finally yielded success when Apollo 11 put humans on the lunar surface in 1969. But soon after the moon landing, public and congressional support for the space program declined sharply.

The Year of Promise

During 1963, John F. Kennedy became, in many ways, a different president than he had been in 1961 and 1962. As the civil rights movement continued to intensify, Kennedy found himself forced to endorse the demands for change swelling from below. Simultaneously, the ethical thrust of the civil rights struggle and the increasing sensitivity of presidential advisors to the economic plight of the poor propelled Kennedy into a far more activist stance on behalf of those Americans bound by the chains of poverty. In foreign policy, meanwhile, the new self-confidence generated as a result of the Cuban missile crisis led to major initiatives for relaxation of tensions with Russia, culminating in the atomic test ban treaty of August 1963. In a career characterized up to that point by moderation at home and Cold War attitudes abroad, such changes seemed dramatic.

No one could ever accuse John Kennedy of having been ahead of his time on civil rights. Through most of his years in the House and Senate, Kennedy appeared oblivious to the issue of racial inequality. When the Senate was considering the 1957 Civil Rights Bill, Kennedy voted "wrong" on two critical roll calls—one sending the bill to the conservative-dominated Judiciary Committee, the other supporting a jury trial amendment which would substantially diminish chances of gaining convictions of white Southerners who violated black civil rights. Only after it became clear that a presidential candidacy was in the offing did Kennedy seek advisors with strong connections to the black community. Even then, most of these were white. "They were [okay]," a black associate later said, "but [they did not know] much at the time about civil rights." Kennedy seemed as intent on winning endorsements from outright segregationists like Governor John Patterson of Alabama as in cultivating black support. Thus, while he advocated compliance with the Supreme Court's desegregation order during a speech-making trip in the Deep South, he was correctly perceived by most Southern political leaders as a moderate on the issue, far less dangerous than Humphrey or Stuart Symington.*

* Kennedy, for example, resisted attending an NAACP dinner in the late fifties because, he believed, it was too obvious a ploy to seek black votes.

Nevertheless, once the Democratic nomination had been won, it became imperative for Kennedy to reach out for black support. Ever since the 1948 election, black votes in the key industrial states of California, Illinois, Michigan, New York, Ohio, and Pennsylvania had assumed decisive importance, with one study estimating that blacks held the balance of power in 61 congressional districts in 21 northern and western states. In a brilliant memorandum to the Kennedy campaign staff, Marjorie Lawson, a black Kennedy advisor, urged the candidate to take explicit steps to overcome the negative image that his past record had generated in many segments of the black community. "Somehow," she wrote, "some warmth has to be added to this image of intellectual liberalism." In particular, she urged Kennedy to pay heed to the new protest movement and its commitment to the protection of basic human rights. "The candidate who wins [blacks]," she said, "will be the one who is most able to make them feel, not only that he understands, but that he cares about human dignity. . . . Nothing short of a *national gesture* will erase the doubts [that now exist] in the minds of rank and file Negro voters."*

With shrewdness and skill, Kennedy took the advice and set out to woo those he had previously ignored. Kennedy both embraced proposals for new civil rights legislation and attacked Eisenhower for having failed to provide executive leadership in enforcing existing legislation. With a "virtual stroke of the pen," Kennedy promised he would abolish racial discrimination in federally aided housing by executive order. But the real coup came when Martin Luther King, Jr., was arrested and sentenced to two months of hard labor in a Georgia prison camp. King's family was gripped by the fear that he would never emerge alive. Millions of other blacks shared the same apprehension. At that moment, candidate Kennedy called Mrs. King to express his concern and ask if there was anything he could do. Simultaneously, his brother Robert contacted the local judge, suggesting—successfully— King's immediate release. Nixon did nothing. Almost overnight, black sentiment swung overwhelmingly in Kennedy's favor. He had, in effect, found the "bold, national gesture," urged by Mrs. Lawson, that would convey to black Americans the gut feeling that he had "genuine concern about [blacks] as people." Reverend Martin Luther King, Sr., who had previously endorsed Nixon because of deep suspicions about Kennedy's Catholicism, dramatically announced that he had seen the light, and that the Lord had found in John Kennedy an instrument for His will. On election day, Kennedy reaped the harvest, his thin margin of victory almost certainly shaped by the last-minute move to his candidacy of black voters grateful for Kennedy's intervention on behalf of their leader.

---

* The same memorandum urged Kennedy to establish close ties with people like Harry Belafonte and Sydney Poitier, to recruit a black reporter as a press aide (Carl Rowan was suggested), and to organize systematic contacts, both through personal appearances and through campaign aides, with major black organizations. Virtually all these suggestions were taken and proved crucial.

Yet on assuming office, Kennedy refused to live up to campaign promises. Urged to give moral direction to the nation through a new emancipation proclamation, Kennedy preferred to keep silent. Sarcastically, he asked which staff members had authored the ill-fated phrase promising to end housing discrimination "with a stroke of a pen." Even after civil rights advocates deluged the White House with ballpoint pens, Kennedy refused to sign the order until November 1962, claiming that precipitate action would sabotage his effort to appoint Robert Weaver, a black man, as head of a new cabinet-level position of urban affairs. There was always an excuse, most often connected to a desire to avoid divisive issues that might interfere with mobilizing a foreign policy consensus. Thus, Kennedy backed away from ordering the integration of the National Guard lest he offend the Southern chairmen of the Armed Services Committees in the House and Senate. When the child of an African ambassador was refused a glass of water in a Maryland restaurant, Kennedy condemned the insult publicly but, in private, wondered aloud why African ambassadors did not simply avoid Route 40 and fly from New York to Washington. While liberals in the House and Senate fulfilled the 1960 Democratic platform pledge to introduce new civil rights legislation, the administration offered only nominal support, refusing to spend any of its political credit for such measures. When challenged on these failures, the president invariably responded that existing legislation was sufficient, and that the real test rested with executive enforcement and the policies of the Justice Department.

Robert Kennedy proved somewhat more responsive than his older brother to the issue of civil rights. Although he later confessed that he had never lain awake at night thinking about civil rights before becoming attorney general, Robert Kennedy was a stickler about law enforcement and was outraged at the failure of the Justice Department to implement existing legislation on voting rights. He surrounded himself at the Justice Department with aides like Burke Marshall and John Doar who shared his conviction that a major new effort at civil rights enforcement was required. By the end of his first year as attorney general, Kennedy had initiated fourteen new court suits on voting rights, had increased the number of black staff members at the Justice Department from ten to fifty, had nominated two Negro district judges, one for the U.S. Circuit Court of Appeals, and had petitioned the Interstate Commerce Commission to desegregate all public accommodations affecting travel across state lines. By May of 1963, the Justice Department had become involved in voting rights issues in 145 Southern counties—nearly a 500 percent increase over the 30 counties subject to federal intervention in 1960. Justice Department attorneys also appeared as "friends of the court" in numerous lawsuits involving employment discrimination, police brutality, desegregation of hospitals, and efforts to reverse the convictions of sit-in demonstrators. Clearly, a posture far different from that of the Eisenhower administration had come into being. Nevertheless, Kennedy and his aides worked strictly within a narrow interpretation of the law and attempted to use persuasion rather than coercion, working closely with Southern law enforcement officials who—as often as not—were part of the problem rather than the solution.

The ambivalent relationship of the Kennedy Justice Department to the civil rights movement was perhaps best manifested during the Freedom Rides in the spring of 1961. So little contact did the Justice Department have with civil rights leaders at the time that Kennedy and his aides knew nothing about the Freedom Rides until they saw a CORE leaflet announcing them. Once the rides began, however, the Attorney General personally took charge of federal efforts to see that the Freedom Riders reached their destination. In endless conversations with the bus company, local law enforcement officials, and the governors of Alabama and Mississippi, Robert Kennedy attempted to guarantee protection for the Riders. "After all," he said in one phone call, "these people have tickets and are entitled to transportation. . . . I am—the government is—going to be very much upset if this group does not get to continue their trip." Initially, Kennedy appeared willing to accept assurances that state authorities could handle the situation. But then came the fire-bombing of the Freedom Riders' bus in Anniston, Alabama, brutal beatings in Montgomery, and the all-night siege of the Freedom Riders and their supporters in a black Baptist Church in Montgomery. The brutal assault on Kennedy's own representative on the scene, John Siegenthaler, finally persuaded Kennedy that the word of Southern law enforcement officials could not be trusted and that federal marshals must be sent. Despite all the promises of Governor John Patterson, Robert Kennedy noted, "twelve hours later Mr. Siegenthaler was lying unconscious on a street in Montgomery. . . . I am therefore not quite so impressed with these words of assurance as I might otherwise be." When the Freedom Riders arrived in Montgomery, not a single city or state policeman was present, despite ample advance notice of when the bus would arrive. The attorney general was appalled when officials in Alabama and Mississippi declared that these "twelve wild-eyed radicals" did not deserve protection.

On the other hand, Robert Kennedy's sympathy did not extend to the demonstrators themselves. While he responded with passion and intensity to the need to protect the physical safety and legal rights of those seeking to travel across the South, he seems to have suffered few qualms when Mississippi law enforcement officials in Jackson prevented violence by simply arresting the Freedom Riders and sending them off to jail. Indeed, the other side of Kennedy's involvement in the demonstrations was his concerted effort to get the protests called off. "This is too much!" Robert Kennedy told Harris Wofford, President Kennedy's civil rights advisor in the White House. "I wonder whether [the Freedom Riders] have the best interest of their country at heart. Do you know that one of them is against the atom bomb—yes, he even picketed against it in jail! The President is going abroad and this is all embarrassing him." The attorney general appeared to believe that his own gradualist policy of litigation offered the only acceptable response to America's civil rights crisis, and that he alone should define the appropriate line between protest and accommodation. From this perspective, civil rights demonstrators were creating disorder and chaos, and in the process impairing the image of the country and the president abroad.

Still attempting to control the civil rights movement from above, Robert Kennedy proposed a "cooling-off period" in civil rights demonstrations and the pursuit of less provocative civil rights actions within the framework of existing law. Working behind the scenes with civil rights leaders and New York foundations, the attorney general suggested that young people committed to civil rights should embark on a massive voter education project, seeking to achieve their goals through registering black people to vote so that they could operate within the established political process. (Ironically, as it would turn out, Kennedy seemed to conceive of voter registration as a "neutral" and peaceful activity that would encounter little resistance from Southern law enforcement officials.) Indeed, he and his aides assured civil rights leaders that if they pursued such a course of action, the federal government would guarantee protection to civil rights workers in the field as they implemented the Voter Education Project. Despite considerable disquiet, especially among SNCC workers, at accepting this effort from above to direct the focus of their activities, the civil rights coalition determined to give the administration a chance, particularly in light of Kennedy's assurances that federal authority would be invoked wherever necessary to provide security for voter registration workers.

Unhappily, Kennedy once again defaulted on his promise. As courageous blacks entered southwest Georgia and the Delta counties of Alabama and Mississippi to educate prospective voters on their rights as citizens, violence greeted them at every turn. In Georgia, four black churches were firebombed after being used as voter registration centers. Sharecroppers and tenant farmers who dared to exercise their basic rights were evicted from the land. Merchants cut off credit, cars followed civil rights workers at night, and beatings occurred constantly. Civil rights workers were assaulted and shot at—systematically, often openly, frequently by law enforcement officials themselves. And through it all, in virtually every case, federal authorities did nothing. Instead of intervening to provide protection, FBI officials stood aside, simply taking notes on the violence and intimidation which greeted voter registration applicants. Only in Greenwood, Mississippi, did the Justice Department file immediate suit to alleviate the situation. Although federal attorneys would later argue that FBI agents were simply doing their job, accumulating information for subsequent legal action, such rationales carried little weight with civil rights workers living on the edge of terror.

For those who believed they had been guaranteed federal protection, the administration's record amounted to outright betrayal. Promises had been made, and then broken. The president's executive order on housing had been promulgated only after an extensive "Ink for Jack" campaign. As early as October 1962, one black newspaper editor concluded that liberals had used up all their credit. It was time, she wrote, to bid them "a fond farewell with thanks for services rendered, until [they] are ready to re-enlist as foot soldiers and subordinates in a Negro-led, Negro-officered army, under the banner of Freedom Now." Even Kennedy's own black campaign aides were disillusioned. Negroes were tired of hearing that "the time is not ripe for a civil rights fight," Louis Martin wrote to Ted Sorensen. "Most Negroes know that the time has never been ripe and perhaps feel that the time will never be ripe." Black leaders could not sustain credibility with their people, Martin explained, "because the pressure for social change comes from the bottom in Negro life." Although Kennedy might cite political obstacles and legislative logjams as restraining forces, Martin concluded, "it has been my experience that the public will accept with more favor a batter who strikes out swinging with all his might than a batter who takes the strikes with his bat on his shoulders."

In almost every respect, the black critique of the Kennedy adminstration record in 1961 and 1962 was on target. When the authority of the federal government was directly challenged, the Kennedy administration responded. In 1961, it sent federal marshals to Montgomery to ensure the safety of the Freedom Riders, and in the fall of 1962, it mobilized federal troops and marshals to guarantee the admission of James Meredith to the all-white University of Mississippi against the defiance of Governor Ross Barnett. But these measures were reactive, coming only after extensive federal efforts to work with local white Southern officials. Despite verbal encouragement, the administration exhibited little support for civil rights workers themselves. To be sure, in its litigation policy, the Justice Department had advanced light years beyond the Eisenhower administration. But the results were far from adequate.* Martin Luther King, Jr., trenchantly summed up the administration's record when he wrote that "if tokenism were the goal, the administration [has moved] us adroitly toward it."

Most distressing of all was the continued absence of any sense of moral outrage about the country's most pressing domestic crisis. During his first two years in office, President Kennedy continued to put civil rights on a back burner while emphasizing foreign policy. The absence of a sense of urgency at the White House was succinctly embodied in the letter of resignation sent by Harris Wofford, Kennedy's civil rights advisor, as he left in March 1962 to join the administration of the Peace Corps. "You should understand," Wofford wrote Kennedy,

> why the larger problem of our integration in this new world represented by Africa interests me, as it does you, more than dealing with the albeit important remaining *rear-guard actions* on the domesic front.

* In addition, the Kennedy administration's successful effort to appoint more blacks to high-level positions was marred by its acquiescence in the appointment of a number of segregationist judges in the Deep South—judges who would become the bane of civil rights litigants for years to come.

Written thirteen months before the Birmingham demonstration, eighteen months before the March on Washington, twenty-four months before Mississippi's Freedom Summer, the letter spoke worlds about the reigning assumptions in the Kennedy White House. For all too many people, civil rights was still a "rear-guard action" even at the moment when black demonstrations were, in King's words, moving from "sporadic, limited actions to broad-scale activities different in kind and degree from anything done in the past."

It was not until 1963 that the Kennedy White House finally heard the message. The new year brought growing frustration in the black community and an increasing intensification of civil rights demonstrations. In Georgia, Alabama, Mississippi, North Carolina, and Florida, blacks took to the streets once again, angry at the refusal of the federal government to act and intent on breaking down, through the force of their own moral commitment, the barriers to equal treatment. "Freedom Now" rang like a clarion call throughout the region. Unavoidably, federal involvement intensified, with memoranda flooding the Justice Department and the White House as one flash point after another exploded.

Nowhere was the crisis greater than Alabama. Led by Reverend Fred Shuttlesworth, the Birmingham civil rights movement had long struggled, through behind-the-scenes negotiation, to loosen the bonds constraining black citizens in America's most segregated and repressive city. Now, Martin Luther King, Jr., and SCLC determined to make Birmingham the Gettysburg of America's new civil war. Mobilizing the black citizenry, King led silent marches through the city to demand that blacks have equal access to public accommodations and to petition the city's corporate leaders for policies that could provide Negroes decent jobs. Confronted by the terror of Bull Connor's police, civil rights demonstrators fought back, with young children joining their parents and elders in the demand for freedom. Refusing to accept even minimal standards of decency and restraint, Connor unleashed massive repression, blasting the demonstrators with fire hoses and siccing vicious police dogs against women and children. The entire nation was transfixed as it witnessed on nightly TV the force of naked racism. "A newspaper or television picture of a snarling police dog set upon a human being," CBS commentator Eric Severaid wrote, "is recorded in the permanent photoelectric file of every human brain."

The Kennedy administration responded with unprecedented pressure on Birmingham's political and economic leadership. Galvanizing cabinet and subcabinet officials, the Kennedys attempted to contact every powerful business official with whom they had any political leverage to urge support of a negotiated settlement. Working behind the scenes, Justice Department officials carried on delicate discussions between civil rights leaders and business officials that finally resulted in a compromise agreement. But even then, the crisis intensified, with Birmingham's mayor denouncing white negotiators as "a bunch of gutless traitors." Birmingham's white reactionaries meanwhile—encouraged by Bull Connor—resorted to bombings, fires, and rioting to disrupt any possibility of permanent progress.

The crisis worsened further when Alabama's governor, George Wallace, refused to admit two black students to the University of Alabama in Tuscaloosa. Flaunting his defiance of a federal court order, Wallace pledged to "stand in the door" and forcibly block the entry of the black students. Afraid that Wallace meant exactly what he said, Kennedy ordered the mobilization of federal troops for deployment at Tuscaloosa if necessary, while having the Justice Department coordinate a massive campaign to enlist the aid of Alabama's business leaders on behalf of compliance with the federal judicial decree.

In the midst of all this, Robert Kennedy met with James Baldwin and twelve other black leaders in New York City. More a confrontation than a conversation, the encounter shocked and stunned Kennedy. Never before had he experienced, firsthand, the depth and intensity of black alienation. While Kennedy counseled patience and pointed to the Justice Department's legal initiatives on behalf of black civil rights, Baldwin, Kenneth Clark, and others vented their rage at white insensitivity and inaction in the face of the brutal beatings and insufferable harassment that were daily fare for civil rights workers. How, they asked, could Kennedy be so smug and self-congratulatory when churches were being firebombed and civil rights workers shot at while federal agents claimed they had no authority to intervene. No longer, Baldwin declared, would black Americans accept white dictation of the pace and substance of progress on civil rights. Although Kennedy's first response was to resent deeply the attack on his own and his brother's integrity, the meeting ultimately helped to generate a new and clearer sense of the dimensions of the crisis and the urgency of a substantive federal response.

By the end of May, events rapidly came to a head. Both Robert and President Kennedy met almost daily at the White House with members of the National Retail Merchants Association, national hotel chains, drug companies, and restaurants, urging them to place pressure on their Southern outlets to desegregate. The combination of leverage from above and mass protest from below began to produce results as cities throughout the South chose desegregation as the only alternative to even greater disruption. The president kept up the pressure, sending letters praising those who had proceeded with integration and using public speeches to urge the nay-sayers to come along. In the meantime, with Governor Wallace pledging to stand in the door "today, tomorrow, forever" to prevent desegregation of the University of Alabama, the administration federalized the Alabama National Guard and prepared to enforce the desegregation order of the courts.

It was at that moment that Kennedy chose—at long last—to go before America and to place himself, for the first time, solidly on the side of those leading the civil rights protests. In a speech delivered largely extemporaneously because the text had not been completed by the time he went on the air, Kennedy told the American people that civil rights was above all "a moral issue . . . as old as the scriptures and . . . as clear as the American Constitution." America, Kennedy declared, had been founded "on the principle that all men are created equal, and that the rights of every man are diminished when the rights of one man are threatened." It should be possible, he said,

> for American students of any color to attend any public institution without having to be backed up by troops. It ought to be possible for American consumers of any color to receive equal service in places of public accommodation, such as hotels and restaurants . . . without being forced to resort to demonstrations in the street, and it ought to be possible for American citizens of any color to register and to vote in a free election without interference or fear of reprisal. . . . But this is not the case. . . . We preach freedom around the world, and we mean it, and we cherish it here at home, but are we to say to the world, and much more importantly, to each other that this is the land of the free except for the Negroes; that we have no second class citizens except Negroes, that we have no class or caste system, no ghettoes, no master race except with respect to Negroes?

With a passion he had rarely shown before, Kennedy asked his audience: "Who among us would be content to have the color of his skin changed and stand in [the Negro's] place? Who among us would then be content with the counsels of patience and delay?" The time had come, Kennedy declared, for "the nation to fulfill its promise. . . . A great change is at hand, and our task, our obligation, is to make that revolution, that change, peaceful and constructive for all."

Although late in coming, the president had offered a ringing endorsement of almost every basic demand pressed by civil rights activists. For many, the commitment was still too little. Kennedy's bill—with its call for an end to employment discrimination, equal access to public accommodations, and a stronger role for the Justice Department in initiating desegregation—had to be strengthened substantially in the course of legislative debate over the next year. Nevertheless, the president was committed as he never had been before. Between May 22 and July 9, he met with nearly 1,600 leaders from religious, labor, business, and women's groups, seeking their support for his legislation and their involvement in establishing biracial committees in their own communities to promote desegregation. Finally, he had placed his own credit on the line. For a man who had always avoided conflict on domestic issues, it was a decisive moment. Kennedy had taken sides—first, because it was right and, second, because he no longer had the option of avoiding a choice.

Just one day before his civil rights speech, Kennedy had made another choice—to embark on a new quest for world peace that would set aside the hysterical slogans of the Cold War and seek a new basis for mutual accommodation with the Soviet Union. Rejecting much of the rhetoric that had characterized his own campaign for the presidency and his first two years in office, Kennedy told an American University audience that the time had come to seek a peace that would allow men, women, and children to live in security—"not merely peace in our time but peace for all time." For too long, he declared, Americans had envisioned "a Pax Americana enforced on the world by American weapons of war." Yet such a view ignored the extent to which conflict was a product of mistakes on both sides. "We must re-examine our own attitudes," Kennedy declared, "as individuals and as a nation—for our attitude is as essential as [that of the Soviet Union]." Both sides, he noted, had been "caught up in a vicious cycle in which suspicion on one side breeds suspicion on the other, and new weapons beget counter-weapons." It was imperative, Kennedy said "not to see only a distorted and desperate view of the other side, not to see conflict as inevitable, accom-modation as impossible, and communication as nothing more than an ex-change of threats. No government or social system is so evil that its people must be considered as lacking in virtue." Instead, Kennedy declared, it was time to start a new dialogue with the Soviet Union, aimed at not only in-creased contact and communication, but also at substantive disarmament. To that end, the president proposed urgent new discussions to outlaw nu-clear tests, promising that the United States would cease its own atmos-pheric testing of nuclear weapons and move quickly toward an agreement that would at least mark the beginning of an end to "an unabated, uncon-trolled, unpredictable arms race."

In effect, Kennedy the quintessential Cold Warrior, was asking Ameri-can citizens to re-examine the very assumptions underpinning the Cold War. Almost as if his confrontation with nuclear holocaust ten months ear-lier had shown him the folly of the trap America found herself in, Kennedy appealed for a new understanding of the bonds that united humankind and the need to avoid using the other side always as a scapegoat. "No nation," Kennedy told his audience, "ever suffered more than the Soviet Union suf-fered in the course of the Second World War." Both sides, moreover, shared a common concern with peace and security. The time had come to put aside the pattern of "seeking to pile up debating points. We are not here distrib-uting blame or pointing the finger of judgment." Rejecting his own image of a world half-slave and half-free, Kennedy told the Irish Parliament two weeks later: "We must remember that there are no permanent enemies. Hostility today is a fact, but it is not a ruling law. The supreme reality of our time is our indivisibility as children of God and our common vulnerability on this planet." With the same eloquence and passion he had once devoted to escalating the Cold War, Kennedy now articulated a different vision. "We cannot end now all our differences," he told his American University audi-ence, but "at least we can help make the world safe for diversity. For, in the final analysis, our most basic common link is that we all inhabit this small planet. We all breathe the same air. We all cherish our children's future and we are all mortal." Just two months later, the United States and the Soviet

Union initiated a treaty banning all atmospheric testing of nuclear weapons. "A journey of a thousand miles begins with a single step," Kennedy observed at the time. A single step had been taken.

Finally, the summer of 1963 brought John Kennedy to a new commitment to take action against the economic inequalities that stood at the heart of so much else that was wrong with America. Moved again by the urgent moral focus of the civil rights movement, Kennedy ordered a complete review on June 4 of all federal construction projects to determine whether blacks were being hired on an equal basis and asked each cabinet member to provide an immediate assessment of what their department was doing to promote equal employment opportunity. The results were startling. Willard Wirtz of the Labor Department pointed out that unemployment was three times higher for Negro male breadwinners than for whites, that only 17 percent of blacks had white-collar jobs as opposed to 47 percent of whites, and that black teenagers suffered joblessness at twice the rate of white teenagers. Instead of improving, average black income had remained almost static in the postwar years—54 percent of that of white workers in 1947, 55 percent in 1962. In 1959, median family income for whites was $5,600, for nonwhites only $2,900. Kennedy was convinced that, in the end, civil rights for blacks would mean little unless they were accompanied by economic gains that made those rights a reality rather than an ideal.

Simultaneously, Kennedy's economic advisors had been working on plans to fuel the economy and provide the basis for offering people at the bottom greater access to the benefits of affluence. While Walter Heller and the Council of Economic Advisors believed that a tax cut in its own right would help the poor by creating new growth and jobs, others pressed for specific programs that would strike directly at poverty. During his 1960 campaign in West Virginia, Kennedy had seen the face of economic suffering personally. Now, reading Michael Harrington's brilliant exposé, *The Other America,* he became more committed to attacking that poverty. Despite all the rosy assumptions of the "liberal consensus," more than one-fifth of the nation lived in conditions that offered no possibility of even minimal decency. While the number of people suffering from poverty had fallen sharply between 1947 and 1957 (from 28 percent to 21 percent), there had been only a 1 percent reduction since 1957.

To attack the problem, Kennedy chose a dual approach. Embracing the advice of his Council of Economic Advisors, he urged Congress to adapt a massive tax cut that would increase consumer spending, create new jobs, and generate sustained economic growth. At a Yale University commencement address in 1962, Kennedy had urged the nation to set aside the economic dogmas of the past lest "[they land] us all in a bog of sterile acrimony" and accept instead calculated management of the economy. The speech was, said Heller, "the most literate and sophisticated dissertation on economics ever delivered by a president." Now, Kennedy ordered his chief economist to proceed as well with a comprehensive plan to wage war on poverty through job training, education, nutrition, and direct aid to the poor.

Three actions on civil rights, peace, and poverty. Three innovative departures on issues that cried out for leadership. Three powerful signals that a new presidency was being born.

In all of this, to be sure, there was continuity as well as change. Kennedy's civil rights package was moderate rather than bold and could easily be construed as the same kind of forced response to crisis that had occurred earlier with the Freedom Rides and the admission of James Meredith to the University of Mississippi. Despite the war on poverty, the tax cut proposal was conservative in its underlying assumptions, as was Kennedy's fixation on more efficient management of the economy. Even the American University speech and the test ban treaty carried some echoes from the past. Moreover, neither departure precluded Kennedy's commitment to the growing involvement of U.S. troops in Vietnam.

Still, it is difficult to avoid the conclusion that 1963 produced a profound change in the political perspective of John Kennedy. He had found his voice. No longer clinging to the shibboleths of the Cold War for protection, he appeared ready to take risks for peace, perhaps based—ironically—on the risk of war that he and the world had survived the previous autumn. Never in the past willing to embrace the civil rights cause as his own or to identify morally with black protestors, he now defined the issue of racial equality as America's number one priority and committed the total resources of his administration to securing racial change. Throughout his political career, including the first two years of his presidency, Kennedy had lacked the vision—either domestically or in foreign policy—to give direction to the brilliant technicians who surrounded him. Now—for the moment, at least—there was a sense of priorities, a willingness to "spend" political credit, and to give structure and order to those pragmatic options his advisors so cherished.

Conclusion

We were never to know, of course, how deep the change really went. Kennedy eagerly anticipated his election year battle with Barry Goldwater, confident that in 1964 he would receive the resounding mandate for his presidency that he had been denied in 1960. His life had been tempered by both triumph and tragedy. The success of the test ban treaty and the acclaim he received for his initiatives on civil rights and the economy gave him a sense of direction and purpose that he had seemingly lacked earlier. Kennedy was also deeply affected, on a personal level, by the death of his third child, Patrick, born prematurely and unable to survive despite heroic medical efforts. Yet if anything, the personal tragedy seemed to reinforce Kennedy's sense of the frailty of life and the importance of working for peace.

Jacqueline Kennedy holds the hands of her children, Caroline and John, after viewing President Kennedy's casket. Robert F. Kennedy is behind Caroline. *(National Archives)*

Supremely self-confident, he embarked on a nationwide speaking tour devoted to the problems of disarmament, delighting in the fervent response audiences gave to his endorsement of détente. Already planning his election year strategy, he even decided to intervene in the divisive political battles of Texas, going to that state in late November to heal party wounds and assure that Texan electoral votes would be part of his mandate in the election a year hence. "This trip is turning out to be terrific," he said. "Here we are in Dallas, and it looks like everything in Texas is going to be fine for us." Less than an hour later the president was dead.

The assassination affected America—and the world—unlike any other single event in modern history. No American born prior to 1960 can forget where he or she was the moment the news came. Most could not believe it until they turned on the TV, saw Walter Cronkite cry as he announced the news, and watched the widow in her blood-stained dress as she departed Air Force One. "I have lost my only true friend in the outside world," Sekou Touré, the President of Guinea, declared. Nikita Khrushchev was stunned, later recalling how he and Kennedy together had avoided world disaster. The Soviets, a reporter wrote, had the feeling that "[here] was the man who understood the problems between the United States and the Soviet Union" and now he was gone. One Washington journalist found the news even harder to take than the death of her own father. For four days, Americans sat before their television sets as the nation collectively shared the grief of a loss that seemed both personal and immediate. "This was the death of a democratic prince," Godfrey Hodgson observed, but a prince who some-how, someway, had become part of everyone's psychic and emotional life. Even among "anti-Kennedy southerners," 62 percent experienced the as-sassination as "a loss of someone very close and dear."

Now, with the passage of more than four decades, it is still difficult to place the Kennedy presidency in perspective. There was something larger than life about the man, his presidency, his death, and his impact on the American people. Part of this he created himself through his extraordinary style and image. With as much artifice as conviction, the Kennedys helped to generate the myth of Camelot—the beautiful and stylish wife, the active and attractive leader, the high culture, the court entourage of brilliant and dedicated public servants—a time that belonged, by design, with the leg-ends of chivalric courts. Americans had found—or were offered—a dashing young monarch who had succeeded in creating a link in the fantasy life of his fellow citizens between their everyday world and the glamour and glitter of the Oval Office.

But there was also something deeply distressing about the Kennedy style and method. Things had always come too easily—the women, the Pulitzer Prize, the victory, the power. Despite his physical condition and the odds he had to overcome simply to survive, Kennedy seemed never to have experienced, in his gut, the travail of ordinary people's struggle to live and overcome. Accustomed to winning and to being surrounded by cool, calcu-lating, and intelligent people, Kennedy embodied in its purest form the view that "the best and the brightest"—those to the manor born—could and should rule. As a result, he helped to create the imperial presidency, as Arthur Schlesinger, Jr., has called it, surrounded by the panoply of power, directing the fate of the universe, unconstrained by the realities and strug-gles of most people's everyday lives.

And yet, in the end, there was something else as well. Pictures of John F. Kennedy still hang on the walls in the homes of black people in America, together with those of Martin Luther King, Jr., and Jesus. Despite himself, he succeeded in conveying to the poor a sense of caring, of commitment. He had, his aide Richard Goodwin wrote, "that rare quality of strengthen-ing men's belief in themselves, in giving them something grand to look toward. . . . He took a country that was on its back, fat and purposeless, lifted it up, gave it momentum, direction, purpose and a sense of its own strength and possibility." If for most of his life he served those who already had power, he also evoked in a new generation a commitment to change the way things were and to work for the way things might be.

And there was always the last year, with its sense of new beginnings. "Government is not a game," John Kenneth Galbraith wrote to Robert Kennedy in 1964.

> Only refugees from the sports pages can settle these matters by the box scores. The proper test is the progress that is made on the truly decisive things—in eliminating those grievances and reversing those trends which could destroy us. When Kennedy came into office there was one such grievance and one such trend—the domestic race crisis and the movement toward nuclear confrontation.

On both, Kennedy had taken decisive action in the months prior to his death, giving new hope to those who believed that he might yet fulfill his potential. The ultimate paradox of Kennedy's life, therefore, was the sense of unrealized possibility. "What was killed [in Dallas]," James Reston wrote, "was not only the president but the promise. . . . the death of youth and the hope of youth, of the beauty and grace and the touch of magic. . . . He never reached his meridian: we saw him only as a rising sun."

8

LBJ
The Trial of Consensus

The years after John Kennedy's death witnessed both the greatest triumphs—and the sharpest defeats—of postwar liberal democracy. Issues of social change exploded into the nation's consciousness as blacks, women, and the economically disadvantaged pressed for reform. Simultaneously, the guardians of the liberal tradition enacted an array of progressive legislation unmatched in the annals of congressional history. Yet the achievement was not enough, and the society's capacity to contain and ameliorate tension burst under the combined pressure of those who insisted on challenging the very premises of liberalism and national leaders who attempted to maintain stability at home while waging war abroad.

In all of this, one man sought to occupy center stage, harnessing all the powers of established authority to direct and mold the history of the era. He wanted, above all, to achieve unity *and* social progress. Ultimately, the events of these years testify to the disappointment of his desire and to the underlying contradictions within the "liberal consensus" which frustrated its fulfillment. But in order to understand fully the external problems that destroyed his dream, it is necessary first to examine the life of Lyndon Baines Johnson, whose personality so thoroughly embodied both the limits and potential of the liberal agenda.*

The Early Years

In her poignant biography of Johnson, Doris Kearns described the conversations she held with the former president: "We talked mostly in the early hours of the morning," Kearns wrote:

> Terrified of lying alone in the dark, he came into my room. . . . Gradually, a curious ritual developed. I would awaken at five and get dressed. Half an hour

---

* This chapter deals with the personality and political philosophy of Lyndon Johnson. Chapters 9 and 10 discuss the Vietnam War, and Chapter 11 explores the emergence of social conflict—from below—which challenged Johnson's assumptions and policies.

later Johnson would knock on my door, dressed in his robe and pajamas. As I sat in a chair by the window, he climbed into the bed, pulling the sheets up to his neck, looking like a cold and frightened child. . . . [Later], he said that all along he had been hiding from me the fact that I reminded him of his dead mother. In talking with me, he had come to imagine he was also talking with her, unravelling the story of his life.

Through these early morning meetings, Johnson tried to sort out the pivotal influences that had shaped his life, and—by extension—the role he would play in leading America. It was an exercise in history, and also, in self-revelation.

The story Johnson told was one of pain, unrequited love, turmoil, and conflict. His mother, he said, was refined and cultured, from a family dedicated to civility and the genteel things of life. When a family financial disaster forced her to leave college, her social aspirations crumbled, and she went on to marry Sam Johnson, a local politician and farmer known more for his raucous language than his high culture. Clearly, she felt that she had married beneath her, and Lyndon, her son, became the vessel through which she sought to rescue, and then achieve, her own, now-deferred dream of a graceful and refined existence.

Inevitably, Johnson's childhood became a battleground, each of his parents warring for his soul. While his mother hovered over him, curling his hair like that of a girl and teaching him the poetry of Longfellow and Tennyson, his father tried to make him a little man and to counter the controlling impulse of his wife. The young boy was torn. He knew his mother needed him. "I liked that," he recalled. "It made me feel big and important. She made me believe I could do anything in the whole world." On the other hand, she froze him out if he did poorly in school or refused to finish his violin lessons; he felt abandoned, bereft, alone. At those times, sharing in his father's gregarious political life seemed particularly attractive. Going out into the countryside, talking with constituents, eating homemade snacks offered by voters, Lyndon—and his father—were in their element. "Christ," he later said, "sometimes I wished it could go on forever."

The tortured conflict seems to have decisively shaped Johnson's life. Although in virtually every way he ultimately followed his father's example—wheeling and dealing in politics, using crude language, intentionally violating "proper behavior" by having aides and government officials accompany him to the bathroom—there remained a longing for his mother, and the security and approval he so desperately craved from her. Johnson seemed to feel that he would never measure up to her elite standards. Displacing his feelings toward her and others, he concluded that intellectuals were contemptuous of him. Yet he never ceased soliciting their favor, perhaps hoping that by possessing his own coterie of "Harvard" types, he could finally achieve the standing, by his mother's criteria, that had always eluded him.

Ironically, it was to Doris Kearns—a Harvard woman—that he bared his most intimate secrets and anxieties.*

Perhaps the greatest impact of Johnson's childhood was to drive him to transcend conflict, to rise above confrontation, to find a way to unite people of opposite persuasions. Unable during his own adolescence to resolve the conflict between his mother's all-encompassing love and his father's crude masculinity, he resorted to physical escape, going off to California. "I must get away," he said, "I must get away." But thereafter, his solution was to poise himself above the battle where he could create consensus, avoid confrontation, and above all protect himself from being torn by competing factions. Significantly, the course he chose was one of cleaving to "father figures" who rose above conflict, and identifying himself with the values of patriotism, prayer, and nationalism, which no one in America could question.

The model for the future rested in Johnson's career at San Marcos State Teachers' College. "The enduring lines of my life lead back to this campus," Johnson later said. Intensely ambitious, Johnson understood that success depended on winning the favor of those with power. In a move that he would repeat throughout the rest of his life, Johnson immediately attached himself to Cecil Evans, the president of the college, making himself indispensable as the college administrator's private secretary. Once he had attained that position, Johnson used the implicit power of his closeness to authority to draw other students into his fold. Handing out jobs, making life easier for students and administrators, Johnson became a central figure at the college. Shrewdly, he patched together a political coalition designed to win all the major college offices for his followers, working tirelessly to court student votes in an election, and to win student respect through his editorials in the campus newspaper. Through it all, he celebrated the virtues of paternalism and patriotism. In times of trouble, he wrote in the student newspaper, it was the father who had to "square his shoulders, resolutely grit his teeth, suppress his emotions and with renewed courage meet the issue." The strong must care for the weak, the older for the young, men for women. If, in his own father, Johnson had not found an adequate model to transcend conflict within the family, at San Marcos he would create his own model, and by service to authorities, such as the president of the college, begin to take part in the image he had created.

* The interpretation of Johnson offered here derives in substantial part from the view presented by Doris Kearns in her biography of LBJ. Kearns's book has been criticized for its emphasis on psychological motives in Johnson's political career. Some have charged that Johnson used Kearns, manipulating his own revelations to her (and perhaps fabricating some) in order to assure that she presented a portrait of him that was sympathetic. While this criticism may be true, and Johnson, on occasion, may have embellished or shaped stories in a manner that distorts the facts, I have found that Kearns evidence, on an overall basis, conforms well to the pattern of findings presented by other observers of Johnson, including George Reedy, Harry McPherson, Eric Goldman, Robert Dallek, and Robert Caro. Hence, the interpretation offered here is consistent with the view of Johnson found in most scholarly works, as well as primary sources.

With astonishing rapidity, Johnson put the lessons of San Marcos to work, moving quickly to become secretary to a Texas congressman, head of the National Youth Administration in Texas, and then, in 1937, congressman in his own right. If, as with other Southerners coming to serve in Washington for the first time, he felt intimidated, apprehensive, and overwhelmed by the big city, he quickly carved out his own niche, meeting every staff person in his boarding house within a week, ferreting out all the information they had to provide, and learning, almost immediately, who to befriend, who to defer to. "The astonishing thing," one of his fellow staff colleagues said, "was that Lyndon made us feel as if we were the pupil and he were the teacher." Both in the Capitol and back home, he impressed powerful people with his ability to get things done, soon winning the approbation of construction companies and big business interests.

During the New Deal, FDR became Johnson's political "daddy," the most important figure in his life. While Johnson confessed enthusiasm and admiration for the populism of Huey Long, and repeatedly demonstrated his ability to work miracles for Brown and Root, a Texas construction company, it was FDR who served as the focal point of LBJ's attention. Running for Congress in 1937 to fill a vacancy left by death, Johnson distinguished himself from a crowd of candidates by making the election a referendum on FDR, labeling himself—inaccurately—the only true supporter of the president's program, particularly his court-packing measure. Assisted at every turn by indirect aid from the administration, Johnson surged to victory, and shortly thereafter was invited to join the president on FDR's return from a fishing trip in the Texas gulf. Johnson ingratiated himself with FDR through flattery and repeated indications of willingness to support the New Deal. As a result, he earned easy access to the president's closest associates, turning his influence to the immediate profit of his chief financial backer in Texas. When one construction project met numerous obstacles from administration officials, Johnson finally importuned the president so energetically that FDR turned to his assistant, and with the nonchalance of a father finally giving in to a persistent child, said "give the kid the dam." Significantly, Johnson managed to serve his conservative Texas supporters even while retaining his intimate relationship with the White House. Frequently, he voted against the president, and only rarely did he speak out on the House floor for New Deal measures. Nevertheless, Johnson retained FDR's confidence and used his access to power as a means of avoiding conflict with those he served. The two men had a special bond. FDR once predicted that LBJ would be president some day. "That's the kind of man I could have been if I hadn't had a Harvard education," he remarked. The ironies were everywhere, and never more so than when, on the occasion of Roosevelt's death, Johnson declared that he felt like he had lost his father.

Still, after FDR's death, Johnson moved to the right ideologically. He supported the Taft-Hartley bill, voted to override Truman's veto of it, opposed antilynching legislation, and defended the Cold War. "I am in favor," he declared, "of letting Stalin know that he cannot run over the world and enslave us . . . and impound our children as captives behind the Iron Curtain." Despite earlier inclinations toward accommodating the Soviet Union and criticizing HUAC's Red-baiting, Johnson now practiced the politics of anticommunism with the best of them. Running for the U.S. Senate in 1948, Johnson ensured that no one could call him soft on communism or labor. Even so, the election turned out to be a draw, and only the discovery of 202 additional votes from Box 13 in Texas (two hundred of them for Johnson, two against) saved the day. By eighty-seven votes, "landslide Lyndon" went back to Washington as the junior senator for Texas.

Johnson dominated the U.S. Senate as no one ever had—before or since. Viewing Richard Russell, the conservative patriarch from Georgia, as the key to his own ascendancy, Johnson argued against any change in the filibuster rules in his initial speech on the Senate floor, thereby winning the support of conservative Southerners. Almost simultaneously, he lambasted the liberal Leland Olds as a "fellow traveler" and potential "commissar," thereby blocking Olds's reappointment to the Federal Power Commission and pleasing his Texas oil and gas friends. As one columnist said in the mid fifties, "the tall traveler [who] came to Congress as a follower of Franklin Roosevelt's . . . [is now] riding in the first-class coach of arch Republicanism." Still, Johnson was more liberal on race than most Southerners, refused to join the Southern caucus, and by getting to know and do favors for virtually all of his Democractic colleagues, soon found himself Minority Leader, and two years later, in 1955, Majority Leader of the U.S. Senate.

All of his previous training had prepared him for the position—his skill at avoiding conflict and forging compromise, his sensitivity to individual personalities, his genius at placating, flattering, wooing—and, yes, bullying potential allies. As he told his aide Harry McPherson, there were two kinds of senators—the minnows and the whales. Johnson knew how to cultivate both, and among the whales, no one was larger than he. Johnson knew every senator intimately, his likes and dislikes, his weaknesses, strengths, family situation, constituency. His skill lay in his ability to seduce those on the margin, persuade those on the other side, and talk into neutrality those who opposed him. He was no orator. As one colleague said, "I never saw Lyndon Johnson win a debate conclusively on the Senate floor, and [I] never heard him lose one in the cloak room." It was off the Senate floor, in his private chambers over drinks, that the Johnson treatment worked its miracles, encompassing, enveloping, overwhelming the recipient with the intense power of personal persuasion. Like a father, Johnson told each senator that the entire future of a given piece of legislation rested with that legislator's response, and like wayward sons, few were able to resist the appeal to join the family. Or, as one recipient of the "treatment" described it: "Lyndon got me by the lapels and put his face on top of mine and he talked and talked. I figured it was either getting drowned or joining."

In everything he did, Johnson was guided by two interrelated objectives: the need to dominate and control, and the use of consensus as a means of doing so—both a product of his obsession with avoiding conflict by rising above it. Even back at San Marcos, the biographer Robert Caro has written, Johnson had exhibited "the desire to dominate. . . . to bend others to his will . . . the overbearingness with subordinates that was as striking as the obsequiousness with superiors." Controlling others offered a means of coping with his own anxieties and insecurities. Unless he were on top, manipulating others, he seemed to feel directly threatened. Even his closest aides noted that, in the words of his press secretary, George Reedy: "he had no sense of loyalty . . . and he enjoyed tormenting those who had done the most for him. He seemed to take a special delight at humiliating those who had cast in their lot with him. It may be that this was the result of a form of self-loathing in which he concluded that there had to be something wrong with anyone who would associate with him."

But the purpose of this domination was to position himself as the only person capable of bringing unity out of division. The whole rationale for the behind-the-scenes "treatment" was to bring together those who would otherwise never share a common position. Johnson told each person something different, and then held his listeners to the personal agreement each had made with him. Nothing could be worse than allowing divisions to surface publicly or different sides to become emotionally polarized. Hence, virtually all of Johnson's public statements invoked ideals to which few would take exception. Americans must support the president in foreign policy, he insisted, and unite behind a position of anticommunism. In almost a parody of this consensus approach, he announced himself in 1958 to be "a free man, a U.S. Senator and a Democrat, in that order. I am also a liberal, a conservative . . . a businessman, a consumer . . . and I am all these things in no fixed order. . . . At the heart of my own beliefs is a rebellion against this very process of classifying, labeling and filing Americans under headings." Indeed, to do so was to acknowledge that there might be divisions worth fighting over.

If this obsession with reconciliation went back ultimately to Johnson's childhood experience with his parents, its most clearcut manifestation occurred on an issue central to the fissures in the American social structure—the question of race. Understanding instinctively that no Southerner could achieve the presidency without breaking with traditional Southern attitudes toward civil rights, Johnson set forth in 1957 to mold a consensus behind civil rights legislation in Congress. Brilliantly, he used his private connections to secure agreement to a bill that could not have secured consensus through public debate. To Southerners like Richard Russell, he argued that the only way to keep "uppity" blacks from wreaking havoc with the Constitution was to give them some reform. Hence, he promised to eliminate the toughest sections of the 1957 civil rights proposal—Title III, authorizing federal intervention in the South to promote voting rights and school desegregation—if Southerners would avoid a filibuster. To Northerners, in turn, he conveyed the impression that he was a "secret liberal," as devoted as they were to racial equality. (When Eleanor Roosevelt was told that Johnson was a secret liberal, she responded "you're crazy.") If liberals really wanted progress on civil rights, Johnson argued, they would accept his compromise measure. The result, of course, was that Johnson was able to take credit for "this long overdue bill for the benefit of Negro Americans," even as those he characterized as "emotional liberals" denounced the measure as an empty shell.

Ironically, Johnson's concern with both dominance and consensus provides a partial explanation for his failure to win the Democratic presidential nomination in 1960 and his acceptance of the vice-presidency instead. While Johnson evidently believed that his behind-the-scenes reign over the Senate would confer on him the legitimacy to lead the Democrats nationwide, Kennedy was out scouring the states for delegate votes. If Johnson was the master of legislative legerdemain, Kennedy understood far better the politics of presidential nominations. Johnson's commitment to private, cloakroom conciliation denied him the public appeal that the Kennedy charisma so quickly evoked. When the former apprentice offered his legislative master the vice-presidential nomination, Johnson in effect had only two choices: he could join Kennedy on the ticket for the sake of party unity and victory, or he could turn down the request, foment bitterness over his rejection, and be left in the potential position of taking orders as Senate Majority Leader from a man who was his inferior in every aspect of legislative politics. In saying no to Kennedy, Johnson would both create division and accept subordination; but if he said yes—even if it involved the temporary ignominy of holding a powerless office—at least there was the possibility of moving up to the presidency when Kennedy's term was over. In effect, there was no option but to accept the vice-presidency.

Predictably, Johnson was miserable in the office. After one or two unsuccessful efforts at securing authority in his own right* he resigned himself to the classic position of the second-in-command—a loyal, powerless, obedient servant. As Johnson later recalled, "The vice-presidency is filled with trips around the world, chauffeurs, men saluting, people clapping, chairmanships of council, but in the end, it is nothing. I detested every minute of it." Only in the trips abroad, sharing the sense of power, dominance, and superiority that his position as the nation's spokesman conferred, did his natural ebullience and sense of authority return. Back at home, in the meantime, he performed loyally and effectively those tasks he was asked to carry forward, frustrated, that with all its rhetoric and style, the Kennedy administration seemed only capable, in one Johnson aide's words, of "racing in neutral." And then came November 22.

---

* Johnson proposed that he become chairman of the Democratic conference in the Senate, giving him control over part of the legislative process. He also submitted a proposed executive order giving the vice-president "general supervision" over a variety of issues. Both attempts were rejected.

A New President Takes Hold

Suddenly, the Oval Office was his. But power had come through such tragic circumstance. How to carry on, how to convey both sadness and leadership, how to sustain and nurture a sense of national continuity and direction, particularly given the aura of romance surrounding the fallen leader and the inevitable bitterness that would follow. As Harry McPherson noted when the phone call came with the news, "Dallas—insane city; insane, wide-eyed, bigoted Dallas bastards . . . a Texan become President after Kennedy is killed in Texas. There would be perilous suspicions." Yet no one was better prepared and more able, based on an entire career of conciliation, to provide the healing hand the country so desperately needed. "I will do my best," he told the mourning crowd at Andrews Air Force Base when Air Force One returned. "That is all I can do. I ask for your help, and God's."

Drawing on every lesson of political coalition-building he had ever learned, Johnson tirelessly set about to bring the country together under his leadership. "Everything was in chaos," he later told Doris Kearns.

> We were all spinning around and around, trying to come to grips with what had happened, but the more we tried to understand it, the more confused we got. We were like a bunch of cattle caught in the swamp, unable to move in either direction, simply circling 'round and 'round. I understand that; I knew what had to be done. There is but one way to get the cattle out of the swamps. And that is for the man on the horse to take the lead, to assume command, to provide direction. In the period of confusion after the assassination, I was that man.

Clearly in his element now, Johnson once again rose above the conflict and confusion, calling labor leaders, civil rights leaders, old political enemies, religious leaders, former friends, exhorting them to join hands in this moment of crisis. "People must put aside their selfish aims," he told each leader, "in the larger cause of the nation's interest. They must start trusting each other; they must start communication with each other; and they must start working with each other."

To forge a new consensus of purpose, Johnson offered himself as an instrument for carrying forward the mission of the slain leader. "Everything I had ever learned in the history books," he said, "taught me that martyrs have to die for causes. John Kennedy had died. . . . I had to take the dead man's program and turn it into a martyr's cause. That way Kennedy would live on forever, and so would I." Whatever past tensions had existed between the Kennedy staff and Johnson, the new president now set them aside, wrapping himself totally in the mystique of the fallen leader, portraying himself as "the dutiful executor" of Kennedy's program. When Kennedy aides offered their resignations, Johnson pleaded with them to stay. "I know how much *he* needed you. But it *must* make sense to you that if he needed you I need you

In the days after John F. Kennedy's assassination, Lyndon Johnson reached out to national leaders of various constituencies seeking support and cooperation. Here he is pictured with Roy Wilkins of the NAACP. *(National Archives)*

that much more. And so does our country." Intuitively, Johnson understood the importance of being linked with Kennedy—to heal the country's anguish, to build unity behind his own legislative commitments, and to win the support of those who otherwise might become his major critics.

Nowhere was Johnson more eloquent or effective than when he brought all these themes together in his first speech to Congress and the nation one week after the assassination. "All I have, I would have given gladly not to be standing here today," he began. Now, he needed their help, their prayers, their support. Kennedy had said "let us begin." Johnson said, "let us continue." "In this critical moment," he declared, "it is our duty, yours and mine, to do away with uncertainty and delay and doubt and to show that we are capable of decisive action; that from the brutal loss of our leader we will derive not weakness but strength, that we can and will act and act now."

If the message were not clear, Johnson underlined it by invoking the rhetorical cadence of another martyred president killed by a bullet of hate one hundred years earlier. "Let us here highly resolve that John Fitzgerald Kennedy did not live or die in vain."

Brilliantly, Johnson yoked the overwhelming emotional intensity of the moment to a plea for action on the country's most urgent social problem. "No memorial oration or eulogy," he told the Congress, "could more eloquently honor President Kennedy's memory than the earliest possible passage of the Civil Rights Bill for which he fought so long." If Johnson faced any single threat to his leadership, it was the suspicion of Northerners and liberals alike that this son of the South would betray Kennedy's leadership on the racial issue. Now, with a passion rarely heard before from any national leader, he swept away that suspicion. "We have talked long enough in this country about equal rights," he told Congress. "We have talked for one hundred years or more. It is time now to write the next chapter—and to write it in the books of law." Johnson would not only seek consensus. He would seek it in the name of racial equality, in the name of abandoning once and for all the teaching and preaching of hate and violence.

Significantly, Johnson had not always been a supporter of Kennedy's Civil Rights Bill. In a series of phone conversations and memoranda to Theodore Sorensen and Justice Department officials in early June, Johnson revealed considerable ambivalence about the president's proposed message. As presently drafted, Johnson claimed, the Civil Rights Bill would cause Kennedy's program to "go down the drain . . . he'll be cut to pieces . . . and he'll be a sacrificial lamb." If the president's legislation was sent to Congress, Johnson colorfully predicted, conservatives like Dick Russell were "going to cut his outfit off and put it in their pocket and never mention civil rights." Instead, Johnson contended, Kennedy should get the rest of his program through, particularly tax legislation. "I'd move my children on through the line and get them down in the storm cellar and get it, lock and key, and then I'd make my attack." The administration had not done its homework on what would be required to enact a Civil Rights Bill, Johnson said, and until it did, it was simply inviting disaster by submitting the bill.

Johnson then gave Sorensen a lesson in legislative strategy. If the Civil Rights Bill were to pass, he noted, it would require twenty-seven Republican votes in support of a motion to end debate. Hence the first person called should be Minority Leader Everett Dirksen, with the promise that Dirksen would get all the credit if he cooperated and all the blame if he balked. Next, Johnson said, all the ex-presidents should be gotten together to issue a statement of support for the principles of civil rights. Third, Kennedy should take his bill to Richard Russell, solicit all of Russell's objections, and then find answers to them before even sending the package to the Hill. That way he could anticipate the opposition and keep from being nitpicked to death. Finally, Kennedy should take his message to the Southern heartland, standing in a place like San Antonio or Jackson, Mississippi, talk about the astronauts, and point out that no one asked the color of a person's skin before they sent him to die in a foxhole. Having put first things first and gotten all the rest of his legislative package through, Kennedy could then "go in for the kill . . . and [not] let anybody deter [him]."

Now, Johnson himself was in a position to carry out his own advice, or at least that part of it that Kennedy had not already taken. Although as vice-president he had urged Kennedy to hold back on submitting the actual Civil Rights Bill, Johnson as president intuitively recognized the urgency of making enactment of the legislation the primary legacy of the Kennedy presidency. Wooing Dirksen, trying to pacify Russell, working hand in hand with Martin Luther King, Jr., and the civil rights coalition, he *used* civil rights as the instrument by which he would seek to transcend once and for all the debilitating effect of regional conflict on his own career. As Tom Wicker observed, Johnson understood "as a *Southerner*" that the South had to be brought back into the union both for purposes of national unity and progress, and for the sake of his own triumph as president.

Johnson also understood the importance of seizing the momentum the occasion offered to make further demands on Congress, building a record of accomplishment that would give him a running start on winning the election in his own right in 1964. There came a time, Jack Garner, Roosevelt's first vice-president had said, when in the game of politics, as in poker, a person had to "put in all his stack." Operating on the premise that pressure on multiple issues could work to his advantage, creating almost a stampede effect, Johnson insisted that Congress also act immediately on Kennedy's economic program, in particular the commitment to a major tax cut to fuel the economy and legislation to combat poverty. Johnson, one Republican chieftain remarked, achieved the coup of being "the only President to have prosperity and poverty going for him at the same time."

The 1964 tax act represented the quintessential instrument of the Kennedy/Johnson effort to "fine tune" the economy. Already the country was in the midst of a boom. By the end of 1963, auto sales were up 10 percent, profits after taxes were up 60 percent, the country was in its thirty-fourth month of unbroken economic expansion, and the cost of living was holding steady. Still, unemployment was over 5 percent, and Kennedy had been convinced by Walter Heller and his Council of Economic Advisors that a tax cut, combined with controlled deficit spending, offered an ideal way of avoiding the cycle of boom and bust, and of setting the economy on the road to sustained long-term growth. Consumers had money to spend, the volume of production would increase, prices could be lowered, unemployment would decline, and additional tax revenues could provide the basis for containing the deficit and funding needed social programs.

Placing himself a hundred percent behind the tax-cut measure, Johnson secured its passage only four months after taking office, thereby triggering the greatest prosperity of the postwar years. The Gross National

Product increased 7 percent in 1964, 8 percent in 1965, 9 percent in 1966. Unemployment dropped below the 5 percent figure, achieving what most experts believed to be the equivalent of "full employment." By 1966, the number of families with incomes of $7,000 a year or more had reached 55 percent, compared to only 22 percent in 1950. The tax measure, by all accounts, proved a brilliant success, and when John Kenneth Galbraith published a new edition of *The Affluent Society* in 1968, the average income of the American family was $8,000, or double what it had been a decade earlier.

Simultaneously, Johnson passionately embraced Kennedy's decision to aid those at the bottom of the economic ladder, telling Congress in his first State of the Union message that it was time for America to declare "an unconditional war on poverty." While the tax cut created more jobs, the poverty program would train those previously left out of the employment market in the skills needed to fill the available positions, and at the same time attempt to deal with the educational, health, and medical problems that perpetuated poverty. Kennedy had been prepared to "run with the program," and now Johnson made it his own, telling Heller, "I'm interested. I'm sympathetic. Go ahead. Give it the highest priority." Within months, the Economic Opportunity Act had also become law, with Sargent Shriver, Kennedy's brother-in-law, heading the Office of Economic Opportunity with a budget of $800 million.

Clearly, Johnson understood how to shape a consensus. Skillfully portraying himself as carrying forward the legacy of Kennedy, he used his own mastery of legislative politics and the art of conciliation to build an overwhelming coalition of support, with each victory snowballing into others. But if Johnson's first task was to implement the legacy of Kennedy, his second objective was to achieve a record in his own name, a vision uniquely his own, a historic place as master of his own administration. To that end, from his first days in the White House, Johnson sought to find a label, a theme, a program that would serve to inscribe his name in even larger letters than those of any of his predecessors. Hence, the evolution of "the Great Society."

Appropriately, Johnson's vision of the Great Society drew on both his own primary identification with the New Deal and his commitment to go beyond the achievement of FDR to create an America worthy of leadership in the twenty-first century. Throughout early 1964, Johnson had inserted the phrase in various speeches, but it was not until a May commencement address at the University of Michigan that the concept took on the meaning of a complete philosophical statement. America had come far, the president told the Michigan graduates. "An order of plenty for all of our people" had become a reality. But was material growth enough? In Johnson's view the answer was no. The challenge of the next half-century was "whether we have the wisdom to use that wealth to enrich and elevate our national life, and to advance the quality of our American civilization." The time had come for America to build a Great Society, "to prove that our material progress is only the foundation on which we will build a richer life in mind and spirit." Clearly, in this "second New Deal," as one columnist called it, there would remain a commitment to social reform. As Johnson said, "the Great Society rests on abundance and liberty for all. It demands an end to poverty and racial injustice, to which we are totally committed in our time." But in the end, the Johnson vision extended further, "to the quality of [our] goals [rather] than the quantity of [our] goods," to a world where "the city of man serves not only the needs of the body and the demands of commerce but the desire for beauty and hunger for community." If, on the one hand, Johnson wanted to embark on a new venture to achieve the reality of equal opportunity for all Americans, on the other hand, he also aspired to a level of civilization and humanity that would enhance the life of every citizen.

Nothing helped Johnson more in his quest for support than the nomination of Barry Goldwater as Republican candidate for president in 1964. Until that moment, Johnson had been able to use the crisis of assassination and his own role as conciliator to push through legislation that, under Kennedy, seemed controversial and divisive. Now, Goldwater's nomination as the self-appointed champion of right-wing Republicanism permitted Johnson to portray his Great Society as the essence of moderation and his own leadership as preeminently centrist. In the Republican convention hall, riven by internecine bitterness between Rockefeller "liberals" and Goldwater "conservatives," the senator from Arizona seized the nomination, defiantly throwing down the ideological gauntlet in his acceptance speech and declaring that "extremism in defense of liberty is no vice . . . [and] moderation in the pursuit of justice is no virtue." Johnson, by contrast, soared to nomination as a fatherly figure and voice of reason who had continued with brilliance the policies of a fallen leader and was now prepared to carry the nation to new heights of glory and progress.

The ensuing campaign reinforced the images projected by the nominating process. Abandoned by whole sections of the Republican Party who denounced his "right-wing extremism," Goldwater exhibited a greater penchant for raising additional questions about his ideological narrowness than for reuniting his divided party. Attacking Social Security before an audience of senior citizens in Florida, he provided ammunition for the Democratic charge that he would abandon the entire structure of social welfare benefits associated with the New Deal. Similarly, his proposal that military commanders be given discretionary power to use nuclear weapons raised the specter of a worldwide atomic holocaust initiated by someone so committed to "victory over communism" that reckless pursuit of military advantage might take precedence over responsible guardianship of world peace. Johnson, meanwhile, campaigned eighteen hours a day as the voice of experience and responsibility, desperately seeking an electoral mandate that would exceed even the victory margin of his hero, FDR. When Goldwater urged American military victory in Vietnam, Johnson responded: "We're not about to send American boys nine or ten thousand miles from home to do what Asian boys ought to be doing for themselves." While Goldwater might dismantle thirty years of social reform, Johnson would carry forward the achievements of the past, and in an era of unbroken prosperity, help to remedy the remaining ills of American society. Even the Goldwater slogan, "in your heart you know he's right," fit perfectly the Johnson strategy. "Yes, far right," the Democrats jeered. As one Maryland voter declared, "If Goldwater is elected, you don't know what to expect." With Johnson, there was stability, continuity, and responsibility. Not surprisingly, election day brought exactly the mandate Johnson had sought. Now president in his own right, the country's thirty-fourth president had won 61 percent of the popular vote, exceeding even FDR's 1936 victory and seeming to confirm that Johnson indeed spoke for a consensus uniting the entire country.

Immediately, Johnson sought to capitalize on his victory. Understanding instinctively the need to strike while the mood was right, he instructed his aides to draw up an arsenal of new legislation. "Look," he said, "I've just been re-elected by an overwhelming majority . . . [but] everyday while I'm in office, I'm going to lose votes. I'm going to alienate somebody. . . . We've got to get this legislation fast. We've got to get it during my honeymoon." When an aide questioned his haste, Johnson responded: "You've got to give it all you can, that first year. . . . It doesn't matter what kind of majority you come in with. You've got just one year when they treat you right, and before they start worrying about themselves." Expending his political capital with the genius of one who knew in his bones how fickle a working congressional majority could be, Johnson established task forces of "the best minds" in the land and drove his staff to come up with the programs and legislation that would make the Great Society a reality.

The results were astounding. A whirling-dervish of energy, Johnson presided over the most extraordinary display of legislative action the country had ever seen—the achievements of the 1965–66 Congress outpacing even the dazzling array of programs enacted during the first two years of the New Deal. The 89th Congress began by enacting long-stalled legislation such as federal aid to education and medicare. But then it moved beyond, into new areas, passing an act for higher education, a housing act that included rent subsidies, a demonstration cities program, aid to urban mass transit, Operation Headstart, manpower training, a teachers' corps, new provisions for mental health facilities, environmental safety legislation, truth in packaging, rent supplements, and high-speed mass transit. In his single most dramatic example of legislative leadership, Johnson even secured congressional approval for the Voting Rights Act of 1965. Confronted by mass demonstrations in Alabama that highlighted the oppressiveness of a social system that refused to give black people even the basic protection of the franchise, the president went to Congress and, in a voice thick with a heavy Southern accent, demanded the enactment of voting rights protection with the promise, "We *shall* overcome."

By anyone's standards, it was a time of extraordinary accomplishment. "Johnson asketh and the Congress giveth," one wag commented. In a performance unprecedented in the annals of American legislative leadership,

Johnson had maximized his moment in the sun, expending his political capital almost flawlessly in quest of his dream to become the ultimate leader of a united nation achieving greatness. The larger question, however, was whether his vision was adequate, whether it realistically addressed the problems of the society, and whether the values and methods of the "liberal consensus" were consistent with the objectives desired. Could Johnson, through his own personal will and obsession with dominance, find the answers to the nation's problems? Or, would that obsession itself become a tragic impediment to success?

The Great Society and the War on Poverty

Perhaps the ultimate test of Johnson's vision was his plan to abolish poverty in America. Notwithstanding his interest in personal power, Johnson felt deeply committed to the poverty program—more committed than to any other issue, with the possible exception of civil rights. Indeed, he frequently connected the two. Addressing Congress on the Voting Rights Bill in 1965, he eloquently recalled his experience teaching Mexican-American children in Cotulla, Texas, in 1928. "My students were poor," he said,

> and they often came to class without breakfast, hungry. They knew even in their youth the pain of injustice. . . . Somehow you never forget what poverty and hatred can do when you see its scars on the hopeful face of a young child. . . . It never occurred to me in my fondest dreams that I might have the chance to help the sons and daughters of those students and to help people like them all over this country. But now I do have that chance—I'll let you in on a secret—I mean to use it. . . . I do not want to be the President who built empires, or sought grandeur, or extended dominion. I want to be the President who educated young children . . . who helped to feed the hungry . . . who helped the poor to find their own way. . . . God will not favor every thing we do . . . but I cannot help believing that He truly understands and that He really favors the undertaking that we begin tonight.

If John F. Kennedy had an intellectual commitment to fight poverty (and he may have had more than an intellectual commitment), Johnson felt the issue in his "gut."

To a large extent, the president's effort to join the issues of poverty and civil rights made sense. In 1965, 43 percent of all black families fell into the poverty bracket, earning under $3,000 per year. Fewer than two out of five black teenagers finished high school; the black rate of unemployment was double that of whites; and black teenage unemployment ran 100 percent higher than black adult unemployment. Nor had blacks benefited substantially from the postwar economic boom. In 1962 the average black income remained at only 55 percent of average white income—approximately the same percentage that had existed in 1947. Blacks owned less than 1 percent of the nation's businesses, and an average black college graduate could expect to earn in his lifetime less than the amount earned by a white person with only eight years of education.

Yet the plight of black Americans provided only the most dramatic example of economic inequalities seemingly embedded in the very structure of American society. Notwithstanding "the postwar boom" that brought new affluence to millions of Americans, there had been no redistribution of wealth or income since the end of World War II, and whole groups of Americans seemed condemned forever to live in "pockets" of poverty. In the early 1960s the top 20 percent of Americans owned 77 percent of the nation's wealth, while the bottom 20 percent owned only 0.05 percent. Income distribution followed the same pattern: the top 10 percent earning twenty-eight times as much as the bottom 10 percent. The poorest half of the nation received 23 percent of total money income; the richest half 77 percent. In short, while prosperity had helped countless individuals to increase their incomes and had even helped to diminish the number of families earning under $3,000 a year, no change had occurred in the overall distribution of dollars. In 1962, 20 to 25 percent of all Americans still lived in poverty.

As government economists and social scientists discovered the dimensions of the problem, it became clear that a vicious cycle of interacting forces operated to perpetuate economic misery for readily identifiable groups in the population. As Robert Lampman noted, over 70 percent of the poor had one or more of the following characteristics: they were over sixty-five, nonwhite, residing in female-headed house-holds, or living in families presided over by individuals with less than eight years of education. Many of these people were caught up in what quickly became known as the "culture of poverty," transmitted from generation to generation. This was the "voiceless minority," the people who had no way of finding a place in the sun. For such individuals, economic growth and increased production offered only a partial solution. Without education or training in technological skills, victims of poverty had no chance of grasping new employment opportunities. In the past, one sociologist noted, the poor had been able to pull themselves up by taking manual or semiskilled jobs. But the new poor, Michael Harrington noted, were "the automation poor," illiterate in the technological language needed to advance. The result was perpetuation of misery and the development of an ever-widening gap between those who shared in the prosperity of economic growth and those on the margin who were barely able to survive. It was, one economist observed, a kind of "colonial situation," with a successful "white economy" leaving far behind a "meager bush economy" in which rarely did the "gains in the main economy . . . trickle down."

Clearly, the problem was profound, representing the complicated intersection of issues involving race, class, gender, power, education, and history. Lyndon Johnson presided over an administration that believed "in doing the greatest good for the greatest number." He wished to educate the young, feed the hungry, and help the poor. But could such goals be achieved without altering the very structure of American society and challenging the consensus Johnson so prized?

Ultimately, the effectiveness of the antipoverty program hinged on which of three possible courses of action the administration adopted. The first option, and the most radical, involved redistributing society's rewards more evenly and embarking on a far-reaching investment of funds in the public sector to create jobs, build new housing, revitalize urban disaster areas, and create a new infrastructure of social welfare institutions. Massive tax reforms and reallocation of economic resources would be essential. The premise of such a program was that the existing social and economic structure had significant flaws. At its root, such an approach viewed the problem as one of power, taking from those who dominated and giving more to those who were "voiceless." By its very nature, however, this approach challenged Johnson's most cherished convictions. "This government," Lyndon Johnson said in June 1964, "will not set one group against another. We will build a creative partnership between business and labor, between farm areas and urban centers, between consumers and producers." Johnson wished unity, not division, and despite his personal commitment to alleviating misery, he was unwilling to accept the notion that improvement for one group meant sacrifice for another. Moreover, in a time of sustained economic boom, where growth promised to provide a vehicle for increasing the well-being of most people, there seemed no compelling reason to promote conflict or to view the poor as anything but an unhappy exception to an overall story of success and prosperity.

The second approach, less radical, viewed the problem of poverty as quantitative in nature. If the poor could be given enough money, either through a guaranteed income or through "income transfers" such as food stamps, health care, and rent supplements, they would eventually be able to rise above the poverty line. As the Council of Economic Advisors said in 1964, the "conquest of poverty is well within our power. The majority of the nation could simply tax themselves enough to provide the necessary income supplements to their less fortunate citizens." Yet this approach also directly challenged the philosophical underpinnings of the existing American way of life. By treating the poor as an impersonal mass, it would contradict the basic premise that each individual was responsible for his or her success or failure. As the Council of Economic Advisors said, "Americans want to *earn* the American standard by their own efforts and contributions." Income transfers would neither motivate the poor to climb out of poverty, nor provide them the skills necessary to maximize their individual talents and abilities. Such aid would be a "handout," something perilously close to the concept of a "dole" that Americans had always rejected as inherently demeaning.

The third approach viewed the war on poverty as simply one more extension of America's liberal reform agenda, emphasizing the central importance of giving *individual* poor people a *chance* to overcome the disabilities that surrounded them and join as full participants in the dominant economic and social life of the nation. Recognizing that poverty was rooted, in part, in substandard education, inadequate job training, and poor health care, this approach sought to embrace specific programs addressed to those problems. Yet it also perceived poverty as a problem of attitude. Too many of the poor, it was thought, lacked incentive. If they could be helped to see a way out, if they could be motivated to try harder, to begin climbing the ladder of opportunity, to see their own future as inextricably tied to full participation in the American dream, then they would solve the problem themselves. Here, the emphasis was, in the CEA's words, on eliminating "the handicaps that [now] deny the poor *fair access* to the expanding incomes of a growing economy." An unfair distribution of power and wealth was not the problem; instead, it was inadequate availability of opportunity.

This third approach drew on two models. The first was that of the early civil rights movement, with its focus on abolishing discrimination and giving blacks the full opportunity, as *individual* citizens, to "make it" in America without having to combat legal barriers based on race. If individual blacks had the right to vote, go to school, and pursue jobs free of legal restrictions based on race, it was argued, they would join other Americans as equals in the race for prosperity and success. By implication, the poor would enjoy the same individual opportunities as the rest of Americans once impediments—rooted in inadequate education, health care, and job training—were abolished. The second model came from social welfare professionals who were convinced that government could intervene in the poverty cycle, break its hold on individuals, and liberate people from a debilitating culture of resignation, indifference, and despair. As described by Daniel Moynihan in his analysis of the poverty program, this approach was popular among liberal New York foundations, manned by upper-class intellectuals, who sought an answer to the alienation and estrangement of the disadvantaged. According to these intellectuals, the poor and the delinquent sought the same rewards as middle-class members of society. When these goals could not be achieved through socially sanctioned avenues, the result was either resignation or deviant behavior. In short, those who were left out *wanted* to conform to the values of the larger society, but were denied the opportunity. Hence, it was imperative to find a way to "provide the social and psychological resources that make conformity possible." By sponsoring programs that offered incentives to the poor, foundations—and government—could turn around the cycle of downward mobility and trigger an upward cycle of confidence, hope, and achievement. As one foundation official put it, the goal was "social application of the art of Jujitsu." By intervening at critical points of the poverty cycle, the whole process could be reversed.

As with virtually all government programs, the war on poverty represented a mélange of the various approaches. Rent supplements, money for model cities, and food stamps reflected at least some of the ideas espoused by those favoring income transfers and the rebuilding of the nation's inner cities. Education received a major boost through the Head Start program that provided nutrition and intellectual stimulation to preschool children; Upward Bound programs sought to aid disadvantaged students; and the Job Corps hoped to retrain drop-outs from school. Much of the focus centered on the young, as in the Neighborhood Youth Corps, which provided inner-city youngsters summer jobs, and in VISTA, a domestic Peace Corps that offered a vehicle for better-off young people to help those less privileged than themselves.

Yet at heart, the war on poverty embodied the most conservative of the three approaches available. The preamble to the Economic Opportunity Act highlighted the choice that had been made. America, it said, would "eliminate the paradox of poverty in the midst of plenty . . . by *opening* to everyone the *opportunity* to live in *decency* and *dignity*." In almost every respect, Johnson's commitment to an unconditional war against poverty reflected the underlying view that the real problem was to give *individuals* access to opportunity so that they could be motivated to climb out of the poverty cycle. As the sociologist Christopher Jencks observed, the administration's premise was that poverty existed "not because the economy is mismanaged, but because the poor themselves have something wrong with them." Character and motivation would provide the key. As Sargent Shriver, OEO (Office of Economic Opportunity) director noted, the government had not embarked on giving "handouts," but rather on an effort to change "indifference to interest, ignorance to awareness, resignation to ambition, and an attitude of withdrawal to one of participation." Not only would such an approach maintain the commitment to consensus so prized by Johnson; it would also offer a way of attacking poverty with the lowest possible expenditure of dollars and the least disruption to the existing social system.

Ironically, one of the administration's primary efforts to encourage a new attitude among the poor—the Community Action Programs (CAPs)—ultimately delivered a body blow to the consensus politics of Lyndon Johnson. Initially suggested as a guarantee that Southern blacks would have a voice in determining policy for their own areas, the CAP segment of the antipoverty legislation mandated "maximum feasible participation" for residents of poverty areas in developing programs affecting their own local communities. At least theoretically, this attempt to mobilize the poor psychologically—overall, a conservative ploy—had a significant potential for radicalization, especially if the poor took seriously the promise that they would share power. Significantly, so little thought was given to the "maximum feasible participation" phrase that the only administration witness before Congress to mention it was Robert Kennedy, who emphasized the importance of giving poor people themselves "a real voice in their institutions." Yet as the poverty program evolved, the CAPs assumed growing importance. Hoping to save money, government officials rejected Sargent Shriver's demand that the OEO focus on a large-scale employment program that would emphasize both creating new jobs and training the poor to fill them. In the resulting vacuum, CAPs became almost a panacea. By involving the poor, giving them a stake in their own future, and providing an instant means for transforming attitude and character, CAPs could provide an inexpensive instrument for turning the cycle of poverty around—an example of the art of Jujitsu—without having to go the whole route of a massive employment program. Hence, instead of being a minor addition to the war on poverty, the CAPs became a focal point, receiving $340 million of the first $500 million of appropriations. Johnson wanted quick results, and this "mobilization of the poor" on their own behalf seemed a brilliant, cost-effective avenue to success. The CAPs, Shriver grandiloquently declared, would be the "corporations of the new social revolution."

Almost immediately, however, the CAP ploy backfired, creating the very intergroup conflict Johnson hoped to avoid. Taking seriously the government's announced intention that the poor should have a genuine voice in shaping all aspects of the poverty program, community members of antipoverty agencies sought actively to shape programs and mobilize community resources in those areas most relevant to their immediate needs. Oftentimes, this involved organizing the poor in rent strikes, picketing City Hall, and attempting to take control over local school boards and antipoverty agencies. Not surprisingly, city mayors and governors responded with outrage. Chicago Mayor Richard Daley declared that putting poor people in control of antipoverty agencies was "like telling the fellow who cleans up [at the newspaper] to be the city editor." The OEO, other politicians insisted, appeared to be "fostering class struggle," with the primary intent to destroy the existing apparatus of political power and representation. Clearly, the CAPs had created a political dilemma. "If the government imposes *any* limits on tactics the poor use," one writer observed, "can it really be said that the poor are making the decisions? or that they have effective power?" On the other hand, if the government retained control and simply used CAPs as a token, was it not being "manipulative and paternalistic."

Before long, contention over the CAPs had transformed the war on poverty into precisely the struggle over power that the administration feared. When Johnson and his aides sought to quell the conflict by siding with City Hall, spokesmen for the poor rebelled. After all, City Hall was the enemy in many cases, and if poor people did not go on strike to force landlords to correct housing violations, or picket the school board to secure decent textbooks, how could they secure redress of their grievances? Confrontation was essential, community organizer Saul Alinsky declared, and if the war on poverty was to avoid simply being "political pornography," seeking to "buy off" community leaders, the struggle would have to continue. Paradoxically, the federal government found itself in the position of paying the salaries of organizers who, by virtue of their constituency and their own mandate, felt compelled to attack governmental institutions. Power *was* the name of the game, one political activist noted, and those who were troubled by agitation "should bear in mind that poverty is a reflection of class differentials in power." The tragedy, of course, was that although some had hoped that the OEO would do for the poor what the Wagner Act had done for labor—give them leverage, recognition, and a voice—the government seemed to have no such intention.

Ultimately, the conflicts that overtook the poverty program reflected the confusion and contradictions inherent in the assumptions of those who initiated it. Failing to address the problem of maldistribution of income, and emphasizing individual opportunity instead of a massive program of employment, the Johnson administration, almost by definition, eliminated the possibility of achieving the goals it had announced. Rejecting more expensive options, it had placed too heavy a burden on those programs—like the CAPs—that it did accept. Yet the rhetoric that accompanied such programs inevitably raised false expectations. As Moynihan noted, "the tendency was to oversell and under-perform," and then, when disappointments occurred, to use words as a substitute for substance. "The program," Moynihan said, "was carried out in such a way as to produce a minimum of the social change its sponsors desired, and to bring about a maximum increase in the opposition to such change." All too often, the result seemed designed to promote the recipe for discontent that one social scientist described: "Promise a lot; deliver a little. Lead people to believe they will be much better off, but let there be no dramatic improvement. Try a variety of small programs, each interesting but marginal in impact and severely underfinanced. Avoid any attempted solution remotely comparable in size to the dimensions of the problem that we are trying to solve."

Despite these problems, the years of the war on poverty witnessed significant success. The number of families living in poverty plummeted from 40 million in 1959 to 25 million in 1968—a decline from 22 percent of the nation's families to 13 percent. Blacks in particular experienced some improvement in their standard of living. By the end of the Johnson administration Negro family income had risen to 60 percent of white family income. In 1965, it had been only 54 percent. While 41 percent of black families had earned under $3,000 in 1960, the percentage had fallen to 23 percent in 1968. As Herman Miller of the Bureau of Census noted, "these changes . . . were primarily associated with the general improvement of economic conditions . . . but who was to say that the anti-poverty programs and the general increase in awareness of the problems of racism and poverty . . . were not also major factors."

Nevertheless, when measured by the expectations set forth by Johnson, the war on poverty remained a disappointment. Almost half of all black families, for example, still earned less than $5,000 in 1968. The number of female-headed families among black Americans increased rather than diminished. Blacks who were concentrated in the poorest neighbourhoods of the nation saw their lives deteriorate rather than improve. Moreover, if one accepted a *relative* standard for measuring poverty—that is, a standard that took into account the rising standards of living rather than an absolute dollar figure—the number of families living in poverty would have been 18 percent, not 13 percent. Three out of every four Americans below the poverty line never received any assistance, and the antipoverty program virtually ignored those poor people—the sick, the elderly, the disabled—who were totally outside the "opportunity structure."

In the end, instead of being "an unconditional war," the antipoverty effort was more like a *Sitzkrieg* or "phony" war. As the historian Mark Gelfand has observed, it represented "a classic incident of the American habit of substituting good intentions for cold, hard-cash." Wherever there existed a choice between substantial expenditures of money to create new jobs and cheaper programs that would generate more publicity, the latter were chosen. Because it cost more than $11,000 per trainee to send a potential worker through the Job Corps, that program never received the support it required if it were to be successful. When the antipoverty program began in 1965, officials projected annual budgets that jumped from $1.4 billion in 1966 to $6.5 billion in 1968 and $10.4 billion in 1970. In fact, OEO appropriations never exceeded more than $2 billion per year under Lyndon Johnson. In the halcyon days of the Great Society, Lyndon Johnson proposed to do everything. He would eliminate poverty, heal the sick, educate the illiterate, restore economic justice to America—all without disturbing the consensus he cherished. "This program," he told Congress in 1964, "is much more than a beginning. It is a total commitment by this President and this Congress and this nation to pursue victory over the most ancient of mankind's enemies." Four years later, the "total commitment" seemed more to describe the press releases and brochures about antipoverty than the programs developed to do the job. During the 1970s and 1980s, it became fashionable to dismiss the war on poverty as a classic example of the inability of government to solve social problems. The war on poverty, it was said, had failed. More to the point, perhaps, was the contention that the war had barely begun. Finding a solution would inevitably have entailed pitting the interests of one group against another. Yet such a conflict was anathema to consensus politics and to the personality of its primary practitioner. The story of the war on poverty thus became a vignette of the problems—social as well as personal—that would ultimately doom Lyndon Johnson's presidency.

Conclusion

Robert McNamara once said to a friend that he would "never work with a more complicated man than Lyndon Johnson." McNamara's words appropriately described both the man and the administration he presided over.

Rarely had any one individual, or any single administration, aspired to so much, generated so many expectations, raised so many hopes, or ultimately suffered so many setbacks. Like the state he came from, Johnson represented a giant presence in American society. He brought the "liberal consensus" to its fullest expression in post-World War II history. Yet simultaneously, and through it all, he also exhibited the limitations, the tragic flaws, and the inherent contradictions of all that he embodied.

No one could gainsay Johnson's achievement. He wanted to be "the greatest of them all, the whole bunch of them," and in many ways he succeeded. As Tom Wicker noted in the *New York Times*, "the list of achievements is so long that it reads better than the legislative achievements of most two-term presidents." In the areas of education, medicare, urban development, social welfare, and above all civil rights, he had achieved what few could even envision. As one civil rights leader noted at the time of Johnson's death, "when the forces demanded and the mood permitted, for once an activist, human-hearted man had his hands on the levers of power. . . . [Lyndon Johnson] was there when we and the nation needed him, and oh my God, do I wish he was there now." In his best moments, Johnson had spoken for a dimension of the American dream rarely articulated by political leaders. "We seek," he told a Howard University audience, "not just equality as a right in theory, but equality as a fact and result." Without overstatement, Senate Majority Leader Mike Mansfield summed up the positive legacy of Lyndon Johnson: "[He] has outstripped Roosevelt, no doubt about that. . . . He has done more than FDR ever did, or ever thought of doing."

Yet in the very course of attempting to realize his dreams, Johnson exhibited fatal flaws of personality and political philosophy that contributed to his undoing. If egomania is an occupational disease of most politicians and virtually all presidents, Johnson carried the illness to its most extreme form. He personally was going to save the nation, right all the wrongs, emulate and then eclipse his mentors. He alone would make it all happen, rising above the conflicts he had been seeking to escape since childhood and imprinting, through personal will, his own brand of dominance on the entire nation.

There was something eerie—almost terrifying—about Johnson's insistence on personalizing the goals he aspired to. "When I looked out at [my cabinet members]," he told Doris Kearns,

> I realized that while all of them had been appointed by me, not a single one *was really mine*. . . . Here I was working day and night to build the Great Society, conquering thousands of enemies and hurdling hundreds of obstacles, and I couldn't even count on my own administrative family for complete support. I felt like a football quarterback running against a tough team and having his own center and left guard throwing rocks at him. It was an impossible situation and I was determined to change it. I was determined to make them more dependent on me than I was on them.

Fantasizing about his role as president, he told Kearns that, "if only I could take the next step and become dictator of the whole world, then I could really make things happen. Every hungry person would be fed, every ignorant child educated, every jobless man employed."

In retrospect, it is difficult to separate Johnson's quest for dominance from his desire to correct injustice. Indeed, helping others often seemed to be the instrument by which he could most directly satisfy his own ego. As William Leuchtenburg has shown, Johnson desperately wanted to overshadow his political father, FDR, and the way to do that was to even more effectively uplift the downtrodden. As one White House correspondent wrote, Johnson saw himself in the "image of a great popular leader something like Franklin Roosevelt, except more so, striding over the land and cupping the people in his hand and molding a national unity that every President dreams about but none is ever able to achieve." If Johnson could achieve what had eluded Roosevelt, then he would occupy the place in history reserved for the noblest and best leaders. Significantly, his moment of greatest triumph came after his landslide victory in 1964 when, he told Doris Kearns, "for the first time in all my life I truly felt loved by the American people." Hence his bottomless depression when, by the end of his administration, he had lost popular support. "How was it possible," he asked, "that all these people could be so ungrateful to me after I have given them so much?"

Yet, Johnson's egomania was also directly tied to maintaining the politics of consensus. A quality of paternalism characterized his approach to people and issues. If, like a generous father, he could give his children the things they wanted and needed, then he could preside over a happy family. The approach pervaded his administration, as with one issue after another he embraced those with grievances, identified their cause as his, and attempted to make things right. In this way, he could both meet urgent needs and simultaneously draw people to him, making them dependent on him. As Eric Goldman has noted, he gave the people everything he had in order to "have them love him." But such a viewpoint allowed no room for the idea that social justice required conflict between different groups or a struggle over power. Moreover, it impelled Johnson to foreswear hard choices in foreign policy that would have challenged or deviated from the historic liberal policy of aggressive containment of communism. After all, no president could sustain the support—and love—of all the people if he broke with the traditional position of paying "any price" or accepting "any burden" to defend freedom. Johnson believed that it was possible to have everything at once: social reform, unity, incremental progress within the structure of a basically sound economic system, and a strong, aggressive foreign policy against worldwide communism. The poor and disadvantaged would feel grateful, the free world would honor him for his courage, and he would go down in history as the ultimate practitioner of conciliation and progress.

The tragedy of Lyndon Johnson was that both his personality and his political assumptions proved inadequate to the dimensions of the foreign policy and domestic tensions that would emerge during his presidency. The final irony, perhaps, was that the man who did more than anyone else to bring to perfection the politics of the liberal consensus ended up presiding over a fragmented nation and ushering in the conservative consensus. At the height of his success, his own commitment to aggressive anticommunism abroad—while seeking to maintain unity at home—would lead to the most severe division in American society since the Civil War.

9

Vietnam—
The Early Years

If the civil rights movement constituted the driving force of domestic history during the 1960s, the war in Vietnam became the focal point for American foreign policy. Taking place 9,000 miles from America's shores, it eventually involved the commitment of 540,000 American troops to a battle where friend and foe were virtually indistinguishable, and where, in the eyes of much of the world, the United States occupied the position of colonialist aggressor, supporting a repressive, totalitarian regime. No one planned the tragedy in Vietnam. Instead, it resulted from two decades of incremental decisions, each of which appeared justifiable as a stop-gap measure to contain an immediate political or military crisis. Only once or twice did any official ask the basic question of whether Americans had any right to be in Vietnam. Yet the war was no accident, nor an aberration. It grew directly from the ideas, values, and policies of the Cold War, and in the end, more than any other event of the postwar years, it became a test case of the shortcomings of America's policy of containment toward world communism.

It would be difficult to overstate the harsh consequences of American involvement in Vietnam. Lush forests were defoliated. Agrarian communes were bombed into oblivion. Whole families and kinship networks were annihilated. Like the illusions one beholds walking through a house of mirrors, America's best intentions became grotesque distortions when imposed on a distant culture. The end result was perhaps best expressed by an Army major after the 1968 battle for Bien Hoa, a town outside of Saigon: "We had to destroy the village in order to save it," he said.

Nor was the destruction limited to Vietnam. Americans turned against each other in bitter conflict over what some called genocide, and what others called a patriotic defense of freedom. The lives of a whole generation were transformed—those at home by having to decide whether to support a struggle many saw as the antithesis of what their country stood for, and those in Vietnam by the brutality of the military combat, the trauma of guerrilla ambush, the escape into drugs, and the knowledge throughout that people in the United States were not united behind them. In addition to all the other casualties, Lyndon Johnson's Great Society became a walking cripple, the president's obsession with consensus shadowed by a foreign power he seemed never able to control or understand. As Johnson said to his wife, "I can't get out, I can't finish with what I've got. So what the hell do I do?" His words bespoke the paralysis, frustration, and confusion of the entire country.

How then did we get into Vietnam? Where and why were steps taken that made withdrawal unthinkable? And how did two decades of America's "best and brightest" leaders manage to avoid the simplest question of whether we ever should have been there in the first place? The questions are difficult, the answers rooted in events that occurred long before the 1960s.

The Cold War and Korea

The starting point came at the end of the 1940s. After enacting the Truman Doctrine, the Marshall Plan, and successfully combating the Soviet Union's attempt to blockade Berlin, American foreign policy seemed to suffer a series of startling setbacks. In August 1949 the Russians had exploded their first atomic bomb, years ahead of the schedule anticipated by American experts. In September communist Chinese insurgents led by Mao Tse-tung finally crushed the Chinese nationalist government of Chiang Kai-shek, forcing him to flee to Formosa. Charges of a communist fifth column at home gained ascendancy with the trial of former State Department official Alger Hiss for perjury, and with the growing recognition that atomic spies had helped the Soviet Union leap-frog ahead in the race for nuclear parity. By early 1950 Senator Joseph McCarthy had seized the headlines with his claim that communist agents occupied sensitive positions throughout the U.S. government, and politicians—including John F. Kennedy and Lyndon Johnson—were echoing the widespread accusation that the State Department was guilty of complicity in the "loss" of China.

The domestic political climate of anticommunism substantially curtailed American flexibility toward the new Chinese government and the Soviet Union. Throughout the 1940s American military and diplomatic officials had maintained friendly communication with Chou En-Lai and other Chinese communists, recognizing that the Chiang regime was rife with corruption and probably doomed to be overthrown. Now, Chou secretly appealed to the United States for foreign aid, suggesting that friendship with the United States was preferable to a reliance on the Soviet Union. But at a time when diplomats who remained in contact with the communists were themselves being blamed for Chiang's defeat, American officials rejected the opportunity to turn China into an independent "Tito-like" state, refusing even to grant diplomatic recognition to the new government. At the same time, Truman administration officials decided to proceed with development of a hydrogen bomb, rejecting the advice of Soviet expert George

Kennan and others that the United States seize the occasion to move boldly for international control over atomic weapons and head off a new arms race.

The ultimate direction of U.S. foreign policy was signaled in April 1950 by the secret promulgation of National Security Council document NSC-68. Based on the assumption that the Soviet Union was engaged in a fanatical effort to seize control of governments wherever possible, the document committed America to assist allied nations *anywhere* in the world which seemed threatened by Soviet aggression. Clearly, the initial sense of containment enunciated by George Kennan had grown by leaps and bounds. Confrontation was now the norm, and NSC-68 urged a 350 percent increase in military spending as a means of combating the perceived Soviet threat.

It was within this context that the Korean War erupted. On Sunday morning, June 25, 1950, Secretary of State Dean Acheson telephoned Harry Truman at his home in Independence, Missouri, to tell him that North Korean troops had crossed the 38th parallel and invaded South Korea. "Dean," Truman said, "we've got to stop the sons-of-bitches no matter what." Hurrying back to Washington, the president ordered an emergency session of his military and foreign policy advisors, intent on establishing America's credibility as defender of the free world. "My father made it clear," Margaret Truman noted, "that he feared this was the opening round in World War III."

From the beginning, Truman viewed the crisis as an outgrowth of the Cold War and a direct test of the views articulated in NSC-68. There was no question in his mind that the Soviet Union had directed the invasion—an instinct subsequently confirmed by Soviet archives. "The conclusion I had come to," he said, "was that force was the only language the Russian dictatorship could understand. We had to meet them on that basis and defeat them." Flying back to Washington, the president ruminated on other examples of aggression that had gone unheeded. "If the Russian totalitarian state was intending to follow in the path of the dictatorship of Hitler and Mussolini," he reflected, "they [had to] be met head on in Korea." With Dean Acheson, the architect of the Truman Doctrine, as his principal advisor, the president concluded that "Korea is the Greece of the Far East." The invasion would measure America's commitment not only to defend a tiny Asian peninsula, but to contain communist aggression everywhere. "If we are tough enough," Truman said, "if we stand up to [the communists] like we did in Greece three years ago, they won't take any next steps. But if we just stand by they will move into Iran, and they'll take over the whole Middle East. There is no telling what they will do if we don't put up a fight now." As Acheson noted, NSC-68 was, until that moment, only a policy. Then, "Korea came along and saved us. . . . In Korea the Russians presented a check which was drawn on the bank account of collective security. . . . The Russians thought the check would bounce, . . . but to their great surprise, the teller paid it." Within three days the United States had secured the endorsement of the United Nation's Security Council to stop North Korean aggression and had committed American troops to bear the major burden of responsibility in implementing that policy. What Averell Harriman later called that "sour little war" had begun.

The fact that North Korean troops had invaded the South was never in doubt. However, the circumstances of the aggression proved far more complicated than Truman or his advisors ever let on. To begin with, South Korea was a nation torn by domestic political dissent and embittered by political repression. It was not a bastion of democracy. As the CIA noted, working-class anger against the South Korean government and the presence of a "restless student class" suggested that people of that divided country were by no means content with the regime that ruled them. Syngman Rhee, the Christian president of South Korea, was described as having a "messianic" complex that led him to override domestic dissent, imprison political foes, and impose the equivalent of totalitarian rule.

The evidence on Soviet responsibility was less clear at the time. In an early version of his memoirs (smuggled to the West for publication), Nikita Khrushchev recalled that North Korea's leader, Kim Il-sung, had consulted Stalin about invading South Korea, arguing that the war would be won quickly, given South Korea's domestic dissent, and that the United States would not intervene (wrong on both counts). We now know from recently opened Soviet records that Stalin did in fact authorize the attack. On the other hand, he did not wish Russia to be blamed for the attack and so withdrew Soviet military personnel from the peninsula. "It's too dangerous to keep our advisors there," Stalin is reported to have said. "They might be taken prisoner. We don't want there to be evidence . . . [of] us taking part in this business." Stalin even went as far as to not have the Soviet delegate to the U.N. take part in the Security Council debate on the invasion, where Russia could have used its veto power to prevent the council from acting on the American request for U.N. support (the Soviets had been boycotting the Security Council in protest against the failure of that body to recognize the Chinese Communist government in Peking). To complicate matters further, some of America's most knowledgeable advisors, including George Kennan, believed all along that the Korean struggle was primarily a civil war.

Still, Truman proceeded on the assumption (which we now know to have been correct) that the Soviets were directly responsible and that the Korean invasion constituted a decisive test of America's will to resist aggression. As soon as the U.N. Security Council condemned the attack, Truman ordered two American divisions into action and authorized Far East commander Douglas MacArthur to coordinate the air, naval, and ground attack, nominally under U.N. command, against the North Koreans. Faced with division among his own advisors as to whether the Soviet Union was actually ready for war, Truman ordered the secretaries of state and defense to make "a careful calculation . . . of the next probable place in which Soviet action might take place," and instructed the military to draw up contingency plans for attacking Soviet air bases if the Russians did become involved. Firm and decisive in his response, Truman drew plaudits from those committed to confronting the Soviet Union on all fronts. "I have lived and worked in and out of [Washington] for twenty years," Joseph Harsch of the *Christian Science Monitor* wrote the next day. "Never before in that time have I felt such a sense of relief and unity pass through this city."

The war itself offered a series of roller-coaster victories and defeats before stalemate finally set in. After U.N. troops were pushed back by North Koreans to a defense perimeter around Pusan at the tip of the South Korean peninsula, Douglas MacArthur launched a brilliant amphibious invasion at Inchon, north of Seoul, the capital of South Korea, which caught the North Koreans in a pincer movement and routed them from South Korea by the end of the year. But then, having restored the territorial integrity of the South, MacArthur—with Truman's permission—proceeded to invade the North to teach the lesson that "aggression doesn't pay." Despite repeated warnings from the Chinese that movement into North Korea would constitute active aggression against the Chinese, U.N. troops surged through the North approaching the Yalu River, which divided China from Korea. True to their word—and in total contradiction to MacArthur's assessment—the Chinese then retaliated, sending hordes of combat troops across the river. In the most brutal fighting of the war, the Chinese decimated U.N. forces, driving them back to the 38th parallel, the original borderline between North and South. At that point, negotiations for an armistice finally began, even as the fighting continued. For eighteen bitter months, the talks went on as countless additional lives were lost. Finally, Dwight Eisenhower, elected on a pledge to "go to Korea" and end the fighting, threatened, through diplomatic channels, to use atomic weapons if peace were not achieved. In the spring of 1953, nearly three years after the war began, the fighting ceased. After nearly 100,000 American casualties, the conflict came to an end with both sides occupying the same territory they had held when the war began.

In retrospect, the Korean conflict represented a decisive moment in American foreign policy history, bequeathing a mixed legacy of precedents that would shape the agenda of subsequent American policy toward the Cold War and Asia. Central to that legacy was the conviction that containment, however painfully implemented, had worked effectively. A line had been drawn, it had been defended, and aggression had been stopped. Whatever the ambiguities of American attitudes toward China and the Far East in 1949 and early 1950, Asia had now clearly become a battleground for the Cold War, with America's commitment to combat the Soviet Union and the Chinese in the Far East now just as firmly embedded as our defense of Western Europe. If nothing else, the Korean War universalized the Cold War, establishing that no geographical region, however distant from our shores, would be seen as exempt from the determination to confront communism.

President Truman pins the Distinguished Service Medal on General Douglas MacArthur on Wake Island, October 14, 1950. Truman later relieved MacArthur of his command in the Pacific because of MacArthur's insubordination. *(Library of Congress)*

Implicit in that legacy as well were a series of historical events that would weigh heavily on America's future conduct of foreign policy. First was the precedent of bypassing Congress and waging a war on executive authority alone. As an aide to Secretary of State Dean Acheson remarked at the time, "the President had done what he did; why open up the question of whether he should have done it? It had been accepted; everyone had overwhelmingly supported it; therefore there was no problem." Acheson feared that, if Congress were asked to declare war or approve Truman's actions, it might lead to divisive controversy. In his words, "both armed services committees would have had great hearings, at which everyone would ask all sorts of ponderous questions; by the time you got through with this you might have completely muddied up the situation which seemed to be very clear at the time." Since no one knew how long the war would take, or how many troops would be required, Acheson believed consulting Congress would simply provide an opportunity to "weaken and confuse [our] will." The result, Senator Robert Taft declared, was "a complete usurpation by the President of authority to use the Armed Forces of this country," a major step toward concentrating control of military and foreign policy in the White House and ignoring the check on executive power through the congressional questioning and debate mandated by the Founding Fathers.

Directly tied to this executive arrogation of authority was the power given the White House to define the issues and control the flow of information to the country on what was actually occurring. Consistently, the Truman administration disguised the nature of American involvement, creating a situation whereby, once the country became aware of the realities, events constituted a fait accompli that could not be reversed. Truman described American involvement as a "police action." When he announced that MacArthur had "been authorized to use certain supporting ground units," his wording totally obscured the fact that his commanding general had been authorized to use up to four divisions, or approximately 40 percent of the total strength of the U.S. Army. By applying phraseology suggesting only small increments of American engagement, the president created a situation where, once the full nature of American participation became clear, Congress had little option but to rally around the flag and support American troops in battle.

Third, the Korean conflict reinforced the tendency already present in American foreign policy to support dictatorship in the name of freedom and to ignore circumstances in local situations that resulted in Americans fighting for governments that systematically denied the possibilities of democracy. In effect, the Cold War became a prism that distorted political realities and defined every battle against communism as a defense of freedom, regardless of how far from the mark that description was. Syngman Rhee imprisoned political foes, slaughtered 27,000 dissidents, was repudiated by many of his own citizens, and refused to accept American injunctions to promote political reform. In the words of America's own State Department, Rhee was "a zealous, irrational, and illogical fanatic," a self-righteous tyrant. But, like Chiang Kai-shek before him, he was also a Christian, and in the words of America's war-time propaganda, he became a "gallant ally" in the battle for freedom. Through such logic, the United States seriously impaired its credibility with Third World countries, neutrals, and even allies. In the process, it moved decisively in the direction of interpreting nationalistic movements and local political dissent as subversive, creating a worldwide frame of reference in which any political force not solidly aligned with us was perceived as solidly against us, and as an ally of the Soviet Union.*

Fourth, the experience of fighting an Asian war highlighted the potential brutalization of American soldiers unable to distinguish friend from foe. Frequently, civilian populations supposedly supportive of the United Nations contained North Korean agents capable of exploding landmines or throwing grenades at allied troops. These tactics, one journalist noted, "forced upon our men in the field acts and attitudes of the utmost savagery . . . the blotting out of villages where the enemy *might* be hiding, the shooting and shelling of refugees who *may* include North Koreans." In one such episode, an American colonel instructed his troops to order a group of several hundred refugees to turn back. "But what if they don't go back," one officer said. "Well, then, fire over their heads," the colonel replied. "Okay, we fire over their heads. Then what?" "Well, then," the colonel said, "fire into them if you have to."

There were, of course, cautionary lessons that emerged from the Korean conflict as well. General Matthew Ridgeway, more responsible than anyone else for containing disaster when Chinese troops threatened to overrun all of Korea, vowed that never again should American soldiers be allowed to fight an Asian land war. The nearly fatal consequence of Chinese intervention also burned itself deeply into America's historical memory, alerting generals and politicians alike to the necessity in any future conflict of avoiding provocative acts that might unleash the "human wave" of Chinese troops.

But to those who chose to do so, these negative lessons could be explained away as the mistakes of General Douglas MacArthur, the reckless, demagogic, and probably pathological figure who conceived of himself as the savior of the Far East. MacArthur cut a dashing figure. As leader of American forces against Japan ("I shall return," he said as he retreated from the Philippines under Japanese attack), he led the island-to-island struggle to repulse Japanese aggression. Remaining as the head of America's occupying forces in postwar Japan, he governed that conquered nation like a dictator and assumed the same realm of authority when the Korean War began. Always stretching his orders to the extreme, he functioned as a power unto himself and felt no compunction about leaking his own views about American policy to reporters and Republican congressmen whenever he felt that he was not getting his own way. Like a spoiled child, MacArthur repeatedly insisted that he alone knew what was best, and that if he did not get his way,

---

* Nevertheless, in its own secret counsels, the U.S. National Security Council was also willing to consider a plan to topple Rhee from power if he proved too obstreperous. Indeed, if the South Korean leader continued to be a problem, he could be "eliminated."

the burden for failure would rest on his superiors. When MacArthur threatened to place "a band of radioactive waste" along the Yalu River and contemplated an atomic war against China, his views finally became so startling that the Joint Chiefs of Staff urged that he be withdrawn from command. According to many, it was MacArthur's stupidity—and, in particular, his total miscalculation of the Chinese—that caused the worst disasters of the war. Supposedly, better generals would fight better wars.*

In the end, the major result of the Korean War was substantially to increase America's resolve to fight communism everywhere around the globe and to bolster the U.S. conviction that containment was the only language the Russians would understand. The price had been exorbitant—more than 23,000 Americans killed, over 100,000 wounded, and bitter division at home by the war's end. In 1949 China had reached out for American help, the United States was weary of Chiang Kai-shek, and throughout the developing world the possibility still existed of American support for indigenous nationalism. By 1953, a viselike rigidity had eliminated all the flexibility of four years earlier with regard to both Asia and the Third World. The United States had committed itself to mortal combat against a monolithic Sino-Soviet bloc, dedicated in Lyndon Johnson's words, to fight "*any* act of aggression, *any*where by *any* communist forces . . . open or concealed." In all of this, Korea proved a decisive turning point, marking the first time America had gone to war in support of containment, but not the last.

The History of American Involvement in Vietnam, 1950–61

In many ways the die was cast for American involvement in Vietnam the day the Korean War began. Simultaneous to deciding to commit American troops in South Korea, Truman accepted Secretary of State Dean Acheson's recommendation that the United States commit $20 million in direct military aid to the French effort to contain Vietminh nationalists in Indochina. The decision reflected a lock-step logic that would increasingly dominate America's perception of the Third World. The United States, Acheson declared, was "convinced that neither national independence nor democratic evolution [can] exist in any area dominated by Soviet imperialism." Since Vietminh leader Ho Chi Minh was a confessed Marxist, he must be a Soviet

---

* In the eyes of many, MacArthur represents a case study of personality disorder. His mother moved to West Point to live near him when he was a student there, and then followed him from post to post. MacArthur came to think of himself as so special that no one could ever question his will. A romantic figure, he loved to be idolized. In Washington before World War II, he maintained an apartment—away from his home—where he would entertain prostitutes. "His idea of a hot time," an aide later said, "was just to bring them in for the evening. He never screwed them; he would just sit there in an arm chair and let the girls admire what a great man he was." The same aide reported that, on repeated occasions, MacArthur would call him to his house, pick up a gun, and threaten to shoot himself, thereby forcing his aide into pleading that the general was so important that the country could not spare him.

puppet. Any question of whether Ho was more a nationalist than a communist was deemed irrelevant. "All Stalinists in colonial areas are nationalists," Acheson averred. It took little effort to reverse the equation and conclude that most nationalists were also Stalinists. In either case, they had to be opposed, lest the United States show weakness and open the flood gates to Soviet aggression.

It had not always been that way. American intelligence officers had worked side by side with Ho in the spring of 1945 to free Vietnam from Japanese domination. They shared the reviewing stand with the Vietnamese leader as he proclaimed independence from French rule on September 2, 1945, quoting Thomas Jefferson's words: "We hold these truths to be self-evident. That all men are created equal." Vietminh leaders spoke warmly of their "particularly intimate relations" with the United States, "which it is a pleasant duty to dwell upon." Over the next few months, Ho Chi Minh addressed eight separate letters to Harry Truman urging him to provide support for the Vietnamese in their effort to build a new nation. The prospect for close ties between the two countries seemed particularly bright given FDR's earlier distrust of Charles de Gaulle, and his oft-expressed desire that colonialism end in Indochina, with America identifying itself with the forces of nationalism.

But the warm atmosphere of Independence Day quickly chilled in the environment of a rapidly escalating Cold War. Roosevelt himself had retreated from full endorsement of independence in Indochina at Yalta when he agreed that trusteeships for former colonies should be established only with the approval of the "mother country." Since France believed that it could "only be a great power as long as our flag continues to fly in all the overseas territories," that seemed unlikely. French colonies in Indochina were among her richest possessions, and having secured control over the southern part of Vietnam, the French preferred to fight rather than concede to the Vietminh's desire for unification and independence. When a French cruiser bombed Haiphong in November 1946, killing 6,000 civilians, full-scale war erupted. While chary of intervening directly on the side of the French in a colonialist war, Truman was intent on doing nothing that would weaken the already fragile relationship that existed between the United States and France. Europe was Truman's first concern, and solid support from France for containment of the Soviets there made it imperative that the United States refrain from any action that would alienate those "European states whose help we need to balance Soviet power in Europe." Ironically, the first step of America's long road toward full-scale war in Vietnam had nothing to do with Indochina itself, but occurred indirectly as a means of containing the Soviet Union in Europe.

Over the next few years, American military and economic aid enabled France to allocate resources for pursuing the war in Indochina that otherwise would have been used at home. Despite State Department acknowledgment that Ho Chi Minh represented a "symbol of nationalism in the struggle for freedom to the overwhelming majority of the [Vietnamese] population," the State Department concluded that America's "immediate and vital interest" lay in bolstering the French regime in order "to assist in the furtherance of our aims in Europe." Through such incremental steps, Americans quickly came to the conclusion that a setback in Indochina would be a setback for freedom everywhere. As one State Department team wrote in 1950, "Indochina is strategically important, for it provides a natural invasion route into the rice bowl of Southeast Asia should the communists adopt this form of aggression. Moreover, it has great political significance, because of its potential influence, should it fall to the communists, on Thailand, Burma, Malaysia, and perhaps Indonesia." Already, what would later be known as "the domino theory" had begun to work its magic.

By the time of the Korean War, the ground had been well prepared for direct military support of the same government that FDR had described as "poor colonizers" who had exploited the people of Indochina. If the Soviet Union were orchestrating a worldwide attack on the bastions of freedom, the United States would have to respond *wherever* the threat appeared, regardless of the local circumstances. Thus, between 1950 and 1954 the United States expended $2.6 billion in an increasingly frustrating effort to "save" Vietnam. With the best of intentions, the State Department urged French leaders to concede independence for Vietnam as an instrument of winning political support from the people against the Vietminh. But the French responded with only the token gesture of appointing a Vietnamese puppet, Bao Dai, who had spent most of the war shooting geese in a Vietnamese resort village. When Americans demanded a greater voice in the French military effort, French pride was wounded and Americans were denounced as interlopers. Yet, the United States could not afford to push the French too far, because French officials had the ultimate weapon at their disposal of threatening to withdraw from the European alliance. Unless Americans continued to accelerate their military aid in Indochina, the French warned, they would be forced to refuse support for the European defense community.

Given such a situation, American involvement in Vietnam inevitably deepened. By 1954 Dwight Eisenhower articulated at length the key reason for trying to contain communism in Asia. "You have a row of dominoes set up," he declared. "You knock over the first one, and what will happen to the last one is a certainty that it will go over very quickly." If the Vietminh won, Ike declared, "the remaining countries in Southeast Asia would be menaced by a great flanking movement. . . . The loss of South Viet Nam would have grave consequences for us and for freedom." Losing Vietnam had become the equivalent of losing China. It was an eventuality America could not tolerate.

The first test of that premise came in 1954 when the forces of Ho Chi Minh isolated 12,000 of France's elite troops at a lonely outpost called Dien Bien Phu. America must come in with troops and planes, the French warned. Generals and admirals drew up contingency plans, and Vice-President Nixon supported dropping an A-bomb on the troops besieging the fortress. But America could get no support from its allies, and this time, consulting Congress in advance, the administration found nothing but hostility toward the idea. As a result, Dien Bien Phu fell, the defeat occurring the same day an international conference of fourteen nations convened at Geneva to consider the fate of Indochina. Reluctantly participating in the conference, the United States struggled to salvage some remnant of a South Vietnamese government that it could support. (John Foster Dulles refused to shake hands with Chou En Lai at the conference on the grounds that one did not engage in diplomatic niceties with the devil.) With Russia in a mood to relax international tensions after Stalin's death, communist participants in the conference persuaded the Vietminh to accept the temporary division of the country into two parts at the 17th parallel, with reunification to take place two years later after national elections. But instead of acceding to the scenario envisioned by Moscow and Hanoi, the United States chose instead to prevent the victory that the Vietminh thought was theirs. In 1947 the British had withdrawn from the Mediterranean, leaving the United States to step in as the guarantor of European stability against the Russians. Now, the French were forced out of Indochina, and once again, America prepared to take the place of a European power, this time in Asia. By 1955 the Vietnam conflict had become an American conflict.

The United States never had any intention of acquiescing in the unification of Vietnam under Ho Chi Minh. Although Eisenhower acknowledged that he could "conceive of no greater tragedy than for the United States to become involved in an all-out land war in Asia," he also affirmed that the United States would "not be a party to a treaty that makes anybody a slave." He thereby justified U.S. refusal to sign the Geneva accords. If the Soviet Union and China had believed that the Geneva agreement would provide a framework for eventual victory by Ho Chi Minh without any further sacrifice of Vietminh lives and money, they had grossly miscalculated. Everywhere in the world the Eisenhower administration seemed intent on successfully combating indigenous insurgency, viewing it as a vehicle for communism. In Guatemala, the CIA successfully sponsored a coup d'état in 1954 against the regime of Jacobo Arbenz who threatened to nationalize United Fruit landholdings. A similar CIA effort overthrew a nationalist government in Iran, restoring the Shah as ruler of that land. When the Lebanese government seemed endangered by domestic civil war, Eisenhower landed American marines on Beirut beaches in 1958 and proclaimed the Eisenhower Doctrine, offering to provide economic and military help to any country threatened by "overt armed aggression from any nation controlled by international communism." In similar fashion, the United States intervened to protect Quemoy and Matsu, Chinese off-shore islands, from the mainland Chinese. Despite a willingness to negotiate with the Russians, exemplified by Eisenhower's summit conference with Russian leaders in

Geneva and in Camp David in 1955 and 1957, it seemed clear that the United States intended to give no quarter to its perceived foe anywhere in the world. In this sense, Vietnam represented one more illustration of a systematic worldwide effort to contain and combat indigenous efforts to challenge pro-Western governments.*

Consistent with overall U.S. policy, the National Security Council in the summer of 1954 urged the United States to "make every possible effort, not openly inconsistent with the U.S. position as to the armistice agreement . . . to maintain a friendly non-communist South Viet Nam and to prevent a communist victory through all-Viet Nam elections." The CIA was instructed to use "all available means" to subvert the Vietminh government in Hanoi, while building South Vietnam as "the cornerstone of the Free World in Southeast Asia." Dulles created the Southeast Asian Treaty Organization (SEATO) in September 1954, to provide a collective security framework within which the United States could counteract "subversive activities directed from without," and proceeded to bolster pro-Western factions inside South Vietnam. Ironically, the United States was convinced that it could avoid the errors of the French experience. After all, the French were a colonialist power; the United States was not. Moreover, the French had botched their military campaign to save Vietnam. American generals knew better how to fight. Hence, the United States could work through "nationalist" pro-Western figures in Vietnam to subvert the Geneva accords, allegedly free of the primary impediments that had crippled the French effort.

Ngo Dingh Diem provided the instrument for implementing American policy. Another Asian Christian, and a staunch nationalist, Diem was given the mandate to bring unity to a country described by the author Frances FitzGerald as a "political jungle of war lords, sects, bandits, partisan troops and secret societies." Although U.S. intelligence sources rated his chances as "poor" at best, Diem became the fragile reed on which America placed its hopes. A scholar and aristocrat, Diem had abstained from participation in the various governments that had ruled his homeland for the past twenty years, spending most of the years of the French-Indochina war in a Catholic seminary in America where he established influential connections with peo-

---

* Eisenhower pursued this policy, it should be noted, within the context of seeking to relax tensions with the Soviets. In an eloquent speech shortly after Stalin's death, the president declared: "every gun that is fired, every warship launched, every rocket fired signifies, in the final sense, a theft from those who hunger and are not fed, and those who are cold and are not clothed." Instead of confrontation, the president urged a "total war, not upon any human enemy, but upon the brute forces of poverty and need." On one level, he seems genuinely to have desired a resolution of the Cold War, proposing an "open skies for peace" agreement with the Soviets, permitting each nation to conduct surveillance of the other's military potential, and working toward treaties on atomic energy and other issues dividing the superpowers; nevertheless, this peace offensive occurred against a backdrop of substantive and systematic opposition to virtually every perceived threat to the West. Just as characteristic of the Eisenhower administration was John Foster Dulles's rhetoric of "massive retaliation" and promises to "liberate" the captive peoples of Eastern Europe.

ple such as Francis Cardinal Spellman, John Kennedy, and Mike Mansfield. Now, this Mandarin ("he always dressed in white and looked as if he were made out of ivory," one journalist said) returned home to try to build a nation.

Diem's chief advantage (and some would say disadvantage) rested in his elite aloofness from the recent history of his native land. As a fresh presence, guided by an almost "divine right" sense of his own destiny, Diem came to the office of Prime Minister free of association with the colonialist French and intent on playing off each other the feudal baronies that controlled most of South Vietnam. With almost unlimited American aid, he attempted to buy off his opponents, while offering a haven for the nearly 900,000 refugees, most of them Catholic, who fled south after the war. Diem even went so far as to put his own family members in charge: his brother Nhu ran the secret police, Madam Nhu controlled the black market currency operation, and his brother was archbishop of Vietnam. Although the remaining French officials in Vietnam viewed him as a disaster, and even American officials doubted his capacity to prevent the country from falling under communist control in the face of sectarian division, Diem had the indispensable asset of complete support from John Foster Dulles and the growing allegiance of American military officers sent to Vietnam to build a new army. When the new ruler proved successful in one pivotal battle against an opposition sect in 1955, he convinced doubting American officials to support him "wholeheartedly" as the only person who could "save South Viet Nam and counteract revolution."

With total American support, Diem proceeded to subvert the Geneva accords attempting to impose unity from above on his divided country. As Eisenhower acknowledged, holding a national election to reunify Vietnam, as mandated by the Geneva treaty, would have resulted in an overwhelming victory for Ho Chi Minh. Hence, Diem refused to permit the election, barred all contacts with the North, and made the 17th parallel a rigid boundary, comparable to the 38th parallel in Korea. With a massive infusion of more than $1 billion in American aid, the new Prime Minister attempted to rebuild the Vietnamese economy, train a modern army, and develop the substance, as well as the appearance, of a viable nation-state. He even held a referendum, at America's urging, to legitimize his authority. While American advisors assured him that a 60 percent vote would be adequate, Diem produced a 98.2 percent margin of victory, including 605,000 votes from the 405,000 registered voters in Saigon.

From the beginning, however, America's hopes for Diem foundered on a dilemma of its own making. Dulles was convinced that the primary requirement for South Vietnamese nationhood was the creation of a strong army. Although the United States made its support for this army conditional on South Vietnamese implementation of political and economic reform, the military side of the equation always came first. Four out of every five

American dollars sent to Vietnam were expended on military activity supervised by America's Military Assistance and Advisory Group (MAAG), and even the economic aid went primarily to flood South Vietnamese cities with Western consumer goods that benefited the middle class, but did little for the vast majority of the Vietnamese living in the countryside. Furthermore, until the end of the 1950s, virtually all of America's military energies were devoted toward transforming the South Vietnamese army into a conventional fighting force, not one prepared for guerrilla warfare. The result, one U.S. official said, was to leave the Vietnamese "pathetically unready for the reality of the Vietnamese countryside. A squad of civil guard policemen, armed with whistles, night sticks, and thirty-eight caliber revolvers, could hardly be expected to arrest a squad of guerrillas armed with submachine guns, rifles, grenades, and mortars." The military buildup seemed more to confirm than to deny that the United States was simply one more Western colonial power.

Nevertheless, most Americans viewed Diem's achievement as an unmitigated success. Observing the thriving economy and the proliferation of Western-style goods, American observers felt reassured about the efficacy of their effort. One Democratic senator urged that Vietnam be used as a "showcase" for American foreign aid, demonstrating to others around the world the "wholesome effect of our efforts to help other people help themselves." Diem appeared to be a hero. "On his record," a Newsweek commentator declared, "he must be rated as one of the ablest free Asian leaders. We can take pride in our support."

Even in the midst of such "success," however, Diem was already sowing the seeds of his own destruction. The very "messianic" complex that made him appear such a strong leader also militated against reform and the sensitivity to political differences that were essential to building a national consensus. Diem would brook no opposition. His government espoused the philosophy of "personalism," the notion that an imperial figure must control everything. In the words of the journalist Bernard Fall, Diem believed that "compromise has no place and opposition of any kind must of necessity be subversive and must be suppressed with all the vigor the system is capable of." Instituting a program of "re-education centers," Diem imprisoned thousands of dissidents, exiling or arresting even ardent anticommunists if they criticized his government. All power emanated from the presidential palace in Saigon and from a government half of whose cabinet ministers were Diem's blood relatives.

Worst of all, Diem greeted with disdain American attempts to promote land reform and a better life for Vietnamese villagers. Despite some gains in dispensing better health care and improved agricultural technology for the countryside, the South Vietnamese government refused to break up the huge land estates of the old aristocracy and give Vietnam's peasants control over the land they farmed. Moreover, in an attempt to centralize further his authority, Diem insisted on appointing village and provincial officials himself, thereby abrogating a centuries-old tradition of local communities choosing their own leaders. Local ties to the national government were also weakened when, in order to combat rising insurgency in the countryside, Diem initiated a program to relocate peasants from their homes, removing them from areas that contained the bones of their ancestors, and from land that they had farmed all their lives.

Not surprisingly, such actions reinforced popular alienation from the government and created a fertile ground for insurrection. During the three years after the Geneva accords, Vietminh supporters remained relatively quiescent, seeking primarily to survive Diem's repression, perhaps still hopeful that the political victory promised in Geneva could be secured. By the end of 1957, however, these Vietminh cadres re-established their political networks and embarked on a campaign to mobilize discontent against the government. As one Vietminh guerrilla later said, the peasants were "like a mound of straw ready to be ignited." Although the North Vietnamese provided little support of any kind until 1959, the rebels in South Vietnam had already succeeded in galvanizing substantial backing for their campaign against Diem, using both political organization and systematic terror to discredit the regime in Saigon. By the time North Vietnam resumed its own campaign of armed aid for insurgents in the South in early 1959, local rebels were already in control of much of the infrastructure of the countryside. Guerrilla terror tactics escalated (approximately 2,500 government officials were assassinated in 1960), and the rebel forces increasingly were ready to engage in full-scale attacks against the South Vietnamese army.

Although it was not yet recognized in Washington, the Eisenhower administration's commitment to making South Vietnam another "showcase" of communist containment was already crumbling. Despite its best intentions, America had become inextricably associated with a repressive government presided over by an imperial tyrant who had little if any contact with his own people. By emphasizing military preparation as its first priority and giving unequivocal support to Diem, the United States made itself a hostage to the Diem regime, mortally undercutting its avowed intention to promote economic and political reform and identify with the forces of nationalism. Supremely confident in 1954 that it could avoid the errors of the French, the United States by 1960 had repeated all of them. As one American said with bitter irony, even before the disasters of the late fifties, "we are the last of the French colonialists." At the end of the decade, most Americans in and out of government still believed that South Vietnam represented a model of success. Preoccupied with a new Berlin crisis, the blowup of Eisenhower's last summit conference because an American U-2 spy plane had been shot down over the Soviet Union, and a growing crisis in nearby Laos, few paid much attention to the rapid erosion taking place in the country that America defined as the "cornerstone of freedom in Asia." But the process was well under way, and it would take a radical reassessment of all America's Cold War assumptions if a greater tragedy were to be averted.

The Kennedy Years

The man who defined his role as "defending freedom at its maximum moment of peril" all around the world was not predisposed to engage in such a reassessment. Although a decade earlier John F. Kennedy had warned that "no amount of American military assistance [in Indochina] can conquer an enemy which is everywhere," he entered the White House convinced that, if America showed weakness, "the whole world, in my opinion, would inevitably begin to move toward the communist bloc." An administration committed to "move forward to meet communism, rather than waiting for it to come to us," could hardly be expected to raise fundamental questions about a policy sanctioned by two previous presidents and consecrated by the litany of containment and the domino theory. On occasion during his thousand days in office, Kennedy exhibited the skeptical good sense of his earlier comments on Southeast Asia. But in the main, his actions simply reinforced and deepened the unfolding tragedy.

The Kennedy policy toward Vietnam emerged during 1961 as a product of four interrelated perceptions, all directly connected to the Cold War itself. First, was the conviction, shared by Kennedy and most of his foreign policy advisors, that communism remained a monolithic conspiracy spearheaded by China and the Soviet Union and committed to newly aggressive efforts to dominate the world. Still traumatized by the "loss" of China, the stalemate in Korea, and the McCarthyite mystique about "softness" in the State Department, the foreign policy establishment was intent on preventing any further defeats, especially in Asia. Dean Rusk, Kennedy's secretary of state, believed that "Peiping" (Rusk always refused to call the Chinese capital Peking, seemingly fixated on the spelling used when the nationalist Chinese were in control) was sponsoring aggression throughout the Asian subcontinent. The new secretary of state, one aide noted, "was possessed of a special mania about China and of a knack for arguing by dubious analogy." For Rusk, compromise in Vietnam was equivalent to appeasement at Munich, with China simply a modern-day surrogate for Hitlerite Germany. Nor was he alone in his perceptions. As Walt Rostow, a White House foreign policy advisor observed in 1961, the situation in the world was exactly comparable to the early 1940s when freedom was suffering setbacks everywhere. It was time to "turn the tide," Rostow declared, and Vietnam was a good place to start.

Second, the perception of communist intentions seemed confirmed by Nikita Khrushchev's endorsement of "wars of national liberation" as a means of promoting communism's global strategy. In a rambling eight-hour speech delivered in January 1961, the Soviet premier had advanced the new doctrine, probably with the intention of warning China that the Soviet Union would not sit idly by while its growing adversary flexed its muscles. But in Washington, the declaration was understood as a clear signal that the Russians were extending their confrontation with the United States into new arenas and, hence, escalating the struggle for global dominance.

Third, a series of reversals in other Cold War crises persuaded the Kennedy administration that a strong stand—somewhere—was imperative, lest the world, and the Sino-Soviet bloc, become convinced that the United States was a weak, waning power. In April 1961 the Castro government in Cuba had humiliated the United States by crushing a CIA-sponsored invasion at the Bay of Pigs. Three months later in Vienna, Khrushchev and Kennedy met at the summit, where the Soviet leader exhibited an attitude of near contempt for his American counterpart, taunting him about wars of national liberation in Southeast Asia and throwing down the gauntlet on Berlin. Some observers noted a "siege mentality" developing at the White House, with the president himself asking his advisors "What's gone against us today?" As Kennedy told the *New York Times* columnist Arthur Krock, it was imperative that Khrushchev not "misunderstand Cuba, Laos, etc. to indicate that the United States is in a yielding mood on such matters as Berlin." In such a context, a strong policy in Vietnam became necessary, not only because the administration believed in the domino theory, but because it needed to take a stand somewhere, even 9,000 miles away, to show the Soviet Union that America was not ready to roll over and play dead.

Fourth, and finally, American involvement in Southeast Asia provided the new administration with a "laboratory" to test its own new strategy of "flexible response" to Soviet aggression. Convinced that the Eisenhower administration's reliance on nuclear deterrence and massive retaliation was inappropriate in a world full of trouble spots of differing dimensions, Kennedy and his foreign policy advisors embarked on a major buildup of conventional forces and counterinsurgent techniques. As Roger Hilsman observed, "The way to fight the guerrilla was to adopt the tactics of the guerrilla." New frontiersmen shuttled back and forth to Fort Bragg, exultant about the possibility that Green Berets—an elite antiguerrilla force—could become the vanguard for turning back insurgent forces in Third World countries. "It is somehow wrong to be developing these capabilities but not applying them in a crucial theatre," Walt Rostow said. "In Knute Rockne's old phrase, we are not saving them for the junior prom." By deploying such forces in areas like Vietnam, General Maxwell Taylor observed, the United States could prove to the Soviets that wars of national liberation were not "cheap, safe, and disavowable [but] costly, dangerous, and doomed to failure."

For all these reasons, the Kennedy administration concluded by the fall of 1961 that America's involvement in Vietnam must be deepened. The "credibility" of the United States as a great power was on the line. As Kennedy told John Kenneth Galbraith, "There are just so many concessions that one can make to the communists in one year and survive politically." Galbraith particularly remembered his saying, "We just can't . . . have another defeat this year in Viet Nam." Clearly, the administration felt on the defensive, needing to find a way of signaling to the Soviets that containment still functioned as an effective policy, and needing a place to demonstrate the new tactics being devised in Washington to forge an aggressive foreign policy. During those first few months in office, McGeorge Bundy recalled, "We [were] like the Harlem Globetrotters. Passing forward, behind, sideways and underneath. [But] nobody [had] made a basket." Partly as an accident, but mostly as a logical extension of everything else that had happened during the first six months of the Kennedy administration, Vietnam became the battleground on which the United States would attempt to make a point with the Russians, demonstrating the administration's commitment "to pay any price, to bear any burden, in the defense of freedom," so that its word elsewhere would not be taken lightly.

What David Halberstam eloquently described as the "quagmire" of American involvement in Vietnam emerged gradually during the first months of 1961, and then accelerated quickly with a November decision to commit substantial American troops for the first time to that distant country. In the process a fateful pattern of bureaucratic compromise and political equivocation developed that would cripple American policy for the next eight years. Ironically, Eisenhower had never mentioned Vietnam to Kennedy in his preinaugural briefing, concentrating instead on the crisis in Laos. But within ten days after taking office, Kennedy received startling information from General Edward Lansdale on the rapid erosion of support for the Diem regime. "This is the worst one we've got, isn't it?," Kennedy replied. By the end of March, intelligence officers notified Kennedy that "an extremely critical period [for Saigon] lay immediately ahead." Establishing a special task force on Vietnam, Kennedy proceeded to order five hundred Green Berets to Vietnam, authorized clandestine operations against the North, and dispatched Vice-President Lyndon Johnson on the first of a never-ending series of fact-finding missions to Southeast Asia. For the first time, active use of American combat troops was considered as a viable option. Still, in Walt Rostow's words, Kennedy was pursuing a policy of "buying time with limited commitment of additional American resources."

By the fall of 1961, such a policy no longer seemed adequate. Rapidly increasing Vietcong attacks appeared to threaten directly the survival of the Diem regime, while the Saigon government itself raised questions about the seriousness of America's commitment. Although Lyndon Johnson had described Diem as the "Winston Churchill of Southeast Asia," it was clear that words were no longer sufficient to stem the deterioration of morale. Many of Kennedy's advisors urged a major new investment of American resources, and the president sent Rostow and General Maxwell Taylor, his personal military advisor, to Vietnam to recommend the steps that needed to be taken. Their report elaborated the chaotic situation in Vietnam, emphasized the Diem regime's uncertainty about the U.S. commitment, and proposed using the occasion of a recent devastating flood in Vietnam to justify sending 8,000 American troops—allegedly for "flood control" work—to South Vietnam to bolster the regime.

Reaction to the report typified the U.S. response in a series of similar situations over the next decade. Fearful of committing combat troops in vi-

As vice-president, Lyndon Johnson toured South Vietnam to offer assurances of American support. Here, he greets South Vietnamese youngsters. *(National Archives)*

olation of the Geneva accords, Rusk initially rejected the suggestions of Taylor and Rostow. Kennedy himself was skeptical. How could the United States justify interfering "in civil disturbances caused by guerrillas," he asked Arthur Krock, noting that "it [is] hard to prove that this [isn't] largely the situation in Viet Nam." In a moment of prophetic insight he told one aide: "The troops will march in; the bands will play; the crowds will cheer; and in four days everyone will have forgotten. Then we will be told we have to send more troops. It's like taking a drink. The effect wears off, and you have to take another." The military, in contrast, recognized that 8,000 troops would be inadequate to the task and estimated that over 200,000 soldiers would be required.

Afraid to do nothing yet wary of doing too much, Kennedy eventually accepted a recommendation for compromise from Rusk and McNamara. The United States would join in a "limited partnership" with Saigon in a "sharply increased joint effort to avoid a further deterioration in the situation in South Vietnam." A combination of additional troops, American technology, and political reform would operate to forestall disaster and create a "turning point" in the struggle. A massive influx of helicopters would give South Vietnamese forces the necessary mobility to contain Vietcong guerrillas. Aircraft manned by U.S. pilots would fly support missions. American advisors inserted at critical points in the Vietnamese bureaucracy would streamline the administration of the South Vietnamese government. And the creation of new schools, better medical service, and land reform would ensure the loyalty of the Vietnamese people to the Diem government. It was all a policymaker's dream, each component designed to achieve, economically and efficiently, U.S. objectives. Although advisors like Harriman and Bowles warned against further support for a "repressive, dictatorial and unpopular regime," Kennedy was ultimately persuaded that American credibility required action. "That son-of-a-bitch [in Moscow] won't pay any attention to words," he had said in the summer. "He has to see you move." By December, the United States had stationed more than 3,000 troops in Vietnam, four times the number there a year earlier. They would serve, in Taylor's words, as "a visible symbol of the seriousness of American intentions." They would also constitute a downpayment on a never-ending demand for more troops in order to preserve the initial investment. Kennedy's initial intuition had been correct, his later decisions a devastating error.

At first, Kennedy's action appeared to pay dividends. South Vietnamese troops launched a major offensive supported by American helicopters and aircraft. "Roaring in over the treetops," Roger Hilsman noted, "[the helicopters] were a terrifying sight to the superstitious Vietcong peasants. In those first few months the Vietcong simply turned and ran—and, flushed from their foxholes and hiding places, and running in the open, they were easy targets." But in a nation full of swamps and forests, hiding places were easy to find, particularly when the local populace offered shelter—even if under duress—to Vietcong guerrillas. "You have to land right on top of them or they disappear," one American remarked. Moreover, South Vietnamese army troops were reluctant to engage the enemy. They relied increasingly on helicopter gun ships, and when they did fight, suffered a startling series of defeats.

In the meantime, the Kennedy policy foundered on the same shoals that had crippled all previous American efforts in Vietnam—the repressive and unresponsive nature of the Diem government. Refusing to insist on political reform and redistribution of land, Washington found itself bolstering a government in Saigon that consistently alienated the Vietnamese people. If Diem was the best that Americans had, he was not good enough. South Vietnamese troops made no distinction between Vietcong and innocent civilians. The use of napalm and chemical defoliants angered villagers, and a new campaign to relocate peasants from land they venerated simply increased popular hostility to the Saigon government. Moreover, most American money for services to the people was siphoned off into the coffers of corrupt Saigon officials, never reaching its intended beneficiaries. Diem, his brother, Nhu, and Nhu's wife—nicknamed the "Dragonlady" after a well-known cartoon character—became increasingly tyrannical and isolated. Although American military reports from the field contained a barrage of statistics that persuaded Washington officials that the war was being won, figures detailing enemy body counts and secure villages bore almost no relationship to reality. When reporters in Vietnam sent back dispatches to their home newspapers detailing the true situation, they were blasted as disloyal. "Why don't you get on the team?," one military official asked a critical journalist.

By the spring of 1963, the rosy optimism of earlier reports began to wane. A new fact-finding mission concluded that the war would "probably last longer than we would like [and] cost more in terms of both lives and money than we had anticipated." Although there were now 15,000 American troops in Vietnam, the war appeared to be stalemated. A massive chasm separated Pentagon reports of success and journalistic accounts of despair and failure. It became increasingly clear that, far from being able to alter the repressive policies of Diem, American aid simply drove him further into his own counsels. Whatever his intentions, Kennedy, like Eisenhower before him, had become hostage to a government in Saigon that in every way gave the lie to American propaganda that this was a battle for freedom and democracy.

The "sink or swim with Diem" policy exploded into crisis in the late spring of 1963 when Buddhists all over Vietnam rebelled against government repression. In response, Diem unleashed brutal reprisals, even ordering troops to fire into crowds of demonstrators. When a number of Buddhist monks dramatized their protest by setting themselves afire on Saigon's streets, Madam Nhu belittled their martydom, calling it a "bonz barbecue." Her insensitivity and contempt simply redoubled domestic anger against Diem and sparked worldwide protest. All over the globe, the CIA reported, governments and protest groups were condemning the United States for supporting a regime that brutally suppressed human rights. No longer was it possible for Washington to delude itself into thinking that victory was at hand.

Kennedy responded by appointing Henry Cabot Lodge to be his new ambassador to Saigon and by sending still another fact-finding mission to Southeast Asia. Lodge, Madam Nhu declared, came almost as a "pro-consul." Indeed, the former ambassador to the United Nations and vice-presidential candidate fit the description. A Boston Brahmin, Lodge coldly and calculatedly assessed the situation, intent on shaping policy in a firm manner that tolerated no equivocation or delay. Kennedy's fact-finding team, in turn, came back to Washington with advice that only reinforced Kennedy's reliance on his new ambassador. While General Victory Krulak assured the president that the war was going well and that Diem posed no serious problem, State Department advisor Joseph Mendenhall reported virtual chaos in Saigon. "You two did visit the same country, didn't you?," Kennedy asked.

Lodge quickly came to the conclusion that Diem had to be replaced. On the eve of his arrival, Diem, in total contradiction to a pledge he had made to outgoing Ambassador Frederick Nolting, ordered a massive assault by special forces units against the Buddhists and then blamed army generals for ordering the attack. Lodge was furious at the betrayal and initiated conversations with Vietnamese generals to determine their willingness to support a coup. When Lodge reported the generals' response to Washington, State Department advisors, with approval by phone from the president, sent back a cable declaring that if "Diem remains obdurate [and refuses to remove Nhu], then we are prepared to accept the obvious implications that we can no longer support Diem. You may tell appropriate military commanders we will give them direct support in any interim period of breakdown [of the] central government mechanism."

Kennedy now entered a period of critical decision-making. Although Kennedy's advisors, upon reconsideration, questioned the wisdom of the earlier cable, Lodge persisted. "We are launched on a course from which there is no respectable turning back: the overthrow of the Diem government," the ambassador cabled. In response, Secretary of State Rusk told Lodge that Kennedy "will support a coup which has a good chance of succeeding but plans no direct involvement of U.S. Armed forces." At the appropriate time, Lodge was given authority to announce suspension of aid to the Diem regime, which in turn would be a signal to the generals of U.S. compliance with their plans. General Paul Harkins was authorized to establish "liaison with the coup planners and to review plans," while Lodge was told to do whatever he had to do to "enhance the chance of a successful coup." Clearly, the United States was intimately involved in the decision to depose Diem.

In the meantime, Kennedy seems to have faced for the first time the possibility that further American involvement in Vietnam would prove disastrous. According to former White House aide Kenneth O'Donnell, the president by late summer of 1963 had recognized the self-defeating nature of American participation in the war. Yet he was unable—or unwilling—to act immediately to extricate the United States from the situation. "If I tried to pull out completely now from Viet Nam," He allegedly told Mike Mansfield, "we would have another Joe McCarthy red scare on our hands." In meetings of presidential advisors in late August, Attorney General Robert Kennedy raised the issue of whether the United States should any longer participate in the Vietnam venture—the first time anyone had asked *the* fundamental question about the war. General Charles de Gaulle simultaneously was pursuing a plan whereby the United States would pull out of Vietnam and sanction creation of a coalition government, including Diem, that would be acceptable to the North Vietnamese.

But for whatever reason, Kennedy rejected the option of withdrawal and proceeded inexorably along a course that would only further deepen U.S. complicity and responsibility for the fighting. Lodge received authorization anew to assure Vietnamese generals of American support in a coup attempt. While Kennedy publicly stated in September that "in the final analysis it is their war" and that, if the Vietnamese were not willing to fight, there was no amount of American support that could win a victory, he also declared that "for us to withdraw from that effort would mean a collapse not only of South Viet Nam but Southeast Asia. . . . I believe [in the domino theory]. . . . If South Viet Nam went, it . . . will give the impression that the wave of the future in Southeast Asia [is] China and the communists." On the night of November 1, 1963, with CIA officers at South Vietnamese army head-quarters, the coup took place, Diem was arrested, and he and his brother were murdered. Just three weeks later, Kennedy himself was assassinated in Dallas.

Conclusion

Although Kennedy supporters continued to argue that the president, had he lived, would never have tolerated a continuation of American participation in the Vietnam debacle, the fact remains that Kennedy and his advisors had charted a course that step by step involved the United States inextricably deeper in the Vietnam tragedy. As Ambassador Maxwell Taylor later recalled, "Diem's overthrow set in motion a sequence of crisis, political and military, over the next two years which eventually forced President Johnson in 1965 to choose between accepting defeat or introducing American combat forces." Whatever the wisdom or error of the decision to depose Diem, American support for the coup carried with it responsibility for standing by those who had promoted it and for providing ever-increasing amounts of support as a desperate way of staving off ultimate defeat. As the authors of one U.S. government analysis reported, "the role played by the U.S. during the overthrow of Diem caused a deeper U.S. involvement in Viet Nam affairs. . . . By virtue of this interference, . . . the U.S. had assumed a significant new responsibility for the new regime, a responsibility which heightened U.S. commitment and deepened U.S. involvement." The die had been cast. However much Kennedy may have started to question the wisdom of the entire Cold War frame of reference, he and his Cold War advisors remained responsible for a fateful and tragic extension of the war—one that would lead to incalculable disaster.

10

"Lyndon's War"

As Lyndon Johnson prepared to take the oath of office aboard Air Force One on November 22, 1963, Henry Cabot Lodge was winging his way across the Pacific for a meeting previously scheduled with John F. Kennedy to assess the consequences of the overthrow of Ngo Diem. Johnson instructed the ambassador to proceed to Washington. Within three days, he had embraced Kennedy's war and made it his own. "I'm not going to lose Viet Nam," he told Lodge. "I'm not going to be the president who saw Southeast Asia go the way China went." When Johnson assumed the presidency, there were 16,000 American troops in Vietnam. When he left there were more than 500,000. The succession of Johnson to the presidency, Godfrey Hodgson has written, "might have made it possible to reverse the direction of [American] policy, and so to avoid a great mistake. . . . A new president . . . could have decided right at the start, before his personal prestige was committed, to cut his losses and get out." But Johnson missed the opportunity. Every bone in his body, every dimension of his political personality, compelled him to proceed. And so the same weekend he authorized Walter Heller to draw up legislation for the war on poverty, he directed Lodge and his foreign policy aides to deepen American involvement in Vietnam. The two wars would become the hallmarks of his presidency, with the tragic paradox that waging one ensured the defeat of the other.

The Johnson Approach to Foreign Policy

Like Harry Truman eighteen years earlier, Lyndon Johnson assumed the presidency with little, if any, firsthand experience in making the momentous decisions of foreign affairs that would so decisively shape the course of his administration. Johnson, wrote a perceptive reporter in 1966,

> was the Riverboat man . . . a swashbuckling master of the political midstream, but only in the crowded, well travelled inland waterways of domestic politics. He had no taste and scant preparation for the deep waters of foreign policy, for the sudden storms and the unpredictable winds that can becalm or batter or blow off course the ocean-going man. He was the king of the river and a stranger to the open sea.

To Johnson, foreign policy had always meant patriotism and bipartisanship. "It is an American, not a political foreign policy that we have in the United States," he said in 1948. "This is a question of patriotism, not politics." Throughout his political career, his first rule was to support the president. "We've got to be for America first," he said when Eisenhower authorized a counterrevolution in Guatamala. "[We have got to] cut out this distrust and hatred of each other." Thoroughly committed to the posture of rigorous anticommunism, Johnson had always rallied behind the flag, supporting— seemingly without question—any and every manifestation of America's containment policy. "When they lead your boy down to that railroad station to send him into boot camp and put a uniform on him to send him somewhere he may never return, they don't ask you whether you are Republican or Democrat," he told one audience. "They send you to defend that flag, and you go."

From Johnson's perspective, foreign policy was a matter of honor, courage, and credibility. America had given its word that it would defend freedom anywhere that freedom was threatened, and it must abide by that commitment. Three American presidents had pledged their support of Vietnamese independence, and Johnson was not about to violate that pledge. If North Vietnam attacked American troops, it was a matter of honor that the United States retaliate and seek revenge. "We're not going to tuck our tails and run home," he once said. "When we are attacked, we must not turn our tail and run, we must stand and fight." Whatever the odds, America must stand behind its commitments. "We love peace," Johnson said. "We hate war. But our course is charted always by the compass of *honor*. . . . We are [in Viet Nam] because . . . we remain fixed on the pursuit of freedom, a deep and moral obligation *that will not let us go*."

Such a sense of commitment had deep personal meaning for Johnson, rooted in his Texas upbringing. As the historian Bertram Wyatt-Brown has written, the code of honor was central to the Southern character—an obsession with personal bravery, profound fear of humiliation and shame, a determination to live by one's word. "If you let a bully come into your front yard one day," Johnson was fond of saying, "the next day he will be up on your porch and the day after that he will rape your wife in your own bed." Texans, of all people, Johnson once said, "should go on record against isolationism and appeasement." Retreat, betrayal of a pledge, cowardice—all were unthinkable. "Hell," the president told the National Security Council, "Viet Nam is just like the Alamo." Texas school children were indoctrinated with the story of how commander William Travis had drawn a line in the dust with his sword, instructing all those who would stay and die not to cross the line. The one defender who chose to escape became the archexample of cowardice and ignominy for all Texans. So closely did Johnson identify with the story that he insisted on telling young soldiers that his own great, great-grandfather had died at the Alamo, even though in fact no relative of his had been there. To Johnson, the idea of retreating in Vietnam was equivalent to "tucking tail and running" at the Alamo. It challenged his most profound sense of identity and personal courage. If he were to accept such advice, then he too would deserve the infamy of being seen as lacking personal courage and skulking away in dishonor.

Johnson's political experience, moreover, taught him the necessity of taking a strong anticommunist stand in foreign policy if he were to sustain the possibility of promoting social reform at home. "Everything I knew about history," he noted,

> told me if I got out of Viet Nam and let Ho Chi Minh run through the streets of Saigon, then I'd be doing exactly what Chamberlain did in World War II. I'd be giving a big fat reward to aggression. And I knew that . . . [there] would follow in this country an endless national debate—that would shatter my presidency, kill my administration, damage our democracy. I knew that Harry Truman and Dean Acheson had lost their effectiveness from the day that the communists took over in China. I believed that the loss of China had played a large role in the life of Joe McCarthy. And I knew that all these problems, taken together, were chicken shit compared to what might happen if we lost Viet Nam.

For Johnson, progress on civil rights, poverty, and health and education issues required a strong position against communism, lest rightwingers begin the kind of witch hunt that had paralyzed Truman's domestic policy. As one Johnson aide wrote, "if [we] wished to pass progressive laws, [we] had to show that [we] were firmly committed against the ultimate 'progressives'— the communists."

All of these personal and political instincts came together in Johnson's obsession with forging unity behind a strong military posture in Vietnam. He hated the war, he understood its devastating potential, yet he saw no choice but to proceed with widening it. Defeat was simply unacceptable. These were "his" soldiers, and as he pored over maps in the White House Situation Room at three in the morning and waited to hear from "his" pilots that they had returned safely from a bombing mission, he came to see the entire war as an extension of his own identification of himself with the country.* Kennedy, after all, had deepened American involvement in Vietnam, and all of Kennedy's advisors supported continuing that policy. How then could the policy be reversed?

At times, the conjunction of personal and political factors seemed almost pathological. Johnson's deepest fears of repudiation focused on the possibility that Kennedy supporters would interpret any softness in policy toward Vietnam as a basis for rejecting *his* presidency. "There would be Robert Kennedy," Johnson told Doris Kearns,

---

* When a military aide at Andrews Air Force base tried to direct Johnson one day toward the correct helicopter, saying "Mr. President, that's not your helicopter," Johnson retorted: "Son, they're all *my* helicopters."

out in front leading the fight against me, telling everyone that I had betrayed John Kennedy's commitment to Viet Nam . . . that I was a coward. An umanly man. A man without a spine. Oh, I could see it coming all right. Every night when I fell asleep, I would see myself tied to the ground in the middle of a long open space. In the distance, I could hear the voices of thousands of people. They were all shouting at me and running toward me: "Coward! traitor! weakling!" They kept coming closer. They began throwing stones. At exactly that moment I would generally wake up . . . terribly shaken.

Thus, Lyndon Johnson did not come to the problem of Vietnam a free man. Haunted by fears of personal inadequacy, profoundly shaped by cultural norms of courage, honor, and manliness, and determined never to allow the right wing to use his policies in Vietnam as an excuse for a new McCarthy era, Johnson approached the horrible dilemmas of Vietnam already wrapped in a straitjacket. He would encourage full discussion of options, he would search for a way out, but ultimately, he could not permit himself to ask the fundamental questions that needed to be asked about the wisdom of American policy. Instead, over and over and over, he would repeat the credo that formed the centerpiece of his entire understanding of foreign policy—"We are there because we have a promise to keep."

The Road to Disaster

During his first few months in office, Johnson concentrated primarily on securing enactment of the Kennedy legislative program and advancing his own congressional agenda. Public opinion polls showed that almost 70 percent of the American public paid little attention to what was taking place in Vietnam, and Johnson, recognizing the importance of mobilizing support for his domestic program, hoped to perpetuate that indifference. Although he urged Lodge to do whatever possible to bolster the stability of the Saigon government, he ordered no major increases in American fighting forces, nor any primary shifts in strategy.

Vietnam would not long remain on the back burner, however. After probing briefly to see whether the post-Diem regime might accept a neutral coalition government, the Vietcong embarked on a vigorous political and military offensive in the winter of 1963–64, scoring repeated successes. In a situation described by Secretary of Defense Robert McNamara as "very disturbing," the military junta in Saigon exhibited almost no capacity for developing popular support or waging concerted warfare. By late January, a new coup had replaced the junta—one of six changes in government that would occur over the next twelve months—and American officials began to despair of any possibility of achieving a popular, efficient, stable ally in Saigon. By the spring of 1964, American intelligence estimates concluded that South Vietnam had "at best, an even chance of withstanding the insurgency menace during the next few weeks or months." The Saigon atmosphere, General William Westmoreland recalled, "fairly smelled of discontent." With Vietcong cadres having virtual free reign in the countryside, and cities in the South taking on the appearance of beseiged fortresses, the crisis in Saigon could no longer be ignored.

Johnson's response to the situation was perhaps best summarized in a phone conversation with Senator William Fulbright in early March. Significantly, Johnson defined the options before him in a manner that clearly precluded flexibility. The United States could withdraw from Vietnam, Johnson told Fulbright. Yet "without our support the government would be unable to counter the aid from the north to the Viet Cong. Viet Nam will collapse and the ripple effect will be felt throughout southeast Asia, endangering independent governments in Thailand, Malaysia, and extending as far as India and Indonesia and the Philippines." Clearly, Johnson totally subscribed to the so-called "domino theory." The president also rejected outright the possibility of neutralization suggested by Senator Mike Mansfield and President Charles de Gaulle, arguing that "any such formula will only lead in the end to the same results as withdrawing support." In such a context, Johnson perceived only two realistic possibilities: either continue present policy, with increases of support for South Vietnam, or embark on a major military escalation. Already anticipating a presidential election campaign against Barry Goldwater who urged substantial escalation, Johnson opted for maintaining existing policy. Prophetically, he told Fulbright that any commitment of major U.S. ground forces could well result in Americans being "bogged down in a long war against numerically superior [forces]." Yet Johnson left open that option. "If we're losing with what we're doing, we've got to decide whether to send [troops] in or whether to come out and let the dominoes fall. That's where the tough one is going to be."

Even as he rejected immediate escalation, however, Johnson took a series of steps that pushed America deeper into the quagmire. In early February, he authorized a series of secret sabotoge operations against Hanoi, including sending clandestine guerrilla teams into the North, engaging in commando raids from the sea against North Vietnamese targets, and bombarding coastal bases, with Vietnamese PT boats operating under a protective umbrella of American destroyers. With the complete support of Kennedy's former foreign policy advisors, the administration in mid-March reiterated its support for "an independent, non-communist South Viet Nam," insisting that failure to achieve such an objective would lead all of Southeast Asia to fall under communist dominance. McGeorge Bundy, Johnson's national security advisor, even urged blockading Haiphong harbor, North Vietnam's major seaport. Although rejecting that suggestion, Johnson authorized an increase in the number of American "advisors" in Vietnam from 16,000 to 23,000, telling Henry Cabot Lodge that "as far as I'm concerned you must have whatever you need to help the Vietnamese do the job, and I assure you that I will act at once to eliminate obstacles or restraints wherever they may appear."

The War in Southeast Asia.

Significantly, Johnson and his aides were already considering far more drastic actions. Administration strategists contemplated direct air strikes against North Vietnam to accompany the "covert" operation already under way. Although only 25,000 Vietcong guerrillas were operating in South Vietnam, and the Hanoi government appeared, in the eyes of some, hospitable toward a negotiated settlement, American policymakers became increasingly convinced that the only way to ensure stability and survival in the South was through carrying the war more aggressively to the North. Bundy suggested the need to obtain a congressional resolution backing future military action, and plans were devised to implement retaliatory action against North Vietnamese targets if the occasion arose. Although Johnson and his advisors rejected explicit endorsement of such a program because of the domestic political uproar it would provoke, the new suggestions clearly indicated the drift of administration thinking. Thus, even as Lyndon Johnson assured the American electorate that he would "never send American boys to do the fighting that Asian boys should do themselves," his own closest advisors were planning substantial escalation of the war.

The occasion for that escalation came with the alleged North Vietnamese attack against American destroyers in the Gulf of Tonkin in August and in the ensuing passage of a congressional resolution authorizing Johnson "to take *all* necessary measures to repel *any* armed attack against the forces of the United States." On the morning of August 1, 1964, the American destroyer *Maddox* was conducting electronic espionage in North Vietnamese waters. Its own activities, plus the bombing of North Vietnamese coastal installations by South Vietnamese PT boats, were a direct outgrowth of covert operations authorized by Johnson in February. Concluding that the South Vietnamese and American ships were operating together, a North Vietnamese torpedo boat fired on the American destroyer. The next day, a second destroyer was dispatched to join the *Maddox* in the Gulf of Tonkin as a show of strength. On the morning of August 4, both destroyers reported they were under attack. Already prepared to retaliate, the Joint Chiefs of Staff argued that the United States must "clobber" the North Vietnamese. "We cannot sit still as a nation," McNamara declared, "and let them attack us on the high seas and get away with it."

In fact, the second attack may never have occurred. Although the destroyers initially reported enemy contact based on sonar and radar evidence, that same afternoon messages from the ships warned that "freak weather effects" on the instruments may have explained the apparent evidence, and that there had been no "visual sighting" of the enemy. A "complete evaluation" of all the evidence was necessary, the naval commander radioed, before any further action was taken. Despite such caution, Johnson proceeded with the air strikes and immediately began to mobilize support on Capitol Hill for his joint resolution. In effect, he and his aides had been anticipating such an occasion for six months and saw no reason to wait further before taking advantage of it. The machinery for expanding the war had been set in place by military and foreign policy leaders. Now the time had come to use it.

Once again, the president chose to define the situation in a manner that precluded consideration of all the evidence, manipulating Congress into an action that was uninformed by any clear understanding of the administration's real objectives. Convening congressional leaders, Johnson presented the North Vietnamese attack as blatant "aggression on the high seas." At no point did he tell any congressmen about the covert operations that American and South Vietnamese ships had been engaged in, nor about the doubts that existed among naval officers about the second attack. A military clash that in reality had occurred as a direct consequence of American aggression against North Vietnam was presented as a wanton violation of international freedom of the seas by reckless North Vietnamese torpedo boats attacking innocent American sailors. In such a context, virtually all congressmen, led by Senator William Fulbright, supported a congressional resolution to demonstrate the resolve of America to defend its freedom and repel aggression.

With patriotism and honor as his rallying cries, Johnson thus secured the congressional support that two months earlier his advisors had told him would be necessary for escalation. So persuasive was Johnson in his appeal that only a few senators raised any cautionary flags. Wisconsin Senator Gaylord Nelson worried that the resolution's blanket terms might be used to "endorse a complete change in our mission," and Maryland Senator Daniel Brewster expressed concern that it might lead to "a situation involving the landing of large land armies on the continent of Asia." But Fulbright assured his colleagues that Johnson had no such intention, and in the end only Senators Wayne Morse and Ernest Gruening cast votes against the Gulf of Tonkin resolution. Johnson had generated massive public support for his strong stance in defense of American independence, even as he continued to portray himself as a "man of peace." The entire country was reassured by the president's sure handling of the situation. Only a few within the administration understood the full significance of what had occurred, or the fact that the August crisis opened the door for a massive increase of American involvement in Vietnam far beyond anything Nelson or Brewster had anticipated—now sanctioned by almost unanimous congressional approval.

"Into the Big Muddy"

By the winter of 1964–65, a pattern had become established in America's relationship to Vietnam so eerie in its rhythm and repetitiveness as to seem, in retrospect, almost frightening. The situation in Vietnam would deteriorate. Successive Saigon regimes would fail to develop support from the people or military effectiveness in the field. American officials would argue the necessity of greater commitment of troops and planes in order to bolster a

South Vietnamese government tottering near collapse. Fact-finding missions would establish a justification for more American involvement, and the troops and money would follow. When all that failed, the cycle would start again.

Only this time the stakes achieved a new dimension. Two policies were at issue: massive American bombing of North Vietnam, and commitment of large numbers of American ground troops to offensive and aggressive combat. The two questions became inevitably linked and served as the occasion for at least the *appearance* of full-scale debate within the Johnson administration about the wisdom of continuing in Vietnam; in fact, the decision seems already to have been made, with Johnson using the illusion of full discussion to achieve the veneer of consensus he so prized. No one could say after the debate leading to the July 1965 decision to increase American troop strength beyond 100,000 soldiers that all the arguments on the other side had not been heard. Yet the process amounted ultimately to what one observer called the "domestication of dissent." Johnson's own options were frozen by the values of honor, patriotism, and fear that he brought to the debate, and he became irrevocably committed to a course that would totally subvert and destroy his presidency.

The primary consequence of the Gulf of Tonkin crisis was to deepen the vicious cycle of American involvement in Vietnam without resolving anything. Shortly after the November election, most American officials concluded that it was necessary to escalate further and proceed with what Maxwell Taylor called "a carefully orchestrated bombing attack" against the North—for the first time engaging in sustained attacks against a nation we allegedly were not at war with. No one knew accurately what would be accomplished as a result. Some believed that Hanoi could be made to pay an unacceptable price for continuing its support of the Vietcong. Others saw the new proposals for bombing as a means of rebuilding the shattered morale of the South Vietnamese government. Only Under-Secretary of State George Ball viewed the proposed course of action as disastrous. In his view, bombing the North could do nothing to solve political problems in the South, while only assuring that Hanoi would redouble its commitment of resources to the South. Ball had a clear recollection of the French experience. No one else did. "Once on the tiger's back," Ball observed, "we can not be sure of picking the place to dismount." But the overwhelming majority agreed with Michael Forrestal's position that bombing was necessary to "delay China swallowing up Southeast Asia until (a) she develops better table manners and (b) the food is somewhat more indigestible."

Although continued instability in Saigon delayed implementation of the new strategy, by February 1965 the administration concluded that the time had come to act. Once again, retaliation against communist aggression served as a rationale. On February 6, Vietcong forces attacked American soldiers at a military base in Pleiku. In defense of American honor, Johnson ordered air raids against the North. But as Bundy observed at the time,

"Pleiku's are like streetcars." There would always be another one coming along, and the primary purpose served by the Vietcong attack was to provide the immediate occasion for a policy long since decided on. Within a week, the Pentagon had launched operation "rolling thunder," America's long planned policy of massive bombing in the North. Almost every advisor endorsed the action, not because they had any sound idea of where it would lead, but because in Johnson's words, "doing nothing was more dangerous than doing something." As McGeorge Bundy observed at the time: "There is one grave weakness in our posture on Viet Nam which is within our power to fix—and that is widespread belief that we do not have the will and force and patience and determination to take the necessary action and stay the course. This is the overriding reason for our present recommendation of sustained reprisal."

The decision to engage in a decisive escalation of the air war led inextricably toward a parallel course of action on the ground. Although Johnson would later claim that the massive buildup of American ground forces in Vietnam occurred only after vigorous debate during the spring and early summer, the president had in fact already cabled Ambassador Maxwell Taylor in *January* that "I am now ready to look with great favor" on sending more troops:

> Everytime I get a military recommendation, it seems to me that it calls for large-scale bombing. I have never felt that this war will be won from the air, and it seems to me what is much more needed and will be more effective is a larger and stronger use of rangers and special forces and marines. . . . Any recommendation that you or General Westmoreland take in this sense will have immediate attention from me, although I know that it may involve the acceptance of larger American sacrifices. We have been building our strength to fight this kind of war ever since 1961, and I myself am ready to substantially increase the number of Americans in Viet Nam if it is necessary to provide that kind of fighting force against the Viet Cong.

Clearly, the president was communicating to his men in the field an unmistakable signal—indeed, a virtual order—that they should come forward with recommendations for increasing American troop strength. In so doing, he appears to have agreed with McNamara and Bundy's assessment that "our current policy can lead only to disastrous defeat."

The initiation of a wider air war against the North provided the immediate justification for deploying American combat troops to Vietnam, just as Pleiku had offered the rationale for operation "rolling thunder." Both events simply represented the occasion to implement policies *already decided* on, while having the public relations advantage of seeming to justify military action in defense of the national honor. In explaining the bombing of the North after Pleiku, Johnson declared: "I can't ask our American soldiers out there to continue to fight with one hand behind their back." Now, in early March, he argued that it was impossible to send American *pilots* into action unless they were protected by American *troops*, thus justifying the decision to send two marine battalions—1,500 men—to defend American air bases. Within six weeks there would be 50,000 American soldiers in Vietnam—a 150 percent increase over the number there in December. Finally, on April 1, Johnson personally authorized those troops to engage *actively in combat* if they or their Vietnamese allies were threatened. Ironically, when the Marines landed at Danang on March 8, they were greeted with flowers and bands, almost as though someone had heard John F. Kennedy's prophecy of such a reception two years earlier, and had acted, with vengeful irony, to fulfill it.

Through all of this, the American people—and even some of Johnson's own advisors—were kept in the dark about the fundamental shift that had occurred in American policy. The day before Johnson authorized American ground troops to engage in offensive action, he told a press conference: "I know of no far-reaching strategy that is being suggested or promulgated." Defense department officials were ordered to "minimize any appearance of sudden changes of policy." When Ambassador Taylor expressed "grave reservations as to the wisdom and necessity" of committing ground combat forces to Vietnam, he was told that they were there only to protect the air fields *even though* Johnson and Westmoreland already knew, in the words of a Pentagon analyst, that "the deployment of the marines [was] the beginning of greater things to come." Indeed, the week after the first marines landed, Johnson ordered the Army Chief of Staff to Saigon to "get things bubbling." Shortly thereafter, the general returned with recommendations for dispatching another U.S. Army division to Vietnam, and for expanding the war against the North. When Taylor protested against the "eagerness in some quarters to deploy forces into [South Vietnam]," he was told in a Department of Defense cable that "*highest authority* believes situation . . . has been deteriorating and that . . . something new must be added in the South to achieve victory." By now Johnson was clearly leading his own advisors in the race for escalation.

Meanwhile, Johnson controlled the public's perception of the war, with a nationally televised speech at Johns Hopkins University in early April 1965. Mentioning neither his authorization for American troops to engage in combat, nor the sustained and systematic bombing of the North, Johnson pledged that America was prepared for an "unconditional discussion" with the enemy in order to end the fighting. Furthermore, he promised, as soon as the war was over that the United States would join with Vietnam in a massive effort to rebuild Southeast Asia. "We are there," Johnson told the American people, "because we have a promise to keep. . . . The central lesson of our time is that the appetite of aggression is never satisfied. To withdraw from one battlefield means only to prepare for the next." But at no time did Johnson let the people know what was already taking place on the battlefield of Vietnam, preferring instead to offer an upbeat assessment of the chances for peace. The Johns Hopkins speech received an enthusiastic response from most Americans who felt reassured by the president's words. Indeed, by the end of the month, the attention of most people had drifted from Vietnam to the Dominican Republic where Johnson ordered several hundred marines to land in order to "guarantee the safety of Americans" and prevent Cuban revolutionaries from engaging in a communist takeover.*

In the privacy of government councils, though, assessments of the situation in Vietnam were still uniformly negative. The bombing had no appreciable effect on the North, infiltration into the South increased rather than diminished, and the Saigon regime entered a new cycle of instability. Instead of seeing such evidence as a reason to pull back and reconsider, most Johnson advisors insisted that the only course available was to pour more money, troops, and energy into the battle. There was "no solution," Westmoreland decided, "other than to put our own finger in the dike." With forceful endorsement from the Joint Chiefs of Staff, Westmoreland requested two additional army divisions amounting to more than 40,000 troops. In June, U.S. forces embarked on their first "search and destroy" mission, taking the war to the Vietnamese. Again, no announcement was made of the change. Nearly 90,000 American troops were stationed in Vietnam, American aircraft flew more than 3,600 sorties per month, and American combat forces had begun to assume a major part of the responsibility for the ground war. Yet according to administration officials, no basic decisions had been made.

In all of this, the role of the dissenter was a perilous one. Important people in the administration *did* disagree vehemently with the emerging administration policy. The dissenters included Under-Secretary of State George Ball, Presidential Press Secretary Bill Moyers, State Department Advisor James Thompson, and Vice-President Hubert Humphrey. But those who disagreed had to function within a maze of bureaucratic politics and with a subtlety of political instinct that oftentimes muffled their disagreement. If a person protested too loudly, or gave offense, he risked being excluded from the circle of advice altogether. According to David Halberstam, Johnson once declared: "I don't want loyalty. I want *loyalty*. I want him to kiss my ass in Macy's window at high noon and tell me it smells like roses. I want his pecker in my pocket." When Hubert Humphrey rushed back to Washington in the midst of the decision to bomb North Vietnam in February and told the president in no uncertain terms that operation "rolling thunder" would be a disaster, he was banished from administration councils for months. Thus, dissenters who wished to be effective had to couch their objections in ways that would assure that they could stay on board and receive

---

* By almost all accounts, Johnson overreacted to the situation in the Dominican Republic. Not only were Americans not in any clear danger; the list of so-called communists allegedly leading the revolution had little if any legitimacy. Despite this overreaction, Johnson seems to have felt enhanced by taking such decisive action and to have viewed it as a plus in his foreign policy record.

a hearing. That very process, however, embodied a debilitating dynamic referred to by Thompson as the "domestication of dissent." Those who wished to have their voices heard had to play within the rules of the game dictated by the president. He, in turn, could use the "freedom" of discussion that resulted as evidence that he had listened to all sides. But if, in fact, the basic decisions had already been made, the entire process became a charade, with dissent—ironically—used to legitimize the policies that would eventually be implemented. Thus, when Johnson referred to Ball as his "devil's advocate" or to Moyers as "Mr. Stop the bombing," he was in fact defining their role as one of deviancy. They would be listened to in order to salve the consciences of the power-makers, but relegated to a position as neutered petitioners who, once their views were heard, could be overridden. It was a tortured, almost impossible role, yet one which had to be played—albeit with fatalism—by those committed to using whatever influence they had to alter the tragic course which they saw their country embarked upon.*

In this context, the dissenters chose two occasions—the bombing decision in February, and the troop decisions in June and July—to raise with prescient insight basic questions about the consequences of American policy. In both instances, they sought to place the burden of proof on those who were advocating further escalation and insisted that the larger issue of where American action would lead must be considered before irrevocable steps were taken. "It seems to me," Thompson wrote in February.

> that we [should] not lose our perspective: in South Viet Nam we have slipped into a gross over-commitment of national prestige and resources on political, military and geographic terrain which should long ago have persuaded us to avoid commitment. Our national interest now demands that we find ourselves a face-saving avenue of retreat—that we marshall our imaginations and those of other powers—to discover such an avenue.

Continued bombing of the North, Thompson pointed out, ran the inevitable risk of leading to further military action that at some point would bring China or the Soviet Union into the war, without offering any possibility of victory. George Ball, in turn, asked that supporters of the bombing look at the situation from the perspective of Hanoi. "For North Viet Nam to call off the insurgency in South Viet Nam, close the border, and withdraw the element that has infiltrated into that country would mean that it had accepted unconditional surrender." Given the sacrifices and the gains that Hanoi had already made, this "unconditional surrender" seemed beyond reach. In such a situation, Ball urged, it made more sense to pursue negotiations, since the other options—given Hanoi's perspective—were unworkable. Continuing the present course of action would simply perpetuate

---

* As Thompson has written, "the inclination . . . to live to fight another day, to give on this issue so you can be effective on later issues . . . is overwhelming. . . . As for the disinclination to resign in protest: while not necessarily a Washington or even American specialty, it seems more true of a government in which ministers have a parliamentary back-bench to which to retreat. To exit is to lose even those marginal chances for effectiveness."

stalemate. Taking over the war, on the other hand, would offer "the worst of both worlds. Our situation would in the world's eyes approach that of France in the 1950s." Hence, unless proponents of escalation could show how their course of action would bring peace and victory, the only option was to find a way out.

Ball and Thompson were, of course, correct in their analysis. As U.S. intelligence would shortly note, the bombing of North Vietnam "had no significantly harmful effects on popular morale. *In fact,* the regime has apparently been able to increase its control on the populace and perhaps even to break through the political apathy and indifference which have characterized the outlook of the average North Vietnamese in recent years." Nevertheless, Johnson refused to accept Ball's insistence that supporters of escalation bear the burden of proving their case and instead accepted what Ball called McNamara's "spectacular display of facts and statistics to show that I had overstated the difficulties we were now encountering and that the situation was much better than I represented." So predisposed was the president to accelerate action rather than withdraw that he could not even conceive of why supporters of escalation should have to prove, step by step, the realistic possibilities for success of the policies they advocated.

The same scenario played itself out in June and July when Westmoreland requested forty-four battalions of American troops in order to begin to accomplish the goals that massive bombing of the North had so woefully failed to achieve. Over 90,000 American troops had already been authorized. Westmoreland now wanted 150,000. The South Vietnamese army was falling apart, the government could not sustain itself, and Westmoreland cabled his "considered opinion that the South Vietnamese armed forces cannot stand up to this pressure without substantial U.S. combat support on the ground. . . . The *only possible response* is the aggressive deployment of U.S. troops," an act which Westmoreland assured the Pentagon would help "establish a favorable balance of power by the end of the year." Although the CIA realistically warned that such action would result in heavy U.S. casualties and would not in any way affect Vietcong determination to continue the war, Ball's "worst case" option of his February memorandum now became the centerpiece of American decision-making.

In response, Ball urged once again that the president consider the consequences of escalation. By sending more than 100,000 American troops to engage in combat, he pointed out, the United States would be initiating a new war—"the United States *directly* against the Viet Cong." If the CIA were correct and this commitment failed to force Hanoi into unconditional surrender, "we may *not* be able to fight the war successfully enough—even with 500,000 Americans in South Viet Nam—to achieve [our] purpose." Here, he insisted, the French experience was directly pertinent. They had sent a quarter of a million troops to Vietnam, only to suffer humiliation. "When we have put enough Americans on the ground in South Viet Nam to give the appearance of a white man's war, the distinction [between us and the French] will have less and less practical effect. . . . Yet the more forces we deploy in South Vietnam—particularly in combat roles—the harder we shall find it to extricate ourselves without unacceptable costs as the war goes badly." Again attempting to place the burden of proof on the proponents of escalation, Ball insisted that "before we commit an endless flow of force to South Vietnam we must have more evidence than we now have that our troops will not bog down in the jungles and rice paddies—while we slowly blow the country to pieces."

Over the next month, Ball persisted in attempting to get the president realistically to assess, with equal scrutiny, the options of negotiated withdrawal as well as massive escalation. "The technique of cutting our losses requires intensive study," he wrote. "*No one has yet looked at the problem carefully since we've been unwilling to think in those terms.*" Warning that the commitment of large American forces would simply generate more pressures for escalation when the war went badly, ultimately risking both domestic division at home and intervention from China or the Soviet Union abroad, Ball urged the president to realize that this was perhaps the last opportunity he would have to exert control over the situation. South Vietnam was now "a country with an army and no government," yet even McNamara acknowledged that, unless "the South Vietnamese hold their own in terms of numbers and fighting spirit," the situation was hopeless.

Although Johnson now promised that each side would have "its day in court," the ensuing debate was shaped from the beginning by the decision for escalation that had already been taken, and by the conviction—shared by most administration advisors—that if the United States did not massively commit troops South Vietnam was doomed. In a "catch-22," McNamara and others argued that expanded troop commitments were a prerequisite for any chance of negotiations. Repeatedly, Johnson was told that continued bombing and escalation of troop deployments would "bring about a favorable solution to the Viet Nam problem." In contrast, Ball argued that "no one has yet shown that American troops can win a jungle war against an invisible enemy." He had no desire, Ball told the president, that the United States should "abdicate its leadership in the Cold War." But a wise general chose carefully "the terrain on which to stand and fight":

> From our point of view the terrain in South Vietnam could not be worse. Jungles and rice paddies are not designed for modern arms and from a military point of view, this is clearly what General de Gaulle described to me as a "rotten country."
>
> Politically, South Vietnam is a lost cause. The country has been bled white from twenty years at war and the people are sick of it. . . .
>
> *In my view a deep commitment of United States forces in a land war in South Vietnam would be a castrophic error. If ever there was an occasion for a tactical withdrawal, this is it.*

At this juncture, McGeorge Bundy played a key role. The president's national security advisor acknowledged that there was "no reason to suppose that the VC will accommodate us by fighting the kind of war we desire." He also recognized that sending American troops to Vietnam represented a "slippery slope toward total U.S. responsibility and recklessness on the Vietnamese side. . . . Any expanded program needs to have a clear sense of its own internal momentum. . . . What is the real object of this exercise? . . . Still more brutally, do we want to invest two hundred thousand men to cover an eventual retreat?" Yet instead of siding with Ball, Bundy promoted the recommendations of his brother, Assistant Secretary of State William Bundy, for a "middle way." The "middle way" would commit increased American troops and test their military effectiveness, without supporting—immediately—the massive deployment urged by McNamara and Westmoreland. As William Bundy wrote, "the middle way avoids clear pitfalls of either of the major alternatives. It may not give us quite as much chance of a successful outcome as the major military action proposed in the McNamara memo, . . . [but it] rejects withdrawal or negotiating concessions."

Ultimately, the "middle way" had two primary consequences. Consistent with the essence of bureaucratic politics, it represented a "compromise" between unacceptable alternatives. And without ever facing up to the fact, it involved precisely the kind of commitment of American troops that would inextricably lead to further escalation. Significantly, McGeorge Bundy embodied the essence of bureaucratic politics in his recommendations to the president. "My hunch," he told Johnson, "is that you will want to listen hard to George Ball and then reject his proposal. Discussion could then move to the narrower choice between my brother's course and McNamara's." Clearly, there was a limit to open debate.

In fact, the discussions convened in July served primarily as a vehicle Johnson could use to ratify commitments he had already made. In his memoirs, the president wrote that "I was not about to send additional men without the most detailed analysis." Prior to a final decision, he even dispatched McNamara to Saigon for another fact-finding mission. Yet the president's instructions to his secretary of defense highlighted the degree to which he had already made up his mind. McNamara's task was not to determine whether troops would be sent, but to determine *how many* were needed. Furthermore, while McNamara was still in Saigon he received a cable from Washington declaring that Johnson had already decided to go ahead with the forty-four battalion request, thus revealing the extent to which the entire notion of "detailed analysis" and debate was illusory. Although Johnson did convene all of his policymakers to discuss McNamara's recommendation upon the secretary's return, the debate served primarily as the performance of a play whose conclusion Johnson had already written. As William Bundy later recalled, "it was a bit of a set piece . . . you felt it had been staged to a degree." Thus, while Johnson put George Ball through the paces once more, and asked all of the key questions, he was essentially enacting a ritual whose purpose was to manipulate the participants into thinking they were all sharing in making a basic decision when in fact the troops were ready to go. In the end, Ball and his allies never had a chance. The deck had been stacked from the beginning.

The one decision that *was* made during July testified eloquently to Johnson's capacity for deceiving himself—and the American people—about the true consequences of expanding America's role in Vietnam. At virtually every stage of the spring and summer debate over America's course of action, Robert McNamara had made his recommendation for a substantial increase in American troop strength contingent on two steps: a call-up of 100,000 reservists to fill the gap in America's defenses being left by troops now deployed to Vietnam; and a substantial increase in taxes to pay for expanded American involvement in the war. Only through such steps, McNamara argued, would it be possible to make the American people and Congress privy to the enormity of the decisions being made. Failure to take such action, he feared, would invite bitter recrimination at a later date, when the true nature of America's role became clear, and would cause economic disaster through uncontrolled deficit spending. At a July 21 meeting almost all Johnson's advisors agreed with McNamara. Yet one week later, when Johnson announced to the nation that American troop strength in Vietnam would increase from 75,000 to 125,000, with more troops to be sent later, he also announced that the major new commitment would take place *without* any new taxes or call-up of reserves or national guard troops.

By his action, Johnson forestalled a national debate on the war and sustained, for the moment, the impression that America could both defeat the Vietcong in South Vietnam and simultaneously create the Great Society at home. Had he gone to Congress, sought a declaration of national emergency, asked for an increase in taxes, and put the nation on a war footing, he could not have avoided alerting the country to the full import of his new policies. But to do so would have shattered the consensus he so prized and endangered the enactment of legislation he most cared about. The very week he announced his decision on troop strength in Vietnam, his medicare and civil rights bills were at a critical stage of deliberation, with a majority of the Great Society agenda still to be acted on. Hence, Johnson intentionally misled the American people about the military decisions he had just taken, instructing his staff to implement his actions in "a low-key manner in order (a) to avoid an abrupt challenge to the communists, and (b) to avoid undue concern and excitement in the Congress and in domestic public opinion." Instead, in his July 28 speech, he denied that there was *any* change in U.S. policy, lied to the American people, and took a gigantic step toward destroying the very fabric of American democracy.

The Quagmire Gets Deeper

When George Ball had raised the specter of half a million American troops in Vietnam during the July debate, Secretary of Defense Robert McNamara dismissed such figures as "outrageous" and accused Ball of "dirty pool." In fact, Ball's prophesy was painfully accurate. Although, in Bundy's words, the commitment of American troops in the summer of 1965 was to be "a test" to determine whether American soldiers could effectively fight a jungle war, the "experiment" never happened. By the end of July, Westmoreland had already requested 179,000 more troops, and by the end of 1965 had secured presidential authorization for a buildup to 450,000 troops by the end of 1966. Johnson had hoped for a quick resolution of the conflict after his July decision. After all, American marines had never suffered defeat. As one marine lieutenant later wrote, "When we marched into the rice paddies, . . . we carried, along with our packs and rifles, the implicit conviction that the Viet Cong would be quickly beaten." But Johnson soon had to face the consequences that he had so persistently refused to confront when Ball had urged him to do so. Caught in a trap of his own making, he found himself on a treadmill of ever increasing escalation. Having raised the stakes once by committing American "honor" and manpower to avert defeat, he saw no option but to continue raising the ante when his initial decisions failed to achieve the results that were promised and his generals came back, repeatedly, for more of the same.

Nothing seemed to work. As the historian George Herring has observed, "the failure of one level of force led quickly to the next, until the war obtained a degree of destructiveness no one would have thought possible in 1965." Because bombing was cheaper and less costly in lives than ground-fighting, the air war grew massively; there were 25,000 sorties in 1965 building to 108,000 in 1967—all this despite intelligence estimates that the bombing did little to impede infiltration from the North and resulted in 1,000 civilian casualties per week. Although the huge B-52s rained terror on the Vietnamese countryside from 30,000 feet, the North Vietnamese proved more than capable of counteracting the damage, digging 30,000 miles of tunnels and mobilizing 90,000 civilians to keep transportation routes open. In one classic example, a bridge totally destroyed by American bombs was replaced almost over night by thousands of Vietnamese villagers recruited to place sandbags where the bridge had been and to rebuild it. "Caucasians," one American noted, "can not really imagine what ant labor can do."

The ground war went no better. Although American planes defoliated the South Vietnamese countryside ("only you can prevent forests," the motto on one plane read), dropped over a million tons of bombs on "free fire zones" in the South, and mounted massive "search-and-destroy missions," the Vietcong refused to be brought to their knees. Pentagon officials, obsessed with body counts and other statistics, insisted that more than 220,000 of the enemy had been killed by the end of 1967 and that the United States was "winning" the war. In the White House, Johnson's national security advisor Walt Rostow insisted on telling the president that everything was going well. (Rostow was a notorious optimist. As one White House aide later said, Rostow, on learning of a nuclear attack on Manhattan, would have told the president that "the first phase of the island's urban renewal had been accomplished in a flash.") But, in fact, the body counts were vastly overestimated, included thousands of innocent civilians, and even if accurate, failed to account for the approximately 200,000 North Vietnamese who each year reached draft age and could be mobilized to match American escalation. Moreover, American generals found, to their repeated frustration, that whenever they succeeded in engaging mainforce Vietnamese troops, the enemy would disappear into the forest just as the Americans were ready to zero-in for the kill.

The result was endless frustration, anger, and bitterness. "A little piss-ant country," as Johnson liked to call Vietnam, was embarrassing the world's mightiest military power. Americans had assumed that their massive tech-nological strength would devastate North Vietnam and the Vietcong; but in-stead, as one journalist observed, every blow from the American military machine "was like a sledge hammer on a floating cork . . . somehow the cork refused to stay down." Whole areas of the countryside were flattened, one American noted, "as if we were trying to build a house with a bulldozer and wrecking crane," but none of the objectives sought by American poli-cymakers was being achieved. Instead, American losses mounted, with no sign of the sacrifice having any tangible consequences. By 1967 nearly 14,000 GIs had been killed in action, more than 600 planes had been shot down, and hundreds of air force crews were POWs in the North, hostages in any subsequent bargaining with Hanoi. American military power, in West-moreland's words, might have turned the South Vietnamese "trees and brush to combustible rubbish," but the enemy remained unbeaten.

In the meantime, the presence of U.S. troops and dollars literally over-whelmed South Vietnam. With U.S. soldiers assuming primary responsibil-ity for the fighting, the South Vietnamese army became a dependent sup-port force, taking on police and supply functions that South Vietnamese generals considered demeaning. Americans mistrusted their Vietnamese al-lies, and as resentment grew, relations between the two countries worsened. Saigon and other cities became outposts of America, with soldiers fre-quenting bars, restaurants, and whore houses, and Vietnamese serving them as pimps, "hoochmaids," and servants. "There evolves here," one jour-nalist noted, "a colonial ambience that can sometimes be worse than colo-nialism itself." Corruption was rampant throughout the Vietnamese bu-reaucracy, with millions of American dollars siphoned into the pockets of a bureaucratic elite instead of reaching the villages they were intended for. While some Vietnamese reveled in the world of rock music, transistor ra-dios, and the easy buck, others became increasingly restive in the face of America's takeover of their country. By 1967 a growing number of proud Vietnamese citizens took part in anti-American demonstrations, carrying signs that read "*End foreign dominance of our country*" and attacking American facilities.

Perhaps the most pernicious consequence of the war was the toll its brutality exacted on American fighting men and Vietnamese civilians. Al-though American soldiers entered Vietnam convinced that the very sight of

Those who suffered the most from the war in Vietnam were innocent civilians who became victims of battles and weapons they could not escape. Atrocities took place on both sides. Here, the attackers were Viet Cong troops. At My Lai, the attackers were American. *(National Archives)*

an American uniform, American tanks, and American aircraft would make the Vietcong cower, they quickly discovered that this was a conflict unlike any other their country had ever engaged in—more vicious, more cruel, more terrifying. The enemy was everywhere, yet nowhere, throwing bombs from a speeding motor scooter into a Saigon cafe, or hiding in the midst of a Vietnamese village preparing to booby trap a trail. "It was always going on," one journalist noted, "rock around the clock, we had the days and he had the nights. You could be in the most protected space in Viet Nam and still know that your safety was provisional, that early death, blindness, loss of legs, arms or balls, major and lasting disfigurement—the whole rotten deal—could come in on the freaky fluky as easily as in the so-called expected ways."

No one knew where the Vietcong would strike next. One American lieutenant asked a Vietnamese peasant—"She wore earrings, I remember"—whether any Vietcong were in the vicinity, and she said no. Then as his platoon walked down the road, they discovered it was mined and were blown to bits. The terror was overwhelming. As journalist Michael Herr has written,

Sachel charges and grenades blew up jeeps and movie theatres, the VC got work inside all the camps as shoe shine boys and laundresses, . . . they'd starch your fatigues and burn your shit then go home and mortar your area. Saigon and Cholan and Danang held such hostile vibes that you felt that you were being dry sniped every time someone looked at you.

Americans coming out of battle looked like "a colony of stroke victims," Herr noted, their eyes sunk into their heads, their faces pasty white, their appearance that of old men. "How do you feel," Herr asked, "when a nineteen-year-old kid tells you from the bottom of his heart that he has gotten too old for this kind of shit?"

Some of them reacted to the constant cycle of death and disfigurement by taking drugs. Others counted the days until they could go home, or at least to Hawaii for R&R—really I&I, one GI remembered, "intoxication and intercourse." Others simply went crazy. One GI, after a vicious battle where Vietcong flung themselves at the barbed wire surrounding his encampment, went out to look at the Vietcong dead after the firing stopped. Then, Herr writes,

> I hear an M-16 on full automatic starting to go through clips, one second to fire, three to plug in a fresh clip, and I saw a man out there doing it. Every round was like a tiny concentration of high velocity wind, making the bodies writhe and shiver. When he finished he walked by us on the way back to his hooch, and I knew I hadn't seen anything until I saw his face. It was flushed and mottled and twisted like he had his face skin on inside out, a patch of green that was too dark, a streak of red running into bruised purple, a lot of sick grey white in between. . . . His eyes were rolled up half into his head, his mouth was sprung open and his tongue was out, but he was smiling.

In part, such insanity emerged as a direct product of the contradictions of American military policy. Simultaneously, the United States seemed committed to ravaging the countryside by dropping more tonnage of bombs than had been dropped during all of World War II and to helping the average Vietnamese villager to achieve independence, health, and self-determination. As one helicopter pilot succinctly summarized it, U.S. policy was to "bomb 'em and feed 'em." Yet it was almost impossible to sustain the "humanistic" side of America's mission when military orders were to "blow the hell [out of the enemy]." The very instruments of American military technology—huge bombers and massive helicopter gunships—militated against any sensitivity to human life. "Air sports," one pilot described his task. "Nothing finer, you are up there two thousand, you are God, just open up the flexies and watch it pee, nail those slime to the paddy wall, nothing finer, double back and get the caribou."

The nature of search-and-destroy missions, moreover, exacerbated the contradiction. Told to go into an area and clear it completely of any Vietcong, platoon leaders quickly lost the patience or wherewithal to distinguish between specific objectives and whole villages.

"That's the general area," said [one] ground commander, apparently tired of trying to pinpoint the one house [where a sniper had been seen]. "Do you want us to pretty well cover this general area?" Captain Reese asked. "Affirmative, hit the whole area. We've seen activity all through this area." "Okay. I'll put in a can of napalm and see what it looks like." . . . "Any civilians in this area are Charleys or Charley sympathizers, so there is no sweat there."

Operating under such orders, soldiers embarked on a campaign of total destruction. "We'd go through and that was it," one GI recalled; "we'd rip out the hedges and burn the hooches and blow all the wells and kill every chicken, pig and cow in the whole fucking village. I mean, if we can't shoot these people, what the fuck are we doing here?"

Implicit in such orders, however, was a poisonous doctrine, a kind of "crypto-racism," as one American called it, that quickly permeated American policy and transformed *all* Vietnamese into the enemy. "What does it matter," one GI said when asked about the danger of killing innocent civilians. "They are all Vietnamese." The only way to win the war, one joke had it, was to "load all the Friendlies onto ships and take them out to the South China Sea. Then you bomb the country flat. Then you sink the ship." No matter that official policy repeatedly emphasized the need to win the "hearts and minds" of the Vietnamese people. "All that is just a *load* man," one battle-hardened veteran said. "We're here to kill gooks, period." After all, even the highest American officials insisted that the Vietnamese placed less value on human life than the Americans. Hence, it did not matter if they died. Even those whose professional calling should have made them most resistant to such attitudes ultimately fell victim to them. When a reporter heard one doctor boast that he had refused to treat wounded Vietnamese, the reporter asked: "But didn't you take the Hippocratic Oath?" "Yeah," the doctor replied, "I took it in America."

The ultimate consequence of such attitudes came in the village of My Lai where an American platoon landed one morning on a search-and-destroy mission. The platoon had suffered severe losses in an earlier engagement, and now was told that it had an opportunity to "get even." "When the attack started," one sergeant recalled, "it couldn't have been stopped by anyone. We were mad and had been told that the enemy was there and we were going in there to give them a fight for what they had done to our dead buddies." No enemy fire was received, but within a matter of minutes, the village exploded in grenade and machine gun bursts. "Off to the right," one observer said, "a woman's form, a head appeared from some brush. All the other GIs started firing at her, aiming at her, firing at her over and over again . . . they just kept shooting at her. You could see the bones flying in the air, chip by chip." The GIs seemed consumed by a raging fever. "People began coming out of their hooches and the guys shot them and burned the hooches—or burned the hooches and then shot the people when they came out," another soldier recalled. "Sometimes they would round up a bunch and shoot them together. It went along like that for what seemed like all day." While some soldiers raped a young girl, others gathered villagers at a canal a short distance away, and when there were 75 or so together, the soldiers opened fire. That day, more than 350 Vietnamese villagers were murdered. There was one American casualty, a GI who shot himself in the foot out of disgust at what he was witnessing. To many Americans later, the My Lai massacre seemed an aberration, an act of total insanity. In fact, it was simply an extension of the horror that consumed Vietnam, and of the policy of massive destruction that had become America's way of winning the war.

Tragically, even those programs most clearly designed to provide health care, education, and "humane reforms" to Vietnamese villagers fell apart under the contradictions of American policy. The Civic Action Program aimed to establish communications with local Vietnamese, to offer medical care and innoculations, and to build rapport between the American military and civilians in the countryside. Teams of volunteers would visit villages, offer agricultural advice, administer to the sick, and attempt to win friends. But from the beginning, the CAP program lacked support from Westmoreland's headquarters while flying in the face of the overwhelming emphasis on destruction that characterized the rest of the American effort. As one marine participant recalled, most of the men in his battalion "considered it a criminal waste of American manpower and resources to try and help 'backward' and 'ungrateful' people like the Vietnamese." The other major program—Rural Development—encountered the same dilemmas. Even where Rural Development teams accomplished their goal of aiding villagers, the positive results of their effort were destroyed when American bombers flattened the very areas that had just been helped.

In the end, American policy foundered on the flaw inherent in its premise—that a modern, industrialized, technological society could "save," through external intervention, a society whose culture and values were totally antithetical to the American way of life. While Americans prized "progress" and looked toward the future, the Vietnamese worshipped traditionalism and the values of the past. While Americans represented the quintessence of individualism, the Vietnamese worshipped the family and the collective, not even having a word for the personal pronoun "I." As author Frances FitzGerald later said, "in their sense of time and space, the Vietnamese and the Americans [stood] in the relationship of a reversed mirror image." Americans insisted that the Vietnamese adopt new technologies and uproot themselves from the land so that they could move to "safe" pacification villages. But the Vietnamese had been using the same technology for thousands of years, and worshipped the land they occupied because it was the burial ground of their ancestors. "I have to stay behind to look after this piece of garden," one grandfather told Americans who had just declared his village a "free fire zone." "Of all the property handed down to me by my ancestors, only this garden now remains. . . . If I leave, the graves of my ancestors, too, will become forests. How can I have the heart to

Although U.S. officials occasionally argued that the Vietnamese did not value human life, and hence that civilian casualties might not mean as much in Asia as they would in the West, this photograph of a family mourning the death of their daughter suggests the depth of pain experienced by those who lost loved ones during the war. *(National Archives)*

leave?" Yet virtually every step the Americans took in Vietnam was designed to destroy Vietnamese culture, to impose, in Fitzgerald's words, American "global strategies [of containment and the Cold War] into a world of hillocks and hamlets." Few, if any, in Washington ever attempted to understand the Vietnamese, their language, their traditions, or their values. The result could not help but be a disaster.

By the end of 1967, more and more Americans were beginning to recognize this fact and to understand the pervasive fallacy implicit in every aspect of American policy. "We seem to be proceeding on the assumption," Assistant Secretary of Defense John McNaughton wrote, "that the way to eradicate the Viet Cong is to destroy all the village structures, defoliate all the jungles, and then cover the entire surface of South Viet Nam with asphalt." Despite the optimism of people like Rostow and Westmoreland, and the insistent claims of the Pentagon that America was "turning the corner" in Vietnam and could now see the "light at the end of the tunnel," others knew better. As early as 1965, Senator Mike Mansfield had warned Johnson that large numbers of U.S. senators were in agreement that America was "deeply enmeshed in a place we ought not to be; the situation is rapidly going out of control, and every effort should be made to extricate ourselves." By 1967, more and more political leaders were saying the same thing in public. A vigorous antiwar movement mobilized more than 200,000 protestors to march against the war in October. And in November, a Gallup Poll revealed that 57 percent of the American people now disapproved of Johnson's handling of the war.* Nearly 10,000 Americans had been killed in action in 1967 alone, with almost everyone now aware that the news would get worse before it got better.

Attempting to deflect mounting criticism of his policies, Johnson authorized a series of peace initiatives that gave at least the appearance of flexibility and commitment to a negotiated solution. Under the urging of McNamara and others, he declared a suspension of bombing on Christmas Eve 1965 and dispatched virtually his entire administration to foreign capitals on a "quest for peace." Averell Harriman journeyed to twelve countries in seventeen days; Vice-President Humphrey went to five; and G. Mennen Williams, Assistant Secretary of State for African Affairs, visited thirteen African nations in four days. But it all seemed too clearly a public relations gimmick ("I guess you would have to say it was about as quiet a peace offensive as a Texan could arrange," one official noted), and once he had given the doves their due, Johnson resumed and expanded the bombing. In late 1966, Polish diplomats tortuously worked out a tentative agreement to begin negotiations in Warsaw, but just before the talks were to begin, U.S. bombers launched air attacks just five miles from the center of Hanoi, sabotaging the effort and causing Hanoi to cancel the talks. The same fate crippled an attempt by British Prime Minister Harold Wilson to establish ground rules for discussions through Russian Premier Aleksei Kosygin, when suddenly without notifying Wilson, Americans hardened their negotiating posture. Troubled, confused, and frustrated, Johnson seemed willing to make gestures toward peace, but not to take any substantive action that would make its achievement more likely.

In fact, Johnson was trapped. Beseiged on the one hand by "hawks" who demanded total victory, and on the other by "doves" insisting on a bombing halt and negotiations, the president "hunkered down" and insisted on staying the course. Although McNamara had now become a "closet dove," beseeching the president to end the bombing, and respected advisors like Bill Moyers, George Ball, and James Thompson had resigned, the president refused to recognize the bankruptcy of his policy and instead flailed out at his critics as "nervous nellies," once calling Senator William Fulbright a "frustrated old woman." While he rejected Westmoreland's demand for 200,000 additional troops, he authorized a buildup of American troop strength to 531,000, with no ceiling on future requests. The war was now "Lyndon's war," and even though all around him his cherished political consensus was

---

* The antiwar movement will be dealt with at length in the next chapter.

shattering, the president determined to "stick it out," in the desperate hope that—somehow—everything would become right again.

Conclusion

There is no way to assess accurately the incalculable damage done to Vietnam, America, or international stability as a result of the war in Vietnam. The wounds go deep and will live for generations—certainly through the lifetimes of all those who were there, and the children and grandchildren who must live with the legacy of what transpired. But if it is impossible to plumb the depths of what Vietnam caused, we can at least venture to understand some of the reasons why a tragedy of such enormity took place.

Without question, the central precondition for American involvement in Vietnam was the set of assumptions that underlay and shaped the entire history of the Cold War. Once committed to the view that the communist world was one, and systematically engaged in a worldwide conspiracy to subvert freedom, any effort in other countries that could be interpreted as hostile to the United States automatically became defined as part of that worldwide conspiracy. In such a context, containment ceased to be a specific and precise response to a particular situation and, instead, became a diffuse, universal rationale for resisting any change in the international status quo. Given such a definition of the world, and the moralistic rhetoric that accompanied it, distinctions between countries and issues became blurred, and it was America's "moral" obligation to defend "freedom" anywhere it was threatened, regardless of how dictatorial, tyrannical, or repressive the regimes on "our" side acted. The result was a massive distortion of reality. Vietnam became Munich; Ho Chi Minh became Hitler; and intelligent disengagement became appeasement.

In Asia especially, such a pernicious misreading of history produced devastating consequences. Fixated by the trauma of having "lost" China, men like Dean Rusk became obsessed with the notion that any nationalist movement would automatically result in further enhancing and solidifying the communist world. Ignoring the fact that Vietnam had been the archenemy of China for two thousand years, Rusk insisted that the Vietnamese quest for independence and freedom from Western colonialism was inspired and controlled by Mao Tse-tung. "The threat to world peace," he declared, "is militant, aggressive Asian communism, with its headquarters in Peking, China. . . . We have proven in Europe that resistance to aggression . . . serves the cause of peace and our own security. The threat to our security is [now] Asia. And we are fighting there not only for the Vietnamese, but for ourselves and the future of our country." In Korea and Berlin, Americans had stood fast in the face of communist aggression. Now they must do the same in Vietnam. It was a world view that no amount of attention to the facts could penetrate.

The tradition of strong bipartisan support for an aggressive anticommunist foreign policy also played a major role in fostering American involvement in Vietnam. After all, Truman, Eisenhower, and Kennedy had endorsed the policy. No American leader could safely contemplate challenging the anticommunist anchor of the "liberal consensus" without worrying profoundly about the domestic consequences. Kennedy and Johnson both feared the revival of McCarthyism if they deviated from any stance sanctioned by Cold War definitions of the world. Moreover, both participated fully in the outlook that spawned such policies, and both were surrounded by advisors who had actively shaped America's posture toward the Cold War. In a government where foreign policy bureaucrats tended to define the options as appeasement and withdrawal on the one hand, or the risk of nuclear confrontation on the other, the only "safe" alternative was to pursue the "middle way" of "reasonable" steps to thwart communist aggression.

Nevertheless, Lyndon Johnson bears substantial responsibility for implementing a radical extension of America's traditional Cold War policies by the actions he adopted in Vietnam. As George Ball has pointed out, Johnson could have overruled his advisors, listened to those in his inner circle who urged alternative courses of action, and found a way to extricate the United States from Vietnam. Although some have argued that Johnson never knew what he was getting into, and that the final disaster of American policy in Vietnam was the accidental result of incremental decisions, each of which was reasonable, the evidence suggests that Johnson had before him accurate assessments of where his policy would lead before he made his basic decisions. All during 1965 members of the Joint Chiefs of Staff, as well as George Ball, predicted that the infusion of American combat troops into Vietnam would lead to unending escalation, with at least 500,000 troops committed to that distant country in a war that would last a minimum of five years. Indeed, Johnson's own national security aide, McGeorge Bundy, prophetically summarized these arguments in a memorandum for the Joint Chiefs of Staff. Critics of American policy, Bundy wrote, will argue that "for ten years every step we have taken has been based on a previous failure and caused us to take another step which failed." They will go on to contend, he wrote, that "we are now doing what MacArthur and others have warned us about. We are about to fight a war that we can't fight and win as the country we are trying to help is quitting." Third, he continued, they will point to our failure "to fully realize what guerrilla war is like. We are sending conventional troops to do unconventional jobs." Fourth, he concluded, they will ask "how long—how much? Can we take casualties over five years—are we talking about a military solution when the solution is really political?"

Yet Johnson ignored such questions. He ordered Bundy to write the memorandum, not with the purpose of considering the issues seriously, but in order to repudiate the criticism. When George Ball argued that sending further troops to Vietnam was "like giving cobalt treatment to a terminal cancer case" and questioned whether "an army of westerners can successfully fight Orientals in an Asian jungle," Johnson used him as a foil. "Wouldn't all these countries [then] say that Uncle Sam was a paper tiger," Johnson asked; "wouldn't we lose credibility, breaking the word of three presidents?" With Johnson setting such a tone, Ball had no chance. Bundy chimed in that "Ball's argument would be a *radical* switch in policy," and Lodge nailed shut the president's case by asking, "Can't we see the similarity to our indolence at Munich?" It was not that Johnson had not heard the other side. He simply had not listened.

Moreover, Johnson compounded his error by consistently deceiving the American people and Congress about his decisions. Rather than inform the public of the dimensions of the enterprise he was embarking upon, the president dissembled, insisted that no major changes had taken place, and buried his announcement of troop increases in a noon-time press conference full of other announcements. By indulging his obsession with retaining total control in his own hands, Johnson thus temporarily held at bay the national uproar over Vietnam that he so feared, even while creating a situation that guaranteed in the long run his total inability to retain credibility with the American people once that debate began.

The ultimate irony was that Johnson ended up destroying himself, and that the very same qualities that brought him greatness in domestic affairs assured failure in his foreign policy decisions. "I knew from the start," Johnson told Doris Kearns in 1970.

> that I was bound to be crucified either way I moved. If I left the woman I really loved—the Great Society—in order to get involved with the bitch of a war on the other side of the world, then I would lose everything at home. All my programs. All my hopes to feed the hungry and shelter the homeless . . . but if I left that war and let the communists take over South Viet Nam, then I would be seen as a coward and my nation would be seen as an appeaser and we would both find it impossible to accomplish anything for anybody anywhere on the entire globe.

Thus, in order to achieve one goal, he embraced another, in the process trying, once more, to rise above contradictions, to put his personal stamp on the world, to transcend all human frailties and impose a solution from above that would bring the consensus he so desperately craved. His own personal sense of honor, courage, and manliness would permit no other course. "After all," he said, "our country was built by pioneers who had a rifle in one hand to kill their enemies and an ax in another to build their homes and provide for their families." But such a vision did not accord with the realities of modern existence, and every dollar that went to Vietnam was a dollar that did not go to fight the war on poverty. Even as he moved to assure consensus, Johnson undermined it, and in the end, by seeking to subjugate the world to his personal vision, he ended up destroying the one thing that he really cared about.

11

Coming Apart at Home

Although the Vietnam war assuredly destroyed Lyndon Johnson's dream of a united America committed to a "Great Society," the dream was already in danger at home as a consequence of internal divisions that challenged the very concept of consensus. Throughout the postwar years, liberal reformers had acted on the belief that the basic economic and social structure of America was sound. Within this framework of beliefs, social categories such as race, class, and gender were perceived as incidental barriers to equity. Once legislation was enacted to abolish discrimination based on such artificial categories, it was thought, individuals would be able to secure equal access to economic opportunity, equal protection before the law, and a full and vital stake in the institutions that made America great.

The experience of the 1960s generated a fundamental challenge to all these assumptions, at least among significant numbers of social activists. Faith in the integrity of American institutions became an anomaly to civil rights workers who repeatedly experienced brutal treatment or indifference from law enforcement officials. To antipoverty workers, the slogan of equal opportunity paled before the persistence of economic inequality and the power of extralegal coercion to negate antidiscrimination statutes. An increasing number of activists even questioned the efficacy of political change from within, since repeated adherence to the "rules of the game" produced little but contempt from those who exercised power. Thus, in one of the most pivotal developments of the 1960s, many who began as true believers in liberal reform became skeptics instead, alienated from their society and committed to revolutionizing its central values and structures. The "liberal consensus" was falling apart.

From Civil Rights to Black Power—A Paradigm

The growing radicalization of the civil rights movement served as a bellwether for incipient domestic tensions. When black students held sit-ins at Woolworth's and elsewhere in the early 1960s, they believed in the essential goodness of American society and were convinced that change would come quickly once white people acknowledged the error of their ways. "We wanted freedom, *now*," one sit-in demonstrator noted, "and we believed we could achieve it." But faith in America's capacity for reform eroded under grueling days of seemingly endless struggle. The young people in the Student Non-violent Coordinating Committee (SNCC) learned quickly how intransigent, brutal, and pervasive were the forces of resistance. Increasingly, they came to question the credibility of the government, their alliance with older, more moderate leaders, and the desirability of "integrating" into a white society that at every turn seemed to betray and subvert them. By 1966, they had broken with King, espoused the doctrine of "black power," and embarked on a campaign of systematic rebellion against the government of the United States and the values and institutions it represented. In their movement from optimistic faith to bitter alienation, the workers of SNCC provided a microcosm of a process that would soon repeat itself with others.

In retrospect, the conflict that ultimately divided SNCC from Dr. King's Southern Christian Leadership Conference (SCLC) was present from the beginning. When Ella Baker, executive secretary of SCLC, convened the first conference of student demonstrators in Raleigh, North Carolina, in April 1960, she was already aware of the potential clash. "Black ministers," Baker later recalled, "always like to be at the center of things, but they tend to be conservative, and have to be prodded." SCLC leaders envisioned SNCC as a youth branch of SCLC, playing a role analogous to that occupied by the NAACP's youth division. But the students, supported by Baker, resisted becoming an appendage of Dr. King. Although they ardently embraced the philosophy of nonviolence, they also asserted their independence, forming their own autonomous organization. Writing about the conference one month later, Ella Baker noted the distinctive qualities of the new group. They had made it "crystal clear," she wrote, " that the current sit-ins and other demonstrations are concerned with something much bigger than a hamburger or even a giant-sized Coke." The students, she observed, had opted for a " group centered leadership, rather than . . . a leader-centered pattern of organization" and had vowed "to keep the movement democratic, to avoid struggles for personal leadership." Fearing "that adults might try to 'capture' the student movement," she noted, "the students showed a willingness to be met on the basis of equality, but were intolerant of anything that smacked of manipulation or domination." In a veiled reference to Dr. King himself, Baker applauded the students' independence as refreshing "to those of the older group who bear . . . the frustrations and the disillusions [which] come when the prophetic leader turns out to have heavy feet of clay." Thus, at its very moment of birth, SNCC determined to forge its own agenda, conceived in a spirit of independence from SCLC.

A second source of contention—money, and the strings it brought with it—quickly became apparent as well. In its fund-raising efforts, SCLC created the impression that it was heavily involved in student protests. Implicitly at least, SCLC pledged that it would give money to finance those activities. Yet SNCC found it difficult to pry loose the promised funds. Although Dr. King had received an $11,000 contribution from a New York labor union—one-third of it earmarked for the students—SNCC received only $1,000. In addition, SNCC was already learning some of the political costs of accepting outside financing. When the American Federation of Labor (AFL) decided to fund a SNCC conference in October 1960, it made its contribution contingent on excluding Bayard Rustin from the conference. Rustin, the AFL said, was too far "left." Although SNCC accepted the funding, one key staff member resigned in protest. Not for the last time, SNCC became sensitive to the effort of liberal "outsiders" to use power and money as a means of imposing political orthodoxy on the young.

It was the direct experience of SNCC workers in the field, however, that contributed most to the growing alienation of the students. In the aftermath of the 1961 Freedom Rides, Attorney General Robert F. Kennedy struck on the idea of channeling student protestors into voter registration work as a means of containing the racial confrontations that inevitably emerged from direct-action demonstrations. As Kennedy and others envisioned it, voter registration would serve as an effective means of social change within traditional and sanctioned avenues of political reform. If civil rights workers used laws already on the books to increase the number of black voters, they could ultimately affect political power, yet in a manner that would minimize the potential for conflict. In return for the cooperation of civil rights groups, Kennedy promised federal protection of voter registration workers. SNCC chose to give Kennedy's proposal a chance, perhaps recognizing that a very thin line separated direct action from voter registration activities, and that securing ballots for blacks in the Deep South constituted as great a confrontation with racism as sitting-in at a five-and-dime.

Almost immediately, that recognition was confirmed by experience. While Kennedy thought that voter registration activities would concentrate on large urban centers, SNCC determined to tackle racism where it was worst—in the delta counties of Mississippi and Georgia. In Amite County, Mississippi, only one black was registered out of 5,000 potential voters. In Walthall County, not a single Negro could vote out of 3,000 eligible residents. SNCC workers quickly discovered that seeking to register blacks under the 1957 and 1960 Civil Rights Acts offered no guarantee of either safety or progress in such counties and amounted to the equivalent of direct action. When John Hardy took two black citizens to register in Walthall County in September 1961, the registrar informed him that he had "no right to mess in the 'nigger's' business," took out a pistol, and cracked Hardy over the head. The sheriff then threatened to beat Hardy "within an inch of [his] life" and arrested him for disorderly conduct. In the tiny town of Mileston, Mississippi, Hartman Turnbow was the first black to try to register. A few nights later, his home was attacked with a Molotov cocktail. When he and his family fled, they were fired on by whites. The next morning, Turnbow, Robert Moses, and three other SNCC workers were arrested by sheriff's deputies. The charge: arson. The violence seemed never to end. Churches were bombed and burned after being the site of voter registration meetings, black homes were riddled with gunfire after SNCC workers stayed overnight, ordinary citizens were beaten and crippled simply for entering the voter registration office. No one was ever arrested for the crimes.

SNCC workers also discovered the subtle ways in which economic intimidation could be used to maintain the status quo, regardless of the law. In Ruleville, Mississippi, one black had worked on a plantation for more than thirty years. "Mr. L . . . never said a thing about nothing I did," the black tenant said. "We would talk and things seemed to be swell between us." But then his wife applied to register. The next day the bossman came and said that if she did not take her name off the rolls, the family would be evicted. In Terrell County, Georgia, a Negro who tried to register had his butane storage tank taken away. The entire crop lien system in the South was based on blacks being furnished with supplies on credit. Now, suddenly, those who went to register to vote had their credit cancelled. Teachers were fired, welfare checks were cancelled, and in one instance, an entire county abolished its free food program to retaliate against voter registration—all of this to give blacks the clear message, in the words of one elderly woman, that "the white man gives and the white man [can] take away."

Frequently, blacks endured a combination of economic and physical coercion. In Ruleville, Mississippi, Mrs. Fannie Lou Hamer heard about SNCC and its effort to teach people how to register. "I had always wanted to do something to help myself and my race," she said,

> but I did not know how to go about it. So I went to one of the meetings. . . . The next day, August 31, 1962, I went to Indianola, Mississippi to fill out a form at the registrar's office. . . . That night, Mr. Marlow [owner of the plantation] where I was staying asked me why I went to register. I told him I did it for myself not for him. He told me to get off the plantation and don't be seen near it again.

Shortly after being evicted, Mrs. Hamer was taken from a bus, jailed, and viciously beaten by police because of her efforts to help others register. Although her injuries were so severe that she never fully recovered, Mrs. Hamer went on to become one of the movement's most eloquent leaders.

In addition to such travail, SNCC workers were also overwhelmed by the poverty blacks faced in the South. SNCC staff members accompanied the people on their chores, slept in their homes, ate their meager food. In the process, they achieved a profound understanding of the ways in which political powerlessness went hand in hand with wretched housing, malnutrition, pervasive illness, and the day-to-day impossibility of being able to see a way out. Writing from Greenwood, one SNCC worker described a typical family situation:

> [Mr. Meek's] wife is thirty-three years old and they have eleven children, age ranging from seventeen down to eight months. Seven of the children are school age, and not one of the ten is in school because they have no money, no

food, no clothes, and no wood to keep warm by. . . . The house they are living in have no paper or nothing on the walls and you can look at the ground through the floor and if you were not careful you will step in one of those holes and break your leg or ankle.

Such experiences inevitably generated a new skepticism among the young civil rights workers. Even as they drew strength and inspiration from the heroism of the people they worked with, SNCC workers also came to understand that the vote—and the law—offered only a partial answer. The real solution was systemic, they came to believe, and required a radical redistribution of wealth, income, and power.

The greatest impetus to SNCC's radicalism, however, came from a profound cynicism about the integrity and good faith of America's white leaders. In the beginning, SNCC had taken literally Attorney General Robert Kennedy's promise to provide protection for voter registration workers, believing that the federal government could be mobilized as an instrument to compel change in the South. At each step of the voter registration campaign, SNCC alerted the FBI and Justice Department to civil rights violations, filed affidavits on the brutality they encountered from Southern law enforcement officials, and beseeched federal agents to act on their behalf. Yet almost always, the response they received was inadequate, sometimes simply reflecting indifference to their plight, at other times communicating callous neglect or even outright sanction of the crimes committed against them.

Stories of the FBI's failure to protect voter registration workers were legion. In the fall of 1962, whites in Ruleville, Mississippi, fired into the homes of two local blacks assisting SNCC workers, hitting two young girls. Yet when the FBI men arrived to investigate, according to a SNCC field report, they "didn't seem to be looking for the person or persons who did the shooting; instead they asked the people if *we* were asking them for money. If they thought *we* did the shooting." In Greenwood, Mississippi, one night, SNCC workers noticed a car full of whites outside their headquarters, with one man holding a pair of guns. They called Burke Marshall, Assistant Attorney General of the United States, at home. He said he could do nothing unless a crime was committed. They then telephoned the FBI agent in Greenwood and asked him to come over. He said he would. When they then heard the sound of men on the steps, they fled through a rear window. Approximately twelve hours later, the FBI agent arrived. As Willie Peacock, a SNCC worker, wrote at the time: "that's when the impact really hit me, how unprotected we really were. Here were our great heroes that we depended on in Washington . . . I had heard that . . . the FBI didn't act when you needed them sometimes [but] I just couldn't believe it; [now] it had happened."

Most galling of all, perhaps, was the passivity of federal agents who stood by and took notes, but failed to act, even as criminal violations of black civil rights took place in their very presence. On Freedom Day in Selma, Alabama, October 26, 1963, SNCC had mobilized more than 300 black citizens to register to vote at the county courthouse, directly across the square from the federal office building. Four FBI agents and two Justice Department attorneys sat at windows overlooking the square. The line moved slowly, and the sun was hot. When SNCC advisor Howard Zinn asked the Justice Department lawyer to go tell the state police that the blacks had a right to get a drink of water, the attorney responded: "I think they do have that right. But I won't do it." Around noon, Sheriff Jim Clark mounted the steps of the federal building to arrest two blacks holding signs saying, "Register to Vote." Federal officials did nothing, even though the arrests took place on federal property and the sign carriers had broken no law. Early in the afternoon, SNCC workers sought to provide food and drink for the long line of blacks still waiting. "If you do [that]," Sheriff Jim Clark said, "you'll be arrested." When SNCC workers attempted to cross the street with the food, state troopers knocked them to the ground, jabbed them with clubs and cattle prods, then dragged them away. As the arrests took place, Zinn wrote, "the Justice Department men hurried in and out of the federal building. The FBI watched." To young blacks who had grown up convinced that the FBI always "got their man," it seemed inconceivable that the most powerful police agency in the world was helpless to act, unless it chose consciously *not* to do so.

Washington, of course, viewed the situation differently. Justice Department officials, particularly Assistant Attorney General Burke Marshall, focused on the limitations of federal police power and were hypersensitive to the charge that the federal government was trying to abolish state's rights and impose external rule on the South. Marshall operated within a strict definition of federalism, concerned that national authorities not supplant local law enforcement officials. Hence, the Justice Department emphasized seeking affidavits and building legal cases that at some future point might be effective in redressing grievances. Moreover, within the Justice Department, there was great fear of stepping on the toes of FBI chief J. Edgar Hoover, who for nearly half a century had exercised almost total autonomy and independence, despite the statutory provision that he was subordinate to the Attorney General. Hoover was intensely loyal to his men in the field—often closely tied to local law enforcement officials—and resisted any efforts to interfere with their prerogatives.

From the vantage point of SNCC workers, FBI inaction and the Justice Department's hesitancy constituted a serious betrayal of the promise made by Robert Kennedy when voter registration activity began. Living day by day in situations that amounted to mortal combat with an unprincipled enemy, the assurance that federal authorities would take action *later* represented the equivalent of the U.S. government siding *now* with the brutality being meted out by white racists. In the eyes of SNCC workers, the gist of FBI policy was exemplified by the response of one federal agent who came to question a white civil rights worker who had been beaten, kicked, and urinated on by four Mississippians. "Well, nigger lover," the FBI agent allegedly asked the civil rights worker, "what seems to be the problem?" In 1961, SNCC had believed the federal government was an ally, but by 1963, SNCC Executive Secretary James Forman wrote, "we [knew] that the FBI was a farce. . . . It was all too clear whose side Uncle Sam was on."

The increasing radicalization of SNCC made inevitable a widening of the split with SCLC that had already been present, in embryonic form, as early as 1960. From the perspective of white America, Dr. King was the pre-eminent leader of the civil rights struggle. Charismatic, eloquent, and brilliantly effective in his ability to portray the civil rights movement in terms that would appeal to white America's conscience, King occupied center stage in the media's coverage of civil rights. As he traveled from city to city, from demonstration to demonstration, TV cameras and journalists focused on this American Gandhi, highlighting his role and dramatizing the contradiction he exposed between the American creed and Southern reality. Wherever King went, his sonorous words appealed to the best part of the American spirit. He became a folk hero, the personal embodiment and symbol of the greatest mass movement for freedom that America had ever seen. Yet the very nature of King's success, and the tactics he employed, ran counter to the lessons SNCC workers learned on the front lines of battle. While King appealed to the "system" for reform, SNCC became disenchanted with the system itself and all it represented. And while the media followed King wherever he journeyed, giving him the credit for victories achieved, all too often SNCC workers were left to pick up the pieces after King departed, suffering the daily indignities and brutality of whites seeking revenge, but with no cameras to record their oppression.

In large part, the growing schism reflected the differing agendas and perspectives of the two organizations. King's audience was the nation as a whole. He understood that, if changes were to take place, they must emanate from Washington through federal legislation designed to correct the inequities from which blacks had suffered for so long. As a result, he concentrated on building a strong coalition, sufficient to generate enough pressure so that Congress and the president would be forced to act. In effect, King stood at the center of a vortex of potentially conflicting political forces. In addition to holding the allegiance of black Americans, he also had to win the support of external groups essential to achieving the victory he sought—organized labor, national religious organizations, intellectuals, white liberals, and the Kennedy/Johnson administrations. King's role at the center of such a coalition caused him to walk a narrow, and sometimes tortuous, line between advocacy and compromise. Even as he criticized the Kennedy administration for its inaction, he had to retain his lines of communication—and friendship—with the president and his brother Robert. Although King, as much as any man, had ample reason to detest the FBI, he had to soften his criticism of that organization lest he alienate those in trade unions and the white liberal community who perceived federal law enforcement officials as an essential ally. Whatever he did, King could ill af-

ford to lose media approval or to communicate an image that would be sufficiently "radical" to bring about the disaffection of white liberals whose political and financial backing he needed to win his goal. In short, the very nature of King's civil rights coalition compelled him to go no further in his
criticisms or demands than was acceptable to the least liberal of his various
constituencies. If he were to secure the legislation he sought, he had to play
by the rules of the game, maximize the political forces that might support
him, and—if necessary—temper his own demands and allow others to
shape his agenda in order not to alienate a potential ally.

SNCC, by contrast, saw little purpose in deferring to groups who had
little awareness of the real conditions in Mississippi and Georgia, and whose
motivation seemed more that of paternalistic control than of solidarity in
the struggle. Just as the nature of King's coalition determined his perspective and options, so the experience of SNCC workers in the most impoverished and racist counties of the South determined theirs. Veterans of Mc-
Comb, Greenwood, and Americus had little reason to place their faith in
the good offices of the Justice Department. Nor did their firsthand encounters with debilitating poverty and malnutrition give them much sympathy for the perspective of wealthy allies who preached the importance of
respectability. Already, SNCC workers were suspicious of white liberals who
funneled their funds through SCLC, or who made their financial backing
contingent on SNCC conforming to a political "means" test that required
the exclusion of "leftists."* From a SNCC perspective, it made no sense to
play by the rules of the game, when those who set the rules more often than
not appeared to align themselves with the enemy—indeed, perhaps were
the enemy. Thus, the preconditions for a radical split within the civil rights
movement were already embedded in the differing vantage points of SNCC
and SCLC. By 1965, these differences had hardened into an unbridgeable
political chasm that divided the movement even as it seemed to be enjoying
its moments of greatest success.

The first public sign of deteriorating bonds between SNCC and SCLC
came with the March on Washington movement of August 1963. All during
the spring of that year, Bull Conners' wanton violence against black demonstrators in Birmingham had seared the nation's conscience and finally galvanized the Kennedy administration into action, culminating in the president's June address requesting major civil rights legislation. Building on the
Birmingham movement, Bayard Rustin proposed a massive march to compel Congress to act on Kennedy's new legislation. As originally conceived,
the march would involve thousands of civil rights demonstrators sitting-in at
the nation's Capitol building until Congress enacted the omnibus civil
rights measure.

---

* Within a civil rights context, "leftists" were either people who in the past had been linked to
communist or "communist front" organizations, or who in the present rejected counsels of patience and expressed doubt about liberal reformers.

By August, however, plans for the march had become a pale shadow of the original proposal. Fearful of the Kennedy administration's hostility to the march, King and more conservative civil rights leaders like Roy Wilkins of the NAACP and Whitney Young of the Urban League agreed to tone down the demonstrations. Seeking to assure the support of labor, church leaders, and northern white liberals, these leaders proposed a series of changes, acceptable to the Kennedy administration, that would limit severely any expression of militancy. The march would occur on one day only. There would be no sit-ins on Capitol Hill. A major effort would be made to have equal numbers of whites and blacks at the rally. And the marchers would come dressed in shirts and ties to prove the "respectability" of the movement. March leaders even agreed to a government order that all liquor stores in Washington be closed on the day of the march, seemingly accepting the implicit message that, after all, blacks might get rowdy if they had access to alcohol. Still, SNCC decided to participate in the march because it would have the opportunity to present its own message to America through the speech of John Lewis, SNCC's chairman.

But when the day of the march arrived, SNCC leaders were told to temper their position even further. In the original draft of his speech, Lewis denounced the Kennedy administration's record of inaction, declared that civil rights workers would "march through Dixie like Sherman," and attacked both major political parties for failing to come to grips with the corrosive racism of American life. Now, Lewis was told that church, labor, and other liberal leaders would not appear on the same platform with him if he insisted on delivering such a speech. Eugene Carson Blake of the National Council of Churches insisted that the words "masses" and "revolution" be deleted from Lewis's remarks. Under intense pressure, Lewis and Forman rewrote the speech, accepting most of the modifications of their position suggested by others. But from their point of view, the changes amounted to censorship.

The day itself was a political triumph. A quarter of a million Americans, black and white, joined hands, sang "We Shall Overcome" with folk artist Joan Baez, and exulted in the soaring words of Martin Luther King, Jr., as he told the American people, "I Have a Dream." By nightfall, all the marchers had left the city, as planned, after their leaders had tea at the White House. From the point of view of King's civil rights coalition, the rally could not have gone better. It reassured white Americans of the peaceful intent of blacks and represented a masterful lobbying effort to secure civil rights legislation. But from the point of view of SNCC, the entire enterprise added new depth to their concern of what could happen when outsiders attempted to shape their agenda and define their options. Not only had the march created an artificially rosy optimism about race relations in America; it had also succeeded in denying SNCC control over its own voice.

All of SNCC's worst suspicions seemed confirmed one year later in Atlantic City when the Mississippi Freedom Democratic Party (MFDP) sought

March on Washington, August 28, 1963. More than 250,000 people gather at the Lincoln Memorial to demand action on civil rights in ceremonies that concluded with Dr. Martin Luther King's "I Have a Dream" speech. *(National Archives)*

recognition from the National Democratic Convention as the authentic voice of the Democratic Party in Mississippi. The MFDP represented a brilliant tactical and strategic effort. In a state where fewer than 5 percent of the black population was allowed to register, SNCC struck on the idea of mobilizing a systematic legal and political challenge to the whites who controlled the Democratic Party in Mississippi. Operating through the Council of Federated Organizations (COFO), they would show that blacks *wanted* to exercise their right to vote and held mock elections to prove it, collecting affidavits from blacks who had been beaten in the quest to exercise their citizenship rights and demonstrating through legal briefs that they were the only Democrats in Mississippi who supported the national party, since white Democrats in Mississippi explicitly supported the candidacy of Barry Goldwater. With the aid of white student volunteers from Yale and Stanford, SNCC conducted a "freedom vote" in the fall of 1963 in which 80,000 blacks cast ballots for MFDP candidates. The election, one SNCC worker wrote, "showed the Negro population that politics is not 'just white folks' business, but that the Negro is also capable of holding political offices. . . . For the first time, since Reconstruction, Negroes . . . [were able to express] their own beliefs and ideas rather than those of the 'white folks.'" To further promote the effort, COFO sponsored the Mississippi Freedom Summer Project of 1964, with more than a thousand northern students—predominantly white—coming to Mississippi to run more than thirty freedom schools and to build support for the MFDP challenge in Atlantic City. SNCC would play by the rules, show that they deserved representation in the national Democratic Party, and with the overwhelming power of the evidence they accumulated, achieve the dignity and participation in the democratic process that blacks in Mississippi had been denied all their lives.

When they arrived in Atlantic City, delegates from the MFDP possessed an extraordinary array of ammunition for their case. In his brief before the credentials committee, lawyer Joseph Rauh emphasized the apostasy of white Democrats and Mississippi's record of violence against blacks. "Are you going to throw out of here the people who want to work for Lyndon Johnson," Rauh asked, "who are willing to be beaten and shot and thrown in jail to work for Lyndon Johnson? Are we for the oppressor or the oppressed?" Dramatically illustrating Rauh's point, Fannie Lou Hamer went before the convention, and on national TV, told of her own experience. "I was beaten until I was exhausted," she said. "I began to scream, and one white man got up and began to beat me on the head and tell me to hush. . . . All of this on account we wanted to register, to become first class citizens. [If] the Freedom Democratic Party is not seated now, I question America." As telegrams poured into the convention from Americans sympathetic to their cause, the MFDP felt confident, assured that at least a minority on the credentials committee would support their petition and bring the issue to the floor of the convention for a vote.

But Lyndon Johnson wanted no one to upstage "his" convention, his moment of glory and acclamation. He called an emergency press conference so that the networks would switch from live coverage of Hamer to himself. Outraged at the support Hamer and the MFDP were receiving, he mobilized all of the forces at his command to frustrate the MFDP's effort. With the FBI bugging MFDP headquarters to alert him of MFDP plans, Johnson mobilized his own coalition to stop the MFDP challenge in its tracks. To build suspense at the convention, Johnson had withheld naming his choice for the vice-presidency. Now, he told Minnesota Senator Hubert Humphrey that Humphrey's selection for the post would be contingent on his being able to stop the MFDP challenge. Using all the IOUs he had collected through his distinguished liberal career, Humphrey recruited Walter Reuther of the UAW, Bayard Rustin, Martin Luther King, and countless others to support a compromise. Even though established journals like the *New York Times* urged that both delegations be given equal seating, Humphrey now pushed through a proposal that would give the MFDP only two out of forty seats in the delegation. Moreover, the credentials committee—not the MFDP—would choose the two delegates. (As it turned out, neither came from SNCC.) Stunned by the rapid developments, and told that the MFDP had accepted the compromise, the convention endorsed the "compromise" of the credentials committee.

But the MFDP refused to play Johnson's game. Victory, which had been in their grasp, had been taken away, and they were angry. Michael Schwerner and Andrew Goodman, two white Northerners, and James Chaney, a black Southerner, had been murdered in June while working for the MFDP. Churches were still being bombed and civil rights workers brutalized. Even as the convention met, MFDP headquarters in Tupelo burned to the ground, set afire by whites carrying cans of gasoline. Now, MFDP was being told that the convention compromise was "the greatest thing since the emancipation proclamation." Bayard Rustin urged the group to go along, because politics, after all, meant compromise and was different from protest. Dr. King chimed in that he had talked personally to Hubert Humphrey and that Humphrey had "promised me there would be a new day in Mississippi if you accept the proposal." But the MFDP had suffered too long and learned too much to just "go along." White Democrats in Mississippi, Forman pointed out, had systematically denied blacks not only the right to vote, but the right to attend any precinct or county meetings of the party. "And now they are asking you," he said, "to agree that in the face of all these injustices you still support this convention and still will agree that these people are entitled to seats no matter what they have done in Mississippi." As one Mississippi black woman declared, "the compromise would let Jim Crow be. . . . Ain't no Democratic party worth that. We've been treated like beasts in Mississippi. They shot us down like animals. We risked our lives coming here. . . . Politics must be corrupt if it don't care none about people down there." Fannie Lou Hamer, who had been told by national Democratic leaders to go back home now that she had made her point, perhaps said it best. "We didn't come all this way for no two votes."

More than any other event, rejection of the MFDP challenge at Atlantic City convinced SNCC workers that they could not trust "white liberals" in the civil rights movement. Blacks had endured viciousness that people from Washington or New York or Detroit could never know. They had done what they were supposed to do in order to claim their just place in American society. And in the end, they had been betrayed—not by white racists in Mississippi but by their liberal allies who presumed to speak for them, yet in the crunch, had marched to a different drummer. While from a liberal perspective the results at Atlantic City represented a major triumph—finally achieving some representation for blacks in a racist state—those who had paid the price on the field of combat could only weep. If politics meant foregoing protest and allowing someone else to tell you what you should want, SNCC would say no.

SNCC'S alienation from King and the white liberal "establishment" in Atlantic City reinforced a separate, but related, resentment against white outsiders that had been festering throughout the Freedom Summer Campaign of 1964. In a calculated and hotly debated move, SNCC had decided to recruit white volunteers to come to Mississippi, knowing that violence—and probably death—would take place, but convinced that only through exposing white America to such suffering could the nation's will to act be mobilized. "We could not bring all of white America to Mississippi," Forman later wrote, "but by bringing in some of its children as volunteer workers, a new consciousness [would feed] back into the homes of thousands of white Americans. . . . We recognized that the results might be great pain and sorrow, but we were not asking that whites do any more than we had done." In many—perhaps most—instances, whites and blacks worked together as part of a "beloved community," finding in their common struggle bonds of solidarity, affection, and communion that transcended anything they had experienced before. Yet problems were inevitable. The white volunteers were economically secure, highly educated, sophisticated in the ways of the world. Without conscious intent or malicious motivation, many found it "natural" to utilize the skills they brought with them to "take over" tasks previously carried out by blacks, whether these involved writing press releases, running freedom schools, or coordinating logistics. Given the psychological and cultural forces at work, anger and misunderstanding were bound to develop. This was a black movement, and most of the workers in SNCC were there for the duration. Whites could leave whenever they wished. Some SNCC staff members, with only a grade school education, felt inferior in the presence of white college students from Yale, Harvard, and Stanford. Tensions developed over interracial sex, as young black men—proud, yet resentful of whites—made the willingness of white women to sleep with them a test of the white volunteer's commitment. Underlying all of these tensions was the fear that whites would attempt to take over a black movement—or worse yet—that they felt entitled to do so on the basis of their superior education and political skills.

SNCC's experience with Allard Lowenstein exemplified these concerns. A charismatic intellectual and politician who had taught at Stanford and North Carolina State and served as president of the National Student Association, Lowenstein was a peripatetic liberal crusader who traveled from South Africa to Spain to Mississippi in quest of social reform, parachuting into trouble spots, sizing up the situation, and immediately coming forward with a hundred ideas on what to do to eliminate inequality. Lowenstein had played a major role in mobilizing students from Yale and Stanford to assist in the freedom elections during the fall of 1963 in Mississippi. He repeated the same process of recruitment for Freedom Summer in 1964. But as time went on, SNCC leaders became suspicious of his intentions. In one instance, Lowenstein ordered a group of demonstrators in Yazoo to "fill the jails" without consulting SNCC's project director in the area. "Where does *he* get off telling people what to do," the director asked. By February, Lowenstein informed students at Stanford that he was singlehandedly responsible for proposing and getting approval for the Freedom Summer idea. Such episodes did not sit well with SNCC veterans, and their conflict with Lowenstein reached a breaking point when—frustrated with the "chaos" of the SNCC operation—Lowenstein proposed moving the headquarters for Freedom Summer from Mississippi to New York City. One of

Lowenstein's primary concerns was the "leftist" tinge in SNCC, particularly its willingness to use legal assistance from the National Lawyers Guild, a group once included on the Attorney General's subversive list. As SNCC perceived the issue, Lowenstein wanted to impose a political litmus test on SNCC, threatening to withdraw his own support—and that of other liberals and labor organizations—if Northern liberals like himself could not control the movement. Lowenstein was also allied with those who supported the MFDP "compromise" at Atlantic City.

The debate over SNCC's autonomy came to a head when liberal organizations and civil rights groups met in New York during the fall of 1964 to discuss the future of the Mississippi project. From the beginning it was clear that SNCC, its "leftism" and its refusal to accept political control by the established civil rights coalition, constituted the primary reason for the meeting. One speaker insisted that the local concerns of people in Mississippi had to give way to "national considerations." Another accused Robert Moses of being a virtual dictator in Mississippi. (Nothing could have been further from the truth.) Joseph Rauh declared that he would "like to drive out the Lawyers Guild." But the gist of the meeting centered on Lowenstein's suggestion that a new, *national* decision-making structure be set in place, giving blacks in Mississippi only a partial say in what would be done. "I have been listening to people from Mississippi for seventeen years," one NAACP representative said. "I don't want to listen to Steptoe [a black grass roots leader in Mississippi]. We need a high level meeting so that we can cut away the underbrush. . . . [In Mississippi] we would have to meet with every Tom, Dick and Harry." The group practically perceived SNCC as an outlaw. The SNCC representative, in turn, perceived the meeting itself as a direct threat to the effort of Mississippi blacks to define their own agenda. "It is unreal," he said, "as far as Mississippi is concerned, for an ad hoc group to meet in New York and determine what should go on." The conflict could hardly have been greater.

By the time of the Selma to Montgomery March in the spring of 1965, the tensions between SNCC and other civil rights groups had become almost irreversible. The scene was eerily familiar. Hundreds of blacks walking quietly to the point of confrontation, the bark of a police command, and the sudden rush of state troopers on horseback trampling demonstrators as TV cameras whirred. SNCC had organized Selma, but Dr. King was the one who brought it to national attention as the pivot for his campaign to secure a new voting rights law. Although SNCC and SCLC supporters marched together, they differed on almost every issue of tactics, from King's insistence on keeping in close touch with the Justice Department and obeying court injunctions, to questions of whether local blacks should be exposed to the brutality of Al Lingo's state troopers. In the end, King's tactics paid off, as they had in Birmingham. People flew in from all over the country to take part in the final march to Montgomery. And the Selma campaign provided the occasion for Lyndon Johnson's greatest speech to congress, in the peroration of which he identified himself totally with the civil rights movement, declaring "We Shall Overcome." From the point of view of King's coalition, it was the ultimate triumph of the civil rights movement. From the point of view of many SNCC activists, however, it represented the nadir. The same president who had sabotaged their efforts to secure representation at Atlantic City now had the arrogance to commandeer the very slogan of the movement itself. It was like being captured and having one's identity obliterated, one SNCC observer noted.

Thus, even as the civil rights movement achieved its pinnacle of success, its foundations were crumbling. Although the nation as a whole saw only unity and triumph, participants in the movement perceived rancor, division, and estrangement. As one Northern white wrote on returning from Montgomery,

> The major gap between King and SNCC is that [SNCC workers] do the grass roots work, prepare the way, clean up afterwards, and get neither the credit nor the results they seek, because King is a political animal, "a white man's nigger," and always compromises. SNCC is the vanguard of a revolution which seeks to transform the system while King seems to be in the middle of an effort to reform it. In the televised proceedings at Montgomery, Ralph Albernathy created the "cult hero" and at no time bothered to thank SNCC for all the organizational dirty work it had done. The liberal, smoothly clad visitors from the North dominated the proceedings and James Forman in his dungarees was given one minute.

However unfair to King, such remarks suggested just how wide and deep the divisions had become.

The final break came a little more than a year later in the state of Mississippi. SNCC had already taken a step toward increased militancy by selecting Stokeley Carmichael, a former Howard University student who had denounced the voting rights act as a "white man's bill," as its new chairman. After agonizing debate, SNCC also determined that henceforth, white staff members should play a peripheral role, concentrating on white communities, with blacks exercising primary decision-making power within the organization. As the liberal press increasingly denounced SNCC's radicalism and placed its imprimatur on King's more gradualist policies, the stage was set for confrontation. James Meredith's solo march across Mississippi to dramatize black rights provided the occasion. After he was struck down by a shotgun blast from roadside bushes, all the major civil rights groups in America determined to complete his march on Jackson.

The resulting drama provided the last act of the civil rights coalition, and the first public declaration of the internal war that had been festering within the movement. In town after town, throughout the countryside of Mississippi, King and Carmichael addressed courthouse square rallies. King exhorted the crowds with the traditional cry of "Freedom *Now*" and pleas for nonviolent action. The response was strangely passive. Carmichael, in contrast, denounced "the betrayal of black dreams by white America." Finally, one day in Canton, Mississippi, Carmichael declared: "The only way we are going to stop them from whuppin' us is to take over. We've been saying freedom for six years and we ain't got nothin'." Then, publicly using for the first time a phrase that had been circulating through SNCC meetings for months, Carmichael declared: "The time for running has come to an end. . . . Black Power. It's time we stand up and take over; move on over [Whitey] or we'll move on over you." Responding, the crowd yelled in rhythmic response: "Black Power! Black Power! Black Power!" A new stage of the civil rights revolution had begun.*

Almost immediately, the slogan became a rallying cry for angry blacks as well as a justification for a white backlash against the civil rights movement. In the summer of 1965, race riots had laid waste the Watts area of Los Angeles, leaving 34 dead, 4,000 arrested, and more than $35 million in property damage. By the summer of 1966—after the Black Power slogan was coined—racial disturbances were occurring almost daily, with 38 separate confrontations taking place in cities like Cleveland, San Francisco, Milwaukee, and Chicago. "Burn, Baby, Burn," cried the rioters. "Get Whitey." White liberals believed that the Black Power movement—typified by SNCC leader H. Rap Brown's statement that "violence is as American as apple pie"—bore a heavy degree of responsibility for the breakdown of civility in America's race relations. According to this argument, Carmichael and SNCC had repudiated the civil rights movement, betrayed Dr. King's commitment to "black and white together," and set America on the road toward racial civil war.

In a more basic sense, however, the Black Power movement was a direct outgrowth of the civil rights experience itself, not a repudiation of it. As the

---

* In the North there had already been a significant shift toward black nationalism and militancy, largely due to the charismatic leadership of Malcolm X, and the influence of the Black Muslim religion. Malcolm X had been a leading disciple of Elijah Muhammed, head of the Nation of Islam in America. Like Elijah Muhammed, Malcolm X had preached the doctrine of black separation from the white devil, of black pride and independence, and of self-defense and self-reliance in the face of white efforts to control and intimidate. Malcolm quickly became more powerful and popular than Elijah Muhammed, and in a dispute over both ideology and power, Malcolm was expelled from the Nation of Islam. He retained an enormous constituency, however, in Northern urban areas such as New York, Boston, Detroit, and Chicago. Over time, Malcolm began to change his viewpoint, and after a trip to several Islamic nations in Africa, proclaimed that differences in color no longer should provide the sole basis for political and religious commitments. Malcolm even talked, albeit cautiously, about working out some form of cooperation with Martin Luther King, Jr., and other civil rights leaders. Although Malcolm X was portrayed in the white press as an apostle of violence against whites, in fact he advocated the use of force only as a means of defense and self-assertion. In the spring of 1965, Malcolm X was assassinated at a New York rally of his followers. The assassins allegedly were followers of Elijah Muhammed, jealous of Malcolm's charisma and appeal. To this day, many believe that a larger conspiracy was at work in Malcolm's death, including some individuals operating as agents of the government. Malcolm's death robbed the black nationalist movement of its most effective leader. It also increased the alienation of many urban blacks in the North, making them even more receptive to the doctrine of Black Power as it emerged from the Southern movement a year after Malcolm's death.

historian Allan Matusow has noted, Black Power "was not a systematic doctrine, but a cry of rage." It had emerged as the inevitable conclusion of Mississippi and Georgia, the March on Washington, and the MFDP experience
in Atlantic City. It flowed from years of day-in and day-out encounters with
the intransigence of white institutions and law enforcement officials, the
crippling horror of seeing poverty in its rawest form, the growing sense that
whites never conceded to black demands except through coercion. As
Roger Wilkins, a government official and nephew of the NAACP leader,
wrote at the end of the sixties,

> In earlier decades, the overwhelming majority of Negroes retained their pro-
> found faith in America, her institutions, her ideals, and her ability to achieve
> some day a society reflecting those ideals. The flaws were in [individual] white
> people . . . but not in the institutions. Now, however, there is a growing and
> seriously held view among some young militant Negroes that white people have
> embedded their own personal flaws so deeply in the institutions that those in-
> stitutions are beyond redemption. . . . There is also, I believe, a subtle, but
> more general and growing Negro skepticism about the commitment and sen-
> sitivity of even "good" white people.

During the March on Washington in 1963, Martin Luther King, Jr.,
had told the assembled throng that "the Negro dream is rooted in the American dream." King offered to America—and to blacks—a glorious vision.
Through the transforming power of Christian love and the redemptive suffering of nonviolent protest, the American people would somehow be able
to transcend their past, to eradicate history, to have a new birth. King held
forth the possibility of a miracle—that through good faith, love, and mutual
commitment, Americans could abolish the significance of race, creating a
situation where black children from the dusty fields of Georgia and Alabama
could walk hand in hand with their white brothers and sisters to the promised land. But history could not be eradicated so easily, nor could the central
significance of race to all American institutions and culture be rooted out
simply through warm feelings. It was that fundamental reality that stood at
the heart of SNCC's rebellion. For too long, blacks had practiced good faith
and accepted the professed intentions of white America to remedy injustices.
Now, an increasing number of blacks concluded that white institutions and
white people could not be trusted, and that their promises were simply another effort to control and define what black America was all about. In response, blacks insisted on controlling their own movement, shaping their
own agenda, defining their own destiny. This nation, Carmichael declared,
"does not function by morality, love and non-violence. . . . [It functions]
by power." And power required that blacks—not "good" whites—control
their own institutions, their own programs, their own demands. In the end,
that was what Black Power was all about. At least some black Americans—as
exemplified in the slogan "black is beautiful"—did not wish to be "assimilated" into a nation shaped by white values and institutions.

By the end of 1967, therefore, the civil rights movement found itself profoundly split over its identity, values, and goals. The civil rights coalition had been a primary engine of social change throughout the late 1950s and 1960s. It had accomplished an astonishing number of the goals it set forth. But even as those goals were achieved, the visions and perspectives of many black Americans were changing, with a growing number concluding that true freedom could be achieved only by challenging the very foundations of American culture and society. The movement of Black Power advocates from conciliation and reform toward confrontation and rebellion represented a visible challenge to Lyndon Johnson's cherished consensus. It was the first, and foremost, declaration of a new radicalism and of the growing impatience among the young. But it would not be the last.

The Student Movement

When the Students for a Democratic Society (SDS) gathered in Ann Arbor, Michigan, in the spring of 1962, they produced a manifesto remarkably similar in its optimism and faith in America to the first statements of SNCC in April 1960. The students were deeply critical of the complacency and indifference of their society. "We are the people of this generation," they declared, "bred in at least modest comfort, housed now in universities, looking uncomfortably to the world we inherit." They were disturbed by the atom bomb, the stultifying impact of bureaucracy, the careerism and conformity of American universities, and above all "the permeating and victimizing fact of human degradation, symbolized by the southern struggle against racial bigotry." Rejecting the passivity of their countrymen in the face of injustice, they pledged to revitalize American democracy, to create communities where work could be meaningful and leisure fulfilling, and to fight for an America where corporations would become more publicly responsible, politics more representative of peoples' needs, and resources distributed in such a way as to make it possible "to establish an environment for people to live in with dignity and creativeness." Yet, through it all, they evinced a faith that America was still an open society, that change could take place within existing institutions, and that their own generation could be the instrument for achieving the social democracy that would enable America to live up to its ideals.

These were the children of the baby boom, the product of America's postwar economic growth and affluence. In unprecedented numbers, they were attending the nation's universities. In 1940, only 15 percent of young hig school graduates from the ages 18 to 22 attended college. By 1965, that figure had mushroomed to 44 percent. By the end of the decade, more than 6 million students would be enrolled in college—four times as many as in the 1940s. The importance of what sociologist Daniel Bell called the "knowledge revolution" had made the university a central institution of American society, with a college degree a prerequisite for a decent job. Futhermore, the prosperity of the postwar years made available an increasing amount of money to be invested in children's education. Approximately 75 percent of the students came from families with incomes above the national median. Having grown up in a world where economic security was a given, they never experienced anxiety over trying to find work or supporting a family that had so decisively shaped the world view of those who had grown up during the Depression.

The very nature of their circumstances, however, helped to make the students of the early 1960s receptive to a more critical perspective on their society. In a world where material comfort was assumed, they were "free" to reflect skeptically on the shortcomings of a consumer society. The hunger for "making it" no longer stood forth as a challenge sufficiently exciting to serve as a beacon for their lives. In schools like Stanford, Harvard, Yale, and Swarthmore, students read the French novelist and philosopher Albert Camus, discussed existentialism, and pondered what to do with their lives in order to become more "human," more "aware," more "honest," and "autonomous." Influenced by sociologist critics who condemned the other-directedness and conformity of American society, they were already wondering whether entering the corporation and donning a "grey flannel suit" was what they wished to do with their lives. These were the "best and brightest" of their generation, told by university officials that they represented the "top five percent" of the nation, with a particular responsibility to make the world they lived in better for the next generation. Yet as they looked around them, some, at least, questioned whether that objective could be achieved by simply doing more of the same. In many cases, they thought, prosperity had been purchased at too high a price. Friendship was undermined by competition, communal loyalties by the drive to get ahead. In America, consumer culture had fostered what psychoanalyst Erich Fromm called "the market personality"—men and women who altered their character to conform to what the marketplace defined as a salable self. To the most skeptical, this was a world to be shunned, not embraced.

This idealism was reinforced by a young American president who exhorted the new generation to "make a difference" in their world and to complete the American revolution. To those who were drawn to his charismatic message, Kennedy's insistent call to the young to fulfill America's unfulfilled promises seemed a mandate for action. In those halcyon days, one student recalled, "vigor and good intentions [seemed to be] in and of themselves invincible. No one's days seemed the least bit numbered. . . . We all . . . pictured dreams of a better world as simple and inevitably redemptive." Anything seemed possible. Whether it be through serving in the Peace Corps, helping the disabled, or becoming active in politics, the young saw an opportunity—perhaps even a command—to escape conformism and complacency through sacrifice. The atmosphere seemed right for a positive commitment. As one student recalled, "disturbed by the hyprocrisy of what was, and unwilling to accept the degradation of making my separate peace with it, I was drawn to the exemplary existential act as a means of transforming both myself and the world around me."

For most students who became activists during the 1960s, the civil rights movement provided the occasion for such an "exemplary, existential" act. In some cases that simply meant joining a local CORE chapter, picketing a Woolworth's in a Northern city, or just following with interest and admiration the courage of civil rights demonstrators in the South. But for many it meant more. Seeing their black brothers and sisters put their lives on the line for democracy inspired some white Northern students to journey South in order to participate in the freedom rides or to join the new civil rights organizations. When SNCC called for students from Yale and Stanford to help with the freedom elections in the fall of 1963, many white students saw the opportunity they had been looking for to take their stand. A thousand more responded when SNCC began recruiting volunteers for the Mississippi Freedom Summer Project. The lessons that SNCC staff members had learned over years of experience were telescoped into days. Whites who had never before seen bathrooms labeled "White" and "Colored" and who had never experienced poverty now had a firsthand look at a kind of oppression they had never imagined. In the beginning, they too had faith in the federal government and in law enforcement officials. But in Mc-Comb, Greenwood, and countless other cities, they repeatedly saw "the law" used as an instrument for repression and violence rather than reform. At first disbelieving, they soon came to share the conviction of their black SNCC colleagues that it was not simply the whim of a few bigoted racists that was the problem, but rather systematic indifference and the complicity of an entire social system that refused to acknowledge, or respond to, the most brutal kinds of oppression.

When these white students returned to their campuses, they brought with them a healthy skepticism—and a growing radicalism—toward all established institutions. With a heightened sensitivity to hypocrisy, it took little time for more militant students to perceive the university itself as a source of repression and manipulation. For some, the college seemed to become a microcosm of society, controlled by a managerial elite, administered by bureaucratic functionaries, and committed to producing robotlike graduates to carry out the task of impersonal corporations. Given such a frame of reference, any violation of student rights easily became an issue of moral significance, in its own way emblematic of the same kind of callous disregard for dignity and democracy they had just witnessed in the South. With a heightened consciousness of "establishment" duplicity and with intense determination to fight injustice wherever it appeared, these students were ready to do battle.

The first public appearance of this new radicalism occurred on the Berkeley campus of the University of California in the fall and winter of

1964–65. Berkeley, in many respects, represented the wave of the future for American universities. It was the best example of what some educators called "multiversities"—huge institutions of higher learning that even proponents sometimes described as impersonal and machine-like in their neglect of individual student needs.* During the fall of 1964, the Berkeley administration ruled that noncampus political literature could no longer be distributed on the Berkeley campus. The ruling seemed arbitrary, a break with tradition and a violation of open political discussion. Led by Mario Savio, a veteran of Freedom Summer in Mississippi, students responded with massive protests. The Free Speech Movement was born, and Berkeley entered a state of extended siege. As each side dug in its heels, the Free Speech struggle took on all of the moral and cosmic dimensions of the civil rights movement itself. It was not only the right to circulate literature that was at stake, Savio declared. Institutions of higher education had become "odious machines which treated students like objects." The only response, he declared, was for students to "put [their] bodies against the gears, against the wheels—and make the machine stop until we are free." Almost overnight, American universities had taken on the character of George Wallace and Ross Barnett, at least in the eyes of militant students.

With Berkeley as a rallying point, campus protests multiplied across the country. In one survey by a presidential committee, "the vast majority" of colleges reported demonstrations of one kind or another. Students for a Democratic Society (SDS) were also embarking on a campaign to organize people of Northern urban areas. Other students spoke of re-enlisting in the ranks of civil rights groups. Yet there were limits to such activities. Most universities would not be so confrontational as to promulgate bans on disseminating political literature on campus. And in the aftermath of Freedom Summer, civil rights organizations—particularly SNCC—increasingly discouraged a white presence in their ranks as they moved toward embracing Black Power. In the absence of a dramatic, overriding issue linking university life to national concerns, the student movement might well have faded with time.

But at precisely that moment, the military escalation in Vietnam occurred, providing the issue that would fuel student activism for the next half dozen years and presenting a problem of such overwhelming moral significance that many students were able to see, for the first time, a direct connection between their own everyday activities and the policies of the national government. Countless universities depended for their survival on federal grants, many of which were directly tied to Defense Department research. Companies that manufactured napalm or chemical defoliants used university facilities to recruit new employees. And through ROTC programs, universities helped to train the military officers who would fight in

---

* Between 1941 and 1958 the number of universities with 20,000 or more students grew from 2 to 31—a partial reflection of the transformation that had occurred in higher education.

Vietnam. In the direct ties between their own institutions and the government, students saw a link that galvanized them into action. After all, this was "their" university. They were of draft age, kept from fighting only by their student deferments.* If they cared about the horrible destruction taking place nine thousand miles away, they had a place very close to home where they could register a protest. As one student observed, the war provided an opportunity to create a new "white SNCC," a "net to pull through the campuses of the country and collect the people you really wanted to work with" to end the war, which symbolized all that seemed to be wrong with American society.

At first buoyed with hope, student activists set out to stop the war through peaceful protest. With an innocence that bordered on naiveté, they believed that simply recording their dissent and highlighting the error of the government's ways would produce a reversal of policy. Twenty thousand mobilized for an SDS-sponsored rally in Washington in April 1965, and another 30,000 marched in a peace parade during the fall in New York City. Convinced that "the truth will set you free," students and faculty members sponsored "teach-ins" in universities across the country, inviting government spokesmen to come and debate the war. They came. But they did not listen. "William Bundy honestly tried to convince an intelligent audience that we were in Vietnam to fight for freedom and democracy," one student observed. "His facts were simply different from those of Gruening and I. F. Stone [an antiwar senator and journalist, respectively], only he would not admit their facts existed, and hence felt no need to answer them." At no point, the same student wrote, would government spokesmen discuss "whether we could win, whether victory was worth the price, whether the price is morally justifiable, and whether a negotiated settlement now would not simply accept the inevitable . . . while saving thousands of lives." The debators simply talked past each other, while in Washington, Secretary of State Dean Rusk denounced "the gullibility of educated men" and their "stubborn disregard of plain facts."

The futility of the teach-in exercise profoundly alienated young antiwar protestors. "I have the awful feeling of being a stranger in the land," one wrote. "The country is at some kind of nadir when a citizen with responsible views feels utterly unable to write to his Secretary of State because there is no common ground of communication and he will immediately be characterized as a confused extremist." The "best and brightest" of one generation sat in Washington making policies that seemed transparently immoral and stupid to the "best and brightest" of the next generation. It all seemed so wrong. Antiwar students had been raised on the conviction that decisions

---

* During the 1960s, the armed forces—under the Selective Service system—drafted young men into service. Everyone was eligible for the draft, but individuals could be given deferments on the basis of responsibilities, physical impairment, or educational activities. Enrollment in college qualified one for such a deferment.

in America were made democratically, based on rational argument and intelligent debate. Now, that conviction lay in tatters, seeming to confirm the radical contention that the very system itself was immoral and oppressive.

By the fall of 1966, many in the antiwar movement were ready to pursue a series of actions that would match, step by step, the government's own policies of escalation in Vietnam. Beginning in California, students announced the formation of a draft resistance movement. "The War in Viet Nam is criminal and we must act together, at great individual risk, to stop it," the resistors announced. "To cooperate with conscription is to perpetuate its existence, without which the government could not wage war. We have chosen to openly defy the draft and confront the government and its war directly." Explaining his own position on the issue, Dennis Sweeney, a leader of the California movement, declared:

> Our lives and our politics will lead only to the despair, fear and impotence we
> see in the American mind unless we develop a resistance which takes into ac-
> count the deep roots of authoritarianism and militarism in the institutions sur-
> rounding us . . . I choose to refuse to cooperate with selective service be-
> cause it is the only honest, whole, and human response I can make to a military
> institution which demands the allegiance of my life.

By the fall of 1966, more than three dozen chapters of the resistance movement had formed, students were burning their draft cards, and plans were under way for civil disobedience at Selective Service headquarters in Oakland.

Throughout 1966 and 1967, the anger, bitterness, and ugliness of antiwar confrontation with the government mounted. When Robert McNamara came to Harvard, his car was surrounded by angry students who beat on its roof. No government official could make a public appearance without having to confront masses of protestors. The president himself became a virtual prisoner of the White House, able to venture forth to speak only at "safe" locations like military bases. Students launched aggressive campaigns to abolish ROTC programs at universities and prevented recruiters from companies with war contracts from appearing on campus. Yet the protest seemed only to produce more confrontation, as though each side saw no option except to polarize the issue further in a vicious cycle of recrimination and righteousness. With a siege mentality, Johnson denounced the antiwar movement as a bunch of "nervous nellies" even as he announced further deployment of troops. Antiwar demonstrators, in turn, were driven to new levels of frustration and anger. As Andrew Kopkind wrote in the summer of 1967, "to be white and a radical in America this summer is to see horror and feel impotent."

The political estrangement of the young had a cultural manifestation as well. Although there was no direct cause-and-effect relationship between the two, the emergence of a "counterculture" in the 1960s testified powerfully to the fragmentation taking place within the society. Writing about students in the 1960s, Paul Goodman observed that "alienation is a powerful motivation of unrest, fantasy, and reckless action. It leads to . . . religious innovation, new sacraments to give life meaning." To those who felt angry at the political direction of America and frustrated by middle-class respectability and the conformity of their elders, it became important to fashion ways of expressing alternative values and attitudes through the rituals of daily life. As a result, the disaffected young of the 1960s developed habits of dress, recreation, and a lifestyle that bespoke their quest for a new culture and that paralleled the emerging radicalism of their politics. Just as SNCC workers donned overalls in order to identify with the sharecroppers and tenant farmers of the rural South, participants in the student movement chose long hair and beards as a way of distancing themselves from traditional norms of middle-class respectability. If individualism, competition, and careerism characterized the dominant culture, the young would embrace communalism, sharing, and harmony. If wearing a three-piece Brooks Brothers suit and living in a suburbia were badges of membership in corporate America, wearing faded blue jeans, endorsing free love, and living on a commune would serve equally well as symbols for those estranged from corporate America.

Music constituted perhaps the most important "sacrament" for the young. Although clearly rooted in the rhythm and blues, rock and roll, and the folk song traditions of the past, the music of the sixties achieved a cultural and political significance that set it apart. Lyrics became important as an expression of young people's concerns. Simon and Garfunkel's "Sounds of Silence" and "Dangling Conversation" spoke eloquently of the emptiness and despair that many of the young saw in the lifestyle of the middle class. Bob Dylan's "Blowing in the Wind" reinforced the belief, widespread by the mid-1960s, that justice would triumph, and the Beatles' declaration that "All You Need Is Love" represented values that challenged directly "establishment" materialism and war-making. Wherever young protestors met, they listened to Dylan, the Beatles, Joan Baez, the Rolling Stones, and Phil Ochs, finding in the alienation and distinctiveness of the music's lyrics an expression of their own sense of being a different generation, with concerns substantially separate from those of their elders.

Drugs represented yet another "sacrament." After marching in protests or picketing a government official, demonstrators would celebrate their distinctive sense of community by listening to music together and lighting up a marijuana "joint" for relaxation. As with music, using drugs quickly became a habit for masses of young people, not just those who were angry or engaged in political activism. Instead of the *individual* escape of alcohol— their parents way of relaxing—marijuana offered a *communal* expression of being different. And so, for millions of young people, social life now consisted of getting stoned together and enjoying the sense of belonging that resulted. "Being" was more important than "becoming," living *now* more valuable than the drive to get ahead. Many adherents of the new ways seemed to believe that they were pioneering, carving out an environment where spontaneity, human intimacy, and love could replace the old values they were rejecting.

By 1967, the new lifestyle had become a national sensation. In the "summer of love," audiences across the nation heard the song "Are You Going to San Francisco" and read news stories about the mass migration of young people to the Haight-Ashbury area of San Francisco, or the East Village of New York City. "Hippies" became a new catchword, LSD and mescaline replaced marijuana, and the Jefferson Airplanes' "White Rabbit" celebrated the extraordinary changes of consciousness induced by taking "acid." Only in the most indirect sense could one define the "summer of love" as political. Yet it represented the flowering of a set of values, a quest for meaning, and a rebellion against conventions that had deep roots in the political disaffection and estrangement that seemed to be developing between the generations. Moreover, to parents of those who used drugs, or took part in radical demonstrations against the war, there seemed little difference between the political and cultural expression of young people's rebellion against the status quo. It all seemed threatening, all part of the turmoil that directly challenged society's definition of what constituted a good and healthy life.

By the end of 1967, the student movement was clearly at a crossroads. In the preceding months, a growing nember of established, respectable political figures had joined the outcry against the war, giving some antiwar protestors renewed hope that change could be won from within the system. "Adult" antiwar activists organized by the thousands, forming lobbying groups such as Women Strike for Peace, mobilizing support for antiwar candidates, both locally and nationally, and providing a critical link among the nonstudent members of the electorate for the growing dissent of mainstream politicians. Arkansas Senator J. William Fulbright denounced the "arrogance of power" that increasingly had come to characterize American foreign policy; Senators ranging from Robert Kennedy (D-N.Y.) to John Sherman Cooper (R-Ky.) voted against appropriations for the war; and the American electorate seemed fed up with Vietnam. In the fall of 1967 less than 30 percent approved the president's war policies. Perhaps—just perhaps—1968 would provide one last opportunity to change American policy through traditional political means.

Operating on that premise, Allard Lowenstein barnstormed the country in 1967 on behalf of a "dump Johnson" movement. "Liberals must begin to act now," Lowenstein and his allies declared. "For at stake is not only the present policies in Vietnam but the political future of the next decade. . . . If there is to be an end to the political polarization that threatens to strain the very foundation of American democracy, it is for the liberal movement to begin to propose another option." Seeking some leading Democrat— Kennedy, McGovern, or Eugene McCarthy—to challenge Johnson, Lowenstein hoped to mobilize antiwar students and reinvigorate their faith in the system.

Yet more radical students had already exhausted such faith. In a debate remarkably reminiscent of the MFDP controversy in Atlantic City, Lowenstein and draft resister David Harris argued out the options. To ask people to reject the "system," Lowenstein said, was "irresponsible." On the contrary, Harris insisted, accepting the dictates of the system meant becoming an accomplice in evil. "While we wait for the system to change itself," he said, "we will be forced to carry out the very [crimes] we are trying to stop. Like 'good Germans' in World War II, having had orders will be no excuse, nor will following proper procedures. Anything less than immediate resistance will amount to collaboration." Thus some students had now reached a point where nothing less than total change in the structure of American society—its values and institutions—was required.

Which way the student movement would go was unclear. Like civil rights demonstrators before them, student activists had begun their quest for a better America convinced that rational discussion and intelligent argument could produce reform within the existing system of government. Now, many had lost that conviction entirely, frustrated by the duplicity, treachery, and condescension they had encountered in their reform efforts. If 1968 did not produce peaceful change from within, some were ready for revolution.

The Emergence of Women's Liberation

Not surprisingly, the civil rights movement also provided the catalyst for the third largest movement of the 1960s—feminism.

Although the actual content of women's roles had changed dramatically in the years after World War II, there had been little substantive progress toward equality and almost no indication of a mass movement to protest that fact. By the 1960s, employment for middle-class white and married women had become the norm rather than the exception; and a two-income household had become almost a prerequisite for the consumer culture. In 1970, for example, 60 percent of all families with an income of more than $10,000 boasted wives who worked. Yet most of these jobs were "women's work"—sex segregated and offering little opportunity for individual advancement or promotion. Despite the large number of women in the work force, assumptions about male and female spheres of responsibility were so deeply ingrained that to question them amounted to heresy. There was no critical mass of protestors to provide an alternative ideology or to mobilize opposition against traditional points of view. Given the absence of a sanctioned feminist alternative and the economic and social circumstances that prevailed, women—and men—tended to perceive the expansion of the female labor force within traditional definitions of sex roles. The wife who held a job was playing a supportive role, not striking out on her own as an "independent" woman. The fact that women were thought to be only "helping out" made it possible for their efforts to receive social sanction as a fulfillment of the traditional family role.

If feminist consciousness itself was slow to develop, however, a process of change was under way that helped to prepare the groundwork for protest later on. The massive increase of women in the work place destroyed the reality behind the traditional idea that a woman's place was in the home. Despite their power, conventional stereotypes no longer corresponded to many women's daily experience. Moreover, some changes did take place as a result of women's employment. Children of parents who both worked grew up with substantially different ideas of what was permissible for men and women to do. Daughters of working mothers indicated that they too planned to seek a life outside the home after marriage. In addition, these same daughters scored lower on scales of traditional femininity and expressed the belief that women and men should share a variety of work, household, and recreational experiences. Despite the seeming entrenchment of traditional cultural norms, sociologists and journalists noted that a latent dissatisfaction existed among women who were told by the media and home economics teachers to do one thing, but who in practice lived lives increasingly divergent from those prescriptions. Many of the objective conditions for rebellion were in place; all that was required to initiate the process was the development of an appropriate context, an alternative set of values and norms, and the social space to embrace the new values.

When the civil rights movement emerged in the early 1960s, it helped to crystallize and formulate a new sense of grievance among women. Because women did not live together in an ethnic neighborhood like minority groups, or share a common political experience on a continuing basis, they had tended in the past to view their problems as individual rather than social. As Betty Friedan observed eloquently in *The Feminine Mystique*, many discontented women talked about "a problem that has no name" and were convinced that their own unhappiness was something personal. Women had been brainwashed, Friedan charged, taught that their entire lives were defined by the condition of their birth and told that "they could desire no greater destiny than to glory in their own femininity." As a result, women were imprisoned in a "comfortable concentration camp," prevented from discovering who they *were* by a society which told them only what they *could be*. What women had to discover, she wrote, was that what had previously been perceived as only an individual problem was in fact a *woman* problem, shared by others and rooted in a set of social attitudes that required change if a better life was to be achieved.

Friedan's book was published in 1963, the same year as the March on Washington and the dramatic media attention focused on the civil rights movement. The two events reinforced each other, because the civil rights

movement also emphasized the extent to which groups of people were oppressed on the basis of cultural and physical characteristics. As women
saw—and participated in—civil rights demonstrations demanding freedom
and personal dignity, they perceived, like their abolitionist forerunners a
century earlier, a connection to their own lives *and* the possibility of acting
for themselves as a group. Although it was true that blacks and women had
strikingly different problems, they suffered from modes of oppression that
in some ways were similar. For women as well as blacks, the denial of equality occurred through the assignment of separate and unequal roles. Both
were taught to "keep their place" and were excluded from social and economic opportunity on the grounds that assertive behavior was deviant. The
principal theme of the civil rights movement was the immorality of treating
any human being as less equal than another on the basis of a physical characteristic. That theme spoke as much to the condition of women as it did to
the condition of blacks.

Through its tactics, its message, and its moral fervor, the civil rights
movement provided a model for political activity and a vehicle for legislative reform for women. When the 1964 Civil Rights Act was passed, Title VII
included a ban on discrimination in employment on the basis of sex as well
as race. (Although the "sex" amendment was introduced by conservative
southerners who were trying to kill the bill, liberal northerners, led by Representative Martha Griffith of Michigan, were able to secure its passage.)
Older women activists—particularly business and professional women, and
veterans of national and state Commissions on the Status of Women—
seized on Title VII as an instrument for change. When the government
failed to act on complaints of sex discrimination, exhibiting the same reluctance it had shown with civil rights violations, these activists formed the
National Organization for Women (NOW) in 1966 to mobilize pressure on
behalf of women's rights. Other groups quickly followed, and the women's
rights wing of the new feminist movement was born, using political pressure, litigation, and mobilization of public opinion to seek justice for
women. Analogous in many ways to civil rights groups like the NAACP and
the Urban League, NOW and its allies worked for reform within existing
structures to secure for women equal protection before the law and equal
participation in the nation's social, economic, and political life.

Just as important, the civil rights movement spurred younger women
who joined SNCC, SCLC, and later SDS to do their part in helping to
change society. As the historian Sara Evans has written, SNCC "created the
social space within which women began to develop a new sense of their own
potential. A critical vanguard of young women accumulated the tools for
movement building: a language to describe oppression and justify revolt,
experience in the strategy and tactics of organizing, and a beginning sense
of themselves collectively as objects of discrimination." Many of the white
women who joined SNCC came from the South. They had been reared in
a culture that celebrated the "Southern Lady," a genteel, elegant, gracious

figure theoretically ordained to represent the pure and spiritual side of life and to occupy a "pedestal" from which she was forbidden to move. But these same young women—people like Casey Hayden, Mary King, and Jane Stembridge—also shared a religious commitment to social activism. Coming from church groups such as the Faith and Life community of Austin, and from universities where discussions of existential commitment were commonplace, they had already developed a profoundly critical attitude toward prevailing middle-class lifestyles in America. Now, by joining SNCC, they were—at least implicitly—declaring war on the culture from which they came, including its venerated ideal of the "Southern Lady." Fired by a vision of "the beloved community" and the idealism of achieving freedom and equality for their generation, they determined to place themselves on the front lines of the civil rights struggle. "I [just] can't sit by any longer," one wrote.

The very process of joining such an embattled movement evoked talents, energies, and independence that many of the women had not even been aware they possessed. One woman who had never before taken part in any political action found herself sitting-in at the Georgia legislature two days after she joined the movement. "To this day I am amazed," she later said. "I just did it." In many field offices, women were the backbone of the staff, coordinating, making decisions, exercising responsibility for the well-being of countless others. "If you are spending your time [doing] . . . community organization, . . . generally lifting or opening people's awareness to their own power in themselves," Mary King observed, "it inevitably strengthens your own conceptions, your own ability." Seeing poverty firsthand, drawing on the courage of local blacks who "put their lives up for grabs every day they spend in Mississippi," women volunteers learned to live with fear and stress they never before had encountered. And every day they gained new confidence from their endurance in the face of such pressures. As one woman later explained, "I learned a lot of respect for myself for having gone through all of that."

The white women volunteers drew particular inspiration from the black women in the movement. In every SNCC project, civil rights activist Charles Sherrod wrote, "there is always a 'momma.' She is usually a militant woman in the community, outspoken, understanding, and willing to catch hell, having already caught her share." Fannie Lou Hamer was one such "momma," inspiring awe in the volunteers by her courage, her suffering, and her refusal to give up. When Mrs. Hamer led a rally, Sally Belfrage wrote, everyone was uplifted.

> The hands hold each other tighter. Mrs. Hamer is smiling, flinging out the words, and crying at once. "Black and white together," she leads the next verse, and a sort of joy began to grow in every face; "we are not afraid"—and for just that second no one is afraid, because they are free.

The younger black women, as well, exemplified a strength and independence that seemed refreshingly at odds with traditional women's behavior—Diane Nash, a former Fisk University beauty queen, who braved brutality to lead the April 1961 freedom rides; Ruby Doris Smith Robinson whose strength and assertiveness became legendary; Anelle Ponder who was jailed and beaten so severely that she could barely talk, but who still managed to whisper to fellow SNCC workers, "freedom"; and Cynthia Washington who singlehandedly organized one of the most racist counties in Alabama riding on the back of a mule. "For the first time," one white woman volunteer in the South observed, "I had role models I could respect."

With their black sisters in the movement, white women also developed a heightened sense of the way in which their own sex was used as a basis for discrimination by men in the movement. Women were expected to do all the typing and clerical work, make the coffee, take minutes at meetings, and play a secondary role in decision-making. "The attitude around here toward keeping the house neat," one white volunteer wrote in 1963, "as well as the general attitude toward the inferiority and 'proper place' of women is disgusting and also terribly depressing. I never saw a cooperative enterprise that was less cooperative." In 1964, black women led a sit-in at SNCC headquarters to protest such conditions and, a year later, insisted that a tape recorder be used so that women would not have to take notes at staff meetings. Women of both races, but particularly black women, were angered further during the Freedom Summer Project of 1964 by the frequency of interracial sexual relationships and the development of "macho" attitudes among men in the movement.

By the fall of 1964, a number of SNCC women prepared a paper on the movement's attitude toward women for SNCC to consider at its fall retreat. Written primarily by Casey Hayden and Mary King, the paper charged that the women in SNCC were often treated in the same way as token blacks in large corporations—barely tolerated, repeatedly made the objects of condescension, paternalism, and ridicule. The "assumption of male superiority [among SNCC men]," they said, "[is] as widespread and deep-rooted and as crippling to the woman as the assumptions of white supremacy are to the Negro." Women helped to keep the movement running on a day-to-day basis, yet were excluded from power. Unless such behavior stopped, the paper concluded, women would have to "force the rest of the movement to stop the discrimination and start the slow process of changing values and ideas so that all of us gradually come to understand that this is no more a man's world than it is a white world." The paper had little effect, and most of the men seemed to feel that however serious the women were, the issue was of secondary importance.

By the following year, as the movement was riven by interracial tensions, Hayden and King made one last attempt to achieve a gender-based solidarity with black women by writing "Sex and Caste: A Kind of Memo." Women had learned from the movement, they argued, a new sense of personal worth and dignity. Yet when applied to women's relationship with men, there seemed little willingness to live up to these ideals. Like blacks, they claimed, women "seemed to be caught in a common law caste system."

In both personal life and public life, women were treated as second-class citizens, yet no one was "organizing or talking publicly" about the issue. In a plea to other women in the movement, Hayden and King proposed that "perhaps we can start to talk with each other more openly than in the past and create a community of support for each other so we can deal with ourselves and others with integrity and therefore keep working." By its very existence, Hayden and King's memo exemplified the lessons of strength, autonomy, and assertiveness that they had learned in the movement; and although the internal dynamics of the Black Power struggle precluded the possibility of achieving the community they desired with black women inside SNCC, the analysis set forth by Hayden and King presented the first public manifesto of women's liberation and would generate a response from women having similar experiences in other New Left movements.

Predictably, assumptions of male superiority also dominated SDS and the antiwar movement. Sometimes, these attitudes were unconscious, as in SDS's Port Huron declaration that "we regard *men* as infinitely precious and possessed of unfulfilled capacities for reason, freedom and love." But sometimes the condescension seemed almost conscious. At the 1965 SDS convention, James Weinstein observed, critically, "women made peanut butter, waited on table, cleaned up, got laid. That was their role." Although women comprised more than one-third of the members of SDS, they occupied only 6 percent of the executive committee seats in 1964. As in SNCC, women frequently bore the primary responsibility for community organization, particularly with the inner-city projects where women staff members worked with welfare mothers to develop political and social programs to address the absence of day care, decent housing, and jobs. Yet the whole intellectual and political style of SDS militated against women's equality being recognized. As Todd Gitlin observed, SDS was characterized by "arrogance, elitism, competitiveness . . . ruthlessness, guilt—replication of patterns of domination and mystification [that] we have been taught since the cradle." Symptomatic of SDS attitudes toward women's role was the antiwar slogan, "Girls say yes to guys who say no." Women were expected to cook, clean up, be supportive, and not be "uptight" about having sex with numbers of different SDS men. But they were not expected to be equal.

With SDS, as with SNCC, women attempted to present their grievances within the existing organizational structure and to secure change through debate, discussion, and intellectual analysis. But whenever they tried to raise the issue, the men resisted—defensive about their own role in women's oppression, arguing, in patronizing tones, that there were other more pressing issues to be solved, and challenging the intellectual framework of the women's presentation as inadequate. More and more, the women were driven to the conclusion that they had to create their own community of support and reinforcement if they were to find a way of acting on their grievances. As they shared their experiences of discrimination, they also developed a new sense of strength and solidarity. "For many women," one participant in a women's workshop said, "it was the first [experience] of caring for other women—the feeling that women should organize women and [that] situations had to be developed so women could support other women." With new excitement and purpose, they discovered the common questions that faced them all: How were women different from men? Why were women different? What explained the fact that women's actions were looked down upon? By 1967, the women of the New Left had decided that only through controlling their own agenda, meeting separately, and seeking to explore the depths of the oppression they suffered could real change come about. Although SDS had approved a resolution endorsing women's rights, the debate accompanying the vote was full of ridicule and contempt, and when news of the SDS action appeared in New Left Notes, it was placed beside a cartoon of a girl wearing a minidress with matching panties. As Sara Evans observed, "SDS had blown its last chance."

The women's liberation movement quickly spread to campuses and cities around the country, using the "consciousness-raising" session as its organizing vehicle. Small groups of women gathered together to explore in a supportive atmosphere what it meant to be female. "I felt like it was almost being back in the South," one participant noted. "I was very conscious that this was a grass roots movement again, and . . . that these were real people, really seriously going to do something about their lives." The consciousness-raising sessions provided what one participant called a "life release":

> One thing became clear: that in the black movement I had been fighting for someone else's oppression and now there was a way I could fight for my own freedom and I was going to be much stronger than I ever was.

As the flood gates opened and women discovered their commonality of experience with sex, jobs, stereotyping, and men's reluctance to recognize women's individuality, they discovered a new sense of energy. "The women's movement really gave me my voice," one participant noted.

Significantly, the consciousness-raising session provided a laboratory for creating both new forms of political expression and new cultural values. If the problem with the society at large was male-dominated hierarchies and obsession with competition, then women could respond by creating their own institutions, operating collectively, sharing decision-making power, and developing a process of interaction in which everyone would have the opportunity to speak and no one would dominate. Every movement of the 1960s eventually arrived at the conclusion that there was a direct link between political goals and the larger cultural values of the society. But women represented the only group that understood, from the very beginning, that there was a place very close to home—in their own personal lives, their own families—where that link existed on a day-to-day basis. As Charlotte Bunch wrote, "there is no private domain of a person's life that is not political and there is no political issue that is not ultimately personal." Public and private lives were inextricably connected, and there was no way that women could

achieve equality in the world at large as long as their personal lives repli-
cated patterns of male domination and gender role segregation.

Although the ultimate impact of the women's movement would come
later, by 1967 women activists had already achieved an independence and
autonomy that challenged some of the basic assumptions of the dominant
culture. Like the supporters of Black Power, women's liberation advocates
sought to define their own goals and to shape their own agenda. No longer
would they accept the ground rules and premises of the larger society. Meeting together offered the "social space" for women to develop a new perception of themselves, to determine where they wished to go. And in challenging the entire spectrum of attitudes and institutions that oppressed
women—from words like "chick" or "girl," to antiquated attitudes toward
marriage and the family—they raised questions similar to those posed by
the Black Power and student movements about the structure of American
institutions, and America's most basic values of individualism, competition,
and achievement. From the perspective of those who exercised power in
America, the women's movement in 1967 represented only a minor concern. But in the end, no movement would prove a greater threat to the perpetuation of the traditional American way of life.

The Counterresponse

Inevitably, the turmoil of the sixties sparked a backlash of resentment. As
one commentator remarked, those who endorsed radical change had forgotten Newton's third law of motion—that for every action there is an equal
and opposite reaction. Even if all the social protestors were grouped together, they still comprised a distinct minority of the country. The majority,
meanwhile, could not be expected to sit idly by as rebels assaulted their values and threatened their self-interest. Millions of citizens had devoted their
lives to playing by the rules of the game—working hard, keeping the family
together, advancing step by step toward a life of security and prosperity.
Now, these same people believed that the rules were being changed and
that a wholesale attack on middle-class respectability was in progress. Blacks
who rioted in America's cities were challenging the concept of law and
order. As antipoverty militants declared war on City Hall, they seemed to be
undercutting all legitimate institutions of political representation. And
when student protestors unfurled the Vietcong flag, called policemen
"pigs," and openly flaunted their sexuality, they were assaulting institutions
and mores that were central to the self-definition of countless citizens. If
radical critics of America were alienated from the values of mobility,
achievement, and respectability that characterized the dominant culture,
many middle-class Americans were equally alienated from those who questioned customs they had been taught to cherish.

Events of the 1960s, and especially the rise of black militancy, galvanized a new self-consciousness among white ethnics. As the plea for black civil rights turned to a clamor for Black Power, members of other ethnic groups felt a challenge to their prerogatives and hard-earned victories. Many white workers had struggled for years to buy a decent house, achieve job security, and give their children an adequate education. Now, blacks seemed to be demanding all of these same things—immediately. To many, it seemed that blacks were seeking an unfair advantage. "The ethnic groups . . . don't want to penalize the Negro," observed political scientist John Roche, but "they feel strongly that the rules they came up by should apply." That meant hard work, sacrifice, and patience—qualities which white ethnics did not perceive in the Black Power movement, or in the activities of rioters in the inner city. "We build the city, not burn it down," one group of white workers declared. In the early 1960s, the vast majority of white Americans had approved of the Negro quest for justice. In 1964, only 34 percent of white Americans believed that blacks were seeking too much, too fast. By 1966, however, that figure had climbed to 85 percent as whites reacted against Black Power and urban riots. "How long," Congressman Gerald Ford asked, "are we going to abdicate law and order—the backbone of civilization—in favor of a soft social theory that the man who heaves a brick through a window or tosses a firebomb into your car is simply the misunderstood and underprivileged product of a broken home?"

Some analysts traced such sentiments to the economic insecurity of those they dubbed the "middle Americans." Earning between $5,000 and 15,000 a year and including many white ethnics, "middle Americans" were estimated to comprise 55 percent of the population. The majority were blue-collar workers, lower-echelon bureaucrats, school teachers, and white-collar employees. Although not poor, they suffered many of the tensions of marginal prosperity, including inflation, indebtedness, and fear of losing what they had worked so hard to attain. From 1956 to 1966, the rate of borrowing to purchase homes and consumer goods had risen by 113 percent, but income had increased by only 86 percent. More than two-thirds of all Americans earned under $10,000 a year by the end of the sixties, and many families were hard pressed to hold onto their "middle-class" status, particularly in an era when Vietnam war inflation brought a sudden end to increases in *real* income. Struggling to get by, many of these white Americans saw black demands and antipoverty expenditures as a direct threat to their own well-being.

But economic vulnerability and ethnic competition could explain only part of the "middle American" protest. More important was a sense of crisis in cultural values, a belief that the rules were being changed unfairly in midstream. Although most whites did not live in neighborhoods immediately threatened by urban violence or student demonstrations, everyday they witnessed on TV and read in the newspapers evidence of a concerted assault on the morals and values that had guided their lives. At just the time when the economic situation began to seem shaky, faith in the old doctrines was also being questioned. "We just seem to be headed toward a collapse of everything," a small-town California newspaper editor said.

From the perspective of such people, the radicalism of blacks, poor people, antiwar demonstrators, and "women's libbers" represented an attack on the very foundations of what they defined as the American way. Everything they had been brought up to believe in—patriotism, religion, monogamy, hard work—seemed under siege. While *their* children were drafted and sent to Vietnam, young radicals were abusing the privilege of a college education to denounce the system that had given them the opportunity to go to college in the first place. Nor were such attitudes limited to the middle-aged. Indeed, if a generation gap did exist in America, it was more likely to be found among the young themselves, between college-educated activists and those without a college degree. The sharp hostility that existed among the young generation was vividly expressed in the attitudes of Vietnam soldiers toward college demonstrators at home. "I'm fighting for those candyasses because I don't have an old man to support me," said one soldier. To many GIs—and their parents back home—the entire antiwar movement represented an act of virtual treason, made even more unacceptable by the implicit assumption that certain people—especially blacks and the young—were privy to a higher code of justice and had no obligation to obey the rules of conventional society.

By the end of 1967, therefore, the shrill attacks on "establishment" values from the left were matched by an equally vociferous defense of traditional values by those who were proud of all their society had achieved. If feminists, blacks, antiwar demonstrators, and advocates for the poor attacked the status quo with uncompromising vehemence, millions of other Americans rallied around the flag and made clear their intent to uphold the lifestyle and values to which they had devoted their lives. Significantly, pollsters Richard Scammon and Ben Wattenburg pointed out, the protestors still represented only a small minority of the country. The great majority of Americans were "unyoung, unpoor, and unblack; they [are] middle-aged, middle class, and middle minded." It was not a scenario from which dissidents could take much comfort.

The White House Response

To all of this, Lyndon Johnson and his White House Staff reacted with bewilderment and anger. "How [is] it possible after all we have accomplished?," Johnson asked. "How could it be?" In Johnson's view he had done so much. In 1965, only 19 percent of black Americans had incomes equal to the national median. By 1967, the proportion had risen to 27 percent. In 1960, the median level of education for blacks had been only 10.8 years. Now it was 12.2 years, only a half-year behind the median for whites. Johnson had secured the Civil Rights Act of 1964, federal aid to education, the Voting Rights Act of 1965, scholarships and loans for the young. "I tried to make it possible for every child of every color to grow up in a nice house, eat a solid breakfast, to attend a decent school, and to get a good and lasting job," Johnson said. "I asked so little in return. Just a little thanks. Just a little appreciation. That's all. But look at what I got instead. Riots in 175 cities. Looting. Burning. Shooting. . . . Young people by the thousands leaving the university, marching in the streets, chanting that horrible song about how many kids I had killed that day. . . . It ruined everything."

Johnson's staff seemed particularly upset by the truculence and ingratitude of blacks. "What really bothered me," one White House aide wrote, "was the Negro's assertiveness—their insistence, their use of the active voice in their own behalf. Demanding rights from the entire society, they were no longer content merely to ask for help from the well-intentioned whites within it." Some in the White House recognized the dimensions of the problem. "The civil rights movement is obviously in a mess," Harry McPherson wrote the president in 1966. "White resentment is great and still growing; the Negro community is fragmented." Part of the problem, McPherson understood, was that the White House was too closely connected to older, established representatives of the movement who had lost credibility with militants. Yet even as he recognized the problem, McPherson betrayed the limitations of the White House viewpoint. His solution was to convene a meeting of blacks to discuss the issue—all of them part of the Negro establishment. "There is no longer any need to have SNCC and CORE," he wrote. In McPherson's view, "the only way to move to the next stage of progress and civil rights [is] to return the leadership of the movement to the sensitive establishment—to business, labor, Wilkins and Young."

There might have been another response. McPherson and others acknowledged that the underlying problem was the economic plight that made it so difficult for black Americans to secure equality with white people. The most effective way of winning over black radicals was not only to show that the federal government cared about civil rights statutes, but also to demonstrate a commitment to eradicate poverty, and to provide jobs, security, and the economic wherewithal for blacks to develop a stake in their society. But that required a break from the politics of consensus. As Doris Kearns noted,

> Some people would have to pay the cost of helping others, shattering Johnson's . . . hopes of sustaining a federal Community Chest joining the blacks and the whites. . . . Once it became apparent that more jobs for blacks meant less jobs for whites, that cheaper housing for the poor meant coming up against the building trade apparatus, that welfare reform meant redistributing income, and that restructuring education meant restructuring neighborhoods, the choices became much harder. The task of creating a social movement dedicated to redistribution and reform was very different from the task of creating a consensus behind a vague set of programs.

Conceivably, Johnson might have considered mobilizing such a movement. But the substantive commitment required could not occur as long as Johnson was spending twenty-five times as much on the Vietnam war as he was on eliminating poverty at home.

The war—somehow it always came back to the war. In his own eyes, Johnson had simply acted on all the lessons he had ever learned from history. He was like Wilson against the Kaiser, like FDR against Hitler. "What I learned as a boy in my teens and in college about World War I was that it was our lack of strength and stamina that got us into that war," he said. Munich and the aggression of Hitler had communicated the same message. Yet no one seemed to understand, and as dissent mounted, Johnson responded not by confronting the problems, but by seeking escape. McGeorge Bundy, George Ball, and Bill Moyers had left, their places taken by advisors more congenial to the president's perspective. Johnson discontinued meeting with the National Security Council because too often it acted like "a sieve" with leaks to the press. Instead, he limited discussions to his Tuesday luncheon group—a small band of top aides who shared completely his own viewpoint. Even there, more often than not he lapsed into extensive monologues of self-justification. Some White House staff members became concerned about "signs of paranoia." "Suddenly in the middle of a conversation," Kearns recalled, "the President's voice would become intense and low-keyed. He would laugh inappropriately and his thoughts would assume a random, almost incoherent quality as he began to spin a vast web of accusations." Surrounded by yes-men whose one purpose, in the words of former White House Press Secretary George Reedy, was "to serve the material needs and the desires of a single man," he found no counterpoint to his ramblings, no check on his obsession with finding a scapegoat.

With such a frame of reference, Johnson quickly concluded that all of his problems could be traced to the jealousy of the Kennedys and his own failure to conform to the "Harvard" model. He was being "done in" by his opponents, not because of the merit of his policies, but because he had supplanted them from power and not gone to the right school. "Two or three intellectuals started it all, you know," he told Doris Kearns. "They produced all the doubt, and then Bobby began taking it up as his cause and with Martin Luther King on his payroll, he went around stirring up the Negroes and telling them if they came out into the streets they would get more. Then the communists stepped in. They control the three networks, you know. . . ." And there was Bobby behind it all. Even McNamara's dissent on the war strategy could be blamed on Kennedy. "Every day Bobby would call up McNamara," Johnson said, "telling him that the war was terrible and immoral and he had to leave." Yet, Johnson knew that *he* was right. "Someone had to call Hitler and someone had to call Ho. We can't let the Kennedys be peacemakers and us war makers simply because they come from the Charles River." Like Lincoln, Johnson would stick it out, be a man. And someday history would acknowledge his achievement. "Deep down I knew—I simply knew—that the American people loved me. After all I had done for them and given to them, how could they help but love?"

Conclusion

The tragedy was so immense. Lyndon Johnson *had* done more than any other president to feed the poor, heal the sick, and bring justice to his fellow men and women. But even as he set out to nourish the real object of his desire—the Great Society—and give her a "chance to grow into a beautiful woman," he deprived her of the energies she needed by committing them to war.

> I figured her growth and development would be as natural and inevitable as any small child's. . . . In the first year, as we got the laws on the books, she began to crawl. Then in the second year, as we got more laws on the books, she began to walk, and the year after that she would be off and running, all the time growing bigger and healthier and fatter. And when she grew up, I figured she would be so big and beautiful that the American people couldn't help but fall in love with her.

But instead, love had turned into recrimination, the money needed to abolish poverty was allocated to search-and-destroy missions, and the support needed to bring Johnson's dream to fruition shattered on the shoals of his commitment to defend "freedom" in Southeast Asia.

Paradoxically, the liberal formula of seeking reform at home while containing communism abroad had reached both its greatest success and its worst failure at the same time. Johnson's vision, like that of countless other liberals before him, was premised on the faith that the economic growth of an energetic capitalism would provide the where-withal for change, without requiring any reallocation of power or resources that might pit one group in society against another. He had made a start toward achieving that vision. Yet the liberal consensus reflected a perspective from above, from the vantage point of those who already exercised control. It showed little sensitivity to the perspective from below, or the vantage point of those who were victims of structural inequalities based on race, class, and gender. For those Americans it seemed increasingly difficult to achieve genuine equality without altering the basic institutions and values of American society, and thereby shattering the consensus that liberals prized. If nothing else, Black Power advocates, student demonstrators, and radical feminists had highlighted the fragility of the liberal consensus, showing that, for some activists at least, incremental reform was not enough.

By the end of 1967, it was all too obvious that the united society Johnson had hoped to achieve was unraveling. As riots swept America's cities, thousands marched against the war, and young rebels flaunted their contempt for America's institutions, the Johnson dream became even more distant. The representatives of the "best and brightest" on both sides indulged in a rhetoric of moralism and denunciation that offered almost no opportunity for dialogue. Some, like Allard Lowenstein, attempted to pick up the pieces, to find some way to achieve reconciliation and change within the established structure of the political system. But momentum rested on the side of confrontation, not healing.

12

1968

"A society is possible in the last analysis," the sociologist Louis Wirth observed in the 1950s, "because the individuals in it carry around in their heads some sort of picture of that society." Through most of their history, Americans had shared such a picture. They believed in "the American Creed"—individual freedom, equal protection before the law, opportunity to advance on the basis of one's merit, and the ability of those on the bottom of society to secure improvement of their lot through hard work and participation in established political processes. Although the Creed was often more honored in the breach than in reality, its hold on the soul and psyche of America was such that even those with the greatest reason for disaffection conducted their struggles for freedom within its framework, convinced, in the words of Martin Luther King, Jr., that "someday, someway," the dream of dignity and justice for all would come true.

Now, the very basis of that shared vision was in question. Racial hatred ran rampant throughout the land. Working-class whites exploded in rage against blacks who demanded immediate access to power, and against a "liberal establishment" that seemed to pamper and indulge the forces of protest. Women's liberation advocates revolted against traditional assumptions of male dominance in the family; student radicals lost faith in a government which they felt had betrayed them; and the very notion that Americans could find a way out of their dilemma through elections and established democratic procedures was greeted with derision by many. In 1948, Arthur Schlesinger, Jr., had issued a clarion call to his fellow citizens to rally behind the "vital center" where all Americans could unite to find answers to their problems. Twenty years later, that center was flying apart, as if uncontrollable centrifugal forces were intent on ripping asunder the social fabric.

Rarely in American history does a presidential election year coincide with the cresting of such powerful social forces, but 1968 consituted such a moment. In a bewildering array of successive crises, each magnified by the overwhelming power of the mass media, Americans witnessed and participated in confrontations that challenged the very viability of their collective identity. It was a time of horror, embitterment, despair, and agony. In the end, all of the conflicts that had emerged out of the postwar years surfaced and came before the American people for a decision. The ultimate conse-

329

quence was defeat for those who sought a new society based on peace, equality, and social justice; victory for those who rallied in defense of the status quo. But in the process, the nation faced, with a brutal candor that had rarely been seen before, the stresses, tensions, and contradictions that lay at the heart of the modern-day American experience.

January and February

As the old year ended and the new year began, Lyndon Johnson and his aides hoped—for the time being—that they had stemmed the tide flowing against them both in foreign policy and at home. In a concerted attempt to deflect antiwar sentiment and the precipitous decline in Johnson's personal popularity, the administration had brought General William Westmoreland home from Vietnam in November 1967 to flood the media with optimistic reports on the progress of the war. The American military, Westmoreland reported, could now see the "light at the end of the tunnel." The North Vietnamese and Vietcong were on the run, and 1968 would represent a turning point toward victory. "The year ended," Westmoreland wrote in his annual report, "with the enemy increasingly resorting to desperation tactics; . . . and he has experienced only failure in these attempts."* On the domestic front as well, things seemed more under control. Robert F. Kennedy had rejected the importuning of antiwar activists to launch a presidential candidacy against Johnson and seemed content to snipe at the president' policies from within the framework of Democratic Party loyalty. Although Martin Luther King, Jr., continued to attack the war and issued increasingly radical calls for fundamental change in the nation's economy, America's crisis in race relations also seemed, for the moment, relatively stable. The president had appointed the Kerner Commission to assess the eruption of racial violence in America's cities, and its report was still in the process of being completed. In the meantime, Johnson aides geared up for the 1968 re-election effort, confident that the president could surmount his difficulties and win.

The only shadow on the political landscape was cast by Eugene McCarthy, the Democratic senator from Minnesota, who on November 30, 1967 had announced his willingness to challenge Johnson's renomination on an antiwar platform. McCarthy's commitment to run had come in response to the frantic efforts of Allard Lowenstein and other liberal antiwar activists to find a nationally known politician with the courage and commitment to risk his own political future in order to rally antiwar Democrats. Never satisfied with no for an answer, Lowenstein had approached Mc-

* Repeated Pentagon attempts to portray America as "having turned the corner," in Vietnam, with the "light at the end of the tunnel" now visible, led Russell Baker, a *New York Times* columnist, to hypothesize that the Pentagon had hidden within its deep recesses a mock, stage-set "corner" that they turned periodically to justify their never-ending optimism.

Carthy, George McGovern, and others after Robert F. Kennedy rejected his pleas. Like the antiapartheid activist he described in his own book on South Africa, Lowenstein dashed "about from meeting to meeting, invariably late, often lost, collecting and forgetting briefcases, documents and bits of paper with notes and addresses, doing alone the work that most men would shy from attempting with half a dozen." Now, he had found his candidate. "There comes a time," McCarthy declared, "when an honorable man simply has to raise the flag." A poet, intellectual, and devout Catholic who once spent nine months in a monastery, McCarthy brought to the antiwar effort an eloquence and biting sarcasm that gave new hope to the political wing of the antiwar movement. Once considered as a potential running mate for LBJ in 1964, he would now lead the fight to prevent the president's renomination.

Yet McCarthy's candidacy seemed a long shot, offering little basis for concern to the Johnson team. Public opinion polls in January showed the Minnesota senator with support from only 17 percent of the Democratic Party. McCarthy had never been a distinguished senator, erratic on domestic issues like civil rights and the oil-depletion allowance, and detached from most of the political battles of the era. "He has wit, charm, and grace," columnist I. F. Stone noted. "But he seems to lack heart and guts. . . . . McCarthy gives one the uneasy feeling that he really doesn't give a damn." When he was "on," McCarthy could transport an audience through his wit and sarcasm. But just as frequently, the Minnesota senator put his audiences to sleep. Perpetually late for appearances, often embroiled in philosophical discussions with poets and intellectuals, he frustrated his own closest supporters. While he claimed to be "pacing himself," others wondered whether the "pacing" did not reflect simply a distaste for battle. "I saw him as a candidate," Lowenstein noted. "He saw himself as a moral protestor for a cause." As the McCarthy campaign floundered during January, Johnson had good reason to feel complacent about his chances for renomination.

Then came the Tet offensive. In the early morning hours of January 30, 1968, the first day of the Vietnamese New Year, a small suicide squadron of Vietcong fighters exploded into the compound surrounding the U.S. embassy in Saigon. For six hours, they held the courtyard of the embassy until all the attackers were killed, leaving behind a scene described by one reporter as "a butcher shop at Eden." Within twenty-four hours, the Vietcong mounted attacks on virtually every significant target within South Vietnam— five major cities, sixty-four district capitals, thirty-six provincial capitals, and fifty hamlets. It required three weeks and 11,000 U.S. and South Vietnamese troops to dislodge 1,000 Vietcong from the Cholon district of Saigon. The ancient capital of Hue was literally razed to the ground by allied troops seeking to retake the city from 7,500 Vietcong and North Vietnamese troops. In the end, one observer noted, the city was left a "shattered, stinking hulk, its streets choked with rubble and rotting bodies." In Ben Tre, more than 1,000 civilians were killed in vicious fighting to expel 2,500 Vietcong invaders. During the three weeks the battles raged, an estimated 33,000 enemy troops were killed. But 3,400 allied forces died as well, including more than 1,600 Americans, with an additional 8,000 U.S. soldiers wounded. Civilian casualties were astronomical, and more than 1 million Vietnamese became refugees. With nearly total surprise, enemy forces had unleashed a massive attack that cast doubt on almost every premise of American involvement in Vietnam.

Although strategic experts still debate whether Tet was a defeat or victory for America in a purely military sense, the most immediate impact of the offensive was to widen the administration's "credibility gap" into a yawning chasm, one that would afflict Johnson for the duration of his term. Throughout the years from 1965 to 1967, journalistic accounts from the field had highlighted the disparity between administration optimism about the war and what was actually taking place in Vietnam. With every passing month, events belied Johnson's 1964 pledge that he would not send American boys to fight in Asia, and his repeated assurances that each increment of American forces would be sufficient to defeat the enemy. Now, all the doubts that surrounded Johnson's rhetoric were multiplied a hundredfold. "What the hell is going on?," Walter Cronkite, the venerable CBS anchorman asked. "I thought we were winning the war!" Typifying the acerbic disbelief of newsmen about Johnson administration practices was a Herblock cartoon two days after the Tet offensive began. Portraying a public relations man churning out optimistic press releases in Saigon as the embassy was surrounded by enemy soldiers, the cartoon's headline blazoned: "Everything's okay—they never reached the mimeograph machine." A week later, columnist Art Buchwald further underscored the administration's dilemma. Westmoreland's claim that Tet represented a military defeat for the Vietcong, Buchwald observed, was like Custer saying at Little Big Horn: "We have the Sioux on the run. . . . Of course we still have some cleaning up to do."

Indeed, the media—especially TV—proved decisive in shaping the American reaction to Tet. More than 60 million people watched network news shows every evening. Editors in New York, choosing five or six minutes of footage out of the multiple stories they had to select from, inevitably exercised profound influence in defining the reality of the war to Americans. Yet the materials from which they chose were so powerful. What were Americans to say about the democracy of their ally when they saw, in glaring color, the chief of South Vietnam's national police execute a Vietcong suspect in the middle of a Saigon street? How could viewers trust assurances from the Johnson administration that progress was being made when TV showed the grounds of the American embassy in rubble? Later, General Westmoreland accused the news media of creating a false impression of defeat instead of victory. Yet if there was distortion, it could hardly match the misrepresentation of the war that had issued from government offices for years. Whether or not Tet represented a military defeat for America, it underscored the disaster of the American presence in Vietnam.

By the end of February, the most respected figures of American journalism had placed themselves on record in opposition to administration policy, creating in the process a sanction for dissent against the war that would ultimately compel the government to reassess its position. "The cities are no longer secure," NBC anchorman Frank McGhee reported; "the Saigon government is weaker than ever. . . . From all this, we must conclude that the grand objective—the building of a free nation—is not nearer, but further, from realization." McGhee's conclusions were echoed by Walter Cronkite, viewed by most Americans as an oracle of truth, dispassionate and nonpartisan in his viewpoint. "It seems now more certain than ever" Cronkite told the nation, "that the bloody experience in Vietnam is to end in stalemate . . . [and] that the only rational way out . . . will be to negotiate, not as victors, but as honorable people who lived up to their pledge to defend democracy and did the best they could." For these high priests of American political culture, Tet had brought home the crushing reality that America was embarked on a hopeless cause, with disengagement the only honorable alternative.

Not surprisingly, Tet also served as a catalyst to those within the administration who had doubted the efficacy of American policy. In the Defense Department, Paul Nitze warned against the "unsoundness of continuing to reinforce weakness," while his colleague Paul Warnke declared that the Tet offensive had shown American military strategy to be "foolish to the point of insanity." As Townsend Hoopes, assistant secretary of the Air Force later wrote, the Tet offensive was the eloquent counterpoint to the effusive optimism of November. It showed conclusively that the United States did not "in fact control the situation, that it was not winning, that the enemy retained enormous strength and vitality . . . [Tet] had made blindingly clear the fatuousness of Westmoreland's ground strategy." Many of McNamara's civilian assistants in the Pentagon had long shared the secretary's concern over the direction of American policy. Now, with McNamara being forced out and replaced by Clark Clifford, these same officials geared up for one last effort to change America's military policy from within. In the aftermath of Tet, Westmoreland requested an additional 200,000 troops, in the meantime repeating his optimistic assurances that the United States had scored a major victory over the Vietcong. But others were far less sanguine and took the opportunity provided by Tet to wage their own battle against Westmoreland's request, and Johnson's hardline determination to continue the war.

Clearly, whatever else it had accomplished, Tet had created a sense of fluidity, frustration, and opportunity in American political discourse that had not been present even a few short weeks before. Despite Johnson's growing unpopularity, a majority of Americans still supported the war itself prior to the offensive. Now, overnight, a majority opposed the war. As one observer noted, the "shock and anger of the first days of Tet soon gave way to a new sense of futility and despair. . . . The feeling grew that the cost of the war was no longer worth the goals for which it was being fought."

In addition to highlighting the dangers of America's policy in Vietnam, Tet also radically transformed the political framework at home, creating for the first time the possibility that antiwar Democrats could succeed in defeating Johnson's campaign for renomination. With Tet in the background, the McCarthy campaign—mired in the doldrums throughout January—suddenly took on new life. Hundreds of college students converged on New Hampshire, seizing upon popular dissatisfaction with the war effort to canvass voters for McCarthy's candidacy. Shaving their beards ("be clean for Gene"), donning suits and ties, the students urged voters to cast their ballots for McCarthy in protest against the disarray and ineffectiveness of Johnson's policies. Two months earlier, White House polls had shown McCarthy receiving only 6 percent of the vote in contrast to Johnson's 76 percent. Now, McCarthy's popularity soared. In the aftermath of Tet, everyone seemed to turn against the president, and on primary day in New Hampshire, the Minnesota senator received 42 percent of the vote and 20 out of 24 Democratic delegates to the national nominating convention. Ironically, many of those who voted for McCarthy actually favored escalation of the war, not disengagement. But whatever their feelings about Vietnam itself, New Hampshire voters clearly saw a vote for McCarthy as a protest against Johnson, and policies which had been cast into total disrepute by the Tet offensive. It was a new day, a fresh chance, a real possibility that, through precisely those electoral processes that so many on the left had come to scorn, America could turn itself around, and choose, through a "new politics" an alternative to the disastrous course that Johnson had been pursuing.

The Struggle of Robert F. Kennedy

Robert F. Kennedy was the politician whose options were perhaps most radically altered as a consequence of Tet. Kennedy had been Lowenstein's first choice to lead the challenge against Johnson within the Democratic Party. The two had met often during the mid-sixties with Lowenstein developing a deep admiration for Kennedy as a politician and as a person. Then, on a late fall evening in 1967, Lowenstein went to Kennedy's house in Virginia to ask his help. With his shoes off and his legs crossed "college bull session style," he implored Kennedy to seize the "moral imperative of stopping the war by dislodging Johnson." Kennedy listened carefully, and even concluded that "Johnson might quit the night before the convention opened. I think he is a coward." All of Kennedy's instincts impelled him to run. As the journalist Jack Newfield noted, "if Kennedy does not run in 1968, the best side of his character will die. He will kill it every time he butchers his conscience and makes a speech for Johnson next autumn." Yet after a tortured debate with himself, and all his principal aides, Kennedy declined.

Now, the situation had changed. Kennedy's primary reason for refusing Lowenstein had been his fear of precipitating a divisive war within the

Democratic Party, which he believed would be interpreted as a personal feud with the president.* "I would have a problem if I ran first against Johnson," Kennedy noted. "People would say that I was splitting the party out of ambition and envy. No one would believe I was doing it because of how I felt about Vietnam and poor people. I think Al was doing the right thing, but I think that someone else would have to be the first one to run." Kennedy was correct, of course, in believing that his candidacy would be "interpreted in the press as just part of a personal vendetta." Everyone knew of the personal animosity between the president and the junior senator from New York. Each man detested the other. Johnson was obsessed with the "Bobby problem," one administration aide noted. "His complaints against Bobby Kennedy were frequent and may have bordered on the paranoid," another said. But Tet had taken the war issue beyond the realm of personal feuding, and McCarthy's candidacy had shown—albeit with fateful consequences for the later relationship between the two antiwar candidates—that the move to unseat Johnson reflected a mass movement of protest against Johnson within the country at large. And so Kennedy was ready to reconsider the possibilities of running just two months after having rejected Lowenstein's pleas.

The road Kennedy had traveled in the four years after his brother's assassination represented, in the eyes of many observers, a remarkable journey toward personal growth and political radicalization. In the years before President Kennedy's death, Robert Kennedy had always been perceived as the "hard-headed" Kennedy, "ruthless" in his single-minded campaign to incarcerate teamster boss Jimmy Hoffa, tough and pragmatic in the machinelike efficiency with which he ran his brother's political campaigns and contested potential adversaries. Although the image reflected as much caricature as reality, and was strongly contradicted by Kennedy's shyness, his warmth toward family and staff, and his growing commitment to civil rights, there had been a cockiness and brashness about his manner that suggested arrogance and a lack of introspection.

November 22, 1963 had dissolved much of that one-dimensional self-assurance, evoking in Kennedy a gentleness, a reflectiveness, and an internal quest for answers to life's basic questions that indicated a new, far more complicated personality. After the assassination, one aide noted, Kennedy seemed to be in constant pain, "almost as if he was on the rack, or as if he had a toothache or that he had a heart attack." His brother's death had been shattering, another aide recalled. "He was virtually non-functioning. He would walk for hours by himself." During those months he read books about philosophy, tragedy, and religion, making notes to himself: "the innocent suffer—how can that be possible and God be just." Or, "all things

---

* There were other reasons as well, of course. Most of JFK's advisors—the "older" generation that surrounded Kennedy—urged Bobby to hold off until 1972 when, in purely political terms, his chances of securing the nomination would be astronomically better. Kennedy had resigned as Attorney General in the summer of 1964 and ran for election to the Senate from New York where he defeated Kenneth Keating.

are to be examined and called into question—there are no limits set to thought." Like so many of the young people with whom he identified, Kennedy became enamoured of the French existentialist Albert Camus, writing in his notebook those thoughts that seemed to mean the most. "Perhaps we cannot prevent this world from being a world in which children are tortured," Kennedy quoted from Camus, "but we can reduce the number of tortured children. And if you believers don't help us, who else in the world can help us do this?" Through such ruminations, Kennedy seemed to find solace and direction—not answers, perhaps, but at least an approach to life that he could live by and that could sustain him.

Kennedy's political views, both on foreign and domestic policy, also underwent a transformation during these years. On one level, Kennedy's outlook was consistent with what he perceived to be the legacy of the New Frontier, and his own responsibility to carry forward the mandate of his brother's administration. But on another level, his views emerged from an emotional commitment to the underclasses of the world, to human beings whose oppression and suffering he identified with, and sought to represent. Personal contact with the human victims of exploitation became a passion, both heightening his own consciousness of poverty and anguish, and informing his political analysis of the individuals and institutions responsible for such suffering. After plunging deep into a dirty and unsafe mineshaft in Chile, Kennedy emerged to say to a reporter: "If I worked in this mine, I'd be a communist too." His anger at the Johnson administration's policies toward Latin America led him to embrace those who urged massive change. "The responsibility of our time," he told students in Peru, "is nothing less than a revolution—peaceful if we are wise enough; humane if we care enough; successful if we are fortunate enough. But a revolution will come whether we will it or not." Reaching out to the radical young of Third World countries, he urged dialogue on the means to change, while identifying totally with the objectives of economic equality and land reform. "Batista, not Castro," he said, "[is] the major cause of communism in the Americas." In Kennedy's view the Johnson administration had betrayed the goals of the Alliance for Progress, substituting commitment to military dictatorship for concern with democratic freedoms and economic reforms. Asked what he thought of Che Guevara, the Cuban guerrilla fighter, Kennedy replied: "I think he is a revolutionary hero." If America rejected the anguished cries of the dispossessed for social justice and identified all insurgency with communism, he concluded, it was aiding the very communist victories it sought to avoid. Kennedy had become, newspaper columnist Murray Kempton wrote, "our first politician for the pariahs, our great national outsider, our lonely reproach, the natural standard held out to all rebels."

On Vietnam, Kennedy also became increasingly critical of administration policies, both on political and moral grounds. As early as 1963 he had begun to question American policy. "He was beginning," Michael Forestall observed, "to have serious doubts about the *whole* effort. . . . Was the

United States capable of achieving even the limited objectives that we then had in Vietnam? Did the United States have the resources, the men and the thinking to have anything useful really to do in a country as politically unstable as South Vietnam was?" Painfully aware of his own and his brother's responsibility for the debacle, he wondered out loud to Arthur Schlesinger how to respond to a question about JFK's role: "to say that he didn't spend much time thinking about Vietnam; or to say that he did and messed it up . . . which, brother, which?" But with increasing frequency, Kennedy raised his own doubts publicly, notwithstanding the fear that his remarks might be interpreted as part of his personal feud with Johnson. By the end of 1965 he had become one of a small group of senators criticizing the war. He defended the moral integrity of those who burned their draft cards, endorsed Americans giving blood for the North Vietnamese as well as the South Vietnamese, and in early 1966, urged Americans to welcome the Vietcong into the political negotiations over Vietnam.

Almost immediately, Kennedy came under vicious attack. "I don't believe in writing a prescription for the ills of Vietnam that includes a dose of arsenic," Vice-President Hubert Humphrey said. The *Chicago Tribune* called him "Ho Chi Kennedy" and the *New York Daily News* declared: "If you feel strongly enough for the enemy to give them a pint of your blood every ninety days, then why not go the whole hog? Why not light out for the enemy country and join its armed forces?" But Kennedy continued his dissent, urging his countrymen to confront the "horror" of American involvement, "the vacant . . . and amazed fear as a mother and child watch death by fire fall from an improbable machine sent by a country that they barely comprehend." Vietnam, Kennedy declared, was "a land deafened by the unending crescendo of violence, hatred, and savage fury . . . Righteousness cannot obscure the agony and pain those acts bring to a single child." The war was America's responsibility, he insisted. "It is we who live in abundance and send their young men out to die. It is our chemicals that scorch the children and our bombs that level the villages."

By the end of 1967, Kennedy's comments had become jeremiads. "Are we like the God of the Old Testament," he asked,

> that we can decide in Washington, D.C. what cities, what towns, what hamlets in Vietnam are going to be destroyed? . . . Do we have a right here in the United States to say that we are going to kill tens of thousands, make millions of people . . . refugees, kill women and children? . . . I very seriously question whether we have that right. . . . Those of us who stay here in the United States must feel it when we use napalm, when a village is destroyed and civilians are killed. This is also our responsibility.

Kennedy even challenged the students at a Catholic university who in a straw vote, voted for more rather than less bombing. "Do you understand what that means?" he asked. "It means you are voting to send people, Americans and Vietnamese to die. . . . Don't you understand that what we are doing to the Vietnamese is not very different than what Hitler did to the Jews?"

The philosophical and religious underpinnings of Kennedy's pronouncements appeared to derive directly from his reading of Camus and of Greek tragedy. On a trip to South Africa, Kennedy articulated explicitly the faith that informed his own political commitments. Eloquently arguing against apartheid, he urged his audience not to give up the battle because of the fear that:

> there is nothing one man or woman can do against the enormous array of the world's ills—against misery and ignorance, injustice and violence. . . . Few will have the greatness to bend history itself; but each of us can work to change a small portion of events, and in the totality of all those acts will be written the history of this generation.
>
> It is from numberless diverse acts of courage and belief that human history is shaped. Each time a man stands up for an ideal, or acts to improve the lot of others, or strikes out against injustice, he sends a tiny ripple of hope, and crossing each other from a million different centers of energy and daring, those ripples build a current which can sweep down the mightiest walls of oppression and resistance.

The words were powerful, but how could Kennedy utter them and still refuse Lowenstein's challenge to run for president?

At home as well, Kennedy increasingly identified with the "have nots" of American society, becoming in Arthur Schlesinger's words, the "tribune of the underclass." Although concern for the poor and minorities appeared to be one area where Kennedy and Johnson shared a common commitment, the years after 1965 witnessed repeated cutbacks in Great Society programs directed toward the disadvantaged, and Kennedy—not Johnson—became more and more the spokesperson for their plight. While other whites expressed concern about Selma, Kennedy asked why they did not pay attention to the "brutalities of the North . . . [the] tenements in Harlem . . . where the smell of rats [is] so strong that [it is] difficult to stay there for five minutes." Unless Americans committed themselves to restore economic and social health *within* the ghetto, Kennedy declared, none of the goals of a truly integrated society could be achieved. Kennedy established a visceral bond with urban blacks who saw his visits to the nation's worst neighborhoods, and his legislation to help those areas, as graphic testimony to his concern. In 1963, when Kennedy had met with James Baldwin, Kenneth Clark, and other blacks in New York, they had been embittered by his failure to comprehend their anger and rebellion. Now, Clark commented, Kennedy had changed. "You know," he said after meeting Kennedy again in 1967, "it is possible for human beings to grow. This man had grown."

Kennedy also became one of the few national politicians to embrace openly the cause of Chicano farm workers in California. Asked by Walter Reuther to support the strike of migrant workers against owners of the grape vineyards, Kennedy journeyed to Delano to hold hearings on conditions among the workers. He immediately met a kindred spirit in César Chávez. Kennedy defended the strikers against the charge that they were communists, endorsed their right to a union, and helped build the political support necessary for the migrant workers to triumph. "Robert didn't come to us and tell us what was good for us," a Chávez aide noted. "He came to us and asked two questions. . . . 'What do you want? and how can I help?' That's why we loved him." Both Chávez and Kennedy shared a belief in nonviolent protest, the struggle for economic justice, and the conviction that Americans must be made to confront the exploitation that existed in their midst. "Today in America," Kennedy wrote, "we are two worlds." On the one side was the comfortable middle class, but on the other the world of "the Negro, the Puerto Rican, and the Mexican American . . . a dark and hopeless place." Kennedy, Chávez said, was able to "see things through the eyes of the poor. . . . It was like he was ours."

Native Americans had the same response. Investigating the poverty, malnourishment, and educational deprivation of Indian reservations in Oklahoma, and New York, Kennedy managed to convey the sense that he cared. "Loving a public official for an Indian is almost unheard of," one Seneca tribesman wrote, "[But] we trusted him . . . we had faith in him." Kennedy had the unique ability, Indian activist Vine Deloria wrote, to "move from world to world and never be a stranger anywhere. . . . Spiritually, he was an Indian!" Marion Wright Edelman, a black activist, noted the same things. "He did things that I wouldn't do. He went into the dirtiest, filthiest, poorest black homes . . . and he would sit with a baby who had wet open sores and whose belly was bloated from malnutrition, and he'd sit and touch and hold those babies. . . . I wouldn't do that! I didn't do that! But he did . . . that's why I'm for him." Even Kennedy's severest critics acknowledged his commitment. "I think he had a real affinity for the hurt people of the world," Gore Vidal wrote, "the blacks, the poor, the misunderstood young."

As America's growing involvement in Vietnam took dollars away from the poor at home, Kennedy's disenchantment with the administration deepened. Despite the urging of White House aides like Harry McPherson, for example, Johnson had refused to respond to urban decay and riots with new programs for employment. When the Kerner Commission released its report in February 1968 declaring that America had become two societies, one white and one black, with the divison widening between them, Johnson ignored its recommendations for massive federal intervention in the areas of jobs, housing, and segregation. In Kennedy's view, Johnson's attitude toward the scandal of America's cities was simply inadequate. "Its over," he told his press secretary. "The President is just not going to do anything more. That's it. He's through with the domestic problems, with the cities."

Why, then, had Kennedy not pursued the logic of his own convictions and challenged the president when asked to? The question tormented

Kennedy and his friends. "He cannot go to South Africa and stay out of New Hampshire," one associate declared in *Newsweek*. Yet Kennedy was confused, torn between his instincts to run and the pragmatic, cold-blooded calculations that told him it would be political disaster. "If [only] one more politician, on [the national] level . . . asks me to run, I'd do it," Kennedy said. "[But] the politicians who know something about it, they say it can't be put together." The popular cartoonist Jules Feiffer posed the dilemma as one between "the good Bobby" and the "bad Bobby." The "good Bobby" was a romantic idealist who condemned the killing of South Vietnamese women and children. The "bad Bobby" declared he was a Democratic Party loyalist who would back President Johnson. The "good Bobby" was a courageous reformer. The "bad Bobby" made deals. The "good Bobby" believed that four more years of Johnson would be a "catastrophe" for the country. The "bad Bobby" wanted to hedge his bets and and wait for 1972.

Like a boat caught in a riptide, Kennedy seemed immobilized by two currents pushing him in different directions. He procrastinated, wavered, seemed ready to take the plunge, then pulled back. Walter Lippmann advised him that "if you believe that Johnson's re-election would be a catastrophe for the country—and I entirely agree with you—then . . . the question you must live with is whether you did everything you could to avert this catastrophe." But the political pollster Louis Harris told him that he didn't have a chance, and New York *Post* publisher Dorothy Schiff asked: "Who is for you? . . . the young, the minorities, the Negroes, and the Puerto Ricans." That was not enough. The Johnson White House believed that Kennedy the political pragmatist would win out. If he ran in 1968, John Roche told Johnson, he "will never be able to put the pieces together for 1972. . . . Does he realize this? Of course he does. He's an arrogant little *schmuck* . . . but nobody should underestimate his intelligence." And so it went during the late fall and early winter of 1967–68. Kennedy was seemingly paralyzed by the scissors hold he had placed on himself, his instincts taking him one way, his pragmatism pulling him the other.

Although the Tet offensive and McCarthy's showing in New Hampshire finally liberated Kennedy, they did so in a way that disfigured his candidacy and evoked old accusations that he was a ruthless opportunist. "All of his own convictions, all of his own statements, all of his own feelings came back to really haunt him," a friend declared. In the fall of 1967, Richard Goodwin had written Kennedy that "your prospects rest on your own qualities: the less true you are to them and the more you play [the political] game, the harder it will be. People can forgive mistakes, ambition, etc., but they never get over distrust." Arthur Schlesinger, Jr., who had changed his own mind about the validity of the Kennedy candidacy, issued a similar warning. If Kennedy did not run, Schlesinger predicted, he would "become the anti-hero of countless Democrats across the country disturbed about the war. . . . If you entered at some later point, there might well be serious resentment on the ground that you were a Johnny-come-lately trying to cash in after brave Eugene McCarthy had done the real fighting."

Thus, when Kennedy declared his candidacy on March 16, he was the first victim of his own earlier indecision. "McCarthy's success had boxed him in," Schlesinger observed. "Obviously he could not now expect Gene to withdraw." Angry and frustrated, McCarthy workers all over the country accused Kennedy of crassly exploiting McCarthy's courage and attempting to usurp—in brutal, calculating fashion—the movement others had created. And there was truth to the charges. When Schlesinger urged Kennedy to endorse McCarthy instead, the senator replied: "I can't do that. It would be too humiliating. Kennedys don't act that way." He would have to bear the price of his own equivocation. But now, he was ready to follow his own impulses, regardless of what others would say about them. "It is a much more natural thing for me to run than not to run," he told friends. "When you start acting unnaturally, you're in trouble. . . . I'm trusting my instincts now and I feel freer."

Thus the choice was made. It meant that Kennedy and McCarthy would compete for the same anti-Johnson and antiwar constituency, taking the risk of dividing those who, under better circumstances, would have united behind one or the other. It also meant that Kennedy had come to a basic turning point in his personal and political life. In effect, he chose the path dictated by the growth he had experienced since his brother's death and the political perceptions that had matured as he embarked on his quest—to embrace the struggle of those who sought to overcome the injustice and intransigence of American institutions. At the end of the 1950s Kennedy had written a book entitled *The Enemy Within,* describing the hidden forces in America that attempted to subvert the country's freedoms. Now, he appeared to have conquered his own "enemy within" with a determination to pursue in the political arena the battles he had identified with over the preceding four years. Whatever the negative consequences of his late decision, the politics of 1968 had been irretrievably altered.

Lyndon Johnson

The third politician deeply affected by the Tet offensive was Lyndon Johnson. Suddenly everything had come unhinged, his own administration fragmenting into polar extremes. On the one side stood the military, led by General Westmoreland and the Joint Chiefs of Staff, who believed that in Tet the enemy had thrown in "all its military chips to go for broke," thereby providing the United States with a "great opportunity" to seize the initiative and win a military victory. The generals had long wanted to mobilize the reserves at home and now mounted new pressure to secure that goal, together with the deployment of 206,000 additional soldiers to Vietnam. On the other side stood the "closet dissenters" against the war within the Defense Department and State Department. "The upper reaches of government were honey-combed," Townsend Hoopes wrote, "with people who were not merely discouraged and disenchanted but deeply angered by the enduring stupidity and the self-protective tenacity of the [president's] inner circle." While some were ready to go the dramatic route of resignation and protest, most prepared for one last effort to fight from within and persuade the president to reverse the disastrous course of American policy. "If we wade in with both feet," Assistant Secretary of Defense Paul Warnke said, "we can perhaps make a difference; and if we fail, maybe they will do us the honor of firing us."

Although the ultimate focus for both sides was the president himself, the immediate object of attention became Clark Clifford, the new secretary of defense. Clifford was generally perceived to be a hard-line Johnson devotee. He was "loyal, well-dressed, and more important, determined to hold the line in Vietnam," *Newsweek* reported when he was chosen. Pentagon insiders, on the other hand, saw Clifford as a tough-minded pragmatist whose commitment to search for the facts created the possibility that the new secretary could be made a powerful supporter of those who sought change. Already uneasy about the precipitous decline in domestic support for the war, Clifford insisted on a wholesale reassessment of the Vietnam policy before acquiescing to Westmoreland's request for 200,000 additional troops—a 40 percent increase in American strength in Vietnam. What difference would the additional forces make, he asked? Would victory be assured? How would the new troops fit into America's long-term strategy, and what would be the consequences for political support at home? In answering these questions, the dissenters mobilized to press for de-escalation.

The stakes were high, the odds unfavorable. Johnson's immediate response to Tet had been strong and aggressive. "There will be blood, sweat, and tears shed," the president declared in Dallas in late February. "The weak will drop from the line, their feet sore and their voices loud . . . [but] persevere in Vietnam we will and we must." Yet despite the president's rhetoric ("free men will never bow to force and abandon their future to tyranny," he said), he too was willing to look hard at the situation. Westmoreland's request had clearly shocked Washington, raising the ante substantially beyond the massive commitment already made. With both Johnson and Clifford providing space for maneuver, civilian dissidents set out to compile a brief for change.

Their campaign proceeded on two fronts. First was the narrow military question of why U.S. forces needed to be reinforced by 200,000 troops when the allies had just killed more than 30,000 enemy troops. Individuals like Paul Nitze urged the administration to place America's involvement in Vietnam within the wider perspective of U.S. interests around the world, particularly the need to avoid direct hostilities with the Soviet Union and China. As summarized by Assistant Secretary of the Air Force Townsend Hoopes, the military case went as follows:

> Anything resembling a clear-cut military victory in Vietnam appears possible only at the price of literally destroying South Vietnam, tearing apart the social and political fabric of our own country, alienating our European friends, and

gravely weakening the whole free world structure of relations and alliances. Russian or Chinese military intervention on the side of North Vietnam, or another geographical point in the world, would be a serious risk if we greatly increase our own effort.

Even if the United States tripled its forces, Hoopes concluded, military victory seemed barely conceivable, with horrendous consequences for everything America stood for in the world.

The second, more important, argument was political. A positive decision on Westmoreland's request would inevitably require mobilizing the reserves, which in turn would send political shock waves coursing through American society. Hawkish Americans would demand the unleashing of all America's military might to end the war, including the potential use of atomic weapons. Doves, on the other hand, would rally to the antiwar movement and take to the streets in even more massive acts of civil disobedience than had already occurred. The American social fabric could never sustain the resulting conflict, and open battle at home might well be the price of seeking military victory abroad. McCarthy's "victory" in New Hampshire in the very midst of these deliberations simply accentuated their relevance.

When Clifford brought his results to the president, it was as if, in Johnson's view, "this Judas [suddenly] appeared." The loyalist whom Johnson had chosen to replace the wavering McNamara had suddenly gone over to the other side. But Clifford was playing for time, noting the tentative nature of his own doubts about the effectiveness of America's military operation in Vietnam, while acknowledging the ongoing support for the president's policy from administration leaders like Rusk, General Wheeler, Maxwell Taylor, and Walt Rostow. Johnson gave mixed signals. In response to U.N. Ambassador Arthur Goldberg's initiative for a bombing pause, he declared: "Let's get one thing clear. I'm not going to stop the bombing. I have heard every argument on the subject, and I'm not interested in further discussion." Yet in preparation for a major presidential address on the war, he was also willing to seek further consultation with "experts" throughout the nation.

In the meantime, the political atmosphere was heating up. In hearings before the Senate Foreign Relations Committee, New Jersey Republican Clifford Case lectured Secretary of State Dean Rusk that "there is a line to be drawn between the honorable meeting of commitments and pig-headed pushing in the direction of a course which has become more and more sterile." George Kennan, one of America's most respected foreign policy experts, described the war as "a massive miscalculation and error of policy, an error for which it is hard to find any parallel in our history." A Gallup Poll in mid-March showed that 49 percent of the American people believed it was wrong for the United States to have become involved in Vietnam in the first place—a result that confirmed the results of the New Hampshire primary. Word had leaked to the press about Westmoreland's request, and the response had been one of outrage. It seemed, Senator Frank Church declared, that the United States was "poised to plunge still deeper into Asia where huge populations wait to engulf us, and legions of young Americans are being beckoned to their graves."

As the debate intensified, Johnson received the harshest blow to date. Dean Acheson, the architect of America's Cold War policy and one of the most revered political figures in Washington, went to the president and told him: "With all due respect, Mr. President, the Joint-Chiefs-of-Staff don't know what they are talking about." Authorized by Johnson to pursue his own investigation of the war, Acheson told the president that Johnson was out of touch with the country, was being led down a garden-path by the Pentagon, and was pursuing a policy that had no chance of success either at home or abroad. Still, Johnson appeared to hang tough. "Your President has come here," he told an audience two days after seeing Acheson, "to ask you people, and all the other people of this nation, to join us in a *total national effort* to win the war, to win the peace, and to complete the job that must be done here at home. . . . Make no mistake about it . . . we are going to win." But behind the rhetoric, Johnson was deeply shaken.

As the scenario played itself out, Johnson convened his council of "Wise Men"—an informal group of prestigious business and foreign policy advisors—to seek their guidance. In the past, the group had endorsed his policies, lending support and legitimacy to American involvement in Vietnam. Now, virtually every man joined the growing dissent. As described by McGeorge Bundy, the group told the president that Acheson was right: U.S. policy was stalemated, victory was impossible without total war, and the administration's policy no longer had the support of the American people. Earlier, Johnson had asked speech writer Harry McPherson to work on a presidential address full of patriotic exhortation and hard-line defense of existing policies, including a proposed call-up of 50,000 reserves. Dubbed by McPherson the "we shall overcome draft," the speech shocked Clifford who called it "everything I had hoped it would not be." But now Johnson was ready to consider a second draft, one that would include a proposal for a partial bombing halt and embrace new initiatives toward peace. Clifford had brilliantly argued for the new approach, and McPherson—sharing fully Clifford's sentiments—composed a new draft pledging a bombing halt at the twentieth parallel and a promise of a complete end to the air war in the North if Hanoi reciprocated by respecting the demilitarized zone and refraining from attacking South Vietnamese cities. When the president later called McPherson and asked him about a comment on page three, McPherson compared his two drafts and discovered that the president was now working on the "peace speech." A decision had been made.

On the evening of March 31, Johnson spoke to the American people. "Tonight," he began, "I want to talk to you of peace in Vietnam and Southeast Asia." It was important, he said, to "no longer delay the talks that could bring an end to this long and bloody war. . . . So, tonight . . . I'm taking the first step to de-escalate the conflict." The president announced the unilateral reduction of hostilities, a cessation of bombing in the areas North of the demilitarized zone, and a plea to Ho Chi Minh "to respond positively, and favorably, to this new step toward peace." Even the limited bombing of the North that remained, the president said, "could come to an early end if our restraint is matched by restraint in Hanoi."

Then, suddenly, came the unexpected peroration to the speech. "I have decided," Johnson told the nation, "that I shall not seek, and I will not accept the nomination of my party for another term as your President." All through the preceding months he had felt trapped, Johnson later told Doris Kearns, as if he were being

> chased on all sides by a giant stampede coming at me from all directions. On one side, the American people were stampeding me to do something about Vietnam. On the other side, the inflationary economy was booming out of control. Up ahead were dozens of dangerous signs pointing to another summer of riots in the cities. . . . And then the final straw. The thing I feared from the first day of my presidency was actually coming true. Robert Kennedy had openly announced his intention to reclaim the throne in the memory of his brother. . . . The whole situation was unbearable to me. After thirty-seven years of public service, I deserved something more than being left alone in the middle of a plain, chased by stampedes on every side.

Now, he had found a way out. He would both initiate the process of peace in Vietnam and leave the presidency, with his gigantic domestic achievements intact. "My biggest worry was not Vietnam itself," he later said. "It was the divisiveness and pessimism at home. . . . I looked on my . . . speech as an opportunity to help right the balance and provide better perspective." He would remove himself from the battle, and thereby take one last step toward reconciliation.

The nation was stunned. Johnson, the "manly" man, who always overpowered people with his strength, his combativeness, his sheer intensity of personality, was withdrawing from the fray. It was difficult to understand. Yet as Doris Kearns later noted, "the predictions that Johnson would stand and fight . . . ignored deeper layers of his personality. They failed to weigh his most consistent pattern of behavior: his profound aversion to conflict." Faced with the demise of the consensus he prized so much, he chose to retreat rather than contribute further to the polarization that was threatening the nation. The legacy of his earlier decision to attempt simultaneously to build a Great Society and wage war had finally taken its toll, with crushing rapidity. Johnson's decision represented, in retrospect, the inevitable outcome of his tragic quest for greatness. But it was not to be the last of the tragedies in 1968.

Martin Luther King, Jr., RFK, and Eugene McCarthy

Johnson's March 31 "peace speech" was the climax of a ten-week series of events bewildering in the speed with which they had occurred and the seismic rearrangement they had caused on the American political landscape. First had come Tet, then McCarthy's "victory" in New Hampshire, then Kennedy's candidacy, and finally Johnson's reversal of policy in Vietnam. It was almost too much to comprehend. Yet in 1968, as the journalist Theodore White observed, "it was as if the future waited on the first of each month to deliver events completely unforeseen the month before." Johnson's retirement from the presidential sweepstakes appeared to set the stage for the victorious ascendancy of a "new politics" that would address the tensions of the country. Three national leaders—Martin Luther King, Jr., Robert F. Kennedy, and Eugene McCarthy—embodied the hopes of those who wished to alter the structure of American society, promote economic reform, and win the battle for peace. Yet during the next seventy days, in a shattering sequence of blows that made the tremors of the preceding ten weeks pale by comparison, two of those leaders would be stricken by assassin's bullets, with the third demoralized and disillusioned by the seeming impossibility of transforming the American system from within.

Martin Luther King, Jr., had experienced his own nightmare of the soul during the 1960s. After skillfully orchestrating the Birmingham demonstrations of 1963, he had galvanized the nation with his "I Have a Dream" speech during the March on Washington and had held together—against great odds—the civil rights coalition responsible for enacting the Civil Rights Acts of 1964 and 1965. But even in the midst of these victories, his base of support was eroding. Lambasted from outside the movement as a radical, he was denounced from within as a tool of the "white establishment." In the face of such attacks, King had struggled, unsuccessfully, to maintain the momentum of his crusade for a just America. Now, increasingly radicalized by the war in Vietnam and the absence of progress at home, he was preparing to mount a new crusade—for economic equality as well as racial justice—in America.

During these same years, unbeknownst to most Americans, King had also faced another, more insidious challenge to his integrity and his sanity—systematic wire-tapping and harassment from the Federal Bureau of Investigation. In the early 1960s the FBI had become concerned about the influence exercised over King by Stanley Levison, a New York attorney who became King's closest personal advisor after 1957. Through reports from a secret double-agent highly placed in the United Nations, Washington officials had learned that during the postwar years—until 1954—Levison had been a top-ranking member of the Communist Party and the conduit through which Soviet money was funneled to the Communist Party apparatus in America. Levison's record raised the suspicion that he was now seeking, on behalf of the Communist Party, to use his friendship with King for subversive purposes. Conveniently ignoring its own information that Levison's contact with the party had apparently ended in 1954, the FBI beseeched Attorney General Robert F. Kennedy to place King and Levison under direct surveillance. In March 1962, convinced by FBI arguments about Levison's influence, Kennedy finally complied with the request.

Although the FBI's Altanta office repeatedly assured J. Edgar Hoover that it could find no evidence of communist infiltration in SCLC, Hoover refused to take the reports seriously, insisting instead that his underlings change their conclusions in conformity with the director's own preconceptions. As a result, King was added to the FBI's "enemies list," and Hoover's closest aides now assured him that "King's advisors are Communist Party members and he is under the domination of the CP."* Indeed, Hoover and his aides singled out King as a primary threat to national security. After King's "I Have a Dream" speech, Hoover aide William Sullivan declared that "we must mark [King] now, if we have not done so before, as the most dangerous Negro to the future in this nation from the standpoint of communism, the Negro and national security." When King charged in the fall of 1962 that FBI agents in the South were often "white southerners who have been influenced by the mores of the community," Hoover considered the allegation an unforgivable affront. Afterwards, one FBI agent noted, "it appeared to me that there was a 'get King' movement in the Bureau." As one FBI source told *Time* magazine, "[Hoover would] do anything to destroy the credibility of a critic." Hoover's lieutenants laid plans to develop information that would destroy King as an effective black leader, and in the words of one memo, "expose [him] as an immoral opportunist who is not a sincere person but is exploiting the social situation for personal gain." Throughout, the FBI investigation was based on the assumption that anything King did represented a threat to the society. "There are clear and unmistakable signs," FBI agents were told, "that we are in the midst of a social revolution with the racial movement as its core."

In all of this, Hoover appears to have been motivated by personal as well as political considerations. In the years after 1963, FBI surveillance had produced no evidence to sustain allegations of communist influence on King. What it had produced was titillating material, composed of photographs and tape recordings, which indicated that King, on occasion, drank to excess and engaged in extramarital sex. Hoover became obsessed with what he called "these entertainments," seeming to treat them as part of his own fantasy life, as well as a volatile source of ammunition with which to undermine his hated enemy. "They will destroy the burrhead," he said. Gleefully sharing his "peeping tom" information with the White House, Hoover made plans to use the material to disgrace King and reveal him "to his Negro followers as being what he actually is—a fraud, demagogue, and moral scoundrel."

---

* Members of the Kennedy administration undertook to warn King about his association with Levison and another staff assistant named Jack O'Dell. The president himself took King aside on a walk in the White House Rose Garden in the summer of 1963 and told him of administration suspicions about his aides: "they're communists. You've got to get rid of them . . . if they shoot you *down*, they'll shoot us down too—so we're asking you to be careful." Government officials never provided King concrete evidence to support their allegations against Levison, and the SCLC director continued to rely on Levison for advice, using third parties to make contact with the New York attorney.

Seemingly consumed by his vendetta, Hoover launched an all-out attack, stooping to tactics so low as almost to defy comprehension. Publicly, the FBI director told a group of women news reporters that King was the "most notorious liar" in America—"one of the lowest characters in the country." Privately, he authorized his aides to compile a tape containing evidence of King's most serious sexual indiscretions and to send it to King with an anonymous letter accusing the SCLC leader of being "a collosal fraud" and "an evil abnormal beast." "You," the letter read, "even at an early age have turned out not to be a leader but a dissolute, abnormal imbecile. . . . You are finished." The letter concluded with an apparent invitation to King either to commit suicide or resign from the movement. "King, there is . . . but one way out for you. You better take it before your filthy, abnormal fradulent self is bared to the nation." Because Coretta Scott King enjoyed hearing tapes of her husband's speeches, the recording was sent by SCLC staff members—unopened—to the King household in January 1965. There, Mrs. King opened the letter and listened to the tape. Simultaneously, FBI officials attempted to disseminate the same material to the news media, first offering it to Benjamin Bradlee of *Newsweek,* and then to reporters from the *Chicago Daily News,* the *New York Times,* the *Los Angeles Times,* the *Atlanta Constitution,* and the *Augusta Chronicle.* Other FBI aides briefed prominent church leaders, such as Cardinal Spellman, and the Atlanta police chief, who conveyed the gist of the information to King's father. There seemed no limit to Hoover's obsession. An FBI document entilted "Martin Luther King, Jr.: His Personal Conduct" was even dispatched to prominent government officials.

Most shocking of all, perhaps, was White House connivance in all of this. When the first tapes of King's indiscretions were brought to Johnson in January 1964, Walter Jenkins, Johnson's aide, declared that "the FBI could perform a good service to the country [if] this matter could somehow be confidentially given to members of the press." To their credit, every reporter who was offered the FBI material turned it down. But Benjamin Bradlee shared his concern over the episode with Assistant Attorney General Burke Marshall. When Marshall then related the episode to Johnson, the president said nothing, as if he were already aware of the FBI's efforts. In fact, he was more than aware; he was an accomplice, instructing his aide Bill Moyers to warn the FBI that Bradlee was not to be trusted. Later, the president would say in response to one advisor's defense of King, "Goddamit, if only you could hear what that hypocritical preacher does sexually."

Inevitably, such harassment took a heavy toll on King. Notified on vacation of Hoover's public attack calling him a "notorious liar," King responded with shrewd irony. "I cannot conceive of Mr. Hoover making a statement like this without being under extreme pressure," King said. "He has apparently faltered under the awesome burden, complexities and responsibilities of his office." But as the private attacks reached home—both literally through Coretta Scott King and his father, and figuratively through word of the FBI's effort to contact newsmen, religious leaders, and allies in the civil rights fight—King became depressed and distracted. An FBI report in early January 1965 noted that King was emotionally distraught. With his leadership under attack from SNCC militants from within, and by FBI sabotage from without, King felt increasingly besieged and helpless. Despite the success of the Selma movement, the next year was a period of self-doubt, questioning, and frustration.

Yet somehow King emerged from the ordeal a stronger, more resolute, more courageous leader. He had always been able to learn from those around him, to be open to new visions, new insights, new departures toward the goals he cared most about. A man of profound faith, he took courage from the support of those closest to him in the face of internal and external attacks, and started to come to grips with his own vulnerability, his own imperfection, his own sinfulness. More and more, he came to see the connection between his commitments to nonviolence and racial justice at home, and the problems of the world—particularly the war in Vietnam.

At great risk to his own position as leader of the civil rights movement, King became one of the first outspoken critics of America's involvement in Vietnam. Beginning in August 1965, and proceeding through the next year, the SCLC leader became an eloquent spokesman for those who insisted that peace in Vietnam was inextricably tied to racial justice in America. "We've got to get out and demonstrate and protest until [we rock] the very foundations of this nation," he told an audience in February 1966. By April 1967 when he preached at Riverside Church in New York, King had moved to the front of the antiwar forces, denouncing the American government as "the greatest purveyor of violence in the world today" and urging all Americans to unite in protest against the war. Although King was denounced by the White House as "the crown prince of the Vietniks," and attacked by *Life* magazine for "demagogic slander that sounded like a script for radio Hanoi," King had clearly crossed a personal watershed. He knew his enemies, was fatalistic about his own political and personal future, and was determined to take a stand he regarded as moral, regardless of the consequences.

At the same time, King substantially broadened his vision of the changes that would be required at home to achieve the goals of racial justice and economic democracy. As early as the 1950s, he had criticized American capitalism. But through the middle of the 1960s, he appeared still to believe in the capacity of the American "system" to reform itself from within, convinced that legislation that outlawed discrimination and guaranteed black voting rights would be a vehicle for achieving major reform. Now, in the aftermath of the Black Power movement and with clear evidence that antidiscrimination legislation meant little unless blacks had the resources to participate as equals in the economy, he moved toward an analysis that directly linked economic and racial issues. "We must recognize," he told his staff in 1967, "that we can't solve our problems now until there is a radical re-distribution of economic and political power." Class was as important to blacks as race, he insisted.

> The black revolution is much more than a struggle for the rights of Negroes. It is forcing America to face all its interrelated flaws—racism, poverty, militarism, and materialism. It is exposing evils that are rooted deeply in the whole structure of our society. It reveals systemic rather than superficial flaws and suggests that radical reconstruction of society itself is the real issue to be faced.

In the early 1960s, King noted, blacks had been engaged in a reform movement. But now it was time to move into an era of revolution, an era that would inevitably "raise certain basic questions about the whole society. . . . We are engaged in [a] class struggle . . . dealing with the problem of the gulf between the haves and the have nots." In a brilliant series of lectures prepared for the Canadian Broadcasting System, King moved toward a position that in substance was inherently radical. Only if Americans understood the inseparable relationship between justice in their own society, peace in the world, and a thoroughgoing reallocation of economic resources, he declared, would it ever be possible to achieve democracy.

To a remarkable extent, King and Robert F. Kennedy had experienced a similar process of growth, rooted for each in having to endure personal agony and suffering, yet resulting in a parallel understanding of the deepest causes of America's crisis of the soul. From different points of departure, both men had arrived at a new comprehension of the importance of class in America—what each called the "gulf between the haves and the have nots"—and the imperative necessity of ending the war in Vietnam if peace and justice were to be achieved at home. Kennedy had traveled far from his cold and unsympathetic confrontation with James Baldwin and other black leaders in 1963 to a new recognition of the need for compassionate identification with blacks and other members of the underclass. King, in turn, had developed a new appreciation for hard-headed, political realism as an essential prerequisite to achieving the radical agenda for America he now envisioned. In Andrew Young's words, "[Martin] saw Bobby as a man of both moral courage and a keen sense of political timing. . . . He admired Bobby's blend of 'crusader' and realistic politician." Both men had also become more fatalistic over the years, conscious of the frailty and weakness of human beings as they sought to achieve their goals. "Neither man," Young said, "could profit . . . from an overt relationship and both avoided any direct association. Yet they continued down parallel paths of opposition to racism, poverty and war."*

---

* Ironically, both men also shared the dubious privilege of being J. Edgar Hoover's most hated enemies. If a streak of vicious racism permeated the FBI's campaign to "destroy [King] the burrhead," the animus toward Kennedy was more personal. After JFK's death, Hoover restored his direct line of communication with the White House, bypassing the Attorney General entirely. The FBI director ordered that the wiretap material gathered on King not be shown to Robert Kennedy except in one instance—when a tape recording revealed King and his aides making obscene references to JFK's sex life and Jacqueline Kennedy's sexual proclivities. When Robert Kennedy announced his candidacy for the presidency, a close Hoover aide declared: "I hope someone shoots and kills the son-of-a-bitch." Thus as King and Kennedy mounted their respective campaigns for change in America, they were united not only by their common vi-

It was in pursuit of his part of their shared vision that Martin Luther King, Jr., had gone to Memphis, Tennessee, in March 1968 to lend his name and support to the strike of Memphis garbage workers for union recognition and better working conditions. Throughout the preceding months, King had spent most of his waking hours attempting to organize a "poor people's march on Washington" that would once again unite blacks and whites, this time on the issues of poverty and economic injustice. By establishing an encampment of tents, mules, and wagons in the nation's capital, King hoped to dramatize the impossibility of resolving America's racial dilemma without eliminating the oppression of class and caste together. King's effort had been stymied by organizational difficulties and internal squabbles over the wisdom of the March, but he was intent on proceeding.

The call from Memphis, though on the surface a diversion of his energies, in fact spoke eloquently to the heart of his concerns. Here, class and race operated together, dramatically illustrating the principal objectives of the entire Poor People's Campaign. In Memphis, King found a microcosm of all the tensions and obstructions that made his effort to rebuild a coalition so difficult. Young militant blacks resisted the approach of nonviolence, urged rent strikes that were opposed by the city's black leadership, and during King's first visit, disrupted a peaceful march downtown with rock-throwing and violence. Profoundly disturbed by the internal divisions in the civil rights movement and the potentially destructive consequences of violence, King poured all his energy into restoring direction and unity to the movement. He was living on the edge of chaos, depressed by tensions that threatened to destroy all he cared about, yet insistent that his own staff—and the Memphis black community—retain a commitment to love and nonviolence as the core convictions of their common struggle.

Returning to Memphis on April 3, King sought to rally his forces for a united march that would redeem his vision. His own internal doubts were revealed in his comments to an aide: "Truly, America is much, much sicker . . . than I realized when I first began working in 1955." In a remarkable, powerful, and poignant sermon he delivered that night, King disclosed to his audience the depth and passion of his own journey through nonviolence. He had experienced other crises like this, he told the congregation, and had faced death many times. But nothing was more important than confronting the enemy and continuing the struggle; no court ruling, not even from the federal government, would stop either him or his followers from completing their march. "I've been to the mountaintop," he declared, and "I've seen the glory" of the vision that was coming. "I may not get there with you," he said, "but I want you to know that we as a people will get to the promised-land." The next night, King was shot dead as he stood on the balcony of his hotel in the all-black section of Memphis.

sion of what America could become, but also by a common enemy who viewed their goals with equal hatred and contempt.

Within hours of hearing the news of King's death, the nation's cities exploded in violence. Black Americans who for years had contained their anger at the brutality that had caged them suddenly erupted in rage at the senseless murder of the man who had attempted to lead them along the road of peace. "What white Americans have never fully understood—but what the Negro could never forget," the Kerner Commission had said one month earlier, "is that white society is deeply implicated in the ghetto." Now, black Americans dramatically verified the commission's conclusion. In Chicago, twenty blocks of the downtown business area burst into flame, set afire by rioters, as Mayor Daley ordered police to "shoot to kill" arsonists. More than one hundred American cities witnessed violence. Soldiers garbed in battle gear set up a machine-gun enplacement atop the nation's Capitol. More than 5,500 troops were finally required to quiet the weeklong expression of screaming fury. As King's body lay ready to be put to rest, those who came to mourn heard a recording of his own eulogy for himself, preached just a short time earlier at his home church: "I want you to say on that day," he declared, "that I tried to love and serve humanity. . . . If you're going to say that I was a drum major, say that I was a drum major for justice. Say that I was a drum major for peace." Yet even as the funeral proceeded, the fires smouldered—as if to say that the dream had been killed along with the dreamer.

Robert Kennedy heard the news as he traveled by plane to Indianapolis where he was to address a rally in that city's black ghetto. He "seemed to shrink back," a reporter said, "as though struck physically." The crowd in Indianapolis had been gathered for more than an hour, awaiting the candidate. They had not yet learned of King's death. "I have bad news for you," Kennedy told them, "for all of our fellow citizens, and for people who love peace all over the world. . . . Martin Luther King was shot and killed tonight." Kennedy continued:

> Martin Luther King dedicated his life to love and to justice for his fellow human beings, and he died because of that effort. . . . In this difficult time for the United States it is perhaps well to ask what kind of nation we are and what direction we want to move in. . . . For those of you who are black and are tempted to be filled with hatred and distrust at the injustice of such an act, against all white people, I can only say that I feel in my own heart the same kinds of feeling. I had a member of my family killed, but he was killed by a white man. . . . We have to make an effort to understand, to go beyond these rather difficult times. My favorite poet was Aeschylus. He wrote: "In our sleep pain which cannot forget falls drop by drop upon the heart until, in our own despair, against our will, comes wisdom, through the awful grace of God." What we need in the United States is not division; what we need in the United States is not hatred; what we need in the United States is not violence or lawlessness, but love and wisdom, and compassion toward one another and a feeling of justice toward those who still suffer within our country, whether they be white or they be black. . . . Let us dedicate ourselves to what the Greeks wrote so many years ago: to tame the savageness of man and to make gentle the life of this

world. Let us dedicate ourselves to that, and say a prayer for our country and for our people.

The next day, in Cleveland, Kennedy attempted once again to address the enormity of the tragedy. The problem, he said, was not simply individual violence. Instead, it was America's acceptance of violence as a way of life. "We calmly accept newspaper reports of civilians slaughtered in far off lands," he said. "We glorify killing on movie and television screens and call it entertainment." But even that kind of violence was not as bad as the violence of American institutions. "This," he said, "is the violence that afflicts the poor, that poisons relations between men because their skin has different colors. This is the slow destruction of a child by hunger." Only if America was willing to root out the underlying causes of violence could an answer be found. "Violence breeds violence," he concluded, "repression brings retaliation, and only a cleansing of our whole society can remove this sickness from our soul."

With King gone, Kennedy became—for many blacks—the only national leader who commanded respect and enthusiasm. "[Kennedy] had this fantastic ability to communicate hope to some pretty rejected people," one black leader declared. "No other white man had this same quality." Kennedy would go into a room of black militants, listen to their angry complaints, accept their criticisms, and then slowly convert them to his cause. "Kennedy . . . is on our side," one angry black told the psychiatrist Robert Coles. "We know it. He doesn't have to say a word." To comfortable whites, in turn, Kennedy carried the message that complacency was not enough. Facing a hostile crowd of medical students in Indiana, he declared: "Let me say something about the tone of these questions. As I look around this room I don't see many black faces who will become doctors. . . . You are the privileged ones. . . . It's the poor who carry the major burden in Vietnam. You sit here as white medical students, while black people carry the burden of the fighting in Vietnam." Those students "were so comfortable, so comfortable," Kennedy later said to a reporter. They had to be moved from indifference to concern, from passivity to activism.

In the early days of his campaign—before King's assassination— Kennedy had been like an uncontrolled rocket, often reckless in his rhetoric, shrill in his speechmaking, demagogic in his appeals. It was as if he had been tethered for so long that he felt he had to make up for lost time by magnifying his appeal and intensifying his indictment of Johnson and America. "As his oratory expanded," one journalist noted, "there seemed to be almost no excellence that the nation had not attained during the regime of his brother, almost no degradation to which it had not sunk in the intervening years, almost no restoration that he could not promise." Others charged that he was deliberately inciting crowds, as if "part of a strategy of revolution, of a popular uprising." With dangerous abandon, he provoked emotional hysteria from his audiences. "They tore the buttons from his shirt cuffs," Jimmy Breslin wrote, "they tore at his suit buttons, they reached for the hair on his face. He went down the fence, hands out, his body swaying backward so that they could not claw him in the face."

In part, Kennedy's excesses could be attributed to his frustration at having entered the race in a manner that almost guaranteed that he would be unable to woo back the supporters of Eugene McCarthy. Kennedy's announcement had deeply angered white liberals like Murray Kempton who declared, in a biting column, that "in the naked display of his rage at Eugene McCarthy for surviving on a lonely road he dared not walk himself, [Kennedy had] done with a single great gesture something very few public men had ever been able to do. In one day, he managed to confirm the worst things his enemies had ever said about him." In his own version of the "good Bobby, and the bad Bobby" scenario, the poet Robert Lowell described Kennedy as having

> a hundred charisma suits. A charisma suit is made of cloth and cardboard; at the touch of a feather . . . it pulls apart. But under the charisma suit is an anti-charisma Bobby-suit. It is made of cloth and steelwool. It doesn't tear at all and leaves metal shreds on the rash admirer for months. . . . It's hard to forgive Kennedy his shy, calculating delay in declaring himself, or forgive the shabby rudeness of his final entrance.

McCarthy himself contributed to the attack, his voice dripping with sarcasm as he denounced those politicians "willing to stay up on the mountain and light signal fires," but afraid to come down and join the fight. The hostility of the young was particularly hard for Kennedy to take. He had prided himself on his sensitivity to their causes, only to find that now McCarthy had the "A students," Kennedy the "B students." "I'm going to lose them," Kennedy told an aide, "and I'm going to lose them forever."*

In fact, a world of difference separated Kennedy from McCarthy. Although the two men shared a common antipathy to Lyndon Johnson and the Vietnam war, their agreement ended there. Kennedy was emotional and evangelical, McCarthy detached and philosophical. While both were devout Catholics, McCarthy was like a Jesuit—the intellectual order of priests who specialize in theology—and Kennedy like a Paulist—those driven by a mission to convert the unconverted. Kennedy appealed to the poor and the blacks, McCarthy to the middle class and the professionals, or, as his wife described them, "[academics] united with a mobile society of scientists, educators, technologists and the new post-World War II college class." McCarthy attacked the institution of the strong presidency, calling for a dismantling of executive authority; Kennedy wanted to use the strong presidency to achieve social transformation. The one relied on biting wit, the other on emotional engagement. As one journalist wrote: "McCarthy speaks

---

* Kennedy's perceived loss was best expressed in a note he gave to Al Lowenstein one night on a bus coming back from upstate New York. The note read: "For Al, who knew the lesson of Emerson and taught it to the rest of us: 'they did not yet see, . . . if a single man planted himself on his convictions and then abide, the whole world would come round to him.' From his friend, Bob Kennedy."

in generalities and Kennedy speaks in specifics. [McCarthy] dwells on himself and his moment in history; Kennedy dwells on the tragedy of the poor. . . . McCarthy soothes; Kennedy arouses."

As the campaign unfolded, the differences between the two men sharpened. In the eyes of many, Doris Kearns later wrote, Kennedy seemed "the only man capable of rebuilding the Democratic Party and bringing back together the blacks and the whites." The Indiana primary offered a test case of Kennedy's appeal. A state full of white ethnic factory workers, inner-city blacks, and rural farmers, Indiana embodied most of the potential constituencies for Kennedy's "new politics." "We have to convince the Negroes and poor whites that they have common interests," Kennedy told one journalist. "If we can reconcile those two hostile groups, and then add the kids, you can really turn this country around." Kennedy took his campaign to these diverse groups, telling white factory workers that he was for "law and order" but also that safety in the cities could only exist when racial justice and equality had been achieved. To blacks, he emphasized passionate commitment to abolish racism and poverty, but urged working within the system for change. McCarthy kept to his high ground of criticizing the war and the imperial presidency, but refused to lower himself to solicit support from the poor. On election day, Kennedy scored a decisive victory, out-polling his foe almost two to one. A similar margin of victory occurred shortly thereafter in the Nebraska primary.

But Oregon was a different story. A middle-class, homogeneous state with only 2 percent of its population consisting of blacks, Indians, and Chicanos, Oregon was fertile ground for McCarthy's political approach. McCarthy was well organized, and his thoughtful statements against the war, his opposition to excessive power in Washington, and his speeches on behalf of the environment evoked an enthusiastic response. Kennedy, in turn, seemed lost, his passionate attacks against poverty and racism seeming to fall on deaf ears. "There is nothing for me to get hold of," he told one reporter. "Let's face it, I appeal best to people who have problems." Tensions between the candidates mounted. McCarthy was outraged by what he perceived as a scurrilous attack on his voting record. Kennedy, in turn, was angered when McCarthy told one audience that Kennedy backers were "among the less intelligent and the less educated people in America." As his sarcasm mounted, McCarthy portrayed Kennedy as a "spoiled child" who had gotten his way for too long. When Kennedy refused an offer to debate McCarthy and ran away from McCarthy supporters seeking to force a confrontation, he seemed ineffectual, and on May 28, McCarthy swept to an impressive victory, defeating Kennedy 44 percent to 38 percent. Never before had a Kennedy been defeated.

The stage was thus set for California, the nation's largest, most important state. Kennedy had accepted defeat graciously in Oregon, and set out to maximize the advantages of his new role as an underdog. César Chávez campaigned through the barrios seeking Hispanic support for Kennedy; Charles Evers of Mississippi and John Lewis of SNCC did the same in black areas; and intellectuals like Arthur Schlesinger, Jr., reached out to the academic community. Kennedy's experience confronting black militants in Oakland, California, typified his ability to convert the disaffected. "It was a rough, gut-cutting meeting," one Kennedy aide said, with blacks denouncing white liberals, and one local figure known as "Black Jesus" declaring, "I don't want to hear none of your shit . . . you bastards haven't did nothing for us." Yet the next day many of the participants in the meeting were handing out Kennedy literature and Black Jesus himself marched at the head of a column clearing a path for the candidate. "What can you call Bobby?," one radical asked, "'the last of the great liberals'? He wouldn't have liked that . . . I guess I have to say he was the 'last of the great believables.'" The press—even those initially skeptical—had increasingly leaped on Kennedy's bandwagon. "Quite frankly," Tom Wicker of the *New York Times* declared, "Bobby Kennedy was an easy man to fall in love with." Even Richard Harwood, one of Kennedy's most scathing critics, changed his mind. "We discovered in 1968," he later said, "this deep, almost mystical bond that existed between Robert Kennedy and the 'Other America. . . .' We were forced to recognize in Watts and Gary and Chimney Rock [Nebraska] that the real stake in the American political process involved not the fate of speech writers and fundraisers but the lives of millions of people seeking hope out of despair."

McCarthy was also in good form. Self-possessed, witty, eloquent, he took his philosophical critique of the imperial presidency and his courageous record of opposition to the Vietnam war to a state only slightly less ideal for his purposes than Oregon. The McCarthy campaign, one aide wrote, was full of "lofty confidence." Many, on both sides, were prepared to say that whoever won in California should go on to secure the support of the other side in order to facilitate a united front at the Democratic Convention in Chicago. McCarthy supporters were convinced that they would be the victors.

By election day, each candidate had done all he could. A straw in the wind had been the first and only debate between Kennedy and McCarthy, which most observers rated as a draw. Yet a draw was in Kennedy's favor, because, as one McCarthy aide wrote, "it was clear that Kennedy could take McCarthy head-on with no fear of his magic powers. If McCarthy had something new and different going for him in American politics, it did not show in open competition with Kennedy." The election results confirmed the assessment, and when the polls closed, Kennedy had scored the most important victory of his political life, out-balloting McCarthy 46 percent to 41 percent. Already making plans to reach out to McCarthy supporters like Richard Goodwin and Al Lowenstein, and to machine politicians like Richard Daley, Kennedy went down to greet the crowds and make his victory pronouncement. "What I think is quite clear," he told the cheering throngs, "is that we can work together in the last analysis, and that what has been going on within the United States over a period of the last three years . . . the divisions, whether it's between blacks and whites, between the poor and the more affluent, or between age groups or on the war in Vietnam—is that we can start to work together. We are a great country, an unselfish country, and a compassionate country. I intend to make that my basis for running." Moments later Kennedy was shot in the head by an assassin. He would never again regain consciousness.

As the country went through one more searing exposure to the anguish of loss in a year full of agony, people groped to make some sense of the meaning of this man who, like King before him, had seemed to embody the hopes of those who wished to transform America within the existing political system. Some would say that the tragedy of Kennedy's death reflected a flaw in his personality—that the Kennedys, Bobby as well as Jack, had created a politics of personalism, using a rhetoric of excess that generated expectations that could never be met. Others—like the columnist Robert Scheer—were convinced that even though Kennedy really "gave a shit about Indians, . . . gave a shit about what was happening to black people," he nevertheless represented "the illusion of dissent without its substance, the danger of [raising] co-optation to an art form"—a man who ultimately would have sold out the causes he believed in for the power he craved.

But there were, as well, those who believed that this shy man, who seemed to combine compassion with realism, represented "the last best hope" for bringing America together in a genuine search for justice and peace. "They think he is cold, calculating, ruthless," the columnist Joe Alsop observed. "Actually he is hot-blooded, romantic, compassionate." "He knew about worlds the rest of us didn't know about," Al Lowenstein observed; and Michael Harrington, author of *The Other America,* declared: "As I look back on the 60s, he was the man who actually could have changed the course of American history." If Kennedy had one commandment, another associate noted, it was that "it really is a secular sin not to try." For these believers, what would remain was a tragic sense of unrealized possibility. In St. Patrick's Cathedral, before Kennedy's funeral, Mayor Richard Daley sat in prayer, his head bowed, weeping uncontrollably. In the same church at the same time, Tom Hayden, the SDS activist also wept. The responses of the two men, so different in background and politics, crystallized Kennedy's appeal and the opportunity he represented. Perhaps the most fitting comment came from columnist Murray Kempton, a friend who had turned bitterly against Kennedy after his decision to run against McCarthy. "I have liked many public men immensely," Kempton said, "but I guess he is the only one I have ever loved." It was an emotion shared by many. And now he was gone.

The Year Comes to a Climax—The Conventions and Election

With Kennedy and King dead, the movement for change within the political system seemed to lose direction and focus. Predisposed by instinct and temperament to avoid the politics of mass mobilization and engagement,

McCarthy retreated to a Benedictine monastery to reflect, write poetry, and attempt somehow to make sense of the chaos around him. In an earlier poem, he had written about politics as involving three acts: "Act 1 states the problem. Act 2 deals with the complications. And Act 3 resolves them. I'm an Act 2 man. That's where I live—involution and complexity." Unable to offer the leadership essential to restore the spirit of Democratic dissenters, McCarthy disengaged. As the journalist Theodore White observed, McCarthy might bear "love in his heart—but it was an abstract love, a love for youth, a love for beauty, a love for vistas and hills and song. . . . All through the year, one's admiration of the man grew, and one's affection lessened." Throughout the preceding months, McCarthy aide Jeremy Larner observed, McCarthy had appeared to possess "a special air of mystery, a hint that he drew strength from a source beyond mere mortals. . . . I thought McCarthy had a secret. One day the secret would explain it all." But in the end, the secret remained a mystery.

In the meantime, the left fragmented in disarray. Among blacks, the pollster Samuel Lubell discovered, there was a sense of fathomless despair, of irretrievable defeat. "I won't vote," one New Yorker said. "Every good man we get they kill." Student movements seemed to explode in a thousand different directions. Columbia University had been shut down all during May as a result of the occupation of administration and classroom buildings by SDS cadres, and a massive confrontation between demonstrators and 900 police resulted in a campuswide strike.* While some student radicals focused on the university as their target, others drifted off into the counterculture or attempted to organize working-class neighborhoods. One splinter faction, the Youth International Party (Yippies), turned its attention to the Democratic National Convention, urging demonstrators to flood Chicago, create chaos, and transform the nation's oldest convention city into a guerrilla theatre, pitting the politics of total freedom and disorder against the politics of machine discipline and stability.

The Democratic Convention of August 1968 brought to a bizarre and brutal climax the churning political emotions of the year. Everyone knew in advance the results of the convention. Hubert Humphrey, Lyndon Johnson's vice-president, had announced his own candidacy for the nomination in late April, proclaiming his theme as "The Politics of Joy" (a singular non sequitur in this year of anguish). With Kennedy now dead and McCarthy possessing only a minority of delegate support, Humphrey was the preordained victor. Thousands of young people had answered the call to come to Chicago, however, either to demonstrate with the Yippies, to take one last stand for the McCarthy peace movement, or simply to testify by their presence to their disaffection from the "old politics." In response, Mayor Richard Daley had turned the city into a virtual fortress, mobilizing almost

* The next chapter will deal more extensively with campus rebellions, including that at Columbia.

12,000 police, preparing to call out 7,500 national guardsmen, and denying demonstrators the right to hold protest rallies, march through the city, or even sleep in the parks. The mayor's reaction fit perfectly the plans of Abby Hoffman, Jerry Rubin, and other Yippies. In a brilliant stroke of guerrilla genius, the Yippies highlighted their contempt for the "pigs" who they claimed were governing America by introducing in the middle of Chicago their own candidate for president—"Pegasus"—a fat young pig who went squealing through the crowds.

What followed was an enactment of Hubert Humphrey's "worst-case scenario," with TV cameras broadcasting the events to a stunned nationwide audience. Many demonstrators had come to Chicago with the clear intent of taunting the police and provoking a violent response. They succeeded. On August 25, police dispersed over a thousand young people from Lincoln park when they tried to hold rallies and make camp. "The cops had one thing on their minds," one journalist wrote. "Club and then gas, club and then gas, club and then gas." The police went berserk, a British journalist wrote; "the kids screamed and were beaten to the ground by cops who had completely lost their cool. Some tried to surrender by [putting] their hands on their heads. As they were marched to vans to be arrested, they were rapped in the genitals by cops swinging billies." By August 28, the fifth anniversary of Martin Luther King's March on Washington, the situation worsened. Delegates at the convention had just rejected by a three-to-two margin an antiwar resolution. As the delegates pondered their action inside, police struck outside against peaceful demonstrators seeking to march on convention headquarters. With no attempt to distinguish bystanders and peaceful protestors from lawbreakers, the police smashed people through plate-glass windows, fired tear gas cannisters indiscriminately, and brutalized anyone who got in their way. "These are our children," *New York Times* columnist Tom Wicker cried out as the violence continued.

In the Convention Hall, delegates divided over how to proceed. The scene was mass chaos. Al Lowenstein demanded that the convention adjourn as long as people were being "maced and beaten unconscious." Abraham Ribicoff, a Democratic senator from Connecticut, denounced the "Gestapo tactics" taking place in the streets, in response to which Mayor Daley could be seen mouthing the words "motherfucker" to Ribicoff. The contrast between what an official commission later called a "police riot" and Hubert Humphrey's acceptance speech endorsing "law and order" underscored how profound the divisions racking the Democratic Party were. It had been a week of shame, violence, and extremism, highlighting, with bitter poignancy, the inability of the "party of the people" to forge a campaign that would address the tensions splitting the country.

If there was one man supremely prepared to exploit those tensions, it was Richard M. Nixon. The perennial Republican campaigner had first come to prominence by exposing Alger Hiss and hyping the anticommunist issue, winning election to the U.S. Senate from California by dubbing Helen

Gahagan Douglas, his liberal Democratic oponent, the "pink lady." He was Eisenhower's "hatchet man," yet had come within an eyelash of winning the 1960 presidential election. Reflecting on that campaign, Theodore White concluded that Nixon was a politician with no roots, no inner security, no sense of identity, integrity, or conviction. When Nixon lost the gubernatorial election in California in 1962, his career seemed finished and he told reporters that "you won't have Nixon to kick around anymore." But if nothing else, Nixon was a survivor and repeatedly over the next six years he campaigned selflessly for Republican candidates. Picking up political credits wherever he traveled, Nixon convinced the party—and reporters as well—that there was now a "new Nixon," reflective, mature, and ideally prepared to turn his years of experience into a new round of service to his country and his party. Easily turning aside challenges from the moderates represented by Nelson Rockefeller, and the "far right" represented by Ronald Reagan, Nixon glided to victory at the Republican Convention in Miami.

But the "new" Nixon quickly was revealed as simply a more sophisticated version of the "old" Nixon. Using South Carolina's segregationist Senator Strom Thurmond as a lieutenant, he set out to capitalize on the country's uneasiness about the "social issues" of race, urban violence, and antiwar protest. Nixon named Maryland's Spiro Agnew as his running mate, seizing on Agnew's reputation for having lambasted Baltimore's black leaders in the spring and having urged the shooting of looters. Nixon himself issued scathing attacks against forced busing of black children to white schools; promised that he had a secret plan to end the war in Vietnam; and wherever he went, wrapped himself in the mantle of patriotism. His top priority at home, the Republican nominee said, was "the restoration of law and order." Pledging to transform the Supreme Court—which he claimed had given a "green light" to American criminals—Nixon concluded his acceptance speech with a ringing appeal to all Americans who felt ignored, stomped on, and abused by blacks and student demonstrators. "As we look at America," he said,

> we see cities enveloped in smoke and flame. We hear sirens in the night. We see Americans hating each other; killing each other at home. And as we see and hear these things millions of Americans cry out in anger: Did we come all this way for this?

Nixon declared that he would speak "for another voice, . . . a quiet voice. . . . It is the voice of the great majority of Americans, the forgotten Americans, the non-shouters, the non-demonstrators . . . those who do not break the law, people who pay their taxes and go to work, who send their children to school, who go to their churches . . . people who love this country [and] cry out . . . 'that is enough, let's get some new leadership.'"

Nixon had found his key to success. By focusing on the discontent of "middle Americans" who were fed up with Hippies, drugs, Black Power, and banners urging victory for the Vietcong, Nixon had located a current of

conservative reaction seeking a spokesman. To Americans who were outraged by radicals who assaulted middle-class respectability and violated all
the rules of the game, Nixon personified America's traditional virtues. He
had raised himself from poverty, he celebrated and embodied the "American dream," and he pledged to lead the way back from chaos and rebellion
to stability and obedience. The average, alienated, white American could
identify with this man.

The only real threat Nixon faced was the appeal of George Wallace. Alabama's segregationist governor had proclaimed his determination in 1963
to "toss the gauntlet before the feet of tyranny" and enforce "segregation
now . . . segregation tomorrow . . . and segregation forever." Wallace
and Nixon drew from the same reservoir of white American resentment
against social protest, but Wallace was even better than Nixon at capitaliz-
ing on raw hatred. Running as a third-party candidate, the Alabama governor denounced the "pointy headed intellectuals" who had taken over Washington and the welfare mothers who he claimed were "breeding children as
a cash crop." Viciously attacking the antiwar movement, he pledged that "if
any demonstrator ever lays down in front of my car, it will be the last car he
will ever lay down in front of." Wallace's campaign burgeoned as he took his
message of revenge and resentment to Northern white working-class neighborhoods. By attacking the "Eastern Establishment," denouncing hippies,
and promising to defend the interests of white people, Wallace soared to
prominence, receiving 21 percent of the nation's support in a presidential
sweepstakes poll in mid-September.

But Nixon had his own Wallace in the person of Agnew. If the Republican vice-presidential nominee was not as folksy as the Alabama governor,
he could still hold his own in any competition for demagogic excess. America's antiwar protestors, Agnew declared, were tools of communist leaders
and to be treated "like the naughty children they are." To those concerned
with the plight of America's cities, Agnew replied: "If you've seen one city
slum, you've seen them all." Moreover, Agnew looked good in comparison
to Wallace's vice-presidential choice, General Curtis LeMay, the former Air
Force General, who urged using nuclear weapons against North Vietnam,
and whose repeated indiscretions in off-the-cuff remarks disturbed even
hard-core Wallace supporters.

Ironically, Nixon probably benefited when the Humphrey campaign
finally took fire and began to eat away at Wallace support. Crippled from the
beginning by his repeated declarations of loyalty to Johnson and his long
record of emotional appeals on behalf of the Vietnam war, Humphrey
seemed dispirited and paralyzed through most of the fall. His old allies in
the civil rights and peace coalitions held back, giving only nominal endorsements to the man who had once been their champion. But Wallace's
appeal galvanized union leaders who were shocked by working-class support for the Alabama governor, and a massive labor campaign for Humphrey started to achieve some success, eroding Wallace's Northern con-

stituency. Simultaneously, Humphrey finally disengaged himself from Johnson's position on the war, announcing his commitment to a unilateral bombing halt in North Vietnam in a Salt Lake City speech on October 31. For a few brief days, it seemed as though the old New Deal coalition would get into harness again and put together a sufficient constituency of blacks, workers, professionals, and intellectuals to put Humphrey over the top. But it was too little, too late. And while Humphrey garnered important support from voters who previously had said they would cast their ballots for Wallace, post-election polls indicated that Nixon had also won critical backing from the "middle American" constituency that had been so pivotal to Wallace. On election day, the Republican candidate squeaked to victory with 43.4 percent of the vote compared to Humphrey's 42.7 percent and Wallace's 13.5 percent. Significantly, less than three out of five Americans eligible to vote had bothered to cast a ballot. Indeed, one pollster claimed 43 percent of the American people preferred none of the three candidates.

Whatever the percentages, the results were clear—and from the point of view of those who had sought major change in American society, they were devastating. The man, whom Theodore White had said had no home and no political center, now had found the domicile he so long had craved—the White House. It was, by any calculations, an extraordinary conclusion to an extraordinary political year. The man who pledged to "bring us together" had won the presidency by skillfully manipulating and exploiting the anger of those Americans who felt that their country, their values, and their own identity were threatened by the forces of social change. In the end, Nixon had won election by securing the votes of only 27 percent of all those eligible to vote. But he was the new president, and his selection, by however small a margin, indicated the political temper of the time, spelling disastrous defeat for those who had attempted to use the political process as a means of achieving economic equality, social justice, and world peace.

Conclusion

Any historian who uses the word "watershed" to decribe a given moment runs the risk of oversimplifying the complexity of the historical process. However, if the word is employed to signify a turning point that marks an end to domination by one constellation of forces and the beginning of domination by another, it seems appropriate as a description of what took place in America in 1968. Just as the onset of McCarthyism brought to a standstill collective movements for social change that had grown out of the World War II experience, the political agonies of 1968 witnessed the cresting of forces committed to social change that had been building since the late 1950s. These forces had failed to triumph in the political arena, and their place was taken by a new political hegemony that fragmented the left and generated a polarization between social activists on the one hand and politicians on the other that would last throughout the 1970s and into the 1980s.

As a result of the politics of anticommunism, political dissent during the 1950s had turned inward, finding expression in individual rebellion against social conformity. The civil rights movement stood alone as a collective expression of protest against the nation's social pratices. Yet a potential constituency for change was developing, particularly in the nation's universities and churches, dramatized in places like Montgomery and Greensboro. The civil rights movement, grounded in the church, turned out to be relatively invulnerable to the charge of communist domination and served as a vehicle for moving people from individual to collective action, reactivating movements for social change that had long been dormant.

Throughout the 1960s these movements experienced their own evolution—caused by both internal conflict and external repression—that led to an increasingly radical critique of traditional American values and institutions. With the civil rights movement as a catalyst and a microcosm, many activists gradually lost faith in the capacity of the American political system to reform itself. The extent to which traditional hierarchies of leadership proved resistant to change persuaded many movement supporters that the only alternative was an outright attack on the nation's institutions. As the civil rights movement pursued its inexorable journey toward Black Power, and as activists in the student movement, the women's movement, and the antiwar movement became disenchanted with the possibilities of incremental reform, the nation witnessed a growing extremism on the left, together with a burgeoning reaction on the right, which called seriously into question the possibility of successfully resolving social tensions through civilized discourse and established political processes.

The protest politics of 1968 represented, for many disaffected critics of America, a last chance to secure their goals through already existing political means. While many were already so thoroughly alienated that they scorned participation in the political process, large numbers of activists saw in the antiwar candidacies of Robert F. Kennedy and Eugene McCarthy, and in the political activism of Martin Luther King, Jr., an appropriate place to concentrate their energies. They hoped—sometimes confidently, sometimes desperately—that if only they worked hard enough, argued well enough, and conveyed their message sincerely enough, the American people would respond and find a way out of the intractable dilemmas that seemed to be propelling the country into chaos and confrontation. Perhaps these hopes were doomed from the beginning. Perhaps the notion of transforming America was a romantic illusion, testifying more to the naiveté of the believers than to their realism. But it was an effort that many were convinced had a fighting chance.

Rarely before had collective movements for social change found such an opportune moment to strike for political realization of their goals. With the exception of the women's movement, almost all of the constituencies committed to social reform in America found a direct outlet for their energies in the turbulent months from January through August of 1968. Even some of those most hardened against the political system—Chicanos, militant blacks, the radical young—saw a reason to act in the campaigns to end poverty, racism, and war led by King, Kennedy, and McCarthy. These men, too—especially King and Kennedy—understood the desperate nature of their quest, the extent to which this might represent the final moment in which social passion and political realism could join to build a viable coalition to achieve the dream they shared, within a social system they cherished. Whatever the feelings of their followers, neither King nor Kennedy were sanguine about the chances for success. But they believed the struggle was worth the effort—and certainly was preferable to the alternatives of resignation, despair, or revolution.

It would be difficult to overstate the dimensions of the tragedies that ensued. The nation seemed to come apart as, one blow after another, it reeled from psychic and emotional wounds unprecedented in the modern era. With the media heightening the impact of each event—the King assassination, urban riots, the Kennedy assassination, the Chicago debacle—many Americans felt that the very fabric of their society was coming unraveled, and that forces of destruction and violence were in the ascendancy. No one could tell whether a different history might have resulted had these events not occurred. But those who *might* have been leaders in that history were now dead, and those who believed in them were crushed by the reality that they were no longer present to provide leadership, direction, and vision.

The important point was that "what might have been" now no longer seemed possible. Those national political leaders who made an effort to achieve a different kind of America through existing political processes were now gone. And with their departure went also—for countless activists—any reason to believe that change was possible. By the end of 1968, it seemed clear that the old order was intact, exhibiting remarkable endurance. To some, the very fact that America was able to hold an election in the midst of such divisions testified to the health and stability of the American system. As one British journalist wrote, "the enormous power of the Presidency passed peacefully from one man to another [despite] the fear that the country was coming apart." That was true. But true also was the enormity of the price that had been paid, causing many to wonder whether there would ever again in their lifetime be another occasion to seek, through political action, the dream of a society committed to genuine social equality and an end to war.

13

"Bringing Us Together"

Richard M. Nixon had been elected president on the promise that he would restore truth and openness to the White House, terminate the war in Southeast Asia, and "bring Americans together again." Over the next five and a half years, unfortunately, he betrayed most of those promises. The president pledged to end the war in Vietnam, then expanded it by the secret bombing of Cambodia. He promised to speak the truth at all times, then lied repeatedly to the American people. He ran an administration rhetorically committed to the principles of law and order, only to have twenty-five of his top aides indicted for criminal activity. By the time Nixon himself finally resigned in disgrace, some of his closest associates even wondered about the president's mental stability.

But there was a perverse logic underlying Nixon's conduct of the presidency. Since the ascendancy of the civil rights movement in the late 1950s, social activists on the left had energized American politics. Now, the politics of the right assumed control. Shrewdly and effectively, Nixon mobilized his constituency of "silent" or "forgotten" Americans around the "social issues" of patriotism, alarm about crime, and traditional middle-class values. Brilliantly pursuing his "southern strategy," Nixon used his opposition to civil rights, his anger at the Supreme Court's liberalism, and his contempt for student demonstrators to forge a new base for the Republican Party in a "Sun Belt"—the states of the Old Confederacy and the American West. In the meantime, the left fragmented into a thousand pieces, destroyed internally by its inability to agree on a common agenda, and externally by the systematic harassment and sabotage of Nixon's counterintelligence agencies.

In the end, of course, Nixon succeeded in his pledge to unite the American people. His direct complicity in the cover-up of Watergate, his seemingly inherent inability to speak candidly to the American people, and his reckless abuse of power finally galvanized a coalition intent on preserving America's constitutional system. Yet if Nixon became the instrument of his own destruction, he could still take some satisfaction from the results of his five and a half years in office. Conservatives had regained decisive power in shaping the political agenda of the country. Social activists had been rendered largely impotent. And it seemed clear that, for the immediate future at least, those who sought to restore and rebuild America would represent traditional and conservative values, not innovative or radical ones. In effect a new conservative consensus had come to dominate the nation.

The Nixon Presidency: Rhetoric and Reality

Richard Nixon's political career represented a bundle of contradictions. Elected to Congress in 1946 and the U.S. Senate in 1950 in vicious Red-baiting campaigns, he had been chosen as Eisenhower's running mate in 1952 largely as a concession to the right wing. Through much of Ike's presidency, Nixon did the president's political dirty work, lambasting Democrats as soft on communism. But Nixon also aspired to the role of statesman, traveling abroad on numerous occasions and displaying his diplomatic panache in the famous kitchen debate with Nikita Khrushchev.* On the one hand, he cared deeply about his place in history, reflecting intently on long-range patterns and his ability to shape them. Perhaps showing the influence of his Quaker upbringing, he spent hours alone in his study contemplating how he could transform the world. On the other hand, he was petty and venal on domestic political issues, frequently vindictive toward those he distrusted. Nixon's long-range vision manifested itself in his carefully plotted effort to break down the wall of hostility that he himself had helped to create between the United States and China. Even before he took office, he told journalist Theodore White that he wished to seek rapprochement with the People's Republic. Yet more often than not, he became mired in short-range details. The president, one aide recounted, had an almost "abnormal" obsession with minutiae, dictating memos on whether the White House curtains should be closed or open, how state gifts should be arranged, whether black or white musicians should play at White House social affairs, and whether the Secret Service should salute during the playing of the National Anthem. When his concern about detail translated into compiling an "enemies list" of domestic political foes to be harassed by the Internal Revenue Service, it quickly became a vehicle for political disaster.

Through it all, many wondered who the "real" Richard Nixon was. "He is the least 'authentic' [person] alive," writer Garry Wills concluded. A loner, Nixon shunned contact with most of his staff and cabinet members, preferring to spend hours in isolated contemplation rather than engage the world around him. Profoundly insecure, he never overcame his resentment against Eisenhower for failing to invite the vice-president to his private quarters in the White House, or his anger at rich Republicans in New York for refusing

---

* Whenever he could, Nixon took the "high ground" and boasted of his experience in shaping policy. Nixon was embarrassed in 1960 when Eisenhower, asked by a reporter to list the decisions that Nixon had played a major role in, paused and responded: "Give me a week to think about it and I will tell you."

to include the Nixons in their social set. Because he was ill at ease with others, Nixon preferred the formal set-pieces of the presidency to informal chit-chat. Once, when a motorcycle policeman was injured in the midst of a presidential trip, Nixon rushed to the injured officer to express his sympathy. Finding nothing else to say, he asked the policeman lying on the ground: "Do you like the work?" As the world was to learn when the Nixon tapes were disclosed, this was not a president of grace, wit, or generosity.

Not surprisingly, the 1968 campaign highlighted the two roads Nixon would travel. Early on, Kevin Phillips, an aide to campaign manager John Mitchell, had shown staff members the draft of a manuscript that would later become *The Emergence of a Republican Majority*. Phillips contended that Americans were sick of New Deal liberalism and ready to rebel against an intellectual and media elite—located in the Northeast—who had come to dominate the Democratic Party. A new conservative majority was in the making, he argued, with members of the Catholic working class, white Southerners, suburbanites in the Sun Belt, and average middle-class Americans sharing a common revulsion against militant minority groups, radical young people, and arrogant intellectuals.

Phillips—and Nixon—had presciently identified as key to their strategy an area of the country that represented the wave of the future in technological and population growth. The Sun Belt—the states of the Old South plus Texas, California, New Mexico, Oklahoma, and Arizona—had become since 1945 a magnet for both the American people and modern industry. In the thirty years after the war these states had more than doubled in population. Cities like Phoenix sky-rocketed from 65,000 to 755,000, Houston from 385,000 to 1.4 million. The Sun Belt also became a haven for the new high-tech industries of aerospace, plastics, chemicals, and electronics. Scientists flocked to industrial research zones in North Carolina, Florida, Texas, and California, and *Fortune* magazine noted that one 25-mile stretch in Santa Clara, California, boasted "the densest concentration of innovative industry that exists anywhere in the world."

Perhaps most important, the burgeoning sunshine states offered a natural home for political and cultural conservatism. The center of evangelical Protestantism, the Sun Belt proved traditional in racial attitudes and deeply suspicious of Northeast elitism. These states thus provided an ideal constituency for Nixon's appeal to "forgotten" and "silent" Americans. Using code words like "law and order," attacking the Supreme Court for its excessive liberalism, and appealing to Western and Southern devotion to the traditional values of hard work, patriotism, and the family, Nixon effectively cultivated the regional distinctiveness of the Sun Belt and began to turn what had been a Democratic stronghold into a Republican base. By zeroing in on cultural values and the emerging power of the religious right, Nixon thus helped shift the axis of American politics away from one that focused on horizontal issues such as income, class, and economic need toward one that focused on vertical issues such as religiosity, anti-elitism, and law and order.

Yet, Nixon also presented himself as a consensus figure—able to overcome domestic division through taking the high road of reform at home
and statesmanlike action abroad. This was the "new" Nixon, whose liberal,
well-argued radio speeches won plaudits from the press, and whose victory
statement the day after the election focused on the sign carried by a
teenager in Deshler, Ohio, that read: "Bring us together." "That will be the
great objective of this administration at the outset," Nixon declared, "to
bring the American people together. To be an open administration, open
to new ideas, open to men and women of both parties, open to the critics as
well as those who support us. We want to bridge the generation gap. We
want to bridge the gap between the races. We want to bring America together." Thus the campaign, like Nixon himself, presented a study in con-
trasts: callous exploitation of polarization for the short run, lofty appeals to
unity for the long run, both existing side by side.

The same division characterized Nixon's first term as president. Nixon
was deeply impressed by Daniel Patrick Moynihan, an Irish Democrat whose
intellectual, yet basically conservative, outlook Nixon found congenial and
entertaining. Drawn to Moynihan's wit and brilliance, Nixon was persuaded
by the former Harvard faculty member that he could become an American
Disraeli. Moynihan gave the new president Robert Blake's biography of the
British prime minister who had been able, in the 1870s, to promote social
reform under the aegis of a conservative administration. Converted to the
notion that this was a way of securing his own greatness in history, the president told Moynihan: "You know, . . . it is the Tory men with liberal policies who have enlarged democracy." With such an historical perspective,
Nixon embraced Moynihan's advocacy of welfare reform, proposing an income maintenance plan whereby each family suffering from poverty would
receive at least $1,600 per year. Indeed, he went beyond Moynihan to em-
brace proposals for tax reform, environmental control, and consumer protection. Just as Nixon could attempt departures in foreign policy that no
Democrat would venture, so in domestic policy, a conservative president
could enter the history books as an effective advocate of social progress.

Yet, on another level, Nixon repeatedly demonstrated his commitment
to the politics of polarization that was at the heart of the Phillips "Southern
strategy." Attorney General John Mitchell, Nixon's primary political advisor,
believed that Nixon's political future depended on holding his own supporters from 1968 and adding to that core those who had supported
George Wallace's candidacy. Civil rights, naturally, played a central role in
this venture. Throughout his 1968 campaign, Nixon had attacked the arbitrary imposition of school desegregation plans on the South, endorsing instead the concept of "freedom of choice" whereby individual blacks could
enroll, through their own initiative, in whichever school they wished to attend. Although such "freedom of choice" plans were notorious for perpetuating segregation (they placed the total burden for change on individual
plaintiffs, denying group redress) and had been invalidated by the Supreme

Court in May of 1968, Nixon continued to embrace them. In pre-inaugural meetings with Senator Strom Thurmond of South Carolina, he pledged to seek the lifting of HEW guidelines that called for terminating federal funds to any school district that refused to desegregate. Since cutting off federal monies had provided the most effective instrument of promoting integration, Nixon in effect was offering the power of the presidency to delay, if not halt completely, federally imposed school desegregation.

Once in the White House, Nixon proceeded to implement his commitment. Thurmond's close aide, Harry Dent, became deputy counsel to the president with the specific assignment of protecting white Southern interests. In January, HEW delayed one desegregation plan for five school districts in South Carolina. Then, in July, HEW head Robert Finch intervened on behalf of thirty-three school districts in Mississippi, requesting that federal courts *slow down* the process of desegregation already agreed to. Six weeks later, for the first time since the *Brown* decision in 1954, the Justice Department entered a federal court, not to argue for school desegregation, but rather to press for delay—all this in violation of the Supreme Court's order a year earlier insisting on immediate school desegregation everywhere. Nixon himself sanctioned the entire process in a September 1968 press conference, declaring that "there are two extreme groups [on this issue]. There are those who want instant integration and those who want segregation forever. I believe we need to have a middle course between those two extremes." What the president had done, of course, was to define obedience to the law as one extreme, and violation of the law as another, thereby aligning himself explicitly with white Southerners who ever since 1954 had been pursuing a strategy of circumventing change by calling integration "extremist."

Simultaneously, Nixon proceeded on the second prong of his Southern strategy—to appoint conservative Southern judges to the Supreme Court while lambasting that court's record as a leading innovator on issues of social justice. Ever since the *Brown* decision, the Warren Court had systematically lowered the remaining legal barriers to racial integration in schools, jobs, and public accommodations. In addition, it had broken new ground in such volatile areas as equal political representation (one man, one vote), guaranteeing the right of the accused to counsel (*Miranda* and *Gideon*), and protecting free speech, even where questions of pornography were involved. From the point of view of Nixon and most conservatives, the court had expanded its purview far beyond the areas assigned it under the Constitution; indeed, conservatives believed that court decisions reflected a near conspiracy of elite, Eastern liberals to impose an alien social philosophy on the land.

Committed to reversing this trend, Nixon successfully nominated Warren Burger, a hard-line conservative, to replace departed Chief Justice Earl Warren in the spring of 1969. Then, when Justice Abe Fortas resigned, Nixon fulfilled his campaign promise to the South, choosing one of Strom

Thurmond's associates from South Carolina, Clement Haynsworth, as Fortas's replacement. Ignoring the fact that the Fortas seat had been held by a Jewish American for fifty-three years, Nixon reached out to his new constituency, choosing a man of his own ideological persuasion who in two critical cases before the Fourth Circuit Court of Appeals had voted on the side of segregationists, and in a bitter labor case had sided with the textile industry.

Although no one questioned Haynsworth's legal credentials, civil rights and labor forces were outraged by the nomination, particularly in the aftermath of Nixon's other activities against civil rights. Nixon's nominee, AFL-CIO chief George Meany claimed, was indifferent to the "legitimate aspirations of Negroes." Northern Republicans like Minority Leader Hugh Scott and his assistant Robert Griffin also were concerned, and after lengthy hearings, the Haynsworth nomination failed on the Senate floor, seventeen Republicans joining the Democrats in overturning the president's recommendation.

Not to be outdone, Nixon immediately insisted on sending to the Senate another nominee of the same political persuasion, only this time far less qualified. "You know," one White House aide said, "the President really *believes* in that Southern strategy—more than he believes in anything else." Nixon's nominee this time was Judge G. Harrold Carswell, a member of the Fifth Circuit Court of Appeals in Florida. As if to flaunt his right to name anyone, Nixon ignored Carswell's disreputable record. Carswell had participated in a scheme by white segregationists to purchase a formerly public golf course in Tallahassee in order to prevent its being integrated, and he had declared his belief in white supremacy during a race for the Georgia state legislature in 1948. Repeatedly his rulings had been overturned by higher courts—a clear mark of judicial inadequacy. Nearly half of his colleagues on the Fifth Judicial Circuit refused to sign a letter endorsing him, and nine out of fifteen professors at the University of Florida law school explicitly opposed his nomination. Even Carswell's advocates were defensive. "There are lots of mediocre judges," one Republican Senator declared. "[Mediocre people] are entitled to a little representation, aren't they?" Although Nixon rallied to the defense of his nominee, the president's shoddy handling of an inferior nomination doomed it to defeat, with thirteen Republicans once again joining in the opposition. Yet, politically, Nixon had advanced his strategy, denouncing Eastern intellectuals and telling the country in a public statement that the real issue behind the rejection of Carswell and Haynsworth was the fact that they came from the South. If Nixon had consciously searched for the most effective way to advance his standing with Southern conservatives, he could not have struck upon a better course.

The final stage of the Mitchell-Phillips strategy involved Vice-President Spiro Agnew's vicious denunciation of the Eastern intellectual elite. Uncomfortable with his administrative duties and disliked by his colleagues on

Capitol Hill where he presided over the Senate, Agnew quickly became Nixon's hatchet man—"Nixon's Nixon." As early as June 1969, the vice-president lashed out at campus demonstrators and antiwar protestors. But in a commencement address at Ohio State University, he saved his harshest words for the "sniveling, hand-wringing power structure [that] deserves the violent rebellion it encourages." If young radicals were the front-line troops, Agnew implied, the Northeastern liberal "establishment" represented the generals sending them into battle. Agnew laced his remarks with scarcely veiled sexual imagery designed to call into question the manhood of those who opposed the president. "A spirit of national masochism" was spreading across the land, Agnew told a New Orleans audience, "encouraged by an effete corps of impudent snobs who characterize themselves as intellectuals." Those who supported antiwar demonstrations, Agnew declared, were "ideological eunuchs." While Nixon on occasion might still take the high ground of national unity, Agnew laid bare the administration's real political strategy. "Small cadres of professional protesters [linked with] avowed anarchists and communists who detest everything about this country," he told a Pennsylvania audience, "are attempting to jeopardize the peace efforts of the President of the United States.":

> It is time to question the credentials of their leaders. And, if in questioning we disturb a few people, I say it is time for them to be disturbed. If in challenging, we polarize the American people, I say it is time for a positive polarization. . . . It is time to rip away the rhetoric and to divide on authentic lines.

Thus, by the middle of 1970, the Nixon administration had explicitly as well as implicitly endorsed a political course of seeking a conservative ascendancy through polarization. There were, to be sure, occasional echoes of the "new" Nixon of the First Inaugural, especially when astronauts Neil Armstrong and "Buzz" Aldrin landed on the moon in July 1969, announcing to a global audience: "that's one small step for man, one giant leap for mankind." Sharing the television screen with the moonwalkers, Nixon declared via telephone connection: "For one priceless moment in the whole history of man, all the people of this earth are truly one." But even the conquest of space fit Nixon's larger effort to rally conservatives and the right, especially in the Sun Belt and among Middle Americans. As *Time* magazine commented of the astronauts: "redolent of charcoal cookouts, their vocabularies an engaging mix of space jargon and 'gee whiz,' the space explorers gave back to Middle America a victory of its own values."

In the meantime, the liberal Republicans in the administration who might have opposed polarization had gone. By the summer of 1970 Finch had transferred from HEW, James Allen was removed as commissioner of education, and Mitchell—called "El Supremo" by his aides—presided over all. Nixon himself functioned in splendid isolation at the White House, cut off from most of his cabinet by personal aides H. R. Haldeman and John Ehrlichman whose primary qualifications were total devotion to the president. Eagle scouts, non-smokers, and nondrinkers, the two veterans of Nixon's California years were alternately dubbed by the press as the "Beaver Patrol," the "Germans," Rosenkrantz and Guildenstern, or "Tweedle-dee and Tweedle-dum." Both men reinforced Nixon's own tendency toward reclusiveness, and with a few others like National Security Aide Henry Kissinger, created a White House structure that fed Nixon's megalomania, and his conviction that he alone could forge a conservative majority that would destroy the liberal opposition.

Foreign Policy

Whatever his concerns about domestic politics, Richard Nixon understood that changing American policy in Vietnam represented the essential prerequisite for his own place in history. Vietnam, a Nixon speech writer noted, had become "a bone in the nation's throat" that had to be cleared away for the Nixon presidency to be successful. "I'm not going to end up like LBJ," Nixon remarked, "holed up in the White House afraid to show my face on the street. I'm going to stop that war. Fast." Throughout his 1968 campaign, Nixon had referred repeatedly to his own secret plan to accomplish his objective. Although he avoided revealing any details of the plan all during the summer and fall of 1968, the time was fast approaching when equivocation must give way to action.

The new president faced a dilemma both in politics and policy. Throughout the Vietnam War, Nixon had advocated increased American involvement in Southeast Asia, frequently urging the Johnson administration to escalate the war, bomb more North Vietnamese cities, and even destroy the dikes and water system of North Vietnam, flooding the countryside. In the president's view, any American withdrawal from Southeast Asia had to be based on preserving an independent, pro-U.S. government in Saigon. "We would destroy ourselves if we pulled out in a way that really wasn't honorable," he told a journalist in May of 1969. Yet, politically, Nixon also understood the necessity of getting American troops out of combat. His own National Security Agency predicted that another eight years of full American participation would be required to eradicate the Vietcong threat. Clearly, *that* route was unacceptable. Furthermore, Secretary of Defense Melvin Laird pushed vigorously for gradual disengagement of American troops. How, then, could Nixon devise a policy that would acknowledge the political imperative of getting American soldiers home, while simultaneously "winning the war."

In fact, Nixon did have a "secret" plan to end the war. During the previous August, in an off-the-record session with Southern delegates to the Republican Convention, Nixon recalled that, when Eisenhower was elected, "we . . . had this messy war on our hands [in Korea]. Eisenhower let the word go out . . . to the Chinese and the North Koreans that we would not tolerate this continual ground war of attrition. And within a matter of months, they negotiated." Eisenhower, of course, had threatened to drop atomic bombs on North Korea, and Nixon, evidently, had the same ploy in mind. In a conversation with H. R. Haldeman in early 1969, Nixon invoked once again the example of Eisenhower's threat, noting that his own plan was based on "the madman theory. . . . I want the North Vietnamese to believe I've reached the point where I might do *anything* to stop the war. We'll just slip the word to them that, 'for God sakes, you know Nixon is obsessed about communists. We can't restrain him when he's angry—and he has his hand on the nuclear button'—and Ho Chi Minh himself will be in Paris in two days begging for peace." Thus, it appeared that Nixon's "hole" card was to threaten the annihilation of North Vietnam.

In the meantime, Nixon recognized the need to proceed—at least publicly—with the appearance of altering the Johnson administration's policy. On May 14, the president addressed the nation proposing a new formula for ending the war, including the mutual withdrawal from South Vietnam of both American and North Vietnamese troops, and an internationally supervised cease-fire. Anticipating what would soon become known as "Vietnamization," Nixon declared: "The time is approaching when the South Vietnamese forces will be able to take over some of the fighting fronts now being manned by Americans." One month later, Nixon journeyed to Midway Island in the Pacific to meet with South Vietnamese President Nguyen Thieu and to announce the "Nixon doctrine." According to Nixon, Asian nations would henceforth be expected to exercise more "self-help." "Asian hands must shape the Asian future," Nixon declared. As American troops withdrew, South Vietnamese forces—reinforced by American matériel and bombing missions—would assume the major burden of the fighting. To implement the plan, the United States provided money to increase the South Vietnamese army to more than a million men and supplied massive quantities of new weapons, including over a million M-16 rifles and 40,000 M-79 grenade launchers. In addition, American forces inaugurated "Operation Phoenix"—a systematic assassination campaign aimed at Vietcong cadres, which resulted in the killing of more than 50,000 suspected communist political leaders. From a purely cynical view, Vietnamization simply meant, in Ambassador Ellsworth Bunker's words, changing "the color of the corpses." Yet from a political standpoint, Vietnamization represented an important first payment on Nixon's promissory note to end American involvement in the war.

Still, Vietnamization was a partial policy, designed, in the words of Secretary of the Army Stanley Resor, to "just buy some time in the U.S." in order to bring the war to a successful military conclusion. The North Vietnamese rejected Nixon's new peace proposal because it denied a political settlement favorable to the Vietcong. As Radio Hanoi declared, "The plan of the Nixon administration is not to end the war but to replace the war of aggression fought by U.S. troops with a war of aggression fought by a puppet army of the United States." If Nixon were to realize his objectives, he would still have to proceed with the "secret" plan he had disclosed to the Republican delegates in August.

Secrecy, however, imposed its own constraints. Any open discussion, even within administration circles, of a proposal to threaten North Vietnam with annihilation would inevitably create division. Always reclusive and suspicious, Nixon distrusted senior cabinet officials like Secretary of State William Rogers and Defense Secretary Melvin Laird, not to mention their respective bureaucracies. Laird and Rogers were "moderates," wary of any action that would destabilize international relations and fearful of domestic political response to belligerency in Vietnam. Hence, from the very beginning, Nixon avoided any forthright debate over his foreign policy objectives with his chief cabinet officials and insisted—with an almost paranoid obsession—on pursuing the *real* objectives of his foreign policy within the narrow confines of the White House, as if the State and Defense departments were enemies within, to be foiled and deceived.

It was here that Henry Kissinger, and the Kissinger-Nixon relationship, became central to Nixon's objectives. On the surface, the two men could not have been further apart. Kissinger was German-born, Harvard trained, and a brilliant intellectual. After serving in World War II, he quickly soared to the top of his profession as an international relations expert. While teaching at Harvard, he served as foreign policy advisor to Kennedy and Johnson, and became Nelson Rockefeller's intimate friend and chief expert on foreign affairs. Witty, sardonic, and given to frequent denunciations of Nixon, Kissinger appeared to be an archetypal example of the Eastern foreign policy elite that Nixon abhorred. Yet as historian George Herring has pointed out, the two men also shared a passionate desire for power and an overriding ambition to make history. "Loners and outsiders in their own professions," each found it easy to set aside their differences in order to indulge a common "penchant for secrecy and intrigue and . . . a flare for the unexpected move." The two men discovered in each other a shared instinct to plot and conspire, seize and guard power. At their best, they made possible remarkable breakthroughs in foreign policy, particularly with regard to China and the Soviet Union. But at their worst (which was simply the other side of their best), they engaged in flagrant violations of constitutional power and reckless use of military force to achieve foreign policy ends.

Perhaps appropriately, Kissinger achieved his entrée into Nixon's inner circle through Machiavellian cynicism and subterfuge. Desperate for access to power in 1968, whichever administration was elected, Kissinger had carefully—and secretly—sent out feelers to both the Humphrey and Nixon camps. Already known in Democratic circles for his contempt of Nixon, Kissinger offered his services to Humphrey, even indicating his willingness to make available to Humphrey's foreign policy advisors all of Rockefeller's private files on Nixon—described by Kissinger as the Nixon "shit files." "Look," Kissinger said, "I've hated Nixon for years." Humphrey told aides that Kissinger was working for him, and that, if elected, he would put

"Henry in the national security spot." Simultaneously, however, Kissinger approached the Nixon camp with a promise to provide classified information on what was taking place in the Paris peace talks. Kissinger had already initiated clandestine meetings with Richard Allen, Nixon's foreign policy advisor, at the Republican Convention and, in September, told Allen that he would contact his sources in Paris and provide Nixon with intelligence that would enable the Republican nominee to forestall, or at least counteract, any dramatic move toward peace by the Johnson administration that would aid Humphrey's campaign.

True to his word, Kissinger returned from meetings with the U.S. peace delegation in Paris to report to Nixon that "something big was afoot regarding Vietnam." In fact, American and North Vietnamese negotiators had achieved a breakthrough, and in a final telephone call before the election, Kissinger told Richard Allen that Ambassador Averell Harriman had "broken open the champagne" because a bombing halt had been achieved, pending approval by the South Vietnamese government. At that point, high officials in the Nixon campaign immediately mobilized right-wing contacts with the Saigon regime to pressure South Vietnam to denounce the agreement, pledging that a Republican administration would be more sympathetic. Humphrey was already closing the gap between himself and Nixon, and when President Thieu publicly repudiated the breakthrough three days before the American election, his action seriously impaired Humphrey's final push. In short, Kissinger's secret warnings had been instrumental in deflecting, if not destroying, Humphrey's possibility of securing victory. Even at *that* time, however, Kissinger was still keeping his options open, writing to Humphrey of his personal dislike for Nixon and his availability to serve the Humphrey administration.

Few people in November 1968, of course, were aware of Kissinger's ploy, particularly given his obsession with secrecy. But he achieved his objective. As Richard Allen later recalled, "My attitude was that it was inevitable that Kissinger would have to be part of our administration. . . . Kissinger had proven his mettle by tipping us. It took some balls to give us those tips." Mitchell and Nixon were fully cognizant of the risks Kissinger had taken—indeed, that he had violated Harriman's confidence, had shared classified information, and had potentially sabotaged a vital agreement in the peace process. Shortly after the election, Nixon called Kissinger to the Hotel Pierre in New York and offered the Harvard professor the prize he so deeply desired. Kissinger would be National Security Advisor in the Nixon administration.*

---

* In the course of these machinations, Kissinger also displayed his skill with the press. During the campaign, Nixon had told columnist Joseph Kraft that Kissinger was a likely nominee for the national security job. Bumping into Kissinger at an airport, Kraft conveyed Nixon's words. Petrified that news of his role with the Nixon camp would leak out, Kissinger called Kraft numerous times the same day urging him to keep the information secret, lest anyone put two and two together and find out about his secret conversations with the Nixon administration.

Quickly sizing up his boss, Kissinger readily became an accomplice in Nixon's "secret" strategy for ending the war. Any "fourth rate power like North Vietnam," Kissinger declared, must have a "breaking point," and the new National Security Advisor immediately endorsed Nixon's plan to threaten escalation in Vietnam in private, even as he adopted a policy of restraint in public. Furthermore, Kissinger saw in Nixon's impulse toward secrecy a ready-made vehicle for enhancing his own personal power over foreign policy by concentrating all decision-making authority in the White House. By forging a personal alliance with Nixon against other foreign policy actors, Kissinger could magnify his own role, aggrandize power for himself, and assure that those who potentially might undermine his influence were denied any audience or consideration.

One immediate consequence of the Kissinger-Nixon modus operandi was the almost total exclusion of the State Department, and particularly Secretary of State William Rogers, from foreign policy decisions. Although Rogers was one of Nixon's oldest and closest friends, he understood from the beginning that Nixon wished to run his own foreign policy. But Rogers had no conception of how far Kissinger and Nixon would go to accomplish that goal. With Nixon's agreement, Kissinger initiated "back channel" contacts with almost all important officials representing the United States abroad. Although regular diplomatic cables continued to go to the State Department, all sensitive and classified material came to Kissinger only, with State and Defense department officials left in the dark. Diplomats and generals cooperated with the secret system as a means of preserving their own access to power; and those who violated the "back channel" by revealing its existence quickly found themselves frozen out. A virtual two-tier system of government thus became established, with those in power making inside jokes about the ineffectual role of State and Defense department officials, and those on the outside increasingly conscious of their isolation and impotence.

By the summer of 1969, Nixon and Kissinger had thoroughly mastered the process of excluding their own professional foreign service from any significant role in shaping policy. Starting in February, Kissinger held a series of private meetings with Soviet Ambassador Anatoly Dobrynin. Secretary of State Rogers was not invited to the meetings, and Dobrynin understood from that point forward that his most important substantive contact would take place through Kissinger. Rogers was not consulted about the first letter from Nixon to Soviet Premier Alexei Kosygin, and when Ambassador Jacob Beam disclosed its contents to the Secretary of State, Nixon and Kissinger admonished him for his indiscretion. All important foreign policy speeches were written at the White House and, whenever possible, were sent only at the last moment to the State and Defense Department for clearance. Rogers was not even aware of Kissinger's secret trips to Paris to negotiate informally with the North Vietnamese. On one occasion when Rogers called Attorney General John Mitchell to complain, Mitchell instructed an aide to tell the secretary of state that he was not in. When Rogers left a message that he wanted information on what was going on in Paris, Mitchell exclaimed: "He's not supposed to know." So complete did White House control over foreign affairs become that the State Department's Romanian desk did not find out until one hour before a formal announcement was made that the president was about to become the first chief executive to visit a communist country.

The principal rationale for such actions, of course, was to free Nixon and Kissinger to pursue more effectively their private strategy of escalating the war in Vietnam. Beginning in February, Kissinger used his "back channel" conversations with Dobrynin to convey America's threat to widen the war if North Vietnam did not become more responsive. Nixon and Kissinger then struck upon the idea of massive bombing raids against communist bases in neutral Cambodia. Knowing that the State Department would raise objections, Kissinger and Nixon devised an intricate plot to accomplish their objective in total secrecy. Kissinger instructed military aides to send B-52 bombers into action over South Vietnam, with a few selected squadrons given orders at the last minute—while in the air—to proceed to new targets over Cambodia and with pilot reports altered, so that no official military record ever existed of the engagements. Although the immediate objective of destroying the North Vietnamese headquarters in Cambodia failed abysmally, Kissinger and Nixon reasoned that the sustained secret air war would help convey to the North Vietnamese the gist of the "madman theory"—that there were officials in Washington willing, without compunction, to use whatever arbitrary force they controlled to coerce a settlement. The entire operation—encompassing 3,630 flights over Cambodia that dropped 110,000 tons of bombs—operated out of Kissinger's office. When the secret bombing was revealed during the Watergate crisis of 1973, Kissinger contended that the White House "neither ordered nor was it aware of any falsification of records" regarding the bombing. "I think it's deplorable," he told one reporter.

After the secret bombing of Cambodia failed to bring the North Vietnamese to their knees, Kissinger and Nixon sought other ways to communicate their intentions to the enemy. Kissinger put staff aides to work on operation "Duck-Hook," a proposed escalation of the war that would involve bombing Hanoi, destroying the dike system that controlled North Vietnamese water supplies, and mining Haiphong harbor. (According to some White House assistants, Kissinger and Nixon also considered using atomic weapons on North Vietnam during the spring and fall of 1969. "The Old Man is going to drop the bomb before the year is out and that will be the end of the war," H. R. Haldeman told Charles Colson.) When Laird and Rogers heard of "Duck-Hook," however, they reacted with vigorous opposition. At the same time, antiwar sentiment in the United States mushroomed, culminating in demonstrations on October 15 that involved more than 2 million Americans. Reluctantly, Nixon concluded that he could not afford the political upheaval that would ensue were he to proceed with

"Duck-Hook" and, instead, went on nationwide TV on November 3 to rally the "silent majority" to his position of standing fast against North Vietnam while gradually withdrawing American troops. For the moment, Nixon's "go for broke" plan of inflicting "savage, punishing blows" against North Vietnam was shelved. But the long-range plan remained intact, confirmed when Nixon and Kissinger decided in October to place the Strategic Air Command on full alert for twenty-nine days. All B-52 planes were taken off routine duty, lined up in take-off positions on runways across the world, fully armed with nuclear weapons. There was no crisis to justify the alert, nor any public announcement of it. Rather, one military aide noted, the purpose was to increase fear in the Soviet Union about the man at the helm of the U.S. government, to give them pause and cause them to ask "what in the hell is [Nixon] doing?"

By the end of 1969, a clear pattern had emerged in the foreign policy apparatus in Washington, with the hard-line impulses of Kissinger and Nixon straining against pleas for caution from Rogers and Laird. After a North Korean fighter plane shot down an unarmed Navy spy plane over international waters in April 1969, for example, Nixon wanted to strike back against North Korea with B-52s. Kissinger, according to H. R. Haldeman, even considered "the possible necessity of nuclear bombing as a bottom line." But the crisis was a public one, triggering four days of intense debate that included Laird and Rogers. Intelligence information revealed that the incident was not preplanned, but rather involved an error on the part of a single North Korean pilot who had misunderstood instructions. Counsels of moderation prevailed, and the administration's response took the form of diplomatic action rather than military reprisal.

A similar scenario developed more than a year later in the Middle East when terrorists of the Palestine Liberation Organization highjacked four Western civilian planes and flew 500 hostages to a Jordanian airport, threatening to kill them unless PLO terrorists were released from prison. The Middle East was one area that Kissinger had left to Rogers and the State Department. Now, with the highjacking, Kissinger reasserted White House control over the area. Nixon, with Kissinger's support, determined to use the crisis as an occasion for destroying the PLO and actually ordered American Navy planes to bomb and destroy PLO bases. Secretary of Defense Melvin Laird refused to carry out the order, telling the White House that "bad weather" in the area made the air strikes impossible. In Laird's view, "conducting an air operation would have been incredibly dumb," having as its only objective confrontation with the Soviet Union. As the crisis evolved, Jordan's King Hussein carried out his own successful military attack against the PLO, but throughout the crucial affair Nixon threatened American military intervention in what he and Kissinger perceived as a direct conflict with the Soviet Union. In fact, Russia appears to have played a moderating role in the crisis, by persuading the Syrians to withdraw their tanks from Jordanian territory and by not intervening to assist the PLO in its battle with Hussein. The crisis ended with the United States, ironically, benefiting from its apparent restraint. But only direct disobedience of an order by Laird, and cautionary advice from Laird and Rogers, prevented military action that could have led to a confrontation with the Soviets.

The election of Salvadore Allende, a Marxist, as Chile's new president in the fall of 1970 provided the most glaring example of Nixon and Kissinger's penchant for intervention. Although the State Department clearly had no desire to see a Marxist regime in such a pivotal South American country, it was willing to abide by the election results. But the CIA, with Nixon and Kissinger's complete support, was intent on preventing Allende from ever taking office. When Edward Korry, the American ambassador to Chile, explicitly opposed any CIA effort to subvert the election results, Nixon and Kissinger united once again in "back channel" efforts in support of CIA activities, unbeknownst to the ambassador. Convening a meeting attended by John Mitchell, CIA Director Richard Helms, and Kissinger, Nixon authorized the expenditure of as much as $10 million and the use of "whatever means necessary" to stop Allende. "If I ever carried the marshall's baton in my knapsack out of the Oval Office, it was that day," Helms later told the Senate Intelligence Committee. Indeed, Nixon appeared to have ordered the "elimination" of Allende.

With virtually no outsiders involved except for Kissinger and his CIA contacts, intelligence officials proceeded to recruit agents in and out of Chile who would coordinate either a miliary coup to prevent Allende's inauguration or accomplish the goal through more direct means. All communications were handled secretly. Following Nixon's orders, Kissinger pushed intelligence officials to provide arms and money to at least two factions in Chile thought to be capable of carrying out the president's orders. Although Nixon and Kissinger would later deny it, CIA headquarters cabled their agent in Chile on October 16 that "it is firm and continuing policy that Allende be overcome by a coup. . . . We are to continue to generate maximum pressure toward this end, utilizing every appropriate resource." Kissinger later wrote that he had ordered a cessation of all coup planning on October 15, but his closest aide, Alexander Haig, met with coup planners as late as October 19. That night, and the next, one of the Chilean groups seeking to prevent Allende's inauguration attempted to kidnap the Chilean general most opposed to a coup, believing that in the general's absence other military officials would be more agreeable to seizing power. Two days later the general was assassinated by the same men who had bungled the earlier kidnapping efforts. Although Allende eventually took office, and the Nixon-Kissinger policy of intervention failed for the moment, plans for the assassination of Allende continued to be updated as late as 1971. Two years later, Allende was murdered, and his government toppled in a military coup. The Nixon administration denied any involvement.

Throughout these years, an "us" against "them" attitude increasingly came to dominate the Nixon White House. Nixon and Kissinger were both obsessed about press leaks. When *New York Times* correspondent William Beecher published accurate accounts of administration deliberations about the North Korean spy plane incident in May, and followed up three days later with information about the secret bombing of Cambodia, administration officials were furious. Nixon himself sent enraged memos to Kissinger demanding further action. "He would read the *Times* or the *Post*," one national security aide later noted, "and he would go through story by story and identify the leaks, and every leak was Laird's. 'I see those God-damned, cocksucking stories about troop levels. This is Laird again. The son-of-a-bitch is up to his old games.' What's he trying to do?" Anxious to protect himself, Kissinger flayed at former associates whose dissenting views might impair his own credibility with the president. Thus, when Daniel Ellsberg, a former Kissinger associate, published the Pentagon Papers providing details of the Johnson administration's policy on Vietnam, Kissinger denounced Ellsberg as a fanatic and a drug abuser who was "always a little unbalanced." Ellsberg, Kissinger said, must be stopped at all costs. In a White House dedicated to secrecy, everyone was suspect. Such an atmosphere, of course, simply reinforced the pattern of surveillance already present. Ironically, even Kissinger himself became a victim when one of his military aides systematically Xeroxed classified documents, purloined papers from Kissinger's desk, and even searched Kissinger's luggage on trips to provide information to the Chairman of the Joint Chiefs of Staff.

Nothing better illustrated this "us" against "them" polarization than Nixon's decision to invade Cambodia with American troops in the spring of 1970. Ever since being forced to back down from the "Duck-Hook" proposals of 1969, Nixon had been stymied in trying to find ways to make credible to the North Vietnamese the essence of his "madman theory." Although the secret bombing of Cambodia continued, the North Vietnamese still used Cambodian territory as a base to attack South Vietnam. With greater numbers of American troops being withdrawn every day, the ability to win the war *and* preserve a pro-American government in the South had become even more problematic. As a result, Nixon suddenly determined to "go for broke" and send American forces into Cambodia to destroy the central headquarters of the North Vietnamese army that had eluded American bombers the previous year. The invasion of a neutral country was a huge risk. Laird and Rogers had been willing to go along with incursions by South Vietnamese troops, but both men resisted emphatically the plan to send large numbers of American troops into a country where previously they had never fought. Both men feared—correctly—the domestic uproar that would ensue. But Nixon was committed to move, believing that the invasion—part of what he called his "big play philosophy"—would be a bold action that would stun the enemy and coerce him into concessions. Furthermore, Nixon was intent on retaliating against those who were attacking him at home. "Those senators think they can push Nixon around on Haynsworth and Carswell," he said at the time. "We'll show them who's tough."

Increasingly defensive and paranoid, Nixon sought to rally the country by throwing down the gauntlet in a nationwide speech. This was to be another of those ritual "crises" where Nixon would show that he could transcend the opposition and achieve greatness. The Cambodian invasion, he declared, was a test of both his own and America's courage under fire. "We will not be humiliated," he declared, "we will not be defeated. If when the chips are down the U.S. acts like a pitiful helpless giant, the forces of totalitarianism will threaten free nations and free institutions throughout the world. It is *not our power but our will* that is being tested tonight." Nixon even claimed that he was putting his own political future up for grabs by the decision. "I would rather be a one-term president than a two-term president at the cost of seeing America become a second-rate power." By personalizing the issue, Nixon attempted to justify both himself and his policies, raising to a level of Churchillian heroics the massive gamble he had undertaken.

As the president himself had predicted, the Cambodian invasion provoked an immediate outcry of anger. Nixon had written his own speech, showing it to only a few associates; but many "cringed" when they saw it, and Secretary of State William Rogers was outraged. "Unite the country!" he fumed. "This will make the students puke." Tony Lake and John Morris resigned from the National Security Council staff in protest, while others beseeched Kissinger to intervene. (Kissinger called them "my bleeding hearts club.") When one Kissinger aide persisted, Kissinger retorted: "Your views represent the cowardice of the Eastern Establishment," and Alexander Haig declared: "you just had an order from your Commander-in-Chief and you can't refuse." "Fuck you, Al," the aide responded. "I just have, and I've resigned." Students across the country took to the streets in protest, and within days the entire nation was rocked by demonstrations more massive than any seen since the most turbulent days of 1968.*

The invasion itself achieved only marginal success. Once again, the central headquarters of the North Vietnamese army escaped American detection. Although allied forces destroyed over 8,000 bunkers and captured huge deposits of enemy weapons, none of the glorious results anticipated by Nixon came to pass. Instead, Cambodia lost its neutrality, North Vietnam became ever more committed to supporting Cambodian rebels in their own revolution, and the United States was condemned throughout the world for its aggression. To be sure, Nixon bought time to solidify the process of Vietnamization, and the Russians, as well as the North Vietnamese, had been given a clear indication of how far Nixon would go to achieve his goals. But in the long run, the basic result was simply more stalemate—in a context of ever-growing polarization at home.

Although increasingly frustrated, Nixon insisted on playing out the same scenario over the next two and a half years, combining withdrawal of American troops with repeated displays of military intimidation. The next major escalation occurred with the Laos invasion of early 1971. Already committed to withdrawing an additional 100,000 troops by the end of 1971

---

* These demonstrations and their aftermath will be discussed in the next section.

(leaving 175,000 Americans there, compared to 543,000 when he took office), Nixon reasoned that an aggressive military campaign by the South Vietnamese army against critical enemy bases in Laos would both buy time for Vietnamization and test the mettle of the South Vietnamese forces. (Use of American combat troops in Laos and Cambodia had been prohibited by Congress after the Cambodian invasion.) Once again, however, the military option failed. As the historian George Herring observed, "the Laotian operation was at best a costly draw, at worst an unmitigated disaster." The South Vietnamese army was riddled with Vietcong agents, and the North Vietnamese learned in advance—to the last detail—every objective of the invading forces. The dense Laotian forest became a trap for the South Vietnamese, and after six weeks of bloody fighting, Saigon forces retreated in disarray, this time with American TV cameras providing vivid pictures of South Vietnamese troops clinging to the skids of American helicopters, desperately seeking escape from the enemy they were supposed to destroy. Back at home, the political response was equally disastrous, with 71 percent of the American people agreeing by the summer of 1971 that the United States had made a mistake in sending troops to Vietnam.

For a brief period, negotiations appeared to have a chance of success. At the secret meetings in Paris, Kissinger offered to withdraw all American troops within six months of an agreement in exchange for the release of all American prisoners of war (POWs). No mention was made of North Vietnamese forces withdrawing, but continued rule by Thieu was assumed. In response, Hanoi proposed the simultaneous withdrawal of American troops and the release of POWs, but insisted that the United States withhold its support from Thieu in the upcoming presidential elections in South Vietnam, thus permitting—conceivably—open elections that could involve the Vietcong as well. On this sticky point, the Americans balked. Thieu had already forced from the presidential race his primary opponents and was the sole candidate. While America was willing to declare its "neutrality," the words meant nothing with Thieu totally in control of the election machinery. The secret talks broke down in late November, and the North Vietnamese prepared to mount a massive new invasion of the South, comparable in intensity to the Tet offensive four years earlier.

When the North Vietnamese struck in the spring of 1972, Nixon returned to his favorite military option, the long delayed "Duck-Hook" operation. Although only 95,000 American troops were left in Vietnam, a massive response, code named "Linebacker," dwarfed all prior attacks on Vietnam. Haiphong harbor was mined, more than 112,000 tons of bombs were dropped on North Vietnam, and in the South, American planes flew nonstop missions against North Vietnamese bases and supply lines. "The bastards have never been bombed like they are going to be bombed this time," Nixon declared. Only this time, Nixon's response appeared to work. Encouraged by the president's successes with China and Moscow (to be discussed shortly), the American people were more patient, perhaps because American combat troops were not heavily involved. The South Vietnamese managed to hold their major cities, and Thieu remained in power. What the *New York Times* described as Nixon's deliberate campaign of "diplomacy through terror" seemed, for the moment at least, to have succeeded.

There then ensued one final cycle of negotiations, terror, and—finally—peace. During the summer and fall of 1972, Kissinger and Le Duc Tho, his North Vietnamese counterpart, engaged in a furious round of negotiations. Increasingly committed to finding peace, Kissinger offered critical concessions to the North Vietnamese. Not only would they be explicitly allowed to keep their troops in the South but, in addition, responsibility for a final political settlement would be placed in the hands of a National Council of Reconciliation in which the Vietcong would play a significant and internationally recognized role. Tacitly, at least, the agreement would acknowledge both the political legitimacy of the Thieu regime in Saigon *and* Vietcong control over the countryside, with the two political entities working through the National Council of Reconciliation to implement the accord. As a North Vietnamese official later said, the pivotal issue was not to have "the Saigon government [be] *uniquely* lawful. . . . There are to be *two* lawful governments and not only one. This was the minimum." Convinced that he had achieved the breakthrough he wanted, Kissinger went to Saigon where he expected to coerce the Thieu government into accepting the agreements, with Nixon's support.

What Kissinger had not anticipated was the intransigence of Thieu and the duplicity of Nixon. Rarely consulted during the negotiations themselves, Thieu reacted with outrage to Kissinger's entreaties for cooperation. Thieu declared he would never accept a peace settlement that permitted North Vietnamese troops to remain in South Vietnam or that acknowledged Vietcong sovereignty. Nixon, meanwhile, had his own doubts. His private polls showed that he would receive a strong reelection mandate regardless of whether peace was achieved before election day. In addition, Nixon had become more and more alienated from Kissinger over the previous few months, jealous of his prestige as National Security Advisor and angry at what he perceived to be Kissinger's obsession with finding peace at any price. Reinforced in Washington by key aides, including Alexander Haig of Kissinger's staff, Nixon suddenly decided to align himself with Thieu and not to apply pressure on Saigon. Thus, while Kissinger returned to the United States declaring that "peace is at hand," the reality was that the agreements had been scuttled.*

---

* In all of this, the internecine squabbling between Kissinger and Nixon appears to have played a significant role. As Seymour Hersh discloses in his book on Kissinger, Nixon had developed a strong dislike for Kissinger and was planning to replace him as National Security Advisor during his second term. Kissinger, in turn, believed that the only way to secure his position with the president and prevent his dismissal was to achieve a Vietnamese settlement, thereby creating a situation where he would become indispensable (and unremovable) in the president's second term. According to Hersh, Kissinger was acutely conscious of his rivals in the administration, and hoped—ultimately—to use his successes as a basis for securing Nixon's support for his nomination as secretary of state.

Determined to play the last card in his "secret strategy," Nixon resorted one final time to the politics of terror. When the North Vietnamese refused to consider substantive changes in the peace agreement, Nixon, bolstered by his overwhelming re-election, determined to make the enemy either settle on his terms or "face the consequences of what we could do to them." Deciding to reinforce the Thieu regime, Nixon sent over $1 billion of military equipment to the South Vietnamese and offered secret assurances that he personally would order "swift and severe retaliatory action" if the North Vietnamese violated the peace accords. Then, to show that his word had substance, Nixon ordered the most massive bombing yet of North Vietnam during Christmas week 1972. "I don't want any more of this crap about the fact that we can't hit this target or that one," he told the Joint Chiefs of Staff. "This is your chance to use military power to win this war, and if you don't, I'll consider you responsible." Sending B-52s directly over Hanoi and Haiphong, Nixon seemed to be trying to bomb the North Vietnamese into submission, laying waste factories, hospitals, residential districts, airports, and bus and train stations. The president was acting like a "madman," critics declared, seeking to "wage war by tantrum."

When North Vietnam returned to the negotiating table in Paris in early January, it took only one week to finalize a new settlement. Almost exactly identical to the one agreed on in October, the new agreement nevertheless contained enough minor changes to permit Nixon to impose it on South Vietnam. It had taken four years for Nixon's "secret plan" to achieve results. During that period, more than 107,000 South Vietnamese soldiers and more than half a million enemy troops had been killed. More than 20,000 additional Americans died as well—more than 50 percent of the total number killed during the entire Vietnamese conflict. In all likelihood, the peace accords that were finally signed in January 1973 could have been negotiated four years earlier. In the name of credibility, honor, and patriotism, hundreds of thousands of lives had been lost. At best, Nixon's secret plan represented the acting out of a bully's fantasies. At worst, it represented a criminal abuse of human rights that in the eyes of some was the equivalent of genocide.

Ironically, what made all of this acceptable to the American people was the brilliance with which Kissinger and Nixon carried out their other long-range plan—rapprochement with the People's Republic of China. Although secrecy and the "back channel" may not have been *necessary* to assure success, the mystery surrounding the sudden announcement that Kissinger had visited Peking and that Nixon would meet Chairman Mao contributed substantially to an aura of romance, excitement, and triumph. In this instance, at least, the private machinations of the Nixon White House seemed to have created a positive result. "You're not going to believe this," one White House aide reported early in the administration, "but Nixon wants to recognize China." With the same sureness of purpose that he had devoted to his secret strategy in Vietnam, but with more intelligence and common sense, Nixon proceeded to achieve his objective.

The history of Chinese-American relations between 1969 and 1972 was like a delicately balanced ballet. At ambassadorial meetings between the U.S. and Chinese representatives in Warsaw, official representatives explored gingerly, then with increasing enthusiasm, the prospect for high-level meetings. From the start, Nixon understood that he would have to agree to withdraw American forces from Taiwan as a precondition for normalization of relations, but Nixon was ready to pay that price, and as a conservative Republican with a long anticommunist history, he was perhaps the only one who could do so with ease. Meanwhile, Nixon and Kissinger established their own secret communications with the Chinese through Romania and Pakistan. During the fall of 1970 and the spring of 1971, the pace of signaling between the two countries accelerated. "If there is anything I want to do before I die," Nixon told *Time* magazine, "it is to go to China." Later in October, Nixon publicly referred to the "People's Republic of China" in a toast to the visiting Romanian president, the first time he had ever used China's official name instead of referring to "Red China."

By 1971, everything seemed to be falling into place, at precisely the moment when Kissinger and Nixon desperately needed a foreign policy success to overcome the humiliation of the Laos invasion and growing domestic anger at their failures in Vietnam. If Nixon could bring off a China summit, then combine it with rapprochement with the Soviet Union, all other foreign policy liabilities would be erased. In January 1971, Chou indicated his readiness to receive a presidential representative. Understanding the political importance to Nixon of a 1972 visit, the Chinese also agreed to consider a presidential trip to China approximately eight months before the election. In a public indication of its new flexibility, China invited a U.S. ping pong team to play in Peking in April 1971. Nixon immediately reciprocated by publicly announcing trade concessions to the Chinese. Two months later, Henry Kissinger boarded an airplane with his staff for a tour of South Asia. Unbeknownst to anyone except his closest aides, the real purpose of the trip was to visit Peking. Pleading illness in Pakistan that required him to rest (and using well the Pakistani "back channel"), Kissinger departed for his meetings with China's leadership. Over the next two days of discussion, the presidential envoy formalized all the prior communications between the two nations. The United States would publicly announce its commitment to withdraw troops from Taiwan; China, in turn, would pledge its cooperation in urging the North Vietnamese to accept a negotiated settlement that would leave Thieu in power. It was a brilliant bargain, consummated amidst an aura of intrigue. Not even Secretary of State Rogers was told of Kissinger's mission until after he had left. When the nation heard the news from Nixon five days later, it was as if a new era of excitement and challenge had opened. The president suddenly had become a bold and imaginative statesman.

By the time Nixon arrived in Peking in February 1972, the stage was set for a masterful triumph. Understanding the politics of America's mass media, the Chinese provided TV facilities for all three networks. Daily reports from the Great Wall, the Imperial Palace, and other sites of legendary glamour flooded American homes. As one reporter declared, "the White House was playing this as a pageant, not as a news story. . . . It was the big social event of the year." No story could be more romantic than America finally achieving reconciliation with an old friend turned enemy. After twenty-five years, ties between the two nations had been renewed. Nixon was the instrument of the reconciliation and, inevitably, the chief beneficiary of all the positive response it provoked. If China was with him, Nixon could afford to risk unpopularity over Vietnam and persist in his secret strategy of intimidation and threat.

With equal skill, Kissinger and Nixon also brokered a new spirit of détente between the Soviet Union and the United States, culminating in a Moscow summit in May 1972 in which Nixon and Soviet leader Leonid Brezhnev initialed a Strategic Arms Limitation Treaty (SALT). The White House understood well the importance of using China and the Soviet Union as levers against each other, correctly perceiving that in a triangular relationship neither communist power would wish to be outflanked by the other entering into a tacit alliance with the United States. By the end of the 1960s, it was clear that China and the Soviet Union viewed each other with greater suspicion and hostility than either viewed the United States. If America could seize the strategic potential implicit in this animosity, it could drive a permanent split between the two communist superpowers and, simultaneously, use its relationship with both as a means of exercising greater control over world affairs.

The summit meeting in Moscow between Nixon and Brezhnev just four months before the 1972 election proved a stunning success, culminating years of informal negotiating. The Kissinger-Dobrynin "back channel" had produced breakthroughs on multiple fronts. The Soviet Union was able to purchase more than 400 million tons of American grain to satisfy a desperate Russian need for more wheat. During 1972 alone, Soviet-American trade tripled, and the New York Times gave its "Businessman of the Year" award to Brezhnev. The new relationship continued despite Nixon's decision to bomb Hanoi and mine Haiphong harbor in the spring of 1972, acts which resulted in the sinking of at least one Russian ship and a loss of numerous Soviet lives. Although some feared that the president's Vietnam action might force a cancellation of the Moscow summit, the Russians decided to proceed, with Brezhnev even fulfilling his promise to exert influence on the North Vietnamese to tone down their demands to procure a settlement in Vietnam. Now, the relationship came to fruition. With furious last-minute negotiations, a SALT treaty was achieved and signed, representing, by anyone's standards, an unprecedented breakthrough in Soviet-American relations.

Nixon's successes with Russia and China helped him retrieve the political popularity at home that seemed so much at risk after the Laos invasion in 1971. A virulently anticommunist president had been able to forge diplomatic agreements that no Democrat would have been able to envision without suffering sharp right-wing assaults. In this instance, at least, diplomacy had proven both effective on the international front and successful in mobilizing political support at home. Yet the price for such successes had been extraordinary. Hundreds of thousands of lives were lost in Vietnam, and, on more than one occasion, irrational and reckless White House actions threatened to produce direct military conflict with the Soviet Union. Nixon and Kissinger achieved their goals with China and the Soviet Union, but the intrigue, paranoia, and reliance on "madman theories" of intimidation that accompanied their success did not bode well for the future health of American foreign policy decision-making. Ultimately, such characteristics would destroy the Nixon presidency. Americans could only feel lucky that, in the process, the same characteristics did not destroy the nation as well.

The Demise of the Left

As might have been expected, Nixon's policies quickly revitalized the antiwar movement. On October 15, 1969, nearly 2 million Americans took to the streets in a nationwide "moratorium" demanding an end to the war. When Nixon responded with his famous "silent majority" speech, railing against the demonstrators and declaring that "North Vietnam cannot defeat or humiliate the United States—only Americans can do that," more than 300,000 dissidents marched on Washington urging immediate action toward peace. Poignantly, more than 43,000 demonstrators paraded silently around the White House to commemorate those Americans who had died in Vietnam. One simple homemade sign read: "All too long I [have] dwelt with those who hate peace."

With increasing frequency, the antiwar movement focused on draft resistance and dissent within the armed forces themselves. According to the Selective Service Center in Oakland, more than half of those called to serve never responded. Another 11 percent who *did* appear refused to serve. The resistance movement spread like wildfire, with protestors burning their draft cards at antiwar rallies and activists conducting raids on Selective Service offices and destroying as many as half a million draft files. Inside the Army, desertions multiplied, until by 1970, almost 70,000 American soldiers fled their assigned duties. One journalist reported that half the members of an American platoon in Vietnam wore black armbands as a sign of their sympathy with the peace movement, and an Army colonel noted that "symbolic anti-war fasts, peace symbols, booing and cursing of officers . . . , are commonplace." One entire battalion conducted a sit-down strike in Vietnam, refusing to go into battle. "By every conceivable indicator," a colonel observed, "our Army that now remains in Vietnam is in a state of approaching collapse."

Students continued to constitute a cutting edge of the antiwar movement. A *Fortune* magazine survey in 1970 reported that three-quarters of a million college students identified with the New Left. According to a second survey 76 percent of American college students believed that "basic changes in the system" would be necessary to improve life in America. When George Gallup tested student viewpoints on the war in December 1969, he discovered that by a ratio of 3 to 1, those who proclaimed themselves "doves" outnumbered "hawks." President Nixon's own Commission on Campus Unrest, created in the aftermath of mass demonstrations in 1970, concluded that "a great majority of students . . . oppose the Indochina war. And if the war is wrong, students insist, then so are all policies and practices that support it, from the draft to military research, from ROTC to recruiting for the Defense industry."

By the end of the decade, the nation was reeling from campus protests against the war and against the university's role as a tool of the government. The new wave of revolts started at Columbia University in the spring of 1968. Columbia's president Grayson Kirk insisted that the university should be "value free" when it came to social issues, although Columbia was tied by university contracts to government policy in Vietnam. In response, radical students denounced the administration. "You say the war in Vietnam was a well intentioned accident," student radical Mark Rudd wrote Kirk, "[but] we the young people who you so rightly fear, say that the society is sick and you and your capitalism are the sickness."

> You call for order and respect for authority; we call for justice, freedom and socialism. There is only one thing left to say. "Up against the wall, motherfucker, this is a stick up."

When Columbia sought to build a new gym in a park overlooking Harlem, with a separate, backdoor entrance for Harlem residents, students protested both the university's racism and its complicity in the war. A small cadre of radicals occupied the president's office and classroom buildings. Files were rifled, research papers destroyed, walls defaced with slogans. After an extended siege, the university finally called in hundreds of New York City police. With blatant disregard for innocent bystanders, the police billy-clubbed their way across the campus to evict the demonstrators. Most students went on strike in protest, and the university shut down for the duration of the semester. Although student militants had acted recklessly and irresponsibly, their excess reflected the extent to which faith in peaceful petition had dissolved and been replaced by bitter alienation.

As if in a Greek tragedy, the same scenario recurred throughout the entire country in 1969, each side seemingly driven to foreclose dialogue, create polarization, and provoke repression. In Cambridge, students occupied Harvard buildings to protest the university's refusal to take a stand against the Vietnam war or to withdraw its investments in racist South Africa. Like Kirk at Columbia, Harvard president Nathan Pusey declared: "Our purpose is . . . to invest in places that are selfishly good for Harvard. We do not use our money for social purposes." As at Columbia, police finally evicted the protestors, only to incite another strike. At Berkeley, Governor Ronald Reagan mobilized a battalion of police to confront more than 5,000 students and community residents who had seized a vacant lot and turned it into a "people's park." Armed helicopters sprayed tear gas on the demonstrators from above, while police shotgun fire killed one student and blinded another. At Cornell, black students with machine guns took over the student union to demand their rights. And at San Francisco State, President S. I. Hayakawa became a folk hero for the right when he called out police and National Guardsmen to suppress student demonstrations. "I enjoyed myself immensely during all the rioting," Hayakawa later said. "Whenever there was any trouble I stocked up for lunch in the office. From then on the biggest problem was whether to have sardines or pâté de fois gras."

The tragedy reached its final denouement at Ohio's Kent State University after Nixon's speech announcing the invasion of Cambodia in May of 1970. Nixon himself had set the tone for the confrontation by referring to student demonstrators as a bunch of "bums" in an informal briefing session at the Pentagon. When Kent State students protested the invasion by rioting downtown and firebombing the ROTC building, Governor James Rhodes called out the National Guard and declared martial law. Student rebels, he declared, were "worse than the brown shirts and the Communist elements" and represented "the worst type of people we harbor in America." Insisting that "we are going to eradicate the problem," Rhodes sent

Ohio National Guardsmen fire on students at Kent State University who have gathered to attend a rally protesting the invasion of Cambodia by U.S. troops. (*National Archives*)

Students at Kent State University in Ohio flee in search of safety after National Guardsmen commence firing on a rally. (*National Archives*)

Guardsmen onto the campus. There, on May 4, students held a peaceful rally to protest the governor's action. Suddenly, with no provocation, National Guardsmen turned, opened fire, shot four students dead, and left eleven wounded. None of the four victims had broken a law; two of the girls killed were simply walking to class. As the president's Commission on Campus Unrest later observed, "Even if the Guard had authority to prohibit a peaceful gathering—a question that is at least debatable—the timing and manner of dispersal was disastrous. . . . The rally was peaceful and there was no impending violence." Even that tragedy was not the end. Just ten days later, two more innocent students were killed at Jackson State in Mississippi when police unleashed a 28-second barrage of gunfire at crowded windows and students gathered in front of a dormitory. It was as if the enemy without had become the enemy within. Horror was everywhere.

Yet even as thousands took to the streets in protest, the New Left was falling apart. No single cause could explain its demise. But as month after month of protest seemed to produce no positive response from those in power, factionalism mounted, some activists resorted to the tactics of revolutionary terrorism, and others concluded that politics itself was an empty charade, with the creation of alternative communities and a new "counterculture" the only hope remaining. Thus, even as protest against the "establishment" seemed to reach new heights, the foundation of collective action on the left was crumbling, with Richard Nixon left to pick up the pieces.

Civil war on the left had already begun as early as 1969. For many radical activists, the primary lesson of the 1960s had been the futility of securing change peacefully. Demonstrations at universities had failed to change the government's Vietnam policy; campaigns on behalf of antiwar candidates proved useless, at least in 1968; and the most bitter activists concluded that revolution was the only answer. SDS shattered into desperate splinter groups, each seeking its own form of extremism to prove itself more radical than its opponents. The "Motherfuckers" and "Crazies" urged anarchy; the Progressive Labor faction sought to impose Stalinist discipline on its followers; and the Revolutionary Youth Movement (RYM) demanded violent revolution. As the SDS national convention disintegrated under the brunt of such infighting, the "Weathermen" seized public attention by endorsing terrorist violence. In October 1969, its members launched the "Days of Rage" campaign in Chicago, seeking to provoke mass violence. According to the Weatherman manifesto ("You Don't Need a Weatherman To Tell You Which Way the Wind Blows"), the main struggle going on in the world was "between U.S. imperialism and the national liberation struggles against it":

> We're within the heartland of a world-wide monster. [Our] goal is the destruction of U.S. imperialism and the achievement of a classless world . . . People, especially young people, more and more find themselves in the iron grip of authoritarian institutions. Reaction against the pigs who are teachers in the schools, welfare pigs or the army is generalizable and extends beyond the particular repressive institutions of the society and the State as a whole. . . . [Hence] the most important task for us toward making the revolution . . . is the creation of a mass revolutionary movement, without which a clandestine revolutionary party will be impossible.

Using the "pig power structure" as its common foe, Weathermen terrorists went underground, seeking to use random violence against establishment institutions as a vehicle for creating revolution. Self-destructive from the beginning, such terrorism provoked a massive backlash from those millions of Americans who believed that, whatever the political issues, law and order represented an essential prerequisite for a civilized society. Ironically, romantic notions of violence in fact helped to destroy the Weathermen. In March 1970, students building a bomb in a Greenwich Village townhouse blew *themselves* up.

For most students, of course, the excessive rhetoric and senseless violence of the radical vanguard proved totally unacceptable. But what to put in its place? To an increasing extent, the counterculture became the answer. Throughout the years of protest on the left, political activism and countercultural experimentation with drugs and alternative living styles had gone hand in hand, the one providing reinforcement for the other. But with a growing sense of resignation and frustration about the efficacy of political activism, the two strands began to diverge, with more and more people convinced that political expression was useless, and that building a new life with different values, mores, and institutions provided the only answer. Appropriately, one of the factions of SDS articulated most clearly this way of thinking. "What we are trying to say," the "Up Against The Wall Motherfuckers" declared, "is that the whole fucking struggle isn't anti-imperialist, capitalist, or any of that bullshit. The whole thing is a struggle to live. Dig it? For survival. The fucking society won't let you smoke your dope, ball your woman, wear your hair the way you want to. All of that shit is living, dig, and we want to live, that's our thing."

But if the whole struggle was "to live," particularly in the manner the "Motherfuckers" described, political action became less important than finding a community, living for the moment, and discovering modes of interaction that would undermine the hierarchical, technological, and money-obsessed lifestyle of the dominant culture. "That high feeling," one counterculture advocate wrote, "when you're relating to each other as brothers and sisters—that's the revolution. That's what's worth living and dying for." In more grandiloquent phrases, Theodore Roszak described the same romantic vision in his popular tract, *The Making of the Counter-Culture*. "Nothing less is required," Roszak wrote,

> than the subversion of the scientific world view with its entrenched commitment to egocentric and cerebral modes of consciousness. In its place there must be a new culture in which the non-intellective capacities of personality—those capacities that take fire from visionary splendor and the experiences of human communism—[become] the arbiters of the true, the good, and the beautiful.

At its root, the social critic Paul Goodman observed, this vision was religious in nature. "I'd imagined that the world wide student protest had to [do] with changing political and moral institutions, to which I was sympathetic," Goodman noted, "but now I saw that we had to deal with a religious crisis of the magnitude of the Reformation." Although such counterculture slogans as "make love not war" retained a link to politics, the counterculture frequently became totally personal and privatistic in emphasis, with liberation in dress style, sex, and attitudes toward respectability taking the place of activism in the public arena. Theoretically, building communes and "getting high" on interpersonal intimacy could have a political consequence. "You can have your cake and eat it too," Bob Dylan's lyrics said. But there was also a tendency for these new cultural forms to become ends in themselves.

Nowhere were the themes of the counterculture more graphically evident than at the Woodstock rock festival of August 1969. Hundreds of thousands of young people descended on the rolling hillsides of upstate New York to baptize their new faith and dramatically affirm their freedom. With Jimi Hendrix galvanizing the audience with his strident, dissonant version of the "Star Spangled Banner"—giving the Woodstock nation its own "national anthem"—and virtually every other major rock band providing free entertainment, Woodstock was literally a festival of life. As Andrew Kopkind wrote, the counterculture was blowing its mind in oceanic communion. "No one in this country had ever seen a 'society' so free of repression. Everyone swam nude in the lake, balling was easier than getting breakfast, and the 'pigs' just smiled and passed out the oats." For three days and nights the young people luxuriated in their new communion of the soul, achieving, for a time at least, a titillating sense of what life would be like totally without restraints. Woodstock almost seemed designed to fulfill the prophetic words of New Left philosopher Herbert Marcuse. "The New Society," he wrote, "will be one where the hatred of the young bursts into laughter and song, mixing the barricade and the dance floor, love play, and heroism."

For some participants in the counterculture, the new way of life certainly produced a sense of fulfillment, identity, and community never before achieved. "It was like awakening to find that you have been reborn and this was your new family," one disciple wrote. Living together on collective farms, trying to grow their own food, refusing to "buy into" the establishment's obsession with grades and careerism, many young people experienced a profound sense of liberation. But the drive to create a new culture was also riven by contradictions. At the Altamont Speedway, a free concert by the Rolling Stones degenerated into chaos, as Hells Angels—hired to enforce security—stomped to death one member of the audience. All too often reliance on drugs led to psychological disarray, a false aura of invincibility, and an inability to deal with the "down" that always followed being "up." Janis Joplin, Jim Morrison, and Jimi Hendrix—all musical heroes of the counterculture—died from drug overdoses, illustrating from the ranks of the famous the social pathology increasingly prevalent in the counterculture as a whole.

Similarly, the passion for communion often generated its antithesis, cheapening rather than enhancing the value of interpersonal contact. It was one thing to prize intimacy, but when the sharing of confidences became the immediate currency of communication instead of the dividend of long-standing relationships, the meaning of friendship was diminished. Some might celebrate open marriage and complete sexual freedom, but what happened to those whose trust and commitment were betrayed as a consequence? Too often, it seemed, the counterculture mirrored the society it was attacking, seeking depth on the surface and lasting ties through transitory "rap" sessions and casual affairs.

In addition, there was something artificial about affluent children of the upper middle class seeking a return to simplicity and nature. As psychologist Kenneth Keniston noted, "the Byronic romanticism characteristic of Roszak's counter-culture has [historically] arisen only among the privileged classes of prosperous societies." Reared in a consumer culture and "glutted with the goodies it provides," many adherents of the counter culture proved unable to shed the impulse to acquisitiveness that had become so internalized during their earlier years. Before long, the dominant culture learned how to make a profit by catering to the new tastes of the young, from blue jeans and counterculture jewelry, to more sophisticated recording and sound systems. "Head shops" sprang up everywhere to provide drug paraphernalia; record companies made a fortune; and manufacturers of stereo equipment found endless ways to entice the young. In its own way, therefore, the counter culture simply became an additional market for corporate America, its own fierce conformity providing a ready outlet for new, up-to-date variants of the old affluent society.

Perhaps most important, the desire to remake the past often went hand in hand with nihilism and intolerance. If *everything* that had gone on before was bad, what materials were left to begin the rebuilding process? "We honor the young," drama critic Robert Brustein wrote, "because without them there is no future. But there will surely be no future . . . unless the more extreme of our young cease trying to annihilate the past." Frequently, the conviction that the whole system was rotten led to disregard of everything that other people believed in or had discovered: the idea that one must read a book or learn an assignment in order to grow became passé, a vestige of an antiquated past. When such attitudes went hand in hand with a celebration of personal indulgence, the result was the direct opposite of the communal, collective values allegedly espoused by the counterculture. If everyone did "his own thing," no one would be responsible for anyone else. At some point, social change required collective action, including the willingness to accept a common discipline and to compromise with others in order to create change. But the counterculture's emphasis on personal freedom and self-expression subverted collective action, reinforcing other obstacles that impeded the realization of a new culture. Prophetically, as the hero of Peter Fonda's counterculture movieparable, *Easy Rider,* concluded: "We blew it."

Thus, in the end, the counterculture's quest for liberation did more to sap the forces of protest than to revitalize them. While the effort to create a new lifestyle exerted a lasting influence on attitudes toward sex, family life, and even the Protestant ethic of achievement, these cultural changes did not result in any significant alteration of the institutions or structures of American society. Moreover, the new emphasis on individual self-expression accentuated the fragmentation already occurring on the left. Although movements for gay rights, Indian rights, Chicano rights, and prisoner's rights all received important sanction from the new atmosphere of freedom, more often than not, these groups worked in isolation rather than in coalition. Of all these, only the women's movement survived and prospered.* Thus by the early 1970s, the "revolution" of the young appeared to have lost its power and been thrown into disarray, bearing little resemblance to the massive political movement that helped force Lyndon Johnson to renounce his chance for re-election. There may have been more freedom; but there was also far less hope that the young could transform their society.

---

* The women's movement, and the experience of other social movements, will be discussed at length in next chapter.

The Nixon administration, meanwhile, contributed to the isolation of the left through a combination of covert counterintelligence operations and overt appeals to "middle Americans" to reject the radicalism and extremism of antiwar dissidents. As the Senate Intelligence Committee revealed in the mid-1970s, the FBI and CIA mounted massive campaigns to subvert left-wing organizations by inserting "deep cover" agents into their ranks, using public statements and internal communications to promote factionalism and provoking violent confrontations that would result in police repression. Operation Chaos, started by the CIA in 1967, eventually collected files on 7,200 Americans. Army Intelligence deployed over a thousand agents to gather information on potentially disruptive groups. Most devastating of all was the FBI's "Cointelpro" operation. Using tactics similar to those employed against Martin Luther King, Jr., the FBI sent anonymous letters to leftist groups designed to trigger internal feuds that undercover agents could then use to foment internecine warfare.

On occasion, government harassment even involved using undercover agents to *provoke* violence to justify using police power to suppress leftist organizations. The Black Panther Party became a primary target in 1969, when an estimated 28 Panthers were killed by police, with hundreds of others imprisoned. Informers and agent provocateurs riddled the Panther Party, providing detailed intelligence, but also "setting up" confrontations where police use of violence could be legitimized. In Chicago, Black Panther leader Fred Hampton was killed in an apartment where he was sleeping when scores of police engaged in a shoot-out during a raid. Subsequent investigation showed that only two shots had been fired from *within* the apartment, while hundreds of bullets came from police guns. More typical, perhaps, was an episode in Greensboro, North Carolina, where an undercover agent attempted to incite black militants to firebomb stores and ambush police. Alerted to rumors of such violence, local police prepared themselves for a showdown in which they would deploy maximum force. When racial demonstrations broke out in a local high school and college, police and National Guardsmen responded as if the long-awaited war against black militants had finally arrived, using Armored Personnel Carriers and tear gas to storm the black college campus. The ensuing battle caused the death of one innocent student, and the complete demolition of black militancy in the community—in large part due to the work of an agent provocateur.

On a more overt basis, the Nixon administration seized on student demonstrations to mobilize a conservative majority among white working-class citizens and middle-class suburbanites who were outraged by radical extremists. Nixon's appeal came at precisely the moment when, on economic grounds alone, many "middle Americans" might have been prepared to return to the Democratic fold. As a consequence of the Vietnam war and Johnson's failure to raise taxes to pay for it, inflation had begun to shoot up and real income to decline. Yet in the context of the times, these same white

Americans proved more susceptible to Nixon's appeal to rally behind traditional American values and against unruly elements of society. Many lower middle-class Americans resented federal programs aimed at blacks and the poor. "Often their wages are [only] a notch or so above the welfare payments of liberal states," one observer noted. "Yet they are excluded from social programs targeted at the disadvantaged." From such a perspective, the Democratic Party's continuing emphasis on helping blacks and supporting the welfare state seemed ill placed. As one white Chicago principal observed, "No one is looking at this side of it at all. We are the forgotten men. We don't get one cent from the government."

At the core of white dissatisfaction was a feeling of being victimized for someone else's advantage. Although statistics indicated that blacks and poor people (the two were often treated as one) still lived an immeasurably more painful existence than lower middle-class whites, the *impression* existed that ghetto dwellers and slum residents were now in the driver's seat. A *Newsweek* poll in 1969 showed that a plurality of middle Americans believed that blacks had a *better* chance than whites of getting a good job, a decent house, and adequate schooling. Almost 80 percent of the same respondents agreed that half or more of the people on welfare could earn their own way if they wanted to. Reflecting such sentiments, one Milwaukee white worker declared: "People on relief got better jobs, got better homes than I've got. . . . The colored people are eating steak and this Polack bastard is eating chicken. Damn right I'm bitter." The same people were infuriated at young students who uttered a stream of obscenities at police and attacked the flag. It was no accident that in the *Newsweek* poll, campus demonstrators, black militants, and people on welfare were all viewed as enemies—with 84 percent believing that campus demonstrators were treated too leniently, 85 percent that black militants were let off too easily, and 79 percent that most people on welfare could help themselves. The poll data suggested the degree to which vertical issues of traditional social values had trumped the more customary pattern of voters choosing their party around the horizontal issues of economic self-interest.

Nixon understood the cultural politics of resentment and, in the aftermath of student demonstrations following the Cambodian invasion, exploited popular anger to obscure the economic shortcomings of his administration. When the killings occurred at Kent State, the White House blamed the slaughter on the victims rather than the perpetrators, with Spiro Agnew calling the slayings "predictable and avoidable," a product of the "politics of violence and confrontation." After New York's Mayor John Lindsay denounced Nixon and declared that "the country is virtually on the edge of spiritual—and perhaps even a physical—breakdown," the White House encouraged New York construction workers to mount counterdemonstrations against Lindsay and antiwar protests. On May 8 workers with hardhats descended on placard-carrying protestors near New York's City Hall and beat them up while smiling police looked on; a few days later, Nixon met

At the height of anti-Vietnam war protests, New York City construction workers attacked student antiwar demonstrators near Wall Street. Here, Richard Nixon expresses his support for the "hardhats" and for their "patriotism." (*National Archives*)

with twenty-two "loyal" union leaders who presented him with his own "hardhat" inscribed, "Commander-in-Chief."

Although for a brief time the president sought dialogue with student protestors (when they gathered in Washington, he went to visit them in the middle of the night, talking to Syracuse students about their football team, and to California students about surfing), he quickly returned to a hard-line posture in the 1970 elections. Using Agnew as his pointman, he believed the time was ripe for solidifying a conservative cultural coalition based on popular anger at student violence, black militancy, drugs, and sexual liberation. "There is a realignment taking place," Nixon told his staff. "If [Agnew] can appeal to one-third of the Democrats, we'll win two-thirds of the races." The next day, adopting with enthusiasm his president's instructions, Agnew defined the issues of the campaign as transparently simple: "Will America be led by a President elected by a majority of the American people or will it be intimidated and blackmailed into following the path dictated by a disruptive radical and militant minority—the pampered prodigies of the radical liberals in the United States Senate?" Appealing explicitly to the "working men of this country," the vice-president described the election as "a contest between remnants of the discredited elite that dominated national policy for forty years and a new national majority, forged and led by the President of the United States."

But Nixon was not content to let Agnew garner all the headlines, and in mid-October set forth on his own 23-state campaign swing. A familiar ritual soon developed. Just enough antiwar demonstrators were allowed into Nixon's campaign rallies to permit the president to use them as a foil for his law and order rhetoric. When one demonstrator hurled a small stone at the presidential party at an airport stop, Nixon quickly exaggerated the incident, claiming that student "rock-throwers" were attempting to assail the president of the United States. Playing his denunciation of permissiveness to the hilt, he declared:

> This is a great and good country. I have flown over it . . . but I also want to say this—there is a small group in this country, a small group that shouts obscenities . . . that throws rocks, as it did in a meeting earlier today, . . . a group of people that always tear America down; a group of people that hate this country . . . that is a minority today; it is not going to be a majority in the future. . . . The way to answer them [is] . . . for the Great Silent Majority to speak out.

By the end of the campaign, Nixon's rhetoric of polarization had reached a fever pitch, culminating with a frenetic, arm-waving denunciation of "the terrorists of the far left" on election eve. "The time has come," he declared, "to draw the line, . . . for the Great Silent Majority . . . to stand up and be counted against the appeasement of the rock-throwers and the obscenity shouters in America."

In the end, Nixon overstepped the bounds. His wild rhetoric contrasted sharply with the calm, Lincolnesque Edmund Muskie of Maine, who on election eve denounced the politics of fear and appealed to reason and calm. On election day, the Republicans succeeded in defeating two of their primary enemies—Gore of Tennessee and Goodall of New York—and added two Republican seats in the Senate. But they lost nine congressional districts in the process, and most observers concluded that the campaign for "realignment" had failed. In fact, however, Nixon had used the election as a laboratory for testing themes that he believed would provide the basis for entrenching, on a long-term basis, the conservative coalition he sought. If the immediate results failed to provide victory, the long-term consequences would prove devastating, both to the Democratic Party and to voices of protest across the land.

Over the next two years Nixon repeatedly demonstrated his intention to solidify his support from the right. When Congress enacted legislation to provide a national system of day-care centers, Nixon vetoed it claiming that it would commit "the vast moral authority of the national government to communal approaches to child rearing, over against the family centered approach." Responding to a burgeoning "right to life" movement that viewed abortion as murder, Nixon took the opportunity to affirm his "personal belief in the sanctity of human life—including the life of the yet unborn." And although the Supreme Court had overwhelmingly endorsed the use of busing as a vehicle to achieve school desegregation, Nixon challenged the court's domain, going on national TV to propose a "moratorium" on all busing.

Nixon's most pernicious appeal to the right, perhaps, came with his intervention in the court martial proceedings of Lieutenant William Calley, the commander in charge of the platoon responsible for the My Lai massacre in Vietnam. After repeated efforts to cover up the slaughter, a member of Calley's platoon—torn by conscience—had disclosed details of the massacre, with investigative reporters following up and creating a national scandal. An army jury of six Vietnam veterans sentenced Calley to life imprisonment. But almost immediately, a conservative furor erupted, treating Calley as a hero rather than a villain. Senator Herman Talmadge of Georgia expressed his sadness "that one could fight for his flag and then be court martialed and convicted for apparently carrying out his orders." Alabama Governor George Wallace, Nixon's primary competition on the right, lionized Calley and announced that he would seek to suspend the draft in Alabama as a result of the verdict. Recognizing an opportunity to mobilize his own right-wing base, Nixon recruited congressional support for leniency on behalf of Calley, and then announced, even prior to the appeals process taking its course, that he would personally review the case "before any final sentence is carried out." On presidential orders Calley was released from a military stockade and returned to his comfortable officer's quarters. Nixon had not only intervened in the legal process—in a manner totally inconsistent with judicial ethics—he also had succeeded in blunting Wallace's demagogic appeal to the right, placing himself instead at the head of the conservative reaction to Calley's sentencing.

The Democratic Party, meanwhile, provided the perfect foil for Nixon's strategy. Four major candidates competed for the 1972 Democratic nomination—George Wallace on the right, George McGovern on the left, and Hubert Humphrey and Edmund Muskie in the middle. Since only a small minority of voters participate in most primary elections, those candidates able to energize the most active voters ordinarily held an advantage. Although Muskie retained a clear lead in the polls prior to the primaries, his moderate policies and calm demeanor failed to excite voters. McGovern and Wallace, on the other hand, appealed to highly vocal constituencies, McGovern to the left through his antiwar position, Wallace to the right through his emotional denunciation of busing, the Eastern establishment, and "pointy-headed intellectuals." Muskie won by a surprisingly narrow margin in New Hampshire, close to his home state of Maine, then proceeded to be swamped by McGovern in Massachusetts and Pennsylvania. His campaign collapsed in the process. Wallace, in turn, swept the Florida primary and appeared to be running well even in Northern industrial states with his calculated racist appeal to white blue-collar workers. But then, in a Maryland suburban shopping center, a crazed would-be assassin shot the Alabama governor, paralyzing him for life and forcing his withdrawal from the campaign. McGovern put together a string of primary victories, culminating in California, and went to the Miami Democratic Convention with a clear majority of delegate support.

But McGovern's strength in the primaries also proved to be his weakness in the general election. The son of a Methodist minister, the South Dakota senator was almost self-righteous in his appeal to left-leaning Democrats. He urged a $30 billion cut in defense spending, amnesty for Vietnam war deserters, total withdrawal of support for the Thieu regime in South Vietnam, and grants of $1,000 to every person in America in order to redistribute income and attack poverty. "Quite frankly," he declared, "I am not a 'centrist' candidate." But while such views appealed to an energetic minority, they offended precisely those segments of the New Deal coalition that Nixon hoped to win to his cause on cultural grounds—white blue-collar workers, conservative Catholics, and the South. The Democratic convention in Miami Beach simply reinforced the alienation of these groups. Under new party reforms, minority groups and women received "quotas" of delegates, urban machines were displaced, and traditional Democrats found themselves in the distinctly unpleasant situation of being a minority. When the party platform took bold positions on the issues of abortion, busing, and the war, many old-line Democrats decided to withhold their support from the party. "There is too much hair, and not enough cigars at this convention," one labor leader declared.

In effect, the vagaries of the primary system had presented Nixon with a scenario almost better than any he could have written himself. Wallace's paralysis created an ideal opportunity for Nixon to fulfill Kevin Phillips's Southern strategy of combining Nixon and Wallace supporters in the eleven states of the Old Confederacy. McGovern's social views, in the meantime, made it easy for Nixon to portray him as a candidate of the counterculture, opposed to mainstream American values. Given the Democratic candidate's position on defense spending, abortion, legalizing marijuana, and ending the war, it became almost impossible for the Democratic nominee to win the support of conservatives and many moderates in his own party. The AFL-CIO remained neutral, and leading Democratic politicians refused to endorse the ticket. McGovern hurt himself further when his choice for vice-presidential candidate, Senator Thomas Eagleton, revealed that he had twice been treated for manic depression and given electric shock therapy. When McGovern first declared that he was "a thousand percent behind Eagleton" and then dumped his running mate in favor of former peace corps director Sargent Shriver, even his sincerity seemed in question. Although the South Dakota Senator portrayed the campaign as "a fundamental struggle between the little people of America and the big rich of America, between the average workingman and woman and the powerful elite," all too many "middle Americans" perceived him as a candidate of the liberal Northeast, intellectual establishment.

The result was a landslide victory for Nixon. Through his highly publicized trips to Peking and Moscow, and his withdrawal of all but a few thousand troops from Vietnam, the president had largely blunted opposition to his re-election on foreign policy grounds. His imposition of wage and price controls during the summer of 1971, and a subsequent upturn in the economy, muted economic discontent as well. All Nixon had to do was reaffirm his support of issues popular among "middle Americans" to both occupy the center and mobilize the right. He did the former by promising to be a president of "peace and prosperity" and by appealing nostalgically to the politics of the fifties, while he strengthened his appeal to the right by pledging to end "the age of permissiveness" and to fight against busing. On election day, the Phillips-Mitchell strategy came to fruition. Nixon swept 61 percent of the popular vote, outpolled McGovern in the electoral college by 521 to 17, and captured the once "solid [Democratic] south." In the process, he won a majority of blue-collar votes, a majority of Catholic votes, and a majority of urban votes. Included in this total were 65 percent of the ballots of middle-income Americans. Once dubbed the "great American loser," Nixon had succeeded in winning a larger majority than any nominee in the history of the Republican Party. Four years earlier, the prospect of breaking the Democratic hold on core members of the New Deal coalition like blue-collar workers, Catholics, and the South had seemed a visionary gleam in the eyes of an ambitious political theorist. Now, the vision had become a reality.* A new "conservative consensus" based on cultural values had received overwhelming ratification by the American people.

Yet even at his moment of greatest glory, Nixon had already embarked on the process of betraying the office he prized so dearly. Despite his almost guaranteed re-election, Nixon's insecurity and paranoia propelled him into authorizing a campaign of subversion against his Democratic opponents that paralleled the FBI's Cointelpro operations against domestic dissidents. Just four months before election day, five burglars—subsequently associated with the Committee to Re-elect the President (CREEP)—had been caught by Washington police as they attempted to break into Democratic National Headquarters at the Watergate Hotel. Throughout the election campaign, Nixon successfully deflected attention from the Watergate break-in. But as he took office for a second term, the web of conspiracy had begun to unravel, and before long, the president's re-election mandate was crumbling in the face of the greatest constitutional crisis the country had faced since the Civil War.

The Downfall of the Imperial President

On the morning of June 17, 1972 Bob Woodward, a new reporter covering the metropolitan desk of the *Washington Post,* was awakened by his city edi-

---

* The sweep did not carry over into congressional races, where Democrats remained in control. Moreover, millions of Americans did not vote at all, unsatisfied with the alternatives.

tor and told to check on a break-in that had occurred the previous night at Democratic National Committee headquarters. He was joined by Carl Bernstein, a high school dropout and "counterculture type" who covered Virginia politics for the *Post*. The two reporters discovered that the five suspects had been arrested carrying expensive cameras and electronic equipment. Among them, the five had $2,300 in cash. All were well dressed, and all had given false names to the police. When they were arraigned, one of the suspects, James W. McCord, Jr., identified himself as a security consultant who had recently retired from government service. "Where in the government?" the judge asked. "The CIA," McCord answered. Subsequent investigation revealed that the other four suspects were all from Miami where they were reported to be heavily involved in CIA anti-Castro activities. The next day, an AP wire story revealed that James McCord was not only a retired CIA officer; he was also security coordinator for the Committee to Re-elect the President (CREEP).

Digging furiously, Bernstein and Woodward soon pieced together information that suggested a story potentially explosive in impact. One of the suspects had an address notebook containing the notation, "Howard E. Hunt, W. House." Another defendant's notebook carried sketches of McGovern headquarters at the Democratic Convention. A call to the White House confirmed that Hunt served as an associate to Charles Colson, Special Counsel to the President. Reached by telephone and asked why his name was in the address book of two men arrested at the Watergate, Hunt replied: "Good God!" Further investigation disclosed that a $25,000 check had been deposited in one of the defendant's Miami accounts with the name of Kenneth Dahlberg on it. Dahlberg, it turned out, was a fundraiser for the Nixon re-election committee. The check was part of a large sum that had been "laundered" through a Mexican bank, to obscure its sources as a political contribution. Later, a frightened secretary from CREEP told the enterprising reporters that three former White House aides now working with the reelection effort knew all about the bugging and break-in at the Watergate, including, she believed, John Mitchell. The pieces were beginning to fall into place.

For the moment, the White House managed to contain the story. At an August press conference, Nixon declared that White House Counsel John Dean had "conducted a complete investigation" of the incident and found that "no one on the White House staff, no one in this administration presently employed, was involved in this very bizarre incident." A federal grand jury indicted only those conspirators already identified in the press. Nixon congratulated Dean for his good work. "You had quite a day today, didn't you?," the president said, praising Dean for "putting your fingers in the leaks that sprung here and sprung there." Although the *Washington Post* reported in early October that Watergate had been only a small part of a "massive campaign of political spying and sabotage conducted on behalf of President Nixon's re-election," the investigative efforts of Woodward and

Bernstein were dismissed by many as an attempt by a vehemently anti-Nixon newspaper to cause trouble. In fact, however, Bernstein and Woodward were on target. Woodward and Bernstein had a secret source they referred to in their subsequent book on Watergate as "Deep Throat"—now known to have been Mark Felt, second in command at the FBI—who systematically pointed them toward the full dimensions of the scandal. The Watergate burglary was just the tip of the iceberg. Beneath the surface lay hidden stories of illegal fundraising, subversion of opposition political candidates, creation of a White House "plumbers" group authorized to conduct break-ins and wiretaps of political enemies, use of the Internal Revenue Service to discredit potential foes, and the mounting of counterintelligence operations against domestic dissidents. Nixon had reason to worry.

The first part of the hidden story involved massive illegal fundraising by CREEP. As early as 1970, the White House had furnished hundreds of thousands of dollars to an effort to defeat Governor George Wallace, the primary obstacle to Nixon's "Southern strategy." When the president's re-election campaign went into high gear, Nixon fundraisers, led by John Mitchell and Secretary of Commerce Maurice Stans, furiously solicited funds from the country's major corporations, asking for a minimum of $100,000 each. If campaign donations were given before April 7, 1972—the day a new campaign finance law went into effect—they did not have to be reported. More than $20 million was raised prior to the deadline, much of it "laundered" through Mexican banks and collected through implied threats that a failure to give would seriously impede a corporation's well-being. George Steinbrenner, a shipbuilding tycoon (and subsequently the owner of the New York Yankees), was told that the IRS, the Justice Department, and the Commerce Department would all be looking into his affairs if he failed to pay up. "You didn't have to draw a map for me to let me know what was going on," Steinbrenner told a friend. "It was a shakedown. A plain old-fashioned Goddamn shakedown." "Pay or die" was the shorthand message, and the scam seemed to be working to perfection.

Of the money collected, over $350,000 was squirreled away in a CREEP office safe for expenditure on "security" operations. Some of the money went to pay for a "dirty tricks" operation against Democratic opponents, orchestrated from the White House with the approval of H. R. Haldeman. Undercover operators purloined confidential documents from the files of Democratic candidates, wrote and distributed anonymous letters accusing Democrats of sexual indiscretions, and infiltrated the campaign staffs of every major candidate. In one bizarre episode, Donald Segretti authored a letter that appeared in New Hampshire's major newspaper two weeks before that state's primary, charging Muskie with making offensive remarks about "Canucks"—French Canadians who lived in the state. So upset did Muskie become in response that he lost his composure, cried in front of TV cameras, and seriously damaged his reputation for self-possession and poise. Other campaign officials including G. Gordon Liddy, another former

CIA agent, sought approval for spending as much as $1 million on projects such as "bugging" the Democratic opposition, seducing Democratic candidates at a yacht party where they would be offered sexual favors, and kidnapping dissident leaders. Told to come up with a less costly plan, Liddy responded with a blueprint for breaking into the Democratic National Committee headquarters, copying documents, and wiretapping phones. John Mitchell okayed the revised plan.

Liddy's ideas were ultimately traceable to the infamous White House Special Investigations Unit, nicknamed the "plumbers," that was created in the summer of 1971 to ferret out and destroy political enemies of the administration. A year earlier, after the Cambodia invasion had led to a series of harmful leaks to the press, Tom Houston, a White House aide, proposed a massive counterintelligence operation that would coordinate the work of the FBI, the CIA, and other intelligence agencies to combat the antiwar movement. Vetoed by FBI Director J. Edgar Hoover as excessive and illegal, the plan lay dormant for a year. But in June 1971, in the aftermath of the disastrous Laos invasion and Nixon's declining political popularity, the idea of a special investigation unit took on new life. The immediate occasion was the publication by the *New York Times* of the "Pentagon Papers," a detailed account of Johnson administration policy in Vietnam up to 1968. Profoundly offended by the role played by former Kissinger aide Daniel Ellsberg in leaking the classified documents, the White House determined to "get" Ellsberg, steal any other classified documents that he or his associates might publish, and stop the leaks coming from various government agencies. Under the ultimate supervision of John Ehrlichman, the "plumbers" included E. Howard Hunt from Charles Colson's office, Egil Krogh from Ehrlichman's staff, and others. Hunt and Colson had already embarked on a campaign to discredit the Kennedys, with Hunt both investigating Edward Kennedy's role in the Chappaquidick drowning of a young woman who had been a Robert Kennedy assistant, and composing fake cables from the State Department seeking to show that John Kennedy had ordered the assassination of South Vietnamese Premier Ngo Diem. Now the plumbers turned to Ellsberg, breaking into his psychiatrist's office to secure potentially damaging information regarding Ellsberg's sexual activities. They even planned to firebomb the Brookings Institution in Washington to obtain other classified documents. The entire operation was run out of the White House, and Nixon feared that any Watergate investigation would inevitably uncover the "plumbers" antics as well.*

As a result of his desire to prevent such disclosures, Nixon intervened directly after the Watergate burglary to divert attention from the crimes that

---

* When Ellsberg was placed on trial for theft of classified documents in May 1973, the judge dismissed all charges after it was revealed that White House "plumbers" had broken into a psychiatrist's office and had attempted to bribe the judge by offering him the directorship of the FBI.

he knew could bring down his administration. On June 20, and then again three days later, Nixon plotted with his chief aides to quash the Watergate inquiry, arranging for H. R. Haldeman to tell Deputy CIA Director Vernon Walters that the FBI investigation of Watergate would compromise sensitive CIA operations. Haldeman then had Walters steer Acting FBI Director L. Patrick Gray off the trail by implying that explosive national security secrets might be exposed if the FBI pursued its leads. The tactic worked, at least for the moment, although various FBI and Justice Department officials—smelling a setup—continued to leak information to Bernstein and Woodward. Politically sensitive Washingtonians sensed a cover-up, but no one fully understood how deep or pervasive the conspiracy of silence went. Still, when Majority Leader Tip O'Neill returned to Congress in January of 1973, he confided to House Speaker Carl Albert: "All my years tell me what's happening. They did so many bad things during that campaign that there is no way to keep it from coming out. . . . The time is going to come when impeachment is going to hit this Congress."

Then, suddenly, the lid blew off. On March 19, 1973, James McCord—former head of security for CREEP—presented a letter to Judge John Sirica prior to being sentenced for his participation in the burglary. The letter was a bombshell, alleging that high-ranking government officials had committed perjury during the investigation, that political pressure had been applied from "high" places to force the defendants to keep their silence, and that numerous participants in the Watergate crime had never been identified during the trial. Immediately, those with the most to lose from McCord's revelations saw the handwriting on the wall. John Dean, White House counsel, whose "investigation" Nixon had cited the previous August (there had never been one) went to the president and told him there was a "cancer" at the heart of the Nixon administration. Simultaneously, Dean started to talk to prosecutors, negotiating for immunity. Acting FBI Director L. Patrick Gray disclosed at a Senate confirmation hearing that he had "deep-sixed" documents critical to the case, allegedly on White House orders. That same day the judge in the Ellsberg case revealed the break-in at Ellsberg's psychiatrist's office. Each morning brought new headlines of scandal, and on April 30, Nixon fired Dean and accepted the resignations of Haldeman and Ehrlichman. While the president self-righteously denounced "any attempt to cover up in this case," the entire fabric of the White House conspiracy had begun to come apart.

The ensuing months produced a bewildering array of startling new revelations, most of them witnessed firsthand by millions of Americans glued to their TV sets. In May, a Select Senate Committee chaired by North Carolina Senator Sam Ervin began televised hearings on Watergate. Although the White House attempted to invoke executive privilege to prevent senior officials from being grilled under oath, the tactic failed, and the nation watched—fascinated—as former Attorney General John Mitchell admitted meeting with the conspirators on three occasions prior to the break-in, and the "Disneyland mafia"—Haldeman, Ehrlichman, Chapin, and others—found themselves caught in embarrassing contradictions as they attempted to stonewall the Senate investigation. Ervin ("I'm just a country *lawyer*") became a national hero with his feigned innocence and rapierlike wit, while Howard Baker, the ranking Republican on the committee, earned his place in history with the repeated inquiry: "What did the President know, and when did he know it." But all the revelations of other witnesses paled into insignificance when suddenly, in midsummer, White House Aide Alexander Butterfield announced that Nixon had installed a sophisticated tape system in the White House in early 1971 that recorded for posterity all the words spoken by the president or in his presence. Now, in addition to all the evidence accumulated on wiretapping, perjury, blackmail, and "dirty tricks," the country learned that there was indeed a source—a very reliable source—that could tell exactly "what the President knew, and when he knew it."

Inexorably, the drama unfolded. With every twist and turn Nixon took to evade accountability, he dug himself deeper into the quagmire. Responding to public clamor, Nixon had appointed a special prosecutor, Archibald Cox, to pursue the Watergate investigation. Both Cox and the Ervin committee subpoenaed critical tapes. Desperately seeking a way out, Nixon claimed executive privilege, arguing that conversations in the White House were as confidential as those between a patient and a doctor. Cleverly, Nixon attempted to work out a compromise with senators friendly to his cause, pledging to allow them to read transcripts of the tapes provided by the White House. But Special Prosecutor Cox refused to agree, petitioning the courts to coerce the surrender of evidence directly pertinent to a criminal investigation. In response, Nixon ordered Attorney General Elliot Richardson to fire the special prosecutor. When Richardson refused, he was dismissed. His deputy, William Ruckelshaus, also refused and he too was fired. Solicitor General Robert H. Bork finally carried out the president's order, but the public was outraged by the "Saturday night massacre" and demanded appointment of a new special prosecutor and release of the tapes.

Everything started to go wrong for Nixon during the fall of 1973. Just ten days before the "Saturday night massacre," Vice-President Spiro Agnew was forced to resign and to plead no contest in federal court on charges of income tax evasion and of accepting hundreds of thousands of dollars of bribes while governor of Maryland. The man who had fulminated against "permissiveness" and who had self-righteously proclaimed the administration's commitment to law and order had now been exposed as a common criminal. By December, Nixon's own personal finances had come under increasingly critical scrutiny. Congressional investigators reported that, although the president had received over $1.1 million in income during his first four years in office, he had paid less than $80,000 in taxes, largely because of a questionable deduction of almost $500,000 for donating his vice-presidential papers to the National Archives. Moreover, investigation of Nixon's personal assets showed that his houses at Key Biscayne and San

Clemente had appreciated enormously in value, largely due to improvements made at public expense. As if all that were not bad enough, Judge John Sirica informed the public in late November that eighteen minutes had been erased from a critical June 20, 1972 tape subpoenaed by the Watergate prosecution. White House assistant Alexander Haig blamed the erasure on a defective recorder; and Nixon's secretary Rosemary Woods explained that she had erased the tape accidently while transcribing it (the journalist Jimmy Breslin later described the posture she would have had to adopt to accomplish the erasure as like that of a runner "sliding into third base"). But subsequent expert testimony disclosed that the tapes had been deliberately tampered with by "manual" erasures. Yet the president proclaimed at a November 17 press conference, "I am not a crook." The country was no longer so sure.

By the spring of 1974, the entire house of cards began to topple. All during the early months of the year, reports had circulated that Special Prosecutor Leon Jaworski (Cox's replacement) had sufficient evidence to indict the president himself for criminal wrongdoing and was restrained from doing so only because he believed that a sitting president was not subject to indictment. When the grand jury completed its work on March 1, seven close Nixon aides were placed on trial, including Haldeman, Ehrlichman, Colson, and Mitchell. Central to the charges against these men was the allegation of perjury, yet as *New Republic* columnist John Osborne observed, "If Haldeman had lied, the President had lied." At issue was the payment of $75,000 in "hush" money to Watergate defendants immediately after a conversation with the president. Having heard the tape, the Watergate grand jury concluded that Haldeman had perjured himself when he swore under oath that Nixon had opposed paying the money. Significantly, Judge John Sirica announced that he would give *all* the evidence pertaining to the president's conversation to the House Judiciary Committee.

With meticulous thoroughness and consummate skill, the legislative branch of government enacted the next to last scene of the Nixon drama. Guided by politically astute Majority Leader Tip O'Neill, the House placed authority for the impeachment investigation with the Judiciary Committee headed by Peter Rodino. Careful, moderate, and above all respectable, Rodino promised to conduct the proceedings in a manner designed to avoid sensationalism and ensure that an indictment of the president would have the maximum opportunity of winning conviction in a trial before the U.S. Senate.*

Wisely, Rodino chose Republican John Doar, a former Justice Department attorney, widely respected for his prudence and restraint, as counsel for the impeachment hearing. From the very beginning, Doar concentrated on the events immediately surrounding the Watergate burglary. "From what

---

* Under the rules governing impeachment, the House of Representatives determines whether an indictment is justified, and the Senate constitutes the jury for the trial.

we've got already," Doar told his associates, "I think the one tape I want to hear, if I had to hear any tape, is June 23." The House leadership understood that to be successful in its investigation of the president, it would need to forge a coalition of moderate Republicans, liberal Democrats, and Southern conservatives so that no one could charge that the proceedings were stacked ideologically against the president. To the consternation of many liberals, Doar and his team—including a young Yale law school graduate named Hillary Rodham—took weeks to amass their evidence. In the meantime, Nixon continued to fight back, appealing to the conservative majority that had elected him and charging that the Watergate investigation represented a conspiracy of the Eastern establishment. Traveling abroad, he sought to use his role as world statesman to counter the political infighting back home and, astonishingly, succeeded in retaining the loyalty of countless millions of Americans who believed the president and were unwilling to acknowledge his complicity in the crimes alleged against him. As yet, no "smoking gun" had directly revealed the president's criminal involvement.

But when the Supreme Court ruled unanimously on July 24 that Nixon had to turn over the tapes of fifty-four conversations, including that of June 23, to the Judiciary Committee, the "smoking gun" finally appeared. The country was already familiar with many Nixon tapes, including the "expletives deleted" that riddled the president's conversations and his ethnic slurs against Italians, blacks, and Jews. But there had never been any hard evidence that Nixon himself had committed a crime. Now, Nixon ordered his counsel, Fred Buzhardt, to listen to the June 23 tapes and determine whether they were as devastating as Nixon remembered them to be. When the answer came back "yes," Nixon still weaseled, asking his colleagues whether there was any "air" in the Supreme Court decision—any way to avoid compliance. Finally, concluding that there was not, Nixon released the June 23 tapes—documenting beyond any doubt that just six days after the Watergate burglary, the president himself had ordered the cover-up and engaged in a criminal conspiracy to obstruct justice. Stunned and disillusioned, White House staff members who had retained their faith in Nixon suddenly understood the enormity of the crime that had been committed. No longer was escape possible. Led by Senator Barry Goldwater, a delegation of the most senior members of Congress waited on the president to insist that he resign. And on August 8, in a rambling, wavering voice that acknowledged nothing more than a "few mistakes of judgment," Nixon announced his resignation as president. At noon the next day, Vice-President Gerald Ford was sworn in as the country's new chief executive. "Our long national nightmare," he declared, "is over."

Conclusion

Ever since the late 1940s, political observers had commented on the dual personality of Richard Nixon. On the one hand, he could appear poised, reflective, statesmanlike—acutely conscious of history and able, in his best moments, to chart brilliant long-range policies. But on the other hand, he seemed deeply insecure, frightened, a petty politician who was resentful of elites and tormented by the thought that he was looked down on. When his first personality was dominant, Nixon could embrace new ideas, cleave to men like Moynihan, and pursue masterful strategies like the breakthrough with the People's Republic of China. But when the second personality took over, he became vindictive, possessed by paranoia, and intent on using whatever means were available—legal or illegal—to "screw" the opposition. Journalists and politicians were admiring of the first Nixon, fearful of the second.

Tragically, it was primarily the second Nixon who controlled the policies and politics of America during his five and a half years as president. Some would later see Nixon as a victim of Watergate, a president trapped by his own inattention to detail who was prevented by a minor error from realizing the grand place in history that his policies merited. Yet from the beginning, this was a president whose positions—both domestic and foreign—testified more to meanness than to enlightenment and restraint. Although Nixon toyed with the rhetoric of a "New American Revolution" and embraced momentarily Moynihan's plea that he become an American Disraeli, his gut instincts drove him to endorse and implement the "Southern strategy" of John Mitchell and Kevin Phillips—a strategy of polarization, racial bigotry, and repression. While on occasion he took the high ground in world affairs, achieving significant successes with SALT and China, more often his foreign policy was one of bluster, intimidation, and reliance on the "madman theory." Only the bureaucratic restraints imposed by William Rogers, Melvin Laird, and others prevented these traits from leading to catastrophic ruin. Symptomatically, he dismissed those in his administration who spoke to the "better" side of his personality—Robert Finch, James Allen, Patrick Moynihan—and sought to exclude from foreign policy deliberations rational voices like those of William Rogers and Melvin Laird. Only with Kissinger, who repeatedly demonstrated his willingness to acquiesce to the president's whims, was Nixon willing to share his most intimate thoughts about "Duck-Hook," the Cambodian bombing, and the destruction of Allende in Chile.

Because of the White House tapes, we now know more of Nixon's crueler side. The "expletives deleted," the intrigue against other politicians, the repeated references to "niggers," "jigs," and "jigaboos"—all these suggest the extent to which meanness and prejudice dominated the Nixon White House. But beyond all this is the further question of Nixon's mental health. The president had a drinking problem. After a few scotches, he ranted and raved—in slurred conversations—against his foreign and domestic enemies. "Henry, we've got to nuke them," Nixon had told Kissinger during a drunken call. One of the reasons for wiretapping Kissinger's aides was the fear that an indiscreet White House official would reveal that, in the middle of the Korean spy plane crisis, the president was uncontrollably inebriated. Kissinger himself, according to National Security Agency staff members, conveyed concern about Nixon's "stability" and often treated him as a doctor would a difficult patient. Frequently, these lapes into irrationality came at moments of crisis. In the midst of the Vietnam offensive in 1972, Press Secretary Ron Ziegler observed to a staff member: "The old man's really high again." During the Cambodian invasion, Nixon seemed incoherent to some officials at the Pentagon. "He was a little bit out of control," one observer noted. "It scared the shit out of me." It was perhaps because of such lapses that Secretary of Defense Laird directly disobeyed the president's order to bomb PLO bases in Jordan.

Toward the end, Nixon's mental state became a source of explicit concern to some. In the midst of a presidential briefing for congressional leaders during the Arab-Israeli war in 1973, Nixon started to giggle and roll his head, making jokes about Kissinger's sex life. "[The] President is acting very strange," Tip O'Neill wrote in his notes. Reporters, in turn, noted Nixon's distracted appearance on his last trip abroad, and some concluded—with corroboration from White House sources—that Nixon's careless disregard of blood clots in his leg might be the president's way of seeking a final exit from the Watergate disaster. Vice-President Gerald Ford believed that Nixon had undergone a significant change of personality in the White House; and a senior official concluded that the president had been mentally ill for years. At the end, Defense Secretary James R. Schlesinger forbade his commanders from obeying any military order from the White House without his permission; and a lawyer who had worked intimately with Nixon during the final months observed: "Mr. Nixon's a very complex man. Who among us would measure up completely to anybody's particular definition of insanity?"

Whether there was a clinical basis for such assessments, the fact remained that Richard Nixon had acted irrationally and had more than once brought the country perilously close to disaster. His complicity in sabotage and spying, and his reckless contempt for constitutional safeguards, exceeded in kind, as well as degree, anything attempted during the Johnson administration. The only thing more frightening than the president's performance itself was how close Nixon came to succeeding in his subversion of the democratic process. Only the persistence of a few reporters and the political wisdom of Republicans and Democrats inside the Congress made possible the unearthing of just how pervasive was the sickness that threatened the nation's political institutions.

Ironically, Nixon finally succeeded—however unintentionally—in his 1968 promise to "bring us together again." Uniting in defense of a government of laws rather than personal whim, people from all walks of life finally rallied to control the excesses of the "imperial presidency."

Yet if the crisis was overcome, the cost was enormous. Nixon had been successful far beyond his fondest hopes in mobilizing a conservative majority, isolating his opponents, and demolishing the potential for protest from the left. Even the Watergate tragedy ultimately worked to the disadvantage of those with a different vision for America by diverting attention from issues of class, race, and inequality, and focusing all energies instead on the constitutional issue of a president abusing power. By 1974, there were few Americans with the psychic or social space to consider economic and social reform. There was a more pressing issue—the very survival of the American system of government. Paradoxically, Nixon had succeeded—despite himself—in achieving many of his most cherished political goals.

14

New Rules, Old Realities

The Continuing Intersection
of Gender, Class, and Race
in the Seventies

Richard Nixon had resigned the presidency in disgrace. American troops withdrew from Vietnam, their departure followed quickly by the total collapse of the Thieu regime. And Middle Eastern nations imposed a complete embargo on oil exports to America, triggering an energy shortage and unending gas lines. For nearly thirty years after World War II, Americans had controlled their own economic destiny and dominated the world. Now, that era appeared to be over. A new sense of limits set in, with Americans forced to confront realities at home and abroad that were frightening. Yet if one era had ended, it was by no means clear what the next would bring. The 1970s thus became a decade of transition—marked by confusion, frustration, and an overwhelming feeling that America had lost its direction, as if the very future of the "American experiment" might be in question.

One aspect of this new era testified to the enduring legacy of the "liberation" movements of the 1960s. Social commentator and pollster Daniel Yankelovich concluded that a new "cultural revolution" was sweeping the country. For two hundred years, he observed, Americans had believed in self-denial and the Protestant ethic. Now, those "old rules" were being set aside, replaced by "new rules" of self-fulfillment, immediate gratification, and personal freedom. The shift, Yankelovich argued, was tantamount to the movement of giant geological plates undergirding the nation, with new attitudes toward sex, family, and work threatening to transform the very structure of America's institutions. In one positive manifestation of the new freedom, hundreds of thousands of women and blacks broke down traditional barriers that had once kept them in their "place," registering dramatic gains in economic status, educational achievement, and social mobility. More ambiguously, family mores also changed. The number of divorces skyrocketed, and the nation seemed embarked on a new cycle of self-absorption and sexual liberation. While commentators bemoaned the "me generation decade," for some Americans at least the seventies represented a time of freedom and progress.

But even as some Americans made good on the promises of the sixties, millions of others became more entrenched than ever in the vicious cycle of poverty. A strange filtering process seemed at work; a growing schism of class divided individual blacks and women who were able to take advantage of the new freedom from their brothers and sisters who entered an ever-deepening spiral of unemployment and hopelessness. Welfare rolls mushroomed, single-headed households multiplied almost exponentially, and social commentators warned that, if present trends persisted, virtually all people classified as poor in the year 2000 would be either women or children. This "feminization of poverty" constituted a striking counterpoint to the liberation trumpeted by Yankelovich and others, portending the development of a "permanent underclass" who would forever be trapped by the circumstances of their birth and station in life.

This "other side" of America during the 1970s reflected the greatest shift of all in the new decade—the halt to economic growth. For most of the postwar period, Americans had lived in the midst of a prolonged boom, taking for granted the endless expansion of an economy fueled by technology, consumerism, and increased productivity. Faith in economic growth had constituted the linchpin of the "liberal consensus." As long as prosperity reigned, there was no need to be concerned about permanent inequality, since in John F. Kennedy's words, a "rising tide lifts everybody." Now, that era of expansion suddenly seemed at an end. Inflation reached unprecedented heights, unemployment swelled, productivity declined, and the economy entered a period of "stagflation." Faced with intractable problems that undercut the whole postwar ethos of consumerism and progress, many Americans became frustrated and restless, bewildered by events that shattered their sense of control and direction. In effect, they were looking for an anchor—a mooring—that would help provide security as they confronted the disarray that surrounded them. More and more, the issue seemed to boil down to one of cultural values, their picture of the country and society they lived in.

The political leadership of the 1970s reflected this malaise. In the aftermath of Watergate and Vietnam, presidential candidates repeatedly attempted to generate a new sense of confidence and purpose. But confusion and indecision prevailed at the ballot box as well. American voters oscillated wildly during the seventies, giving the Democrats their greatest majority in the postwar era in 1974, and then in 1980 doing the same for the Republicans. Moreover, almost half the potential electorate felt so alienated from the political process that they failed to vote at all, even in presidential elections. No one seemed able to find answers capable of forging a new consensus. While some subscribed to the liberation ethic that Yankelovich described, others rallied to the New Right, using issues like abortion, the

Equal Rights Amendment, prayer in the schools, and busing to build a political coalition commited to returning to the "old rules" of a bygone era. To a growing extent, politics became less about alternative economic programs and more about the "culture wars" between those who believed in an ethos of personal liberation and those who cleaved to traditional values, reinforced by the evangelical fervor of the New Right.

Ultimately, then, the 1970s became a microcosm of the unresolved conflicts within America society. No longer infused with the faith and optimism of the postwar years, Americans faced a frightening array of prospects—permanent economic stagnation, the presence of an "underclass" that directly challenged the essence of the American dream, and bitter division over fundamental cultural values. By the early 1980s, the only thing that seemed certain was how critical were the issues left still undecided.

The Positive Legacy of the 1960s

Of all the social movements of the 1960s, the ones that retained the most strength in the 1970s were the struggle for women's rights and the newly empowered movement for gay liberation. As its foundation, the women's movement called on men and women to fashion a new definition of human identity—one which would no longer rely on traditional conceptions of masculinity and femininity. In consciousness-raising sessions throughout the country, feminists drew strength from each other as they united in demanding an end to class treatment, to the idea that women—as women—should automatically be expected to take minutes at meetings, get lower pay than men, wash dishes, get up with the baby at night, or place their aspirations behind those of their husbands. By the early 1970s, the movement had become a national sensation, its advocates picketing professional meetings to demand equal employment opportunities, boycotting the Miss America contest to protest the treatment of women as sex objects, and demonstrating before state legislators for the repeal of abortion laws. Although the media ridiculed and caricatured its demands, there was virtually no household in the land that had not become aware of the movements' insistence on a radical re-examination of what it meant to be male and female in America.

The women's movement of the early 1970s differed from its predecessors in two primary ways: it drew its strength from the grass roots' energies of women in local communities working to improve their own immediate lives, and it pursued a variety of objectives, each in its own way pivotal to attacking the pervasive presence of sex discrimination. Some observers criticized the movement for its lack of focus and organization, but its alleged weaknesses were in fact the source of its greatest strength. Women in countless towns and cities organized in small groups to deal with the reality of discrimination in their own lives and to devise strategies to combat it. One group might come together to work with public school teachers on eliminating sexism in the classroom. Others organized for political action, published children's books that avoided invidious sexual stereotypes, started abortion and birth control clinics, or established day-care centers. Support groups for lesbian women, widows, divorcees, or battered wives occupied other activists. The extent to which the movement grew out of, and related back to, the immediate experience of large numbers of women made unnecessary the centralized and hierarchical structures of the past. The absence of these structures, in turn, encouraged the development of multiple activities, each dealing with a particular aspect of sex inequality. Although such issues as the Equal Rights Amendment drew the most national attention, supporters of women's liberation understood that the problem they confronted had many dimensions and ultimately required parallel action against sex discrimination wherever it manifested itself.

Inevitably, the most profound consequence of the women's movement occurred in the individual lives of those who enrolled in the struggle. "Ten years ago," Robin Morgan wrote in 1975, "I was a woman who believed in the reality of the vaginal orgasm (and had become adept at faking spiffy ones). I felt legitimized by a successful crown roast and was the fastest hand in the east at emptying ash trays." But then came the movement,

> a blur of joy, misery, and daily surprise: my first consciousness raising group. . . . the guerrilla theatre, the marches, meetings, demonstrations, picketing, sit-ins, conferences. . . . and all the while, the profound "interior" changes: the tears and shouts and laughter and growth wrought in the struggle with my husband; . . . the detailed examination of life experiences, of power, honesty, and commitment.

With each passing year, such stories multiplied a thousandfold as women shared together intimate details of their lives and created a new sense of purpose and determination. The result was new personalities, new values, new commitments to self-development and collective action. "I have learned to love that women's movement," Morgan concluded; "I want to say to [every] woman: we've only just begun; and there's no stopping us."

Since feminism challenged the entire structure of society, the women's movement was bound to provoke hostility and resentment. Its very decentralization and diversity generated internecine conflicts. Lesbian women expected "straight" women to identify with their cause; more "mainstream" feminists like Betty Friedan viewed gay activists as "the lavender menace." Marxists believed that only a revolution of the entire social structure could bring equality; middle-class professionals sought reform within the existing structure. Ideological polemics occasionally threatened to sabotage the entire possibility of achieving "sisterhood," with groups contending against each other in an effort to become more "pure" in their feminism. Nonmovement observers, meanwhile, responded to feminism's more strident appeals with dismay and anger. Many men felt that their authority, their strength, and their very identity were under attack. And many women who had devoted their lives to fulfilling the culturally sanctioned role of home-maker believed that the movement was judging and indicting them as failures.

But astonishingly enough, the movement succeeded in bringing about substantial change in American attitudes toward gender roles. Although opinion surveys in the early 1970s showed that many women continued to harbor antagonism toward the movement per se ("it's too extreme"; "it goes overboard"), the same women in a majority of cases endorsed feminist positions on day-care centers, repeal of abortion laws, equal career opportunities for women, and a greater sharing of household tasks. Whatever the acceptability of the movement as a movement, its message and ideas were making an impact. When a Gallup Poll asked American women in 1962 whether they felt themselves victims of discrimination, two out of three said no. Eight years later, in response to the same question, half of the women declared that they were victims of discrimination. And when the question was asked yet again four years later, American women by a margin of two to one asserted that they *were* treated unequally and that they supported efforts to improve their status. Significantly, the changes coincided almost exactly with the emergence of the women's movement as a central force in American society.

Not surprisingly, the movement exerted its greatest influence on college students. At the end of the 1960s, Daniel Yankelovich reported, the woman's movement had made virtually "no impact on youth values and attitudes." But by the early 1970s Yankelovich noted a "wide and deep" acceptance of women's liberation arguments. In just two years, the number of students who viewed women as an oppressed group had doubled. A large majority of women endorsed equality in sexual relations, the importance of women's relationships to other women, and the idea that men and women were born with the same talents. Over two-thirds of college women, moreover, agreed that "the idea that a woman's place is in the home is nonsense," an idea that would have been unheard of twenty years earlier. A 1970 survey of college freshmen had indicated that half the men and more than one-third of the women endorsed the idea that "the activities of married women are best confined to the home and the family." Five years later, only one-third of the men and less than one-fifth of the women took the same position.

Such changing attitudes coincided with and reinforced the accelerating pace of women's entry into the paid labor force. Throughout the post-World War II era, employment rates for women had climbed steadily upward, constituting what labor economist Eli Ginsburg called "the single [most] outstanding phenomenon of our century." The spiraling increase represented an essential ingredient in the expansion of middle-class households in the 1950s and 1960s; it also reflected an underlying cultural logic. During the 1950s, most women joining the labor force were over the age of thirty-five and had children who were in high school or out of the home. During the 1960s, in turn, the greatest employment increase took place among women between the ages of twenty-five and thirty-five—generally after their children entered school. (By 1970, more than 50 percent of mothers whose children were six to seventeen were employed.) In short, the women who pioneered the postwar increase in the female labor force avoided directly challenging the societal prescription that mothers should stay at home to care for young children. In almost all cases, women's jobs were seen as helping the family, not as expressions of feminist independence or autonomy. Now, however, the greatest employment increase occurred among younger women of child-bearing age. The proportion of women in the twenty to twenty-four year old age group who worked increased from 50 percent in 1964 to 61 percent in 1973. Among college women the employment rate in that age group was 86 percent. Most startling of all was the change among women with young children. By 1980, more than 50 percent of mothers with children under six were in the labor force. To an ever-increasing extent, female employment had been redefined as a life vocation, with time taken out for childbearing and only a few years of childrearing. Almost all women expected to be employed for most of their lives—a radical contrast to the situation that existed just thirty-five years earlier.

Perhaps most important, the college women who had proven most receptive to the ideology of women's liberation now seemed intent on moving forcefully into careers historically restricted to "males only." In a 1970 survey of freshmen college students, men outnumbered women eight to one in expressing an interest in the traditionally "masculine" fields of business, engineering, medicine, and law. By 1975, the ratio was down to three to one. During the same years, moreover, the number of women expecting to enter the "feminine" professions of elementary and secondary school teaching plummeted from 31 percent to 10 percent. Reflecting these trends, the proportion of women entering law school during the 1970s mushroomed 500 percent, with most law schools—and an increasing number of medical schools—boasting entering classes that were 40 percent women. (The figures had been 5 to 8 percent during the forties, fifties, and sixties.) During the same decade, the number of women earning doctorates increased from 11 percent of the total to more than 25 percent. No longer, it seemed, did women college students expect to secure a degree and then get married. Instead, the ideology of feminism had converted them to the belief that women—no less than men—should expect to have full access to careers defined as prestigious and important. One survey of eight colleges in 1973 showed that 82 percent of the women students considered a career important to their self-fulfillment, while only 67 percent put marriage in the same category.

Partly as a consequence of these changes, the composition of the typical American family also changed dramatically. As late as the 1950s, more than 70 percent of all American families consisted of a father who worked and a mother who stayed at home to take care of the children. By 1980, that description applied to only 15 percent of all families. In the same years, birth rates declined precipitously. At the height of the "baby boom," the average family had more than three children. By 1980, that figure had fallen to less than 1.6 children. Demographers in the 1960s attributed the decline to oral contraceptives and economic changes, predicting a new "baby boom" in the 1970s. But rather than rising, the birth rate reached an all-time low in the 1970s, achieving the reproduction level required for zero population growth. The crucial variable that demographers had underestimated was the influence of cultural values. In fact, the declining birth rate of the 1960s and 1970s could be traced to the "multiplier effect" of changing attitudes toward gender roles and women's new economic aspirations. Women married later, delayed the birth of their first child (often their only child), and bore their last child at an earlier age. Whether as cause or effect, this trend coincided with many women finding careers and interests outside the home. Two Gallup polls in 1967 and 1971 sharply revealed the shift in values. The 1967 survey showed that 34 percent of women in the prime childbearing years anticipated having four or more children. By 1971, the figure had dropped to 15 percent.

Changes in family composition also testified, at least in part, to the "new rules" that Daniel Yankelovich saw as so pervasive among the young. In an age that emphasized personal happiness and immediate gratification, millions of Americans no longer were willing to sacrifice self-fulfillment to maintain marriages or relationships that failed to meet their demands. The divorce rate climbed almost 100 percent during the 1960s, and after a brief period of stability in the early 1970s, increased another 82 percent by 1980. More than two out of five marriages initiated during the 1970s would end in divorce. The number of individuals living in "single households" sky-rocketed from 10.9 percent in 1964 to 23 percent in 1980. And although there was no direct cause and effect, social scientists noted a clear correlation between the increase in the divorce rate and the number of women entering the labor force.

The same "new morality" seemed to be reflected in attitudes toward sexuality. Prior to the late 1960s, rates of premarital intercourse conformed to the patterns established in the 1920s, with engaged women having the highest frequency of premarital sex. From the late 1960s onward, however, a major increase occurred in the number of women having intercourse while in a "dating" or "going-steady" relationship. A nationwide sample of freshmen college women in 1975 disclosed that one-third endorsed casual sex based on a short acquaintance, and that over 40 percent believed a couple should live together before getting married. Most indicative of changing mores, perhaps, was a mid-1970s survey of eight colleges that showed that 76 percent of women had engaged in intercourse by their junior year (the male figure was 75 percent), and that women were appreciably more active sexually than men. Other poll data suggested that college students, in particular, had changed their underlying approach toward sexual behavior and attitudes. Only a minority of women disapproved of premarital sex, homosexual relationships between consenting adults, or abortion. Although such attitudes sometimes became a trap in which women were victimized as sex objects under the guise of sexual freedom (for example, the TV ad featuring a beautiful woman who says that "All my men wear English Leather"), a veritable seachange had clearly occurred in the rules governing sexual behavior.

By the 1980s, therefore, it was possible to conclude that for some women—particularly the college-educated young—important breakthroughs had taken place in the realm of personal freedom, self-realization, and autonomy. Informed by changing attitudes toward individual fulfillment, hundreds of thousands had charted a new course, free of constraints that in the past had assigned women to prescribed roles. It was still too early to conclude that these changes meant significant progress toward equality. Most professions were still controlled by men; professional women received only 73 percent of the salaries paid to professional men; and while a record number of women were entering junior levels of medicine, law, and business, it was by no means assured that they would receive promotions and rewards comparable to those awarded their male counterparts. Nevertheless, it remained true that many women had achieved a level of independence and freedom that would have been unheard of just two decades earlier, building on the advances of the feminist movement to record far-reaching and impressive personal gains.

The gay rights movement also boomed during the 1970s. For years dominated by small cell-like gatherings and seeking respectability through organizations like the Mattachine Society (male) and the Daughters of Bilitis (female), gay Americans found a new voice of assertive self-affirmation after the Stonewall Riots in New York City in 1969. All along, gay bars had been the gathering places where men and women who were homosexual could find the freedom to express themselves uncircumscribed by having to role-play in a "straight" world. Like churches in the black community, gay bars provided the organizing base for a new insistence on equal rights. One night, when New York City police for the umpteenth time chose to raid the Stonewall, a gay bar in New York's Greenwich Village, the patrons decided to rise up as one and fight back, hurling bricks at police cars, jousting with their tormentors, and forcing the police to retreat.

A new sense of pride and militancy then spread among gays throughout the country, manifesting itself in annual gay rights parades, a new willingness to "come out of the closet" and celebrate their homosexuality, and a determination through political and legal activism to enhance their power as gay Americans and their status as equal citizens before the law. An American who had erotic feelings toward members of the same sex and who grew up in the '30s, '40s, and '50s had almost no opportunity to express those feelings publicly and felt compelled to conform to the norms of the dominant culture, even when that meant listening to, and laughing at, jokes about "fags" and "dykes." But now there was a new willingness to stand up and fight back, demand equal respect, and publicly proclaim one's pride at being gay, celebrating a different sexual identity than that which had previously dictated social norms. Anti-gay discrimination remained powerful, particularly in New Right religious groups; but more and more, gays won "domestic partner benefits" at the workplace, legal reforms in employment statutes, and a political seat among those wielding power.

Hundreds of thousands of black Americans also seized on the advances of the 1960s to move energetically into the mainstream of American economic and social life. The Civil Rights Act of 1964 and the Voting Rights Act of 1965 had swept away any laws that sanctioned political discrimination against Negro citizens. The Housing Act of 1968, in turn, removed the last legal obstacle to black citizens who dreamed of moving to a better neighborhood or wherever they could afford a house. By 1971, the Supreme Court's pathbreaking decisions on racial balance and busing had created a situation where virtually every school system in the Old South was thoroughly integrated. With the way cleared for black citizens to claim their birthright of full participation in the benefits of the American way of life, those in a position to move ahead maximized the opportunity to transform the conditions of their lives.

Economic statistics provided one index of the progress that some Afro-Americans made as a consequence. The proportion of black families earning more than $10,000 a year (in constant dollars) leaped from 13 percent in 1960 to 31 percent in 1971 (it had been 3 percent in 1947). While income for white families increased 69 percent in the 1960s, income for black families leaped 109 percent. On the average, black Americans still earned only 61 percent of what white families received, but that represented a substantial increase over the 48 percent of a decade before. Moreover, in many areas of the country, the gap narrowed still further. Outside of the South, husband and wife two-income families earned 88 percent of what white two-income families received. Simultaneously, black political clout increased substantially, bolstered by advances made possible through the Voting Rights Act. During the 1970s black mayors were elected in Los Angeles, Detroit, Cleveland, Birmingham, Oakland, and Atlanta. The number of blacks in Congress, meanwhile, increased from 4 in 1959, to 10 a decade later, and to 18 by 1980.

The sharpest gains took place in the educational arena. The median number of school years for black citizens increased from 10.7 in 1960 to 12.2 in 1970, only half a percentage point less than whites. In 1960, only 227,000 black Americans were enrolled in the nation's colleges. By the end of the 1960s, that figure had increased by 100 percent, and in 1977, 1.1 million blacks attended America's universities (a 500 percent increase over 1960). Indeed, the U.S. Census Bureau concluded that "among high school graduates, blacks and whites [were] attending colleges at about the same rate (32 percent)." As corporate recruitment of black college graduates increased in response to affirmative action mandates, many well-educated black Americans entered professional and technical jobs previously set aside for whites only. In the North, black college graduates could even expect to earn slightly more than their white counterparts at entry-level positions.

All of this amounted, in the eyes of some observers, to a story of "massive black success." With school desegregation and better jobs, hundreds of thousands of blacks moved out of black ghettos into middle-class neighborhoods. Ben Wattenberg and Richard Scammon estimated that as many as half of all black families had risen to join the middle class. Although such statistics may have been debatable, there could be no gainsaying the fact that substantial numbers of black Americans had seen their lives transformed. The civil rights struggles of the 1960s *had* made a difference, resulting in progress that would have been unthinkable just a few years earlier.

The Other Side of the Coin

Such "success stories," however, described only one aspect of American society during the 1970s. If a person were bright, talented, and from an economically secure background, liberation from the encrusted traditions of racism and sexism could indeed spell a life of unparalleled new opportunity. But there were millions of other blacks and women whose stories represented the direct antithesis of upward mobility and economic advancement. For these people, the 1970s produced massive suffering—a downward spiral into deeper poverty and the experience of being trapped by circumstances that seemed totally outside any individual's capacity to change. This "other side" of the picture was one of despair, hopelessness, and chronic misery. For its victims, the social changes of the 1960s meant nothing. Instead, they found themselves more buffeted than ever by the triple whammy of race, class, and gender oppression.

For women, one source of continued discrimination was the type of jobs set aside for female workers. Despite well-publicized examples of individual women scoring significant gains in male professions, the overwhelming majority of women workers occupied positions in the labor force that were deadend, low paying, and sex segregated. Over 80 percent of all women workers, for example, clustered in 20 of the 420 occupations listed by the Census Bureau. The areas of personal services and clerical work were defined almost exclusively as "women's jobs"; yet it was precisely such occupations that suffered the most dramatic decline in real earnings during the inflationary cycle of the seventies. Even within these categories, women experienced substantial sex discrimination. Women salesworkers, for example, earned only 52 percent as much as male salesworkers; furthermore, they tended to be assigned to those customer areas where commissions were not offered on sales. One economist estimated that 70 percent of all the new private-sector employment positions created between 1973 and 1980 were in the low-paid retail and service areas. As higher-paid skilled jobs disappeared, women flooded into the jobs at the bottom—jobs that paid the minimum wage or only slightly above. Thus, although women experienced an employment "boom" in the late 1960s and 1970s, the work most entered offered almost no possibility for upward mobility. "We may be approaching a situation like that in some industrializing third world countries," one economist declared, "where there has been a big increase in jobs for women . . . but the jobs don't lead anywhere, they don't lift women out of poverty." Ironically, women's work frequently meant marginal survival instead of the liberation so often trumpeted in the media.

Divorce, separation, or desertion compounded women's economic plight. While a few may have gained from the "new morality" of tolerance toward divorce and family breakup, for many more women the departure of a male breadwinner spelled disaster. In her compelling narrative of "the nouveau poor," historian Barbara Ehrenreich described in graphic detail the stories of such women. Avis Parke had been the wife of a Unitarian minister, devoting her days to raising six children and helping her husband's "mission" to his parishioners. She was almost fifty years old when he announced he wished a divorce. With few marketable skills, Avis Parke and her children ended up on the welfare rolls, buying clothes at the Salvation Army, using food stamps to secure their daily nutrition, suddenly catapulted from middle-class comfort into deep poverty. One of Parke's friends, a woman named Carla, was forced to leave her affluent Long Island home because her husband systematically battered her and her child. She, too, ended up on welfare, making a few extra dollars by working as a cleaning woman. Ehrenreich estimated that 85 percent of all American women could expect to support themselves at some time in their lives without the aid of a husband or male job holder. Although many of these women did find work, most frequently the jobs they entered fell into the category of "women's work," paying a minimum wage that left a woman and her children still poor. Approximately 25 percent of all working women who were heads of households with children received incomes beneath the poverty level. By 1980, more than 2 million other women were either working part-time "involuntarily" or could not find a full-time job because of "home responsibilities." For these people, the new "liberation" of women was laughable. As one of Ehrenreich's "working poor" observed: "I work in an office with fifteen fantastic women who are suffering exactly as I am. You want to talk about mad? Everyone of these women is divorced. We come home with a hundred and twenty-three dollars a week. We don't even know how we are going to eat . . . how the kids are going to be fed."

Underlying the rapid acceleration of the "feminization of poverty" was a massive increase in female-headed households during the 1960s and 1970s. At the end of the 1950s, 3 million Americans received welfare assistance under the program of Aid to Families with Dependent Children (AFDC). By 1980, that figure had soared to 11 million—8 million children and 3 million women—almost all in female-headed households. During the 1970s alone, the number of women heading families with children increased by 72 percent. The correlation with poverty was direct and startling. A child born into a family with no father in the house had one chance in three of being poor; if a family was headed by a man alone, the chances of being poor were one in ten; and if both parents were present, the chances were only one in nineteen. With each passing year, moreover, the problem deepened. During the 1970s the number of poor families with a man present *declined* by 25 percent; but the number of poor families headed by women *increased* 38.7 percent. By 1980, 66 percent of all adults officially classified as poor were women. The "feminization of poverty" reflected not only low-paying and unskilled jobs, but also inadequate training for better jobs. More than half of all single-parent families were headed by people who had never completed high school. The problem was compounded further by a soaring increase in teenage pregnancies. One of every six children born in America during the 1970s had a teenage mother. Most frequently, these mothers were unmarried, had dropped out of school in order to raise their children, and thus became even more deeply trapped in the cycle of poverty.

Perhaps most dramatically, the phenomenon of female-headed households reflected the intersection of race and gender. While the number of white families headed by women increased from 9.4 percent in 1970 to 14 percent in 1980, the number of black families headed by women skyrocketed to 47 percent (for Puerto Rican families the figure was 40 percent), constituting a virtual epidemic. (In 1970, the figure for black families had been 30 percent; in 1950, 17.6 percent.) Black women also experienced most severely the debilitating consequences of new sexual mores. One out of every three black children was born to a teenage mother, and 55 percent of all black babies were born out of wedlock. In inner-city ghettos, the figure often climbed above 70 percent. The consequences were devastating. "You can't underestimate the stress of raising a child in the ghetto by yourself," Eleanor Holmes Norton, a black lawyer and civil rights advocate observed, "without a grandma, without an aunt, with no one you can turn to."

A direct correlation existed between such statistics and the increasing impoverishment of millions of black families. A female-headed black family earned a median income of less than $6,000 in 1978—compared to $16,000 earned by two-parent black families. Yet one of the reasons black women lived alone was because there were no jobs for black men. The unemployment rate for black male teenagers reached the astronomical figure of 50 percent during the 1970s, helping to explain the number of black female teenagers who bore their children out of wedlock and without financial support from a father. Furthermore, welfare laws in many states required that no male be present if AFDC payments were to be received, thus

424 THE UNFINISHED JOURNEY

creating an incentive for black men to live apart from their children, particularly if they were unemployed. It was all a vicious cycle. Young men in the ghetto could not find jobs. Young women in the ghetto needed welfare to support their children. Welfare rules discriminated against those who had a husband present. The end result was that black women became heads of families, descending further into poverty and starting the entire cycle all over again.

One of the primary consequences of this process was the increasing bifurcation of black America into a two-class society. While 35 to 45 percent of black families succeeded in achieving a middle-class lifestyle during the seventies, another 30 percent of the black population experienced a steady decline into ever deeper poverty. "As [some] Negro families succeed," one commentator noted, "they tend to move out of these economically and socially depressed areas to better neighborhoods where they and their children have a better opportunity to lead a better life. They leave behind the least educated and the most deprived—unwed mothers, deserted wives, the physically and mentally handicapped, and the aged. As a result there is a concentration of misery in the very hearts of our largest cities." Significantly, black families living on the margins of the nation's urban ghettos made substantial gains during the 1960s and 1970s; but in the heart of the ghetto, every indicator of poverty showed deterioration. In the past, blacks from all classes had been united by neighborhood bonds, common institutions, and a shared commitment to self-help and progress. Now, the middle-class leadership of those communities moved into desegregated suburbs, leaving the least well off to endure crime, massive unemployment, malnutrition, and urban chaos. In the past, the majority of poor families had lived in rural areas of America. Now, more than 70 percent lived in inner cities.

As a consequence of such bifurcation, the lives of inner-city blacks became a montage of unmitigated blight, depression, and hopelessness. More than 50 percent of black teenagers in New York City dropped out of school before receiving their high school diploma. Drug addiction, crime, and alcoholism entered an upward spiral. Overall, black family income declined from 60 percent of white family income in 1971 to 58 percent by 1980, while the share of low-income households headed by blacks increased by almost a third. "We're not born to be where we are," the psychiatrist Robert Coles observed. "We *become* what we are. We are raised to expect a lot or to expect virtually nothing. We are given hope or taught fear. We live in a time of progress, or we live amidst . . . chaos." For most inner-city blacks, the seventies became a decade of expecting "virtually nothing," being "taught fear" and living amidst "chaos." A black child was twice as likely to die before reaching age one as a white child, more than twice as likely to drop out of school or be suspended, and more than four times as likely to be murdered between the ages of one and four.

For the millions who endured such conditions, the worst-case scenario was rapidly becoming a reality—a life sentence of impoverishment. "The great unmentioned problem of America today," Senator Edward Kennedy declared in 1978, "[is] the growth, rapid and insidious, of a group in our midst, perhaps more dangerous, more bereft of hope, more difficult to confront, than any for which our history has prepared us. It is a group that threatens to become what America has never known—a permanent underclass in our society." Of the approximately 30 million Americans classified as "poor" in 1980, at least 9 million fit Kennedy's category. Welfare mothers, ex-drug addicts, habitual criminals, or simply societal "drop-outs," these individuals represented the ultimate intersection of race, class, and gender. Approximately 70 percent were nonwhite, 50 percent came from female-headed households, and two-thirds were children under eighteen. There were no jobs for such people. In New York City, 40,000 youngsters dropped out of high school each year; but of the 105,000 annual job openings in New York, only 9,000 were for messengers, janitors, bus boys, or maids—those occupations available for people without skill or education. The result was an ever-burgeoning group afflicted by chronic hopelessness. According to one survey of the "underclass," virtually none of the teenagers had completed high school, more than half had been arrested, and a third of those who received AFDC had been on public welfare for more than eight years.

Ironically, the welfare system itself became part of the problem, its dehumanizing processes breeding dependency, helplessness, frustration, and lowered self-respect. Barbara Ehrenreich described two typical cases. In one, a woman who had fled a husband who battered her arrived at the welfare office at eight-thirty in the morning, dressed neatly in an attempt to impress welfare officials. She waited for eight hours, skipping lunch because she had no money. Still she was not seen by social workers. The same delays occurred the next day, until finally she exploded and was granted an interview. Another woman described the repeated assaults on her dignity that occurred whenever she went to ask for additional food stamps or clothing allowances. "I would cry whenever I came home," she said, "and my kids would ask 'momma, what's wrong?' I just had to be alone for awhile afterwards because it was so degrading. . . . I felt like a hungry dog going to get a very small bone." According to one social scientist, welfare workers all too often acted like "colonial administrators" handling the "natives." The poor were always being "caught up in someone else's social reality." They had no input of their own and were treated with constant condescension. In most European "welfare states," almost all citizens received public health care and child assistance, with no stigma attached to the process; but in America, those who sought help were viewed with suspicion, their need for assistance taken as a sign that something was wrong with them, that they were "less worthy" than others, and hence deserved to be treated as wayward children.

In the face of such attitudes, many welfare recipients became locked into the system, angry and cynical about its abuses, yet unable to see any way out. Ultimately, they came to devalue themselves. With few support groups to draw on, welfare became the only answer. "You get into security and hate to lose it," one welfare recipient observed. "You're afraid to let go, for fear of not being able to support your child." In rural areas, there were relatives to turn to during the hardest times. "In the South," one woman declared, "we [had] more unity—family unity. It's like being rooted. Your grandparents done it this way, your mama done it this way, and you in turn take it that way." But once such people migrated to the North, these support systems evaporated, leaving helpless individuals alone to cope with realities beyond their comprehension. "Many are illiterate, unskilled, without health care," Marion Wright Edelman of the Children's Defense Fund wrote. "This is compounded by unemployment, and by the language problem if they are Puerto Rican. I think about how hard it would be to raise a child if I were fifteen and I had an eighth-grade education and I didn't speak much English and I were in a big city. I can't imagine it. I can't imagine the isolation, the feeling of hopelessness and fear."

For many of these people, welfare became a way of life, perpetuated from generation to generation. As one welfare mother said: "A lot of those on welfare stay on welfare cause they say, 'Why work? Someone is going to take care of me. As long as Uncle Sam will do it, why not?' Then they instill it in their children: 'Why should I have to go out there and bust my behind and have them take it out of my taxes?'" The result was what experts and welfare recipients alike referred to as a "welfare mentality." With no real jobs available, what was the alternative? As a consequence, the whole system began to feed on itself, becoming a given from which there was no escape. "The child's being around people who [are] just cursing all day, getting high and drinking," one welfare recipient observed. "That kid don't get a chance to see nothing else. So its like what the child learns." The end result was always more of the same—more illiteracy, more drug addiction, more crime, more dependence on welfare. Some called the results a "culture of poverty," but whichever label was used, the reality was a world in which the sole focus was on how to survive, not how to break the cycle. Perhaps most frightening of all, the situation seemed destined to become worse. In 1940, fewer than one child in ten was supported by welfare; by 1970, the figure had risen to one in three, and it was getting higher.

Whatever the ultimate explanation, it seemed clear by the end of the 1970s that America was quickly on its way to becoming a two-tiered society. For those with a decent education, technological skills, a secure family background, and an aptitude for those jobs most prized by a post-industrial society, a decent chance existed for advancement, comfort, and prosperity, with race and gender becoming increasingly less an obstacle to success. But for those on the bottom, the 1970s brought alienation, hopelessness, dependency, and an ever-deepening immersion in poverty. With neither education, decent health care, minimal nutrition, or an environment that gave hope for escape, the shackles of gender joined those of class and race to create a world totally at odds with that of middle-class existence. Few talked about the problem; and an even smaller number attempted to do anything about it. But in the long run, there was no single phenomenon that more directly threatened the cohesiveness of American society.

A New Economy

At about the same time that some Americans first noted the appearance of an "underclass," the economic foundations of America's postwar boom also began to erode. Rapid growth had been the wellspring of America's startling prosperity after World War II. The number of businesses in the United States had increased sevenfold. Exports boomed from $4 billion in 1945 to $180 billion by the 1970s. Average family income (in real dollars) more than doubled in the same years. Unemployment steadily declined until it reached 4 percent in the 1960s, with inflation held constant. The Gross National Product had increased by more than 100 percent, and in the early 1960s American workers produced four times as much as Japanese workers and twice as much as German workers. Such prosperity constituted the underpinning for America's faith that economic progress for *all* people—especially the poor—could occur without any conscious effort to redistribute income. Now, in the early 1970s, all these indicators of progress began a startling and sustained decline. For the first time since World War II, Americans faced economic realities that undermined rather than reinforced traditional optimism. "What happens to society's unity when the self-denial ethic is no longer reinforced by an expanding economy?," one observer asked. "What happens when the . . . growth machine begins to falter at the very moment that the population's appetites have been whetted and its expectations have reached unprecedented heights? . . . What happens when economy and culture are reversed."

Although the declines of the 1970s reflected a series of mutually reinforcing causes, experts unanimously agreed that the origins of the crisis lay in political decisions made by Lyndon Johnson and Richard Nixon. Unwilling to face the threat to his Great Society programs that would have occurred if the Vietnam war had been funded on a "pay as you go" basis, Johnson refused to raise taxes and insisted that the country could have both "guns and butter." As a result, government deficits caused by the war increased dramatically, while consumer spending power—unreduced by increased tax levies—overheated the economy at home. Politically, Johnson had succeeded in obscuring—for the moment at least—the inherent contradiction between greater social welfare expenditures and an astronomical rise in military spending. But, inevitably, deficits weakened the dollar and, by 1971, inflation had reached an unheard of postwar rate of 4.5 percent. Initially, Nixon responded to the inflationary cycle by increasing interest rates, lowering the money supply, and promoting a planned recession. But he, too, placed political self-interest ahead of economic common sense, and to bolster his chances for re-election, suddenly imposed wage and price controls in the summer of 1971 in an effort to restrain inflation and restore prosperity prior to the 1972 presidential election. Successful in the short term, his policies proved disastrous in the long run. Once wage and price controls were removed, inflation skyrocketed, reinforced by OPEC's decision to increase oil prices substantially. Held to well under 5 percent between 1955 and 1972, inflation suddenly exploded to 8 percent at the beginning of 1973 and to nearly 10 percent by the end of the year. Nixon's 1972 budget deficit was $40 billion—more than 300 percent larger than he had forecast—and the economy reeled into disarray.

When the Arab oil embargo began in 1973, it simply confirmed the extent to which Americans no longer exercised complete control over their own economic destiny. American devaluation of the dollar in 1971 had sharply reduced the incomes of oil-producing nations, and to recoup their losses as well as to protest American support of Israel, Arab nations imposed an embargo on oil shipments to the United States. As late as the middle 1960s, such a boycott would have made little impact, since America was largely self-sufficient in energy production. But to an increasing extent, Americans had become dependent on Middle Eastern oil reserves. As a result, when the embargo finally ended, OPEC nations had quadrupled the price of oil. During the winter of 1973 and 1974, heating oil and gas prices in America shot up as much as 33 percent. Yet Americans continued to increase rather than diminish their dependency on Arab oil. In 1970, the United States had spent only $4 billion for imported oil; in 1980, the figure was $90 billion. Although some economists believed that the increase in oil prices explained only a small portion of the overall rise in inflation, the real significance of the oil boycott was to drive home—in unmistakable terms— the extent to which America's economic dominance in the world had been undermined. Arab sheiks may not have singlehandedly caused inflation or monetary instability, but they confirmed the extent to which Americans no longer could shape their economic future alone. In this sense, one commentator concluded, "the year 1973 should probably be taken as a watershed, sharply dividing the second half of the 20th century." Prior to that year, America had exercised virtually unchallenged economic and military dominance in the world. Afterward, it became a dependent nation.

In the wake of the Arab oil boycott, economic distress multiplied dramatically, with almost every indicator testifying to the depth and pervasiveness of the crisis. Inflation hit double digits in 1973 and 1974. During the period from 1972 to 1978, industrial productivity rose only 1 percent per year (the average had been 3.2 percent from 1948 to 1955) compared to a 4 percent average increase in West Germany and over 5 percent in Japan. The standard of living in the United States fell to fifth in the world, with Denmark, West Germany, Sweden, and Switzerland surging ahead; Switzerland's per capita Gross National Product (GNP) was 45 percent larger than America's. In the past, unemployment had been a cure for inflation, with government-manipulated recessions helping to bring down prices, and employment resuming its growth once inflation was under control. Now, unemployment and inflation increased simultaneously, as if they were symbiotically related. When inflation reached 11 percent in 1975, unemployment swelled to nearly 9 percent. None of the old policies seemed to work, at least in part because U.S. dependency on foreign oil and its continually declining competitive position against foreign firms had created economic pressures hitherto unknown.

By the 1980s, changes in the domestic job market had further deepened the economic crisis. Throughout the postwar years, blue-collar jobs had expanded only 19 percent—well below the 32 percent average growth rate for all jobs, and four times less than the growth rate in clerical positions. Yet industrial workers were the first to be laid off. With capital expenditures declining, there were simply no *new* jobs in those fields that most directly occupied the working class. Companies that did modernize relied on automation. With robots and computers increasingly taking the place of skilled workers, structural unemployment soared, debilitating the working class. As one expert noted, "The re-organization of work that occurs with the introduction of new automation equipment tends to eliminate jobs at the center of the skilled spectrum. We call it the case of the disappearing middle. You have more low skilled jobs at the bottom, jobs that are likely to be slotted for women, and then you have managerial jobs—and a growing polarization between them."

In the face of these developments, worker alienation and discontent multiplied. When the productivity of American labor declined, corporate leaders placed the blame on worker laziness and lack of motivation. From a worker perspective, however, the problem was one of management insensitivity, and what appeared to be a calculated effort to displace workers, destroy trade unions, and limit, wherever possible, labor participation in management decisions. "The leaders of industry . . . have broken and discarded the fragile, unwritten compact previously existing during past periods of growth and progress," United Automobile Workers' President Douglas Frasier declared in 1978. Instead of seeking cooperation with workers, Frasier charged, business leaders were waging a "one-sided class war." In Lordstown, Ohio, for example, General Motors attempted to double the output of cars on its assembly lines, giving workers only 36 seconds to perform their tasks and imposing harsh new work rules that required union members to secure permission to leave their posts for only one or two minutes. When the workers went on strike in protest, the episode became what one journalist called an "industrial Woodstock," and what another labor relations authority portrayed as "the explosion of youth in its rebellion against the management and union Establishment." Products of the cultural revolution of the 1960s and the demoralizing effects of the Vietnam War, younger workers were primarily interested in self-rewarding and interesting jobs; they sought greater participation in decisions affecting their workload, more informality at the workplace, and a larger responsibility for establishing their own goals. Yet at precisely that moment, management seemed determined to promote routinization, impersonality, and a rigid distinction between supervisors and workers. As absenteeism and drug addiction increased and productivity declined, one sociologist concluded that "the sky has finally fallen. Workers in virtually all occupational demographic categories [are evidencing] appreciable and unmistakable manifestations of rising discontent."

With signs of economic distress increasing, "stagflation" took an ever deeper toll. By the early 1980s real discretionary income per worker had declined 18 percent since 1973. In the meantime, inflation continued unabated. The average price of a new single-family home more than doubled in the seventies, while the cost of basic necessities rose 110 percent. Worker morale also continued to deteriorate. In 1969, 79 percent of non-college-educated young people agreed that "hard work always pays off"; by the mid-1970s the figure had fallen to 56 percent. Union membership declined to less than 25 percent of the nonagricultural work force (it had already fallen from 35 percent in 1954 to 28 percent in 1966), and management intensified its efforts to decertify already existing unions. (More than 330 decertification cases were filed in 1979 compared to 136 in 1956.) Besieged by inflation, unemployment, and loss of control in the workplace, the average blue-collar worker, for the first time since the end of World War II, seemed to face a future that contained little basis for optimism or faith.

By the end of the 1970s, all these accumulated reversals had caused a significant erosion of buoyancy and confidence among Americans. Throughout the 1950s and 1960s, Americans enthusiastically embraced the notion that the future would be superior to the past. But the new economy of limits radically altered that. By 1979, 55 percent of all Americans believed that "next year will be worse than this year." Nearly 90 percent feared that inflation was a permanent presence. (The figure had been 38 percent in 1975.) As real income dropped by 2 percent each year from 1973 through 1981, the average workers' real spending power fell to its lowest level since 1961. Federal Reserve Board Chairman Paul Volcker observed at the end of the 1970s that "under [present economic] conditions the standard of living for the average American has got to decline," and most Americans appeared to accept the verdict. Nearly two-thirds of the population agreed that the country was entering an era of enduring shortages, that "our current standard of living may be the highest we can hope for," and that "Americans should get used to the fact that our wealth is limited and most of us are not likely to become better off than we are now." As if to confirm these instincts, a massive study of "Who Gets Ahead" in America concluded that the "luck" of the family into which one was born proved the only reliable predictor of success. For most of their history, Americans had believed in the Protestant ethic, confident that hard work, talent, and creativity would produce upward mobility and ever-expanding economic security. Now, nearly three out of four Americans agreed with the statement: "We are fast coming to a turning point in our history. The land of plenty is becoming the land of want." The economic wellsprings of the American dream appeared to be drying up, with Americans of all backgrounds responding with confusion, frustration, and uncertainty.

The Political Malaise

Significantly, the nation's political processes both mirrored and reinforced the confusion and pessimism of the society at large. Throughout the postwar era, American politics had rested on two pillars: sustained economic growth and a position of leadership and dominance in the world. Now, the economy was faltering and the country endured a series of diplomatic reversals that directly challenged the nation's sense of self-confidence and well-being. Within the overall context of the "conservative consensus" that had been established with Richard Nixon's victory in 1968, voters see-sawed between the two major parties, and no politician seemed able to offer a new program that would respond to the erosion of America's once-vaunted power. It was an era that seemed to fit perfectly the definition of political crisis advanced by Italian theorist Antonio Gramsci—a time when "the old is dying and the new cannot be born."

When Gerald Ford took over the Oval Office in August 1974, he brought with him substantial political capital based on his own reputation for decency and the nation's relief that the Watergate tragedy had finally come to an end. But within weeks after taking office, that political capital had been frittered away by a single presidential action. While most of Nixon's chief political aides were serving jail sentences for carrying out presidential orders to obstruct justice, Ford pardoned the president for all wrongdoings, freeing him forever from being brought before the bar of justice to answer for his crimes. The nation was stunned. Ford undermined his popularity further by becoming the most conservative president since Herbert Hoover. In one year, he vetoed thirty-nine measures—including federal aid to education and health-care bills—even as the country entered its worst recession since the 1930s. Instead of stimulating the economy, Ford brought it to a crushing halt by driving interest rates to all-time highs and vetoing a tax cut designed to give consumers more money to spend.

In a post-Watergate backlash, the voters expressed their verdict on Republican leadership in the congressional elections of 1974. Nearly 60 percent of all voters supported the Democrats. Republicans lost 48 seats in the House, and even Ford's own Grand Rapids district elected a Democrat for the first time since 1910. It was the second largest Democratic congressional victory of all time and seemed to bode well for the resumption of Democratic rule in the White House in 1976. While Ford scored some foreign policy successes—most notably through the Middle Eastern shuttle diplomacy of Henry Kissinger and with a new arms control agreement with the Soviet

Union—he also had presided over the humiliating withdrawal of all Americans from Vietnam when the South Vietnamese crumbled before onrushing North Vietnamese forces in the spring of 1975. As TV audiences witnessed the frenzied flight of the last Americans from the rooftop of the American embassy, the realization dawned that America had lost its first war to a nation Lyndon Johnson had once called a "tenth rate piss-ant" country. As the 1976 presidential campaign approached, Democrats were ebullient. As one said, "We could run an aardvark this year and win."

Jimmy Carter seemed ideally suited to take advantage of America's post-Watergate political atmosphere. A deeply moral, "born again" Christian who prayed daily and cared deeply about his faith, Carter journeyed tirelessly across the country telling audiences in small towns that they deserved a government as good, as competent, as moral, and "as filled with love as are the American people." Although the former one-term governor of Georgia began his campaign with a name-recognition factor of only 2 percent, he soon cut a swath through the precincts of Iowa, New Hampshire, and Florida. Here was a man who understood that government had betrayed the people, a person who could offer an almost religious salve designed to heal the damage. Carter trumpeted his credentials as an outsider, attacked the "bloated bureaucracy" of the federal government, and pledged to restore simplicity, decency, and efficiency to the American political process. As if to show his own vulnerability and fragility, he even confessed in an interview published in *Playboy* to having sinned against the Fifth Commandment by looking upon women "with lust." Rarely had America seen such a candidate. In his personality, his convictions, and his concern for basic American values, Carter succeeded in creating a new image and a sense of fresh hope. During his acceptance speech after winning the Democratic nomination, Carter even sounded like an old-time Populist, inveighing against corporate corruption and theft, pledging to stand up for the "little man" and to cleanse the American system of its tax loopholes and vestiges of racial and economic discrimination. With Martin Luther King, Sr., at his side, Carter ended his race for the nomination in a scene from the civil rights movement, with blacks and whites holding hands together at Madison Square Garden and singing "We Shall Overcome."

By election day, however, Carter's weakness had already begun to appear. He squandered a 33-point lead in the polls, seemingly unsure of the direction he should take and thus losing the direct and simple appeal he had used to garner successive victories in the primaries. "He wavers, he wanders, he wiggles, and he waffles," President Ford charged, and there was truth to the accusation. Only Ford's reputation as a bumbler (on the comic TV review, "Saturday Night Live," Ford was repeatedly shown stumbling and falling) and his gaffe in a televised debate (Ford said "There is no Soviet domination of Eastern Europe") prevented the incumbent from squeaking out a victory. Neither candidate was perceived as having "presidential" qualities; 80 percent of the American voters gave a negative assessment of

Carter's leadership ability, 76 percent of Ford's. On election day, Carter won narrowly with 51 percent of the votes, and the Democrats secured more than two-thirds of all seats in Congress. But Carter's victory contained a warning. Nearly 70 percent of all voters identified economic issues as their basic concern, with 31 percent emphasizing unemployment and 26 percent choosing inflation. Carter won 75 percent of the votes of those Americans whose primary worry was jobs. The key question was whether he could answer these economic concerns, and whether his presidency could forge a new consensus on how to function within a world of limits. While Carter had the numerical majorities in Congress to support such a consensus, it was by no means clear that he possessed the vision or leadership to create it.

Carter began his administration by continuing to project a "populist" empathy for the average American. The president walked down Pennsylvania Avenue on inauguration day in a business suit (not a cutaway), wore a cardigan sweater for a televised "fireside" chat, and made a habit of holding "town meetings" in small American communities where he stayed with "average" families. He excelled at the politics of gesture, nominating a record number of women and blacks to administration posts. But he failed to make a dent in the underlying economic crisis that was of most concern to blacks, women, and white blue-collar workers. Jettisoning the radicalism of his nomination acceptance speech, Carter preferred instead to center himself, in James Reston's words, "in the decisive middle ground of American politics." Most important, Carter showed a complete inability to function effectively in the political whirligig of Washington. Having run for president as an "outsider," he never learned how to become an "insider" once elected. Arrogant and insensitive toward Congress, self-righteous about his own position, he entered into a permanent deadlock with the major political institutions of America. His own staff treated congressional leaders with condescension. Three years after the election, House Speaker Tip O'Neill noted that he still would not recognize Hamilton Jordan, Carter's chief aide, because Jordan had never bothered to introduce himself to the Speaker. The episode symbolized the standoff that increasingly paralyzed the internal machinery of government during the Carter years. "If the Carter administration were a television show," political commentator Russell Baker acidly noted, "it would have been cancelled months ago."

Nothing illustrated both the struggles and weaknesses of the Carter presidency better than the energy crisis. To his credit, Carter confronted the issue directly, pointing out that Americans consumed 40 percent more energy than they produced and that, by importing oil, they were also importing inflation and unemployment. But when Congress refused to respond to Carter's legislative proposals, the president retreated to the style of his campaign, attempting to reach over the head of Washington officials by delivering a sermon to the American people. Having gone off to a mountaintop retreat to hear the advice of religious leaders, historians, poets, and psychiatrists, he returned with a diagnosis that blamed America's malaise not on energy itself, but on the "crisis of confidence [in the American people] . . . a crisis that strikes at the very heart and soul and spirit of our national will." In the past, Carter declared, Americans had "believed in something called progress," characterized by "a faith that the days of our children will be better than our own." Now, he said, the country had lost its bearings:

> In a nation that was proud of hard work, strong families, close knit communities and our faith in God, too many of us now tend to worship self-indulgence and consumption. Human identity is no longer defined by what one does but by what one owns.

With shrewd insight, Carter delineated the sources of America's troubled spirit—a narrow concern with self over community and a loss of faith in institutions because of political assassination, Vietnam, and the shame of Watergate. But having described the problem, Carter proposed no solutions. Instead, he simply asked Americans to reject the "mistaken idea of freedom" and to restore their "faith and . . . confidence" in traditional American values. The speech was a brilliant jeremiad, the words of a preacher and a therapist attempting to express and resolve the uncertainty that gripped the population. But the words failed to break the political stalemate that existed. Indeed, Carter's subsequent dismissal of half his cabinet simply seemed to confirm his ineffectuality as a politician and his utter inability to break the "paralysis and stagnation and drift," which, in Carter's own words, had come to characterize the American government.

At the root of Carter's problems was his sense of the presidency as a "trusteeship." Reflecting his religious and family background, this concept of being a steward in charge of the nation's well-being led Carter to forswear political negotiation as somehow being equivalent to betraying his mandate. Instead, he saw his role as studying the nation's problems, gathering all the facts, and then rendering an Olympian judgment that, by virtue of the process that had led to it, could not be questioned. Hence, on the energy issue, Carter developed legislation with 113 separate parts, but *insisted* that the entire package be accepted in toto, since by his lights, the solution represented Solomonic wisdom, arrived at in a manner that made any change an assault on the integrity of the process. The result, one historian has written, was that Carter tended "to equate his political goals with the just and right, and to view his opponents as representative of some selfish or immoral interest." From civil service reform to foreign policy initiatives, Carter's presidential agenda was suffused with questions of morality and ethics; in this world, political give and take was somehow sordid. Such an approach, however, ran so counter to the ground rules of Washington that Carter had almost no chance of communicating—or working effectively—with those whom he had to enlist as allies in order to make his presidency effective. Dependent on cooperation to implement his goals, he instead guaranteed by his methods that such cooperation would never be forthcoming.

Within five months of his July 1979 energy speech, Carter—and his administration—received the cruelest blow yet when Iranian revolutionaries, encouraged by Ayatollah Khomeini, seized and occupied the American embassy in Tehran. The Shah of Iran, America's chief ally in the Near East, had already been overthrown a year earlier, in part because he had proved too slavish to Western ideas and was perceived more as an instrument of U.S. imperialism than as an autonomous leader of an Islamic nation. When Carter agreed to let the deposed Shah come to the United States for medical treatment, many Iranians took the act as a direct insult. In protest against American hospitality to a man most Iranians viewed as a murderer, student radicals seized fifty-three Americans and held them hostage in the American embassy for more than 400 days. Coming at the end of a decade that had witnessed American defeat in Vietnam, the constitutional crisis of Watergate, and the OPEC oil embargo, the hostage crisis reinforced and deepened America's sense of having lost control. Humiliated, embarrassed, and powerless to do anything about it, the United States seemed, in the eyes of many of its citizens, to have become second-rate and indecisive, a helpless pawn of external forces that treated the former "leader" of the free world with scornful contempt.

As a result of such misfortunes, the Carter presidency became permanently disabled. A pervasive sense of impotence spread through the nation, obscuring many of the positive achievements of the Carter presidency. In foreign policy, Carter had scored significant triumphs, by bringing Egyptian President Anwar Sadat and Israeli Premier Menachem Begin to Camp David to forge an historic peace agreement in the Middle East, by pushing through Congress a long overdue Panama Canal Treaty that restored Panama's eventual sovereignty over its own territory, and by reaffirming American commitment to human rights as a foreign policy principle. In Latin America and Africa especially, Carter's dedication to preserving and protecting the freedom of peoples too often oppressed by totalitarian right-wing regimes had made a significant difference in America's reputation. But none of this could overcome the cumulative frustration, distress, and anger of the American people. The economy was in a shambles, with inflation rates once again hitting double digits, unemployment threatening to reach 8 percent, and the whole nation watching, night after night for twelve months, as TV commentators dissected the latest stories of America's national humiliation in Tehran. Carter had come into office pledging to restore decency, pride, and integrity to the American political process. Instead, he seemed utterly incapable of moving even the Congress of the United States, let alone a fanatical religious leader in Iran. As much a victim of circumstance as anything else, Carter felt—and acted—like a man under siege. Many of his own party, long alienated from the Georgia mafia at the White House, turned against him. Senator Edward Kennedy mounted a primary campaign to challenge the president's renomination, accusing him of being a Republican "clone" with his tight money policies, his failure to do anything about the economy, and his betrayal of the campaign promises made four years earlier. "We've exchanged radicals and wits for Jesus and grits," one liberal wag commented. To Democrats as well as Republicans, it seemed time for a change, time to make one more effort at finally reversing the long nightmare of the seventies with its litany of defeat, humiliation, and decline.

The Republican who rode in from the sunset to turn America around was Ronald Reagan. Known throughout America for his movie performances and his TV role as the host of both "Death Valley Days" ("brought to you by forty-mule team Borax") and "GE Theatre," he had also been an effective and popular governor in California. Throughout most of the 1970s Reagan had devoted his energies to mobilizing Republicans with lecture appearances on the "rubber chicken" circuit. But despite Reagan's reputation as a "right-winger," his appeal in 1980 was remarkably akin to that of Carter in 1976. With great shrewdness, Reagan played to traditional American values and offered America still one more attempt to recover what had been lost, this time by going back to a rhetoric and program that reminded the United States of its former power. Reagan was brilliant at presenting his programs as simple verities. America was strong, great, and free. The American people believed in self-reliance, individualism, and patriotism. Communism was a false God; democracy the wave of the future. If America would only respond to Reagan's leadership, it could stand tall against its foreign foes, recover the faith that Carter had found missing, and achieve once again the buoyancy of spirit and confidence of character that had distinguished the postwar era until 1973. Reagan offered a message of revival, as Carter had done in 1976, but this time with buoyant optimism rather than moralistic judgement and the American people—once again desperate for a leader to carry them out of the wilderness—responded.

In retrospect, it seems that Carter never had a chance. By 1980, according to a Gallup Poll, 46 percent of all Americans viewed his performance in office as either "poor" or below average—more than twice the percentage giving the same response to Gerald Ford in 1976. While Carter symbolized pessimism and gloom, Reagan exuded optimism and hope. It was almost a replay of the 1932 election, only this time the Democrat played the role of Herbert Hoover, the Republican the role of Franklin Roosevelt. Significantly, Carter suffered his greatest losses on economic issues—ordinarily the mainstay of Democratic support. Only 55 percent of those voters who said they were primarily concerned about unemployment voted for a Democrat, while Reagan won 67 percent of those concerned most about inflation. Carter, whom one political scientist called "the most conservative Democrat since Grover Cleveland," had lost credibility on the primary rallying point of the New Deal coalition—the notion that the Democrats were the party of the "common man" and cared most about economic problems.

International events, meanwhile, worked decisively in Reagan's favor. Two-thirds of the voters agreed that Reagan would be much more likely to maintain a strong posture against the Soviet Union. Only 27 percent felt the same way about Carter. Three out of four Americans believed that Reagan would ensure that the United States was respected by other nations. The major obstacle that Reagan faced—a popular belief that he would be more likely to get us into war—evaporated in the aftermath of the Carter-Reagan debate two weeks before the election. Prior to the debate, 43 percent of potential voters expressed concern that Reagan would lead us into war, while only 19 percent expressed the same concern about Carter. After the debate, only 35 percent still believed that Reagan would be dangerous. But above all, the election was decided by public frustration and anger at the ineffectuality that Carter seemed to represent. Nearly 40 percent of those who voted for Reagan gave as their primary reason that "it's time for a change." As one political scientist noted, the 1980 election represented more than anything else a "landslide vote of no confidence in an incompetent administration."

Nevertheless, the results were devastating for Democrats. Not only had Reagan won the presidency by a massive margin (Carter took only six states), but the Republican Party swept twelve Senate seats, defeating some of the best-known Democratic liberals in the country, and won 33 seats in the House of Representatives. By contrast, Nixon's landslide in 1972 had brought virtually no gains in either House. Just six years after the Republican Party had suffered its worst defeat since the Depression, it scored its greatest victory. In the eyes of some, the Reagan triumph symbolized a profound realignment of the American political landscape, representing a final and definitive shift to the right and institutionalizing the new Republican majority anticipated by Kevin Phillips twelve years earlier. But just as eloquently, the Reagan victory spoke to the continued confusion and uncertainty of the American political process, as Americans thrashed about trying to find *some way* out of the frustrations of the seventies.

In fact, if there was one single lesson to be learned from the politics of the 1970s, it was the substantial loss of faith in voting and in politics itself as a vehicle for securing change. Just as impressive as Ronald Reagan's lopsided margin of victory in 1980 was the fact that he had been chosen president by only 28 percent of the potential electorate. Nearly 47 percent of those who might have voted failed to go to the polls, making the party of "nonvoters" the single most dominant group in the American political spectrum. In Sweden, West Germany, Italy, and France, more than 85 percent of those eligible to vote took part in national elections in the 1970s. In the United States in 1980, only 53 percent did so. Such political passivity had not always been true of America. In the late 1880s, approximately 90 percent of the potential electorate had gone to the polls. Even as late as 1960, nearly two-thirds of America's potential voters had cast ballots. If the same proportion had voted in 1980 as cast ballots in 1888, more than 40 million additional votes would have been cast. And even if the 1940 percentages had held up, another 19 million votes would have been counted. Compared

In the election of 1980 Ronald Reagan swept to victory over Jimmy Carter, resuming the conservative Republican ascendancy that had commenced with Richard Nixon. Nancy Reagan stands between the two presidents on Inauguration Day, 1980. *(Diego Goldberg, Sygma)*

to only eighteen years earlier, the figures represented a startling decline, with nearly 30 percent of those who had voted in 1962 having ceased to participate in the political process.

Most striking of all, perhaps, was the class distribution of those who had stopped going to the polls. "When people ask 'where have all the voters gone?,'" a political scientist observed, "they should really be asking where all the working class Democrats have gone." To a remarkable extent, withdrawal from the political process was concentrated among the less well-off. Of those Congressional Districts where voter participation declined more than 20 percent between 1968 and 1976, nearly half were in the nation's three largest urban centers—precisely the areas most victimized by poverty, crime, and unemployment. The two Congressional Districts with the lowest turnout were both in New York: Bedford-Stuyvesant, with an 18.8 percent voter participation rate, and the South Bronx, with a 21.8 percent rate. The highest turnouts, by contrast, occurred in the wealthy suburbs of Chicago and Minneapolis—over 70 percent. In cities like New York, with a heavy proportion of lower-class voters, electoral participation plummeted from 63 percent in 1960 to 42 percent in 1976. As the political scientist Walter Dean Burnham has noted, far from ameliorating, "The massive class skew in electoral participation, which is America's chief peculiarity, [became] more and more accentuated." By the time Jimmy Carter was elected, blue-collar and service workers constituted 75 percent of the "party of nonvoters." The figures were even more appalling when contrasted with those of Western European democracies where there was little if any variation in the participation of different classes in national politics. In Italy, for example, 75 percent of those with less than five years of formal education still voted. In America, the figure was 8 percent. In short, not only were American officeholders being chosen by an increasingly small segment of the American public; they were also being chosen by an electorate increasingly dominated by middle- and upper-class citizens, with those at the bottom of society choosing to withdraw completely from the political process. If lower-class voters had participated in the Ford-Carter election at the same rate as their participation in 1960 and 1964, Carter would have won in a landslide.

One of the causes of the rapidly accelerating decline in voter participation was clearly a growing sense of alienation and disaffection from government itself. "The changes move in only one direction," the pollster Daniel Yankelovich observed, "from trust to mistrust. They are massive in scale and impressive in their cumulative message. In the course of a single generation Americans have grown disillusioned about the relation of the individual American to his government." Between the end of the 1960s and the end of the 1970s, the number of Americans who agreed that government will "do what is right most of the time" fell from 56 percent to 29 percent. In the same years, the proportion believing that government officials were "smart people who know what they are doing" fell from 69 percent to 29 percent. Simultaneously, those who agreed that the country's affairs were run for the benefit of just a few big interests, rather than for the benefit of all the people, leaped from 28 percent to 65 percent. Similar results appeared in Harris Polls. In 1966, only 45 percent of Americans believed that "the rich get richer, the poor poorer." By 1977, the figure had increased to more than 75 percent of the population. In the same years, those agreeing that the "people running the country don't really care what happens to you" shot up from 26 percent to 60 percent; and those who confessed to feeling "left out of things" increased from 9 percent of the population to 35 percent. "Why don't people vote?," one welfare worker asked. "Because it doesn't make a difference." More and more Americans, it seemed, had come to the conclusion that political decisions were made by a small elite, and that elections had little chance of changing "what really happens." If politics represented an accurate barometer of society, the poll data suggested a massive disaffection and resignation on the part of the American people—and especially working-class people—toward their entire system of government, a sense that things really were out of control, and that political institutions no longer represented the interests of the people they allegedly served.

Just as important, voter decline seemed to reflect the extent to which the Democratic Party had abandoned its roots as the voice of the common people. According to Walter Dean Burnham, the history of recent American politics has been one of "excluded political alternatives," with voter passivity corresponding directly to "the degeneration of [American] political parties" and their irrelevance to "any possible, potentially organizable needs of the lower classes in the American society." In Burnham's view, one of the reasons for the severe decline in voter participation was the failure of the Democratic Party to speak on behalf of those at the bottom of society. Instead of mobilizing and educating a cohesive working-class vote, as Social Democratic parties in Europe did, Democrats in the United States had abandoned their natural constituency, moving so strongly to conservative positions on economic issues that they offered no appeal to blue-collar workers or inner-city ghetto dwellers. Hence, the party of nonvoters was actually comprised of former Democrats—once the core of the New Deal coalition—who now no longer saw any political party that represented their economic interest.

In a modification of Burnham's analysis, Thomas and Mary Edsall have argued that the Democratic party lost its ability to reconcile competing interest groups in the 1970s and 1980s. In the past the party had succeeded in mediating conflicts between groups—for example, white ethnics and inner city minorities—by recognizing each of their concerns, while focusing on economic interests they shared in common. It was always a delicate balancing act. Getting Polish-Catholic workers in Gary, Indiana, to join together in the same party with women activists who opposed the Catholic position on birth control and with black civil rights groups who wanted to open up unions to black membership was no easy task. But the party of Franklin Roosevelt, John Kennedy, and the early Lyndon Johnson had somehow managed to sustain the tension between supporting dissident causes and pacifying the mainstream. Now, the Edsalls argued, that delicate balance had been lost.

Although such an explanation was inherently speculative, it fit well the history of the Democratic Party during the late 1960s and 1970s. In 1968, perhaps only Robert Kennedy could have held together the New Deal coalition on economic issues while also appealing to antiwar sentiments. With Kennedy's death, the possibility of such an alliance was shattered. Although Hubert Humphrey retained enough of the working class vote to give Richard Nixon a close race, many Democratic voters—particularly of the antiwar stripe—failed to vote. By 1972, Democratic Party strength was further splintered, with George McGovern associated more with counterculture issues like abortion and the antiwar movement than with the blue-collar core of the party's traditional base. Trade unionists and big-city ethnic bosses felt completely excluded from the party and, for the first time, white working-class voters began to associate the Democrats with "special interests" like minorities and feminists. "Fairness" had come to mean quotas for dissident groups instead of equal access for all. While Carter squeaked to victory in 1976, he was an "outsider," not only to Washington but also to the Northern urban industrial heartland that had been the party's primary source of strength ever since the 1930s. Furthermore, Carter pursued economic policies hardly distinguishable from those of the Republicans. He was part of the "conservative consensus." In perhaps his worst political mistake, Carter had given away the economic issues that had always been central to the Democratic Party's appeal and that had been essential to his own election. In the meantime, Reagan made substantial inroads among voters primarily concerned with unemployment and inflation. Significantly, Carter's greatest losses were among white "middle Americans"—blue-collar workers, members of labor union families, Catholics, and high school graduates—people who in the Kennedy and Johnson eras would have been certain supporters of a Democratic candidate.

It made sense, then, to attribute much of the Democratic Party's weakness in the 1970s—and the deep decline in voting rates of lower-class citizens—to the party's failure to concentrate on traditional economic issues of greatest concern to the "common people." At the same time, the Democrats allowed Republicans to take over the cultural issues of law and order, religion, and mainstream morality. By ignoring their natural constituency and becoming increasingly identified with controversial liberal positions on issues such as abortion and affirmative action, the Democrats had narrowed their electoral base, making it possible, in Burnham's words, for "conservatives who occupied only a minority position in the whole population [to] prevail at the top of the political vacuum that [was] thus created." In effect, many of those who had suffered most from the economic reversals of the 1970s no longer had a party. Hence they increasingly withdrew from the political process, making it possible for those who remained to dominate. As a result, Ronald Reagan was chosen president by the same proportion of the potential electorate that had voted for Wendell Willkie in 1940 when he suffered overwhelming defeat at the hands of Franklin Roosevelt. While some might attribute the Reagan triumph to a massive conservative switch among voters, it could also be explained as the logical consequence of the withdrawal from the electoral arena of Americans who felt that the Democratic Party no longer spoke for their interests. In this context, Reagan's election represented both a victory for conservative Republicans and a self-inflicted defeat by Democrats who had abandoned their historic constituency. Most lower-class Americans simply had lost faith in the political process.

What made this apparent loss of faith even more devastating for Democrats was that it occurred simultaneously with the second major political development of the 1970s—the *increased* mobilization of conservative voters by the "New Right" around volatile social issues. If millions of Americans "dropped out" of politics because of disillusionment with the alternatives offered by major parties, millions of others were galvanized into action by their outrage at the excesses of the 1960s and at what seemed to be a concentrated assault on the most basic values and institutions of the society—the family, the church, patriotism, and sexual morality. First identified as the "middle American" revolt of the late 1960s, this rebellion accelerated and deepened in the midst of the political malaise of the 1970s. Although it had roots in traditional conservatism—notably through its strong anticommunism—the "New Right" drew its primary strength from *anger against* policies that had only recently been introduced to the national agenda: busing, affirmative action, feminism, the Supreme Court's 1973 decision sanctioning abortion (*Roe v. Wade*), abolition of prayer in the schools, and new attitudes of "permissiveness" toward pornography and sexual freedom. Ironically, most of those who participated actively in the conservative response to these issues were traditional Democrats; yet it was now the Democratic Party that was identified primarily with the "liberal" stance on such questions, and the Republicans who grasped the dimensions of popular anger and seized the opportunity to capitalize on it. In effect, the Republican Party had claimed the right to speak on behalf of the "average American" while the Democrats had become the voice of "special interests."

One of the cornerstones of the New Right revolt was the strength of traditional personal morality, along with the conviction that actions by a distant government bureaucracy were threatening directly the survival of the family. For conservatives, the 1970s were a culture war, with liberal technocrats attempting to invade the private domain of the family and destroy America's most cherished values, while conservatives rushed to defend the bulwarks of traditional morality. Conservative supporters of the New Right devoted countless hours and money to opposing the Equal Rights Amendment, defending the "right to life" of fetuses, and seeking to ban homosexuals from teaching in the schools. More than 50,000 joined Phyllis Schlafly's Eagle Forum, bombarding legislators with mail insisting that the Equal Rights Amendment would sanction homosexual marriages, inaugurate unisex toilets, lead to the drafting of women, and destroy the traditional authority of the family. (One woman earned $2,000 at a bake sale for the anti-ERA movement by selling 450 coconut layer cakes she had made.) Countless others rallied to the National Right to Life Committee, besieging legislators with pictures of unborn children and calling supporters of abortion "murderers."

What united these single-issue campaigns was an overwhelming sense that—in the words of one New Right leader—there existed a "master plan to destroy everything that is good and moral here in America." One letter from a New Right group symbolized the confluence of these issues under the pro-family banner. "Dear friend," it read:

> *I am rushing you this urgent letter because the children in your neighborhood are in danger.* How would you feel if tomorrow your child . . . was taught by a practicing homosexual? . . . was bused twenty to thirty miles away to school every morning? . . . was forced to attend classes in a school where all religion is banned? If you think this could never happen . . . you are in for a shock!

According to such arguments, a conspiracy existed among the liberal elite to subvert and destroy the values taught in the home and to sanction a "new morality" of individual license and excess. Why busing?, one conservative leader asked. Because, he answered, busing "maximizes the amount of time the child is away from his home, promotes race mixing, and destroys the authority of parents." Access to abortion accomplished the same conspiratorial goals, with federal regulations allowing teenagers to terminate their pregnancies without telling their parents. Not only was life no longer sacred, but the government was now taking control of the sexual behavior of the nation's children. Millions of Americans who supported these "anti" campaigns expressed "liberal" views on economic questions; but for them, the word "liberal" had now become associated with an assault on the most sacred private relationships—parenting, sex, prayer, family discipline—and on these issues, they were determined to fight.

A second pivot for the New Right revolt was the remarkable growth of evangelical Christianity during the 1970s. Significantly, depth of religious commitment constituted the only variable that correlated directly with opposition to the Equal Rights Amendment and abortion. Other indicators— social status, education, employment, region—proved completely secondary. The number of Americans who reported that they were "born again" and had personally experienced salvation increased from 24 percent in 1963 to nearly 40 percent in 1978. By the end of the 1970s, evangelical Christianity claimed the support of more than 50 million Americans.

Many subscribers to this "new faith" were ardent supporters of TV preachers. Each week, Reverend Jerry Falwell's "Old Time Gospel Hour" was broadcast on 225 television stations and 300 radio stations. Fundamentalist talk shows like the "700 Club" or the PTL (Praise the Lord) hour reached millions more. All told, these broadcasts had an audience of almost 100 million Americans each week. Such "electronic evangelism" had a clear political message. Falwell's Moral Majority attempted to mobilize millions of believers to "fight the pornography, obscenity, vulgarity, [and] profanity that under the guise of sex education and 'values clarification' literally pervades the literature [of the public schools]." Pat Robertson, another charismatic TV preacher, urged his listeners to condemn the "humanistic/atheistic/ hedonistic influence on American government." "We have enough . . . votes to run the country," Robertson declared, "and when the people say, 'we've had enough,' we're going to take over." By the end of the 1970s, leaders of the new Evangelical Right had clearly put behind them any compunction about mixing politics and religion, seeking in sermons, as well as literature, to mobilize support for candidates who would fight abortion, defeat the Equal Rights Amendment, wage war against homosexuality, and restore prayer to the schools. "We're going to single out those people in government who are against what we consider to be the Bible, moralist position," Falwell declared. Explicitly as well as implicitly, religious leaders like Falwell expected their church followers to make "pro-family" and extreme anticommunist positions the sole criteria for choice when they entered the voting booth.

The third strength of the New Right—and the critical vehicle for translating diffuse concern over social issues into direct political action—was the use of direct mail as a tactic for recruitment and fund-raising. Pioneered by Richard Viguerie, a former Texas lawyer and admirer of Douglas MacArthur and Joseph McCarthy, direct-mail businesses developed in the aftermath of a 1974 finance reform law that limited the amount of money any individual could contribute to a political campaign. Rather than see this as an obstacle to fund-raising, Viguerie and his associates viewed it as a massive opportunity to mobilize grass-roots support for the right-wing causes they cared most about. Over the next few years, Viguerie's firm, RAVCO, developed into a multimillion-dollar business, sending out 100 million pieces of mail each year to names garnered from over three hundred lists. Serving virtually all the single issue causes of the New Right, direct mail threatened to revolutionize the politics of the seventies. Each piece of mail appeared to be a personal letter seeking support for a campaign or individual, and re-questing a small donation. One letter from right-wing congressman Philip Crane, for example, asked more than 80,000 citizens to join his *personal advisory* committee, as well as to make a financial donation. Direct mail, Viguerie commented, "allows a lot of conservatives to by-pass the liberal media, and go directly into the homes of the conservatives in this country. . . . There really is a silent majority in this country, and the New Right now has learned how to identify them and communicate with them."

Voter mobilization represented the primary goal of the direct-mail campaign. "Our purpose," one New Right leader declared, is "to organize discontent." Most direct-mail letters were consciously strident, seeking to make voters angry. "The shriller you are," another fundraiser declared, the easier it was to recruit supporters. "That's the nature of our beast." Thus, one anti-abortion mailing called on voters to "stop the baby killers."

> These anti-life baby killers are already organizing, working and raising money to re-elect pro-abortionists like George McGovern. . . . Abortion means killing a living baby, a tiny human being with a beating heart and little fingers . . . killing a baby boy or girl with burning deadly chemicals or a powerful machine that sucks and tears the little infant from its mother's womb.

Frequently accompanied by graphic pictures, such literature almost inevitably compelled a response. Although direct mail often did not prove cost effective (expenses frequently consumed 80 percent of the money raised), the larger purpose was to activate the anger of potential right-wing voters and bypass the media—generally seen by the right as biased toward liberals. While critics described New Right fund-raising as a "rape [of] the public," and an effort by "quasi-political entrepreneurs [to discover] commercial opportunities by merchandizing discontent," the recruitment efforts paid off. A study by the National Right to Life Committee showed that 70 percent of those contacted had voted in the congressional election of 1978 (nearly double the overall percentage), with another 50 percent giving at least $25 to a "pro-life" campaign. By sharing mailing lists and repeatedly contacting potential recruits, New Right direct-mail operations reached approximately 10 percent of the total population at the end of the 1970s, striking fear in the hearts of politicians who found themselves on a New Right "enemies list."

The final asset of the conservative revival was provided by the new legitimacy conferred on right-wing positions through conservative think tanks and intellectuals. For most of the 1960s and early 1970s, liberals were able to control the national agenda, with studies from the Brookings Institution, the Ford Foundation, and the Rockefeller Foundation shaping debate on critical national issues. Now, funded by millions of dollars from individuals such as Joseph Coors (of Coors Brewery) and institutions like the Scaif Foundation, conservatives developed their own brain trust of ideas, threatening to compete with and overwhelm liberal think tanks. The Heritage Foundation, founded by Coors in 1973, generated most of the task force ideas of the new Reagan administration. The American Enterprise Institute, committed to conservative positions on both domestic and foreign policy, increased its budget by 1,000 percent in the 1970s. Such groups seized the cultural initiative, mobilizing a powerful arsenal in defense of the family, traditional middle-class values, and a strong anticommunist foreign policy. They were aided, in turn, by "neo-conservatives" who controlled critical media instruments such as *Commentary* magazine and *The Public Interest.* While attempting to dissociate themselves from the far right, these neo-conservatives—most of them former liberals—offered substantial intellectual ammunition to those seeking to reverse liberal "excesses," such as affirmative action and busing, and return to hallowed values of individualism, family togetherness, and community morality. Their authority and reputation ensured that conservative ideas would receive respect and attention, and that the New Right would not be dismissed as a lunatic fringe.

With all these ingredients in place, the New Right became one of the most visible and powerful political forces in America by the late 1970s. The American Conservative Union claimed over 300,000 members and spearheaded the drive to defeat the Panama Canal Treaty in 1977–78, raising more than a million dollars in the process. The National Conservative Political Action Committee (NCPAC) targeted numerous "liberals" for defeat in 1978 and 1980, using strident ads accusing opponents of favoring a weak defense and submitting to communism. Jesse Helms's National Congressional Club did the same. Anti-abortionists claimed credit for defeating liberal Iowa Senator Dick Clark in 1978, and the Moral Majority took credit for stalling repeated efforts to ratify the ERA. The Conservative Caucus headed by Richard Viguerie and Howard Phillips attempted to coordinate the activities of all New Right groups. Indeed, an interlocking directorate wove together the leadership of virtually every conservative organization, from the National Right to Work Committee to the Committee for the Survival of a Free Congress. By 1980, the New Right had embraced the candidacy of Ronald Reagan and claimed direct responsibility for the defeat of such liberal giants as Gaylord Nelson in Wisconsin, Birch Bayh in Indiana,

John Culver in Iowa, Frank Church in Idaho, and George McGovern in South Dakota. "[We aim] to take control of the culture," one New Right leader declared, and the election results seemed to suggest that the aim had been accomplished.

In fact, such a claim was a vast overstatement. Not only had Reagan received only 28 percent of the total potential vote; the Republican landslide represented primarily a rejection of an incumbent who had lost virtually all support in the population at large. As the historian William E. Leuchtenburg has pointed out, most liberals ran far ahead of the president. Frank Church and Gaylord Nelson each received 49 percent of the vote in their states, compared to Carter's showing of 25 percent in Idaho and 43 percent in Wisconsin. Bayh, Culver, and McGovern were all narrowly defeated, victims less of a Reagan landslide than of a Carter disaster. Elsewhere, liberals triumphed despite the most arduous efforts of the New Right. Gary Hart received 55 percent of the vote in Colorado (compared to 31 percent for Carter), and Alan Cranston survived a vicious New Right attack in California. Only 11 percent of the voters interviewed in a *New York Times* CBS poll asserted that they had chosen Reagan because he was "conservative," while more than three times that number gave as their reason the fact that it was "time for a change." Nevertheless, the fact remained that many commentators *interpreted* the results as an apparent right-wing sweep. As Democratic Senator Paul Tsongas said, "Basically, the New Deal died yesterday." If Reagan could exploit popular impressions of a conservative mandate, there was at least a possibility that he could transform appearance into reality.

Conclusion

In retrospect the social complexities and cultural contradictions of the 1970s can be traced to two preeminent realities—the postwar world of abundance and optimism appeared to have ended, while a new world of confused cultural ideas and widely disparate social values had been born. For most of their history, Americans had been, in David Potter's words, a "people of plenty." With endless resources and an inexhaustible potential for growth, there had always been room for upward mobility, always faith in the chance for a new start. As a consequence, Americans had been able to avoid dealing with the problem of how to define equality by substituting in its place a belief in "equal opportunity." According to the American creed, every individual was free to maximize his or her talents, to secure a decent education, to gain access to the political and economic mainstream. Even those who were left out continued to believe in the goals and values of this creed, seeking through political and economic reform to secure their piece of the pie. That had been the essence of the "liberal consensus."

Now, the very underpinnings of that faith had been eroded. Instead of growth, there were limits. The economy seemed stagnant, and despite the creation of some new jobs, high unemployment was seemingly endemic. Through automation and technology, countless positions were permanently lost. An international energy crisis—apparently unsolvable—crippled America's chances for continued growth and expansion. One of every six jobs in America was tied to the automobile industry which, in the face of energy shortages and a declining competitive position vis-à-vis foreign manufacturers, seemed on a permanent down-hill slide. International politics, meanwhile, imposed new constraints on America's sense of dominance in the world. No longer could Americans glibly assume that foreign foes would meekly back down before American power, or that "our" wishes would automatically prevail in the international arena. It was a new world, full of frightening uncertainties.

At precisely the moment when American self-confidence began to decline, it also became apparent that many Americans had lost faith in their political institutions and leaders. In the aftermath of Vietnam and Watergate, trust in the fairness and judgment of politicians plummeted. "The majority of Americans," Yale psychologist Kenneth Keniston noted, "now believe that government serves the interests of big business rather than of all the people, that birth and connections matter more than effort and ability in getting ahead." Nearly half the potential electorate saw no reason to cast a ballot, and more than three-quarters of the respondents to a Harris Poll affirmed that politicians did not care what people felt or believed. Nor were political institutions the only ones subject to the new skepticism. More than 90 percent of all young people believed that business was too concerned with profits. And nearly two-thirds of Americans in the 1970s responded "no" when asked whether married people could expect to spend the rest of their lives in a permanent relationship. By the end of the decade, 40 percent of all households consisted of individuals living alone, with others to whom they were not related, or in single-parent families. The upsurge of teenage pregnancies and suicides, divorces, drug addiction, and alcoholism suggested a profound deterioration in the social fabric, a frightening dissolution of the bonds that held communities together. At the same time, a powerful New Right, conceived out of the fervor of evangelical fundamentalism, insisted that all of these social problems reflected a falling away from religious faith. With single-minded intensity, the New Right campaigned to return America to an ethos that forbade homosexuality, abortion, and all other forms of "deviant" behavior.

In the face of such new realities, experts tended to divide in their diagnosis of what was wrong—some focusing on social and economic issues, others on cultural ones. Economists like Lester Thurow emphasized the structural sources of America's crisis—the "deskilling" process in American industry and the precipitous decline in blue-collar jobs. Such problems brought to center stage for the first time in American history the question of social equity. "Whose income ought to go up and whose income ought to go down?" Thurow asked. "What is a fair or just distribution of economic resources." What did equality mean? And who was going to pay? "When there are economic *gains* to be allocated," Thurow noted, "our political process can allocate them. [But] when there are large economic losses to be allocated, political processes paralyze. And with political paralysis comes economic paralysis."

For Thurow and others, the history of America during the 1970s was the history of that paralysis. Many observers, for the first time in American history, acknowledged class as a permanent dividing line in American society, with millions of blacks and women—unable to take advantage of the individual opportunities available to their better off brothers and sisters—permanently consigned to poverty. From this perspective, America threatened to become divided into two parts, each growing ever more separate from the other. On the one side were the well-educated, upwardly mobile, individual beneficiaries of the changes wrought during the postwar era—including hundreds of thousands of women and blacks. But on the other side were the millions trapped in inner cities, caught in the permanent vise of race, class, and gender victimization, and utterly unable to see any future of promise and possibility without far-reaching structural changes in the economy and society.

Much more prevalent than such social and economic analysis, however, was an assessment that saw America's crisis as one of cultural values and spiritual decay. "Throughout much of this century," Daniel Yankelovich wrote, "Americans believed that self-denial made sense. . . . But doubts have now set in." According to Yankelovich, Americans had forsworn the old ethic of social responsibility, and in pursuit of the liberation ideology of the sixties had embraced a new ethic of personal self-indulgence. According to his data, between 70 and 80 percent of the American people were now saying: "Forget the family, to hell with my obligation to others." Historian Christopher Lasch and political commentator Kevin Phillips offered complementary views. According to Lasch, America had become a narcissistic society, celebrating the "liberated personality of our time, with his charm, his pseudo-awareness of his own condition, his promiscuous pan-sexuality." Kevin Phillips blamed the decomposition of the body politic. "Small loyalties are replacing larger ones," he wrote. "Small outlooks are also replacing larger ones. The country is becoming Balkanized."

What united each of these viewpoints was the conviction that America had lost its sense of common purpose. As three Michigan sociologists declared after examining survey data from more than twenty years, "There has been a shift from a *socially* integrated paradigm for structuring well-being, to a more *personal* or *individuated* paradigm for structuring well-being." Old standards had collapsed, traditional role models no longer described reality, emphasis on the self had taken the place of sacrifice for the community. Even those sixties radicals who had been most committed to social change were now "doing their own thing." Bob Dylan and Eldridge Cleaver had become born-again Christians; Yippie leader Jerry Rubin was a Wall Street broker; and SDS leader Rennie Davis was selling insurance and emphasizing the importance of the "inner self."

Significantly, the politics of the 1970s focused much more on these cultural cleavages than on social and economic issues. Political conflicts revolved around the "vertical" axis of disputes over spiritual and moral direction rather than the "horizontal" axis of economic and class conflicts. Traditional political constituencies fragmented, with the greatest realignment generated by the cultural war between right and left over such issues as abortion, homosexuality, feminism, and prayer in the schools. Those who were most offended by the "new morality" Yankelovich described sought to coerce the "enemy" by banning abortions, putting a halt to "busing," restoring prayer to the schools, and outlawing pornography. Their adversaries, in turn, preached the libertarianism of individual freedom, seeking to make personal choice rather than community consensus the basis for social behavior. The poorest and most alienated members of society, meanwhile, simply withdrew from the political arena.

Yet in the end, the two manifestations of America's crisis of faith were more related than separate. One of the principal reasons for the deterioration of confidence in America's institutions was a pervasive sense that the old answers were no longer adequate to new economic and social realities, and that political leaders were systematically ignoring the concerns and problems of the average citizen. Clearly, heated debates over "social issues" such as personal lifestyle and individual morality were symptomatic of profound divisions in American society over the values the culture should embrace and the moral direction it should pursue. But part of the reason for the primacy of such issues was the failure of the country to address the social and economic dilemmas of a new age and unite Americans in support of a new social compact. Indeed, some argued that the cultural conflicts of the seventies were taking the place of attention to economic issues, thereby preventing concerted action to resolve them. "At times," Daniel Yankelovich wrote, "our narrow self-concern threatens to get out of hand . . . [making us] less sensitive to the plight of the most vulnerable citizens in our economy [and] bored . . . with the problems of race and unemployment."

What remained most clear as the nation entered the eighth decade of the century was that no one had yet found a way to resolve the cultural and social conflicts that besieged the society. A new era had dawned, lacking the confidence, optimism, and sense of national purpose that had dominated the immediate postwar period. The problems were huge, demanding a response as creative and imaginative as any that had been called for in the past. Yet, there was little evidence—despite the 1980 election—that America's political leaders were ready to provide solutions, or even, perhaps, to ask the right questions.

15

The Reagan Years

To a degree unmatched in any era since Franklin Roosevelt's New Deal, Ronald Reagan imprinted his personal brand on the decade of the 1980s. It was not that Reagan possessed a master blueprint that would determine, in detail, the shape of a new society—he did not. Rather, he possessed a simple vision, uncluttered and pure, which could not be penetrated either by dissenting voices or contradictory facts. The country was in trouble, he believed, let down by leaders too prone to worry about nagging dilemmas, too obsessed with limits rather than possibilities. And so the voters "rounded up a posse, swore in this old sheriff, and sent us riding into town." In those words, Ronald Reagan described how he defined his presidential role—to rescue America, restore confidence, and sweep away all the doubters and skeptics who insisted on talking about "problems."

Appropriately enough, Reagan came to the White House determined to emulate Franklin Roosevelt, his only real political hero. His generation too, Reagan said, "had a rendezvous with destiny." In simple phrases reminiscent of FDR, Reagan spoke of America "standing tall" once again, overcoming fear and insecurity, winning the "big ones" for the good side—except that Reagan's goal was to dismantle the political legacy of his hero, and to use the commanding power of the presidency to undermine the welfare state. Thus, while paying lip service to his hero, Reagan excoriated the Great Society, denounced environmentalists, condemned welfare recipients as too "lazy" to get a job, and lambasted the Soviet Union as an "evil empire." More to the point, he acted on these pronouncements, and, to a degree that astonished even his closest allies, succeeded in getting his way.

By the end of his second term, the Reagan bubble seemed ready to burst. The two issues that had propelled Reagan into the White House—Iran and economic crisis—reappeared with a vengeance, threatening to topple his administration, as they had once toppled the presidency of Jimmy Carter. But then, in the height of ironies, the Reagan presidency was "saved" by the emergence of another visionary, the "evil empire's" Mikhail Gorbachev, whose ascendancy allowed Reagan, the ultimate Cold Warrior, to leave the White House claiming to have presided over the dissolution of Soviet-American tensions. A man introduced on the national political stage as the clarion voice calling for the election of Barry Goldwater in 1964, Reagan brought the politics of the "Old Right" to a new level of ascendancy and simultaneously was able to pronounce a proud benediction on the Cold War. It was left to George Bush, his successor, to deal with the paradoxical legacy of the Reagan revolution—a country able to bestride the world with unsurpassed military power, yet so weak from economic stagnation and out-of-control deficits at home as to seem in free-fall decline.

The Reagan Credo

The essence of Ronald Reagan's success lay in two qualities—the overwhelming intensity with which he believed in a few basic ideas, and the extraordinary capacity he had to communicate those beliefs to the American people. The ideas themselves were simple, perhaps even trite: the "monkey" of big government was bad and should be lifted from the American people's backs; the military was good, the sole exception to the evil of government, and merited unlimited support; the purpose of foreign policy should be to fight and defect communism, whenever and wherever it appeared (hence, the need for a strong military); and slashing taxes would accomplish the dual goals of making America rich and abolishing deficits. These ideas became a religious catechism. As items of faith, they were infallible, impervious to argument, evidence, experience, or reality; and precisely because they were matters of faith, Reagan's advocacy of them was powerful, persuasive, and inspiring.

The depth of Reagan's commitment to his credo liberated him from the need to become embroiled in the day-to-day development of policies and programs. The ideas themselves were sufficient; it only required the right staff to carry them out. From the very beginning, insiders at the White House recognized that the president would remain detached from the details of the decision-making process. Reagan was a "delegater" of authority, his admirers said. Thus it was no surprise when he made errors of fact such as saying that ICBMs could be called back after launching, or that submarines did not carry nuclear missiles. Although some columnists might comment sarcastically about the president's "data bank" problem (David Broder wrote that "when someone approaches Reagan bearing information, he flees as if from a leper's touch"), those who believed in Reagan knew that detail was not his strong suit, and that vision was.

Not surprisingly, Reagan's daily conduct of the presidency reflected these strengths and weaknesses. Washington pundits marveled at how relaxed the president was, at how lightly the burdens of office weighed on him. Unlike Jimmy Carter, who seemed almost masochistically devoted to eighteen-hour days, Ronald Reagan was customarily fresh, buoyant, and ebullient. As his former aides later revealed, the president's schedule was designed to assure such results. He read the newspapers over breakfast, went to his office at 9 (where he fed the squirrels outside in the Rose Garden), received a security briefing at 9:30, had "personal time" from 10 to 11 to read and answer mail, ate lunch at 12, napped briefly, then conducted whatever business was on the schedule until 5 when he retired to the family quarters with his evening reading and to watch television. Wherever possible, the schedule was shaped to conform to the president's desire for order, and for a positive, upbeat atmosphere. The staff's job was to conserve Reagan's energies for the tasks he *had* to carry out, to arrange his day so that they could be completed as efficiently as possible, and to present the "big" decisions in a sufficiently clear-cut way that they would require as little detailed involvement by Reagan as possible. The key to such a system, of course, was the quality of the people the president called on to implement his program.

When it came to appointing these officials, however, Reagan displayed the same passivity and detachment that he demonstrated toward the details of decision making. He named Alexander Haig Secretary of State, for example, without ever exploring Haig's ideas on foreign policy. The two men had dined together once prior to the presidential campaign, but Reagan spent the whole evening reminiscing about his show business friend Edgar Bergen, who had just died. Donald Regan, the new Secretary of Treasury, was named to his position after one brief phone conversation and neither saw nor talked to the president again until after the Inauguration. "From the first day to the last at Treasury," Regan later wrote, "I was flying by the seat of my pants. The President never told me . . . what he wanted to accomplish in the field of economics."

In the end, such an approach created an extraordinary dependency on the few White House aides who *did* have his ear—Edward Meese, an old California friend who was deeply ideological (a "movement conservative," insiders said), Michael Deaver, Reagan's long-time public relations advisor, and James Baker, former campaign director for George Bush. Together, these men, in effect, ran the government. They sat *at* the Cabinet table with the president (a fact that profoundly offended Alexander Haig's sense of hierarchical etiquette); Meese, not the president, defined the Cabinet's agenda and moderated its discussions; and no one, not even the National Security Advisor, had direct access to the president without their approval. In theory, good advisors could make such a system work. But it was clear that Reagan himself was not going to ask the searching questions that would control the dangers inherent in the process. And there lay the Achilles heel, for as White House economic advisor Martin Anderson noted, "if any of his personal staff chooses to abuse his or her position, and deliberately withholds key information or misleads him, Reagan is helpless and disaster can strike."

At the moment, however, such dangers seemed real only to Democratic Cassandras who were jealous and resentful of Reagan's triumph. What mattered was not the President's executive style, his personnel policies, or his abhorrence of "hands-on" government; rather, it was Reagan's burning conviction that if only the country would support the simple verities that constituted his credo, America *would* come back, the nation would once more stand tall, and no one, anywhere, would ever again think about challenging the strongest country in the world.

The Domestic and Foreign Policy Agendas

To the consternation of some liberal Democrats who had insisted that there was no significant difference between a reactionary Reagan and a conservative Carter, the new president moved quickly to implement his credo for a new America. Compiling legislative victories at a speed that threatened to challenge even the epoch feats of FDR and LBJ, Reagan proceeded to perform radical surgery on the American economy and welfare system. In 1981 Congress agreed to cut more than $25 billion from welfare programs (with hundreds of billions more planned for future years), while slashing taxes over five years by $750 billion. Simultaneously, Reagan won Congressional approval for a staggering $1.2 trillion five-year increase in defense expenditures, thereby presumably making good on his promise that never again would America be subject to humiliation at the hands of the Soviet Union.

Reagan also delivered on his pledge to combat the social philosophy, programs, and regulations of the Great Society. Although affirmative action had produced significant gains for both blacks and women, Reagan ordered his attorney general to fight such programs in the federal courts, and packed the Civil Rights Commission and EEOC with individuals dedicated to reversing the racial policies of previous administrations. Reagan slashed food stamp benefits, eliminated 300,000 CETA jobs, cut AFDC funds—leading to a reduction of more than 10 percent in the welfare rolls—and lowered the benefits of an additional 300,000 families receiving welfare assistance. Reagan's appointees, meanwhile, carried out his injunction to dismantle environmental strictures on private developers. EPA administrator Anne Burford delayed imposing penalties on chemical companies responsible for toxic waste dumps, and Secretary of the Interior James Watt embarked on a campaign that virtually gave away mineral rights to oil and coal developers. Only on the "social issues" of the New Right did the Reagan administration fall short, but even there—on questions such as abortion, prayer in the public schools, and busing—the president enthusiastically embraced New Right positions, frequently using his executive power to back up his words. New federal rules prohibited the circulation of birth control information or abortion advice without parental consent and, wherever possible, Justice Department lawyers argued the New Right position on social issues that came before the federal courts. As a result of such actions, the Supreme Court by the end of Reagan's second term had substantially eviscerated previous rulings on "set aside" programs for minority and women contractors, while threatening to overturn the *Roe* vs. *Wade* decision protecting women's right to have an abortion. Still, Reagan turned out to be more a devotee of the "old right" than of the "new." Although he gave his rhetorical embrace to the anti-gay, anti-abortion, and anti-feminist positions of Jerry Falwell and other members of the evangelical right, more often than not he retreated from programmatic follow-through. Throughout, the administration's agenda reflected two fundamental convictions of Reagan's credo: that the least government was the best government, and that giving economic power to the private sector offered the surest guarantee of sustained prosperity and growth.

Perhaps appropriately, the architect who designed the administration's fiscal and economic policy was not a cabinet member, but David Stockman, an ideologue whom Reagan named as head of the Office of Management and Budget. While Donald Regan, the Secretary of Treasury, was desperately trying to ferret out the president's economic wishes, Stockman was plotting a five-year plan that would transform the government and the economy. Using the theories of economist Arthur Laffer (the "Laffer curve" would soon take on a double meaning), Stockman proposed a series of far-reaching initiatives—dubbed "supply-side economics"—to solve America's problems. Sharp reductions in personal income taxes, Stockman believed, would encourage savings and investments; deregulation of industry, in turn, would free business to compete more efficiently in the marketplace; rolling back environmental protection measures would release energy and resources for private development; and cutting back social expenditures to the old and the poor would bolster self-reliance and initiative. The overall goal, Stockman later said, was "a minimalist government . . . a spare and stingy creature which offered evenhanded public justice, but no more." Millions might suffer in the short run, but in the long run, America would be strengthened "by abruptly severing the umbilical cords of dependency that ran from Washington to every nook and cranny of the nation." Enthusiastically endorsing Stockman's proposals, Reagan predicted that within three years, an unfettered economy would produce a balanced budget based on sustained growth. The American spirit of individualism, competition, and personal pride would be restored, and with the shackles of government bureaucracy removed, individual citizens would once again be liberated to maximize their abilities and aspirations.

Not all economists, of course, accepted the ideological assumptions of Reaganomics. The president and his advisors had blamed America's economic decline on social welfare expenditures, yet each of the three Western countries with the highest average expenditure on social welfare—the Netherlands, Belgium, and Sweden—outstripped the United States in economic growth during the 1970s. Reagan also insisted that America's high rate of personal taxation had contributed to its economic decline. But eight other Western countries had a higher tax rate than the United States, and these countries, on average, grew 10 percent faster than America each year and enjoyed a 13 percent greater increase in productivity. Countries like Germany and Japan boasted considerably more national planning than the

United States and had a far less sharp dividing line between public and private sectors. Yet each consistently exceeded America in growth and productivity. Indeed, America's own economic history belied Reagan's assertions, since the greatest economic growth in the United States had occurred during the early 1940s, when a wartime government virtually managed the economy, and during the 1960s, when social welfare programs expanded rapidly. As the economist Lester Thurow observed: "The American problem is not returning to some golden age of economic growth (there was no such golden age), but recognizing that we have an economic structure that has never in its entire history performed as well as Japan and West Germany have performed since World War II. We are now the ones who must copy and adapt policies and innovations that have been successful elsewhere. To retreat into our mythical past is to guarantee that our days of economic glory are over."

Of more immediate concern were the practical contradictions that ran through the Reagan economic policy. On the one hand, the president endorsed the Federal Reserve Board's tight money policy that raised interest rates in order to lower inflation and discourage consumer spending; on the other hand, the president pushed tax cuts to accelerate economic growth and encourage spending. The result of such policies, one economist noted, was analogous to running a railroad train with "one engine heading west to New York, the other east to Boston." It was simply not possible to have a government both tighten and loosen the purse strings simultaneously.

Even worse, Reagan's own advisors knew that the figures did not add up. Stockman's entire plan was premised on more than $100 billion in cuts in social welfare including social security and medicare. In Stockman's own words, "the success of the Reagan revolution depended upon the willingness of the politicians to turn against their own handiwork." But that was suicidal. No one in Congress was going to slash senior citizen benefits. When Stockman realized the dilemma he had created, he tried to trim the increases in the defense budget, and persuade Reagan to raise revenues. Convincing other White House advisors of the need to revise the President's economic plan—"You mean it really is voodoo economics after all," Jim Baker said—Stockman mobilized what he later called his bipartisan "Gang of Seventeen" to support new taxes and lower defense expenditures. "Everyone was ready," he said. "But Reagan said no. He wouldn't allow it. He didn't believe there was a problem. That was his selectivity on the facts of life. The whole thing got turned into a cynical, politicized, surreal substitute for sane fiscal government." As a result, Reaganomics became an exercise in self-contradiction. One could not massively *expand* military spending, *cut* taxes sharply, *and still* have a balanced budget. The futility of such efforts quickly became apparent as budget deficits soared to over $100 billion in 1982—more than three times the largest deficit incurred during the Carter years—and eventually to nearly $300 billion, a ten-fold increase. "No one imagined how bad the outcome would be," Stockman later said. "It got away from us."

By the second year of the administration, the worst recession to hit the country since the 1930s made the critics of Reaganomics seem prophetic, at least temporarily. Although inflation had fallen to less than 6 percent by 1983, unemployment mushroomed, reaching almost 11 percent by the end of 1982. Real income continued to fall, and the gap between potential and real Gross National Product reached a Depression level of 9 percent. Savings and investments remained either steady or declined, confounding all of Reagan's predictions. Moreover, as interest rates remained high, America's European allies screamed in pain because of the outflow of capital from their own countries to American banks. The resulting strong dollar, meanwhile, led to cheap imports, a decline in exports, and the shutdown of at least some American industries. The economy, David Stockman later said, was an "utter, mind-numbing catastrophe." The worst news for Reagan came with the 1982 congressional elections, when the Democrats unseated twenty-five Republican Congressmen in what appeared to be a clear rejection of supply-side economics. "The great majority of voters saw yesterday's Congressional election as a referendum on President Reagan's economic program," a *New York Times/*CBS poll concluded.

But then the stormclouds disappeared. By 1983, prosperity had returned, and with it the widespread belief that Reagan's economic policies had indeed finally worked their magic. The recovery was by no means universal, and blacks especially continued to suffer, with their income declining relative to whites, and the percentage of those living in poverty climbing. But blacks were not Reagan's top priority, and for much of the rest of the nation the economic indicators were positive. Unemployment steadily fell, returning by 1984 to the 7.5 percent that it had been in 1980, while inflation continued downward. In the meantime, the automobile industry recovered its vitality, housing starts boomed, and consumer spending soared to new heights. It was the most vibrant economy since the early 1960s, and despite continued high interest rates and deficits that threatened to vault into the stratosphere, people felt good. Continued growth seemed likely, and the nation acquired once again a sense of confidence and buoyancy. Although Stockman and others understood that nothing had changed to alter the long-term economic devastation that would be wrought by continued deficit spending, for the moment at least the bad news seemed beyond the horizon, while the good news made the economic part of Reagan's vision appear to be a blinding success.

In foreign policy also, many Americans felt a new sense of pride and direction, a tribute—Reagan supporters believed—to the president's bold and clear-cut policies of military strength and strident anticommunism. Proclaiming that America's "Vietnam syndrome" was over, Reagan aggressively defended America's right to intervene anywhere in the world to combat communist insurgency, and then proceeded to act on his commitment. Giving content to what would later be dubbed the "Reagan Doctrine," the administration embarked on a concerted effort to roll back communism in the "third world," providing financial and military support to "freedom fighters" in Angola, Ethiopia, and Afghanistan. Dearest to Reagan's heart, though, was Central America. With single-minded purpose, Reagan insisted on committing military advisors and millions of dollars to bolster a reactionary regime in El Salvador, while making the overthrow of the Sandinistas by Nicaraguan "contras" his top foreign policy objective.

The premise of all of this, of course, was the need to lead the forces of freedom against the Satanic forces of Communism. To the Soviet Union, Reagan declared a new policy of moral superiority. The arms race, he declared, was a struggle of "good versus evil, right against wrong." Acting as though an entire nation was affected with a genetic disability, he accused the Russians in one of his early press conferences of being accustomed, by nature, to lying and cheating. Indeed, Reagan charged, the Soviet Union was the "focus of evil in the world." To give substance to his rhetoric, the president encouraged a 41 percent increase in defense spending during his first administration, and pledged to build 17,000 new nuclear weapons. In the face of such actions, and the president's persistent refusal to engage in arms control negotiations, the Soviets concluded that American intentions had turned dangerously hostile and upgraded the alert status of their own armed forces. The chasm separating the superpowers seemed unbridgeable after Soviet jets shot down a civilian Korean airliner in the fall of 1983. Although American intelligence officials knew within hours that the tragedy was a product of incompetence and confusion by Soviet military officials who actually believed the airliner to be a spy intruder, Reagan ignored that information, seizing on the event to lead a worldwide chorus of condemnation, labeling the Soviets as "inhumane," "barbarous," and "uncivilized," and accusing them of a "massacre," with all the implications that word carried of premeditated murder of innocent civilians.

There was good reason to criticize Reagan's monolithic worldview and the consequences it produced. In El Salvador, for example, "death squads" assassinated thousands of civilians (transposed to U.S. population figures, the death toll would have been 4,500 victims per week), including the Roman Catholic Archbishop of San Salvador. Many believed as well that the Sandinista regime in Nicaragua had far more popular support than the contra "freedom fighters," many of whom were associated with a prior right-wing dictatorship that had been overthrown. And more than a few experts in the Middle East questioned Reagan's decision to send American marines to war-torn Lebanon on a peace-keeping mission, a venture that alienated many of America's long-time friends in the region and pleased practically nobody.

Yet for the most part, Reagan put these problems behind him, achieving instead a reputation for strength, independence, and leadership. As the political commentator Elizabeth Drew observed, "Reagan is a political phenomenon—a man who by force of personality and marvelous stage management super-imposes himself over his own mistakes." Notwithstanding weaknesses in his policies, Reagan appeared to the American public as a hero rebuilding America's vaunted strength and dominance in the world. He seemed capable of doing no wrong, an impression highlighted by the events of a single week in October 1983. One day, a terrorist attack in Beirut murdered 274 marines, a tragedy that a blue-ribbon investigation later blamed on politicians in Washington who overrode Pentagon recommendations. Yet Reagan escaped criticism. A few days later, 10,000 American paratroopers landed on the small Caribbean island of Grenada, allegedly to protect the lives of American medical students threatened by a Marxist dictatorship, but in fact to eliminate Cuban influence on the island. After a day of skirmishing with 750 Cuban laborers constructing a new airport (only 110 of them soldiers), the paratroopers prevailed.

By any objective standard, Reagan should have been severely criticized for the tragedy in Beirut, with serious questions asked as well about the need to invade a tiny island. Instead, the president rallied the nation in a tour de force television appearance in which he joined together the two events of the week and used each to identify his own policies with American patriotism and bravery. It was as if the "victory" in Grenada had erased the disaster of Beirut. Reagan's peroration focused on a wounded marine in Lebanon, unable to speak, who scrawled the marine motto, "Semper fi," on a pad and handed it to a visiting general. The president had attempted to tell the story twelve times before he was able to complete it without choking up. Finally, he used it to end his exhortation, in the process fusing his own leadership with the courage of the troops he commanded, celebrating their shared pride, honor, and patriotism. So vividly did he communicate his own burning convictions of 100 percent Americanism that all other emotions or criticisms fell away, as if trivial and selfish. The next day, Reagan's approval rating rose 15 points. This would not be an easy man for any Democrat to defeat.

The 1984 Election

In another age and time, Walter Mondale might have been a sure bet to win the presidency. The son of a minister and piano teacher, descendant of Norwegian stock, and the anointed heir of Hubert Humphrey, Mondale embodied the midwestern ethos of hard work, compassion, and public service. His political career represented a lifetime of preparation for the nation's highest office. A student leader at Macalester College, he became Humphrey's protege as attorney general in Minnesota, then moved on to the U.S. Senate to carry forward the New Deal/New Frontier program of liberal democracy. Mondale was bright, he worked hard, and his colleagues respected him. After Jimmy Carter chose him as his running mate in 1976, Mondale became a full partner in the new administration, playing—with

Carter's encouragement—an active and daily role in all major decisions. He knew the tensions, the ambiguities, the challenges of the Oval Office better than any person except the president himself. Mondale was ready.

In 1984 the Minnesotan also believed he could win—not easily, to be sure, but if Mondale could draw together the New Deal coalition, add a few allies, and appeal to America's sense of "fairness," maybe he could do it. After all, even Reagan's budget director, David Stockman, had admitted that the Reagan tax program was simply the old Herbert Hoover "trickle-down" theory revisited. If one gave enough to the rich, it would eventually have some impact on the poor. "I mean," Stockman told a reporter, "[our proposals were] always a Trojan Horse to bring down the top tax rates." The result, Yale University economist James Tobin noted, was the redistribution of "income, wealth and power—from government to private enterprise, from workers to capitalist, from poor to rich." Mondale believed that the country would reject this "class struggle on behalf of the rich."

With these concerns as a base, Mondale was convinced that he could put together a coalition that would successfully challenge the president. Political scientists had blamed Democratic failures in the 1970s on the party's inability to retain traditional Democratic constituencies. Now, Mondale sought out these constituencies, going to the AFL-CIO, the National Education Association, civil rights groups, and women's organizations for support. According to public opinion polls, the most significant new political phenomenon in America was the "gender gap." Women differed from men by 10 to 15 points when asked about war and peace, or social justice at home. If he could cultivate the support of groups like the National Organization for Women, go back to the trade unions, and sell his case on fairness at home and relaxation of tensions abroad—then, Mondale believed, he could line up the troops and begin a march to victory.

In this election year, however, even a good idea turned on itself. Critics charged that the former vice-president was *too* subservient to special interest groups. He seemed to *pander* to the unions, the teachers, the blacks. Mondale was running on a platform of "fairness," but the word "fair" had become identified, in the eyes of many working-class white Democrats, with inordinate sensitivity to blacks and Chicanos, and with race-based policies like affirmative action and busing. In 1980, 22 percent of formerly Democratic voters had switched to the Republican banner, with the highest percentage coming from those who opposed special government intervention on behalf of minorities. Since then, Reagan had succeeded even further in persuading people that *he* was the "equal opportunity" candidate; a believer in "conservative egalitarianism," he trumpeted his identification with the average citizen, and his opposition to "special treatment" for blacks. Ironically, Mondale played into Reagan's strategy with his own attempt to cater to Democratic interest groups. Although Jesse Jackson was clearly the most dynamic Democratic contender prior to the convention—"our time has come," he announced, "from freedom to equality, from charity to parity

. . . from welfare to our share, from slave ship to championship"—Jackson also symbolized a Democratic philosophy that many working-class whites now rejected. When Mondale gave Jackson centerstage at the Democratic convention, and then boldly chose Geraldine Ferraro as the first female vice-presidential candidate in history, he may have solidified his ties to the liberal base of the party, but in the process he also reinforced the impression held by many disaffected white and working-class Democrats that they no longer represented a primary constituency for the party.

In retrospect, of course, the very idea that anyone could have defeated Ronald Reagan seems bizarre. The economy was booming, inflation was down, America was strong again. In the summer of 1980, before Reagan was first elected, Americans had been held hostage in Iran, United States athletes had boycotted the Moscow Olympics, the economy was paralyzed, and American morale had sunk to its lowest level since the Great Depression. Now all that had changed. Americans swept the gold at the Los Angeles Olympics (helped no small amount by the nonparticipation of Soviet and Eastern European athletes), a new patriotism permeated the body politic, and America had demonstrated its strength—once and for all—in Grenada. Nothing seemed impossible any longer. "Just about every place you look," said one Reagan ad showing a man painting a white picket fence, "things are looking up. Life is better—America is back—and people have a sense of pride they never thought they'd feel again." As one Reagan advisor observed, "I almost feel sorry for Mondale having to go up against this . . . it's like running against *America*."

As if by magic, Reagan remained untouched even by his mistakes. He was a "Teflon president," Congresswoman Pat Schroeder of Colorado said. Nothing stuck to him. Americans had long since accepted Reagan's unfamiliarity with facts, one presidential advisor noted. "What's wrong with it if the system works and people are happy. Ronald Reagan is part of the mythology of what America likes its leaders to be." If Reagan had been Nixon, one Republican wag commented, he would have been dead because people blamed *everything* on "Tricky Dick." But Reagan was the "gipper." He "never lost that quality of next-door neighborliness and never became part of the system," a journalist noted. He was a "cultural democrat," still "playing best friend, a citizen cast up among politicians." Reagan had been made into "the personification of America," *The New Yorker*'s Elizabeth Drew commented. In that context, "to suggest that anything is wrong with him is to run down the country." Indeed, it was precisely that chemistry that made the president invulnerable. As one of Mondale's leading advisors observed, "you couldn't touch Reagan without hurting yourself."

In the end, there was no gainsaying the president's popularity. In a devastating landslide, he rolled to re-election with 59 percent of the vote and 49 of the 50 states. In almost every single category where Reagan appeared vulnerable, he triumphed instead. Women gave him 57 percent of their vote, the elderly 61 percent, the young—for the first time in decades—voted Republican. Catholics voted for the president; more Jews voted Republican than ever before; and even union households—where Mondale hoped for his strongest support—split almost down the middle. No electoral result better typified what had happened to Mondale—and the party—than the returns from Macomb County, a white working-class suburb of Detroit. In 1960, Macomb had been a bastion of Democratic strength, giving John F. Kennedy a 63 to 37 margin of victory over Richard Nixon. Now, stunned by recession and angry about blacks, this union enclave reversed itself completely, giving Reagan 63 percent to Mondale's 37. It was a night, *Newsweek* said correctly, "that Ronald Wilson Reagan became Mr. America."

Whatever the momentary analyses of the pundits, the 1984 election ultimately was as much about traditional values—and America's sense of confidence in itself—as about the prosperous economic state of the union. The two were clearly connected. If America in 1984 had been where it was in 1982, with a 10 percent unemployment rate and little prospect of recovery, Reagan might well have been defeated. But instead the economy was on the move and there was a new sense of pride and confidence about the nation's stance in the world. This latter mood was difficult to quantify, but in many ways it held the key to the election. At the end of the Carter years, 75 percent of Americans said they no longer felt confident that the future would be better than the past. Now, after four years of Reagan, more than half had returned to their traditional optimism. In 1980 only one-fifth of all Americans said that the government was run for the benefit of all. Now, in 1984, that figure had more than doubled, notwithstanding the redistribution of wealth that had taken place *away* from the poor and *toward* the rich. Reagan's campaign slogan, "We Brought America Back," seemed to resonate. His ability to link the Olympic triumphs of Los Angeles with a new sense of national assertion in the world appeared to make sense. "Let's take our cue from our . . . athletes," he declared. "Let's go for growth, let's go for the gold." And Americans responded. There was, one commentator said, "a new patriotism" abroad in the land, "growing out of a natural desire to *feel better* about things after Watergate, Vietnam and the hostage crisis." Reagan embodied this new patriotism, and brought it to fulfillment in his campaign, from the speech he gave on the beaches of Normandy commemorating the sacrifices of American soldiers on D-Day, to his proud display of America's Olympic triumphs, telling the voters that their athletes were "living proof of what happens when America sets it sights high." Whatever its intrinsic shortcomings, the Reagan credo had succeeded in winning the ardent support of millions of people inspired with a new faith in themselves and in their country. Even if based on an illusion, this new era of good feelings was one that people wanted to celebrate and savor for as long as possible. The question at the beginning of the second term was how long it could continue, given the flawed foundation on which it rested.

Falling Apart

One of the lessons of twentieth-century political history is that a regime may be most in danger of overreaching itself at precisely the moment when it appears most completely in control. FDR's New Deal started to disintegrate in 1937 after the president had won a resounding mandate, which he then used to justify an attempt to pack the Supreme Court—a step that precipitated a powerful rebellion by conservative Democrats and Republicans who resented the president's effort to tamper with the constitutional structure of the nation. LBJ's political consensus began to crumble when, in the midst of his most dramatic success in passing civil rights and social welfare legislation, he decided to engage in a massive military build-up in Vietnam, all the while lying to the American people about his intentions. And Richard Nixon's overwhelming triumph on behalf of a new Republican majority started to unravel at its peak of success when his administration resorted to the "dirty tricks" of Watergate. What each of these moments shared was the seduction of power, a willingness to engage in deceit or illegal actions to accomplish a hidden objective; hubris generated in each case its own antidote, bringing tragic failure.

Now it was Ronald Reagan's turn to experience the same fate—or to at least come close to doing so. For four years, he had escaped accountability for the flaws of his style and his politics. Although his passive mode of executive governance had not led to disaster, it was only because of extraordinary good luck and the skill of his immediate staff. After the election, however, those staff roles altered. Jim Baker and Donald Regan engaged in a swap, Regan moving to the White House as Chief of Staff and Baker becoming Secretary of the Treasury. National Security personnel also changed. With a new lineup of people and continued frustration at the administration's inability to completely get its way in the face of Congressional and bureaucratic obstacles, at least some of Reagan's aides decided that they had the authority and the right to take the law into their own hands. Uninvolved, as always, in the details of setting policy, Reagan became an accomplice in his administration's descent into hubris. In the meantime, the economic time bombs planted by his own ideas on the budget and taxes began to explode. And by the fall of 1987, the Reagan Administration, like so many of its predecessors, seemed poised to self-destruct, a victim of its own excesses.

The pivotal event in this process was the development of what became known as the Iran-Contra scandal. The chronology of the affair is simple, the subterfuge involved in carrying it out both murky and complicated. In the spring of 1985, American contacts with Israeli intelligence produced a suggestion that Israel provide American arms to Iran in return for which Iran would facilitate the release of American hostages held in Lebanon by a pro-Iranian terrorist group. Although Israel would supply the weapons, America would replace them, so that, in effect, the American government would be trading arms for hostages. Frustrated by the intractability of the hostage problem and impelled by a desire to secure the release of an American CIA officer who was among the hostages, aides in the White House national security office encouraged the scheme. Although the president himself had always insisted that America would never negotiate with terrorists, or ransom the hostages, he evidently failed to understand that this was exactly the nature of the bargain being proposed. According to the then national security advisor, Robert McFarlane, Reagan in August authorized the initial transfer of arms, despite the fact that both his secretary of state (George Shultz) and his secretary of defense (Caspar Weinberger) were vehemently against the idea. In fact only one hostage was released, but the process had been set in motion, and in November another arms deal was broached, this time involving Hawk missiles.

Already in violation of a law requiring that Congressional intelligence oversight committees be apprised in "timely fashion" of all covert activities, some intelligence officials now requested a presidential "finding" that would legally justify these activities as necessary to the "national security." On December 5, unbeknownst to relevant Cabinet officials, Admiral John Poindexter, McFarlane's successor, secured the president's signature on such a "finding." The issue of an arms deal surfaced for more complete discussion in December and January, with Shultz and Weinberger once again in strong opposition. Weinberger believed that "this baby had been strangled in its cradle," but in fact, Reagan sided with his NSC aides, and in January 1986 once again signed "findings" that authorized further transfers—even though former NSC advisor McFarlane came back from a European meeting with an Iranian intermediary to advise calling a halt to the entire affair.

For the first time also in January, a link was made between arms sales to Iran and funding for the Nicaraguan contras. Ever since 1984, the administration's commitment to overthrow the Sandinista regime had been hamstrung by the Boland Amendment, a Congressional act that forbade any aid to the contras by the CIA, Defense, or any other intelligence agency of the government. Desperate to circumvent the Congressional restraint, NSC staffers had repeatedly sought third-country funds for the contras (receiving $32 million from Saudi Arabia over 18 months) as well as private contributions. The private funds, in turn, were generated though passionate "briefings" for prospective donors by NSC staff member, Colonel Oliver North, who would leave the room just before a nongovernment person made the "pitch" for money. Now, the suggestion was made that Iran be overcharged for the weapons it desired, with the excess profits siphoned off to the contras so that they could purchase weapons and continue their "freedom fight." The problem was that the entire scheme involved precisely the U.S. intelligence officials who were prohibited by the Boland Amendment from providing any aid to the contras.

As the intrigue deepened and more and more players of dubious repute became involved, it became almost inevitable that word of the chicanery would leak. A Beirut newspaper first published a story about the

Iranian arms deal; later, a leading Iranian official confirmed that weapons had been exchanged. Reagan at first denied the entire story, then insisted that no third country (Israel) had been involved, and finally acknowledged that the whole venture had occurred, but as part of a strategy for developing ties with "moderate," anti-Khoumeni Iranians. Eventually, of course, all the "cover" stories were punctured, the plan to divert money to the contras was revealed, and an administration that had railed against its allies for talking to terrorists was exposed as having both betrayed its own exhortations and violated its own laws.

Although a blue ribbon commission consisting of former senator John Tower, former Secretary of State Edmund Muskie, and former NSC advisor Brent Scowcroft exonerated the president from knowing about the Iran-Contra link in advance of its public disclosure, the commission stunned Americans with its stark portrait of a chief executive so far removed from decision-making responsibility that he was almost a president in absentia. Reagan "did not seem to be aware" of either what policy was being implemented, or its consequences, the Tower commission said. Indeed, according to one reporter, commission members came close to describing the president as "a man who sometimes inhabited a fantasy island." Not only were they dismayed by Reagan's lack of knowledge, but also that he knew so little—and seemed to care so little—about what the commission had found. In a comment that could have won an award for oblique understatement, commission member Scowcroft concluded that "the system [of decision making at the White House] did not compensate adequately for the management style of the president." In fact, it appeared that Reagan's staff could function with total freedom simply by phrasing memos or briefings so that the president would never know the full extent of the illegal actions they were undertaking in his name. Indeed, *they might even find ways of securing his approval for such illegal activities* as long as they did not confront him explicitly with the fact that he was breaking the law.

Most frightening of all was the dawning realization that a few of these staff members saw themselves as empowered to create a secret government beyond the control of laws or institutions, free to pursue a hidden agenda that they alone would have the right to define. The Tower Commission had talked about Admiral Poindexter, Colonel North, and others functioning "largely outside the orbit of the U.S. government," but it was not until the televised Congressional Iran-Contra hearings that the full nature of that "outside" operation became more clear. Poindexter, for example, declared that it was his right to lie to Congress and the press on his own authority, without going to Reagan, since *he knew what the president wanted, and, after all, the people had chosen the president.* It was more important, he said, to refuse to inform the president of details, so as to guarantee him "plausible deniability," than to bring important issues for decision to him. Senators were "astonished" and "terrified" by Poindexter's presumption that he could act as president, without the president's knowledge.

President Reagan receives the Tower Commission Report on February 26, 1987 in the Cabinet Room with John Tower and Edmund Muskie. (Courtesy Ronald Reagan Library)

But North's testimony was even more terrifying. According to North, CIA director William Casey, together with North and Poindexter, aimed ultimately to use the funds from the Iranian arms sales not only to fund the contras in violation of the law, but to finance "an overseas entity capable of conducting activities similar to the ones we had conducted here"—in short, a CIA outside the CIA. (Casey had been stricken by a cerebral hemorrhage the morning of his testimony before Congressional intelligence committees and, after several months of hospitalization, died without ever being questioned about his role.) When challenged as to how he could be confident about the wisdom of such an operation, North replied that such ventures could be trusted because they would be led by patriots like himself. "What we see [here]," one columnist wrote in response, "is a combination of right-wing fervor, militaristic nationalism, and religiosity . . . reminiscent of the stirrings of authoritarianism in Europe." Blithely, North acknowledged that he had lied repeatedly to the Congress on behalf of the contra venture; he seemed to take particular glee in recounting how he had shredded reams of incriminating documents while Attorney General Edward Meese stood fifteen feet away interrogating another staff member about North's illegal activities. With the likelihood that the surface had only just been scratched, the country was witnessing what could happen with a government out of control, presided over by a chief executive who had neither the will nor the ability to enforce accountability. Perhaps most distressing, North was initially treated like a national hero by an American public more impressed by his protestations of patriotism than by his reckless disregard of the law.*

As if chaos in national security affairs were not enough, the world soon learned of an insidious new disease called AIDS (acquired immunodeficiency syndrome). Initially striking primarily gay males, the disease destroyed the capacity of the body to fight infections and once contracted—usually through sexual intimacy—led rapidly to fatal illnesses like skin cancer and pneumonia. By 1982 the Centers for Disease Control identified 853 Americans who had died of AIDS, the numbers exponentially accelerating year by year. Yet, not until 1985 did Ronald Reagan even mention the word, even though thousands were dying, including the romantic film hero, Rock Hudson, and international conferences were being convened to assess how to deal with the spreading epidemic.

The economy also began to display some of the long-term consequences of Reagan's tax and fiscal policies. Despite constant warnings that massive increases in military expenditures would generate excessive deficits, Reagan refused to propose new taxes and continued to act as if there were no problem. Although he systematically blasted Congress for *its* role in creating deficits, he seemed congenitally incapable of acknowledging that *he* was to blame for 95 percent of the problem, since it was his budgets that created the dilemma. The Reagan tax cuts, combined with a 41 percent real increase in the defense budget, caused the federal deficit to soar from $90 billion in 1982 to $283 billion in 1986—nearly ten times the highest deficit under any previous president. To finance the debt, America had to borrow, raising interest rates to attract capital. What that did, in turn, was to generate a flow of foreign money into America, which then caused the value of the dollar to rise dramatically, out of all proportion to its true worth. As the dollar skyrocketed, imports became cheaper—forcing many American industries either to relocate to third-world countries or go out of business—and the nation's trade imbalance also went haywire, since foreign markets could not afford to buy American goods at the inflated dollar value that now prevailed. The world's largest creditor nation in 1980, America now became the world's largest debtor nation, with a trade imbalance that soared to $170 billion by 1987. It was all a vicious spiral downward, fueled by in-

* According to investigative reporter Seymour Hersh, the same men had plotted the assassination of Libyan strongman Mu'ammar Gadhafi. Casey allegedly had manufactured intelligence data stating that Ghadafi had dispatched "hit" squads to the United States to kill Reagan. Casey also insisted that Libya was responsible for the bombing of a disco in Berlin (later evidence indicated it was the Syrians) where American soldiers were killed, so that Reagan could be persuaded to bomb Libya. When that bombing occurred in early April 1987, North used a secret channel of communication to target the planes to attack Gadhafi's home and family. Although Gadhafi survived, one of his children was killed, while other members of his family were injured. United States law at the time also expressly prohibited efforts to assassinate foreign leaders by intelligence officials.

debtedness. The interest on the national debt alone took as much money as it cost to run *nine* departments of government, including Labor, Commerce, Education and Agriculture; and the more the budget and trade deficits grew, the harder it would be for the American economy to reclaim its independence and self-sufficiency. It required the output of 1.5 million American workers simply to pay America's interest on the debt it owed to the rest of the world. In the face of such realities, one economist concluded, "the potential for disaster is very great."

Even more disturbing were some of the deeper structural changes that flowed from these realities. More and more American workers, for example, were forced to seek employment in low-wage service industries. Although more new jobs were created in the 1980s than were lost, half of those that were lost were in relatively high-paying industries; on the other hand half of the *new* jobs *paid wages below the poverty level for a family of four.* Hence, the number of low wage earners increased substantially during the 1980s at the expense of high wage jobs that either disappeared or moved overseas. Given existing conditions, some economists predicted, every new job created in America for the foreseeable future would be in the service sector of the economy.

In such circumstances, the trend toward a two-tiered society accelerated. The proportion of blacks and Hispanics who were poor continued to grow, in both instances exceeding one-third of the total black and Hispanic population. High school dropout rates in the inner cities exceeded 50 percent; the number of female-headed households jumped to nearly 60 percent among blacks and 50 percent among Hispanics; and children born to these families ran a better than even chance of being poor. (Almost 90 percent of black female heads of household under 25 lived below the official poverty line.) The problem of homelessness spiraled in small and large cities alike, with hundreds of thousands of Americans sleeping on sidewalks, in doorways, on subway platforms, over heating grates, and in the nation's parks because they had no other place to go. While Ronald Reagan dismissed the problem as one limited to the emotionally disturbed, the facts were that the majority of the homeless—many of them children—came from families that simply had *no place* to go in the larger society.

At the root of all of this was the lack of decent jobs. Unskilled work was being mechanized out of existence. Skilled work was either moving out of the country or to the suburbs. Inner city residents lacked the education or the mobility to compete for jobs far removed from their own neighborhoods. And their own neighborhoods offered only minimum wage work or none at all. In such a context, drugs or crime offered some of the only options available. (The problem was compounded, unfortunately, by one of the positive results of the civil rights revolution—the fact that middle-class blacks, the leaders of the community, had for the most part moved from the inner city to more comfortable housing, thereby depriving ghetto neighborhoods of stability and direction.) If decent paying jobs existed in the inner city, the sociologist William J. Wilson observed, then young people would have a reason to stay in school, and would have the wherewithal to support nuclear families. Without such jobs and the institutions they would reinforce, the country seemed destined to experience an ever widening gulf between the haves and the have nots, a gulf that, in the words of one Urban League official, was going to "produce an individual that you're not going to be able to do anything with no matter what you do, someone who has been completely severed from what we consider normal relationships, someone who's outside the pale."

Although most Americans may have remained unaware of these structural problems, the whole world jolted awake to the perilous state of the American economy when the stock market crashed in October 1987. Like a bolt of lightning, the Wall St. debacle glaringly illuminated the fundamental weakness of Reaganomics. In one week, the Dow Jones industrial average lost 13 percent of its value, plummeting almost 800 points. One day alone, $500 billion of losses occurred in the market value of U.S. securities. And with remarkable unanimity, economists throughout the world agreed on the cause: the deficits in the budget and in the trade balance had cast profound doubt on America's ability to sustain itself in the world economy. The United States, one Republican economist pointed out, had been borrowing from abroad at twice the rate of its previous high mark in the 1800s when the nation was industrializing. But the "unprecedented consumption and borrowing binge" could not continue. America had to display "self-denial, collective discipline" and the same willingness to pay the price for its own excesses. Sounding the same theme, Texas billionaire Ross Perot declared that everyone had to realize the lessons of the crash: "It's outrageous that our elected officials say the fundamentals of our economy are sound; *none of the fundamentals are sound*" (italics added). The problem, *Newsweek* concluded, was "this Rube Goldberg structure" of indebtedness that Reaganomics had foisted on the nation; the economic miracle of the Reagan revolution, it now appeared, was a big bust.

By the late fall of 1987, commentators from virtually every political perspective concluded that the Reagan presidency had imploded, a victim of its own excesses and of the president's inattentive and erratic ways. "No sadder tale could be spun in this holiday season," David Broder noted, "than the unraveling of yet another presidency." Adopting the same theme, a Republic leader observed that "we have as weak a cast of political characters as anyone in the Western world, [and] this government still has fourteen months to go." Pundits searched for parallels in history, most settling on Reagan's similarity to Warren Gamaliel Harding, with his amiable but ineffectual style. But more disturbing was the *Financial Times of London*'s observation that "historical comparisons with previously incapacitated chief executives like Woodrow Wilson may now seem relevant."

For the time being, at least, it seemed that the "Teflon" had disappeared, with each embarrasing episode exposing what some now saw as a persistent pattern of manipulation and malfeasance. Thus, when Poindexter confessed to Congress that he had lied to them, James Reston declared: "You shouldn't be surprised. This administration has been living a life of pretense, cheating and borrowing for over six years." Even Republic stalwarts such as Richard Cheney of Wyoming, former chief of staff for President Gerald Ford, found the revelations astonishing. "You have to say it's a pretty fundamental flaw," Cheney observed, "that would allow a lieutenant colonel on the White House staff to operate in defiance of the law." With little more than a year to go in the Reagan presidency, the White House seemed overwhelmed by its own misfortunes, paralyzed by the president's detachment and indifference, and without the will or the way to turn things around. As *The New Yorker*'s Elizabeth Drew commented, "It is hard to see how [things] could change sufficiently to give us a presidency that is not— and does not put the country in—danger."

Reaching New Heights

Ironically, the Reagan administration was rescued from lassitude and despair by the leader of the president's arch-nemesis, worldwide communism. If there was one single theme that had dominated Ronald Reagan's public pronouncements from 1947 until the end of his second term in office, it was his evangelical denunciation of communism. Reagan talked as though every misfortune America had ever suffered since World War II emanated directly from the "uncivilized" leaders of Moscow. Consistent with that almost religious conviction, Reagan refused to meet Soviet leaders during his first term, avoided making any major decisions on arms control policy, and acted as though the sheer force of weaponry was the only way to deal with Russia. But now, suddenly in his second term, there was a new leader in the Soviet Union—Mikhail Gorbachev—who not only challenged all of Reagan's preconceptions, but accepted Reagan's ground rules for devising a new system of superpower cooperation. As in a conversion story, the archtypical anticommunist became a defender of detente, while the leader of totalitarian communism became a champion of democracy. For the average mortal, it was a miracle almost too extraordinary to contemplate.

The turnabout on the Soviet side was so startling because during the early 1980s, there seemed so little vitality and imagination in Soviet policymaking circles. Leonid Brezhnev had played his last international card with the SALT II arms limitation treaty he had signed with Jimmy Carter, but the Soviet invasion of Afghanistan, plus the American response with the grain embargo and Olympic boycott, had destroyed any possibility for ratifying that instrument. Reagan refused to resume arms control talks, and the Soviets appeared to hunker down for a long siege of an ever more chilly cold war. Yuri Andropov, Brezhnev's successor, seemed to some Westerners a more cosmopolitan, creative individual, but he had serious health problems and died after a short reign, only to be replaced by an elderly apparatchik, Konstantin Chernenko, whose flexibility and imagination appeared to be nonexistent. Afflicted by emphysema, Chernenko seemed to exemplify in his health and his personality the arteriosclerosis of the Soviet system. But even as Chernenko's health problems became more visible, a new member of the politburo began to make his mark felt. Traveling to London to meet Margaret Thatcher, the young (mid-50s) Gorbachev displayed a flair, an openness, and a freshness that caused the British prime minister to declare, even then, "This is a man we can do business with."

In fact, Gorbachev's agenda, when he took over as Soviet Premier and then President, was to transform both the internal politics and economy of his own country, and to revolutionize Russia's relations with the rest of the world. The first objective depended on the second, since the Soviet economy could not generate growth and productivity as long as the nation's resources were harnessed to an out-of-proportion military budget. More than 10 percent of the Soviet GNP went to defense, and while Soviet consumers waited hours for a scrap of meat, billions of rubles were being spent producing new tanks and rockets. Foreign and domestic policy, therefore, had to be mutually reinforcing, and reforms in each had to proceed simultaneously. Thus Gorbachev announced his commitment to glasnost and perestroika (openness, freedom, and decentralization) at home at the same time that he startled the world by proposing massive cuts in Soviet arms and a new policy of close cooperation with the United States and its western allies.

While many Americans were deeply suspicious of Gorbachev's motives (wasn't this just one more classic Soviet trick, lulling the West into complacency as the Russians prepared to strike?), the evidence that Gorbachev meant what he said slowly accumulated. Dissidents like Andrei Sakharov were released from prison and restored to positions of prestige, all the while remaining free to speak out against the regime; groups of Soviet scholars displayed new openness in confessing the errors of their own past, while accepting critical perspectives from the researchers of other countries; art and theatre blossomed in Soviet cities, often with a politically explosive message; and at least some steps were taken to encourage private initiatives in the Soviet economy, whether these were "cooperative" restaurants run by individual citizens for a profit, or farmer's markets where people sold their home-grown produce on a private basis.

Initially, the Reagan administration refused to deal with this strange, but exciting new phenomenon. The president had declined to choose between the competing arms control positions of Weinberger and Schultz during his first term, with the result that there were no significant initiatives by the United States. When Reagan finally did articulate a policy in response to the clamor of West European countries for *some* leadership, it was his proposal for a "zero option" agreement in which the Soviets would give up their overwhelming predominance in missiles in the European theatre in return for the Americans not deploying (or later removing) the Pershing missile. To most observers, the plan seemed unworkable because it placed such a disproportionate burden on the Soviets.

In the meantime, Reagan had started to champion a brand new idea that he had never even cleared with Defense, State, or the Joint Chiefs of Staff—namely, creation of a Strategic Defense Initiative (SDI, or "star wars") that would use laser-beam technology, à la Buck Rogers, to build an umbrella of protection that would destroy any incoming missile. Most of Reagan's own aides thought the idea unworkable, but he glommed onto it and would not let go. To the Soviets, in turn, the suggestion smacked of a violation of the 1972 Anti-Ballistic Missile Treaty between the two countries, and seemed designed eventually to make them vulnerable to an all-out American attack, with their own deterrent rendered ineffectual by SDI.

How, then, to end the stalemate? Desperate for a foreign policy breakthrough, Gorbachev seized the initiative by accepting Reagan's "zero option" proposal for intermediate nuclear forces (INF) as a basis for discussion, hoping in the process to win American acquiescence to defer testing of SDI. Under pressure from his European Allies and from Nancy Reagan to make some concession toward peace, President Reagan agreed to meet and talk with Gorbachev. The man who had refused even to consider arms control initiatives at the beginning of his administration now proceeded to have four summits with Gorbachev in two and a half years, breaking even Nixon's record with Brezhnev.

Not all summits went well. When the two leaders met in Reykjavik, Iceland, in the fall of 1986, they almost struck an accord that would have abolished all nuclear weapons. In a scenario that seemed to reflect more a Hollywood fantasy than a shrewdly plotted, diplomatic chess game, the two world leaders entertained visionary agreements on destroying weapons that left most governments aghast when the deliberations were made known. But in the end, the pot of gold at the end of the rainbow eluded the leaders. Reagan would not compromise on SDI, nor would Gorbachev. But the talks had been a beginning. Now, there was a foundation—and a sense of how much *could* be done if only a way could be found to avoid the insuperable obstacle of star wars.

Ultimately, it was that beginning that rescued the Reagan presidency. By the next year, mired in the scandal of Iran-Contra, stunned by the stock market crash, and humiliated by the indictments and betrayals of his official family, Reagan desperately needed a victory to clear the slate and restore his own personal magic. American and Soviet diplomats delivered that victory. In October, November, and December 1987, almost every Washington observer had concluded that the Reagan presidency was over, with most deeply anxious over what would transpire during the lame-duck period to follow. By April, the same observers were returning from the Moscow summit where Reagan and Gorbachev had signed an INF treaty, the two first families had gone to the Bolshoi, and the Reagans had paid a late night visit at

Red Square to nostalgically commemorate the coming together in friendship of two mortal enemies. The president's luck had returned, and Ronald Reagan could leave the White House as the man who presided over the greatest step toward world peace since World War II, instead of as a leader, like Johnson and Nixon before him, embarrassed and humiliated by his own errors of judgment.

But whatever Reagan's part (and it should not be ignored), the triumph was above all a gift of Gorbachev, who for his own reasons had entered onto the world stage with a commitment to radical change. In the Soviet Union, the newspaper *Izvestia* announced cancellation of a world history examination because the textbook was full of lies. "Today," the paper editorialized, "we are reaping the bitter fruit of our own moral compromises and we are paying for those things that we mutely accepted and supported and do not know how to explain to our children. . . . But no one has the right to cancel history itself, no matter how painful. It continues and everyone now living must take part in its creation." Through elections, more open debate, and further reforms, the Soviet Union seemed prepared, at least potentially, to pursue the path of radical change, with all the consequences that would have for the United States as well. "We are going to do something terrible to you Americans," one Soviet leader humorously announced, "we are going to deprive you of an enemy." As a result, the first two-term president since Dwight Eisenhower could leave the White House proclaiming himself a man of peace, not an advocate of conflict. History had indeed produced change.

If there is any way to make sense of the Reagan era, it must ultimately involve the president's sense of his own identity and mission. When Reagan described his presidency as that of a sheriff who had come to town to clean up a mess, he evoked an image of himself that almost always astonished European sophisticates: how, they asked incredulously, could an actor who played cowboys in the movies ever become president? Yet in the deepest meaning of the word, it was Reagan the actor who held the key to the political history of the 1980s. He himself wondered out loud how any president who had *not* been an actor could survive the presidency. In his daily routine he carried out the role assigned to him. At moments of the highest drama, he aspired to Academy Award levels of performance; in his worst parts, he played a role so unrelated to reality that he ran the risk of endangering the entire nation; and in the parts he cared about most, he conveyed the identification, vision, and intensity that could alter the stage of history.

Whether for good or ill, the metaphor of acting permeated the description of the Reagan White House offered by presidential aides and cabinet officers who published their memoirs before Reagan even left the Oval Office. When Donald Regan became Chief of Staff, he was astonished to see how meticulously Deaver, Baker, and Meese had "scheduled" Reagan to maintain an upbeat environment and control that environment. "Every word was scripted, every place where Reagan was expected to stand was chalked with toe marks." And Reagan seemed to take it with such good nature—until Regan realized that his boss had been "learning his lines, composing his facial expression, [and] hitting his toe marks for half a century." This was Reagan's profession, the schedule his "shooting script," his performance of the daily routine a familiar task that gave him "a tangible sense of accomplishment." In fact, Reagan was so much into the script that he remained passive, awaiting direction, even when confronted with such strange circumstances as a smoking fireplace in his office. Without his lines, the president was lost. It was difficult, Sam Donaldson said, to ask Reagan a question that he knew the answer to; and Elizabeth Drew commented that "he treats knowledge as if it were dangerous to his convictions." But given a part to play, he was superb. Thus, one White House aide declared, "the whole thing was PR. This was a PR outfit that became president and took over the country."

A profoundly negative consequence of approaching the presidency as a "role" was the detachment that occurred between appearance and reality. The president was not *connected* on a daily, engaged basis with the complexities of government issues and decisions. "Aloof," "remote," "passive" were all words used repeatedly by memoirists to describe the president. He communicated an air of familiarity, intimacy, and affability; but by all accounts, he was completely impersonal in his private life—with his staff, his closest aides, even his children. "He is a friendly man with few close friends," George Will observed. "Perhaps only one. He married her." Nancy Reagan was his link to reality, not only the confidante who prompted him on the answers he should give to reporters at "photo-opportunity sessions," but also the advisor who dealt with personal conflicts in his official family (getting rid of troublesome cabinet members). It was Nancy Reagan who pushed her husband to pursue peace with the Soviets, who served as his navigator when political stormclouds gathered.

Some speculated that the president's detachment was a product of his hearing problem. Peggy Noonan, his speechwriter, commented that:

> There was a quizzical look on his face as he listened to what was going on around him, and I realized: He doesn't really hear very much, and his appearance of constant good humor is connected to his deafness. He misses much of what is not said straight to him, and because of that, he keeps a pleasant look on his face as people chat around him.

Others attributed Reagan's inability to deal with problems to a personality trait associated with unhappy childhoods, in this case, Reagan's unreliable alcoholic father. Thus, he distanced himself from bad news, or uncomfortable facts, denying he had cancer ("I didn't have cancer. I had something inside of me that had cancer in it, and it was removed"), and refusing to face up to the deficits he had caused.

But whatever the explanation, Reagan remained a loner, shutting out even the closest of his aides from his personal confidence. Perhaps it was inevitable that they should turn on him, and in a display of pique and retribution unheard of in any previous administration, portray their leader in such unflattering terms. Press Secretary Larry Speakes confessed to making up quotes and putting them in Reagan's mouth; Michael Deaver, the gentlest of the lot, described a White House out of touch with reality; and Donald Regan depicted a puppet, controlled by his wife, Nancy, who consulted astrologers before allowing her husband to travel or hold a press conference. "The [likeness] they paint is appalling," Frances FitzGerald observed, "of a president almost devoid of curiosity, reflectiveness, energy or purpose, a man full of his own preconceptions, yet easily manipulated and fooled by others." What did it say of this Administration, so devoted to a rhetoric of morality, patriotism, and fidelity, that so many of its members betrayed their leader, engaged in criminal acts, and ended up being indicted by panels on ethics?

Yet there was another side to Reagan's perception of the presidency as a role to be acted. A good performer identified with his character, infused the part with vibrancy, rose to the occasion when called upon, and communicated intensity and passion. Reagan may have had only a few simple ideas, and they may have come from a primer on laissez-faire government, or a General Electric propaganda tract. But he conveyed them with the conviction of a true believer. His presidency was unexcelled. Precisely because he believed so strongly in the ideas that were his credo, he could override anyone who quarreled with them or attempted to present contrary evidence. He needed to believe in SDI, and so he ignored the scientists who insisted it was a Hollywood fantasy. He adamantly refused to choose between taxes and deficit spending, and so he pretended the deficit did not exist, or that it was solely the creation of the Democrats. He desperately wanted the hostages to come home "on his watch," and so he blotted out all negative questions that might stand in the way of plans to release them. All that mattered were his convictions. As long as they were consistent with the role he envisioned himself playing, he would let nothing get in their path.

But he was also prepared to rise to the occasion. He could take leaps of imagination, as in the nearly realized fantasy at Reykjavik, and in the INF summit in Moscow. He might oversimplify, Elizabeth Drew observed, "but his oversimplification allowed him to send powerful messages [in Moscow] as it does here." Appropriately, Reagan's gift to Gorbachev at the Moscow summit was the movie *Friendly Persuasion* which depicted the Civil War in America, and how patriotism and peace could both be noble.

It was in Moscow that Reagan, perhaps unintentionally, disclosed the most about his own view of the presidency. Speaking to a group of intellectuals and artists, he declared that acting had helped him greatly "in the work I do now." Citing the Russian director Serge Eisenstein, he went on: "The most important thing is to have the vision. The next is to grasp and hold it. . . . To grasp and hold a vision, to fix it in your senses, that is the very essence, I believe of successful leadership." In many ways, Reagan had grasped and held onto his vision. He had gotten "inside a character, a place, and a moment." And because he was so successful at playing the part, he had been able to make a mark on history. Never one to let a good metaphor go, Reagan told reports on the way back that the trip to Moscow had been like a "Cecil B. DeMille production," and he, the president, had "dropped into a grand historical moment." The evil Empire? "That was a different time and place."

At the end of the script, it was difficult to know where to place the critical emphasis. As Reagan supporter George Will noted, the president had produced an era of good feelings. Rhetoric had been essential to his presidency, because "Reagan has intended his statecraft to be soulcraft." Yet Will also acknowledged that Reagan's cheerful facade had been "a narcotic, numbing the nation's senses about hazards just over the horizon." For six years after AIDS was discovered and the number of U.S. deaths from the disease soared to more than four thousand per year, the president acted as though no national epidemic existed. By ignoring economic realities, disguising portents of disaster like AIDS, and glossing over the rising presence of poverty, homelessness, and alienation, Reagan had bought time, for the moment, from the harsh consequences that flowed from implementing his credo. He had played his part. But, as *Newsweek* observed in its valedictory on the Administration, "buried in the [economic] numbers was an almost Edwardian sense of decline, in industrial wealth, moral fiber, and imperial sway. . . . The long Reagan spring had been a holiday from all that—from leaders who talked about malaise and sacrifice and what the country couldn't do. But his hour was passing, and at the dawn of [the next presidency], Americans for the first time in years were apprehensive about tomorrow again."

Whether that tomorrow produced a new engagement with politics and the abiding realities of economic decline and social inequality—or a continued reluctance to address such issues—would in large part determine the state of the nation at the end of the century, and on the eve of a new millennium. What remained clear was that Ronald Reagan, with the enormous help of Mikhail Gorbachev, had brought an end to more than forty years of bi-polar confrontation. The Cold War was coming to a close, and with its demise would also come the end of a political paradigm that had used the Cold War as its anchor and controlling principle. Whether one believed in the "liberal consensus" or the "conservative consensus" (and the major difference was whether one saw the need for incremental reforms on issues of social inequality), unanimity on the importance of fighting communism at home and abroad shaped every other dimension of American political discourse. Now, with the Cold War about to be declared over and done with, the question was whether a new consensus would emerge, or whether the '90s would instead be an era of polarization.

16

The 1990s

A Referendum on the
Post–World War II Years

In the period from the early 1960s to the late 1980s, Americans had experienced a wrenching and dislocating series of changes. The optimistic activism of the civil rights movement, the Peace Corps, and a youthful chief executive mythologized as the leader of Camelot had given way to racial polarization, assassination, a brutal war, and massive civil unrest. The brief period of triumph signaled by the Nixon presidency and his foreign policy breakthroughs with China and Russia had barely taken hold before the devasting constitutional crisis of Watergate occurred, threatening to undermine the very structure of the American political system and people's confidence in it. Followed quickly by the nation's first defeat in war and the humiliating experience of long lines at the gas pumps brought about by the OPEC oil embargo, Watergate contributed to a creeping erosion of faith in the well-being of the American system. The Iranian hostage crisis in 1979–80 simply reinforced that growing sense of demoralization. During the same years a deep fissure developed within the ideological underpinnings of American culture, pitting those who believed in individualism, liberation, and cultural diversity against those committed to traditional definitions of the family, patriotism, social hierarchy, and evangelical fundamentalism. Although Ronald Reagan momentarily revived American spirits, the underlying feeling of being buffeted to and fro remained.

In this roller-coaster sequence of ups and downs, there were a series of abiding issues—all interrelated—begging to be resolved. One was the role of the State in shaping and defining the social and economic arrangements of the nation. What part should government play in directing the economy, intervening in social relationships, promoting equality, or preserving the environment? A second, related issue centered on inter-group relationships in America. Was the nation a conglomerate of individuals, each to be treated alike, or did "group rights" exist that might justify special recognition and protection for minorities, women, or others who by virtue of a collective characteristic had become victims of discrimination? Was race still the central issue of American history, or could some way be found to address its pernicious consequences? Could those who believed in the free-dom of sexual choice, including gay marriage, and the right of each woman to control her own reproductive choices co-exist with those who sought to forbid homosexuality and wished to outlaw abortion? Finally, there re-mained the crucial question of whether the social welfare "safety net" es-tablished by the New Deal should be expanded, maintained, or perhaps even terminated. What should the nation's attitude be toward welfare, na-tional health insurance, protection of children, the aged, and the disabled?

Interestingly, the political history of the 1990s evolved into a successive series of referenda on these issues. Notwithstanding enormous changes and advances in civil rights protections for African Americans, race resumed its pivotal position in American culture, painfully manifest in phenomena as diverse as the police beating of Rodney King, the Los Angeles race riot that followed the acquittal of his assailants, and the O. J. Simpson trial. The gov-ernment's responsibility for economic regulation and control became criti-cal for two national elections, in 1992 and 1996. And the issue of what should constitute a social welfare "safety net" shaped the volatile politics of health care reform, on the one hand, and the Gingrich Republican coun-terrevolution of 1994 on the other. In the meantime, the cultural schism di-viding the New Right from liberalism continued to widen.

With all these issues, the roller-coaster cycle of the previous decades continued, a seemingly decisive movement in one direction followed almost immediately by a complete turnabout in the other direction. Perhaps ap-propriately, the 1990s embodied a summing-up of what had occurred in the preceding decades, as if the country were searching to find some way through the maelstrom of conflicting currents to a final sense of direction that might represent a new consensus on how to proceed. If the journey re-mained unfinished, the 1990s at least seemed a time when some conclu-sions could be ventured as to the rules that would prevail in the journey's next stage.

The Reagan Legacy—George Bush

The person who politically would bridge the decades of the 1980s and the 1990s was George Bush, Ronald Reagan's vice-president. It was his good for-tune to preside over the final dissolution of the Cold War and the unchal-lenged rise of America to military supremacy in the world; it was his bad for-tune to inherit an economy wasting away under bloated deficits (the national debt had tripled from $1 trillion when Reagan took office to $3 tril-lion in 1988) and industrial inertia.

Bush succeeded to the presidency in one of the least inspired and meanest campaigns of recent memory. Despite having served eight years as the malleable and devoted servant to Ronald Reagan, Bush seemed a mys-tery to most people, tagged with the label of "wimp" by a *Newsweek* cover story. The descendant of a quintessentially WASP, Eastern establishment family, he had gone to Yale, then moved to Texas after serving in World War II, where he subsequently boasted of having Western roots. Others were not so sure. "All hat and no boots," John Connally said of Bush's claim to be a Lone Star native. Furthermore, although he had served as ambassador to the U.N., America's envoy to China, the head of the CIA, and Reagan's vice-president, Bush seemed to have no core political identity. He had been elected in his own right only once—to Congress.

The Democrats, on the other hand, faced even more serious problems. Not only had they lost their demographic stronghold among blue collar, industrial, and Catholic workers; they had also lost their geographic base, being able to count for sure only on Minnesota, Massachusetts, and West Virginia; by virtue of their identification as the party of civil rights, they had almost automatically lost the white South. The Democratic primary campaign was notable primarily for the fact that Gary Hart, the Colorado senator, was driven from the race by reporters who probed his sex life and produced photographs of Hart and a model (not his wife) aboard a yacht called *Monkey Business;* also impressive was the surprisingly strong showing of Jesse Jackson, who won states like Michigan and for a period of time boasted the most delegates. But in the end, the victor was Michael Dukakis, the serious, dry, "high-tech" governor of Massachusetts who declared that "competence," not ideology, was the primary issue of the campaign, and whose triumph could be attributed more to a superior campaign organization than to any charismatic qualities.

The electoral race that followed said less about the profound issues facing the country than it did about the extraordinary hold that appeals to law and order, "negative images," fear, and patriotism still exerted on the American public. "One of the rules of the [political] business," John Sasso, Dukakis' campaign manager said, "is that somebody gets to fill up the cup. If you want to be successful, you have to fill it first," creating the public's impression of what the campaign is about. By those criteria, Dukakis never stood a chance. Although initially Bush's "negatives"—the "suspect" qualities people associate with a candidate—were nearly three times as high as Dukakis', Bush campaign operatives soon turned the situation around. They discovered that when voters were told that Dukakis had vetoed a law requiring school students to pledge allegiance to the flag (he had been advised by his attorney general that the law was unconstitutional), that he opposed the death penalty, and that he had authorized weekend furloughs for prisoners who had committed violent crimes, they turned against Dukakis and toward Bush. Nothing crystallized this approach better than the infamous ad focusing on Willie Horton, a black inmate who had been convicted of rape and assault and who, on a weekend furlough, had terrorized a Maryland couple, raping the woman. The Willie Horton TV ad depicted a revolving door letting people out of prison (black people), and accused Dukakis of pampering criminals and endangering law-abiding citizens.

"Never had the appeal to racism been so blatant and raw," the *New Yorker*'s Elizabeth Drew wrote. "If I can make Willie Horton a household name," Bush's campaign aide Lee Atwater said, "we'll win the election." He was right.

In the end, the 1988 election campaign ended up more as an exercise in media manipulation than serious dialogue. "Sound bites" became the object of the day, and "spin doctors" wielded the ultimate power. In 1980, the average time devoted to a candidate's thoughts had been 45 seconds per network news broadcast; in 1984 that plummeted to 15 seconds, and in 1988 to 9 seconds. Any less, and the screen would have shown only images, perhaps subliminal; but in a sense, that was the whole point of the Willie Horton ad. Little if any attention was devoted to issues like the greenhouse effect, the globalization of the economy, the proliferation of homelessness, or even the implications of Gorbachev's revolution in the U.S.S.R. When, as the polls predicted, Bush swept to a massive victory, it seemed to say more about the nadir to which presidential campaigns had fallen than about any decisions on the future course that America would chart in an increasingly troubled world.

Despite this fact, George Bush was in many ways as well prepared to be president as anyone could be. His CIA and ambassadorial experience provided him with a wealth of foreign policy expertise to enable him to deal with the ongoing turbulence occasioned by the Gorbachev revolution. Bush preferred policy-making to politics; he had told Mikhail Gorbachev "not to listen" to what he said in the campaign—that was just for domestic political consumption. Indeed, when Bush spoke after the election of moving Americans toward being a "kinder, gentler" people, and evoked the image of people helping their neighbors through volunteer work, creating "a thousand points of light," he seemed to be signaling a desire to break from the harsh social policies of the Reagan years. The question was whether he would—or could—deliver on both a foreign and domestic agenda of change.

Not surprisingly, Bush deftly and purposefully handled most of the foreign policy crises that came his way. While many might criticize the positions he took on specific issues, even his foes agreed that Bush was sure-handed and effective in pursuing his goals.

The first and most obvious challenge he faced was the continuing disintegration of the Soviet bloc. With bewildering speed, democratic struggles for autonomy and self-determination swept through Eastern Europe. In a world made more open by Gorbachev's policies of glasnost and perestroika, the demand for freedom exploded in 1989 and 1990. The Berlin Wall toppled in November 1989, Solidarity won free elections in Poland, Hungarians thronged their capital to celebrate a new multi-party constitution, and the people of Czechoslovakia mobbed Wenceslas Square in Prague to celebrate the return of a democracy that had been so brutally crushed by Communist tanks in 1948 and then again in 1968. Even Romania—the harshest of the hard-line Stalinist states—appeared to be swept along by the tide of change, its tyrannical dictator unable to retain control despite his attempt to massacre his own people.

Although a few critics attacked Bush for not responding more boldly to these dramatic changes, in fact his careful approach made eminent sense. To have reacted precipitously might well have created greater instability, more violence, and a stronger likelihood of counter-democratic action, especially from the armed forces within the Soviet Union. Gorbachev was embroiled in his own desperate attempt to survive politically, bobbing and weaving between hard-liners urging him to suppress dissent within the Soviet Union and reformers who advocated privatization of the economy and democratic reform. Gorbachev had played a crucial role diplomatically in undermining the East German regime and supporting the independence of Solidarity in Poland. Were he to lose power, it might reverse many of the positive changes that had already occurred. Hence, Bush devoted most of his energies to bolstering Gorbachev. He responded to the USSR's initiatives on arms control by cancelling the nuclear-alert status of U.S. bombers, and agreed to terminate plans to build mobile long-range missiles. Through a series of summits, the two superpower leaders arrived at stunning breakthroughs on new arms control treaties that promised to reduce dramatically the nuclear weapons arsenals of the world.

Then, the most unthinkable event of all happened. The Soviet Union itself disintegrated, victim to the same forces of nationalism, democracy, and anti-authoritariansim that had engulfed the rest of the Soviet empire. In a last-ditch effort to reassert control, Soviet military leaders attempted a coup in August 1990, only to have their authority flaunted by Russian citizens rushing to mobilize behind their own nationalist leader, Boris Yeltsin. Once an ally and now a foe of Gorbachev, Yeltsin stood atop a tank in Red Square and courageously defied the Soviet military, in the process sowing fear and confusion among the coup plotters. Rescued from his fate, Gorbachev returned to Moscow seeking one last time to assert control and save a socialist regime. But by then, he had lost all credibility and within weeks, the Union of Soviet Socialist Republics had disappeared, replaced by fifteen different nation states. By now more a bystander than a player, Bush had committed his only major error—recognizing too late the ascendancy of Yeltsin and the decline of Gorbachev. Recovering quickly, the American president sought to make Yelstin into an ally, beginning a new coalition wherein both world powers would act in concert to enforce peace in the world.

The fruits of that cooperation became visible for all to see in Bush's greatest foreign policy achievement, the three-day ground war of March 1991 that liberated Kuwait from Iraqi occupation. "Operation Desert Storm" represented the culmination of eight months of military and diplomatic consultation among Arab states, Western allies like France and England, and America's newest partner, Boris Yeltsin's Russia. Iraq's leader Saddam Hussein—armed and supported by the United States throughout the 80s—thought he could seize the oil fields of Kuwait with impunity and on August 1, 1990, had invaded that country, sending its elite rulers and monarch into exile. The United States, however, refused to countenance the takeover, and, during the next eight months, Bush pieced together a multi-national coalition that initially imposed economic sanctions on Iraq, and ultimately used lightning and overpowering military force to crush Iraqi tanks and soldiers. When the attack finally came, it devastated Iraq. More than 300 Iraqi soldiers died for every allied casualty, with thousands of civilians killed and millions made homeless. In a television war that witnessed CNN reporters broadcasting live from a Baghdad hotel room while the first allied bombs fell on the Iraqi capital, the whole nation participated in a patriotic frenzy, capped by a victory that to even optimists, seemed extraordinary in its swiftness and efficiency. (What no one realized at the time was the fateful consequence of George H. W. Bush's decision not to pursue the enemy into Baghdad and topple Saddam Hussein.) To some, it was as though the shame of Vietnam had finally been exorcized. Within weeks, George Bush's popularity reached an all-time high of 91 percent.

Yet as Winston Churchill had learned in the summer of 1945, success on the battlefield could be short-lived, especially if not accompanied by parallel progress in other arenas of political importance. Bush's triumph had come in the face of profound division within the country over whether military force should have been used. The Senate split 52-48 on a resolution to authorize armed action, as opposed to continued sanctions. The lightning victory appeared to vindicate Bush, with many suggesting that anyone who had opposed the war faced political extinction. Indeed, given the resounding popularity the president enjoyed through the early summer of 1991, many prospective Democratic presidential candidates decided to give 1992 a bye, assuming that no one could challenge Bush's entrenched power. But all of that was based on a short-term perspective. The divisions visible earlier would not disappear. And the popularity of a triumphant commander-in-chief could fade in the face of other discontents, whether in foreign policy matters or at home.

One of Bush's weaknesses in the foreign policy field was the degree to which he had been part and parcel of virtually every major decision of the Reagan/Bush terms. Thus, even if Bush was not directly associated with an event at the time, subsequent disclosures could place him at the scene, playing a role he would rather never have discovered by others.

Such was the case in the Iran-Contra scandal. Throughout the investigations by the Tower commission and by Congressional committees, Bush had been portrayed as a bystander to the Oliver North plan to sell arms for hostages. Over and over again, Bush claimed to have been "out of the loop," hence not accountable for the errors made by others. Even though his chief foreign policy advisor as vice-president—Donald Gregg—had conferred with participants in the Iran-Contra scandal at the time it was occurring, Bush succeeded in conveying the story that he had never been informed. By the end of his own presidency, however, Reagan administration cabinet members such as George Shultz and Caspar Weinberger had begun to speak out. Both were clearly angry that Bush had gotten away with what they considered to be a fabrication. Moreover, Weinberger had kept contemporary notes of meetings held at the White House. It was clear from both these notes and the recollections of Shultz and Weinberger that not only was Bush "*in* the loop"; he had also been a strong advocate of the policies Reagan pursued, arguing *for* the arms sales. Although for the moment, these revelations did no dramatic harm to Bush—he continued to stick by his "out of the loop" story—what they did do was raise questions about his candor and integrity.

In similar fashion, journalistic investigations soon raised the issue of how much George Bush had himself been responsible for Saddam Hussein's power in Iraq, and the degree to which the Iraqi ruler was led by Bush to believe that he could get away with his aggressive stance toward Kuwait. American cooperation with Iraq had begun during the Carter administration in the midst of the Iranian crisis. Under Reagan it had extended to sharing intelligence information during the Iraq-Iran war, providing satellite photos, and sending arms. Subsequently, billions of dollars were channeled to Iraq through the Export-Import bank, with vice-president George Bush twice intervening to get loans approved. As president, Bush continued such support, opposing a Congressional move to impose sanctions on Iraq for its use of chemical weapons against the Kurds, and arranging for $2 billion more in agricultural credits. As late as October 1989, 10 months before the invasion of Kuwait, Bush issued a National Security directive ordering all government agencies to strengthen their ties with Iraq. Just a few short days before the invasion, the U.S. ambassador in Baghdad reassured Saddam Hussein once more that the U.S. wanted good relations with him, and had no opinion about Iraq's territorial dispute with Kuwait. Conceivably, then, Saddam Hussein had every reason to feel stunned when Bush suddenly turned against him on August 1. As one reporter noted, "During a decade of extensive contacts with Washington, nothing whatever had occurred that could have led him to expect it."

Far more important than miscues in foreign policy, however, was Bush's lassitude and ineffectuality in domestic matters. Seeking to insure his election, he had uttered repeatedly the ill-advised and demagogic phrase, "READ MY LIPS! NO NEW TAXES." Once in office, however, he had to find some way to deal with the ballooning deficit, and in a package similar to that put together seven years earlier by David Stockman (and then nixed by Reagan) he agreed to a bipartisan plan of spending controls and higher taxes. In fact, it was quantitatively the largest tax increase in history. Once again, the message was confusion and incoherence.

That message was reinforced when the nation entered a prolonged recession in the months after "Desert Storm" and Bush had absolutely no response. In fact, Bush cared little if anything about domestic policies, had no ideas on how to proceed, and appeared content to mouth platitudes about things not being *that* bad. "Where was the guiding concept," a Bush administration official asked. "There was none. It's been a problem for the whole Bush presidency." Pollsters for the Republican Party began to pick up disquieting evidence of disaffection and concern in the body politic, notwithstanding "Desert Storm." Unemployment was over 7 percent; new jobs were concentrated in service industries; and even huge firms like IBM and Xerox were beginning to flounder. Yet instead of alarm, the administration responded with indifference—even complacency. "I don't think it's the end of the world even if we have a recession," Treasury Secretary Nicholas Brady said. "We'll pull out of it again. No big deal." Rather than devise a new approach, presidential advisors recommended standing pat. "Frankly," John Sununu said in November 1991, "this president doesn't need another single piece of legislation."

Lulled by a 91 percent approval rating and paralyzed by its own lack of direction in domestic matters, the Bush administration thus ignored the realities of a major sea change in people's attitudes toward politics, even as all around it the tide was rushing out. Eight months after the Gulf War, fewer than 40 percent of the American people felt comfortable with the way the country was moving. A deep-seated malaise seemed to sweep the land: there were problems no one was addressing, issues that for too long had been swept under the rug. Los Angeles had been engulfed by race riots after the verdict acquitting the police who had been shown beating black motorist Rodney King on a videotape. Government officials and corporate executives were going to jail for betraying their obligation to the people. Suddenly, an election that had looked like a ritual coronation of the incumbent became a wide-open contest, evoking images and passions not seen in the political arena for three decades—not since the 1960s.

The 1992 Presidential Election

At its most basic level, in fact, the 1960s was what the election of 1992 was all about. Not simply the romantic image of a 16-year-old Bill Clinton shaking the hand of his hero John F. Kennedy in the White House Rose Garden, or the links that connected Kennedy's archfoe Richard Nixon to George Bush, his CIA director. Nor the Vietnam war, and how symbolic it—and attitudes toward fighting the war or not fighting it—became in the course of the 1992 election. Rather, the underlying theme of the campaign was whose 1960s would triumph: the 1960s of idealism and energetic faith in the capacity of government to make life better, or the 1960s of rancor, counterculture alienation, and hateful rhetoric pitting one self-righteous perspective against another in a civil war. For Bill Clinton, the 1960s represented a moment of hope, a surge of moral commitment to make the world better. To George Bush, they represented a display of excess, a deviation from the

American way, an explosion of unwarranted government intervention and special favors on behalf of the poor and the black amidst carping criticism of the traditional values and institutions that made America great. Two realities, two different decades. The American people would decide which version of the 1960s they wished to honor and remember in 1992.

Before that could happen, of course, there were the endless preliminaries. Once again, a flood of Democrats entered the fray, ranging from the investment-oriented Paul Tsongas, who hoped to "grow the economy" through private initiative, to the antiestablishment Jerry Brown, former governor of California, who wanted to give politics "back to the people." At the middle of the pack stood Arkansas governor Bill Clinton, elected six times to be chief executive of that small and poor southern state. A former Rhodes scholar who studied at Oxford after completing his undergraduate years at Georgetown, Clinton represented as vivid and dramatic a personality as had ever run for president. His mother, a strong, vivacious woman, had been widowed three months before his birth. Her husband, it later was revealed, had been married at least three times before and had fathered numerous children. When Clinton's mother remarried, she chose a man who soon became both alcoholic and abusive, forcing young Bill into the role of protecting and defending the family. (The theme of the absent father became a leitmotif of Clinton speeches.) Incredibly bright, talented, and charismatic, Clinton rose to the top of every group he was in, including the national governors' conference, where he preached his litany of investing to create jobs, supporting new technology, rebuilding the nation's infrastructure, and creating a new partnership between management and labor to increase American productivity and competitiveness in world markets. Young—in the summer of 1991 he was only 45—handsome, and articulate, Clinton was a superb politician in public with a sure grasp of issues and a winning campaign style, while in private he appeared to understand well the tactics of putting together a winning coalition of supporters.

In the early stages of the marathon for the presidency, two major stories dominated the news. First was the third-party candidacy of Texas billionaire Ross Perot. With a pithy, down-to-earth style, outspoken views on everything, and a remarkable capacity to be in the right place at the right time, Perot professed to speak for the forgotten Americans who were sick of government, tired of political manipulation, and ready for a take-charge kind of guy who could look under the hood, tell them what was wrong, and proceed to fix it. Perot's flair was legendary. He had sent a rescue mission into Iran to save employees of his company who had been arrested; he spearheaded a movement to locate and recover American troops thought to be still alive in North Vietnam and Laos; and now, on behalf of his own citizens' group, "United We Stand, America," he was prepared to clean house at home, focusing special attention on the need to cut the deficit and balance the budget. Although Perot had no particular political philosophy, his "rough-hewn candor" appealed to people across party lines and threatened to upset all traditional political calculations on both sides. Further-more, he had the wealth to guarantee that his message would be heard. As the *New Yorker* editorialized, "to paraphrase Al Capone you can do more with an air of rough-hewn candor and a billion dollars than with an air of rough-hewn candor alone."

Directly related to the Perot phenomenon was the amazing new power of talk-show journalism to shape political dialogue and activity—in effect, the media equivalent of Richard Viguerie's direct-mail campaigns. With none of the political analysis or careful questioning of media outlets like the *New York Times* or NBC's *Meet the Press*, talk shows hosted by such celebrities as Oprah Winfrey, Geraldo Rivera, and Phil Donahue provided a direct out-let for politicians to reach the American heartland via TV. At the center of this galaxy was *Larry King Live*, the one-hour nightly interview program on Cable News Network that became the prize media site for any aspiring can-didate. Not by accident, Ross Perot notified the nation of his availability to be president by persuading his friend Larry King to let him go on the air to say that the American people could draft him for national service—a dra-matic tour de force, all sans tough adversarial questions, engaged debate, or informed rebuttal. Media control—or control of the media—suddenly took on new meaning.

The new journalism also played a major role in creating the second major story of the preelection period, the intense interest of the media in probing a candidate's personal life and especially his or her sexuality. Fu-eled by the multiple scandals that had emerged about John F. Kennedy's sexual escapades, this new passion for connecting the personal to the polit-ical could be justified where there was a clear link between how a person be-haved in private and what that person did in the public policy arena. Ar-guably, Kennedy's attitude toward women and sexual conquest could help explain some of his arrogance toward those around him, and his assump-tion that he could always get his way. But journalists could also be sensa-tionalists, reducing complicated political lives to intrusive questions about private matters. That had happened with Gary Hart in 1988 when an entire presidential candidacy came down to a reporter asking Hart, "have you ever committed adultery?" It was now about to happen again to Bill Clinton.

The Arkansas governor and his wife Hillary knew the issue would arise. Whenever Republicans or Democratic competitors ever talked about a Clin-ton candidacy, some said, the first word that was uttered was "Women." In various gubernatorial campaigns in Arkansas, allegations had been made about "womanizing," though never with corroboration or devastating con-sequences. Still, the Clinton campaign prepared to address the issue. In a reporters' breakfast early on, Clinton initiated a discussion about the charges that had been made in the past, and in the eyes of most of those present, did a good job of putting the issue behind him. But then came the allegations made in a national tabloid (*The Star*) that Gennifer Flowers had engaged in a twelve-year affair with Clinton. Claiming to have taped conversations, Flowers held a live CNN press conference, the "respectable" media picked up the story making it front-page news, and the entire Clinton candidacy seemed ready to implode. At the time a front-runner in New Hampshire, Clinton entered "free fall" in the polls. Despite evidence that the Flowers tapes were doctored, and that the charge had already been dismissed in an Arkansas campaign, the media engaged in its own feeding frenzy about the story.

Clinton and his wife Hillary finally chose to confront the issue directly, accepting an invitation to appear on CBS's *60 Minutes*. There, they did what no American political couple had ever done before—confess that they had experienced marital problems, and that they had now worked them out. "I think the American people—at least people who have been married a long time—know what [that] means," Clinton observed. "Listen to what I've said. . . . I have acknowledged causing pain in my marriage. I have said things to you tonight . . . that no American politician ever has. I think most Americans [will] . . . know what we're saying; they'll get it, and they'll feel that we have been more than candid." Hillary Clinton then added: "You know, I'm not sitting here—some little woman standing by my man, like Tammy Wynette. I'm sitting here because I love him, and I respect him, and I honor what he's been through and what we've been through together. And you know, if that's not enough for people, then, heck, don't vote for him." It was an amazing commentary, both on what had happened to the political media and what it took to survive that development. The Clintons had no choice but to place themselves at the mercy of the American people and hope they understood. In this instance they did. The free fall stopped; by sheer tenacity and persistence, Clinton climbed back into second place in New Hampshire; and his candidacy endured, though not without having to survive another hour-long exploration of his sexual habits on the *Phil Donahue Show*. But both the Larry King phenomenon and the focus on politician's sex lives represented benchmarks in the American electoral marathon that were as frightening as they were powerful in their implications for the democratic process.

By the late spring, Clinton had succeeded in wrapping up the Democratic nomination. He won most of the head-to-head races against his major competitors, put together a superb campaign staff, and began to secure backing from top party people. But was it a nomination worth having? Bloodied and bowed, Clinton seemed incapable of rising above the attacks that had so preoccupied him. By June he was running third in the polls, behind both George Bush and Ross Perot. How could he make this candidacy more than that of another sacrificial Democratic lamb? How could he define himself, and his program, in such a way that the American people would have a positive reason to support him?

First, Clinton put together a campaign team that streamlined its message and with discipline, stayed on target. The Clinton campaign staff acted on the premise that the candidate had to focus his message on the issue or issues that had the greatest likelihood of grabbing the attention of the American people. In 1992 America, it was not difficult to see what that issue was. As the sign in Clinton's Little Rock campaign "war room" blared, "IT'S THE ECONOMY STUPID."

Second, that simple message had to be delivered in a context of reaching out to Democratic voters who had defected to Ronald Reagan and George Bush, but were now sufficiently angered by what they considered a Republican betrayal that they might be ready to return to the Democratic camp. To win back the Reagan Democrats, Clinton needed to recover and reassert as his own philosophy what the Democratic party had meant to people in the early 1960s, and demonstrate that he rejected the Republican definition of the party as a tool of the "special interests." To do that, he emphasized repeatedly his commitment to help the middle class—not only the largest voting bloc in the country, but people who Clinton insisted had been ignored and victimized by a Reagan revolution that gave a 100 percent increase in income and wealth to the top 1 percent of the country, while allowing the middle class to see its earning power atrophy. In the new Clinton litany, "fairness" meant respecting the hard work and values of the middle class, getting able-bodied people off of welfare, and assuring that everyone, but especially the well-off, paid their fair share of taxes. The entire focus on the economy occurred within a framework of emphasizing investment, accountability, and shared responsibility. To punctuate that commitment, and illustrate his own independence from "special interests," Clinton went to a Jesse Jackson conference and openly criticized Sister Souljah, a black rap singer who had used lyrics that attacked white people, thereby underlining the extent to which he saw himself as a "new" Democrat.

Finally, Clinton offered this formula for governing as part of an effort to restore a sense of community and mutual caring to America. If Republicans had chosen to run against Democrats as the party associated with the social chaos and polarization of the late 1960s, Clinton would offer a party committed to the collective hopefulness of the early 1960s. Like John Kennedy, he emphasized getting the country moving again economically, not just so that the rich could benefit, but so that everyone could improve their lot. Tolerance for people of different backgrounds and lifestyles became a positive value, strengthening the common identity of Americans by using the resources of diversity, rather than seeing the existence of multiple cultures as negative and un-American. In effect, Clinton sought to re-invent the tension and dialectic that had made the Democratic coalitions of Roosevelt, Kennedy, and Johnson possible in the first place—a commitment to respect each group within the coalition, while holding it together by devotion to a common set of rules and economic priorities.

The Republican Party even helped in the process. By the midpoint of the Bush administration, all the zip had gone out of the Reagan boom. Not only was real income declining for the lower middle class and working class, but Republicans as well as Democrats were expressing dissatisfaction with

Bush's failure to do anything about it. By the end of 1991—notwithstanding the triumph of "Desert Storm"—Republican conservatives started to wage war against the man they never believed to be a true conservative anyway. Patrick Buchanan, former Nixon and Reagan speechwriter, decided to challenge Bush from the right in the primaries. Lashing out at the president as timid, indecisive, and without a plan—the "vision thing," as Bush called it— Buchanan promised a Reagan-like revitalization of the party. Never a real threat to Bush, Buchanan nevertheless won more than one-third of Republican votes in New Hampshire, and did almost as well in other primaries he entered. Instead of being invulnerable, Bush now appeared weak and defensive.

Then, trying to make peace with the conservatives, the Bush forces literally turned over the opening night of the Republican convention to Buchanan and his religiously fundamentalist colleague, Pat Robertson. The two engaged in rhetorical overkill of the Democrats, calling for a cultural and religious war against feminism, homosexuality, and any other point of view that deviated from 100 percent Americanism. There was no gentleness, no tolerance, and no humor. By contrast to the Democratic emphasis on community, inclusiveness, and warmth, the Republicans conveyed a message of narrowness, mean-spiritedness, and anger. Even Ronald Reagan could not rescue the evening. Under the circumstances, only a "speech of a lifetime" by Bush accepting the nomination could have made a difference. Instead, the president arrived at the convention with two contradictory drafts that he then tried unsuccessfully to combine into one, ending with a text that offered neither vision nor hope for the party.

At the core of Bush's problem was his own failure to find a reason to run and to win. "His re-election campaign lacks direction because he does," The New Yorker's Elizabeth Drew wrote; "he seems to have no clear idea why he should be re-elected." For months the president had shooed away those who were urging him to come up with a campaign strategy. He insisted he could win with an organization that moved into full gear only after Labor Day. To some, Bush acted as though he deserved reelection simply on the basis of having been president. He could run on his laurels, invoke the pride of "Desert Storm," and be returned to office by acclamation. Finally, by mid-summer the truth began to dawn. Fifteen points back in the polls, he now knew he was in trouble and determined to right things by asking Jim Baker to leave the State Department and take over management of his campaign. But even Baker could not do anything without the president having a message he wanted to deliver, and that remained a mystery. "I still can't tell you what he stands for," a highly placed staffer said, "and I've worked for him for ten years."

Eventually, Bush returned to some of the campaign tactics he had used four years earlier against Dukakis, impugning Clinton's patriotism, even suggesting that while a student in England, Clinton might have made a trip to Moscow for nefarious purposes. Clinton had picked up "foreign" ideas

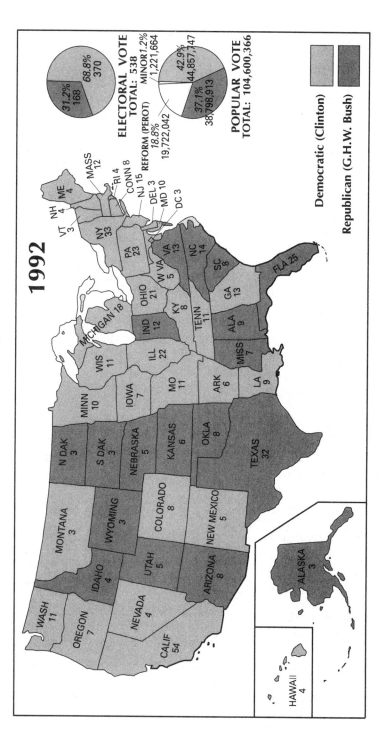

1992

ELECTORAL VOTE
TOTAL: 538

31.2% 168

68.8% 370

POPULAR VOTE
TOTAL: 104,600,366

MINOR 1.2%
1,221,664

42.9%
44,857,747

REFORM (PEROT)
18.8%
19,722,042

37.1%
38,798,913

Democratic (Clinton)

Republican (G.H.W. Bush)

WASH 11
OREGON 7
CALIF 54
NEVADA 4
IDAHO 4
MONTANA 3
WYOMING 3
UTAH 5
ARIZONA 8
COLORADO 8
NEW MEXICO 5
N DAK 3
S DAK 3
NEBRASKA 5
KANSAS 6
OKLA 8
TEXAS 32
MINN 10
IOWA 7
MO 11
ARK 6
LA 9
WIS 11
ILL 22
IND 12
MISS 7
ALA 9
MICHIGAN 18
OHIO 21
KY 8
TENN 11
GA 13
W VA 5
VA 13
NC 14
SC 8
FLA 25
PA 23
NY 33
VT 3
NH 4
ME 4
MASS 12
RI 4
CONN 8
NJ 15
DEL 3
MD 10
DC 3

ALASKA 3
HAWAII 4

A weak economy and Bush's failure to rally the conservative base allowed a well-defined Clinton campaign to break the Republican hold on cultural issues through a focus on renewed community and fairness to a working middle class. Democrats since Clinton have not been able to repeat his victory in the South and Midwest. (*National Atlas of the United States, http://nationalatlas.gov*)

about "social engineering" while at Oxford, Bush said, ideas that had failed "from Warsaw to Prague to Moscow." If such allegations constituted "subtle red-baiting," as one reporter said, the Bush campaign's attempt to investigate Clinton's passport files and get the British foreign office to do the same (both illegal acts) descended to a level where subtlety was a stranger.

On the other hand, Bush had a legitimate point when he raised the "character" issue by challenging Clinton to "come clean" about his draft record during the Vietnam war. While acknowledging that he had opposed the war, Clinton had obfuscated the question of his draft status when asked about it, on one occasion saying he had never received an induction notice, on another admitting that he had. There were times when Clinton became his own worst enemy (as Bush was), taking so many approaches to the same issue that he became almost a caricature of the "slick Willy" portrait his adversaries painted of him. Despite his campaign staff's advice, Clinton too often seemed to want to be all things to all people. "We can be pro-growth and pro-environment," he told one audience, "we can be pro-business and pro-labor . . . we can be pro-family and pro-choice." Yet whenever Bush pressed too hard on the character issue, the question came back to his own complicity in the Iran-Contra scandal. Moreover, hard as he might try to make Vietnam an issue, polls showed that most Americans were prepared to leave that tortured squabble behind them and not punish someone who twenty-three years earlier had been against the war.

In the end, Clinton won because he possessed a strategy, a vision of renewed community, and a campaign apparatus prepared to implement a winning plan. By contrast, Time observed, Bush was "feckless, confused, whining and rudderless." Clinton had set out to redefine the Democratic Party, to win back Reagan defectors by giving a new meaning to "fairness." Reflecting that philosophy, Clinton called his triumph "a victory for the people who work hard and play by the rules . . . a victory for the people who are ready to compete and win in the global economy but who need a government that offers a hand, not a hand-out." Bush, on the other side, seemed oblivious to the average people Reagan had so skillfully cultivated. Never a "cultural democrat" like Reagan, Bush seemed unable to escape his own persona as an aristocrat. As a result, he won a lower percentage of votes than Barry Goldwater, Herbert Hoover, or George McGovern. No incumbent since William Howard Taft had fared so poorly.

On the other hand, William Jefferson Clinton by no means could claim a mandate. "Landslide" Bill had won with 43 percent of the popular vote. Unlike Reagan, he did not sweep into office with a dozen new Senators and Representatives dependent on him for their own victories, and hence prepared to support his every whim. Ross Perot's 19 percent of the vote suggested a huge number of Americans were still disaffected from traditional party politics and viewed both mainstream candidates as little better than fraudulent manipulators. Notwithstanding Bush's abysmal showing, then, Clinton himself was a minority president who began by having to persuade voters and Congress that he deserved a measure of support he did not yet have.

That made all the more difficult the high expectations with which a Clinton presidency was greeted by many Americans. Here was a youthful, exuberant, thoughtful activist. His wife Hillary, an accomplished attorney and distinguished political figure in her own right (she had chaired the board of the Children's Defense Fund), promised to be a full partner in the White House, perhaps more powerful in the public arena than any First Lady since Eleanor Roosevelt. It was almost as though the best parts of the 1960s had come together to make a reappearance—feminism, a commitment to fairness, a modern marital relationship, but one framed by devotion to family, an energetic excitement about the ability to use government to make people's lives better. "What excites most people about Clinton," one magazine said, "is precisely the degree to which he speaks to their hunger for meaning and purpose, their half-conscious and often inchoate desire to transcend the selfishness and meaningless of materialistic and narcissistic society." *Time* was equally elegaic. "For years," it said in its Man of the Year issue, "Americans have been in a kind of vague mourning for something that they sensed they had lost somewhere—what was best in the country, a distinctive American endowment of youth and energy amid ideals and luck: the sacred American stuff." And now here was Clinton, with the potential of providing the answer. "[His] victory," *Time* enthused, "places him in a position to preside over one of the periodic reinventions of the country—those moments when Americans dig themselves out of their deepest problems by reimagining themselves." Clinton was, another writer rhapsodized, "our generation's second chance."

The new president himself contributed to such romantic expectations. "Today," Bill Clinton said in his Inaugural Address in January 1993, "we celebrate the mystery of American renewal. . . . In the depth of winter, we force the spring. . . . This is our time. Let us embrace it." Whether any president could live up to this mission represented both the challenge and the Achilles' heel of the new administration. Would it be possible for Bill Clinton to validate and recover his version of the 1960s and move toward fulfilling the legacy of Roosevelt, Truman, Kennedy, and Johnson? Or would he founder, overwhelmed by the immensity of the problems facing America and victim to his own capacity for self-destructive behavior?

The First Clinton Administration

Finding a safe passage through such shoals would have tested the helmsmanship of even the greatest political captain. Although the problems he faced were not as desperate or severe as those that had confronted Franklin Roosevelt in the midst of the Great Depression, they were in many ways far more complicated and intractable, calling upon the same breadth and depth of leadership skills that FDR had deployed in the 1930s. Indeed, given the array of structural dilemmas Clinton faced—the underclass, the de-skilling of industry, racial polarization, a runaway health care system, a broken welfare state, and a widespread loss of faith in the American political process—the comparison with the Roosevelt years made eminent sense.

Perhaps appropriately, Bill Clinton brought to these issues a personality and set of character traits as complicated, colorful, vivid, and contradictory as any occupant of the White House before him. "He is the most seductive and persuasive person I have ever met," one White House aide declared, summarizing—almost in understatement—the impact Clinton had on those around him. Yet if he was "one of the biggest, most talented, articulate, intelligent, open [and] colorful characters ever to inhabit the Oval Office," *New York Times* reporter Todd Purdum wrote, he could "also be an undisciplined, fumbling, obtuse, defensive [and] self-justifying rogue." Purdum's colleague Maureen Dowd described the same paradox another way: "[Clinton] is naive and sophisticated, thin-skinned and self-assured, bold and hesitant, genuine and glib." There was no way to separate the good from the bad. Few if any presidents before him had demonstrated such a capacity to master the details of the most complex policy dilemma, or articulate a vision of how to deal boldly with it. Yet few among his predecessors displayed so much slickness, expediency, and disingenuousness. The irony, as Todd Purdum wrote, was that "his strengths and weaknesses not only spring from the same source, but could also not exist without one another. In a real sense, his strengths are his weaknesses, his enthusiasms are his undoing, and most of the traits that make him appealing can make him appalling in the flash of an eye." Such a man clearly had the capacity to rise to the challenge facing him, as FDR had done. But he also had the capability to destroy his own best impulses and visions, giving vent to the undisciplined, careless, and self-indulgent side of his personality.

The first nine months of the Clinton administration dramatized brilliantly this tendency toward political schizophrenia. Clinton had used an economics "teach-in" in Little Rock to bring together industrial leaders, financiers, and academics to educate the American people and his own team of advisors about the appropriate combination of deficit reduction and stimulus in the economic package he would introduce once he became president. But almost immediately after entering the White House, Clinton got "off message," making his first major pronouncement not on taxes or deficit reduction, but on the need to end discrimination against homosexuals in the military. Clearly, Clinton believed in civil rights for gays; his campaign had endorsed such measures more openly than any previous presidential candidacy, and now he was delivering on his pledge. Yet he had not done his homework. A simple proposed executive order encountered massive opposition from military leaders like Colin Powell, from prestigious senators like Armed Services Committee chair Sam Nunn, and from out-

William Jefferson Clinton being sworn in as president. Clinton's daughter Chelsea and his wife Hillary stand beside him. *(Clinton Presidential Materials Project)*

raged middle-American citizens who saw Clinton embracing a constituency that they defined as "deviant." When Clinton hemmed and hawed, and finally came up with a policy of "Don't ask, don't tell," his actions profoundly alienated liberals and gays, even as it gave the message to moderates that Clinton was a "waffler."

The same sense of indecisiveness characterized other Clinton moves. The Clinton cabinet never lived up to its aspiration to be a microcosm of America in its diversity—despite including blacks, women, and Latinos, it still represented primarily establishment lawyers—and Clinton was forced to withdraw two female nominees for attorney general because they had technically violated IRS and immigration laws in their hiring of household help. When he subsequently withdrew the nomination of Lani Guinier, an African-American law professor from Pennsylvania and an old FOB (friend of Bill's), for the post of assistant attorney general for civil rights—she had defended proportional representation for minorities in some situations, rather than the doctrine of one-person, one-vote—many liberals became convinced that Clinton had no backbone at all.

Even Clinton's most notable success came wrapped with controversy and derogatory sniping from people who otherwise would be counted as his chief supporters. Courageously, Clinton had concluded that he must place deficit reduction ahead of the middle-class tax cut he had promised voters in the campaign. The result was a carefully crafted economic package that would cut in half the annual deficit as part of total expenditures, raise taxes on the wealthy, and put in place a mechanism for sustained economic growth. To sweeten the package and help create new jobs, Clinton offered an economic stimulus program that would inject $30 billion into the economy through various federal programs and incentives. Despite their own avowed commitment to deficit reduction, the Republicans refused any cooperation with Clinton; Senate minority leader Robert Dole told Clinton he would not get a single Republican vote. The Republicans then successfully filibustered against the stimulus package, and in order to secure a one-vote victory in the Senate for the overall deficit-reduction bill, Clinton sacrificed an energy tax that he had insisted Democrats in the House must support as a litmus test of their loyalty to him. In the end, the legislation turned out to be a great success—even if it did pass by only one vote. But in the process liberals felt they had once again been sold out by the president. The appearance, at least, was of a White House that even in the midst of victory seemed weak, inexperienced, and temporizing. "It was the grimmest start of any presidency in generations," the *New Republic*'s TRB declared in August 1993.

From the very beginning, however, everyone understood that Clinton's presidency would rise or fall on his success in passing health care reform that would guarantee insurance to every American citizen. In 1992, the United States remained the only developed industrial nation in the world without such a system. Most of Europe had instituted national health programs in the immediate aftermath of World War II if not before. Franklin Roosevelt had toyed with the idea of making national health insurance a part of his Social Security legislation, but decided to defer it until later. When Harry Truman attempted to follow through with such a plan in 1947, on the other hand, it immediately fell victim to Cold War politics. National health insurance, it was claimed, was communistic, "socialized medicine," a step toward extinguishing the individual rights of patients and the freedom of physicians in service to a state behemoth.

Now, with the Cold War over, it seemed possible for the first time in almost 50 years to revisit the issue. Health care consumed one seventh of the nation's goods and services, far more than in any other industrialized country. Health care costs skyrocketed throughout the 1970s and 1980s, double or triple the rate of inflation, eating away completely any increases in real income. Furthermore, by virtue of the private nature of the existing insurance system, and the numbers of workers who were denied access to fringe benefit packages, nearly 40 million Americans were totally without health care coverage. They could neither secure preventive care nor afford timely attention to medical problems that without attention threatened to become disabling or even life-threatening. The loss of labor hours, a healthy citizenry, and a sense of security in dealing with fundamental physical problems was impossible to calculate. In 1990, Harris Wofford had won a Senatorial contest in Pennsylvania, where no one had given him a chance, by making health care reform his central issue. The right to health care, Wofford had declared, was as fundamental in a democracy as the right to vote. By 1992, health care reform had become the centerpiece of the presidential primary campaign, with Bill Clinton focusing ever more of his energies on advocacy of major change. In effect, economic reform and health care reform were two sides of the same coin. A permanent cure for huge deficits required harnessing the explosive rate of inflation in health care costs. Accomplishing both would put Clinton's presidency in the same league with that of FDR.

Clinton instinctively understood the parallels. "There's no example since the Depression and [World War II]," he said, "when something [so] sweeping was [attempted] in as short amount of time as I was trying to do." In the mind of West Virginia senator Jay Rockefeller, Clinton's approach to health care reform represented the most massive, important social legislation in all of American history, making even Social Security look small. Moreover, the political consequences were enormous. If Clinton could tie the middle class to the Democratic party through providing universal national health insurance, he would solidify for at least another generation the dominance of his party. The Republicans, of course, also understood that fact. Hence, from the very beginning Newt Gingrich—minority leader in the House—determined to resist, defeat and kill the Clinton effort, knowing that if the Republicans could achieve that goal, and in the process portray Clinton as the president of excessive liberalism and big-government intervention, the GOP could emerge triumphant. That made the presentation and definition of the issue absolutely critical to success or failure.

Although arguably there were a thousand reasons why health care reform eventually went down to crushing defeat, the first—and perhaps fatal—error occurred when Clinton chose to give responsibility for drafting his health care reform to a task force directed by his wife, Hillary, and administered by his old friend and fellow Rhodes scholar, Ira Magaziner. By everyone's account, Hillary Rodham Clinton was brilliant, hard-driving, a master of detail, and a charismatic leader. A feminist with a distinguished legal career, she was the first presidential wife to exercise, publicly and explicitly, a major policy role.

As an engaged activist on both children's issues and health concerns, Hillary Rodham Clinton seemed ideally suited to lead such an effort, especially given the fact that it was her husband's chief legislative goal and she was his partner, both in politics and in marriage. The president chose her, he later told Haynes Johnson and David Broder, because "she cared enough about it, had enough talent, and had enough understanding that if anybody had a chance to do it, she had the best chance." The other side of the picture, unfortunately, was that precisely because of her marital and political partnership with the president, she could just as easily become a lightning rod for hostility as for praise. A person of strong opinions (some called her dogmatic), she did not easily accept criticism or tolerate dissenting views. As one Cabinet member reported, "You make your point once to the president's wife, and if it is not accepted, you don't press it." With such a person in charge, the policy-making process might well be less sensitive than normal to political negotiation and barter.

The task force operation itself represented another deviation from the regular political process. Ira Magaziner represented the quintessential "policy wonk," Connie Bruck wrote in a *New Yorker* article; he believed that mastery of incredibly complex data could lead to legislative solutions that—even if complicated themselves—could win the day. Hence, Magaziner set out to recruit more than 600 experts to work on 34 different issues—issues such as health care alliances, managed competition, and caps on health care premiums. Moreover, all the work of the various groups would take place in secret until final proposals were developed. It was policy-making by expert fiat, led by a man who, like Hillary Clinton, was often seen by others as arrogant, dismissive of viewpoints contrary to his own, and intent on riding roughshod over those less bright and competent than he.

The fundamental problem with such a process was that it left out Congress—and the political wheelers and dealers who make what Broder and Johnson called "the system" work effectively. By choosing the "expert" approach of a task force, Clinton committed himself to presenting a finished package to Congress. Yet that would take time and risk the loss of momentum. Furthermore, it meant that participants in the congressional committee process—the staffers and political leaders who would eventually be responsible for *enacting* the legislation—would not be involved in its drafting. Nor were members of the administration itself, who ordinarily would have been part of the policy-making process. Neither Donna Shalala, Secretary of Health and Human Services, nor Lloyd Bentsen, Secretary of the Treasury and former chair of the Senate Finance Committee who had handled more health care legislation than anyone else, took part in the task force process. Suspicion mounted, among both members of Congress and some of the administration, that their own, customary role in making policy was being ignored. The Magaziner operation seemed eerily similar to when "the best and the brightest"—David Halberstam's phrase to describe the Ivy League elite—took over the planning of the Vietnam war in the Kennedy years. As Illinois Congressman Dan Rostenkowski, chair of the House Ways and Means Committee, said about Magaziner, "I wish he had some dirt under his fingernails." Instead, the health care proposal to be submitted by Clinton was developed behind closed doors with no input from the hands-on political managers who in the end would be pivotal to any bill that had a chance of being enacted.

Not surprisingly, the measure produced by this process was extraordinarily complicated, sophisticated beyond belief—with a provision for any and every eventuality—and inaccessible to the average citizen. Nearly 1350 pages in length, the Clinton health care measure arrived on Capitol Hill almost a full year after the president had taken office. Immediately, it drew criticism, Utah Republican senator Bob Bennett denouncing it as "incredibly bloated, complex, unresponsive, [and] incomprehensible, . . . [symbolic of] everything people hate about government." Even supporters expressed anxiety, and the lobbyist for America's senior citizens openly worried "about the complexity of this [plan] and the ability of people to feel comfortable with something that is so complicated. If you're explaining it, people's eyes glaze over." How much better it might have been had the president gone to the American people with the broad outlines of a program and worked from the beginning with congressional committees to draft legislation appropriate to implementing those goals.

The potential of such an approach became manifest when Bill Clinton went before Congress and the nation in September 1993 to deliver his vision of health care reform. The speech was the most important of his presidency. Clinton had mastered the subject, synthesized its complexity, and knew the importance of focusing on the principles he and Hillary had agreed to—quality care, savings, simplicity, and security. Although for a minute or two at the beginning of the speech Clinton seemed a bit uncertain (the wrong speech had been scrolled onto the teleprompter, and it took time to insert the correct one), the president was clearly in his element, rising to the occasion with a memorable address that galvanized even his opponents in the audience. One Republican senator called Clinton's speech "the most comprehensive, brilliantly presented analytical dissection of everything that is wrong with the present health system" that he had ever heard. If, as Haynes Johnson and David Broder noted, "the great moments of the modern presidency are closely associated with memorable presidential addresses," Clinton had made a fine start.

Yet almost immediately, he allowed the momentum he had created to dissipate. Other issues took center stage—NAFTA, the effort to create a free trade zone between Mexico, the United States, and Canada; a military crisis in Somalia where U.S. troops were bogged down in a United Nations effort to end a civil war. The Magaziner task force was still laboring away trying to produce a legislative draft—a process that would take two more months. Suddenly the stiff wind that Clinton had seemed to run with on health care disappeared, to be replaced by inaction, confusion, and demoralization, especially among advocates of reform who saw passing from their control perhaps the best chance they would ever have to secure success.

Into the vacuum strode the Republican opposition, who had been waiting to savage the president's plan precisely because of its elephantine size, its incomprehensibility, its apparent threat to small business and individual choice. "There must be a better way," announced a series of TV ads featuring Harry and Louise sitting around the kitchen table pondering the fate of health care. Certainly there was a problem, the ads avowed, but was more big government the solution? Clinton was losing the battle of defining the issue for the public. Immediately after his speech, public approval for the Clinton initiative exceeded disapproval by 32 points. Just three weeks later, the gap had dwindled to 12 points, the decline a product of lassitude by the Clinton forces, brilliant media manipulation by the "No-name coalition" of insurance and small business lobbying groups, and the adamant refusal of Republican congressional leaders to consider compromise. Senator Phil

Gramm of Texas announced that the Republicans were going to "blow this train up." Newt Gingrich insisted on total opposition lest his plans for a Republican revolution "be cooked" by a Clinton foray into guaranteeing new middle-class entitlements. And Bob Dole, seeing which way the wind was blowing, saw no reason to jeopardize his hopes for the Republican presidential nomination in 1996 by holding out an olive branch to the president.

Early on, it seemed to some optimists that a middle ground of leadership in the House and Senate would produce victory, even if they had not been consulted in the process of drafting the legislation. People like John Chaffee of Rhode Island, James Cooper of Tennessee, John Breaux of Louisiana, Fred Grandy of Iowa—all thought that once congressional leaders took charge of the negotiation process, success was still possible. Now, however, with Clinton's forces losing focus and momentum, and the Republican leadership empowered by the success of its negative message, that likelihood faded. As one moderate House Republican noted, "it's disappointing, but we have a leadership that preempts policy with partisanship."

For a brief period at the end of Clinton's first year, prospects again briefly brightened. Clinton had scored a major legislative success in getting the NAFTA treaty ratified; in addition, he achieved a notable "moral" victory by getting Congress to pass the Brady bill, the first legislation in years that attempted to place restrictions on free access by Americans to handguns and assault weapons. Together with passage of the Clinton deficit-reduction package, creation of a national service corps (Americorps) of young people volunteering to work among America's disadvantaged populations, and a new, more liberal voter registration bill, these legislative victories gave the Clinton administration a sense that the worst might be over, with better days ahead.

Then Whitewater, sex scandals, and the suicide of White House aide Vincent Foster exploded in the national press, setting Clinton on the defensive and crippling any chance that his primary political objective could be achieved. The stories of Clinton and his sex life had been the grist for late-night TV humorists for months, but now new reports surfaced of Arkansas state troopers procuring women for Clinton when he was governor, including a former state employee named Paula Jones who announced at a press conference convened by a conservative Republican group that Clinton had asked her to perform oral sex. At the same time new allegations emerged about the legality of the Clintons' role (here, both Mrs. Clinton and the president were under siege) in the Whitewater real estate venture in Arkansas, with accusations flying that Governor Clinton and his wife had used improper influence with state regulatory bodies and a savings and loan association to protect and maintain their private investment. When Vincent Foster, Mrs. Clinton's former law partner and counsel to the president, took his own life—protesting in a suicide note the degree to which "getting people" had become a sport in Washington's political culture—the scandal mongering and personal attacks reached new heights. Talk show host Rush Limbaugh accused the Clintons of being involved in Foster's "murder"; a cottage industry developed around rumors that Foster's death related directly to his having handled Whitewater files; and demands accelerated for a full-scale Watergate-type investigation around the Whitewater matter. By March of 1994, there were more Whitewater stories published in major newspapers in America than the combined total of stories on health care, welfare, and crime legislation.

The damage to health care was enormous—both directly and indirectly. Placed totally on the defensive, Clinton struggled just to keep his political balance, with conservatives linking the personal with the political. "I think Whitewater is about health care," Rush Limbaugh pronounced. Perhaps even more to the point was the change in political tone and dialogue that occurred. In effect, respect between politicians and recognition that there should be limits to the terms of political discourse had completely disappeared. No calumny was out of bounds. Bumper stickers proclaimed, "Where is Lee Harvey Oswald now that we need him?" Hillary Clinton was accused of being a lesbian power-monger. Hecklers greeted a bus tour of health care advocates. In response, Mrs. Clinton bemoaned "the way a lot of unbalanced, alienated, mean-spirited people are being given a license to be very disruptive. . . . There isn't any counter-balance to this incredible twenty-four-hour-a-day hate that is being spewed out." The vicious and uncivil political environment helped explain why a record thirteen U.S. senators—eight Democrats and five Republicans—announced that they would not run for reelection in 1994. The group included majority leader George Mitchell.

Notwithstanding a determined last-minute effort by Senate moderates to come up with a compromise plan, the Clinton health care initiative was doomed. By March, the 17-point margin of approval for health care that had existed as late as December had disappeared, with a new majority now saying they opposed health care legislation. Clinton had lost his moment to become another Franklin Roosevelt and to redefine the politics of America.

To a large extent, Clinton himself was responsible for the defeat of health care, and he openly admitted as much to reporters. "We made the error of trying to do too much, took too long, and ended up achieving nothing," he declared in an interview with Haynes Johnson and David Broder. The president had failed to "stay on message," as he had done during the campaign. He made the error of going outside the regular system of congressional consultation to use task forces administered by nonpoliticians to devise his plan. And he failed on the critical terrain of timing and momentum.

Yet Clinton also faced an implacable opposition that brooked no dissent and set out from day one to demonize and personalize the debate. If he knew the stakes when he began his campaign to finish the social revolution started by Franklin Roosevelt, Newt Gingrich knew them even better. Health care reform, he had declared, was the Democrats' "Stalingrad, their Gettysburg, their Waterloo." As the general of the opposition, he would defeat Clinton, giving no quarter, and proceed to lead a Republican counterrevolution that would attempt to destroy the social welfare state that the Democrats had built over the preceding six decades.

Topsy-Turvy: The 1994 Elections

In a parliamentary system, the Clinton years would have constituted the shortest presidency on record. Two years after *Time* magazine had called him the "second chance" for the sixties generation to prove itself, Bill Clinton received a thrashing at the hands of the American people that could be interpreted only as a personal repudiation. The Republican party gained 9 Senate seats, 52 House seats, and 11 governorships, winning control of both houses of Congress in the process. As one leader of the Democratic Leadership Conference observed, "The New Deal era is over. . . . The nails are in the coffin. . . . New Deal liberalism . . . is dead and buried." Not only could Bill Clinton no longer aspire to be another FDR; the Roosevelt coalition seemed finished, with even the Roosevelt social welfare legacy gravely imperiled. And health care reform had been the key. As another Democratic observer noted in the aftermath of the election, "The Republicans enjoyed a double triumph, killing reform and then watching jurors—the American people—find the president guilty. It was the political equivalent of the perfect crime."

Newt Gingrich presided as architect, builder, and salesman for the new Republican edifice in power. Early in the campaign, he took the bold risk of announcing a Republican "Contract With America." Consisting of ten items, the contract pledged to cut taxes, pass a balanced budget amendment, reduce government size, promote radical welfare reform, and begin the process of dismantling the New Deal state. Pronouncing Clinton Democrats "the enemy of normal Americans," he defined the election as a referendum on big government—as represented by health care reform. Foolishly, Bill Clinton took up the Gingrich challenge, making himself the issue of the campaign, and campaigning ardently in states across the country. At that time, and under those terms, Clinton was doomed. "It's over," said Democratic consultant Ted Van Dyk. "The president is done. He's finished. He's like that old . . . cartoon where the guy has just had his head sliced off in a fencing match. He just hasn't noticed it yet, but as soon as he tries to turn or stand up, his head's going to topple right off his neck." Appropriately, Gingrich headquarters on election night was "filled with vengeful glee," the *New York Times* reported.

In fact, many forces were in play in the election. Certainly, Clinton himself stood at the center of the contest. Bruised, battered, the subject of endless gossip, most of it malicious, he was part and parcel of a surge of disappointment in how much the promise of his presidency had failed. Claiming to represent a new Democratic party of smaller government, targeted reform, and far greater reliance on private initiative, he had allowed himself to be tarred as the quintessential apostle of big government. The scandals hurt. People's trust in government reached an all time low. Only 38 percent of the eligible voters even turned out at the polls. But did that mean that the American people embraced the Gingrich revolution and the Republican Contract With America?

Clearly, Gingrich himself believed that the voters had made such an ideological choice. Just as he had wielded power with an iron fist when head of the Republican minority, he now sought to whip his minions into a phalanx of united, disciplined commitment to enact within their own first Hundred Days—once again, the Rooseveltian metaphor—the contract they had made with the American people. One after another, bills were brought to the floor for votes. There were no hearings; often, legislators did not even know what they were voting on. Clinton was an object of ridicule, someone not even considered relevant. One after another, items in the Republican contract were enacted. Dazed, Clinton watched in silence. The counterrevolution appeared to have been unleashed and triumphant. "We are finally seeing where [the Republican contract has] been carrying us," Russell Baker acidly noted in the *New York Times*. "Dr. Kevorkian is now waiting in the parlor. He's about to be shown upstairs to finish off the government we have known for sixty years."

Yet the very act of seeking so much so completely reflected a hubris not dissimilar from Clinton's belief that a task force of experts could come up with a plan to save the health care system. Both approaches ignored the larger politics of Washington and the reluctance of the American people to take radical leaps, either backward or forward, without adequate discussion and negotiation. In commenting on Clinton's health care proposal, Robert Reischauer, head of the Congressional Budget Office, had made a comment that applied as directly to the Gingrich contract with America as to Clinton's 1350-page bill. "Our institutions," he said, "were created to stop things from happening, and they're very good at it." The Robert Dole-run Senate, for example, operated on a different set of assumptions and procedures than the Gingrich-led House. "There's a way to use power when you get it," Dole commented, "and my view was that maybe they've just been a little too much in a hurry [in the House]. You don't undo 40 years or 20 years or 30 years in 100 days or [even] four years." Moreover, as Russell Baker noted, what was the end game? "Do the designers of the post-government age know what they're doing? In a matter of days they have been dismantling and redesigning structures that took years to put up. . . . Who really has the vaguest idea what the results will be? Best Bet: Nobody."

It was the absence of answers to such questions that planted the first seeds of doubt among the voters who ostensibly had chosen this counterrevolution. What were the consequences of private lobbyists working hand in glove with congressional committees to draft legislation dismantling procedures for protecting the environment? Were there not some government programs worth preserving and even expanding? Surveys showed that half the new Republicans in Congress had no prior elective experience, with a significant number defining their politics primarily through their ideological connection to groups like the Christian Coalition. But what did this mean about their other constituents? In whose interests were they acting? Perhaps because of such questions, the American people began to reverse their position on the new Congress, just as they had on Clinton's health care reform package. By September 1995, 58 percent expressed disapproval of the job Congress was doing.

In the meantime, Clinton—known throughout his career as "the come-back kid"—returned to the political wars, armed with a new strategy for reclaiming and redefining the vital center of American politics. Ultimately, Clinton had lost the 1994 congressional elections because his health care proposals had alienated the middle class. Clinton knew that his 1992 victory had hinged on his ability to win back Reagan Democrats and middle-class voters by portraying himself as a "new" Democrat with fresh ideas, a willingness to take a hard look at the excesses of big government, and a person receptive to experimentation—in short, someone not harnessed to, or caged by, old Democratic shibboleths. As a result of the health care fight, on the other hand, Republicans had succeeded in casting Clinton once more as a quintessential "old" Democrat. Now, he needed to escape that straitjacket while putting the Republicans in one of their own.

Clinton received help in that venture from two sources. The first, and perhaps most critical, was the aid provided by the Republicans themselves. As part of their plan to strip back the welfare state and ensure budgetary integrity, the Republicans proposed cutting projected expenditures on Medicare by $270 billion over five years. Nearly everyone agreed that curbing the ever-rising cost of Medicare was essential to securing a balanced budget. Indeed, Clinton had used the out-of-control rise in Medicare expenses as a primary argument for his health care plan. But the Republicans not only proposed this major reduction in the rise of Medicare expenses. They also proposed a tax cut for the wealthy that would return to the rich almost exactly the same amount of money that was to be cut from Medicare. They thereby allowed Clinton to contend, with apparently impeccable logic, that what the Republican counterrevolution was really about was taking money away from senior citizens who needed it and putting it in the pockets of the rich, who did not.

In perhaps the most astonishing self-inflicted wound by the Republicans, Newt Gingrich even stated that Medicare would "wither on the vine." Although he later claimed to have been talking only about the Medicare bureaucracy, the impression given by the Republican leader—and continuously reinforced by Clinton—was that Republicans intended to kill the entitlement program of greatest importance to middle-class citizens over 65, while at the same time making the rich richer. That was a straitjacket that Clinton could never have put on the Republicans by himself. Instead, in their fiery enthusiasm and the pureness of their own ideological assumptions, the Republicans had donned it on their own, apparently oblivious to the consequences.

What Clinton could do, on the other hand, was to recast his image back into the new-Democrat mold that had secured his election in the first place. As early as 1993, the *New Republic* had offered Clinton a strategy for building a new "center" on the American political spectrum. Clinton's goal, the magazine said, should be to create "a liberalism that can learn from its past excesses, restore faith in the actions of a prudent, effective government, and build a constituency among the American middle class" through deficit reduction, carefully targeting limited resources to achieve specific reforms, and using decentralization and the marketplace to encourage new solutions to social problems like health care. Now, Clinton took up this strategy with a vengeance. "We need a dynamic center," he told the nation in an April 1995 speech, "that is not in the middle of what is left and right, but that is way beyond it." As an indication of his primary audience for this new "dynamic center," Clinton had already proposed a "middle-class bill of rights," including selective tax cuts, an education credit for young people going to college, "a leaner, not meaner" government, and a commitment to advance the fortunes of "hardworking Americans" who had earned their opportunities and were not seeking giveaways.

Guiding Clinton through this process of redefinition was Richard Morris, a political consultant with a variegated past. Beginning as the chieftain of a Democratic political organizing group in Manhattan while a student at Columbia—his elders called the group the "young Mafia"—Morris had gone on to become a political *wunderkind*, masterminding election victories of Republicans and Democrats alike. He had worked for Clinton in Arkansas, helping Clinton come back from his only electoral defeat as governor, also through recasting his political image. In later years, Morris had worked more closely with conservative Republicans, including Trent Lott of Mississippi. But behind the scenes, he now came back to the Clinton camp, at first holding secret consultations with the president, feeding him ideas, writing drafts of speeches—for example, the call for a new "dynamic center"—and plotting a strategy for Clinton's reelection; then, more and more becoming the acknowledged chief strategist of Clinton's return to the political attack, as the champion of limited governmental reforms on behalf of the middle class instead of chief spokesman for a massive new governmental health program.

Morris identified the areas where Clinton could be pinned to the wall by Republicans unless he preempted them: high taxes, crime, welfare, the federal budget, and affirmative action. To make himself invulnerable on those issues, Morris advised, Clinton should take the initiative in defining positions that would seem reasonable to middle-class voters. At the same time, he should paint the Republicans as radicals seeking to overturn 60 years of progress, and advance his own agenda on issues that cut in his direction such as education, the environment, and women's rights.

Focused and rarely if ever "off message," Clinton responded brilliantly. He boasted a crime bill passed under his leadership that would put 100,000 new police on the streets; he endorsed the strategy of "three strikes and you're out," giving life sentences to criminals convicted three times of felonies; and he cultivated (and secured) endorsements from major police organizations in support of his anti-crime and anti-assault weapons measures. He embraced the principle of setting a two-year limit on how long a person could remain on welfare, while supporting as well a jobs program to help take people off the relief rolls. He proposed tax cuts that targeted the middle-class, while opposing those directed primarily to the wealthy; and he continued, with the help of a booming economy, to cut the federal deficit. Even on the controversial issue of affirmative action, he claimed the middle ground, defending the concept of correcting centuries of discrimination by seeking to aid minorities who had been victimized, but agreeing that some excesses had to be controlled—"mend it, don't end it."

At the same time, Clinton took the initiative in doing battle with the Republican opposition, seeking to define them in the public eye as a threat to middle-class stability. Endorsing an unprecedented series of TV ads in critical states nearly a year before the election, Clinton and the Democratic National Committee pilloried the Republicans for trying to destroy Medicare and other basic entitlement programs. In a dramatic reversal of the "Harry and Louise" health reform ads of only eighteen months earlier, it was now the Democrats painting Republicans as extremists, and asking, "isn't there a better way?" By the end of 1995, Clinton's poll ratings were soaring, while those of Gingrich and the Republican Congress plummeted. The roller coaster had gone through one more loop, and it was now time to see which direction it—and the country—might take next.

Clinton/Dole—A Decision or a Stand-off?

For many observers, the presidential election of 1996 ended the day of the State of the Union address in January 1996. Bill Clinton, buoyant with his recovery from the political equivalent of cardiac arrest, and brimming with ideas for how to implement Dick Morris' strategy of outflanking Republicans on issues that were popular, delivered a masterful speech to the nation, highlighted by the message: "The era of big government is over." Responding to the president, Senate majority leader Bob Dole—the frontrunner for the Republican nomination—came across as mean-spirited, crabby, old-fashioned, and unfocused. "That was the worst performance I've ever seen," arch-conservative Senator Jesse Helms observed. If the election, in fact, were to be between these two men, there appeared little doubt of who would come out on top.

Bob Dole found himself in a position as a potential candidate that on the surface seemed optimal, but underneath was crammed with pitfalls. On the plus side, Dole had earned the respect of legions of Republicans, in and out of office, by virtue of his distinguished record of service to the party and the country. In contrast to Gingrich, his image shone. People trusted him (he had a 62 percent approval rating in 1995, compared to 35 percent for Gingrich and 45 percent for Clinton); he appeared to put country over partisanship; and his wife Liddy was one of the most attractive political spouses in the nation, as well as a political career person in her own right, having served in two cabinet positions.

On the other side, however, he faced substantial—though often intangible—obstacles. If nominated, he would be the oldest person ever to run for president. A product of the World War II generation, he seemed, despite his good health, to represent a step backward. Even more important, polls suggested that no Republican could be nominated without support from such conservative groups as the Christian Coalition—a reality that might well force Dole to take positions on issues such as abortion rights and other women's issues that would feed perfectly into the Democratic strategy of portraying Republicans as a party of reaction and extremism. Never a person given to soaring rhetoric, Dole seemed more a pragmatic "pol" than a person of vision and inspiration. As his own chief campaign strategist observed, "Dole's strength is [that]what you see is what you get. Dole's weakness is [that] what you see is what you get."

In that contest, the younger, more energetic, more charismatic Clinton possessed a clear advantage. Dole might try to paint Clinton as a classic liberal, but Clinton could point to deficit reduction, a tough crime bill, the family leave act, and a commitment to welfare reform to argue that it was he—not Dole—who occupied the center. On the other hand, with brilliant advertising, Clinton and the Democrats portrayed Dole as Gingrich's clone, always picturing the two together, suggesting by association that Gingrich was Dole's true running mate, not Jack Kemp, the surprise selection Dole had made before the Republican convention. Although Ross Perot's repeat third-party candidacy certainly constituted a thorn in the side of both major parties, the Republicans were hurt most. By election day, it was a foregone conclusion that Clinton would triumph in one of the most amazing political comebacks ever seen. Winning nearly 50 percent of the vote, Clinton swept the electoral college, having succeeded in his fundamental strategy of portraying himself as a dynamic centrist, running against a Republican candidate who represented narrow interests and extremism. Women supported Clinton over Dole by 59 percent to 35 percent; Catholics, self-described moderates, and single people by similar margins. In a booming economy, with a focused message dedicated to the middle class, Clinton had done what he needed to do to recapture the support he had lost in 1994.

But was this a Clinton mandate? It hardly seemed so in an election where one third of the voters split their tickets, voting for one party in one race, and a second party in another race. Despite some loss of seats in the House, the Republicans retained control of Congress, and even gained additional seats in the Senate. As experts read the election returns, they concluded that if the voters had made a decision, it was for divided government, not for one party over another. Only by ensuring that one party could balance and counter the other, they seemed to be saying, could the nation be protected from moving too far either toward liberalism and big government on the one hand, or toward conservatism and the end of entitlements on the other. Reforms, yes, if targeted to specific problems and limited in expense; a leaner government, yes, but not at the expense of the environment, entitlements like Medicare, or government guarantees of fundamental rights.

In the end, it appeared that the electorate opted for neither a decisive victory for one side nor a stand-off. Instead, the American people seemed to be directing their political leaders to proceed on a middle path that would preserve government's freedom to intervene on issues of basic national interest but constrain "social engineers" from using government intervention to enlarge the public sphere or limit the flexibility of the private sphere. It may not have been a *clean* resolution of the debates that had been going on over the preceding decades, but it seemed to be a *clear* message as to how politicians should proceed to deal with those debates. The question was whether the framework the voters had chosen would be sufficient to deal with the ongoing problems that challenged the nation's ability to survive and prosper.

The Second Clinton Presidency

Unfortunately, Clinton's own actions ensured that the nation would never discover whether the newly reelected president could traverse successfully the middle ground of targeted reforms and modest state intervention for which the voters had seemed to call. If Clinton's first term represented a roller coaster of triumph and failure, highlighted by economic recovery, health care reform, and the Gingrich revolution, his second term was more like a jetliner plunging 30,000 feet and nearly crashing, only to stabilize and climb temporarily, and then plunge again. Never had the American people witnessed such an extraordinary political spectacle. Their president, by nearly all estimates one of the most talented and politically shrewd men ever to occupy the White House, engaged in repeated acts of self-destruction and public deception that held the country transfixed in two years of pre-impeachment and impeachment trauma. The result was to ruin any chance of redeeming an already flawed presidency and to minimize the significance of even Clinton's positive accomplishments in domestic and foreign affairs.

The drama began at the height of Clinton's confrontation with Gingrich over the national budget in 1995. The government, in effect, was shut down because of the failure to pass a yearlong appropriations measure. In a crisis-style mode, the White House was operating around the clock, staffers and politicians running in and out with the latest news and strategies. One night, a 23-year-old intern named Monica Lewinsky brought pizza to the president. Long attracted to the president, Lewinsky initiated what became a torrid mutual seduction that never culminated in intercourse but did involve repeated instances of oral sex, which on one occasion resulted in a semen stain on the blue dress Lewinsky was wearing. Although Clinton broke off the affair a year after it started, there were frequent phone calls, notes, and presents. Furthermore, Lewinsky began to share her excitement, anxiety, and fear about the secret in meetings with Linda Tripp, a recently acquired friend, who, unbeknownst to Lewinsky, tape-recorded her conversations. Almost exactly a year after Clinton's second inauguration, the whole world began to learn, piece by piece, all the lurid details of Bill Clinton's tryst with a White House intern barely older than his own daughter.

Coming on the heels of the Whitewater allegations and the charges by Paula Jones of sexual misconduct by Clinton when he was governor of Arkansas, the Lewinsky story exploded into national headlines. Attorney General Janet Reno had already named a special prosecutor, Robert Fiske, to investigate Whitewater. A federal court, in turn, replaced Fisk with Kenneth Starr, a Republican with strong conservative credentials. In the meantime, Paula Jones had filed a federal lawsuit against Clinton, and, over the president's strong objections, the Supreme Court unanimously ruled in May 1997 that the Jones lawsuit should not be deferred until Clinton left office, arguing that it would not sufficiently preoccupy the president to prevent him from conducting his presidential duties. (In retrospect, virtually every legal source has seen *that* decision as absurd, and a failure to acknowledge the realities of the chief executive's responsibilities).

Now the vise started to close. On January 17, 1998, in testimony under oath in the Paula Jones case, lawyers surprised the president by asking if he ever had sex with Monica Lewinsky. Clinton said he had not. At the same time, a federal appeals court granted Kenneth Starr's request that his investigative purview in Whitewater be expanded to include the Monica Lewinsky case. On January 21, Clinton flatly denied the affair. "There *is* no sexual relationship," he said before the TV cameras. And later: "I never had sex with *that* woman." Hillary Clinton not only told NBC's *Today* show that the story had no validity, but also went on to add that, in fact, it represented a "right-wing conspiracy" to destroy her husband.

The scenario was thus created for a national tragedy—or tragic comedy—to unfold. While Clinton swore to all his closest staff and Cabinet associates—and to his wife and daughter—that no affair had taken place, evidence continued to emerge that eroded the president's credibility. Many of Clinton's allies wanted and needed to believe this was a right-wing plot. After all, the judges who had selected Starr were themselves known to be conservative; they even had lunch with Jesse Helms just before naming Starr. There had always been an irrational hatred of the Clintons, as if their very presence in the White House symbolized a defamation of conservative

On January 26, 1998, President Bill Clinton insisted, "I did not have sexual relations with that woman, Miss Lewinsky." (Reuters/Win McNamee/Archive Photos)

values. Moreover, the leaks from Starr's office, and the shoddiness of Linda Tripp's behavior, reinforced a sense of scheming by reactionaries out to "get" the president. But then there was the blue dress, and the DNA test that showed the semen stain *did* come from Bill Clinton; all of this, like water torture, undermined, drip by drip, Clinton's stature, making even his most ardent defenders suspicious that, once again, the Republican caricature of "Slick Willie" had more truth than falseness to it.

By August 1998, the final acts of the drama started to unfold. Called to testify before a federal grand jury that Starr had convened to consider Whitewater related allegations, Clinton finally acknowledged what had now become almost a given, namely, that "I did have a relationship with Ms. Lewinsky that was not appropriate." Even then, if Clinton had gone to the American people, confessed his sin, and asked for forgiveness, he might still have achieved some sense of absolution. Instead he went on television and, while admitting he had dissembled, offered a truculent and aggressive defense of himself, portraying Bill Clinton as the victim and Starr and his Republican allies as the perpetrators of wrongdoing. It was an awful—and unsuccessful—effort to displace the blame onto someone else. By September, Starr told Congress that he possessed "substantial and credible information" that Clinton had committed offenses that constituted grounds for impeachment. For the next three months, the nation watched as Congress heard and debated four different counts under which Starr wished Clinton indicted. On two of those four counts, most importantly that of perjury, the House of Representatives voted for impeachment. In the end, the United States Senate, acting as the jury of Clinton's guilt or innocence, acquitted him of the charges, allowing Clinton to remain in office. But forever he would be tarred with the knowledge that he was the first American president since Andrew Johnson to be impeached and that even if his offenses did not rise to the level of "high crimes and misdemeanors," he had disgraced the office of the presidency of the United States.

In the meantime, Clinton missed the opportunity to build on and claim credit for the record of tangible achievements he had begun to accumulate. The economy entered its fifth, sixth, and seventh years of unparalleled growth—an unprecedented era of prosperity for which most presidents would give anything to be able to claim credit. At the same time, with support from Congress, Clinton put into place a budget process that promised to substantially reduce the federal deficit, producing the first surpluses in post–World War II history, and offered the prospect that in a few years, the entire federal debt could be retired. Continuing to target popular, previously "Republican" issues like crime and welfare, Clinton saw murder and arrest rates go down in municipalities across the country and welfare rolls plummet as the welfare reform bill, for which he took credit, sent people off to jobs rather than onto relief rolls. Even if many felt that welfare reform inappropriately and cruelly ended a 50-year commitment by the federal government to provide for those least able to provide for themselves, the statistical results of the new welfare rules made this reform seem like a stunning success. In foreign affairs as well, Clinton made important inroads. He vigorously promoted reconciliation and peace in Northern Ireland, sending former Senator George Mitchell as his personal envoy to try to bring warring Catholic and Protestant parties together. In the Middle East, Clinton devoted endless hours and days to trying to forge the foundations for lasting peace between the leaders of Israel and Palestine. For the first time, he created the possibility that North Korea and South Korea might become friends rather than enemies and that North Korea might cease to be a missile-toting "rogue" nation. In Kosovo, Clinton finally engaged in a strategy of intervention that ended Serbian genocide and provided the possibility of peace in the Balkans. And in Africa and Latin America, Clinton created the kind of foreign policy of friendship for democratic regimes that promised a new partnership between the United States and the developing world.

But the impeachment process, in many ways, rendered immaterial whatever else Bill Clinton had been able to do. For the average president—his term unmarred by scandal and disgrace—the Clinton record might well have qualified for a grade of B or B minus. He secured the enactment of NAFTA, the free trade accord that significantly increased trade, industrial productivity, and prosperity between the United States, Mexico, and Canada.

In winning passage of the Family and Medical Leave Act, he provided a start at least toward governmental recognition of the human cost of caring for children and the elderly. His triumph with the Brady Bill, banning assault weapons, represented the first successful breach in the otherwise impregnable domination of the gun-control debate by the National Rifle Association. Welfare reform, it seemed, did more good than harm, providing incentives for hundreds of thousands to go to work rather than the welfare office. Clinton's deficit reduction package, even if enacted by only one vote, proved critical to ending the seemingly interminable round of huge federal deficits, while encouraging record-setting economic growth and prosperity. And even if the rhetoric was greater than the reality, he conveyed a message of caring and commitment to minorities, women, gays, and the historically disenfranchised.

Clinton also showed that he could learn politically from his defeats. At the beginning of his presidency, he envisioned change on a grand level, especially health care reform that would have eclipsed even Social Security as a giant legislative achievement. But when that failed, he lowered his sights, and taking Dick Morris' advice, devised a seemingly never-ending list of smaller achievements from adding 100,000 officers to the police rolls to mandating 48-hour hospital stays for women giving birth, all of which conveyed a sense of doing something tangible for people who needed assistance. Precisely because he responded with such shrewdness and creativity, he trumped the Gingrich revolution, creating the possibility at least of a new paradigm for incremental governmental activism.

Yet there could have been so much more. Bill Clinton had the potential to become a great president. His political capacity was boundless. Clinton was "the ultimate postmodern political practitioner," Joe Klein wrote in the New Yorker, "a fabulous communicator." Political scientist Larry Sabato agreed. "Clinton seems to reach right into your heart," he wrote. "He pierces you with his eyes. He knows your emotions. He cares about you. Personally. It may be totally phony, or it may not, but he really seems to love you. It may be the rhetorical equivalent of cotton candy, but it works." Clinton cried easily, identified with those who were hurting, and created bonds of intimacy with those who reached out to him.

Nowhere was that more true than in the black community. "He used surpassing gifts of innate empathy," New York Times reporter Todd Purdum wrote, "to find a new presidential style of relating to the public, and to forge an extraordinary connection with ordinary Americans, especially minorities." Novelist Toni Morrison called Clinton "our first Black President," someone who seemed instinctively to understand the oppression that black Americans had experienced and who identified totally with their cause. His true eloquence, Joe Klein said, was "physical, the body language he can deploy at crucial moments. The two steps he took toward a black woman questioner who was concerned about the economy during the second presidential debate in 1992 may have been the most important 'statement' he made during that campaign (especially when contrasted with the detachment of George Bush who was caught by the television cameras that same evening checking his watch)." And when he initiated a "national conversation on race" at the beginning of his second term—a program headed by Clinton's good friend and renowned African American historian John Hope Franklin—he seemed poised to bring America face to face with its longest standing national shame.

Indeed, so skilled was Clinton in conducting the public policy part of his presidency that his opinion polls ratings went up even as his legal troubles multiplied. People might not have approved of his sexual proclivities, but they liked his policies. While a lightning rod for obsessive personal hate on the part of many conservative Republicans, Clinton was like a box office matinee idol for those who responded positively to his personal message. "Everything about such people is big," wrote one citizen who described Clinton as a classic hero, "their loves, their eagerness to do spectacular things, their deep understanding of how the world works and also their moral failings and their need to win. Clinton's enemies never grasped this; they measured him according to their own smallness."

Still, it was Clinton's "moral failings" that made tragic what might have been triumphant. "This is a tale of two presidencies," White House counselor Leon Panetta observed, "one obviously brilliant and extremely capable, with the ability to help produce the greatest economy in the history of this country and to focus on major domestic priorities, and the other . . . the darker side, the one that made a terrible human mistake that will forever shadow that other presidency." The tragedy was that the two could not be separated, the good side reflecting the same qualities and passions that shaped the bad side. The Greeks called it *hubris,* an arrogance that knows no bounds and whose ambitions almost always turn into excess and wanton self-destruction. Summarizing all that had happened, Todd Purdum wrote: "For eight years, Bill Clinton has been the bright sun and the bleak moon, embodying much of the best and the worst of his times." The tragedy was that so much more could have happened and that Clinton killed his own potential for greatness.

The Basic Issues

Even as politicians sought to redefine, then occupy, the center of American political viewpoints, that center itself threatened to disappear, eroding under the impact of multiple changes in the broader society. At best, one could characterize the 1990s as a period of "no consensus," at worst, as a time of rapidly growing polarization. Some of the fault lines were old, like the central theme of America's quest for democracy, the "color line." Others reflected more recent changes, such as dramatic shifts in family composition, gender relations, and immigration patterns. And still others suggested the divisive, as well as unifying, consequences of the digital revolution and a new economy based on knowledge, technology, and cybernetic communication. Finally, there was the festering culture war between New Right advocates of evangelical fundamentalism, who insisted that abortion and homosexuality had no place in America, and "moderate" or "liberal" Americans, who sought a society tolerant of diverse lifestyles. Together, these issues offered a challenge that even the most far-sighted politicians might be incapable of mastering.

A new flood of immigration posed potentially the most dire threat to a sense of civic unity and coherence. Arriving at a rate of more than 1 million a year—the same numbers that had transformed America in the early twentieth century before immigration restrictions were imposed—the new immigrants provided both new vitality and essential service and industrial labor for the economy and also a linguistic and cultural counterpoint to the still dominant Anglo society. Unlike their earlier twentieth-century predecessors, the new immigrants were primarily Asian and Hispanic. Los Angeles became a microcosm of the larger changes, Korea Town, Japan Town, the barrio, and South Central L.A. taking over the inner city, while ever wealthier whites, often serviced by the new immigrants, took to the hills and suburbs. Hispanics grew 300 percent in America between 1970 and 2000, constituting nearly 30 million people, including one-third the population of Los Angeles and Miami. While the country continued to be dominated, politically as well as demographically, by whites of European descent in the nineties (76 percent), census experts predicted that by 2050 whites would constitute only half the country.

Such shifts rang warning bells for many observers. Harvard political scientist Samuel P. Huntington warned of a "clash of civilizations" based on multiple groups demanding their own languages and values. "Will the new immigrants be assimilated into the hitherto dominant European culture of the United States," he asked, "[and] if they are not, . . . will it survive as a liberal democracy?" Immigrant historian John Higham observed that "ethno-racial tensions are acute and in some ways growing. . . . Are we witnessing an approaching end of nation-building itself?" Similar specters, of course, had frequently been raised in the past, helping to fuel the xenophobia of the 1920s, including the Ku Klux Klan, the eugenics movement, and immigration restriction. Yet the potential for seismic changes in the body politic as well as the economy could not be understated. In the 1990s, it was estimated that 4 out of 10 New York City children over the age of five did not speak English in their homes, and the New York telephone company provided customer service in more than 100 different languages. How to sustain and nurture civic solidarity in the face of such diversity would severely test both average citizens and their social and political representatives.

At the same time, many of the traditional institutions associated with building and preserving social stability were themselves undergoing dramatic change. Large public school systems were racked with high teacher turnover, low pupil scores, and epidemics of antisocial behavior. The murder of students at Columbine High School in Colorado by hate-filled and gun-fixated classmates did not speak to the overall health of the educational system, but it seemed to symbolize for many the chaos and unreliability of the public school as a positive agent of socialization. More and more parents, minority as well as white, endorsed the possibility of using tax-paid "vouchers" to send their children to private academies, notwithstanding the likelihood that such private schools would undermine the value of assimilation historically associated with public education.

It was the family that exhibited the most change, however. By the 1990s, it was expected that half of all new marriages would end in divorce. Moreover, fewer people were marrying and the age of marriage was growing older (25 for women, 27 for men, up from 20 and 23, respectively, in 1960). More than 30 percent of all births were to unwed mothers (compared to 4 percent in 1940), and half the children born in the 1990s were expected to spend at least part of their childhood in a single-parent home. Indeed, nearly 30 percent of the adult population had never married at the beginning of the new century, and married couples who were rearing children now composed less than 25 percent of all households. The figures were startling, as much for what they portended for future developments as for what they said about the present. Clearly, one of the institutions that had most reliably provided an anchor during periods of instability in the past now seemed to have lost its mooring.

The implications of the new immigration and shifts in family composition became crystallized when looking at economic developments. Without question, the 1990s represented a time of unprecedented prosperity. Corporate profits more than doubled, the value of Dow Jones stocks exploded almost 400 percent, and many youthful entrepeneurs became overnight millionaires (even if only briefly for some!) by starting dot-com companies that took advantage of the Internet for sales and marketing. As a result, the *New Republic* editorialized, "the 1990s will be seen in future decades as a golden age in American history."

Still, the major lesson of 1990s prosperity was how uneven it was and how "left out" of the boom millions of citizens affected by the social and demographic changes discussed here were. For example, Hispanic unemployment was twice that of whites. While the income of the top 40 percent of Americans increased dramatically in the nineties, that of the lowest 60 percent, when adjusted for inflation, actually declined. Furthermore, those struck worst by the disparity were children in single-parent households. Children born to unwed mothers or living with divorced parents were almost twenty times as likely to end up on welfare as those living in two-parent homes. Moreover, in two-thirds of poor families, even if a single parent worked full time his or her income still fell below the poverty level. Not only did the rich get richer and the poor get poorer, but those left at the bottom, even if they did everything they were supposed to do to "make it" according to the American dream, fell beneath the poverty level.

Of all these problems, the longest-standing and most profound remained the issue of race. From the very beginning of white European settlement of America, race had defined power, control, status, economic opportunity, and freedom. As Edmund Morgan eloquently demonstrated, even the concept of democracy in the new colonies—especially Virginia— owed its genesis to the paradoxical coexistence of slavery and freedom. The presence of African-American chattel enabled whites of widely disparate wealth to talk about the fact that they shared equality of political rights— notwithstanding their class differences—*based* on the fact that they were neither black nor slaves. From that point forward, race constituted what one scholar called "the central theme" of American history. Its existence contradicted both the spirit and letter of the Declaration of Independence and the Constitution, bedeviling those who sought a way to reconcile the noble ideals of equality and freedom with the existence of trade in human bodies. Even a war that killed nearly three quarters of a million Americans failed to extirpate the problem.

One hundred years after the Civil War, a second national crusade set out to finish the job that the first one had left undone. Finally, laws were written providing guarantees of equal protection, including the right to vote, the right to hold a job without being subject to racial discrimination, the right to enter the restaurant, hotel, railroad car, plane, or theater of one's choice without being segregated or treated unequally. For a period, that revolution seemed to have taken hold. Millions of African Americans joined the middle class, competed for decent jobs, secured a college education, and won election to political office. Millions of white Americans, in turn, believed that the issue of racial discrimination had disappeared as a matter of public concern, convinced that there was no longer a reason to think of blacks and whites as having different life chances, no longer a basis for public policies that focused specifically on helping to secure equal treatment for blacks. According to this viewpoint, whites and blacks were the same, and should be treated that way. Significantly, even many of those who still focused on problems afflicting African Americans talked more in terms of the problems being "class"-based rather than exclusively race-based.

Tragically, the 1990s revealed the degree to which all such discussions represented an illusion. Notwithstanding the progress that had been made—and it was critically important to acknowledge that progress—it became glaringly obvious during these years how fundamental race was to defining worldviews, first-hand experiences, cultural attitudes, and political assumptions. Far from having become more alike, it seemed that blacks and whites—or at least *many* blacks and whites—were becoming ever more polarized in how they experienced and perceived the world around them. In 1968, at the height of the nation's descent into the contagious madness of multiple race riots, the Kerner Commission, established by President Lyndon Johnson, had evoked the spectre of America becoming two separate nations, one black, one white, forever divided by the ever-growing chasm of suspicion, hatred, and inequality. Now, after so much that had seemed positive had occurred, that spectre came closer to reality than ever.

The first sign of the abiding centrality of race came with the arrest and beating of black motorist Rodney King in Los Angeles. The largest city in California, Los Angeles in many ways embodied the multiracial demographic complexity that in the twenty-first century promised to become the picture of America as a whole. With Koreans, Chicanos, Vietnamese, Japanese, Chinese, and African Americans living in the same urban metropolis as whites—and in a state that boasted of its tolerance—it seemed that this was a place that might offer hope for the future rather than fear. Yet Los Angeles was also the site of the Watts riot in 1964, a city where police chief Darryl Gates frequently indulged in remarks contemptuous of blacks, and where police on the beat often acted without restraint or ignored the rules. Thus it happened that in the city of angels, police stopped Rodney King for driving erratically and, when he protested and perhaps even resisted, threw him to the ground and mercilessly stomped and punched him for what seemed like an eternity. The same scene had presumably occurred countless times before, but this time an onlooker videotaped the entire episode, providing vivid, indisputable evidence of what had transpired. Even in the face of such evidence, however, an all-white jury acquitted the officers accused in the beating, finding that they had done nothing criminal in hammering a human being who was lying helpless on the street.

The number of frightening messages conveyed by the Rodney King case exceed the grasp of any single storyteller. But three stood out. First, in a supposedly civilized and sophisticated area of America on the eve of a new century, police acted like a white Southern lynch mob of the 1890s or 1910s. A "nigger" had given offense by failing to act in a compliant manner, and he had to be taught a lesson. Second, like the all-white juries in those same Southern towns of a century earlier, the jury in Los Angeles County saw a reality totally different from that presented to them in stark black-and-white footage of an actual event. It was as though the jury had taken a hallucinogenic drug that altered totally what others saw as reality—and the drug was race. Third, because that perception of reality confirmed so totally African Americans' understanding that whites *never saw* black people, a scream of protest erupted in the form of the race riots in South Central Los Angeles in 1991.

Appropriately, the same issue of perception lay at the heart of the second episode that dramatized the degree to which race persists as America's central dilemma. Again, Los Angeles was the scene, with video—in this case television cameras—a primary means by which the entire nation became transfixed. The wife of former football all-American and sports-caster O.J. Simpson had been brutally slain at her condominium, along with a male friend who was returning some eyeglasses to her. Her two children slept upstairs as the crime was committed outside their home. Simpson, who had flown to Chicago shortly after the crime, became a prime suspect, especially after it was discovered that he had physically abused his wife. On one such occasion, she had called 911. Recordings existed of her terrified voice. With the police ready to arrest Simpson, he fled in a white Bronco, driving for hours on Los Angeles freeways with police in pursuit and television helicopters broadcasting the scene live into homes across the country. He was eventually arrested.

The trial went on for months. It featured bizarre interchanges between lawyers for both sides who seemed more intent on billing themselves in future starring Hollywood roles than in proceeding with the business of the court (many of them subsequently started their own talk shows). Each day, audiences across the country watched obsessively as the courtroom drama unfolded on live TV, and each night millions more tuned into Larry King, Geraldo Rivera, or other talk shows for their daily fix on what was occurring in the trial of the century. The prosecution portrayed Simpson as a jilted and jealous lover, who had been spurned the day of the murder in his latest effort to seek a reconciliation. He had been driven—according to the prosecution—to the same rage that had possessed him repeatedly before to beat his wife, but this time he murdered her because she had rejected him forever.

From one point of view, the evidence was clear. DNA tests linked blood from the crime scene to blood in Simpson's car, on his gloves, and on socks found in his bedroom. Police records on the history of spouse abuse verified Nicole Simpson's fear of her husband. A limousine driver, called to take Simpson to the airport the night of the murder, testified that no one was home when he arrived, and that lights came on only after he had seen a figure approximately Simpson's size cross the lawn and enter the house.

But there was another story as well. Police had handled the evidence carelessly. The vehicle with the blood stains had not been guarded. The glove with blood on it had been found by a detective who was thought to have been by himself at the time; later, the glove was transported to police headquarters by a circuitous route. The sock failed to be visible on police photographs of Simpson's bedroom when they were first taken. And the crucial glove—in some ways the most direct piece of evidence linking Simpson to the crime scene—apparently was too small for Simpson's large hand when he tried to put it on in court.

But disputes over the evidence meant nothing until the factor of race was read into the proceedings. Race was everywhere. The jury was predominantly black. The defendant represented an authentic black athletic hero, known affectionately as "O.J." to a generation. His wife had been a beautiful, blonde white woman, the pictures of them together bound to evoke countless fears, anxieties, or desires on the part of observers black and white, male and female. But most pivotally, the policeman whose testimony lay at the heart of the case—who had found the bloody glove, who had been to Nicole's house on one of the domestic abuse calls—turned out to be a "rogue" cop who, witnesses testified, frequently used the "N" word, and who had a track record of manipulating evidence in order to secure convictions of those defendants he passionately disliked. At the end of the trial, in his closing statement, defense lawyer Johnny Cochran, a black man, explicitly played what critics called "the race card," apparently appealing to jurors to identify with Simpson as a fellow African American. But Cochran did not have to play the race card. The entire trial—the entire deck of cards—had race written all over it.

When the case went to the jury, most "experts" anticipated that deliberations would last for days. There were mountains of evidence, documents galore. But within hours, the jury foreman announced that they had reached a verdict, which would be announced the next day. Virtually the entire country turned on their television sets at 1 o'clock the next afternoon, tension thick and pervasive everywhere. Calmly and deliberately, the jury delivered its verdict—not guilty on all counts.

Once again, the world was stunned—or at least part of the world was stunned. Because at the heart of the Simpson trial, as with the Rodney King police trial, was the presence of two different worlds, eons apart, almost as separate—or maybe even more separate—than the Kerner Commission had predicted a quarter of a century earlier. One world—the white world—trusted the system of justice and believed in the integrity of law enforcement agents and the sanctity of due process. The white world believed in evidence based on modern science and technology. DNA tests, this view claimed, never lied. When blood matched up the way it had in this crime, on the car, the socks, the glove, and at the scene of the murders themselves, it constituted irrefutable evidence of guilt—just as irrefutable as if there had been a video camera recording the murders and showing the perpetrator.

But there was another world—a world that had seen the Rodney King beating, and the acquittal of his assailants. This was a world that had little if any experience that provided justification for trusting the police. For black Americans, the judicial process had more often been a vehicle for persecution and discrimination than for the achievement of justice. Moreover, many an African-American family—no matter how rich or well placed—had a male who could testify to having been stopped by a white policeman who used racist language and stereotypes, and many had a first-hand experience with being terrorized. From this perspective, it was totally credible that Mark Fuhrman, the racist detective, had planted the evidence that prosecutors now sought to use to convict Simpson. Even those African Americans who were convinced that Simpson *was* guilty also believed that a conspiracy existed to destroy him. As one noted black writer observed about the trial, "They framed a guilty man."

Not all whites, of course, believed that Simpson must be guilty; nor did all blacks insist he was innocent. But the most dramatic confirmation that two different worlds *did* exist came in the form of public opinion polls on the case. Consistently, white Americans, by a three-to-one margin, said that they believed Simpson to be guilty of murder. By contrast, black Americans, by the same three-to-one margin, said that they believed Simpson to be innocent. The stark statistical contrast powerfully confirmed just how far apart the races were in America in their perceptions of power, politics, culture, and experience.

Tragically—and also logically—the persistence of the cancer of race within America carried its malignancy into a series of related and equally intractable problems. The "two worlds" that the Kerner Commission had talked about increasingly described a divide that was economic as well as racial. To be sure, the majority of poor people were not black; and a growing number of black people had entered the ranks of the nonpoor. Yet the percentage of African Americans and Hispanics who lived in poverty continued to grow, accompanied by startling increases in the number of female-headed households, children growing up without fathers, and high school dropout rates that in the nation's inner cities threatened to make it increasingly more likely that a black teenager—especially a male— would leave school rather than graduate. More than one third of African-American families lived in poverty; the unemployment rate for young black males approached 50 percent; and in the most devastating statistic of all, by 1990 there were more black males between 18 and 22 in jail than in college.

As William Julius Wilson, the black Harvard sociologist, pointed out, much of this could be traced to the fact that upwardly mobile black families had left the inner city for new jobs, better housing, and a different lifestyle. Their departure deprived inner city neighborhoods of leadership, institutional vitality, and a stable presence able to generate community resources. Here, class and race became intertwined. Yet beneath the growing class divisions within black America there existed the fundamental reality that those blacks left behind in the inner city had no basis for believing in the viability of the promise of equal opportunity. The lesson of the inner city was that the only way to acquire the material symbols of having "made it" in America was through dealing drugs or engaging in other illegal activities.

Compounding the problem was the degree to which the 1980s and 1990s had brought the most radical reallocation of wealth and income in the twentieth century. The richest 5 percent of American families benefited enormously from the Reagan tax cuts and the growth of the economy. The top 1 percent saw their wealth skyrocket. At the same time, however, the bottom 20 percent saw their share of national income and resources steadily dwindle, while even the middle class suffered a relative loss of real income. It was as if, one Washington analyst said, American were moving "toward the Third World . . . where there are explosive sanctioned differences between classes in the basic opportunities of life: education, health care, welfare, you name it." And race was there at the center of this new two-tier system.

Even on issues seemingly unrelated, race played a major role. The greatest health crisis of the late twentieth century was AIDS, the insidious virus that destroys the body's immune system and brings on a painful process of steady deterioration and eventual death. Although associated initially in the public mind with gay men, the infected population included large numbers of women as well. Black men and women were prominent among the victims; moreover, even when progress finally occurred in the 1990s in the development of more effective drugs to fight AIDS, blacks failed to benefit from the new treatments in the same proportion as whites, again due to their lack of resources to pay and to the more generalized reality that blacks remained relatively invisible as objects of public concern and government health programs. (Worldwide, the death total from AIDS had reached over 6 million, with more than 20 million other people infected—largely poor black and brown people who lived in Africa and Asia.) On the other hand, when it came time to identify locations to build chemical waste dumps or dispose of other toxic materials, it was black-populated counties that most often ended up at the top of the list for environmental waste disposal.

Finally, there existed the challenge of creating a civil discourse about values in a society where a large minority of the people believed in absolutist moral standards that brooked no compromise. Whether members of Jerry Falwell's "Moral Majority," Pat Robertson's PTL Club, countless evangelical churches, or the most conservative wing of the Roman Catholic church, millions of Americans insisted that abortion was murder, that homosexuality was a sin, and that only those who supported a "culture of life" perspective could sit on the Supreme Court, be elected to Congress, or occupy the White House. Sometimes the issue was stem-cell research, using discarded embryos that could never become a human life; at other times the issue was public policy on birth control. But the dividing line precluded almost any possibility of mutual respect for alternative viewpoints, and it threatened to create its own form of religious civil war.

Underlying all other issues facing the nation, therefore, was the fundamental question of whether it was possible any longer to speak of Americans as a common people who share the same values, goals, and institutions. Could there exist a renewed commitment to provide a shared experience of educational opportunity, economic progress, and decent health care for all citizens? In his 1937 inaugural address, Franklin D. Roosevelt had articulated such a concern when he declared that he "saw one third of a nation ill-housed, ill-clothed, and ill-fed," and challenged his fellow citizens to end such an anomaly once and for all. Was it possible for the American people at the end of the twentieth century to accept—and act upon—a similar set of challenges, particularly in an era where common goals and values seemed so hard to find?

17

2000 and Beyond

As the nation prepared to enter a new century and a new millennium, one fact seemed clear. The American people appeared uncomfortable with the idea of rapid or radical change, especially if that change involved a major increase in the size of government. They had indicated as much by the way they responded to the Clinton health care plan—or at least to the Republican portrayal of it as unbridled state intervention into family and private lives. On the other hand, they had responded even more vehemently when Newt Gingrich sought to implement the Republican Contract With America to dramatically curtail government regulation of the economy and the environment.

The search for a middle ground had characterized the end of the nineties. Clinton had successfully fought off Republican efforts to impose a budget that in his view would have destroyed many essential programs. On the other hand, he had finally signed a welfare reform act that went a long way toward ending the 60-year-old commitment of the federal government to provide basic support for the poor, including mothers of dependent children. Turning most of the responsibility for welfare back to the states through block grants, the new legislation also pledged to put welfare recipients back to work under the penalty of losing their benefits—including health care—if they refused. Based on the first years' experience with the new legislation, it appeared that as long as the American economy prospered, a lesser government role in welfare was workable.

The difficulty, of course, was that most of the grievous problems facing the nation required approaches and solutions that depended on a strong federal role. On the basis of what happened during the 1990s, it seemed possible that new federal programs, if limited and well defined, could be acceptable. But were such limited programs adequate to deal with the de-skilling of industry, the export of manufacturing jobs abroad, the pernicious effect of a health care system that left 40 million people uninsured and senior citizens with huge prescription bills, and the reality of a two-tier economy where the young, the black, the female, and the poor had little prospect for upward mobility? Even a booming economy could not save those who had never acquired skills, notwithstanding John Kennedy's aphorism that "a rising tide lifts all boats." And what would happen if the tide stopped rising?

Behind all these issues lay the larger and more fundamental question of defining successfully a new vision for uniting Americans. The times, and the problems, required a president who could not only reach out and speak on behalf of all the American people, but also effectively define the two or three priorities around which the nation could cohere in a sense of common purpose. Such a role involved discipline, insight, and above all the ability to transcend traditional divisions and point to the "common wealth" that might inspire a commitment on the part of all factions of the American people to come together on behalf of values they shared. The burdens of such an assignment were overwhelming, particularly in light of the culture wars between the New Right and liberal/moderate Americans, yet the ability of the United States to move forward together rested on the assignment being fulfilled successfully. This was the challenge facing the American political system as it prepared for the first presidential election of the new century. It was also a challenge that, before the new century was very old, would take on wholly different and tragic dimensions of urgency and crisis.

The 2000 Election

Ironically, Bill Clinton's personal flaws created a circumstance in which the presidential candidates of both parties in 2000 had to run against him. Notwithstanding Clinton's abiding popularity in the polls and the likelihood that he would have been reelected had he been able to run, Democrats felt they had to distance themselves from their president, almost as if he were a moral leper. In the case of Vice-President Al Gore, that dynamic was exacerbated by a sense of personal betrayal. Gore had stood by Clinton 100 percent, defending his denials of an affair and praising his leadership, only to be shown as a naif when the truth emerged. Gore's wife Tipper was even more angry, appalled by the absence of a moral core in the president and bitter at his deception. Thus even if Gore deserved enormous credit for many of the accomplishments of the Clinton administration, from the economy to the Kyoto treaty on global warming, he literally ran away from Clinton's record. The Republicans, of course, had only to talk about restoring integrity and decency to the nation's capital to remind people of Clinton's moral lassitude. They didn't even need to mention Monica Lewinsky's name.

With varying degrees of difficulty, Al Gore and Texas governor George W. Bush moved to the nominations that everyone thought would be theirs. Both, in fact, faced the same kind of foe. Bill Bradley, a former New York Knicks basketball star, Rhodes Scholar, and senator from New Jersey, possessed an almost Abe Lincoln–like modesty and simplicity. Expert on many issues and passionately committed to racial justice, he presented himself as a serious thinker, different from the normal politician. In a series of debates, however, Gore aggressively exposed Bradley's weaknesses and systematically won primary elections. Senator John McCain, Bush's leading opponent, also represented a challenge to politics as usual. A former prisoner of war in Vietnam, he had moved to the forefront of politics by his advocacy of campaign finance reform, including legislation that would cap soft money contributions and the influence of big donors on the political process. He was "wickedly impolitic," one observer noted, winning the praise of skeptical reporters for his unvarnished candor, his willingness to speak his mind on any and every issue. Like Bradley, McCain seemed a breath of fresh air to programmed politicians whose every word was scripted by political consultants. McCain gave Bush a real scare, his integrity and honesty shining through for Democrats as well as Republicans, but in the end, Bush rallied the support of party professionals as well as strong conservatives on issues like abortion and successfully compartmentalized McCain as a maverick, too independent to be trusted.

All of which made for a presidential campaign singularly lacking in freshness, spontaneity, and color. By most people's accounts, Gore had a striking lead on the issues. A "policy wonk," he had written a scholarly book on the environment, knew economics inside out, and seemed particularly well schooled on issues of health care, information technology, and diplomacy. He also had 8 years of experience in the White House and 14 more in Congress. Bush, by contrast, had a relatively spotty career as a businessman and, as governor of Texas, where the chief executive actually enjoyed less power than the lieutenant governor, was known primarily for his joviality and success at developing good relationships across party lines. He had vetoed a patients' rights bill as well as a hate crimes measure. With no foreign policy experience (he had been abroad only twice, and George Kennan, the octogenarian sage of postwar diplomacy, called him "intellectually juvenile"), Bush seemed singularly unprepared for international leadership; many observers commented on his apparent lack of intellectual curiosity or "capacity for original thought." Indeed, by the end of the summer of 2000, Gore seemed to have a well-ensconced lead, based on his greater appeal to the electorate on issues of medicare reform, Social Security, taxation, and the environment. To be sure, Bush and Gore sounded very much alike on education, prescription drugs for senior citizens, and Social Security reform, with Gore, ironically, more critical of the status quo than Bush. Overall, though, Bush seemed deficient on mastery of those issues where presidential leadership would be essential.

The "intellectual gap" on policy substance, however, soon took a distant second place to voters' judgments about the character and personality of the two men. George W. Bush managed successfully to transfer doubts about President Clinton's personality to Al Gore, who allowed himself to get caught in a series of exaggerated statements that suggested carelessness with the truth. At one point, Gore seemed to say that he had "invented" the Internet—an obviously inflated statement—and even though Gore had done more than perhaps anyone else in Congress to recognize the value of information technology and to support it with federal programs, he was portrayed as someone who tried to deceive people into believing what was not true. Often ponderous and "school-marmish," Gore seemed heavy-handed in his approach to Bush's positions on taxes and health care. In many instances, Bush was vulnerable on such issues—claiming to have pioneered a patients' bill of rights in Texas when in fact he was largely resistant—but Bush came off, overall, as more genuine, less contrived in his responses. Bush seemed more gracious, less officious, and occasionally able to depart from his script, as when he told one harsh questioner who asked what should be done about all those "bastards" born to women on welfare: "First sir, we must remember that it is our duty to love all the children." Only rarely did Gore express such spontaneity, and when he did, he quickly repaired to his script, as though anything he said that the political consultants had not approved might be hurtful. In private someone who was described as having a "wicked, impolitic sense of humor," Gore, in public, rarely let himself go.

More than anything else, the debates crystallized a focus on personality. The written transcripts suggested that on the issues, as one might have expected, Gore did significantly better than Bush. But the real drama lay in Gore's Jekyll and Hyde demeanor. Aggressive and domineering in the first debate (too much so, many said), he became a "yes" man to Bush in the second, refusing to draw any differences or to challenge Bush on any issue. The transposition from "lion to lamb" caused one columnist to ask, "How could we trust a man who reinvented himself so readily?" Given the opportunity to share his passion for gun control and to talk poignantly, as he often had in the past, about the horrible murders that had taken place in Columbine High School, Gore instead acted as though he and Bush had no significant disagreements on the issue. "He was too passive, too constricted, too malleable," one reporter wrote, "too willing to trim his persona to 'match' the research. As a result, almost everything he said seemed calculated, and the calculations were often so transparent as to be embarrassing."

Largely through a failure to be himself, therefore, Gore lost a lead that had seemed solid and transformed the campaign from one about issues to one about character, where style, not substance, became the criterion for voting. "The wasting of Gore," Joe Klein wrote in the *New Yorker*, "has been a stunning and quite unexpected phenomenon." Convinced that running on Clinton's record would make him indistinguishable in character from the president, yet unable or unwilling to present his own unvarnished personality for voters to assess, Gore took on the appearance of a detached puppet, pulled one way or another by what the political consultants said on any given day, but unable to convey a sense of being his own person with a vision he passionately cared about. The result was not only a campaign that was boring, but one that created a race too close to call, when most people two months earlier had predicted a runaway.

The 2000 Post-Election Debacle

One could get a sense as election night unfolded that this would be one for the history books. Early on, Gore's lead in the popular vote seemed confirmed in the electoral college margins as well. Key states like Missouri, Pennsylvania, and Illinois popped up in the Democratic column. Then, shortly before 8 P.M., with some voting places in the state still open, all four networks—using their vaunted exit poll data—declared Florida to be in Gore's column. With California a virtual certainty for Gore, it looked like an early election evening. A Bush relative conducting poll research at the Fox network, told his cousins that it did not look good. Then, suddenly, lights started going on at network research stations. Reversal, they counseled, reversal. Quickly, the networks put Florida back in the undecided column, joining other states like Washington, New Mexico, and Tennessee. The evening wore on, becoming early morning in the East, when the networks cautiously made another leap, this time calling Florida for Bush at 2 A.M. Gore made an initial concession call to Bush and was on his way to talk to his supporters and the nation when his staff aides called and said, "Wait, it's not over." Gore called Bush again, withdrawing his concession, and at 3 A.M. the networks retracted once again. The Bush margin was less than 2,000 votes in a state with more than 2 million ballots cast. It began to dawn on the American people that this election might not be over for weeks!

Almost immediately, rumors spread of voter suppression, fraud, and manipulation. In Palm Beach County, a Democratically controlled election board had used a "butterfly ballot" that so closely aligned candidates from different parties with each other that a confused voter, unwilling to ask for assistance, might well cast a ballot for someone other than his or her choice. Indeed, that seemed to have been the case. In a Democratic county, Pat Buchanan, the right-wing Republican running as an Independent, received 3,407 votes, 1600 percent above his average in other counties and 250 percent higher than his total in Broward and Dade counties, whose combined population was three times greater than Palm Beach. It turned out that Buchanan's name was lined up so close to Gore's that a voter with poor eyesight might easily punch the Buchanan button, thinking they were voting for Gore. Hundreds came out of the booth distraught that this was exactly what had happened. "It was the kind of week," a New Yorker writer said, "when the free world contemplated the interesting possibility that the identity of its maximum leader would be determined by the fact that a couple of thousand sweet little old Jewish ladies in West Palm Beach retirement communities accidentally voted for a Holocaust denier."

Allegations of black voter suppression were even more serious. According to many reports, inaccurate lists of former felons were used to prevent hundreds of black voters from casting their ballots in Duvall County. In Palm Beach and Miami-Dade County, hundreds of additional black voters—particularly college students who had responded to a massive voter registration drive—were told that their names were not on the voting list when they went to the polling place. Even more distressing, votes in predominantly black precincts were invalidated at a rate four to five times greater than was the case in white counties. Finally, dilapidated punch card voting machines—those whose age and condition are most often associated with machine malfunction and large numbers of "undercounted" ballots—were three times as likely to be located in black precincts as in white precincts.

If, as seemed to be the case, African Americans were treated systemwide in a different manner than white voters, there could be profound implications for a sense of fairness, equal protection, and justice in the overall electoral process—especially since nationwide Gore's popular vote lead over Bush was more than 500,000, with Florida the only path Bush could find to victory.

Complicating matters further was the fact that Katherine Harris, Florida's Republican secretary of state, held the power—pending judicial review—to certify the election results as well as determine what would and would not be accepted from county election commissions. Although Democrats protested that as a co-chairperson of Bush's Florida campaign she should recuse herself, Harris insisted she would and could perform her duties without prejudice.

That, of course, made the strategems of both camps critical as they contemplated how to navigate the terrain of recounts and challenges. In the first critical decision to be made, the Gore campaign considered, then rejected, the possibility of calling for a statewide hand recount of all ballots. Instead, they chose—in what would later seem a fatal error of judgment—to focus on three counties, Palm Beach, Miami-Dade, and Broward, all Democratic, where reports of disputed ballots were most frequent. There then ensued an invasion of all of Florida by lawyers and volunteers from the Bush and Gore campaigns, arguing, often contentiously, over election law, with the greatest intensity of debate focused on how to determine a voter's intent, particularly with voting machines that used a stylus to punch out a piece of paper beside the name of the preferred candidate. What should happen if the hole was not completely punched through but there was evidence of voter intent? There thus evolved what became the stock in trade of late night TV comedy—the meaning of the "hanging chad," and how a presidential election could be determined by whether or not a piece of paper was barely attached to a ballot.

One line of battle derived from the recount process in the three counties, the decisions by Secretary of State Katherine Harris about those recounts, their review by the Florida Supreme Court, and then the ultimate review by the United States Supreme Court. Initially, the Florida Court had ordered by a 6-1 vote that the recount should proceed in the three counties specified by Gore's lawyers, with a deadline of November 18. Under intense time pressure, one county failed to meet the secretary of state's deadline for reporting its recount, and another suspended the recount in midstream because it recognized the impossibility of completing the task within the appointed time frame. Even so, Bush's margin fell to under 400 votes, and Gore's attorneys went back to the Florida Supreme Court, seeking an order to complete a manual recount in all precincts of the three affected counties. By a four to three margin, the Florida Supreme Court ordered a statewide

Palm Beach County Supervisor of Elections Theresa LePore, County Court Judge Charles E. Burton, and observer Mark Wallace (representing the Bush campaign), examine a questionable ballot during the hand counting of the first precinct. LePore and Burton are members of the county Canvassing Board. (Lannis Waters/ *The Palm Beach Post*)

recount in sixty-six counties (Volusia had already been recounted). Now, more than three weeks after the election, Gore's team could feel the rush of victory.

In the meantime, the other line of battle proceeded, far out of the public eye, but equally important to the final outcome. Here, the central issue involved the standards that would be used for counting—or not counting— overseas absentee ballots and military ballots. Florida's election rules required a postmark on or before election day, as well as the signatures of witnesses. Katherine Harris' office had always insisted that the rules be applied uniformly, but in fact, the opposite occurred. As uncovered by a *New York Times* investigating team, there appeared to be a significant discrepancy between how the rules were applied in Republican counties and Democratic counties, and an equally significant difference in the tactics employed by the two camps. While the Gore lawyers practiced a relatively uniform policy of challenging and/or counting votes in counties across the state, the Bush team pursued a tactic of severely questioning absentee and military votes in Gore counties, while pushing for a waiver of the rules in Bush counties—a waiver that, in fact, revised instructions that Katherine Harris' office encouraged. As a result, the *Times* concluded, "under intense pressure from the Republicans, Florida officials accepted hundreds of overseas absentee ballots that failed to comply with the laws." Thus in counties that Gore carried, canvassers accepted only 2 in 10 of ballots that showed no evidence of having been mailed before election day, while in Bush counties, 6 out of 10 such ballots were counted. All in all, the *Times* found that more than one quarter of the ballots it reviewed were flawed, with 4 out of 5 of those in counties controlled by Bush. Moreover, Bush counties were four times more likely to count ballots that lacked witness signatures and addresses than Gore counties. The *Times* concluded that without the absentee ballots counted after election day, Gore would have won by 202 votes.

Pivotal to this second line of battle was the shrewdness of Republicans in publishing a memo by a Democratic lawyer highlighting legal reasons that Democrats could use to challenge overseas and military ballots. With righteous indignation, Republicans accused the Democrats of trying to disenfranchise men and women who were risking their lives by serving in the nation's armed forces, claiming that Democrats had "gone to war" against soldiers. Adding to their ammunition, General H. Norman Schwarzkopf, head of allied forces during the Persian Gulf War and a national hero, called it "a very sad day for our country" when soldiers facing "danger on a daily basis" are denied the vote on a "technicality." Thrown totally on the defensive, Joe Lieberman, Gore's vice-presidential running mate, publicly urged canvassers to bend over backward to count military ballots, even when they were illegal. (In fact, one-third of those interviewed whose ballots had come in late or without postmarks acknowledged mailing them after the election.) By raising the flag in this manner, Bush officials persuaded three counties to disregard entirely the postmark rules. Again, the discrepancy between counties was striking. While Bush counties accepted 70 of 109 ballots that arrived without postmarks two days after the election, Gore counties accepted only 17 of 63. In what turned out to be a decisive line of battle, the Republicans won going away, essentially by employing significantly differing standards of judgment between Republican counties and Democratic counties, with the Democrats displaying far less aggressiveness and tenacity on their own behalf.

That left only the Supreme Court to decide the final act of the election drama and give the Republicans total victory. Exhilarated by the Florida Court's ruling ordering a completion of the recount, Gore's team counted, confidently, on the U.S. Supreme Court to not interfere. The Bush appeal for intervention, *Newsweek* speculated, had low odds for success because "federal courts generally do not like to second-guess state courts on election matters like ballot counts." Yet this court was different. Already unhappy with the Florida Supreme Court's earlier decision to intervene and change the calendar of reporting election returns, the U.S. Supreme Court by a 5-4 vote ordered a halt in the vote recount until it could hear the full case. Now, with the entire country holding its breath, the Court heard skilled attorneys for both sides argue why the uncounted Florida votes should or should not be tallied.

The week before Christmas, the Court finally rendered its decision. Once again splitting 5-4, the Court determined that no further vote counting should take place in Florida, ensuring that George Bush would be declared the winner by 540 votes (his margin had gone down to 154 before the Supreme Court intervened and stopped the recount). Intriguingly, the Court's majority argued that the equal protection clause of the Fourteenth Amendment required that the vote-counting process stop because voters were being treated unequally. Not only were different standards being used in different counties ("hanging chad or no hanging chad"), but only certain counties had been singled out—recalling the critical, and ultimately fatal, decision the Gore campaign had made not to ask for a total manual recount of the entire state return but to concentrate on only three counties—making their votes count unequally compared to those of other counties. In effect, the Supreme Court, by the slimmest margins, had bought the Bush attorneys' argument that it was not fair to change the rules and standards governing the counting of votes once the election was over.

From a Democratic perspective, of course, the reality was that it was the Republicans who had changed the standard. Their entire post-election operation seemed to discard the rules governing the legitimacy of absentee and military ballots, treating Republican counties totally differently than Democratic counties, and, as the *New York Times* showed, producing just enough votes to win the election for Bush. Perhaps more to the point, the Court had used the "equal protection" clause, created for the explicit purpose of ensuring equal voting rights for black citizens, to justify an election that had revealed systematic discrimination against black voters. The ironies were overwhelming. On the other hand, subsequent review by news organizations of all the actual votes—not those absentee and military ballots assessed by the *Times*—showed that a recount of the entire state may well have not changed Bush's victory over Gore in Florida by a couple of hundred votes.

Still, the Supreme Court had prevented such a recount, and rarely had a decision so intensely divided the Court or the nation. "The franchise, it turned out, was limited to certain members of the Supreme Court," one legal journalist wrote. The dissenting judges wrote with disdain and contempt of the Court's majority decision. Justice John Stevens declared that the decision "can only lend credence to the most cynical appraisal of the work of judges throughout the land." Justice David Souter joined in, saying "there is no justification for denying the State the opportunity to try to count all disputed ballots now"; and Justice Stephen Breyer, recalling the bitterness created in America by the Court's *Dred Scott* decision in 1857 upholding the notion that escaped slaves should be treated as property, called the *Bush v. Gore* decision another "self-inflicted wound—a wound that may harm not just the Court, but the Nation." The Court, according to the dissenters, had violated "the basic principle, inherent in our Constitution and democracy, that every legal vote should be counted." The depth of feeling dividing the judges one from another could not have been more intense or deep; the same could be said for the country at large. An election that for most of its days had featured a nearly total absence of fire had become a torrent of passions. And now it was over.

The First Bush Administration

Notwithstanding the absence of an electoral mandate, George W. Bush came into the White House acting as though he had won in a landslide. As Dick Cheney, his vice-president, observed, Bush was determined to throw political caution to the wind: "[the] notion of a . . . restrained presidency, because it was such a close election . . . lasted maybe 30 seconds. We had an agenda, we ran on that agenda, we won the election—full speed ahead." Within days, the American people knew that this president would neither equivocate nor shy away from long-range objectives that were intended to transform American policy both at home and abroad. Almost reflexively committed to doing the exact opposite of whatever Bill Clinton might have done, Bush set out to revamp America's domestic policy by pursuing both "old right" objectives on economic policies such as tax cuts and the environment and "new right" objectives on social issues such as abortion and homosexuality. In foreign policy, meanwhile, he jettisoned the multilateral approach of both Bill Clinton and his father, George H. W. Bush, and adopted an "America first" unilateralism that soon left traditional allies gasping in disbelief. And all of this before the world was transformed by 9/11.

But first came the start-up. In a remarkable display of the personal features that had won such support in the campaign, Bush brought to the creation of his administration the same kind of healing balm that had characterized his approach to governing Texas and that had helped make issues of character and personal style so decisive in the presidential election. A startling contrast to Clinton, Bush displayed a low-key, relaxed understated persona. "There is nothing wrong with a guy who's been around power long enough not to be too impressed by it," one journalist observed, "nothing terrible about someone who relies on human instincts rather than set dogmas; and something pleasing about a man who is less concerned with making history than with making it home." Bush surrounded himself with his father's friends and advisors, as if to suggest that he would continue a beneficent, stewardship-style government, like that of the first Bush presidency. Colin Powell, who had presided over the Joint Chiefs of Staff during his father's days in the White House, became Secretary of State. Donald Rumsfeld returned for a second turn at being Secretary of Defense. James Baker, one of his father's chief advisors, guided the new president in selecting both Cabinet members and policy priorities.

Nothing better illustrated Bush's inclusive approach than his Inaugural Address. Gracious and elegantly written, the speech sounded the themes of compassionate conservatism, signaling Bush's intention to be president of all the people. At least one longtime critic called it "by far the best [inaugural] in forty years, . . . tightly constructed," its rhythms flowing "pleasingly." Bush seemed intent on persuading those at the bottom of the society that he cared. "We know that deep, persistent poverty is unworthy of our nation's promise," he declared. "And whatever our views of its cause, we can agree that children at risk are not at fault. Abandonment and abuse are not acts of God, they are failures of love." And as if to demonstrate his commitment to inclusiveness, Bush named more African Americans, Latinos, and women to senior positions than had any of his predecessors.

When it came to setting actual policies, on the other hand, Bush soon abandoned inclusiveness and showed just how profoundly he was committed to serving the interests of his conservative base. George W. Bush was the first president to embrace not only the language of the New Right but also its exhortations to make New Right ideals the basis for action. Ronald Reagan had always pleased evangelical conservatives with his speeches denouncing abortion, but only rarely had actions followed. In his first executive order, on the other hand, George W. Bush terminated U.S. aid to international family planning agencies, thereby pleasing anti-abortion groups in the United States who viewed such agencies as part of a pro-choice cabal. Bush lashed out at gay rights groups who demanded "domestic partner" benefits and same-sex marriage. He launched "faith-based" initiatives as the best way to deal with people who were poor and disabled; and he pushed for major federal financial support of church-related organizations. Repeatedly, he nominated judicial candidates known for their hostility to abortion rights and government intrusion into "family" issues. Although use of condoms had long been recognized as the best way to combat the soaring proliferation of AIDS, especially in Africa and other Third World countries, the Bush administration endorsed abstinence instead. On almost every issue of importance to conservative evangelical fundamentalists, George W. Bush not only "talked the talk"; he also "walked the walk."

The same steel-like determination could be seen in Bush's pursuit of "old right" policies toward the economy, energy, and the environment. Until 2001, Ronald Reagan had seemed the epitome of "old right" economic conservatism, passing huge tax cuts, deregulating the economy, and liberating individual entrepreneurs to "make their mark." But George W. Bush made Reagan look like a moderate Democrat. Bush's tax plan most dramatically highlighted the policy splits between his administration and that of Bill Clinton. Under Clinton, the share of taxes paid by the top 20 percent of the people—and especially the top 1 percent—rose significantly, with the tax rate going from 31 to 39 percent, while taxes went down for the other 80 percent of the population. Working people especially gained help through measures like the child credit and earned-income tax credit. Overall, the middle class had benefited substantially from Clinton's tax changes. Now, Bush proposed a $1.6 trillion tax cut (eventually, as passed, a $1.3 trillion cut) that dramatically reversed that pattern, with the top 1 percent of taxpayers getting 43 percent of the tax break. Under the Bush initiative, the bottom 20 percent of taxpayers would receive an additional $15 the first year and $37 in the third year, while the top 1 percent would get $13,469 the first year, rising to $31,201 in year three. Moreover, the beneficiaries of eliminating the estate tax (called the "death tax" by Republicans) would be primarily 2,400 families per year, who would receive half the income freed up. Enacted primarily in anticipation of a dramatic new surplus envisioned by 2010 (if the Clinton budget policies had continued), in fact the tax cut used up much of that money, transforming a $200 billion surplus in Clinton's last year to a $450 billion deficit in Bush's second year and a multi-trillion-dollar projected deficit by 2010. The Bush tax cut made it virtually impossible to pass any new programs, such as health care. One tax research group suggested that the Bush tax plan would give the richest 1 percent of the country a bonus of $774 billion by 2010, approximately the same amount that would be required to provide a high-quality prescription drug plan. In his first major economic act, therefore, Bush had turned on their head the budgetary projections of just one year earlier, creating a degree of indebtedness almost unprecedented in the nation's history, with all the implications that fact had for future generations and for U.S. dependency on foreign investment. (It was foreign dollars that bought most of the bonds used to finance the deficit.)

Nor was the economy the only indication of Bush's devotion to "old right" conservatism. Bush quickly rescinded a series of executive orders handed down by Clinton on such matters as levels of arsenic allowable in water supplies and prohibitions of logging in Western forests. Millions of acres of land that Clinton had removed from economic development now were again available. Snowmobiles were permitted again in national parks, and regulatory agencies in the Department of Interior and the Department of Energy reverted to a laissez-faire approach to individual entrepreneurs seeking to invest in public lands. Bush also proposed an energy package largely geared to the interests of big oil producers and endorsed drilling for new oil supplies in the Artic National Wildlife Refuge, a sanctuary that most environmentalists, and many average citizens, viewed as inviolable. Although the final version of the law that was eventually passed precluded drilling in the Alaskan refuge, the remainder became a boon for energy and oil developers, many of whom had been part of Vice-President Cheney's "team" of advisors who drew up the legislation.

The final distinctive aspect of the Bush administration's first year was its total repudiation of foreign policy assumptions that had guided American approaches to other nations since World War II. Although Bush's father had brought to new heights the doctrine of multilateralism in his strategy for the Persian Gulf War and his collaboration with China and Russia, his son forswore multilateralism, severing—unilaterally—many of the commitments that had served as cornerstones of American foreign policy through the eighties and nineties. Reviving Ronald Reagan's desire to build Star Wars, a ballistic missile defense system, Bush announced that he would abrogate the ABM (anti-ballistic missile) Treaty that Richard Nixon had negotiated with Russia in 1972. (That decision, interestingly, led China and Russia—recently antagonists—to sign a new "friendship" treaty.) Bush then announced that the United States would not participate in the Kyoto Global Warming Treaty that Al Gore had been so instrumental in bringing about, even though 178 other nations—seeking to accommodate American objections—had already agreed to implement the treaty. As a result, one columnist noted, America became "the haughty sole hold-out" on fighting global warming. In the same spate of unilateral actions, Bush declared that the United States would reject a treaty banning land mines and withdrew its support of the Comprehensive Nuclear Test Ban Treaty. Finally, Bush turned his back completely on the Clinton-sponsored effort by South Korea to seek rapprochement with North Korea. As many of America's traditional allies viewed these actions, it seemed that a new arrogance had asserted itself in American foreign policy, making the United States, not Iraq or North Korea, a "rogue" state. Reflecting this concern, one pro-American British newspaper declared that "Mr. Bush's America seems in danger of convincing itself that it can force everybody to make concessions, while itself remaining impervious to change." Whatever the merits or demerits of specific decisions, the administration had clearly embarked on a radical new course, undermining the very framework of multilateral and collective security pacts that had provided the foundation for American foreign policy since World War II.

Within just a few months, therefore, George W. Bush had shown his determination to pursue fundamental but transformative policies. He would both embrace and implement programs sought by the New Right. He would reframe American foreign policy. And he would enact an economic program more dramatic in its departure from the status quo than even anything envisioned by Ronald Reagan. In all of this, he was remarkably successful. He succeeded in passing the largest tax cut in history. He secured educational reform, renounced Clintonian policies on the environment, and gave notice to the world that no longer could America be counted upon to follow a course of unity and collaboration with allies. Profound divisions remained. Moderate Republicans felt betrayed by the president's failure to follow through on his rhetoric of inclusion, and one of them—Jim Jeffords of Vermont—bolted from the party, saying that Bush's policies on withdrawing U.S. support for international family planning had hit him like a "kick in the stomach." Still, a direction had been charted. Bush had clearly shown how different he was from his predecessors, including his father. The question was whether the rest of his administration would display the same degree of determination to pursue foreign policy and domestic agendas so much at odds with the rest of post-World War II history.

September 11, 2001

And then came September 11. It was a day that would transform forever America's sense of invulnerability and innocence. With the weather brilliantly clear up and down the East Coast, four planes prepared to take off for California. All were jumbo jets, flying with full tanks of fuel for a transcontinental journey; each carried a passenger load far below normal. But on board each of the planes—American Airlines flight 11 and United Airlines 175 from Boston, American Airlines 77 from Washington, and United Airlines 93 from Newark—were groups of terrorists. Seizing control of each aircraft shortly after it reached cruising altitude, the hijackers killed or disabled pilots, took control of the cockpit, and steered the planes—now deadly missiles—toward their targets. The first plane, American 11, struck the North Tower of New York's World Trade Center at 8:48 A.M. Exactly 15 minutes later, at 9:03, United Airlines 175 smashed into the South Tower. One minute before 10 o'clock, the first tower—110 stories high—collapsed in a heap. Just half an hour later, the second tower fell. In the meantime, American Airlines 77 dive-bombed into the Pentagon just outside the nation's capital. Only United Airlines 93 was still aloft. There, a heroic band of passengers—knowing from cell phone conversations what had happened in New York—refused to let their plane become another enemy missile and instead assaulted the terrorists and forced their plane to come crashing to earth just outside of Pittsburgh.

Almost as one, people sensed the bottomless horror of what had just occurred. A journalist heading for a meeting inside the Trade Center suddenly found himself on an observation deck halfway up the tower. "I didn't know it wasn't an exit," he said. "And it was just covered with dozens of shoes. High heels. Strapons. . . . There were bodies, luggage, torsos. People were jumping [leaping from flames]. At first, I didn't know they were people, but I realized they were flailing on the way down . . . people lining up and dropping, too many people falling." A short distance away, novelist John Updike stood on a Brooklyn Heights roof with his wife, watching as "the South Tower . . . fell straight down like an elevator, with a tinkling shiver and a groan of concussion distinct across the miles of air. We know we had just witnessed thousands of deaths; we clung to each other as if we ourselves were falling." Millions watched on television as repeatedly, hour after hour, newscasts showed pictures of the second plane penetrating the North Tower and exploding in flames, each time experiencing anew a profound awareness that someone, some extraordinary force, had grabbed hold of America's consciousness and twisted it in ways that would never permit the old ways of doing and thinking to return.

As soon became clear, these terrorists were not maverick individuals acting out of desperation or futile rage. Most had been in training for years. Many were well educated, middle class, even with families. Some had lived in the United States for up to a decade, "sleepers" inserted into a culture, carrying on normal lives, buying cars, getting jobs, mixing with neighbors, awaiting the signal to activate the plans for destruction that had been generated in their training camps years earlier. They functioned in small "cells" of four or five, one person serving as the link to a larger structure. A few key

Firefighters make their way through the rubble of "ground zero" after two airliners crashed into the World Trade Center in New York on Tuesday, September 11, 2001, bringing down the landmark buildings. (AP Photo/Shawn Baldwin)

individuals enrolled in flying schools, learning the methods of turning a plane in midair. Unconcerned with mastering how to take off or land, they surprised flight instructors who, in retrospect, admitted to having been puzzled by students who "wanted to bypass primary training and go right to flying Boeings." One or two attended planning sessions in Kuala Lumpur or Hamburg, where they met higher-ups in the terrorist network known as Al Qaeda. But only at the last minute did most know the exact date and flights, and only those piloting the planes understood that their own deaths were part of the plan to achieve the goals being sought. To those who later analyzed what had happened, the genius of the planning was almost eerie. As one retired CIA officer declared, "I've never seen an operation go that smoothly."

The success of the terrorist mission reflected in large part the strategic skill and charismatic leadership of Osama bin Laden, the leader of Al Qaeda. One of 54 children fathered by a Yemeni construction billionaire, bin Laden, unlike many of his brothers and sisters, chose not to adopt Western lifestyles or establish residency in Western countries (15 of his siblings settled in Europe, 4 in the United States). Instead, bin Laden used his engineering education and his substantial inherited wealth to support Islamic rebellions against foreign rule. As a major figure in Islamic fundamental-ism, in 1979 he devoted his energies to freeing Afghanistan from Soviet in-vasion, joining the mujahedin in their successful guerilla war against Russia. For the moment, he was on the same side as the United States, but that po-tential alliance soon ceased.

When Iraq invaded Kuwait in 1990, bin Laden went to King Fahd of Saudi Arabia, offering to mobilize 100,000 Muslim fighters to liberate Kuwait. When asked how he would defend his troops against biological war-fare, bin Laden responded: "through faith." He became infuriated when King Fahd turned him down and instead welcomed American troops as leaders of the Persian Gulf War. As a result, bin Laden dedicated his life, and that of his growing Al Qaeda network, to the destruction of the American infidels who dared to occupy the sacred home of Islam. Relocating to Af-ghanistan, bin Laden built a worldwide network of terrorist cells, sustained their operations with millions of dollars from his own family fortune and funds donated by nations supportive of his mission, and proceeded to train bands of new recruits and then send them to more than 40 countries throughout the world to await the signal to activate their terrorist plans. Al Qaeda members launched the first truck bombing attack on the World Trade Center in 1993; perpetrated the explosions that ruined American embassies in Nairobi, Kenya, and Dar es Salaam, Tanzania, in 1998; and or-ganized the deadly sea assault on the *U.S.S. Cole* in October of 2000—all of this in pursuit of bin Laden's "Ladenese Epistle" of 1996 declaring that pushing America out of the holy land was his top priority and his declara-tion of 1998 that "to kill Americans and their allies, both civil and military, is an individual duty of every Muslim who is able, in any country where this is possible."

The genius of bin Laden was his ability to combine the meticulous planning of an engineer with the religious authority of a mystic. Drawing on a deep sense of grievance in the Muslim world that Western greed, secular-ism, and culture were destroying Muslim traditions, bin Laden conveyed to his followers the belief that they were part of a divinely ordained mission to save Islam from the corruption of Satan. Each of his targets embodied the supposed majesty and invulnerability of the enemy, none more so than the World Trade Center. When bin Laden set his sights on New York's landmark skyscrapers, one reporter noted, "the attack was not only against a nation or government, but against a symbol, the twin towers of Sodom and mam-mon." Most terrifying of all, it was an attack carried forward with the preci-sion of a scientific mind. "We couldn't do this," one military expert said. "It was an incredible operation that was pulled off perfectly."

Although most Americans were oblivious to bin Laden's role in or-chestrating worldwide terrorism, intelligence experts in Washington knew better. The CIA had followed bin Laden's insidious plots for years, and law enforcement agencies brought to trial bin Laden followers who had been responsible for the first World Trade Center bombing. After the attack on

America's embassies in Nairobi and Dar es Salaam, Clinton ordered a missile attack against bin Laden's presumed headquarters in the Afghanistan mountains (he allegedly left the site an hour before the missiles struck). George Tenet, director of the CIA, warned that bin Laden was the nation's number one enemy; Clinton's Sectretary of Defense, William Cohen, predicted in an op-ed piece for the *Washington Post* in the summer of 1999 that a terrorist attack was imminent in the United States; a national commission headed by former Senators Gary Hart and Warren Rudman declared that terrorism represented the most dire threat America faced; and the Federal Aviation Administration warned that hijackers from Al Qaeda might seize an American plane and fly it into a national landmark.

Despite these warnings, the Bush administration was slow to get up to speed on the dimensions or imminence of the bin Laden threat. Repeatedly, Tenet and others insisted on the urgency of confronting bin Laden. The leading official responsible for countering terrorism—a career officer— pleaded with Condoleezza Rice, Bush's National Security Advisor, to convene a meeting of leaders from all security agencies to engage the mounting evidence of an ominous threat. Rice failed to do so. A military intelligence team had even identified Mohammed Atta as the leader of a terrorist cell committed to attacking America—but that information, too, never reached the president's desk. Indeed, even when such information did get to the commander-in-chief, he seemed to ignore it. An August 6, 2001, presidential intelligence summary specifically headlined the possibility of terrorists using hijacked airplanes as missiles to assault American cities. But the president was on vacation in Crawford, Texas, at his ranch, and nothing happened. Other issues seemed of higher priority, including tax cuts, shifts in environmental policy, and new initiatives in military strategy. As former State Department official Leslie Gelb noted, despite repeated warnings "that the terrorist threat to America was far greater and more imminent than any missile attack to be defended by [President Bush's] proposed missile-defense system . . . very little [had] been done."

September 11 changed all that, providing a dramatic wake-up call to a nation engaged in what one security expert called a "lengthy sleepwalk." President Bush heard the news while reading a story to an elementary school class in Florida. He continued his reading for another few minutes, then excused himself and left. The White House had been evacuated. No one knew what would come next, and the Secret Service, fearful that *Air Force One* might be a potential target, insisted that the president get airborne and not return to Washington until it was safe. (It turns out that the White House may well have been in danger, with the glare of the sun making it hard for terrorists to identify—hence their decision to hit the Pentagon instead.) Shaken, Bush nevertheless understood that this was the most critical test any leader could face.

Initially, Bush seemed to flounder. His comments lacked compelling vision, and he used colloquial phrases, such as getting bin Laden "dead or alive," that scared suspicious Europeans fearful of another gun-toting LBJ. But as the week wore on, Bush rose to the occasion. He gave a moving address to a national prayer service at the National Cathedral and then an eloquent speech to a joint session of Congress, where he demonstrated a gravitas that conveyed to the American people the sense that a sure hand was at the helm. Bush was not Churchillian, nor like Roosevelt or Kennedy during World War II or the Cuban Missile Crisis. But he communicated a confidence suggesting that he was up to the task, and when he visited Ground Zero and exhorted rescue officials through a bullhorn to keep up their spirits, the response of gratitude and confidence was palpable.

The heart of Bush's message was that the war on terrorism was a totally new phenomenon, unlike any other war the nation had ever fought. There would be no unconditional surrender, no decisive victory as over Japan and Germany—indeed, perhaps not even evidence of battles fought. Instead, this would be a war of covert missions and secret forays, which might or might not lead to visible achievements such as the capture of bin Laden. It might also go on for years, with no endpoint defined in advance. Yet Bush remained clear on the objective: "Our enemy is a radical network of terrorists and every government that supports them," he told Congress. In that context, "every nation in every region now has a decision to make. Either you are with us, or you are with the terrorists." Within that framework, Bush pledged that America would wage unrelenting war until the specter of terrorism was eliminated from world politics.

Tellingly, the "you are either with us or against us" language recalled the rhetoric of the Cold War, evoking a Reaganesque image of an "evil empire" and a battle of good against evil. Except that there were important differences—and it was not yet clear that either Bush or his advisors understood them. First, in this instance, there was no Soviet Union, no superpower nation that embodied the mortal threat—instead, there was a worldwide band of fervent "cell" groups located in multiple nations, committed to a totally new kind of unpredictable terrorism; and second, unlike the Cold War, with its nation-state alliances, a policy of "containment" could not work. There was no visible enemy to contain, only an ideology sustained by religious fervor.

Thus, although on the surface a simple conflict, the war on terrorism involved an enemy more diffuse and complicated than one would ever find in a traditional war—an enemy rooted in volatile cultural, economic, and religious undercurrents that affected millions of people in countless countries. From the beginning, for example, bin Laden tied his attacks on America to the explosive Israeli-Palestinian conflict, insisting that his ultimate objective was not only to remove the infidels (America) from the homeland of Mecca (Saudi Arabia), but also to end what he described as the oppression of Palestinians by the "petty state of the Jews." No region of the world more embodied ancient grievances. Although President Clinton had brought Israel and the Palestinians to the brink of peace in the months before he left office, the proposed settlement fell apart, largely due to Yassir Arafat's cowardice in refusing to embrace the agreement. In the aftermath of that failure, violence and terrorism multiplied. Ariel Sharon, soon to become Israel's prime minister, provocatively visited—with an armed entourage—one of the holiest mosques in East Jerusalem, outraging Palestinians. A new intifada, featuring suicide bombing missions by Palestinians aiming to secure immediate salvation, quickly accelerated polarization. More than one thousand lives were lost in the fall of 2001 alone, eight times, in terms of proportional populations, the losses of September 11. Too many of the victims were children.

The Arab-Israeli conflict simply mirrored deeper tensions. Bin Laden insisted that at its foundation, the Middle East crisis reflected a battle between Christians and Jews on the one hand and Muslims on the other. Many individuals, including President Bush, pointed out that Islam is a peaceful religion that forbids suicide and the killing of innocent civilians. Yet a number of Americans, reciprocating the hatred found in the jihads of Islamic fundamentalists, agreed that this was a battle between faiths and became deeply suspicious of Muslims. One professor at a prominent American university rejected applications for post-doctoral study from Pakistani students, accusing them of being Islamic terrorists in the making. Many followers of Islam retorted that the United States was engaged in a worldwide conspiracy to exterminate their religion. When George W. Bush used the word "crusade" to describe America's effort to bring down bin Laden, he inadvertently resurrected the image of Christians seeking to annihilate Muslims in the holy wars of the thirteenth and fourteenth centuries and thereby helped support bin Laden's protrayal of himself as a new Saladin who would save Islam by expelling the "crusaders and Jews." In the eyes of at least some, both Muslim and Christian, the developing conflict seemed all too much like the "clash of civilizations" that political scientist Samuel Huntington had predicted in 1993 as "the next world war."

As if such tensions were not enough, lurking just beneath the surface were the enormous fissures of wealth and status that fed Islamic revolutionary discontent and threatened to bring to power in the Muslim world fundamentalists who opposed all forms of modernity and cooperation with the West. Poverty pervaded the Arab world. In nations like Egypt, unemployment reached 30 percent. While princes in Saudi Arabia built $300 million palaces and took huge bribes from Western corporations, the poor became poorer. Islamic fundamentalists provided a simple explanation for these profound inequalities: America, with its culture of consumerism, materialism, and capitalist greed, was seeking, arrogantly, to take over the world, destroy all in its way, and create corrupt puppet states like Egypt and Saudi Arabia to carry out its wishes. In the face of such a threat, Islamic scholar Fouad Ajami wrote, "fundamentalism . . . connects people to a tradition" and points a way toward salvation and empowerment. In this worldview, bin Laden's attack on America could be seen as retribution, striking down the devil and exacting justice. "At last," said one Arab to another, "a new balance of terror has been struck. After a decade in which America could do as it pleased anywhere in the world, from Iraq to Serbia, the poor and disenfranchised are finally rising up against her." No matter how wrong-headed and ill-informed such a reaction might be, it nevertheless pointed out the depth and complexity of the challenges America had to deal with if it were not only to defeat bin Laden, but also to address the deep springs of discord, anger, and oppression that for so long had fed his apocalyptic vision and that continued to fuel the spread of that vision everywhere that immiseration and anger existed in the Muslim world.

The problem the Bush administration faced in mounting its "war on terrorism," therefore, was far different from that faced by Harry Truman when the Soviet Union stifled freedom on Poland and Hungary. This was a far more nuanced, far more complicated cultural and ideological battle, confronting the Bush administration with a series of challenges that called for an imagination and a creativity very different from those of another era. Whether those challenges could be met effectively would eventually determine the success or failure of George W. Bush's presidency.

Yet however these dilemmas were resolved, the most compelling legacy of September 11 remained the human resilience, courage, and love that were expressed that day. Like a chorus of affirmation about the capacity of the human spirit to survive and overcome even the worst of tragedies, the voices of that day conveyed a new sense of common humanity and concern. It was heard in the hushed tones of a daughter on the telephone, hearing, then understanding, what had happened, grateful to be alive and to know that her loved ones were also; in the solicitude of a car rental agent at a Chicago airport trying to put together teams of riders to travel together to Seattle, or Dallas or Norfolk; in the hugging that said yes, there was something to live for; in the bells that tolled for the dead as hundreds of students, holding hands, gathered in total silence to grieve for the lost.

Never before had America, collectively, experienced this kind of coming together. From up and down the hundreds of floors of the Twin Towers at the World Trade Center, husbands called their wives, lovers called their partners, mothers called their children, daughters their fathers. A chef at the Windows on the World restaurant told his partner on his cell phone "that he loved me. . . . He just said, 'I'm okay—don't worry. I love you no matter what. I love you." Another worker wrote a last e-mail: "I don't think I'm going to get out. You've been a really good friend." And the phone calls from the airplanes: Cee Cee Lyles, a flight attendant on UAL 93, calling Lorne her husband "to tell me that she loved me, loved me dearly, and to tell the boys that she loved us," all with screams in the background. Or Jeremy Glick calling his wife Lyzbeth just before he and other passengers rushed the hijackers to prevent them from aiming their plane at another terrorist target: "We said 'I love you' a thousand times, over and over again, and it just brought so much peace to us. . . . He said 'I love Emmy' who's our daughter and to take care of her. And then he said, 'whatever decisions you make in your life, I need you to be happy, and I will respect any decision that you make.' I think that gives me the most comfort."

As stories like these filled the airwaves and the newspapers, Americans discovered a feeling of family and support across social, ethnic, economic, and international lines that had not been seen or experienced since World War II. Only now it was so immediate. "All this time," *New Yorker* sports writer Roger Angell wrote, "we've forced ourselves to imagine what it was like to be there—in Guadalcanal, in Stalingrad, at KheSanh, in Sarajevo and Belfast and Palestine. . . . Now that's over. Now we're all the same age together. None of us is young this week, and with death and calamity just down the street, few of us is vicarious any longer." American Middle East negotiator Dennis Ross walked back to a seminar in Washington after the Pentagon attack and saw the look on people's faces that on so many occasions he had seen on the faces of Israelis. And from a Jerusalem coffee shop, journalist Aharon Applefield wrote: "In modern Jewish mythology, America is the father figure who saved many Jews from the cruel Bolsheviks and Nazis by giving us a home. Now the father is united with his sons in a Jerusalem coffee shop, in grief over the evil that refuses to disappear from the world."

New York exemplified the miracle that accompanied the tragedy. Its mayor, Rudy Giuliani, spoke for the world in acknowledging that the losses "are more than we can bear"; but at the same time he became the legion-bearer for the hundreds of firemen and policemen who had given their lives in the rescue effort and for the hundreds of other victims who could not speak for themselves, but had, so many of them, spoken for their sense of community by going back to try to help others escape, or leaped to their deaths holding hands with a comrade. For more than three months, the *New York Times* performed a service to the world that no one could gainsay— publishing each day vignettes about the human characteristics that distinguished each of the victims: the firefighter who, in his private papers, left his wife a note saying that if he died in the course of duty, he was proud to have been a firefighter, and asking her to carry on; the father who each day told his five-year-old daughter not to grow old on him while he was away at work and who each night took down the American flag outside the house with her; the brothers, each devoted family members who fished and coached with their children, who, as fate would have it, both perished when the towers crumbled. All of this, the *New York Times* editorialized in eloquent understatement, helped Americans "to recognize . . . how interchangeable we might have been with those who died. Their lives resembled ours more closely than we can let ourselves imagine. . . . The result of [September 11's] destruction is that we have been given a privileged glimpse into the interior of one family after another. . . . For now, we have a remarkable precious opportunity to witness a portrait of this nation assembled out of memories and pictures, out of the efforts of everyday people to explain in everyday words who it is they lost."

Thus, in the end, the most enduring legacy of September 11 was the sense of common humanity that survived and that flourished. The stories of courage in the face of death, of love in the face of parting, of togetherness in the face of terrorists who sought to divide, provided the best hope that people from different backgrounds, faiths, and cultures could nevertheless find a way to live together.

The Bush Response

Whatever the capacity of the American people after 9/11 to rise above petty distractions in the face of tragedy, George W. Bush now faced a series of critical questions: first, how should the world's most powerful nation respond to an attack on its most cherished institutions—surely, it *had* to respond; second, should that response reflect the unilateralism of the administration's first seven months or revert to the multilateralism that had characterized the senior Bush's prosecution of the Persian Gulf War; and third, what was the long-term strategy for not only destroying the immediate threat of terrorism, but also addressing the underlying causes that continued to fuel the recruitment of new terrorists? There were no easy answers, and as time would show, answering one question one way could lead to complications that created a thousand new questions and controversies.

For a significant period of time after 9/11, the United States enjoyed a degree of support and empathy around the world that was unprecedented. "We are all Americans," proclaimed the leading Parisian newspaper, *Le Monde.* Vladimir Putin called the president and pledged his support; so, too, did Mubarak of Egypt and leaders of China, India, and Pakistan; farmers in Italy and factory workers in Japan all greeted Americans with a new measure of warmth and appreciation. Most of the world's leading powers were fully prepared to endorse what most saw as inevitable—a military assault on Afghanistan, bin Laden's home-in-exile and a country that had already displayed deep hostility toward the United States through its ruling regime, the Taliban. Moreover, most of those world powers trusted Colin Powell, Bush's Secretary of State (and commander of the military during the Persian Gulf War) to ensure that multilateralism would prevail in the coming months.

Powell had been fighting a rearguard action against many of the Bush administration's unilateral policies. He understood the dismay with which Europeans viewed U.S. dismissal of the Kyoto Accords and the International Criminal Tribunal. Now, Powell set out to galvanize his friends, starting with Putin, and European allies like Blair of England, Chirac of France, and Schroeder of Germany. In perhaps the most delicate task before him, Powell presented Pakistan's president, General Pervez Musharraf, with a demand that Pakistan unconditionally support America's struggle, providing military bases, full intelligence briefings (since the Pakistanis knew more about Al Qaeda than anyone else), and hand-in-glove cooperation on day-to-day tactics—this from a government notorious for having supported the Taliban and itself deeply worried about an internal Islamic fundamentalist revolt. Musharraf agreed to cooperate on all points, completely embracing Washington's agenda.

The first stage of Washington's response could not have gone better. With support from traditional allies as well as world powers such as China and Russia, the United States unleashed in early October—only four weeks after 9/11—an ambitious bombing campaign against the Taliban. Well before troops were ready to land, the bombing attacks were far more successful than even the most ardent optimist had predicted. Confounding skeptics who believed that the United States might suffer the same fate in Afghanistan as the Soviet Union had when it invaded, Taliban forces started to crumble. The capital of Kabul fell to anti-Taliban, Northern Alliance forces, and in quick succession so, too, did other large Taliban outposts. The United States had deployed stunning new technologies of war. Unmanned "drones" flew over the countryside using scanning cameras to identify prospective targets. Under instruction from ground controllers, the drones would then "paint" targets with lasers and, using global positioning systems (GPS), guide weapons and bombs to their specific objective. Special forces from the U.S. Army and Marines traveled on horseback to help coordinate the bombing attacks. Similarly equipped with GPS monitors and laser designators, they used their laptop computers and radios to talk to pilots overhead and zero in on targets to be hit. Over 60 percent of the air missions in Afghanistan utilized such high technology—two times the percentage of bombing sorties that had used the same methods in Kosovo and four times the percentage used in the Persian Gulf War. Al Qaeda and Taliban forces fleeing the caves said they were stunned by the overwhelming and unseen weapons unleashed upon them, panicking and seeking surrender in response. At the same time, effective political action by the United States and its allies resulted in the creation of a new coalition government in Afghanistan seeking to work across tribal and ethnic divisions to forge a government that might, for the first time in decades, bring stability and human rights, especially for women, back to their country. There was even good reason to hope that with adequate troops and the ingenious technology already displayed, Osama bin Laden could be smoked out of his hiding place in the impenetrable cave structures on the Pakistan-Afghan border and brought to justice.

Yet even before victory in Afghanistan had been solidified or the attack on bin Laden focused, the Bush administration diverted its attention from Afghanistan and embarked on a second, divisive, and ultimately fateful venture: a plan to attack Iraq and depose Saddam Hussein. Bitterly contested from within and without the administration, the decision to invade Iraq crystallized the long-simmering tensions over unilateralism versus coalition-building. It pitted Secretary of State Colin Powell against Secretary of Defense Donald Rumsfeld and Vice-President Dick Cheney (and ultimately President George W. Bush) in a bitter civil war over intelligence data and policy; and ultimately, it created a degree of domestic dissent in the United States and anti-Americanism abroad that approached in fervor the polarization that had occurred over Vietnam thirty-five years earlier. Instead of rooting out terrorist insurgency, the Iraq invasion appeared to redouble it. Rather than build on the foundation of empathy that the world displayed toward America after 9/11, the invasion undermined and destroyed it. And the entire process was premised on a series of intelligence assessments that a national commission on U.S. intelligence services later found to be "dead wrong." How did such a decision happen? And what did it mean for the future of the war on terrorism as well as the Bush administration?

As reconstructed by journalists and two national commissions—the 9/11 bipartisan commission chaired by Governor Thomas Kean and former Congressman Lee Hamilton and a national commission on intelligence created by the president—the impulse to go after Iraq was born long before 9/11, though ultimately 9/11 provided the occasion for pursuing a pre-existing determination to "get" Saddam. Like a bone stuck in the throat, the continued presence in Iraq of a ruthless dictator who had in the past practiced genocide infuriated people who eleven years earlier, in the first Bush administration, had been party to a decision not to "go to Baghdad" and get Saddam after Kuwait had been liberated. In 1998 Congress had passed unanimously a resolution declaring it U.S. policy to seek regime change in Iraq. Now, the horror of 9/11 provided the occasion for finishing a job that had been left incomplete a decade earlier. Yet tragically, the wish to depose Saddam preceded the existence of evidence that might warrant his being deposed. Moreover, the will to find that evidence created a process whereby intelligence was fudged, declarations that something was true were made without findings of fact, and a nation was mobilized for war on the basis of claims that within two years were shown to be without any foundation. In effect, the country was driven to war by arguments that turned out to have no justification whatsoever.

The process had a fascination—and a momentum—all its own. From the beginning of the administration—long before 9/11—a cohort of Bush officials perceived the elimination of Saddam as a top priority. The cohort included Vice-President Dick Cheney, his chief of staff Lewis Libby, Secretary of Defense Donald Rumsfeld, and Assistant Secretary of Defense Paul Wolfowitz. In all likelihood, it included George W. Bush as well. Significantly, the first briefings on national security that the new administration received from George Tenet in January 2001 focused on Al Qaeda, China, and weapons of mass destruction (WMDs). Iraq was not mentioned. Yet as early as 9/11 itself, Rumsfeld raised with his staff—and eventually the president's inner circle—the idea of going after Saddam *as well as* Osama bin Laden, *as though the two were equally dangerous and responsible for 9/11*. Although initially a decision was reached not to make Iraq an immediate target, the idea took on a life of its own. Just five days later, Bush told Condoleezza Rice, "We won't do Iraq now, we're putting Iraq off. But eventually we'll have to return to that question." Powell could not believe the interpretations Rumsfeld and Wolfowitz were putting on partial intelligence. Rumsfeld contended that dump trucks newly purchased by Iraq were intended to be used as launching points for rockets. "This is lunacy," Powell said.

But it was a lunacy that Bush himself was quickly ready to believe, and to act on. On November 21—just ten weeks after 9/11—the president told Rumsfeld to make an updated war plan on Iraq a top priority. The venture was to be conducted in total secrecy, lest other nations, or even America's own generals, resist the idea (the Joint Chiefs of Staff were not told about any of this until six months later). Work on the new war plan was assigned to General Tommy Franks and a small number of assistants, with strict orders to discuss the results only with Rumsfeld—who insisted on a weekly update—and the president. Subsequently, opponents of Bush's policy, using CIA sources, would argue that sending American troops to ferret out Osama bin Laden in the underground caves around Tora Bora in Afghanistan in the winter of 2001 had a strong possibility of success. Indeed, in early December 2001, military intelligence experts believed they had bin Laden cornered, and an American general requested permission to deploy four thousand marines to go get him. But the request was denied. At precisely the time when such a search-and-destroy mission could have worked, attention shifted to putting in place a plan to invade Iraq. Now, getting Saddam had replaced getting Osama as the top priority.

The direction in which Bush was heading was heralded in his State of the Union speech in January 2002. Five months after 9/11, Bush told the American people they were threatened by "an axis of evil." The three nations Bush mentioned as comprising the "axis" were Iran, North Korea, and Iraq, but some observers thought they knew what was really coming. The State of the Union speech, conservative columnist Charles Krauthammer declared, was in fact all about Iraq. Ruminating on the speech later, Bush told *Washington Post* reporter Bob Woodward, "Freedom is God's gift to everybody in the world . . . and I believe we have a duty to free people." Like Reagan's speech about "the evil empire," Bush's tirade against the "axis of evil" created the ideological framework for zeroing in on a specific enemy—the one for which he had asked Rumsfeld to develop a "plan of attack" just two months earlier.

Now, the administration had to come forward with a rationale. In the past, Saddam Hussein had used chemical and biological warfare, against both his enemies in the Iran-Iraq war (where the United States supported Saddam against Iran with billions of dollars in agricultural aid and millions of dollars in weapons) and against his own people. Throughout the '90s, as consequence of its defeat in Kuwait, Iraq was subject to intensive U.N. inspections to try to locate any remaining WMDs, as well as to U.N. sanctions designed to punish Saddam for his brutality toward minorities and Kurds in his own country. But in 1999, Saddam expelled the U.N. arms inspectors from the country. Their absence permitted pro-war officials in the Bush administration to claim that Saddam was engaged in developing WMDs, with the ultimate threat that he would share them with terrorists and attack the United States.

At the same time, Bush proclaimed a new American doctrine of pre-emptive war. "We must take the battle to the enemy," he told a University of Michigan audience, "disrupt his plans, and confront the worst threats before they emerge." Never before had the United States suggested that it would initiate a war or fail to secure multiple alliances before it responded to an enemy. By this new reasoning, on the other hand, the chance that Saddam possessed WMDs and might share them with terrorists made him a logical—indeed a necessary—target for pre-emptive war. As the *New York Times* editorialized, this was a doctrinal "shift with profound implications," potentially putting the United States "in the business of unilaterally invading other countries or toppling other governments."

With the new "pre-emptive" strategy as a context, pro-war Bush administration officials ratcheted up the case for an invasion, while Secretary of State Colin Powell fought desperately to forestall unilateralism and create a multilateral, U.N.-based alternative. In Powell's view, an invasion would alienate most of America's allies, provoke hostility throughout the Middle East, and destabilize regimes otherwise friendly toward the United States such as Egypt and Saudi Arabia. "You will be the proud owner of 25 million people," he told Bush in a rare private session with the president (*Time* magazine had described Powell as being frozen out of the White House), "you break it, you own it," with all the negative consequences. Urgently, Powell asked the president to go to the U.N., build a coalition, and find a peaceful solution—or if military action became necessary, at least to have international backing. Brent Scowcroft, the national security advisor for the first President Bush, weighed in with a *Wall Street Journal* op-ed article arguing that the real enemy was Al Qaeda, not Iraq, that there was no connection between bin Laden and Saddam, and that a unilateral attack against Iraq would be completely counterproductive. (The first President Bush was shown a draft of the article and made no comment.)

By now, Cheney and Powell were completely at odds. Powell believed Cheney was so committed to war that he would oppose any diplomatic solution. Cheney believed that going to the U.N. was a way to start an endless debate and suck the wind out of America's determination to act decisively. To bolster his case, the vice-president went public with a new set of charges, well beyond what any intelligence findings justified. He invoked the specter that Iraq was seeking nuclear weapons and for the first time declared on the record—and without corroborating evidence—that "there is no doubt that Saddam Hussein *now* has WMDs and that he is amassing them to use against our friends, our allies, and against us." It was a breathtaking allegation—almost as though Cheney had taken the words of Bush's pre-emption speech and created the exact scenario for applying them. WMDs in the hands of a "murderous dictator," he argued, constituted "as great a threat as can be imagined. The risks of inaction are greater than the risk of action." Combined with the claim that Saddam was pursuing "an aggressive nuclear weapons program," Cheney was essentially telling the public—and the president—that Bush had no choice but to go to war. By this reasoning, Saddam was a far bigger threat than Osama. In Powell's view, Cheney was acting like "he had a fever," "fixated" on going to war. The dispute between Powell and Cheney had now reached the point where rapprochement seemed impossible. Their debate, Bob Woodward wrote, "pulled apart the last fraying threads of what had connected them for so many years." Cheney even went so far as to say that the return of inspectors to Iraq would make Saddam even more dangerous because they would be fooled, and their presence would make it more difficult to "take" Saddam out.

Even though military and intelligence officials still qualified their assessments of whether Iraq had WMDs with words like "might" or "perhaps" (General Tommy Franks said they had been looking for SCUD missiles for years and had found nothing), the president now emulated Cheney, declaring unequivocally in September 2002 that "Saddam Hussein possesses weapons of mass destruction." Moreover, leading administration officials, including the president, continued to claim that Iraq was buying equipment—aluminum tubes—to enrich uranium for an A-bomb. Invoking the danger of doing nothing, Condoleezza Rice told CNN television, "We don't want the smoking gun [proving Saddam's evil intentions] to be a mushroom cloud." In fact, the CIA had doubts about the aluminum tubes, and Department of Energy intelligence experts were adamant that the tubes could not be used to enrich uranium. Nevertheless, the seed had been planted, by no less a personage than Bush's own national security advisor, and the momentum toward war grew apace.

Powell made one last intervention, pleading with Bush to demand from the U.N. a resolution requiring compliance with all weapons restrictions and the reintroduction of inspectors. Any violation by Iraq would be a "material breach" of the U.N. resolution and a justification for war. Bush agreed, at the last minute inserting into a speech he was giving at the U.N. the statement that America was willing to work with other nations and the U.N. to disarm Saddam. Left ambiguous was whether a second Security Council meeting would be required to declare the "material breach" and authorize war, as had happened in the first Gulf War under Bush Sr. But for the moment, Powell had won a major victory, and as testimony to the skill with which he had navigated the diplomatic waters, the resolution was approved unanimously by the Security Council, with even Syria agreeing. A whole new weapons inspection team, led by Sweden's Hans Blix, prepared to search out sites far and wide in Iraq to find and destroy any WMDs that existed.

In the meantime, the pro-war Bush forces on the home front mobilized further support. Bush went to Congress for a resolution authorizing him to use force if he found Iraq in violation of the U.N. resolution, assuring Congressional leaders that "Saddam Hussein is a terrible guy who is teaming up with Al Qaeda." He went on to state unequivocally that "[Saddam] has weapons of mass destruction. . . . He still needs plutonium and he has not been shy about trying to find it. Time frame would be six months," he said, for Iraq to get a nuclear weapon. All the cards were now being played. Although no evidence existed of any relationship between Iraq and 9/11, Bush fudged the connection by calling Saddam a terrorist and saying that the worst thing that could happen would be for Saddam to make his WMDs available to Osama (in fact Saddam was deeply hostile to Islamic fundamentalism). And even though senators like Bob Graham of Florida—one of the most knowledgeable people in government about intelligence matters— were profoundly skeptical that any evidence existed that Saddam had WMDs, Bush packaged his appeal so effectively that the resolution approving war, if necessary, passed by overwhelming margins.

The Joint Chiefs of Staff were finally brought into the planning for a war in October (eleven months after Bush had given the order to draw up war plans). The army chief of staff publicly declared that any successful invasion would require a minimum of a quarter of a million troops on the ground (Powell agreed, especially given his experience in the first Gulf War), but the Army chief's objections were ignored, and shortly thereafter he left his post. Responding to Rumsfeld's pleas for a quick and lean fighting force, Tommy Franks declared that an initial invasion force of under 130,000 could do the job. Meanwhile, the CIA came forward with a new national intelligence estimate that started out saying that Saddam had WMDs and then equivocated on every specific, using words like "could," "probably," or "might," and acknowledging that the CIA had "low confidence" that Saddam would ever give Al Qaeda assistance in waging chemical or biological warfare against the United States. Instead of the six months that Bush had said might be necessary for Iraq to get nuclear weapons, the CIA estimated it would take five to seven years. Even then, the State Department's intelligence office dissented strongly from the CIA report, although its disagreement never reached the public or Congress. At no point did the Bush administration ever acknowledge that there was no smoking gun. Instead, Bush insisted, "facing clear evidence of peril, we cannot wait for the final proof, the smoking gun, that could come in the form of a mushroom cloud." Such inflammatory language inevitably made an impact.

By December, the U.N. inspectors were in Iraq pursuing their work, while Bush was under pressure from the military to invade by March lest the summer heat cripple the possibility of quick success. At a critical meeting in December 2002, intelligence officials presented their best-case scenario for proving that Saddam had WMDs. "Is this the best we've got?" Bush asked.

And responding with all the authority he possessed as the nation's number one intelligence official, George Tenet responded, "It's a slam dunk." It was the last time within pro-war administration circles that any skepticism was expressed about the intelligence data. Bush now told Powell of his decision to go to war. The Secretary of State repeated his question: "You know you're going to be owning this place?" but never told Bush he opposed the decision. All the momentum was now on the side of the pro-war group. When State Department officials said they were "appalled" by the use of evidence that had not been corroborated, Wolfowitz responded, "Lack of evidence [does] not mean something [does] not exist," thereby making a weakness in his argument into a strength. Hans Blix issued a tough report in January, citing the absence of evidence of WMDs, criticizing Saddam's evasiveness, and asking for additional time to come to a final judgement. But Bush had no desire to play. He was ready to go to war.

Perhaps the most poignant personal episode of the prewar build-up occurred when Bush asked Colin Powell to make the case for war before the U.N. Only Powell had the respect and stature to convince those who doubted the wisdom of America's actions. Everyone knew he had been opposed to the unilateralism of Rumsfeld, Cheney, and Bush and had profound doubts about the evidence of WMDs, an Iraqi nuclear program, and any ties between Saddam and Osama. And a few knew that he saw Cheney as having a "fever" for war. Now, like the good soldier he was, he agreed to make the case. But first, he insisted on going to CIA headquarters and poring over the evidence he was being asked to use before the Security Council. What he found was more chaos than clarity. The sources, he told Bob Woodward, "had been masticated over in the White House so that the exhibits didn't match the words." He totally rejected the material he found on a supposed connection between the 9/11 conspirators and Iraq. "That was worse than ridiculous." And he remained convinced that "Cheney took intelligence and converted uncertainty and ambiguity into fact." But he was intent on making the best case he could. Tragically, one of the pieces of evidence he relied on most—supposed evidence of an effort to hide WMDs—came from a source in Germany known as "Curveball." Powell questioned the veracity of the evidence. He was assured it was reliable. No one told him that not a single CIA officer had ever interviewed "Curveball" or that the German intelligence services, who had done the research, had concluded that "Curveball" was a "mental case" who was not to be trusted. One of Tenet's assistants called Tenet the night before the speech to warn about the validity of the section using "Curveball's" intelligence. Tenet never passed the information on to Powell. And so the government official most dubious about the course his country was about to follow went before the world and put his credibility on the line by stating why making war on Saddam was unavoidable. "The cumulative effect was stunning," said one anti-war columnist. "I'm not ready for war yet, but Colin Powell convinced me that it might be the only way to stop a fiend, and that if we do go, there is a reason." Looking back two and a half years later, Powell said he was "devastated" by the degree to which he had been deceived by the CIA; his appearance at the U.N., he commented, was a permanent "blot" on his record, a source of "pain" and embarrassment. The ironies were in some ways beyond comprehension.

With Powell having laid the groundwork, Bush gave the order to invade. Saddam, he told the country, "continues to possess and conceal some of the most lethal weapons ever devised"; moreover, "nuclear weapons obtained with the help of Iraq" could kill hundreds of thousands. "We choose to meet that threat now, where it arises, before it can appear suddenly in our skies and cities." It was all there: the doctrine of pre-emption, the certainty about WMDs, the specter of nuclear holocaust, the implicit ties between Saddam and 9/11. Ever since 9/11, Cheney told a close friend, he had been confident that the discussions on Iraq "would come out okay." Now, they had.

Using the tactics of "shock and awe" that Rumsfeld found so compelling, American troops scissored through Iraq in March 2003, their smart bombs and lightning forays shearing Iraq's weak defenders (the Iraq Army had diminished by more than a third since 1992). Most Iraqi forces fell back to Baghdad, then splintered and melted into the countryside. Pulling down a giant statue of Saddam in the capital, throngs of Iraqi citizens cheered the American forces as liberators. With remarkably little loss of life, America's army had freed the country, apparently vindicating Rumsfeld's belief that a lean, sharp fighting force could sweep the country and achieve victory. Indeed, so thrilled was the Bush team that on May 1, 2003—just six weeks after the invasion—George W. Bush put on his pilot suit and landed a fighter plane on a U.S. aircraft carrier anchored off San Diego. Against a backdrop of a huge banner declaring "Mission Accomplished," the president told the Amerian people: "Major combat operations in Iraq have ended. The tyrant has fallen and Iraq is free. In the image of falling statues, we have witnessed the arrival of a new era. . . . We have seen the turning of the tide." It had all been so easy.

The Aftermath

Or so it seemed.

The first indication that things might not be as rosy as they appeared came when widespread looting occurred across Iraq days after the invasion, but especially in Baghdad. Ancient treasures were left unprotected, the archaelogical museum—home to countless relics—totally open for street corner thugs. Munitions dumps had no protection, with armed groups from numerous factions stripping them of weapons, bombs, grenades, and armored vehicles. When asked how it could be possible that an armed force so lightning quick on the battlefield seemed so "hands-off" and incompetent when it came to securing invaluable assets, the military responded that

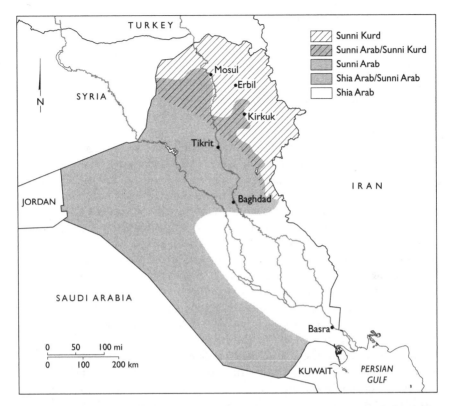

When American forces invaded Iraq in the spring of 2003, they proceeded quickly to Baghdad. They did not anticipate either the mass looting that occurred or the popular insurgency that soon developed. *Source:* Charles W. Kegley and Gregory A. Raymond, *After Iraq* (Oxford University Press, 2007).

"pacification" and protection had not been part of its game plan. The American occupying force seemed confused, uncoordinated, without either direction or plans. Initially, a military official was placed in charge, but soon thereafter, Paul Bremer, a former ambassador, took over. But neither seemed to have a blueprint or any sense of how to address the multiple constituencies, ethnic factions, or fundamental infrastructure needs of the country. Electricity and water were available only sporadically. There were no police, no firefighters, no bureaucrats to distribute food, arrange for repairs, engage the citizenry.

Part of the problem was that no one in Washington had drawn up an adequate plan for the postwar era. Douglas Feith, a Wolfowitz ally in the Defense Department, was placed in charge of figuring out the postwar world. The State Department, under Powell's direction, had already completed a "Future of Iraq" project that anticipated every problem, from oil to food to agriculture. Indeed, virtually every practical dilemma encountered by the occupying Americans had been predicted by the State Department document, with a series of contingency plans laid out. But when Powell sent over the two leading drafters of the State Department document to help out Feith at Defense, Rumsfeld ordered them to leave by sundown, saying he needed people who were "believers," not "doubters." Powell, Bob Woodward writes, "wondered if things could get weirder." The answer was yes. When State sent over seven more experts, Feith declared he did not want insiders, only outsiders.

The second problem went back to the size of the occupying force. Based on his experience in the first Gulf War, Powell had always believed that at least a quarter-million troops were needed to conduct "pacification" missions. The same figure had been used by the Army chief of staff in testimony before Congress, before he was shunted from office. Rumsfeld insisted that his "lean" force of 130,000–140,000 could do it all. But the troops were overwhelmed. Not only could they not protect museum treasures from looters, but also they had no experience in providing the massive infrastructure needed to keep a country on the edge of disintegration from falling apart. Perhaps if the Iraq Army had been kept intact (and there were many Iraqi generals ready to cooperate with the United States), it could have provided the personnel to keep the peace and distribute food and water. Or the police could have been kept whole. But neither happened because the administration was determined to clean out all members of Saddam Hussein's Baathist Party and all remnants of his military forces. Thus it was like being present at the creation of a new society and a new structure of power—except that only half the troops necessary had been sent to do the job, and the Iraqis who might have served as their surrogates were purged.

The third problem was that within a matter of weeks, the Iraq insurgency was born. Saddam Hussein escaped capture for nearly nine months after the invasion, and he and his closest aides mobilized forces loyal to the old regime to begin attacks on American forces and those Iraqi citizens allied with them. But Saddam was only a small part of what became, within a year, an insurrection out of control. The "liberators" soon came to be "occupiers"; efforts at outreach were perceived as intrusive attempts to control. Electricity and water still were not available. Revolutionary rhetoric against the pro-Israeli invaders turned a younger generation of Iraqis into guerrilla fighters. The Americans came ill-armed for resisting attacks from lightning strikes by insurgents who could melt into the populace. Whole cities came to be ruled, unofficially, by anti-American insurgents. The humvees that Americans drove lacked protective armor, making them totally vulnerable to IEDs—improvised explosive devices—that soon made American casualty totals start to climb. Not only were the body bags of the dead coming back with a regularity totally inconsistent with the notion of "Mission Accomplished," but also many times more soldiers lost their limbs because of IEDs and could expect to spend months, if not years, trying to learn how to live with prosthetic devices like artificial hands and legs. Worst of all, literally hundreds of Iraqis were persuaded that the highest service they could perform to their God and their country was to wrap themselves in dynamite and blow themselves up, usually in the midst of Iraqi citizens being recruited to join the police force or army or in a car or truck that rammed into an American roadblock or convoy and then detonated its explosives. Nothing could be predicted. The "enemy" looked no different than one's "friends." It became a nightmare, with a growing sense among many that this looked all too familiar—almost like Vietnam.

The contrast between the "Mission Accomplished" speech of George Bush and what ensued thereafter could be seen by comparing statistics between August 2003 and August 2005. U.S. troop fatalities went from 36 in August 2003 to 90 in August 2005; troops wounded leaped from 181 to 608; fatalities among Iraqi security personnel soared, from 50 to 280, while those among Iraqi civilians went from 225 to 600 (or 1,600 if one included victims of a stampede on a bridge during a religious pilgrimage); perhaps most disturbing of all, the estimated size of the insurgency had skyrocketed from 3,000 in August 2003 to 18,000 in August 2005.

To make matters worse, it became increasingly clear that the arguments the Bush administration had made for going to war in the first place were flawed, if not totally ill-founded. The United States sent David Kay, a veteran arms inspector, to lead an aggressive and well-informed team of experts to find Saddam's WMDs. Five months later, Kay gave his first and tentative report: "We have not yet found stocks of weapons," he declared. But he continued to look. Finally, nearly a year after the war had been started because it was a "slam dunk" that Saddam had WMDs and imperative to disarm the murderous tyrant, Kay announced, "We were almost all wrong." From his searches, and from countless interviews with former Saddam officials, Kay concluded that Saddam had destroyed all his WMDs in the mid- to late '90s. Even Tenet now "went soft," claiming there had always been doubts about the solidness of the evidence.

The news got worse. Investigations disclosed that there had been neither a nuclear program in Iraq, nor any evidence of Saddam having tried to buy unenriched uranium to turn into A-bombs. The 9/11 commission, after months of hearings and an extraordinary degree of bipartisanship, concluded that the United States had overlooked countless indications that a terrorist attack like that unleashed on 9/11 was being planned. As important, the commission declared, unequivocally, that there was *no* connection between Saddam Hussein and 9/11. Finally, the bipartisan commission on national intelligence that the president had appointed concluded that the entire intelligence apparatus had been weak and inefficient and that the assessments that the apparatus gave to the administration to provide the basis for going to war were "dead wrong." In short, two years after the invasion, not only was the Iraq insurgency out of control, but also it now seemed that every argument used to justify the war—Saddam's aggressive nuclear program, his multiple WMDs, and the allegation of a direct link between

Saddam and Osama—had no basis in fact. The United States had lost more than two thousand lives—and the Iraqis countless more—for a war that lacked a persuasive rationale.

The 2004 Election

Halfway through the disclosure of these depressing developments, the nation held its quadrennial presidential election. The country remained incredibly divided. Bush had successfully pursued his domestic agenda of tax cuts, environmental deregulation, and education reform. More importantly, he had risen in stature and become a national leader after 9/11, rallying a stunned people and providing a model of purposeful determination to prevent any subsequent attacks while battling worldwide terrorism. Even the war in Iraq—initially very much debated—seemed in the first months to work to his advantage because the early results were so positive. Still, much of the country felt otherwise. Millions continued to resent the 2000 election results, which, they believed, had defrauded the Democratic Party of a victory it had earned. Many Americans also disagreed bitterly with Bush's economic agenda, which they correctly saw as more radically conservative than anything Ronald Reagan had proposed; and they felt embattled by Bush's social agenda, with its commitment to the "culture of life," anti-choice ideology of evangelical fundamentalists. In a political environment still basically divided 50-50, Democrats faced the delicate dilemma of finding the right candidate and platform to take on a wartime commander-in-chief. Bush, in turn, faced the necessity of expanding his base from 2000 so that a successful re-election bid could have a legitimacy that his 2000 popular vote did not allow.

The choices facing the Democratic field of candidates were not easy. Notwithstanding the fact that Bush's tax cuts primarily benefited the super-rich and created a soaring national deficit, it was suicidal—as Walter Mondale had learned in 1984—to run a campaign urging tax increases. In addition, by the time potential Democratic candidates were preparing to take the field for the spring primaries in 2004, the war in Iraq had not yet disintegrated to the point it reached a year later, so how to position oneself in the ongoing controversy over Iraq posed a difficult problem, especially for members of a party most of whom had voted *for* Bush's war resolution in 2002. Finally, the Democratic Party faced its own long-standing division between centrists, à la Bill Clinton and the Democratic Leadership Coalition, who cleaved to mainstream social and economic programs, and more liberal critics who argued for a "new politics" that would reach out to minorities, the economically disenfranchised, and those who never voted because they felt they had no one to vote *for.*

The last group found a powerful champion in Vermont Governor Howard Dean. Although his record as governor had been more centrist than left, he vigorously denounced the mealy mouthed rhetoric of mainstream Democrats and offered himself as a vocal critic of the war in Iraq as well as a rallying point for all those who wished to throw out the old politics of compromise and bring in a new politics of principle. (In 2002, he displayed a characteristic boldness, telling a gay fundraising party on Fire Island in New York: "if Bill Clinton could be the first black president, I can be the first gay president.") Through brilliant staff work and an amazing proficiency with Internet fundraising and organizing, Dean soon leapt to a strong lead in the early contests in Iowa and New Hampshire. One of Dean's chief opponents was John Kerry, the aristocratic, Purple Heart Vietnam veteran who had galvanized the anti-Vietnam war movement when he came back from Southeast Asia and who had served three terms in the U.S. Senate from Massachusetts. Kerry was a mainstream liberal whose strongest suit was his military background, his "character" as one who had been willing to risk opprobrium in order to stand up for principle, and the degree to which he personified the Kennedy-like appeal of Democrats from the '60s and '70s. His primary weakness was the degree to which he had vacillated on Iraq, on alternative days supporting, then being critical of Bush's policy. The final major contender was John Edwards, a trial lawyer by training and a textile millhand's child by birth. Edwards embodied the rags-to-riches appeal of the American Dream. Although new to politics (he had been elected U.S. senator from North Carolina only five years earlier), Edwards soon earned the respect of his fellow senators. He distinguished himself during the Clinton impeachment hearings and quickly carved out a niche as the only Southerner in the race, with a populist message that resonated particularly well with minorities, workers, and the middle class. On message all the time, Edwards delivered the powerful sermon that there were now "two Americas," one whose citizens were wealthy and surrounded by privilege, the other whose citizens were hard-working, struggling, and trying to find a government that would deal with them fairly, enable their children to do better than they had, and restore the sense of "common wealth" that the party of Franklin Delano Roosevelt had stood for. It was a talented pool, though remarkable for its lack of experience in presidential politics.

Initially, it looked like Howard Dean had the nomination wrapped up, something that Karl Rove, Bush's political "guru," devoutly hoped for. What could be better from a Republican perspective than an opponent who, like George McGovern in 1972, was known for being a darling of the left and an acid critic of the center? It was always critical in the primaries for a candidate outside the mainstream to rally a new base and demonstrate credibility. Dean had done that, to the point that he earned the endorsement of former Vice-President Al Gore. But ironically, from that point forward Dean's campaign started to crumble. As his campaign manager Joe Trippi noted, "The guy is not ready for prime time. I mean he's just f__king not ready . . ." Dean had peaked too early. And like most "dissident" candidates, he faced the always delicate conundrum of appealing to his ideological base without alienating middle-of-the-roaders. For most of his campaign, Dean had walked that line brilliantly, but now he started to give speeches that seemed too far "left" and that caused stirrings of discontent in established party leaders. At the same time, Dean's front-runner status meant that all the other candidates ganged up on him, zeroing in on contradictions in his record and exploiting weaknesses in his past. Why did his wife never campaign with him, they asked. Meanwhile, John Kerry, whose campaign had been floundering amidst staff disorganization and a tendency to say something different every day—often on the same issue—finally took on direction, spark, and energy. Picking up some of the populist rhetoric of Edwards and the anti-war rhetoric of Dean, Kerry suddenly spurted to the front of the pack. Edwards, a tireless and brilliant campaigner, kept gaining ground with his "two Americas" campaign theme, but he never quite sprinted into the lead. The result was that Kerry surged to victories in both Iowa and New Hampshire, Edwards came in a strong second in both, and Dean essentially plummeted from first place to a distant third. It was an extraordinary drama, but with the exception of an impressive win by Edwards in South Carolina, the results defined the terrain the Democrats would occupy from that point forward. In July, in his native Boston, John Kerry was crowned the Democrat nominee, and the young, handsome, vibrant newcomer, John Edwards, was chosen as his running mate.

There then ensued a tough, sometimes bitter, often exhausting campaign, with polls never giving one candidate a lead of more than four or five points, and virtually every expert predicting a re-run of the excruciatingly close 2000 race. In his re-nomination convention—held in New York City—Bush effectively rang all the patriotic chimes, invoking 9/11 wherever possible, singing the praises of the heroes of both New York City's firefighters and America's infantry troops in Iraq, conflating wherever possible patriotism, fear of terrorism, and the war in Iraq. Powerful, moving, and infused with feelings of national pride, the Republican convention showed just how compelling Republican appeals to national solidarity could be. In his own convention, Kerry, too, had highlighted his record of military service; his shipmates from the swift boat he commanded in Vietnam praised his heroism and thanked him for risking his life to save theirs; and the convention placed a spotlight on his courage in protesting the Vietnam war—as now he was protesting the war in Iraq. But in any comparison of the two appeals to military power and patriotism, Kerry came up short, his message less clean and focused than Bush's, more open to misinterpretation or contention, as soon would become obvious.

Nevertheless, Kerry entered the campaign with significant advantages. The economy was in the doldrums. Thousands of workers had lost their jobs, many of them to foreign countries because manufacturers and high-tech companies had "outsourced" their businesses to India, Thailand, and China. With some justification, Democrats blamed the Bush administration for creating this employment "drain" through its tax and trade policies.

Whereas the Clinton years had produced 22 million new jobs, the first Bush term generated fewer than 3 million. Moreover, the fact that many of these new jobs were in the service sector, paying the minimum wage or barely above, made Bush vulnerable to the charge that millions of Americans were worse off than just four years earlier. Average incomes were either stable or going down; high-paying and high-skilled jobs were leaving; and there seemed no viable plan for recovery. The ongoing crisis in health care was also a "Democratic" issue. More than 40 million families lacked any form of health insurance, with medical costs outpacing every other sector of the economy in their inflationary spiral. Finally, there was a growing sense of disenchantment with the war in Iraq. As casualty figures rose, and the insurgency in Iraq gained strength, there seemed less and less reason to be sanguine about where the country was going and why it was going there.

Significantly, all these issues were most pivotal in large states like Ohio, Pennsylvania, New Jersey, and Illinois. Ohio, in particular, looked more and more like the bellwether state that would determine the election. Proportionately, it had lost more industrial jobs than any other. A representative amalgam of urban and rural populations, different racial and religious groups, and Southerners as well as Northerners, the state also seemed to crystallize the tensions dividing the nation as a whole. Of these, none was more important than the cultural battle between the New Right—embodied primarily in the religious tenets of evangelical fundamentalists who bitterly opposed gay rights, same-sex marriage, and abortion—and the liberal tolerance associated with Supreme Court decisions on *Roe* vs. *Wade*, government prohibition of discrimination against gays, and ardent support for gender and racial equality.

It was in this context that Kerry made his most critical mistake. Instead of zeroing in on the economic issues—putting a magnifying glass on his running mate John Edwards' discussion of "two Americas," one middle income and getting poorer, the other rich and getting more privileged—Kerry chose to take on the president on Bush's strongest turf, the Iraq war itself. However contentious the war in Iraq was becoming, it still did not constitute the central dividing issue that the war in Vietnam had become in 1968. In that context, no political strategy was more difficult than that of attacking the commander-in-chief in the midst of an ongoing military conflict. One could be accused of undermining the troops, of betraying the flag, of aiding and abetting the enemy. It might have been possible to critique the war and its rationale—even then wide open to debate—if one's *primary* focus was on leadership in general, and in particular on the failure to preserve and protect the economy and the society's well-being. But Kerry did not go that route. Instead, he chose to take the case of Iraq aggressively to the president.

In the meantime, Kerry's own military credentials came under attack. A group of Vietnam veterans unleashed a series of TV spots called the "Swift Boat" ads that essentially called Kerry a coward who had lied about his service in Vietnam. The advertisements were scurrilous, lacked substance, and represented a new low in political mudslinging. But they undercut Kerry's effort to make military leadership, and Bush's conduct of the war, the central issue of the campaign. For too long, Kerry let the ads go unanswered; and when he did respond, it was too late to minimize their impact. Instead, the focus of attention became his own experience in Vietnam and his record of "waffling" on Iraq—at one point voting for the war, at another point voting against appropriations to support the war—rather than on Bush's failures in Iraq. Had Kerry made jobs and the Clinton record versus the Bush record on the economy his primary line of attack, the attention of voters might have focused on issues where Bush was most vulnerable. As it was, the economy took second place, Bush was able to campaign on terrain most favorable to his national leadership role, and Kerry had given away his strongest weapon.

Still, as the campaign wore on, no one gained a decisive advantage. In state after state, the candidates waged toe-to-toe battle. New political organizations, from Move On on the liberal side to religiously based political action groups on the conservative side, generated massive get-out-the-vote campaigns, registering millions of voters for the first time. Never before had so many volunteers become involved in door-to-door canvassing; they hosted house parties, sponsored fundraising events, sought ways of galvanizing previously unengaged citizens into realizing that this was a pivotal election. Even though the candidates initially seemed boring and tedious— neither was known for captivating audiences with his rhetoric—people followed the campaign with intense preoccupation. The Internet reinforced this involvement. "Blogs" associated with different candidates or perspectives hyped the issues dividing people. Each day voters who were invested in one candidate or the other logged on to a liberal or conservative Web site to see the latest poll data and projections of how the electoral votes would divide between the "red" (Bush) states and the "blue" (Kerry) states.

Many observers believed that the televised debates between the candidates would be decisive. Both sides in fact were apprehensive about the strengths of their respective combatants. Kerry seemed unable to discipline his thought process and delivery, and Bush's syntax was infamous for its false starts; but given his performance against Gore in 2000, he was expected to be the person in charge. In fact the debates surprised everyone, and the first one in particular gave Kerry his first big break. Instead of wandering, Kerry was sharp, on target, and totally disciplined. He knew the points he wished to make, he made them concisely, and he demonstrated a masterful control of the facts and issues. Bush, by contrast, seemed out of his element, distracted, confused, without focus. Even on issues that should have been to his advantage, the president appeared unsure and indecisive. By everyone's assessment, including the instant polls taken immediately after the debate, Kerry had won and won big. And even though the next two debates were less one-sided, it was common wisdom that Kerry had won all three, both intellectually and politically.

As the election approached, the contest became tighter and tighter. Public opinion polls showed gaps of 51–49 or less, with successive days showing first Bush, then Kerry on top. By late October, it was clear that just a few states would hold the key—Florida, Ohio, New Jersey, Pennsylvania, Missouri, New Mexico, Michigan, and Wisconsin. Although multiple issues could conceivably shape the outcome, two questions seemed of particular importance: which party would be most successful in turning out its base, bringing to the polls the millions of new voters who had been registered by groups like Move On and the religious right; and which issue was most salient with the American people—fear of terrorism, successful prosecution of the war in Iraq, cultural issues like gay rights and abortion, or the weak state of the American economy? In either case, the turnout proved spectacular, rising to 59.4 percent, compared to 51.2 percent in 2000 (it had hovered around 50 percent since 1976).

Early returns filled Democrats with hope. Exit polls suggested that Kerry would sweep Florida, New Jersey, Pennsylvania, and Ohio. But as the evening wore on, those polls looked less and less viable. Although Kerry won Pennsylvania and New Jersey, it was by far less than the exit polls had suggested. Bush narrowly won Florida, but by a margin that would not invite the kind of challenge that had happened four years earlier. In the end, it all came down to Ohio, the state where political action groups had spent so many resources registering new voters. Back and forth the vote went, cities like Cleveland bringing in large Democratic majorities, southern Ohio doing the same for Republicans. By daybreak it was clear that Bush had won. The state that had lost the largest number of jobs and that also had a substantial number of troops in Iraq had decided to stick with the commander-in-chief.

Two reasons primarily explain Bush's re-election. First, to the dismay of political action groups on the left, voter mobilization by the New Right turned out to be even more effective than that of groups like Move On. More Democrats voted in 2004 than ever before, with registration figures reaching new heights. But the New Right did even better and proved more successful at turning out its voters. In post-election polls, large numbers of voters declared that "moral values" were central to their choice; columnists noted the degree to which New Right activists had made same-sex marriage, abortion, and cultural permissiveness their major reasons for supporting George W. Bush, and a referendum prohibiting same-sex marriage was on the Ohio ballot, pulling out conservative voters. (Prohibition of gay marriages appeared as a constitutional amendment in eleven states in 2004, winning in each state by margins ranging from 57 to 77 percent.) Whether or not "moral values" had won the election for George Bush, it seemed clear that the "vertical dimension" of politics—a focus on cultural and social values—had trumped the "horizontal dimension" on issues of economic status and jobs.

But that shift, which had been going on since 1968, reflected the second reason for Bush's election. John Kerry had failed to make jobs, eco-

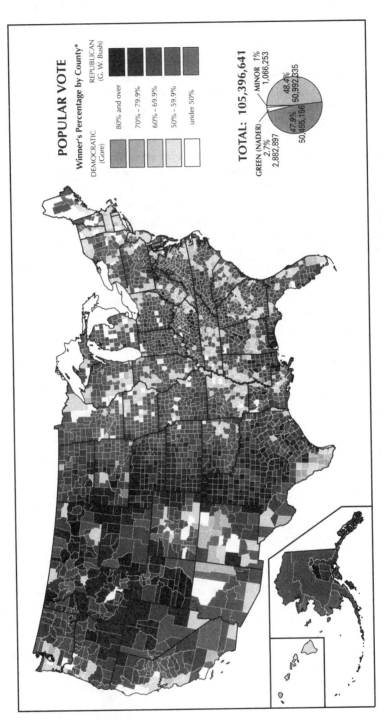

POPULAR VOTE

Winner's Percentage by County*

DEMOCRATIC (Gore)	REPUBLICAN (G. W. Bush)
80% and over	
70% – 79.9%	
60% – 69.9%	
50% – 59.9%	
under 50%	

TOTAL: 105,396,641

MINOR 1%
1,066,253

48.4%
50,992,335

47.9%
50,455,156

GREEN (NADER)
2.7%
2,882,897

This election map demonstrates the degree to which the country was divided into dark (Republican) and light (Democratic) zones. Note the extent to which Democratic strength was concentrated on the coastlines and large cities of the country. (*National Atlas of the United States, http://nationalatlas.gov*)

nomic growth, and health care the primary thrust of his campaign; instead he chose to engage Bush primarily on the president's responsibility for the war in Iraq. Yet in 2004, discontent about Bush's leadership was only beginning to crest—it had not yet reached flood stage. Had the campaign taken place a year later, Kerry might well have triumphed. But in 2004, Bush effectively conflated fear of terrorism with his decision to invade Iraq, and in that battle, Kerry did not have a chance. Fear of terrorism dwarfed all else, and Bush was the president who had brought the country through 9/11.

The Second Term

Yet as Bush entered his second term as president, that political equation ceased to work. Within weeks after his re-election, skepticism about his leadership grew. Already beginning to appear as the Iraqi insurgency grew in 2004, it now multiplied. Casualties continued to mount, the number of suicide bombers failed to diminish, and the prospect for political stability and reform in that distant country seemed bleak at best. Repeatedly, Bush administration officials had insisted that after the Iraqis created their own constitution—guaranteeing rights for women and ensuring an effective sharing of power among the Sunnis, Shiites, and Kurds—and trained a new army and police force to take responsibility for Iraqi security, Americans could withdraw their troops, having made a major stride forward for democracy in the Middle East.

Yet by the fall of 2005, the constitutional process had fallen apart. Sunnis abandoned participation, the draft written by Shiites and Kurds left women unprotected, and civil war seemed a real danger. Although Donald Rumsfeld talked about 150,000 Iraqis being trained to take responsibility for maintaining domestic peace, realistic estimates put the figure of trained soldiers at under 10,000. Other Arab countries showed little if any sympathy for the new Iraqi government. Nowhere in Baghdad was security a given, except perhaps in the Western fortified and totally shut-off "Green Zone," and the road to Baghdad airport was a gauntlet. Suicide bombers in Baghdad and elsewhere killed up to seventy-five people a day. Everything seemed to disintegrate. And as things got worse, the insurgency seemed to grow, almost as if the very presence of American troops in Iraq served as the major recruitment tool for Al Qaeda. In the end, said one writer in the *New York Times Magazine,* it seemed as if America had ended up fighting the very kind of war Al Qaeda wanted the United States to engage in—one that would mobilize support to Islamic fundamentalism, not erode that support. Just as the Soviet Union found itself surrounded by enemies each day it occupied Afghanistan in the 1980s, the United States now occupied the same dismal position with almost no way to reach across the divide of cultures and religions and roll back the tide of hostility.

Not surprisingly, Bush's standing at home suffered as his leadership abroad came into question. The president started his second term with a determination to build on the economic policies he had charted over his first four years. Most significantly, he made the centerpiece of his domestic program the privatization of Social Security. According to Bush, the maturation of the baby boomer generation would create a circumstance in the future when the Social Security trust fund would no longer be able to pay the benefits promised by the program. Hence, he proposed that taxpayers invest part of their Social Security payments into private funds, which, he presumed, would grow at a faster rate than government bonds. There were three problems with the Bush proposal. First, it assumed a degree of peril for Social Security that was far greater than most experts foresaw—certainly far greater than was true for even larger entitlement programs like Medicare; second, the cost of bridging the transition between the old system and a privatized system would be more than $2 trillion added to the national debt at a time when the debt was already soaring out of control; and third, privatization was more than an amendment to Social Security—it gutted the very heart of the oldest entitlement program in the nation and, if enacted, threatened to crumble the foundational legacy of the New Deal. Most Americans reacted negatively to the plan. Indeed, the more the president took his plan to the people and proselytized on its behalf, the greater the opposition became. Republicans in the Senate and House did not support the plan, fearing that they would be politically vulnerable were they to do so. Within a year of its being proposed, there seemed little if any support for the most radical proposal Bush had ever made.

Bush also proposed that the government eliminate entirely the estate tax, or the "death tax" as Republicans called it. Amounting to over $700 billion over a ten-year period, elimination of the estate tax would benefit primarily a few very wealthy families per year. Although some Democrats declared their willingness to modify the tax, raising the exemption level from $600,000 per person to $2–3 million, there appeared little enthusiasm to do away with the tax entirely, particularly given the very small number of rich people it would benefit and the degree to which the tax loss would accelerate the deficit. The same dilemma surfaced in response to Bush's proposal to make permanent a series of tax cuts that had passed during his first administration on the condition that they would expire in a few years. Once again, the issue was the lopsided distribution of benefits—toward the rich, away from the middle class—and the degree to which, budgetarily, making the tax cuts permanent endangered fiscal stability. What made all of this even more difficult was that Bush had gone to war, at the cost of more than $100 billion per year, but had never asked the American people to do a single thing to sacrifice for the cause. No taxes were raised, no fuel rationed, no bond drives mounted. It was as though one could fight a war on terrorism but no one had to pay—except the troops and National Guardsmen who were placing their lives at risk. Democrats protested the inequalities of the entire process, with working people doing most of the fighting and rich people getting most of the advantages of the tax breaks. But Republicans were upset as well, because Bush seemed to be on a fiscally irresponsible disaster course. The greater the national debt, the more the country placed itself under the ownership of foreign investors.

The event that crystallized all these concerns was the domestic equivalent of a terrorist attack—Hurricane Katrina. For days in early September 2005, meteorologists issued bulletins about the raging tropical storm that was heading first for lower Florida, then across the Florida Panhandle, and finally to the Gulf Coast of Mississippi, Louisiana, and Alabama. For years, federal emergency officials had talked about three potential doomsday events: a terrorist attack on a major U.S. city, an earthquake in Los Angeles, and a hurricane that would swamp New Orleans, break through the levees, and leave hundreds of thousands homeless. The terrorist attack had come; so had a major California earthquake (though not the one experts feared the most); and now every knowledgeable official in the nation warned that the ultimate hurricane was rushing toward New Orleans. So dramatic and dire were the warnings that New Orleans' mayor ordered a mandatory evacuation of the city. A category 5 hurricane, Katrina threatened Louisiana and Mississippi with winds of over 150 miles per hour and a flood surge twenty-eight feet above normal. The entire city of New Orleans was below sea level, and the levees protecting the city could cope with no more than a thirteen-foot storm surge.

When the storm hit, the damage at first seemed less than had been feared. But then the levees broke, flood waters covered the city, and disaster took over. "Problems cascaded and cascaded," *Newsweek* reported. Tens of thousands of New Orleans residents had no cars, had no way of obeying the mayor's mandatory evacuation order and exiting the city. Now, they either huddled together in their attics to escape the rising waters or crowded into the Convention Center downtown or the Superdome. Initially, food, water, and sanitation facilities were adequate. Then the food gave out, there was no more water, and the toilets overflowed. Bodies floated in the streets, the stench of urine and feces was suffocating, there was nowhere to go, and, worst of all, no one to provide help. The Federal Emergency Management Administration (FEMA) had been given full warning of what was to happen but sent only a few staff members to be onsite. No massive food supplies, no emergency water, no temporary toilet facilities were in place.

Above all, there were no federal officials to do what Mayor Giuliani and New York's firefighters and police had done in 9/11. Those FEMA officials who were on hand seemed more an obstacle than a help. Wal-Mart sent six trailer trucks full of drinking water to the city, and FEMA officials turned them away. The Coast Guard had thousands of gallons of fuel oil it was ready to deliver, and FEMA ordered them to take it back. When a local sheriff called FEMA for assistance, he was told to send an e-mail—this at a time when he had no electricity and his office was under water. Day after day after day, people waited to be rescued. One woman called her son each morning for five days in a row to ask when help would come, and each day her son told her help was on the way, someone would be there tomorrow. On the fifth day, when there was still no help, she died, drowning in the rising water. People watching the horrific scenes from around the world could not believe this was the famous New Orleans, jazz capital of the world, a place where celebration and culture existed in tandem. To them it looked like Mogadishu in Somalia or Darfur in the Sudan. An American jewel now seemed like a Third World slum.

The news media were astounded. Reporters from every major newspaper and network quickly told the world what was happening, with television cameras showing the grisly scenes of people perched on rooftops, bodies floating in the street, houses broken apart into a thousand pieces of kindling. And they could not understand why help had not come. *They* had reached the city. Why had the federal government not? Brian Williams, the NBC anchor who reached New Orleans on Saturday before the storm and stayed for five days, reported with outrage about "rescue workers overwhelmed, food and water scarce, people left behind, becoming more and more unglued. . . . Where is the help?" Paula Zahn, the CNN anchor, could barely contain her disbelief when she interviewed Michael Brown, the head of FEMA, about the thousands of New Orleans citizens packed into the Convention Center with no toilet facilities, inadequate food, and the stench of garbage all about—a scene broadcast for hours on national television—only to find that Brown knew nothing of their plight. "You mean you do not know about these people," she asked Brown, "when their pictures have been on television for twenty-four hours?" To which Brown responded weakly, government officials did not watch television. As the local head of emergency planning in New Orleans acidly noted, "It's like FEMA has never been to a hurricane."

But worst of all, the president of the United States seemed not to know. Despite the fact that every expert in government was predicting the worst, Bush declared that no one had anticipated the breaking of the levees; in fact *everyone* in government had anticipated exactly such an eventuality under such a storm surge. Bush stayed at his Texas ranch on vacation as the storm hit, then two days later boarded a plane to go to San Diego for a speech about Iraq—in the midst of the horrific pictures of what was happening in New Orleans. (Vice-President Cheney was on vacation in Wyoming and remained there.) Only on the fourth day after the hurricane did Bush take notice. Because the president neither watched television nor read newspapers (he boasted about getting his information only from government briefings), he had not seen what the rest of the country had seen, and now his staff put together a DVD of television coverage so he could witness how bad it was and had been. As *Newsweek* asked, "How could this be—how the president of the United States could have even less [awareness] . . . than the average American about the worst natural disaster in a century . . . [It is] a national disgrace." But even then, Bush did not go to New Orleans. He simply flew over the flooded areas on his way back to Washington. Only on Friday, nearly six days after the disaster, did Bush visit the Gulf area. Yet even then he met no victims, never went into New Orleans, made no direct contact with people who were sick and dying, as he had the rescue workers at Ground Zero after 9/11. Instead, he engaged in small talk, reminisced about his days partying in New Orleans, and talked about the fact that Trent Lott, the senator from Mississippi, had lost his home—but it "will be replaced by a fantastic house." "He didn't get it," one reporter observed. Indeed, the atmosphere at the White House was "strangely surreal and almost detached," one official who was there said. "Mr. Bush's performance last week," wrote one columnist, "will rank as one of the worst ever by a president during a dire national emergency . . . What we witnessed . . . was the dangerous incompetence and . . . indifference to human suffering of the president and his administration."

Finally, more than a week after Katrina hit, the president began to recognize the political explosion he had touched off. Bush acknowledged what Louisiana's Senator Mary Landrieu called the "staggering incompetence" of the federal response. Michael Brown, FEMA's head, was relieved of duty in Louisiana and two days later resigned. Bush further announced that he was personally responsible for the failure of the government to respond efficiently and with speed. The president journeyed to the Gulf area twice in the next week, mobilized Bill Clinton and his father, George H. W. Bush, to lead a national fundraising campaign, and—belatedly—tried to make right what had gone so wrong. But he could only begin to come to grips with the enormity of what Katrina revealed. It was not just the dimensions of the hurricane tragedy itself, but rather what the government's response highlighted about the fault lines in the entire Bush presidency, and the country as a whole.

First, Katrina had laid bare the schisms of race and class that continued to define America. No one watching television pictures of the destruction in New Orleans could *not* be aware that virtually all the people crowded into the Convention Center and the Superdome were black—black and poor. "It takes a catastrophe like Katrina," Jonathan Alter wrote in *Newsweek*, "to strip away the old evasions, hypocrisies, and not-so-benign neglect." Black people could not escape because only 35 percent had cars. They could not escape because they were the poorest of the poor. New Orleans itself had a 28 percent poverty rate—double the national average—but 85 percent of the poor people in New Orleans were black. They could not escape because they were crowded into Ward Nine, the warehouse district, the farthest below sea level, the poorest, the least served by public transport. As Illinois Senator Barack Obama declared, "the people of New Orleans weren't just abandoned during the hurricane. They were abandoned long ago—to murder and mayhem in the streets, to substandard schools, to dilapidated housing, to inadequate health care, to a pervasive sense of hopelessness."

Also highlighted was the degree to which New Orleans simply exemplified problems besetting the rest of the country. America's poverty rate was twice as high as that of any other industrialized society. Nationwide, only 8 percent of whites were poor. In contrast, 25 percent of blacks were poor. Racial stereotyping persisted. Whites who were photographed with food bags in the flood waters of New Orleans were described as "carrying" food. Blacks in the same circumstance were called "looters." Nationwide, half of all black and Latino teenagers never graduated from high school. Only 15 percent of low-income fourth-graders achieved proficiency in reading, with the average low-income fourth-grader reading three grade levels behind non-poor students. In the meantime, maldistribution of income accelerated. In 1965, the chief executives of America made 24 times as much as the average worker in their companies. By 2003, CEOs made 185 times as much. It was not a pretty picture.

More to the point was how much the Bush administration could be blamed. Poverty had gotten worse since Bush took office, up more than a million people in 2003 alone. Almost 3 million manufacturing jobs had left the country since 2001. Some of the gains made in the '90s had been rolled back. The Clinton administration's support for "scatter-site" housing—helping the poor get homes in middle-class neighborhoods, which particularly helped young people—was cancelled. So, too, was the Youth Opportunity Grant program focused on partnering with the private sector to help disadvantaged teenagers. And the Bush administration had tried to cut by 40 percent after-school programs, which had been almost universally praised for helping poorer families. Then there were the tax cuts, with the glaring discrepancy between those who walked away wealthier than ever and those who received little or nothing.

In the eyes of many, the lessons of New Orleans had a significance that went far beyond a tropical storm in one particular city. David Brooks, the conservative columnist, wrote about New Orleans: "the rich escaped while the poor were abandoned. Leaders spun while looters rampaged. Partisans squabbled while the nation was ashamed. . . . Leaving the poor in New Orleans was the moral equivalent of leaving the injured on the battlefield." But he then went on to make an even larger point. "This is a huge cultural moment," Brooks wrote. "Confidence in civic institutions is plummeting . . . [The] national humiliation [of New Orleans] comes at the end of a string of confidence-shaking institutional failures that have cumulatively changed the nation's psyche."

As Brooks and others assayed what had taken place with Katrina, it was more than simply a tragedy within a vacuum. Instead, it reflected a systematic disintegration of institutional confidence—in the country, its leadership, its policies, its direction. Brooks cited the linkage between the massive failures of leadership in Katrina and the intelligence failures in Iraq, "incompetent postwar planning," Wall Street corruption, the prison abuses at Abu Ghraib (where Americans tortured Iraqi prisoners), the seemingly endless insurrection in Baghdad, and the countless suicide bombings. "Each institutional failure and sign of helplessness," he wrote, "is another blow to national morale." Some might see no connection, but for Brooks—and many others—this was a seamless portrait, and one that did not bode well. "The scrapbook of history accords but a few pages to each decade, and it is already clear that the pages devoted to this one will be grisly. There will be pictures of bodies falling from the twin towers, beheaded kidnapping victims in Iraq and corpses still floating in the waterways of New Orleans five days after the disaster that caused them."

So, in the end, the real question was whether any connection existed between the cataclysm of 9/11, on the one hand, and the carnage of Katrina, on the other, and how the Bush administration handled both. In part the answer had to do with style and management. Columnist Paul Krugman perceived a profound connection, observing that "at a fundamental level, our current leaders just aren't serious about some of the essential functions of government. They like waging war, but they don't like providing security, rescuing those in need, or spending on preventive measures. And they never, ever ask for shared sacrifice." From Krugman's perspective at least, the key linkage was the absence of long-range planning, with a readiness to provide the resources necessary to carry out policies once decided. Not only did government bear the responsibility for ensuring that its decisions were well-informed; but also it carried the burden of implementing those decisions through effective fiscal and tax policy, a responsive bureaucracy, and a commitment to serve all the people with equal attention.

In that context, it appeared that there was a connection. "If 9/11 is one book-end of the Bush administration," Thomas Friedman wrote, "Katrina may be the other." Bush and Cheney had initially seemed the right people to handle Osama. But it was not clear that they had carried through on that promise, and the hurricane had helped highlight why they "seem exactly the wrong guys to deal with Katrina—and all the rot and misplaced priorities it's exposed here at home." In fact, Friedman noted, "besides ripping away the roofs of New Orleans, Katrina ripped away the argument that we can cut taxes, properly educate our kids, compete with India and China, succeed in Iraq . . . and take care of a catastrophic emergency—without putting ourselves in the debt of Beijing."

In the end, therefore, many believed that a linkage did exist between a rising insurrection in Iraq and the incompetence with which the government responded to Katrina. The failure to investigate carefully the intelligence used to justify the war, the decision not to pursue Osama bin Laden as a first priority, the reluctance to provide the troop strength necessary for success in Iraq, the absence of intelligent post-invasion planning, and the refusal to provide financial resources sufficient to meet both domestic and foreign challenges—all these seemed connected to the failure to plan adequately for economic growth, health-care reform, a reduction in poverty, and efficient emergency management. Drastic tax cuts did not comport with waging war. "Shock and awe" did not necessarily guarantee an infrastructure to ensure stability and peace.

Thus, for many Americans, there appeared a direct connection between what was going wrong in Baghdad and what was going wrong in New Orleans. By the early fall of 2005, Bush's approval rating had fallen below 40 percent, and his disapproval rating had risen above 50 percent. Significantly, the figures were virtually the same for confidence (or lack of confidence) in Bush's handling of Iraq and his handling of domestic emergencies like Katrina. By the fall of 2005, 52 percent of all Americans endorsed an immediate withdrawal from Iraq, 60 percent disapproved of Bush's handling of the war, and only 44 percent believed that the United States had made the right decision in taking military action against Iraq. (As one index of the racial divide, only 10 percent of black Americans—versus 50 percent of whites—were "proud" of what the United States had done in Iraq.) Bush's troubles seemed to compound when he had to withdraw the nomination of his longtime associate Harriet Miers to be a Supreme Court justice (senators questioned *her* competence) and when Vice-President Cheney's chief aide, Lewis Libby, was indicted for allegedly lying before a grand jury about his involvement in disclosing the identity of CIA agent Valerie Plame, wife of a major critic of Bush's Iraq policy. If it turned out that Thomas Friedman was correct—that 9/11 and Katrina were the two bookends of the Bush administration—the likelihood that historians would view the Bush presidency in a positive light seemed minimal.

Reflections

As the first presidency of the new millennium drew to a close, the country seemed as divided and troubled as at any time since the presidency of Ronald Reagan ended. The underlying problems of inequality—whether defined in racial, gender, or economic terms—appeared worse rather than better. American school children ranked twenty-fourth out of twenty-nine advanced nations in math literacy. More and more high-tech jobs were flying to India and China. When American customers phoned an 800 number for assistance with a reservation or a computer problem, it was as likely that the call would be answered in Bhopal as in Bangor. Income disparities dramatically expanded, providing further corroboration of John Edwards' claim that the United States was becoming "two Americas." In the meantime, public policy seemed unprepared to deal with the complexities and urgent crises of the new world. FEMA had deteriorated dramatically from the '90s under Clinton, when experts were in charge. The first FEMA director under Bush had been a college buddy, the second a friend whose past experience was primarily in running international horse shows. Most of the talented bureaucrats left, as had happened to other agencies such as the Federal Drug Administration and the Environmental Protection Agency, where political appointees ruled the roost. By the fall of 2005, *Time* magazine was headlining the degree to which the issue of "cronyism" had become a signature of Bush administration staffing decisions.

George W. Bush had started out with something few recent presidents had demonstrated—a clear vision and a steely determination to bring that vision to fruition. In his determination to slash taxes, roll back environmental regulations, and privatize Social Security, Bush was, literally, the most radical president to hold office in a hundred years—"radical" being defined as someone who seeks to change dramatically the status quo. Similarly, in his insistence on forging a foreign policy in which the United States would call the shots and pursue its policies unilaterally if necessary, Bush turned his back on fifty-five years of precedent in foreign policy in which collective security and partnership with allies provided the hallmark of America's leadership.

In crafting this vision, Bush displayed a self-assurance and a single-mindedness that also were different from those of prior presidents. He had not always been so purposive. For two decades after college, Bush was a "party boy." By his own admission, he drank too much and played too hard. His record as a business executive was at best mixed, at worst a story of repeated failures. Then he had what he himself called an epiphany. His wife, Laura, insisted he stop drinking; he joined a Bible study group; and he experienced a religious conversion, becoming a "born again" Christian. The result was an individual with a new sense of direction, poise, and self-certainty, all reflected in how Bush conducted his presidency.

On the negative side, Bush's new "core" self perceived the world in Manichean terms—everything was either "good" or "evil." An analysis of Bush's speeches after 9/11 would show that he used the word "evil" or "evil-doers" more often than any other. Bush's worldview provided little room for nuance or complexity. He settled on a course of action, made sure that it was consistent with his religious convictions, and pursued it with single-minded intensity. Hence, it was not surprising that Bush, as early as 9/11, and in all likelihood before that date, had made up his mind to "get Saddam." The evidence did not have to be overwhelming, just usable. And if he did not exactly have the "fever" about Iraq that Colin Powell attributed to Dick Cheney, his fixed focus on Saddam (and Iraq) came close. The problem was that having single-minded vision could easily become indistinguishable from wearing blinders, and like a horse with no peripheral vision, lead to a failure to see alternative arguments and evidence or different roads to pursue.

On the positive side, such a sense of direction made it easy to make choices and, after having made them, to persist in achieving success, regardless of the opposition. One of Bush's greatest strengths was the resolve he brought to the post-9/11 world. He knew what he needed to do and where he wanted to go; that intensity of vision, in turn, communicated itself to allies and the American people alike. On the one hand, it inspired them to follow his direction; on the other hand, it discouraged them from proposing alternative courses of action because it seemed impossible that Bush would listen. Thus arose the contentiousness between Western allies (like France and Germany) and Bush over whether to invade Iraq without U.N. sanction and the poisoned relations between Colin Powell and Bush's favored associates like Cheney and Rumsfeld over the importance (or "evil") of listening to other nations and pursuing multilateral coalitions. Still, Bush's forte was his ability to pursue his own tack, giving little heed to the arguments of those who disagreed with him. His strength as a leader derived from this self-certainty, enabling him to carry the day on issues as diverse as drastic tax cuts to how America should wage the war on terror.

In the end, the one thing that was clear was that Bush's character proved to be both his greatest strength and his most severe weakness. On the one hand, if the government's policies in Iraq led to stability and the spread of democracy to the entire Middle East, especially to peace in Israel and Palestine, Bush's single-mindedness would deserve a large part of the credit. On the other hand, if the Iraqi insurgency persisted, civil war erupted, and America found itself having to withdraw its forces; and if it turned out there were never enough troops to start with, and Iraq represented an inappropriate target in the war on terrorism, then the same single-mindedness and Manichean worldview would constitute the primary source of blame. As the Bush administration came to an end, the one thing that seemed most clear was that profound divisions in the American polity were likely to persist and that the lessons provided both by the events in Iraq after Bush's "Mission Accomplished" speech and by Katrina would have to be carefully learned if any successor hoped to overcome those divisions and restore a sense of "common wealth" to the nation as a whole.

Epilogue

Roads Taken—
And Not Taken

In looking back, we inevitably try to find patterns and meaning in our experience. What has all this history meant? Where have we been during the past two-thirds of a century? And, just as important, where are we going?

So much has happened that the task of making sense of it all seems daunting. First, there is the depth and breadth of the change that has occurred in America since World War II. Suburban homes, VCRs and DVDs, shopping malls, the Internet, personal computers, television shows with women lawyers and black doctors, automobiles getting 30 miles to a gallon—how incredible this would seem for anyone whose last look at America was in 1940.

Events in the world outside the United States have been no less mind-boggling. American military bases around the globe, space shuttles and moon walks, star wars technology and laser-guided missiles, counterinsurgency, terrorism, the Cold War—what extraordinary developments. In 1940 the average American taxpayer spent $75 (in constant dollars) for national defense. Today, the figure is nearly $1,000. Could anyone five decades ago have foreseen such change? Or even more astonishing, could anyone in 1984 have anticipated that the Cold War would end, the Iron Curtain fall, a Russian leader be seen as our ally, and the United States' worst enemy become a terrorist named Osama bin Laden?

In a very real sense, this period has witnessed more progress and achievement than any comparable era in American history. During the past 50 years average incomes have increased by more than 100 percent. Home ownership has grown by half. Ancient barriers of discrimination have toppled. Black Americans have succeeded in eliminating virtually all rules and regulations that in the past denied them equality before the law. A majority of the population—women—have seen the content of their daily lives profoundly altered as well. Now, not only does the average woman participate in a variety of social and economic roles; she also views her "public" responsibilities and activities as a primary source of self-gratification and fulfillment. For millions of Americans, higher education has become the norm rather than the exception. In 1950, 15 percent of young people went to college. Today, more than three times that number do so. For whole segments of the population, therefore, opportunities are available today that would have been unthinkable just a few decades ago. And despite (or because of?)

the terror of mutual assured destruction, there has been no worldwide conflagration. The world has *survived* almost six decades of the nuclear age.

But what of the roads not taken? Or those that still remain to be explored? Choices are the essence of history, and while different historians will emphasize different turning points, it is important to think about those moments of decision and about the possibilities not pursued as well as about those that were followed.

There have been countless such "moments of possibility" or turning points in America since 1940, but five in particular stand out, especially in light of the conceptual framework offered in these pages about America's unfinished journey. The first came in the immediate aftermath of World War II. At that time, women war workers hoped to build and expand upon the gains they had made during the war; black Americans sought to sustain the momentum toward achieving democracy at home that had developed during their "double-V" campaign; and CIO unions worked to create a political and economic base for industrial and social democracy. Success in any of these ventures would have required a combination of political leadership from above, tacit approval of a broad segment of average citizens, and active organization by those groups most immediately involved.

In the end these elements failed to coalesce. Women were not sufficiently organized politically or ideologically to define or seek action on their agenda; civil rights groups worked effectively, but with inadequate support from Washington; and labor groups split apart over internal political tensions and which issues to pursue most vigorously in negotiations with management. Casting a pall over all efforts at social activism was the politics of anticommunism that emerged in tandem with the Cold War and that made suspect any social message that conveyed criticism of American institutions and values. In light of this new Red Scare, and the active engagement of millions of Americans in the pursuit of postwar prosperity, the possibility of concerted action in pursuit of greater social and economic equality faded away.

A second moment of possibility occurred in 1963–64, during the last few months of John Kennedy's presidency and the first year of Lyndon Johnson's. The civil rights movement had compelled the American people—and especially the American president—to face directly the country's legacy of racism. The movement's energy also focused renewed attention on issues of economic inequality and poverty. In the aftermath of the Cuban Missile Crisis, and with a sharpened sense both of human frailty and the chance for new leadership, John Kennedy embraced the objectives of racial equality, initiated planning for a war on poverty, and systematically questioned many of his own most deeply rooted assumptions about the Cold War. Speaking of Russia and the United States, Kennedy declared: "We are both caught up in a vicious and dangerous cycle, in which suspicion on one side breeds suspicion on the other." Such a situation had to end, Kennedy concluded, "for in the final analysis our most basic common link is that we all inhabit the same planet. We all cherish our children's future." On that basis, Kennedy campaigned for world peace and initialed the nuclear test ban treaty of 1963, even as he lobbied intensively with Congress for support of his civil rights legislation and prepared to submit his antipoverty program.

When Lyndon Johnson took office after Kennedy's assassination, he endorsed with passion the quest for greater racial and economic equality, using his extraordinary legislative skill to secure a statutory framework for achieving social justice in America. But simultaneously, he expanded massively America's involvement in Vietnam, believing that he had no other choice given Kennedy's commitment of troops there and the nation's dedication to containing "communism." In implementing his policy, Johnson refused to tell the American people the truth, expended resources on a hopeless war that should have gone toward accomplishing his domestic objectives, and ultimately destroyed not only his presidency but also the opportunity to achieve more equality at home than had occurred at any other time in the twentieth century.

A third moment of possibility came in 1968. Largely a product of the polarization that followed Johnson's Vietnam war policies, it provided the most clear-cut and dramatic moment of choice during the entire postwar era. Once again, as on the other two occasions, foreign and domestic issues were totally intertwined. At home, social activists pressed for changes that entailed far more than the simple reform of existing institutions. Together with antiwar and student protestors, supporters of Black Power and women's liberation seemed to be demanding a change in the basic structure, direction, and values of the society, calling into question the extent to which it was possible to achieve *real* equal opportunity and peace within the existing social and economic system. In response, those who cherished traditional values rushed to defend *their* America from assault. There were two individuals whose talent and vision might have offered a basis for achieving some of the goals of social activists within the established framework of American society. The assassinations of Martin Luther King, Jr., and Robert F. Kennedy devastated those who hoped for peaceful change and helped to create the circumstances that led to the revitalization and triumph of conservatism.

A fourth turning point occurred at the end of the 1980s and the beginning of the 1990s. The end of the Cold War and the disintegration of the Soviet empire produced a sea change in world politics, utterly inconceivable even a half decade earlier. The results were stunning—vibrant new economies in Prague and Budapest, thriving political debates in Warsaw over how to reconcile private enterprise and social democracy. Other consequences were more depressing—ethnic cleansing and virtual genocide in Bosnia, despair and disintegration throughout the Balkans. Yet for the first time in decades, the United Nations had the opportunity to fulfill its original mission as a vehicle for collective security and peacekeeping, this time with Russia and the United States working in concert—as in the Persian

Gulf War—rather than in opposition. Perhaps most importantly, the changes that had occurred had emerged largely as a result of people acting together, taking control of their own lives in the name of freedom and self-determination, just as countless black Americans, women, Latinos, and gays had asserted control over their lives during the preceding decades in the United States. Thus in the midst of tension and crisis, there was also in the mid-1990s a sense of possibility in the world that had not been present, in so many places, or with such intensity, for almost half a century.

In the United States that same sense of possibility blossomed as well, only to wilt in the debacles surrounding Bill Clinton's "character." For decades, the country had functioned within a political framework shaped by the Cold War and the passionate anticommunism that used the Kremlin as its primary foil. Not only did the Cold War define America's stance in the world, from Southeast Asia to Latin America; it defined the contours of domestic politics as well. Discussion of issues such as national health insurance or day care centers inevitably became contaminated by allegations that the United States was moving toward socialized medicine or the antifamily practices of Soviet collectives. In the early 1990s, for the first time in almost five decades, questions of health care and family leave policies could become important topics of debate. A new freedom existed within which to discuss the appropriate size of government, the meaning of entitlements, the definition of a welfare "safety net," and the best course to pursue in trying to bring the multiple ethnic groups that constituted America into some form of common union. Yet the potential for resolving such questions never came to fruition during the presidency of Bill Clinton, with partisan recriminations over personality and morality taking the place of enlightened public policy debate.

September 11, 2001, brought such partisan recriminations to an end, at least for a moment. This fifth turning point—the assault of worldwide terrorism against the Twin Towers, symbols of American hegemony and capitalist values—placed in perspective all the pettiness of the political battles of the 1990s, even as it ushered in a new awareness of how complicated, dangerous, and culturally divided the global village of the twenty-first century had become. How was it possible to understand a family in Palestine who viewed a suicide bombing mission by their child in downtown Jerusalem as justifiable martyrdom? What were the links between worldwide poverty and a rising tide of hatred against America? Why were the divisions among the world's religions suddenly more salient than the common beliefs in a moral and just God that previously had brought people of different faiths together? And how could America respond, providing protection for its citizens and other citizens of the world without sacrificing fundamental freedoms or the ongoing quest for greater social and economic justice at home? How to strike the balance between weapons and educational opportunities, between "homeland security" and the security at home that comes from decent jobs and health care?

As a result of this fifth turning point, the nation entered a new century and a new millennium facing challenges even greater and more unprecedented than those of any of the prior six decades. So much positive change had occurred—the material progress of prosperity, victories against discrimination, new instruments of technology, education, and creativity. Yet so much remained to be done, not only in an America where homelessness, poverty, and discrimination persisted, but also in the larger world where divisions based on class, ethnicity, gender, and religious identity threatened perpetual warfare and violence. In effect, the country—and the world—faced a new day needing to define a framework of communal vision and shared responsibility adequate to guide governments, religious groups, and political organizations to a place where the goal of a "beloved community," once identified with the civil rights movement in America, could become a goal uniting peoples around the world.

At times we may be tempted to think that we have no control over our history, that everything is determined, that our will and choices are irrelevant. But in such moments, it is well to remember what has happened even in this last half century. The four freshmen who entered the Woolworth's in Greensboro in 1960 had no idea that by week's end they would be joined by 1,000 others, or that within two months similar demonstrations would occur in 54 other cities. Casey Hayden and Mary King did not know, when they wrote their memorandum insisting that women no longer be treated as sex objects, that they would help to transform the thoughts of a generation. And Lech Walesa could not conceive, when he and other workers at the Lenin Shipyards in Gdansk went on strike in 1980, that they would set in motion a movement destined to shatter the tyranny of Stalinism and eventually bring down the Soviet empire. Yet each of these people acted because they believed they had to—*in* history, in order to *make* history.

Speaking to the spirit that animated all of these actors in our time, Robert Kennedy said in South Africa:

> Few will have the greatness to bend history itself; but each of us can work to change a small portion of events, and in the total of all those acts will be written the history of this [next] generation.

It was a message that would be renewed with each act on behalf of human dignity and self-determination.

BIBLIOGRAPHICAL ESSAY

In recent years the literature on America since World War II has increased significantly. Among the best overviews of the period are Richard Polenberg's *One Nation Divisible* (1980), which emphasizes class and ethnic differences; William E. Leuchtenburg's *A Troubled Feast* (1982), which focuses on the emergence of a consumer culture and the travails of liberalism; Lawrence Wittner's *Cold War America* (1979), which offers a new-left critique of corporate hegemony in modern America; Godfrey Hodgson's *America in Our Time* (1976), a provocative assessment of the achievements and limitations of what Hodgson calls the "liberal consensus" in America; John Blum's *Years of Discord: American Politics and Society, 1961–1974* (1991); John Diggins' *The Proud Decades: America in War and Peace, 1941–1960* (1988); and Martin Jezer's *The Dark Ages* (1982). Other books that survey the postwar years include James T. Patterson's recent Bancroft prize–winning narrative *Grand Expectations: The United States, 1945–1974* (1996), Frederick F. Siegel's *A Troubled Journey: From Pearl Harbor to Reagan* (1984); Emily Rosenberg and Norman Rosenberg's *In Our Time* (1982); Alonzo Hamby's *The Imperial Years* (1976); Carl Degler's *Affluence and Anxiety* (1975); Howard Zinn's *Post-War America, 1945–1971* (1973); and Eric Goldman's *The Crucial Decade and After* (1961). Numan V. Bartley's *A History of the South, Volume II: The New South, 1945–1980* (1995) is an excellent overview of the postwar years for the South. See also James T. Patterson, *Restless Giant* (2005).

The nation's domestic experience during World War II has been the subject of several books. The best general volumes on the war are John M. Blum, *V Was for Victory: Politics and American Culture during World War II* (1976); and Richard Polenberg, *War and Society* (1972). James M. Burns examines the life of the president in *Roosevelt: The Soldier of Freedom* (1970). More recent is William O'Neill, *A Democracy at War: America's Fight at Home and Abroad in World War II* (1993). American culture during the war is examined by Lewis A. Erenberg and Susan E. Hirsch, *The War in American Culture: Society and Consciousness during World War II* (1996) and George H. Roeder, *The Censored War: American Visual Experience during World War II* (1993). Allan Winkler's *The Politics of Propaganda* (1978) deals with the Office of War Information and the overall propaganda effort. John Dower's *War without Mercy: Race and Power in the Pacific War* (1986) explores American and Japanese racial propaganda in the Pacific theater and its impact on both societies. On the specific issue of war bonds, see Robert K. Merton, *Mass Persuasion: The Social Psychology of a War Bond Drive*

(1946). The impact of the war on class and income is assessed in numerous volumes, including Gabriel Kolko, *Wealth and Power in America* (1962); Robert J. Lampman, *The Share of Top Wealthholders in National Wealth, 1922–56* (1956); and Simon Kuznets, *Shares of Income Groups in Income and Savings* (1955); On labor, see Nelson Lichtenstein, *Labor's War at Home* (1983); and Matthew Josephson, *Sidney Hillman* (1952). The general issue of mobilization is treated in George Flynn, *The Mess in Washington: Manpower and Mobilization and World War II* (1979). On the Communist Party during World War II, see Maurice Isserman, *Which Side Were You On* (1982). Neal R. McMillen, ed., *Remaking Dixie: The Impact of World War II on the American South* (1997), focuses specifically on the war's impact on the South, with a particular emphasis on women and African Americans. The impact of World War II on the American West is discussed by Gerald D. Nash, *The American West Transformed: The Impact of the Second World War* (1985).

Women's experiences during World War II have been the subject of a number of books. D'Ann Campbell's *Women at War with America: Private Lives in a Patriotic Era* (1984) looks at poll data as a measure of women's reactions to the war. Karen Anderson's *Wartime Women* (1981) charts the changes that occurred during the war and concludes that continued discrimination constituted the greatest legacy of the war years. Susan Hartman, *The Homefront and Beyond* (1980), looks at the entire decade of the forties. Maureen Honey, *Creating Rosie the Riveter* (1984), assesses class differentials in the propaganda campaigns aimed at women. William H. Chafe, *The Paradox of Change: American Women in the Twentieth Century* (1992), sees the war as a partial breakthrough for women, albeit in a context of continued inequality and discrimination. Also see Alan Bérubé, *Coming Out Under Fire: The History of Gay Men and Women in WWII* (1990).

The black experience has also received significant attention in recent years. Gunnar Myrdal's *An American Dilemma* (1944) is a classic sociological work on the status of black Americans at the time of the war. On Myrdal and American race relations, see Walter Jackson, *Gunnar Myrdal and America's Conscience: Social Engineering and Racial Liberalism, 1938–1987* (1990). The condition of blacks during the 1930s, especially in the South, is dealt with in John Dollard, *Caste and Class in a Southern Town* (1937); Hortense Powdermaker, *After Freedom* (1939); Raymond Wolters, *Negroes and the Great Depression* (1970); and Harvard Sitkoff, *A New Deal for Blacks* (1979). Nancy Weiss, *Farewell to the Party of Lincoln: Black Politics in the Age of FDR* (1983), argues that blacks voted for FDR in support of their economic interests despite the shortcomings of the New Deal's racial policies. Different aspects of the wartime experience are covered in Richard Dalfiume, *Desegregation of the United States Armed Forces 1939–1953* (1969); Neil Wynn, the *Afro-American and the Second World War* (1976); Lee Finkle, *Forum for Protest: The Black Press during World War II* (1975); and Louis Ruchames, *Race, Jobs, Politics: The Story of FEPC* (1948). Racial violence during the war is discussed in Robert Shogan and Tom Craig's *Detroit Race Riot* (1964) and Dominic J. Capeci, Jr.'s *The Harlem Riot of 1943* (1977). Jervis Anderson offers a detailed description of one of the primary leaders of the civil rights movement during the war in *A. Philip Randolph: A Biographical Portrait* (1973). On the war and postwar black migration to Chicago, see Nicholas Lemann, *The Promised Land: The Great Black Migration and How It Changed America* (1991). The Native American experience during the war is explored by Alison Bernstein, *American Indians and World War II: Toward a New Era in Indian Affairs* (1991). On Hispanics, see George Sanchez, *Becoming Mexican American: Ethnicity, Culture and Identity in Chicano Los Angeles, 1900–1945* (1993); and David G. Gutiérrez, *Walls and Mirrors: Mexican Americans, Mexican Immigrants, and the Politics of Ethnicity* (1995).

The best treatments of America's response to the Holocaust are David Wyman, *The Abandonment of the Jews: America and the Holocaust, 1941–1945* (1984); and Leonard Dinnerstein, *America and the Survivors of the Holocaust* (1982). Other studies of the same subject include Henry Feingold, *Politics of Rescue* (1970); Saul Friedman, *No Haven for the Oppressed* (1973); and Wyman's earlier work, *Paperwalls* (1968). Treatment of Japanese Americans is discussed in Peter Irons, *Justice at War: The Story of the Japanese American Internment Cases* (1982); and Roger Daniels, *Concentration Camp U.S.A.: Japanese Americans in World War II* (1971).

Few issues have received more sustained attention than the emergence of the Cold War. The best general surveys include John L. Gaddis, *The United States and the Origins of the Cold War, 1941–1947* (1972); Walter LaFeber, *America, Russia, and the Cold War, 1945–1996*, 9th ed. (2002); Daniel Yergin, *A Shattered Peace: The Origins of the Cold War and the National Security State* (1977); Stephen Ambrose and Douglas Brinkley, *Rise to Globalism: American Foreign Policy Since 1938*, 8th rev. ed. (1997); and Thomas Paterson, *On Every Front: The Making and Unmaking of the Cold War* (1992). Other books on the Cold War include Lawrence Wittner, *American Intervention in Greece* (1982); Fraser Harbutt, *The Iron Curtain: Churchill, America and the Origins of the Cold War* (1986); and Melvyn Leffler's prize-winning *A Preponderance of Power* (1992). American diplomacy before and during the war is chronicled in numerous books, the most noteworthy of which are Robert Dallek, *F.D.R. and American Diplomacy* (1979); Robert Divine, *The Reluctant Belligerent: American Entry into World War II* (1955); Gaddis Smith, *American Diplomacy during World War II* (1955); Donald Drummond, *The Passing of American Neutrality: 1937–1941* (1955); Herbert Feis, *The Road to Pearl Harbor* (1950); Paul Schroeder, *The Axis Alliance and Japanese-American Relations, 1941* (1958); John Toland, *Infamy: Pearl Harbor and Its Aftermath* (1982); and Roberta Wohlsetter, *Pearl Harbor, Warning and Decision* (1962).

The orthodox school of Cold War historiography is represented in Adam Ulam, *Containment and Co-existence* (1974); Herbert Feis, *From Trust to Terror: The Onset of the Cold War* (1971); and Marvin Herz, *Beginnings of the Cold War* (1966). A more revisionist approach can be found in Joyce and Gabriel Kolko, *The Limits of Power: The World and U.S. Foreign Policy, 1945–1954* (1972); D. F. Fleming, *The Cold War and Its Origins* (two volumes, 1961); Richard Barnett, *Intervention and Revolution* (1969); and David Horowitz, ed., *Containment and Revolution* (1967). The historiographical controversy between revisionists and traditionalists is dealt with in Robert W. Tucker, *The Radical Left in American Foreign Policy* (1978); and Robert James Maddox, *The New Left and the Origins of the Cold War* (1979). Autobiographical accounts can be found in George Kennan's *Memoirs, 1925–1950* (1967), and *Memoirs, 1950–1963* (1972);

and Dean Acheson's *Present at the Creation: My Years at the State Department* (1969). On legal issues, see Stanley J. Kutler, *The American Inquisition: Justice and Injustice in the Cold War* (1982).

Specific aspects of Cold War policy have been the focus of other books. George Herring has written about the Lend-Lease program in *Aid to Russia, 1941–1946* (1973). The issue of atomic policy is discussed in Martin Sherwin's *A World Destroyed: The Atomic Bomb and the Grand Alliance* (1975) and in Gar Alperowitz's *Atomic Diplomacy: Hiroshima, Potsdam* (1965, rev. ed. 1986). On the development of the atomic bomb and the politics involved, see Richard Rhodes' exhaustive *The Making of the Atomic Bomb* (1986), and on the H-bomb, see Rhodes, *Dark Sun: The Making of the Hydrogen Bomb* (1995). John Gaddis discusses the emergence of containment as a policy in *Strategies of Containment: A Critical Appraisal of Post-War American National Security Policy* (1982). Bruce Kuniholm writes about *The Origins of the Cold War in the Near East* (1982). On the cultural and psychological impact of the A-bomb, see Paul Boyer, *By the Bomb's Early Light: American Thought and Culture at the Dawn of the Atomic Age* (1985), and Boyer, *Fallout: A Historian Reflects on America's Half-Century Encounter with Nuclear Weapons* (1998); see also Allan Winkler, *Life Under a Cloud* (1993). On the secret government-sponsored human radiation experiments during the Cold War, see Eileen Welsome, *The Plutonium Files: America's Secret Medical Experiments in the Cold War* (1999).

The relationship between the Cold War and the politics of anticommunism at home is discussed in David Caute, *The Great Fear: The Anti-Communist Purge under Truman and Eisenhower* (1978); Allen D. Harper, *The Politics of Loyalty: The White House and the Communist Issue, 1946–1952* (1959); and Michael Belknap, *Cold War Political Justice: The Smith Act, the Communist Party, and American Civil Liberties* (1977). Athan Theoharis is sharply critical of Truman's role in *Seeds of Repression: Harry S. Truman and the Origins of McCarthyism* (1972). The perjury trial of Alger Hiss is discussed in Allan Weinstein, *Perjury: The Hiss-Chambers Case* (1978); and Alistair Cooke, *A Generation on Trial* (1950). Covering the general issue of anticommunism is Earl Latham, *The Communist Controversy in Washington: From the New Deal to McCarthy* (1956), while Walter Goodman writes about the HUAC in *The Committee* (1968). Richard Rovere's *Senator Joe McCarthy* (1960) is still a fine book on the junior senator from Wisconsin. Also excellent are Robert Griffith's *The Politics of Fear* (1970); David Oshinsky, *A Conspiracy So Immense: The World of Joseph McCarthy* (1983); Richard Fried, *Nightmare in Red* (1990); and Thomas Reeves, *The Life and Times of Joe McCarthy* (1982). The opposition to McCarthyism is covered in Richard Fried, *Men Against McCarthy* (1976). Numerous books treat the phenomenon of McCarthyism in general, including Daniel Bell, ed., *The Radical Right* (1963); Michael Rogin, *McCarthy and the Intellectuals* (1967); and Richard Hofstadter, *The Paranoid Style in American Politics* (1971). A conservative perspective is offered in William F. Buckley and L. B. Bozell, *McCarthy and His Enemies* (1954), while that of the victims of the HUAC is available in James Wechsler, *The Age of Suspicion* (1953), and Victor Navasky, *Naming Names* (1980). Some of the best essays on McCarthyism appear in Robert Griffith and Athan Theoharis, ed., *The Specter: Original Essays on the Cold War and the Origin of McCarthyism* (1974). Recent works on McCarthyism include Ellen Schrecker's important *Many*

Are the Crimes: McCarthyism in America (1998) and Joel Kovel's critical *Red Hunting in the Promised Land: Anticommunism and the Making of America* (1994), which argues that anticommunism has been about persecution of outsiders in U.S. history, be they Communists or Native Americans. See also Athan Theoharis and J. S. Cox, *The Boss: J. Edgar Hoover and the Great American Inquisition* (1988).

On American communism see Harvey Klehr and Kyrill M. Anderson, *The Soviet World of American Communism* (1998). Based on research in the newly opened Soviet archives in the early 1990s, the authors cite strong evidence for the tight control of the CPUSA by the Comintern. In comparison, see Robin G. Kelley, *Hammer and Hoe: Alabama Communists during the Great Depression* (1990), who argues that the loosely controlled CP in Alabama's backwaters gave the black working class for the first time a political voice that challenged black middle-class organizations such as the NAACP. For Soviet activities in the United States, see also Allen Weinstein and Alexander Vassiliev, *The Haunted Wood: Soviet Espionage in America—The Stalin Era* (1999). Earlier works on the state of the Communist Party include David Shannon's *Decline of American Communism* (1959); Joseph Starobin's *American Communism in Crisis 1943–1957* (1972); and Irving Howe and Lewis Coser, *The American Communist Party* (1972). And on the varied cultural and multiethnic politics of the American left in the 1930s and its legacies, see Michael Denning, *The Cultural Front: The Laboring of American Culture in the 20th Century* (1996).

The Cold War as a cultural and social phenomenon has received increasing attention over the past decade and is the subject of Christian Appy, ed., *Cold War Constructions: The Political Culture of United States Imperialism, 1945–1966* (2000), a collection of essays that occupies a middle ground between cultural studies and traditional diplomatic history; see also John Fousek, *To Lead the Free World: American Nationalism and the Cold War* (2000); Walter L. Hixson's interesting *Parting the Curtain: Propaganda, Culture, and the Cold War, 1945–1961* (1997); Frances Stonor Saunders, *The Cultural Cold War: The CIA and the World of Arts and Letters* (1999); Reinhold Wagnleitner, *Coca-Colonization: The Cultural Mission of the United States in Austria after the Second World War* (1994); and Wagnleitner and Elaine Tyler May, eds., *"Here, There, and Everywhere": The Foreign Politics of American Popular Culture* (2000).

Nancy E. Bernhard explores *U.S. Television News and Cold War Propaganda, 1947–1960* (1999). Michael Hunt was one of the first diplomatic historians to explicitly analyze the ideological and cultural bias of U.S. foreign policy in *Ideology and U.S. Foreign Policy* (1987). On the role that expertise gained in psychological warfare played in civilian areas, see Ellen Herman, *The Romance of American Psychology: Political Culture in the Age of Experts* (1995); the impact of the Cold War on universities and academics is examined by Noam Chomsky, ed., *The Cold War & the University: Toward an Intellectual History of the Postwar Years* (1997); Christopher Simpson, ed., *Universities and Empire: Money and Politics in the Social Sciences during the Cold War* (1998); and Jessica Wang, *American Science in an Age of Anxiety: Scientists, Anticommunism and the Cold War* (1999), who offers a social history of politically active scientists during this era. See also Paul Boyer, *By the Bomb's Early Light* (1985); Ellen Schrecker, *No Ivory Tower: McCarthyism and the Universities* (1986); Alex Bloom, *Prodigal Sons: The New York Intellectuals and Their World* (1986); Peter J. Kuznick and James Gilbert, eds., *Re-*

thinking Cold War Culture (2001), a collection of essays that deals with domestic Cold War culture; Lary May, ed., *Recasting America: Culture and Politics in the Age of the Cold War* (1989); and Steven Whitfield, *The Culture of the Cold War* (1987). The role of women and families is explored by Elaine Tyler May, *Homeward Bound: American Families in the Cold War Era* (1988), who depicts women as domesticized homemakers of nuclear families in an age of anxiety, and Joanne Meyerowitz's anthology *Not June Cleaver: Women and Gender in Postwar America, 1945–1960* (1994), which challenges May's portrayal by illustrating the social diversity of gender roles in postwar America. See also Daniel Horowitz, *Betty Friedan and the Making of* The Feminine Mystique: *The American Left, the Cold War, and Modern Feminism* (1998), who explores the links between 1930s Popular Front activism and the feminism of the 1960s.

The best single-volume biography of Harry Truman is Alonzo L. Hamby, *Man of the People: A Life of Harry S. Truman* (1995). For a discussion of one liberal's experience during the postwar years, see Steven M. Neuse, *David E. Lilienthal: The Journey of an American Liberal* (1996). The most comprehensive political overview of the postwar years can be found in Alonzo Hamby, *Beyond the New Deal: Harry S. Truman and American Liberalism* (1973). See also Cabell Phillips, *The Truman Presidency* (1956); Bert Cochran, *Harry Truman and the Crisis Presidency* (1973); Robert Donovan, *Conflict and Crisis* (1977); and Robert Ferrell, *Harry Truman and the Modern American Presidency* (1982). Samuel Lubell, *Future of American Politics* (1952), presents a provocative interpretation of the political climate of the postwar years, and Barton Bernstein, ed., *Politics and Policies of the Truman Administration* (1970), surveys the accomplishments and goals of the administration. An acerbic, more critical view of these years appears in I. F. Stone, *The Truman Era* (1953); and Paul G. Pierpaoli, *Truman and Korea: The Political Culture of the Early Cold War* (1999).

Numerous books focus on more specific issues of the Truman years. These include R. Alton Lee, *Truman and Taft-Hartley* (1966); Allen J. Matusow, *Farm Policies and Politics in the Truman Administration* (1967); Maeva Marcus, *Truman and the Steel Seizure Case* (1977); Steven Bailey, *Congress Makes a Law* (1950), a study of the full employment act; Richard O. Davies, *Housing Reform during the Truman Administration* (1966); and Davis R. B. Ross, *Preparing for Ulysses* (1959), a study of the veterans' issue. Susan M. Hartman looks at executive-congressional relations in *Truman and the 80th Congress* (1971); while James T. Patterson examines Truman's major opponent in *Mr. Republican: A Biography of Robert A. Taft* (1972). See also Richard Kirkendall, *The Truman Period as a Research Field* (1972).

Truman's civil rights policies are the subject of several good books, particularly Steven Lawson, *Black Ballots* (1977); William Berman, *The Politics of Civil Rights in the Truman Administration* (1970); and Donald R. McCoy and Richard Ruetten, *Quest and Response: Minority Rights in the Truman Administration* (1973). For the activities of specific civil rights organizations, see Wilson Record, *Race and Radicalism* (1954) on the NAACP; and August Meier and Elliot Rudwick, *CORE: A Study of the Civil Rights Movement, 1942–1968* (1973).

The issue of labor is best treated in David Brody, *Workers in Industrial America: Essays on the Twentieth Century Struggle*, 2nd ed. (1993). See also Irving Howe and B. J. Widick, *The U.A.W. and Walter Reuther* (1949); Sydney Lens, *Left, Right, and Center* (1949); and C. Wright Mills, *The New Men of Power* (1948). James A. Gross, *Broken*

Promise: The Subversion of U. S. Labor Relations Policy, 1945–1994 (1995), reviews the history of the National Labor Relations Board. Kevin Boyle, *The UAW, and the Heyday of American Liberalism, 1945–1968* (1995), represents an excellent survey of the legacy of New Deal social democracy as it encountered a more conservative politics in postwar America. The life and times of Henry Wallace provide the focus for Edward L. and Frederick H. Schapsmeier, *Prophet in Politics: Henry A. Wallace and the War Years, 1940–1965* (1971); Norman D. Markowitz, *The Rise and Fall of the People's Century; Henry A. Wallace and American Liberalism, 1941–1948* (1972); and Carol A. Schmidt, *Henry A. Wallace: Quixotic Crusade* (1960). The Dixiecrat challenge in 1948 is the subject of William Barnard's *Dixiecrats and Democrats: Alabama Politics, 1942–1950* (1974). For a cultural perspective on labor, see George Lipsitz, *Rainbow at Midnight: Labor and Culture in the 1940s* (1994).

The 1950s have always been difficult to describe with brevity, but perhaps the best place to start is with some works on economic developments and thought during that era. See, for example, John Kenneth Galbraith, *The Affluent Society* (1958); R. W. Davenport and the editors of Fortune, *U.S.: The Permanent Revolution* (1956); and Walt W. Rostow, *The Stages of Economic Growth* (1959). The political emphasis on consensus and moderation can be traced in Daniel Bell, *The End of Ideology* (1958); Seymour Martin Lipset, *Political Man* (1960); Arthur Schlesinger, Jr., *The Vital Center* (1949); Peter F. Drucker, *The New Society* (1940); and Chaim Waxman, ed., *The End of Ideology Debate* (1960). Critiques of the new managerial style and its political consequences appear in C. Wright Mills, *The Power Elite* (1956); William H. Whyte, *The Organization Man* (1955); and G. William Domhoff, *Who Rules America* (1967). See also David Halberstam's entertaining *The Fifties* (1993).

The emergence of suburbia is covered in both popular and scholarly treatises. Perhaps the best study of suburbanization is Scott Donaldson, *The Suburban Myth* (1969). Other excellent scholarly works are William M. Dobriner, *Class in Suburbia* (1953); William M. Dobriner, ed., *The Suburban Community* (1958); Herbert Gans, *The Levittowners* (1957); and Bennett Berger, *Working Class Suburbs: The Study of Auto Workers in Suburbia* (1960). John Keats, *The Crack in the Picture Window* (1957), and Richard E. Gordon et al., *The Split Level Trap* (1960), are both critical of the cultural impact of suburbia. The phenomenon of politics in suburbia is dealt with in Frederick Wirt et al., *On the Cities Rim* (1972). The automobile in suburbia is covered in John B. Rae, *The Road and the Car in American Life* (1971). Robert Andrew Greeley writes about ethnicity in *Why Can't They Be Like Us? America's White Ethnic Groups* (1975), while the exclusion of blacks in suburbia is discussed in Michael Danielson, *The Politics of Exclusion* (1976). The role of the church in suburbanization is the subject of Gibson Winter's *The Suburban Captivity of the Churches* (1960) and Andrew Greeley's *The Church in the Suburbs* (1959). See also Barry Schwartz, ed., *The Changing Face of the Suburbs* (1976); Philip Dolce, ed., *Suburbia: The American Dream and Dilemma* (1976); and Kenneth Jackson, *The Crabgrass Frontier* (1985).

The best place to read about the emergence of the mass media is in Erik Barnouw's classic history of television, *Tube of Plenty* (1982). See also Alexander Kendrick's *Prime Time* (1973) and Robert McNeil's *The People Machine* (1977). Mass culture is discussed in Bernard Rosenberg and D. M. White, eds., *Mass Culture* (1957), and Eric Larrabee and Rolf Meyershon, eds., *Mass Leisure* (1958). American literature is discussed in Marcus Klein, *The American Novel Since World War II* (1970); Howard M. Harper, Jr., *Desperate Faith* (1968); Marcus Cunliffe, *The Literature of the United States* (1967); and Richard Pells, *The Liberal Mind in a Conservative Age: American Intellectuals in the 1940s and 1950s* (1984). American movies are discussed in Michael Wood, *America in Movies* (1975); Molly Haskins, *From Reverence to Rape* (1978); and Pauline N. Kael, *I Lost It at the Movies* (1965). A more recent assessment of the relationship between the media and American politics is David Thelen's *Becoming Citizens in the Age of Television: How Americans Challenged the Media and Seized Political Initiative during the Iran-Contra Debate* (1996). Michael Kammen's *American Culture, American Tastes: Social Change and the 20th Century* (1999) explores the growth of mass culture and the debates over popular and mass culture over the past century.

Postwar art developments are covered in Richard Kostelanetz, ed., *The New American Art* (1965); Barbara Rose, *American Art Since 1900* (1967); and Serge Guibaut, *How New York Stole the Idea of Modern Art* (1983). The emergence of rock and roll is covered in Greil Marcus, *The Mystery Train* (1982); Jerry Hopkins, *The Rock Story* (1970); and Carl Belz, *The Story of Rock* (1969).

Some of the most powerful criticisms of American society and culture during the postwar years appear in David Riesman's *The Lonely Crowd* (1958); Erich Fromm's *Man for Himself* (1947); and the books of C. Wright Mills mentioned earlier.

Most studies of politics during the 1950s focus on the presidency of Dwight Eisenhower. Biographical treatments include Peter Lyons, *Eisenhower: Portrait of the Hero* (1974); Stephen Ambrose, *Eisenhower, Vol. 1, Soldier, General of the Army, President-Elect, 1890–1952* (1983), and *Vol. 2, The President* (1984); Herbert Parmet, *Eisenhower and the American Crusades* (1972); and Robert J. Donovan, *Eisenhower* (1956), a campaign biography. See also Richard Burk, *Dwight D. Eisenhower: Hero and Politician* (1986); and for a view of the liberal side, Steven Gillon, *The ADA and American Liberalism* (1987). Other assessments of Eisenhower from close associates include Sherman Adams' *First Hand Report* (1975) and Arthur Larson's *Eisenhower: The President Nobody Knew* (1958). Eisenhower's own memoirs appear in two volumes entitled *Mandate for Change* (1963) and *Waging Peace* (1965). Relationships between Eisenhower and Nixon are discussed in Richard M. Nixon, *Six Crises* (1962); and Garry Wills, *Nixon Agonistes* (1974). The general politics of the era are discussed in Samuel Lubell, *Revolt of the Moderates* (1956); Charles Alexander, *Holding the Line: The Eisenhower Years, 1952–1961* (1975); and I. F. Stone, *The Haunted 50's* (1963). Relationships between business and government are covered in David Fryor, *Conflict of Interest in the Eisenhower Administration* (1970); and Aaron Wildavsky, *Dixon-Yates* (1962). E. Frederic Morrow discusses what it was like to be the president's only black advisor in *Black Man in the White House* (1963). Eisenhower's secretary of state for most of his administration is the topic of Townsend Hoopes' *The Devil and John Foster Dulles* (1973). Other general works on the fifties include John Diggins, *The Proud Decades: America in War and Peace, 1941–1960* (1988); and William L. O'Neill, *American High: The Years of Confidence, 1945–1960* (1986).

It was during the 1950s, of course, that the civil rights issue became central to America. Richard Kluger's *Simple Justice* (1976) is a classic chronicle of the *Brown* decision. The legal aspects of that decision are also discussed in Albert Blaustein and Clarence Clyde Ferguson, Jr., *Desegregation and the Law* (1962). Jack Bass, in *Unlikely Heroes* (1981), tells the story of judges in the Fifth Circuit who attempted to implement the *Brown* decision. Melvin Tumin assesses the overall response of public opinion in his book *Desegregation* (1957), while Numan P. Bartley traces the emergence of a white opposition in *The Rise of Massive Resistance: Race and Politics in the South during the 1950s* (1959). Overall background on the racial question is provided by Thomas F. Pettigrew, *A Profile of the Negro American* (1964); and Talcott Parsons and Kenneth Clark, eds., *The Negro American* (1957). Other overviews include Anthony Lewis' *Portrait of a Decade* (1971) and Benjamin Muse's *The American Negro Revolution* (1970). The response of the Eisenhower administration is treated in J. W. Anderson, *Eisenhower, Brownell, and Congress* (1964). Harvard Sitkoff provides an assessment of the entire civil rights movement in *The Struggle for Black Equality* (1983; rev. ed., 1993). See also Robert Weisbrot, *Freedom Bound* (1991); Steven Lawson, *Running for Freedom: Civil Rights and Black Politics in America Since 1941*, 2nd ed. (1997); and Manning Marable, *Race, Reform, and Rebellion: The Second Reconstruction in Black America, 1945–1982* (1984). See also James T. Patterson, *Brown v. Board of Education* (2001).

Other works on the civil rights movement include Vicki L. Crawford et al., *Women in the Civil Rights Movement: Trailblazers and Torchbearers, 1941–1965* (1993); Aldon Morris, *The Origins of the Civil Rights Movement* (1984); Mary King, *Freedom Song* (1987); Robert Norrell, *Reaping the Whirlwind: The Civil Rights Movement in Tuskegee* (1985); Steven Lawson, *In Pursuit of Power: Southern Blacks and Electoral Politics, 1965–1982* (1985); and Adam Fairclough, *To Redeem the Soul of America* (1987), a history of the SCLC. Charles W. Eagles, *Outside Agitator: Jon Daniels and the Civil Rights Movement in Alabama* (1993), is a fascinating story of one white civil rights activist murdered during the movement. Taylor Branch's *Pillar of Fire: America in the King Years, 1963–65* (1998) is the second volume in Branch's monumental study of Martin Luther King and the civil rights years in America. Branch's *At Canaan's Edge* (2006) concludes the trilogy. As a mixture between investigative journalism and personal memoir, Diane McWhorter's *Carry Me Home: Birmingham, Alabama: The Climactic Battle of the Civil Rights Revolution* (2001) explores the segregationist resistance to the movement.

Martin Luther King, Jr., describes the emergence of the Montgomery bus movement in *Stride Toward Freedom* (1959). Later stages of King's activities are described in his *Why We Can't Wait* (1964). David L. Lewis, *King: A Critical Biography* (1970), presents an overview of the civil rights leader's life. On J. Edgar Hoover and King, see *The FBI and Martin Luther King, Jr.* (1983). See also Stephen Oates, *The Trumpet Sounds* (1982), and Vincent Harding's essay in Michael Namoroto, ed., *Have We Overcome?* (1981). Howard Zinn's *The Southern Mystique* (1962) provides the perspective of a Northern white civil rights sympathizer, while Morton Sosna's *In Search of the Silent South* (1977) describes the role of white dissenters in the South. More recent works on King include David Garrow, *Bearing the Cross* (1986) and Taylor Branch, *Parting the Waters: America in the King Years, 1954–63* (1988).

The emergence of the direct action movement provides the theme for numerous books. William Chafe, *Civilities and Civil Rights: Greensboro, North Carolina, and the Black Struggle for Freedom* (1980), traces the growth of the sit-in movement and the transition to black power in one community. Howell Raines, *My Soul Is Rested* (1977), offers oral testimony from multiple participants in the movement. Clayborne Carson's *In Struggle: SNCC and the Black Awakening of the 1960s* (1981) is a history of the leading direct action group of the civil rights forces. Charles Payne emphasizes SNCC's crucial role in the civil rights movement in *I've Got the Light of Freedom: The Organizing Tradition and the Mississippi Freedom Struggle* (1995).

Perhaps the most eloquent testimony on the civil rights movement comes from participants themselves. First-person accounts include James Peck, *Freedom Ride* (1962); James Forman, *The Making of Black Revolutionaries* (1975); Sally Belfrage, *Freedom Summer* (1965); Howard Zinn, *SNCC: The New Abolitionists* (1965); Anne Moody, *Coming of Age in Mississippi* (1970); Cleveland Sellers, *River of No Return* (1976); and Elizabeth Sutherland, ed., *Letters from Mississippi* (1973).

Recent scholarship has set the civil rights movement in an international context of decolonization and the Cold War. Some notable titles include Penny von Eschen, *Race Against Empire: Black Americans and Anticolonialism, 1937–1957* (1997) and Mary Dudziak, who argues in *Cold War Civil Rights: Race and the Image of American Democracy* (2000) that the Cold War helped facilitate desegregation as the U.S. government sought to polish its international image. On the connection between Cold War commodities, race, and foreign relations, see Thomas Borstelmann, *Apartheid's Reluctant Uncle: The United States and Southern Africa in the Early Cold War* (1993).

Books on other minorities include works by Ronald Takaki, *A Different Mirror: A History of Multicultural America* (1993) and *Strangers from a Different Shore: A History of Asian Americans* (1989). In recent years, historians have increasingly focused on Hispanics; see George Sanchez, *Becoming Mexican American: Ethnicity, Culture and Identity in Chicano Los Angeles, 1900–1945* (1993); David Gutierrez, *Walls and Mirrors: Mexican Americans, Mexican Immigrants, and the Politics of Ethnicity* (1995); and David Montejano, *Anglos and Mexicans in the Making of Texas, 1836–1986* (1987). The history of Native Americans after World War II is discussed in Donald L. Fixico, *Termination and Relocation: Federal Indian Policy, 1945–1960* (1986); and Vine Deloria, *American Indian Policy in the Twentieth Century* (1985), which explores the relations between the government and Native Americans and related legal issues. For Native Americans' urban experiences, see Fixico, *The Urban Indian Experience in America* (2000). On contemporary issues of ethnicity, see David Hollinger, *Postethnic America: Beyond Multiculturalism* (1995; rev. ed., 2000).

The Kennedy involvement in civil rights is chronicled in Carl N. Brauer's *John F. Kennedy and the Second Reconstruction* (1977). Victor Navasky's *Kennedy Justice* (1971) is a study of Robert F. Kennedy's tenure as Attorney General. JFK's economic policy is the topic of Seymour Harris' *Economics of the Kennedy Years* (1966) and Hobart Rowen's *The Free Enterpriser* (1964). David Knapp and Kenneth Polk assess the president's decision to attack poverty in *Scouting the War on Poverty: Social Reform Politics in the Kennedy Administration* (1971). Kennedy's relationship with business is analyzed in Jim F. Heath, *John F. Kennedy and the Business Community* (1969).

Most books on the Kennedy years focus on the president himself. Laudatory biographies include Arthur Schlesinger, Jr., *A Thousand Days* (1965); Theodore Sorenson, *Kennedy* (1965); Pierre Salinger, *With Kennedy* (1966); and Kenneth O'Connell and David Powers, *"Johnny, We Hardly Knew Ye"* (1972). Far more critical are Garry

Wills, *The Kennedy Imprisonment* (1983); Bruce Miroff, *Pragmatic Illusions: The Presidential Politics of JFK* (1976); and Henry Fairlie, *The Kennedy Promise* (1976). Herbert Parmet's *Jack* (1983) is an effective discussion of Kennedy's life prior to assuming the presidency, while his *JFK* (1983) discusses the time in the White House. Nigel Hamilton discusses Kennedy's earlier years in *JFK: Reckless Youth* (1992), while the best recent book on the Kennedy administration is Robert Dallek, *An Unfinished Life* (2003). See also James Giglio, *The Presidency of John F. Kennedy* (1991); and Thomas Reeves, *A Question of Character: A Life of John F. Kennedy* (1991). The election of 1960 is the topic of Theodore White, *The Making of the President 1960* (1961), the best of White's many election-year volumes. Other studies of that election include Angus Campbell et al., *American National Election Study, 1960* (1974), and Lucy S. Davidowicz and Leon J. Goldstein, *Politics in a Pluralist Democracy: Studies of Voting in the 1960 Election* (1963). Kennedy's Catholicism is treated in Lawrence H. Fuchs, *John F. Kennedy and American Catholicism* (1967), and Garry Wills, *Bare Ruined Choirs: Doubt, Prophecy, and Radical Religion* (1972).

Kennedy's foreign policy has also attracted significant attention. Peter Wyden's study *Bay of Pigs* (1980) is a classic of investigative reporting. The missile crisis is the topic of Robert A. Divine, ed., *The Cuban Missile Crisis* (1969); see also Robert F. Kennedy, *Thirteen Days* (1969); and Graham T. Allison, *Essence of Decision: Explaining the Cuban Crisis* (1971). Other foreign policy ventures are discussed in Walt W. Rostow, *View from the Seventh Floor* (1964); Robert McNamara, *The Essence of Security* (1968); and Jack M. Shick, *The Berlin Crisis, 1958–62* (1971). David Burner et al., *A Giant's Strength* (1971), is an overview of foreign issues; and Aida Donald, ed., *John F. Kennedy and the New Frontier* (1966), assesses domestic issues. For a critical view of Kennedy's foreign policy, see Richard Walton's *Cold War and Counter-revolution* (1972) and Louise Fitzsimmons' *The Kennedy Doctrine* (1970). Another study of Kennedy's foreign policy is Michael Beschloss, *The Crisis Years: Kennedy and Krushchev, 1960–63* (1991). The Kennedy assassination is the topic of William Manchester's *Death of a President* (1966). On the paradoxes of Kennedy liberalism in foreign policy, see Michael E. Latham, *Modernization as Ideology: American Social Science and Nation Building in the Kennedy Era* (2000). Latham explains how modernization theory became the basis for some of the administration's best known anticolonial yet imperialistic innovations in foreign affairs: the Alliance for Progress, the Peace Corps, and the strategic hamlet program in Vietnam.

Like Kennedy, Lyndon Johnson has been the subject of controversial biographies. Among those most critical of Johnson are Robert Caro, *The Years of Lyndon Johnson: The Path to Power* (1982), and *The Years of Lyndon Johnson: Means of Ascent* (1990); and Ronnie Dugger, *The Politician* (1982). Doris Kearns is more sympathetic in *Lyndon Johnson and the American Dream* (1977). So too is Caro's third volume, *Master of the Senate* (2002). See also Eric Goldman, *The Tragedy of Lyndon Johnson* (1969), and George Reedy, *The Twilight of the Presidency* (1971). The best recent studies are Robert Dallek's two volumes, *Lone Star Rising: Lyndon Johnson and His Times* (1991) and *Flawed Giant: Lyndon Johnson and His Times, 1961–1973* (1998). One of the best books on Johnson is Harry McPherson, *A Political Education* (1975). Tom Wicker assesses both Johnson and his predecessor in *JFK and LBJ* (1968). Johnson's Great Society legislative program has also been the focus for many books. One of the best studies of politics and public policy during the 1960s is James Sundquist, *Politics and Policy: The Eisenhower, Kennedy, and Johnson Years* (1968). Allan Matusow offers a biting critique of liberalism in *The Unraveling of America* (1984). Other Great Society legislation is the topic of Sar Levitan and Robert Taggert, *The Promise of Greatness* (1976); Theodore Marmer, *The Politics of Medicare* (1973); Daniel P. Moynihan, *Maximum Feasible Misunderstanding* (1970); and Stephen M. Rose, *The Betrayal of the Poor: Transformation of Community Action* (1972). The issue of poverty is also addressed in Michael Harrington, *The Other America* (1962); James Patterson, *America's Struggle Against Poverty, 1900–1980* (1983); Harry Caudill, *Night Comes to the Cumberlands* (1963); Oscar Lewis, *La Vida: A Puerto Rican Family and the Culture of Poverty* (1966); Peter Marris and Martin Rein, *Dilemmas of Social Reform* (1973); James Sundquist, ed., *On Fighting Poverty* (1969); Chaim Waxman, ed., *Poverty* (1972); and Charles A. Valentine, *Culture and Poverty: Critique and Counter Proposals* (1968). For an overview, see Marvin E. Gittleman and David Mermelstein, eds., *The Great Society Reader: The Failure of Liberalism* (1975). Charles Murray offers a critical view of Great Society legislation in *Losing Ground* (1984). For a more sanguine view, see Jonathan Schwarz, *America's Hidden Success* (1983).

Johnson's involvement with the Dominican Republican episode is treated in John Barlow Martin, *Overtaken by Events* (1966); Theodore Draper, *The Dominican Revolt* (1968); Tad Szulc, *Dominican Diary* (1967); and Abraham Lowenthal, *The Dominican Intervention* (1972).

It was Vietnam, of course, that constituted the major foreign policy crisis of the Kennedy and Johnson years. The best single book on Vietnam is George Herring, *America's Longest War: The U.S. and Vietnam, 1950–1975* (1981, 2002), a survey of U.S. involvement from the earliest postwar years through 1975. See also George Herring, *LBJ and Vietnam: A Different Kind of War* (1994). A good complement to Herring is Larry Berman, *Planning a Tragedy* (1982), a chronicle of debates within the administration in 1965. Everyone will want to consult Neil Sheehan's *The Pentagon Papers* (1975) for what they reveal about the perceptions that shaped government decisions. Also valuable are the early works of Bernard Fall, *The Two Vietnams* (1967) and *Street Without Joy* (1964). See also David Halberstam, *The Making of a Quagmire* (1965); Gunter Lewy, *America in Vietnam* (1978); and Stanley Karnouw, *Vietnam: A History* (1984). For an insider's perspective, see Robert McNamara, *In Retrospect* (1995).

Any assessment of the Kennedy-Johnson administration policies must begin with David Halberstam, *The Best and the Brightest* (1972). The work of other journalists is also critical to understanding the war. See, for example, Gloria Emerson, *Winners and Losers: Battles, Retreats, Gains, Losses and Ruins from the Vietnam War* (1976); Alexander Kendrick, *The Wound Within* (1974); Michael Herr, *Dispatches* (1977); Robert Shaplen, *The Road from War: Vietnam, 1965–1971* (1971); Philip Caputo, *A Rumor of War* (1977); and Frances FitzGerald, *Fire in the Lake* (1972). Recently, David Kaiser published *American Tragedy: Kennedy, Johnson, and the Origins of the Vietnam War* (2000) on the decisions made by the Eisenhower, Kennedy, and Johnson administrations leading the United States to disaster in Vietnam. Atrocities in the war are covered in Richard Hammer, *One Morning in the War* (1971); Seymour Hersh, *Mylai: A Report on the Massacre and Its Aftermath* (1971); and Jonathan Schell, *The Military*

Half (1968). On the Tet offensives, see Don Oberdoffer's *Tet* (1971) and Peter Braestrup's *Big Story* (1978). The media is also discussed in S. J. Epstein's *News from Nowhere* (1973) and David Halberstam's *The Powers That Be* (1979). The perspective from government officials is available through Chester Cooper, *The Lost Crusade: America in Vietnam* (1970); Walt W. Rostow, *The Diffusion of Power* (1972); Roger Hilsman, *To Move a Nation* (1971); Leslie Gelb and Archie Betts, *The Irony of Vietnam* (1979); and Roger Morris, *Uncertain Greatness* (1978). See also Kathleen J. Turner, *Lyndon Johnson's Dual War: Vietnam and the Press* (1981), and for poll data, Milton Rosenberg, Sydney Verba, and Philip Conyers, *Vietnam and the Silent Majority* (1975).

Other recent books on Vietnam include Marylin Young, *The Vietnam Wars: 1945-1990* (1991); for two contrasting approaches on the Vietnam war, see Frederick Logevall, *Choosing War: The Lost Chance for Peace and the Escalation of War in Vietnam* (1999), and Rhodri Jeffreys-Jones, *Peace Now! American Society and the Ending of the Vietnam War* (1999). Logevall explores how other countries provided the United States with face-saving ways to escape its commitment in Vietnam and how LBJ's largely solitary decisions contributed to the deteriorating situation in South Vietnam. In contrast, Jeffreys-Jones argues that citizens influenced foreign policy. Students, African Americans, women, and labor initially supported the war to achieve acceptance by "insider" groups, then turned against the war once their goal was achieved. See also Gabriel Kolko, *Anatomy of a War: Vietnam, the United States, and the Modern Historical Experience* (1986); and Loren Baritz, *Backfire: A History of How American Culture Led Us into Vietnam* (1985). See also Nancy Zaroulis and Gerald Sullivan, *Who Spoke Up? American Protests Against the War in Vietnam, 1963-1975* (1984); Timothy Lomperis, *The War Everyone Lost—and Won* (1984); and Harison Salisbury, ed., *Vietnam Reconsidered* (1984). Neil Sheehan, *A Bright Shining Lie: John Paul Vann and America in Vietnam* (1988), narrates the story of one soldier's experience in Vietnam, using it as a window to view what went wrong both in Vietnam and in America during these years. Other recent books on Vietnam include Fred Turner's *Echoes of Combat: The Vietnam War in American Memory* (1996), a study of both individual experiences and the cultural framework around the war, and Tom Holms' *Strong Hearts, Wounded Souls: Native American Veterans of the Vietnam War* (1996).

Escalation of the war in Vietnam coincided with increasing fragmentation at home, the most notable instance of which was the emergence of the Black Power movement out of the civil rights struggle. The forerunner of Black Power, Malcolm X, is the subject of Alex Haley, *The Autobiography of Malcolm X* (1966); Archie Epps, *Malcolm X and the American Negro Revolution* (1969); and Peter Goldman, *The Death and Life of Malcolm X* (1974). Michael Eric Dyson, *Making Malcolm: The Myth and Meaning of Malcolm X* (1995), explores the legacy of Malcolm X and the myth that grew up around him after the years of his assassination. The doctrine of Black Power itself is explicated in Charles Hamilton and Stokely Carmichael, *Black Power* (1967); Julius Lester, *Look Out Whitey! Black Power's 'Gon' Get Your Momma* (1968); Eldridge Cleaver, *Soul on Ice* (1968); Bobby Seale, *Seize the Time* (1974); and Floyd Barbour, ed., *Black Power Revolt* (1968). See also William L. Van Deburg, *New Day in Babylon: The Black Power Movement and American Culture, 1965-1975* (1992); and Timothy Tyson, *Radio Free Dixie: Robert F. Williams and the Roots of Black Power* (1999), which argues that the civil rights movement and the Black Power movement were much closer than previously suggested. On race relations and the cash value of whiteness, see George Lipsitz, *The Possessive Investment in Whiteness: How People Profit from Identity Politics* (1998).

The urban revolts that occurred in the late 1960s are chronicled in numerous books, including Joe F. Feagin and Harlan Hahn, *Ghetto Revolts: The Politics of Violence in American Cities* (1973); Robert M. Fogleson, *Violence as Protest: A Study of Riots in Ghettos* (1969); Paul Jacobs, *Prelude to Riot* (1969); John Hersey, *The Algiers Motel Incident* (1971); Tom Hayden, *Rebellion in Newark* (1970); and Robert Conot, *Rivers of Blood, Years of Darkness* (1968). Other books on racial violence include Jack Bass and Jack Nelson, *The Orangeburg Massacre* (1970); Michael Wallace and Richard Hofstadter, eds., *American Violence: A Documentary History* (1970); and Hugh Davis Graham and Ted Robert Gurr, *The History of Violence in America* (1969). See also the Kerner Commission's *Report of the National Advisory Committee on Civil Disorders* (1968) and Tom Wicker's powerful chronicle of the Attica prison riot, *A Time to Die* (1975).

The relationship between the emergence of Black Power and the women's movement is effectively chronicled in Sara Evans' *Personal Politics* (1975). See also William Chafe, *Women and Equality* (1977); Jo Freeman, *The Politics of Women's Liberation* (1975); Leslie B. Tanner, ed., *Voices from Women's Liberation* (1970); Robin Morgan, *Sisterhood Is Powerful* (1970); Shulamith Firestone, *The Dialectic of Sex* (1972); Kate Millett, *Sexual Politics* (1971); Barbara Moran and Vivian Gornick, eds., *Woman in Sexist Society* (1971); Betty Friedan, *The Feminine Mystique* (1963); Gayle Graham Yates, *What Women Want: The Ideas of the Movement* (1975); Ellen Levine and Judith Hole, *Rebirth of Feminism* (1974); and Michele Wallace, *Black Macho and the Myth of the Super Woman* (1970).

More recent books on feminism and women's liberation include Ruth Rosen, *The World Split Open: How the Modern Women's Movement Changed America* (2000); Alice Echols, *Daring to be Bad* (1989); Cynthia Harrison, *On Account of Sex* (1988); and Jane Sherron DeHart and Donald Mathews, *Sex, Gender and the Politics of the ERA* (1990). For the role of black women in both feminism and the black freedom struggle, see Kay Mills, *This Little Light of Mine: The Life of Fannie Lou Hamer* (1993); Elaine Brown, *A Taste of Power: A Black Woman's Story* (1992); and Paula Giddings, *When and Where I Enter: The Impact of Black Women on Race and Sex in America* (1984). Nancie Carroway, *Segregated Sisterhood: Racism in the Politics of American Feminism* (1991), assesses the dilemmas that the women's movement has faced in trying to overcome barriers of race and class. Daniel Horowitz's study *Betty Friedan and the Making of* The Feminine Mystique: *The American Left, the Cold War, and Modern Feminism* (1998) sheds light on the previously obscure links between labor activism and left-wing politics of the 1930s and 1940s and the women's movement of the 1960s.

The literature on the antiwar movement, student protest, the New Left, and the counterculture is voluminous. For a general overview of the period, see William L. O'Neil, *Coming Apart* (1974); John Diggins, *The American Left in the 20th Century* (1972); Irwin Unger, *The Movement: A History of the American New Left* (1974); and Christopher Lasch, *The Agony of the American Left* (1969). See also Allen J. Matusow, *The Unraveling of America: A History of Liberalism in the 1960s* (1984).

The origins of the student movement are explored in a variety of books. Seymour Lipset and Sheldon Wolin, eds., *The Berkeley Student Revolt* (1965), offer one starting place. Other collections dealing with student revolts include Samuel Lubell and Irving Kristol, eds., *Confrontation: Student Rebellion in Universities* (1971); and Seymour Lipset and P. Altbach, eds., *Students in Revolt* (1969). For coverage of the Columbia story, see Jerry Avorn et al., *Up Against the Wall* (1969); and James Kunan, *The Strawberry Statement* (1968). Steven Kellman describes events at Harvard in *Push Comes to Shove* (1971).

For more books on the student left, see James Miller, *Democracy Is in the Streets: From Port Huron to the Siege of Chicago* (1987); Todd Gitlin, *The Sixties: Years of Hope, Days of Rage* (1987); and Maurice Isserman, *If I Had a Hammer: The Death of the Old Left and the Birth of the New Left* (1987). A very critical look at the New Left appears in Peter Collier and David Horowitz, *Destructive Generation: Second Thoughts About the Sixties* (1989).

A good beginning place for assessing the New Left is Kirkpatrick Sale, *SDS* (1973). See also Michael Fervor and Staughton Lynd, eds., *The Resistance* (1973); Mitchell Goodman, ed., *The Movement Toward a New America* (1971), a collection of underground press articles; Todd Gitlin, *The Whole World Is Watching: The Mass Media in the Making and the Unmaking of the New Left* (1980); and M. Teodori, ed., *The New Left: A Documentary History* (1969). In *Dreams Die Hard* (1983), David Harris presents a portrait of three individuals involved in the student movement. A biographical approach also appears in Paul Cowan's *The Making of an Un-American* (1970) and in Abbie Hoffman's *Revolution for the Hell of It* (1968). See also Kenneth Keniston's two volumes, *The Uncommitted* (1965) and *The Young Radicals* (1968). For the tragic climax of student protest, see I. F. Stone, *The Killings at Kent State* (1970). The culture wars are also explored in Maurice Isserman and Michael Kazin, *America Divided: The Civil War of the 1960s* (2000); and Todd Gitlin, *The Twilight of Common Dreams: Why America Is Wracked by Culture Wars* (1995), which examines the origins of the culture wars of the 1990s.

There are many different perspectives on the counterculture, rock music, and drugs. Phillip Slater's *The Pursuit of Loneliness* (1970) represents the best work at the time on the motivations of those who chose the counterculture. See also Theodore Roszak's *The Making of a Counterculture* (1969) and Charles Reich's *The Greening of America* (1970). Another excellent introduction to the relationship between culture and radicalism is Morris Dickstein, *Gates of Eden: American Culture in the Sixties* (1977). On drugs in the counterculture, see Tom Wolfe, *The Electric Kool-Aid Acid Test* (1969); D. Salamon, ed., *The Marijuana Papers* (1970); Harrison Pope, Jr., *Voices from the Drug Culture* (1971); and Timothy Leary, *The Politics of Ecstasy* (1973). On the music of the time, see Ralph Gleason, *The Jefferson Airplane* (1972); John Landau, ed., *It's Too Late to Stop Now* (1973), a book on the Rolling Stones; Hunter Davies, *The Beatles* (1978); Michael Lydon, *Rock Folk* (1971; 1991); R. Serge Demiroff, *Great Day Coming* (1971), and Jon Wiener, *Come Together* (1983).

The political and cultural reaction of white ethnics and "middle-Americans" to the turmoil of the 1960s has provided the subject for numerous sociological studies. Among the best are Richard Lemons, *The Troubled Americans* (1970); Andrew Levison, *The Working Class Majority* (1974); Sar Levitan, ed., *Blue Collar Workers: A Symposium of Middle Class America* (1971); Louise K. Howe, ed., *The White Majority: Between Poverty and Affluence* (1970); Murray Friedman, ed., *Overcoming Middle Class Rage* (1971); Patricia Cayo Sexton and Brandon Sexton, *Blue Collars and Hard Hats* (1971); Jan Erickson and Robert Coles, *Middle Americans* (1973); Richard Scammon and Benjamin Wattenberg, *The Real Majority* (1974); Michael Novak, *The Rise of the Unmeltable Ethnics* (1973); Peter Binzen, *Whitetown, U.S.A.* (1970); and Michael Wenk et al., eds., *Pieces of a Dream: The Ethnic Workers' Crisis with America* (1972). See also Dan Carter, *The Politics of Rage: George Wallace, the Origins of the New Conservatism, and the Transformation of American Politics* (1995).

The issues of affirmative action and the meaning of equality are discussed in Nathan Glaser, *Affirmative Discrimination* (1975); Allan P. Sindler, *Bakke, DeFumis, and Minority Admissions: The Quest for Equal Opportunity* (1978); J. Harvey Wilkerson, *From Brown to Bakke: The Supreme Court and School Integration, 1954–1978* (1979); More recently, Richard J. Herrnstein and Charles Murray's Social-Darwinist *The Bell Curve: Intelligence and Class Structure in American Life* (1994) has rekindled intense controversies about the connections between race, intelligence, and class. Steven Fraser, ed., critically responded in *The Bell Curve Wars: Race, Intelligence, and the Future of America* (1995). See also Herbert Gans, *More Equality* (1973); John Rawls, *A Theory of Justice* (1971); and Christopher Jencks, *Inequality* (1976). An important recent book on the underclass is William J. Wilson, *The Truly Disadvantaged* (1987); One of the best books on the use of race in politics is Mary and Thomas Edsall, *Chain Reaction* (1992). See also John Micklethwait and Adrian Woolridge, *The Right Nation* (2005).

Many groups in America that had been oppressed came to new prominence during the 1960s and 1970s. Among the books dealing with these groups are Alvin Josephs, *Red Power* (1972); Stan Steiner, *The New Indian* (1968); Stan Steiner, *LaRaza: The Mexican Americans* (1970); Matt S. Meier and Feliciano Ribera, *Mexican American, American Mexicans: From Conquistadors to Chicanos* (1972; rev. ed. 1993); Joan London and Henry Anderson Crowell, *So Shall Ye Reap* (1972); and Dick Meister and Anne Loftis, *A Long Time Coming* (1977), the last two books on César Chavez. Armando Navarro, *Mexican American Youth Organizations: Avant-Garde of the Chicano Movement in Texas* (1995), is a case study of the Chicano movement of the 1960s. The history of gay Americans is discussed in John D'Emilio's *Sexual Politics, Sexual Communities* (1984) and Jonathan Katz's *Gay American History* (1972). Martin Duberman, *Cures, a Gay Man's Odyssey* (1991), combines memoir with history in a powerful portrayal of the cultural climate surrounding homosexuality in 1950s. The emergence of a shift in cultural values and the new concern with self are the topics of Peter Clecak, *America's Quest for the Ideal Self* (1982); and Daniel Yankelovich, *New Rules: Searching for Self-Fulfillment in a World Turned Upside Down* (1982). For a superb historical overview of sexuality, see Estelle Freedman and John D'Emilio, *Intimate Matters* (1988). Excellent personal memoirs on what it means to be gay include Martin Duberman, *Cures* (1992); and Paul Monnette, *Becoming a Man* (1992). For recent titles on the history of homosexuality and the gay/lesbian movement, see Marc Stein, *City of Sisterly and Brotherly Loves: Lesbian and Gay Philadelphia, 1945–1972* (2000); John Howard, *Men Like That: A Southern Queer History* (1999); John-Manuel

Andriote, *Victory Deferred: How AIDS Changed Gay Life in America* (1999); Elizabeth Lapovsky Kennedy and Madeline D. Davis, *Boots of Leather, Slippers of Gold: The History of a Lesbian Community* (1993); and Esther Newton, *Cherry Grove, Fire Island: Sixty Years in America's First Gay and Lesbian Town* (1993); see also Allida M. Black, ed., *Modern American Queer History* (2001).

The politics of the late 1960s and 1970s can be understood in part through biographical portraits of the principal figures involved. Robert Kennedy's life is chronicled in Arthur M. Schlesinger, Jr., *Robert F. Kennedy and His Times* (1978), and Jack Newfield, *Robert F. Kennedy: A Memoir* (1976). Joseph A. Palermo's *In His Own Right: The Political Odyssey of Senator Robert F. Kennedy* (2001) explores the significance of the civil rights, antipoverty, and peace movements in RFK's political journey. Eugene McCarthy is the subject of Jeremy Larner, *The Man Nobody Knows* (1974). William Chafe studies the most influential "moderate" leader of student activism in his biography of Allard Lowenstein, *Never Stop Running* (1993). Marshall Frady writes about Alabama's governor in *Wallace* (1970). The campaign of 1968 is the topic of Jules Witcover's *Eighty-Five Days: The Last Campaign of Robert F. Kennedy* (1970). James Wooten writes about Jimmy Carter in *Dasher* (1978), while the 1976 campaign is discussed in Jules Witcover, *Marathon* (1977). Gerald Ford is the topic of Richard Reeves' *A Ford, Not a Lincoln* (1975) and of Gerald TerHorst's *Gerald Ford and the Future of the Presidency* (1974).

Richard Nixon, of course, has been written about more than any other recent president. He describes his own life in *Six Crises* (1962; rev. ed. 1978) and in *RN: The Memoirs of Richard Nixon* (1978). One of the early biographies of Nixon is Earl Mazo, *Richard Nixon: A Political and Personal Portrait* (1958); Rowland Evans and Robert Novak are the authors of *Nixon and the White House: The Frustration of Power* (1973); and Bruce Mazlish attempts a psychohistorical portrait in his book, *In Search of Nixon* (1972). See also Jonathan Schell, *Observing the Nixon Years* (1989); and Anthony Summers, *The Arrogance of Power: The Secret World of Richard Nixon* (2000). The presidential campaigns of Nixon are covered in Timothy Crouse, *The Boys on the Bus* (1976); Joe McGinnis, *The Selling of the President* (1969); and Hunter Thompson, *Fear and Loathing on the Campaign Trail* (1972); Lewis Chester, Godfrey Hodgson, and Bruce Page, *An American Melodrama* (1970); and Theodore White, *The Making of the President, 1968* (1969).

The most searching book on Nixon's foreign policy and his relationship to Henry Kissinger is Seymour Hersh, *The Price of Power: Kissinger in the Nixon White House* (1983). See also Walter Isaacson, *Kissinger* (2004). Also on foreign policy, see David Landau, *Kissinger: The Uses of Power* (1972); Stephen Graubard, *Kissinger: Portrait of a Mind* (1973); Henry Brandon, *The Retreat of American Power* (1973); and William Shawcross, *Side-Show* (1979), a study of American policy in Cambodia.

The best book on Republican strategy during these years is Kevin B. Phillips, *The Emerging Republican Majority* (1969). Samuel Lubell describes the background of American politics in his work *The Hidden Crisis in American Politics* (1970). Nixon's economic policy is presented in Leonard Silk's *Nixon* (1972), while the attempts at welfare reform are portrayed in Daniel Moynihan's *The Politics of a Guaranteed Income* (1973).

Much of the bibliography of Nixon revolves around Watergate. Memoirs from those closest to the president include H. R. Haldeman, *The Ends of Power* (1978); John Dean, *Blind Ambition: The White House Years* (1976); John Ehrlichman, *Witness to Power: The Nixon Years* (1982); and Maurice Stans, *The Terrors of Justice: The Untold Story of Watergate* (1984). Other participants in the drama have also written about it. See, for example, Leon Jaworski, *The Right and the Power: The Prosecution of Watergate* (1976); and John Sirica, *To Set the Record Straight* (1979). The best books, however, come from journalists, including those who helped to break the story in the first place. Carl Bernstein and Robert Woodward's *All the President's Men* (1974) describes the process of uncovering the conspiracy. Jonathan Schell, *The Time of Illusion* (1976), does the best job of presenting the entire drama in a tight narrative. See also J. Anthony Lukas, *Nightmare: The Underside of the Nixon Years* (1976); Theodore H. White, *Breach of Faith: The Fall of Richard Nixon* (1975); and Jimmy Breslin, *How the Good Guys Finally Won* (1975). For particularly insightful writing about Nixon, see the multivolume series by John Osborne entitled *The Nixon Watch* (1971, 1972, 1973, 1974), a compilation of Osborne's columns for the *New Republic*. Some more recent books include Stanley Kutler, *The Wars of Watergate: The Last Crisis of the Nixon Presidency* (1990), and Michael Schudson, *Watergate in American Memory: How We Remember, Forget, and Reconstruct the Past* (1992).

Political trends during the 1970s and early 1980s provide the subject for Everett Ladd, Jr.'s *Transformation of the American Party System, Political Coalitions from the New Deal to the 1970s* (1978). Dealing with the legacy and end of the New Deal order in labor and politics is Steve Fraser's and Gary Gerstle's, eds., essay collection, *The Rise and Fall of the New Deal Order, 1930–1980* (1989).

The white backlash against racial equality and the emergence of a new conservatism are explored in Dan Carter, *The Politics of Rage: George Wallace, the Origins of the New Conservatism, and the Transformation of American Politics* (1995); Godfrey Hodgson, *The World Turned Right Side Up: A History of Conservative Ascendancy in America* (1996); and William C. Berman, *America's Right Turn: From Nixon to Clinton*, 2nd ed. (1998); in *Populist Persuasion: An American History* (1995) Michael Kazin explains how American Populism changed from a politics of the left to a politics of the right. Thomas Sugrue, *The Origins of the Urban Crisis: Race and Equality in Postwar Detroit* (1996), examines how the Great Migration to the Urban North influenced urban race relations and contributed to the white backlash; see also Nicholas Lemann, *The Promised Land: The Great Black Migration and How It Changed America* (1991); on the relation between race and religion in the urban North see John McGreevy, *Parish Boundaries: The Catholic Encounter with Race in the Twentieth Century Urban North* (1996). Earlier books on the rise of conservatism include Allan Crawford, *Thunder on the Right: The New Right and the Politics of Resentment* (1980); and George Nash, *The Conservative Intellectual Movement in America* (1979). See also Peter Steinfels, *The Neo-Conservatives: The Men Who Were Changing American Politics* (1979). On the rise of the Sunbelt, see Kirkpatrick Sale, *Power Shift: The Rise of the Southern Rim and Its Challenge to the Eastern Establishment* (1975). For the reorganization of business after the economic crisis of the 1970s, see Louis Galambos, *The Rise of the Corporate Commonwealth* (1988).

In the 1970s, the oil crisis highlighted the importance of environmental policy. Energy is discussed in Barry Commoner, *The Closing Circle* (1971), while environmental issues in general are the topic of Paul Ehrlich, The *Population Bomb* (1968); and Paul and Anne Ehrlich, *The End of Affluence* (1974). Rachel Carson's *Silent Spring* (1962) is the first widely read account on the role of toxic chemicals in the environment. See also Frank Graham, Jr., *Since Silent Spring* (1970); James Ridgeway, *Who Owns the Earth* (1980); and Martin Melosi, *Coping with Abundance: Energy and Environment in Industrial America, 1820–1980* (1983). More recently, see Samuel P. Hays' collection of essays, *Explorations in Environmental History* (1998), his *A History of Environmental Politics since 1945* (2000), and Hal Rothman's short *The Greening of a Nation? Environmentalism in the United States Since 1945* (1998), all of which provide good overviews of the topic.

While science and technology were often viewed with suspicion in the 1970s, this changed in the 1980s particularly with the advent of the personal computer. For a contemporary account of the early developments in computing, see Steven Levy's entertaining *Hackers* (1984). Clifford Stoll's *Silicon Snake Oil: Second Thoughts on the Information Highway* (1995) takes a more skeptical view on the subject. Biology and medicine were the sites of some of the most controversial developments. Shane Crotty, *Ahead of the Curve: David Baltimore's Life in Science* (2001), provides a biographical perspective on the enormous changes and challenges of microbiology and medicine. On the search for the cause of AIDS, see Randy Shilts, *And the Band Played On: Politics, People, and the AIDS Epidemic* (1987). In the field of American science and technology in general, Thomas P. Hughes is arguably the dominant intellectual figure. He applies his model of large-scale technological systems to the twentieth century in *American Genesis: A Century of Invention and Technological Enthusiasm* (1989). Carroll W. Pursell takes a social perspective in *The Machine in America: A Social History of American Technology* (1995), and in Pursell, ed., *Technology in America: A History of Individuals and Ideas* (1990); see also Ruth Schwartz Cowan, *A Social History of American Technology* (1997). David E. Nye explores the cultural implications of American technology in *Narratives and Spaces: Technology and the Construction of American Culture* (1997) and in *American Technological Sublime* (1994); for a useful overview, see Alan I. Marcus and Howard P. Segal, *Technology in America: A Brief History* (1989). Merritt Roe Smith and Leo Marx, eds., *Does Technology Drive History? The Dilemma of Technological Determinism* (1994), address the general question of the extent to which technology determines a society's political, social, economic, and cultural changes.

The economic and political crisis of the 1970s and 1980s has generated some thoughtful commentary. See, for example, Robert L. Heilbroner, *An Inquiry into the Human Prospect* (1975); Ken Auletta, *The Underclass* (1981); William J. Wilson, *The Declining Significance of Race* (1978); Lester Thurow, *The Zero Sum Society* (1979); Robert Reich, *The Next American Frontier* (1983); and Samuel Bowles, David M. Gordon, and Thomas E. Weiskopf, *Beyond the Wasteland* (1983). For a penetrating analysis of the relationship between American politics and economic issues, see Walter Dean Burnham, *The Current Crisis in American Politics* (1982).

Many books on Ronald Reagan have recently been published. Among those worth consulting are Michael Schaller, *Reckoning with Reagan: America and Its President in the 1980s* (1992); Lou Cannon, *President Reagan: The Role of a Lifetime* (1991); Sydney Blumenthal, *Our Long National Daydream: A Political Pageant of the Reagan Era* (1988); Haynes Johnson, *Sleepwalking Through History: America in the Reagan Years* (1991); Barbara Ehrenreich, *The Worst Years of Our Lives* (1990); Paul Boyer, ed., *Reagan as President* (1990); and Michael Rogin, *Ronald Reagan the Movie, and Other Episodes in Political Demonology* (1987). For excellent critical essays on American politics in the contemporary era, see E. J. Dionne, *Why Americans Hate Politics* (1992); and William Greider, *Who Will Tell the People* (1992).

The meaning of the Cold War, its end, and the beginning of a new era in international relations are discussed in John Lewis Gaddis's controversial and orthodox *We Know Now: Rethinking Cold War History* (1997); John Lewis Gaddis, *The United States and the End of the Cold War: Implications, Reconsiderations, Provocations* (1992); Michael Hogan, ed., *The End of the Cold War: Its Meaning and Implications* (1992). On the foreign policy in the post-Cold War Bush-Clinton era, see David Halberstam's *War in a Time of Peace: Bush, Clinton, and the Generals* (2001).

The contested presidential election of 2000 gave rise to a number of books examining the election itself and its aftermath in the courts. Comprehensive in covering the election itself are Jeffrey Toobin, *Too Close To Call: The Thirty-Six Day Battle to Decide the 2000 Election* (2001) and the political staff of the Washington Post, *Deadlock: The Inside Story of America's Closest Election* (2001). For the Supreme Court's role in ruling on the Florida vote recount, see Alan Dershowitz, *Supreme Injustice: How the High Court Hijacked Election 2000* (2001); for a view opposed to Dershowitz's see Richard Posner, *Breaking the Deadlock: The 2000 Election, the Constitution and the Courts* (2001). Perhaps more balanced accounts and assessments of Election 2000 may be the views found in two collections, Jack N. Rakove, ed., *The Unfinished Election of 2000: Leading Scholars Examine America's Strangest Election* (2001) and Cass Sunstein and Richard Epstein, eds., *The Vote: Bush, Gore and the Supreme Court* (2001). For an account of George W. Bush's rise to the presidency and his first year and a half in office see Frank Bruni, *Ambling Into History: The Unlikely Odyssey of George W. Bush* (2002).

The events of September 11, 2001, needless to say, also resulted in a huge outpouring of books and articles on the World Trade Center towers and their collapse, the threat of terrorism in the U.S., Islam, Afghanistan, the Muslim world in general, and the escalating tension in the Middle East. As of this writing, the publications dealing with these issues continue to roll off the presses; these suggestions should be considered partial at best.

Accounts of the events of September 11 and the days that followed can be found in all the major metropolitan newspapers, especially the *New York Times* and the *Washington Post*, as well as news magazines such as *Time* and *Newsweek*. One of the more gripping descriptions of and reflections on the events of that day can be found in the essay by novelist Don Delillo, "In the Ruins of the Future: Reflections on Terror and Loss in the Shadow of September," Harper's Magazine (December 2001). *Washington Post* writers Bob Woodward and Dan Balz provide a vivid account of the federal government's response to the attacks in "Ten Days in September: Inside the War Cabinet," their ten-part series, beginning in the January 27, 2001 issue of the paper. Their account is based on interviews with President Bush, Vice President Cheney, and other key National Security officials. Two other excellent sources for an account of what happened are *Inside 9/11: What Really Happened,* by the editors of the German magazine *Der Spiegel* (2002) and Dennis Smith, *Report From Ground Zero: The Story of the Rescue Efforts at the World Trade Center* (2002). Finally, William Langewiesche, *American Ground: Unbuilding the World Trade Center* (2002), based on his three-part *Atlantic Monthly* series, details the actual collapse of the buildings and the mechanics of the clean-up which ensued.

Interest was immediately piqued in Osama bin Laden, the leader of the Al Qaeda terrorist organization and the man widely suspected of being behind the attacks, as well as in the Taliban, the former ruling regime of Afghanistan that harbored and supported him. British journalist Peter L. Bergen, *Holy War, Inc.: Inside the Secret World of Osama bin Laden* (2001) provides a detailed account of bin Laden and his terrorist network. Ahmed Rashid, *Taliban: Militant Islam, Oil and Fundamentalism in Central Asia* (2001) explains the history, nature, and rise to power of the regime ultimately toppled by American military forces in the conflict which followed on the heels of September 11. For an account of how and the extent to which terrorists, including the perpetrators of the attack on the World Trade Center, have managed to infiltrate American society, see Steve Emerson, *American Jihad: The Terrorists Living Among Us* (2002). Finally, for a more general account of the historical and cultural circumstances which precipitated and led to the Middle East's antagonism toward the West, see Bernard Lewis, *What Went Wrong: Western Impact and Middle Eastern Response* (2002). On the build-up to the war in Iraq, see Bob Woodward, *Plan of Attack* (2005).

INDEX